D0501011

BROKEN LIVES

BROKEN LIVES

How Ordinary Germans Experienced the Twentieth Century

KONRAD H. JARAUSCH

Princeton University Press
Princeton and Oxford

Published by Princeton University Press,
41 William Street, Princeton, New Jersey 08540

In the United Kingdom: Princeton University Press,
6 Oxford Street, Woodstock, Oxfordshire OX20 1TR

press.princeton.edu

Jacket photographs: (*top*) Courtesy of the Prussian Heritage Image Archive, Berlin;
(*bottom*) Courtesy of Isolde Stark

ISBN 978-0-691-17458-7

Library of Congress Control Number: 2018932868

British Library Cataloging-in-Publication Data is available

This book has been composed in Minion Pro

Printed on acid-free paper. ∞

Printed in the United States of America

1 3 5 7 9 10 8 6 4 2

Contents

Cast of Characters vii

Introduction: Narratives of German Experiences 1

PART I: PREWAR CHILDHOOD

1. Imperial Ancestors 17
2. Weimar Children 42
3. Nazi Adolescents 66

PART II: WARTIME YOUTH

4. Male Violence 101
5. Female Struggles 147
6. Victims' Suffering 190

PART III: POSTWAR ADULTHOOD

7. Defeat as New Beginning 237
8. Democratic Maturity 279
9. Communist Disappointment 320

Conclusion: Memories of Fractured Lives 360

Acknowledgments 381

Notes 383

List of Sources 431

Index 437

Cast of Characters

1. Key Individuals (more than eighty mentions)

Angress, Werner "Tom," *1920 in Berlin into a wealthy Jewish family, expelled from high school, learned farming at Gross Breesen, escaped from Germany in 1938, worked at Hyde Farmlands in Virginia, joined US military intelligence, parachuted into Normandy, went to college on GI bill, became German historian, retired to Berlin.

Baehrenburg, Ursula (name changed on request of author), *1927 in Pomerania into baker's family, was raped by Red Army soldiers, expelled to West Germany, studied education, worked in various schools as special education teacher outside Frankfurt, had difficulty with personal relationships, retired to live with childhood friend.

Bulwin, Ruth, *1922 in Kassel, father an abusive traveling salesman, enthusiastic BdM member, married a Hitler Youth leader and SS soldier during the war, lived in occupied Prague, fled from East to West Germany, worked in government office, helped husband build a house and create an independent business firm.

Fest, Joachim, *1926 in Berlin, father a conservative Catholic high-school teacher critical of the Third Reich, avoided the Hitler Youth, volunteered for the German military in 1944, released from US captivity, studied law and art history, worked for Radio in the American Sector, became a noted journalist and historian.

Frenzel, Paul, *1920 in Leipzig into lower-middle-class family, served in construction battalion in Wehrmacht, fled dramatically from Russian imprisonment, learned accounting, joined SPD, worked as banker and financial expert, had conflict with SED, became critic of planned economy, was Stasi target, as retiree was allowed to move to FRG.

Grothus, Horst, *1925 in Essen, stepfather successful lawyer, member of air Hitler Youth, enthusiastic supporter of Third Reich, captured at end of war, lost both feet in Russian POW camp, served as manager in uncle's firm, became independent management consultant, turned into a liberal democrat, pacifist, and social activist.

Härtel, Karl, *1923 in Breslau into working-class family, served in Wehrmacht, escaped from French prison camp, trained as electrician and mechanic, studied engineering in night school, worked in chemical triangle of GDR, fled to West Germany before the building of the Wall, began new career in FRG nuclear facility.

Helmer, Erich, *1922 in Braunschweig, father a critical Protestant pastor and opponent of Third Reich, avoided Hitler Youth, served in air force, escaped imprisonment, lived in East but completed Gymnasium in the West, studied theology, had run-ins with nationalist church hierarchy, became a critical clergyman and left the official church.

Joachim, Gerhard, *1926 in Stettin into half-Jewish business family, joined air force, tried to desert, was imprisoned, succeeded in reaching Russian lines, turned into a socialist idealist, became cultural functionary, ran afoul of party line, was disciplined, lost son to suicide in the West, hoped for Gorbachev, was disappointed in unification.

Johannsen, Horst, *1929 in Barmbek, father unskilled worker, Communist, as child sent to Transylvania, drafted at end of war, left unit and went home, slave laborer for SED, musical entertainer, studied engineering, worked as shipping clerk at railroad and dispatcher for chemical combine, critic of planned economy in GDR.

Klein, Fritz, *1924 in Berlin into upper-class nationalist publishing family, stepfather educator, served in military without enthusiasm, converted to Communism, studied Marxist history, served as editor of professional journal, was disciplined and sent to Academy of Sciences, became prominent GDR historian and Gorbachev supporter.

Krapf, Gerhard, *1924 in Meissenheim, father charismatic Protestant clergyman, patriotic youth, served as artillery officer in Wehrmacht, was imprisoned by Russians for several years, studied music at Karlsruhe, became organist and composer, due to exchange year emigrated to US, became University of Iowa professor.

Mahlendorf, Ursula, *1929 in Strehlen into middle-class family, supported the war, was caught in Silesia in the final fighting, expelled by the Poles, finished high school in the West, studied languages and enjoyed exchange year in US, emigrated there and became professor of German studies, fierce critic of National Socialism.

Neumaier, Robert, *1924 in Lahr into binational Swiss-German trading family, Catholic milieu, apprenticed as metal worker, air force volunteer, survivor of Stalingrad and Normandy, studied engineering after the war, specialized in circular-pump design, wrote several books and became international authority in his field.

Raschdorff, Hellmut, *1922 in Kassel into Catholic merchant family, skeptical of the Third Reich, apprenticed in business, volunteered for army, was wounded, sent to Channel Islands, started own textile business selling door to door, succeeded through hard labor typical of Economic Miracle, enjoyed car, house, mountain hikes, and travel.

Schöffski, Edith, *1928 in Berlin into sectarian Protestant family, poor household, limited schooling, cared for younger sister, worked as telephone operator, experienced saturation bombing, survived Russian occupation and postwar hunger and cold, met refugee husband, started her own family in spite of dire need.

Schultheis, Heinz, *1921 in Giessen, father wealthy store-owner, Hitler Youth member, drafted into Labor Service, construction soldier, survived combat, studied chemistry, worked as university research assistant, joined leading chemical company BSAF and had a successful business career.

2. Secondary Protagonists (more than forty mentions)

Andrée, Horst, *1927 in Pomerania, father forester, Wehrmacht service in Italy, POW, flight from East to West Germany, trained in forestry, forester in Rhineland-Palatinate.

Baucke, Gerhard, *1919 in Berlin, father baker and Nazi, Wehrmacht survivor, GDR journalist, West Berlin anti-Communist, successful printing company owner.

Debus, Hermann, *1926 in Buer, patriotic Navy SEAL, Rhine River captain, chemical shift worker, local real-estate official, disability retiree, amateur theater actor.

Eyck, Frank, *1920 in Berlin, father prominent Jewish lawyer and politician, sent to UK boarding school, served in British occupation force, European historian in Canada.

Feigel, Werner, *1924 in Plauen, military truck driver, East German police officer, despite problems with SED an unregenerate Communist, spokesman for ex-GDR elite.

Finckh, Renate, *1926 in Ulm, League of German Girls leader, study of German and history, mother of eight children, youth author, moved to southern France.

Gay, Peter, *1923 in Berlin as Peter Fröhlich into an assimilated Jewish family, escaped Nazi Germany 1939 via Cuba, arrived in the US 1941, distinguished historian.

Gompertz, Albert, *1921 in Gelsenkirchen, father wealthy Jewish furrier, émigré to US, served in the US Army, US citizen, successful businessman.

Grothus, Gisela, *1920 in Berlin into upper-class family, critical of Third Reich, trained as medical technician, management consultant assistant, feminist activist.

Huber, Anneliese, *1920 in Waldshut, father Communist, trained in fashion sales, war widow, worked for insurance company, second husband policeman, housewife.

Hübschmann, Klaus, *1932 in Thuringia, father doctor, studied medicine, became director of pediatric clinic in Potsdam, after retirement amateur musicologist.

Klüger, Ruth, *1931 in Vienna, father Jewish doctor, survivor of Theresienstadt and Auschwitz, emigrated 1947 to US, author and professor of German literature.

Mandelstam, Lucy, *1926 in Vienna into Jewish family of modest means, deported to Theresienstadt and Auschwitz, survived death march, emigrated to Israel.

Queiser, Hans R., *1921 in Oberstein, Hitler Youth leader, air force volunteer, tail gunner, NS war reporter, postwar democratic journalist.

Sieg, Martin, *1927 in East Prussia, Wehrmacht soldier, studied theology, Protestant pastor in Osnabrück, theological author and critic of Nazi regime.

Sternheim-Peters, Eva, *1925 in Paderborn, enthusiastic Hitler Youth leader, postwar study of pedagogy, worked as high-school teacher and later as psychologist.

Taubhorn, Erika, *1928 in Barmen, poor family, BdM member, apprenticed as seamstress, overcame postwar privation, working-class housewife.

Tausch, Hans, *1922 in Wildstein, Sudeten German, military officer, POW, expelled by Czechs, high-school classics teacher in Bavaria.

Thamm, Gerhardt B., *1930 in Jauer, boy soldier in Silesia, Soviet slave laborer, expelled by Poles, emigrated to US, intelligence analyst and author.

Walb, Lore, *1919 in Alzey, enthusiastic Hitler Youth leader, wartime study of German, postwar journalist and feminist, worked for SWF and Bavarian Radio.

Weigelt, Ruth, *1922 in Schreiberhau/Silesia, family restaurant owners, Reich Labor Service, wartime marriage, released by Poles 1957, difficult new beginning in Swabia.

3. Minor Individuals (more than five mentions)

Alenfeld, Irene, *1933 in Berlin, half-Jewish survivor, translator, émigré in France.

Bässmann, Joachim, banker, SS perpetrator in Auschwitz.

Beilmann, Christel, *1921 in Bochum, Catholic youth activist.

Berger, Gabriel, *1944 in France, Jewish physicist, GDR refugee.

Bork, Ingrid, *1928 in Berlin, housewife.

Braune, Werner, *1936 in Berlin, East German Protestant pastor.

Busch, Marianne, Auschwitz teacher, NS accomplice.

Buschmann, Heinrich Johann, *1922 in Essen, East German agronomist.

Ehrle, Gustav, *1927, World War II soldier, Bundeswehr member.

Elias, Ruth, *1922 in Mährisch-Ostrau, Holocaust survivor in Israel.

Fehr, Bettina, *1922 in Frankfurt am Main, bookseller, housewife.

Ganor, Niza (Anna Fränkel), *1925 in Lviv, slave laborer and Auschwitz survivor in Israel.

Greiffenhagen, Martin, *1928 in Bremervörde, West German political scientist.

Gros, Günter, *1920 in Giessen, POW escapee, eye doctor.

Groschek, Christel, *1928 in Königsberg, expellee, housewife.

Hagemann, Günter, *1921 in Hamburg, worker and Social Democratic politician.

Hecht, Ingeborg, *1921 in Hamburg, author, half-Jewish survivor.

Homeyer, Wilhelm, *1913 in Hameln, Wehrmacht soldier, Russian POW.

Iggers, Georg, *1926 in Hamburg, Jewish émigré historian in US.

Keil, Jack Baruch, *1926 in Berlin, Jewish refugee, accountant in US.

Koch, Gertrud, *1924 in Cologne, Communist resistance fighter, housewife.

Kolesnyk, Sonja, *1928 in Letnia, Ukrainian slave laborer.

Kolesnyk, Wilhelm, *1927 in Vienna, Ukrainian Nazi accomplice.

Kosing, Alfred, *1928 in East Prussia, East German Marxist philosopher.

Krause, Günter, *1920 in Gera, mechanical engineer, GDR refugee.

Leithold, Albert, *1923 in Delitzsch, chemist and GDR critic.

Manz, Günter, *1922 in Berlin, East German economist.

Meyerstein, Heinz Jehuda, *1920 in Göttingen, Jewish escapee to Israel.

Moosmann, Agnes, *1925 in Bodnegg, Swabian housewife and official.

Mueller, Irmgard, *1920s in Halle, Auschwitz survivor, secretary in USA.

Neglein, Hans-Gerd, *1927 in Westphalia, Siemens board member, environmentalist.

Polak, Ilse, *1927 in Papenburg, Jewish survivor, émigré to USA.

Schirmer, Hans-Harald, *1924 in Wolfenbüttel, worker, SPD politician.

Schoenhals, Dieter, *1926 in Giessen, émigré Germanist in Sweden.

Schöffski, Benno, *1923 in Pillau, East Prussian refugee.

Scholz-Eule, Eberhard, *1921, in Reichenbach in Silesia, refugee.

Seelmann-Eggebert, Will, *1923 in Berlin, officer, Bundeswehr.

Simon, Marie Jalowicz, *1922 in Berlin, Holocaust survivor, professor.

Sölle, Dorothee, *1929 in Cologne, Protestant theologian and activist.

Stern, Carola, *1925 in Ahlbeck, liberal journalist in West Germany.

Stern, Fritz, *1926 in Breslau, Jewish émigré historian in US.

Warmbrunn, Werner, *1920 in Frankfurt, Jewish émigré, Germanist in US.

Witolla, Jakobine, *1923 in East Prussia, Red Army refugee to FRG.

Zöger, Heinz, *1915 in Leipzig, Communist journalist, refugee to FRG.

BROKEN LIVES

INTRODUCTION

Narratives of German Experiences

Conversations with older Germans about their pasts trigger amazing stories whose alleged facts are often stranger than fiction. For instance, during the night of March 16, 1945, Toni Schöffel huddled with her three small children in a shelter during a British bombing raid on the medieval city of Würzburg. When an air shaft was hit, "panic broke out since smoke spread through the room." After digging through the blocked entry, they faced an inferno of flames that made the front of their apartment building collapse. "The firestorm was so strong that Toni had to hold onto the children to keep them from being swept away." With the smallest girl sitting in a handcart, the bedraggled survivors had to walk twenty-five kilometers until a friendly farmer finally took them in. But there was no news of their father Paul, who served at the front: "Was he fallen, had he died?"[1] Beneath the veneer of postwar recovery, almost every family has such tales of lives disrupted or lost, showing the devastating impact of dictatorship and war.

Listening to such life stories greatly expands one's perspective on the twentieth century, since it puts ordinary people back into the well-known narrative of major events. Instead of concentrating on the course of high politics, this reverse angle illuminates the human dimension, revealing an extraordinary mixture of prolonged suffering and surprising happiness. As Bettina Fehr recalled: "Only by retelling an individual fate can one really understand the thousandfold misfortunes that befell people." On the one hand, many people struggled with forces beyond their control, becoming complicit with the demands of the Nazi or Communist dictatorships. On the other, the survivors who emerged from these disasters rebuilt their lives in spite of the Cold War confrontation between the liberal West and the socialist East. A sustained look at unexceptional lives therefore dissolves the grand story of calamity and reconstruction into countless individual tales of survival and recovery that reveal the irresistible impact of political conflicts that ruptured peaceful existences but also offered new opportunities.[2]

In these personal accounts, the Nazi dictatorship, World War II, and the Holocaust emerge as the central vortex that irreparably altered millions of life trajectories. While the suffering of the First World War and hyperinflation seemed bad, the Weimar Republic provided a beacon of hope that progress would resume. But the devastating effect of the Great Depression created the mass disappointment upon which the novel National Socialist movement rode to power, renewing German pride by providing a warped sense of a national community. Though these stories attest to Hitler's initial popularity, they also demonstrate how the criminal war of annihilation eventually came back to haunt the German people themselves through mass death in military battle, civilian bombing, and ethnic cleansing. The drama of the final war years that turned erstwhile perpetrators into victims has deeply engraved itself in people's minds, since it cost many lives and scarred even those fortunate enough to survive.[3]

These life histories also suggest that the more peaceful second part of the century offered some relief by allowing individuals to rebuild their broken lives and get on with their private affairs. But many postwar decisions consciously or unconsciously tried to avoid the potential repetition of past disasters. During the Cold War, the personal and collective attempt to restore a degree of normalcy required an enormous effort that focused on the present. The pursuit of material wealth in the West and social equality in the East absorbed much attention for several decades. Many people succeeded in forgetting their nightmares, resuming personal relationships, basking in professional success, and reaping the spoils of prosperity by buying cars, building houses, and traveling abroad. But for some, with retirement, the terrible memories of defeat, flight, and expulsion and postwar hunger returned, forcing a delayed reckoning. It is that painful process of self-examination that ultimately transformed many Germans into peaceful democrats.[4]

ANALYTICAL PERSPECTIVES

Making sense of such disparate narratives requires a collective biography involving more than a single individual but less than an entire society.[5] One way of limiting the scope is to focus on a specific age cohort, such as the children born during the 1920s whose life stages were particularly shaped by historic events.[6] While their parents faced World War I and their childhood took place in the Weimar Republic, they were affected severely by the Nazi dictatorship because their adolescence coincided with the first years of the Third Reich, forcing them to take a stand on Hitler's rule. Their coming of age was further complicated by the hazards of military or civilian service, as well as persecution and mass murder, in the Second World War. Surviving defeat and destruction allowed them to begin their lives anew, reaching adulthood in the Federal Republic of Germany or German Democratic Republic, only to be surprised by the overthrow of Communism in the end. Rather than pretending to a nonexistent generational uniformity, it is the diversity of the entanglements between private affairs and public events that sets them apart.

The age cohort born between the end of World War I in 1918 and the Nazi seizure of power in 1933 contained numerous illustrious figures who left their mark on the twentieth century. In politics, they ranged from Chancellor Helmut Schmidt (born 1918) to his successor Helmut Kohl (1930) and included President Richard von Weizsäcker (1920), Foreign Minister Hans-Dietrich Genscher (1927), GDR spymaster Markus Wolf (1923), Premier Hans Modrow (1928), and US Secretary of State Henry Kissinger (1923). In culture, it comprised writers such as Heinrich Böll (1917), Günter Grass, and Martin Walser (1927), as well as Christa Wolf (1929). Among social thinkers, Niklas Luhmann (1927) and Jürgen Habermas (1929) are the most significant. Other celebrities include soccer player Fritz Walter (1920), artist Joseph Beuys (1921), film star Hildegard Knef (1925), and conductor Kurt Masur (1927).[7] While most of these people's lives are already quite well known, they share with ordinary Germans many of the formative experiences detailed below.

The more than six dozen accounts selected include a broad spectrum of reactions to National Socialism, ranging from enthusiastic support to courageous opposition. The most difficult to find were those of fanatical Nazis who supported Hitler, because they did not want to write about their complicity in crimes. More forthcoming are the dozen or so nationalist collaborators who celebrated their military success until 1942. The majority of memoirs are by apolitical folks who merely took pride in surviving the Third Reich through ingenious stratagems. Less numerous, at about one-tenth the total, are the critics of Nazi rule who recount their small acts of noncompliance as proof of decency. Only a few accounts stem from the small minority who actively resisted the blandishments of the Third Reich. Since the voices of Jews or other Nazi victims were largely silenced by mass murder, only a dozen accounts by survivors of the concentration camps (KZ) or people rescued by timely emigration could be incorporated. These written testimonies therefore reflect a somewhat truncated set of responses that characterize the experiences of the majority.[8]

Another cluster of responses to politics had to be chosen for the second half of the century, because Nazi defeat sorted people's life chances anew, turning allegiances topsy-turvy. One key difference involved adherence to the conflicting sides in the Cold War—either joining the capitalist reconstruction of the Federal Republic or the socialist experiment of the GDR. In the majority of accounts from the West, the texts show that economic success inspired people to accept democracy at least nominally, while only a critical minority pushed for further reforms. By contrast, the two dozen East German autobiographies reveal that the anti-Fascism of the SED (Socialist Unity Party of Germany) initially attracted much support, but the imposition of a new Marxist dictatorship created another set of victims and forced critics to flee. As a result, the East Germans eventually overthrew Communist rule and joined the Western system, reunifying their country.[9] These contrasting stories of material prosperity and ideological disappointment add a different postwar trajectory to the narratives.

In order to go beyond the elite bias of most written accounts and recover the voices of ordinary people, this study attempts to present wider segments of the German population.[10] Autobiographies from various social strata are included, with about half hailing from the upper middle class, one-third from the petite bourgeoisie, and one-tenth from the working class. Texts from various regions were chosen in order to reflect the wide geographical range of German society: two dozen individuals came from the West, eighteen from the East, and one dozen from Berlin. The book incorporates different religious perspectives, since confessional affiliations retained a powerful force in Central Europe: the majority were Protestants, a substantial minority Catholic, and the rest Jewish. Whenever possible, accounts have been picked that cover an entire lifespan so as to combine narratives of earlier events with subsequent reflection on their meaning. In contrast to more limited studies, this stratified sample of more than six dozen individuals represents a broader range of personal and collective experiences.[11]

Because popular life courses were highly gendered during the twentieth century, the distinct if related experiences of men and women must also be represented. The men who make up two-thirds of the sample tend to write about their job histories and their military service on the front or in POW camps in the tone of adventure stories. They openly engage political questions, describing how they collaborated with or tried to escape from the reach of National Socialism. By contrast, the women report more on their families, relatives, and friends, reconstructing a dense network of human relationships. Especially in difficult times, their stories center on providing food, clothing, and shelter—that is, the basic survival of their own family unit. Politics rarely makes an appearance, viewed generally as an intrusion from the outside. Of course, in some areas such as courtship, marriage and children, or absence and death, the two strands are closely intertwined. But it often appears as if the sexes lived in different worlds, divided not only by age or occupation but by gender.[12]

AUTOBIOGRAPHICAL SOURCES

Promising sources for such a cohort biography are the autobiographies written in retirement during the 1990s as retrospective accounts after German unification. Some writers composed them for their grandchildren in order

1. An author's self-portrait. *Source*: Deutsches Tagebucharchiv.

to portray the background of their ancestors or communicate exciting experiences, formalizing oral stories by writing them down. Others had a psychological compulsion to justify problematic decisions by explaining past circumstances, the books serving as a form of personal therapy. Still others responded to increasing media interest in German suffering after President Richard von Weizsäcker's injunction in 1985 to engage popular memories.[13] Many of the narratives, like that of Ursula Baehrenburg, are richly illustrated with family snapshots, personal drawings, maps of battles, and newspaper clippings concerning civic engagements (image 1).[14] Though directed primarily toward creating private family memories, these amateur accounts also offer a public substitute for the disappearance of oral testimonies due to the passing away of the eyewitnesses.

Finding life histories composed by ordinary Germans turned into a voyage of discovery that went beyond the customary sources of historical scholarship. The project started with an effort to recover stories told by friends such as composer Gerhard Krapf, Jewish émigré Tom Angress, and East German historian Fritz Klein. An inquiry by hairdresser Brigitte Stark about whether her mother's memoirs might interest historians propelled the effort further; her text and pictures turned out to be a treasure trove of popular experiences. From there the search ventured into a realm of similar grey literature by authors such as river captain Hermann Debus, published by small vanity presses. The effort to obtain permissions for citations and images from persons such as engineer Karl Härtel triggered a surprisingly positive response that led to phone calls, emails, and touching interviews with two protagonists, businessman Hellmut Raschdorff and pastor Erich Helmer, already in their mid-nineties. All of these respondents were delighted to have a professional historian take their stories seriously.

Though many manuscript autobiographies remain in private possession, others are located in public repositories. On hearing about the project, descendants such as Katharina Hochmuth and Ulrich Grothus offered access to unpublished recollections by their parents or grandparents. Moreover, beginning in 1955 the Leo Baeck Institute in New York has made a systematic effort to preserve the culture of German-speaking Jews by archiving approximately two thousand personal narratives.[15] In the late 1970s the writer Walter Kempowski also started to collect such accounts as material for his social novels and assembled over eight thousand volumes that are now housed in the literary archive of the Academy of Arts in Berlin.[16] Similarly, in the late 1990s Frauke von Troschke began a parallel project to create a German Diary Archive in the small Badensian town of Emmendingen. This now contains more than fifteen thousand entries, about two-fifths of which are autobiographies.[17] With other accounts published by small presses, these texts constitute a veritable archive of popular memories, so far largely ignored by professional historians.[18]

The subjectivity of such ego-documents is both their weakness and their strength for analytical purposes. Of course, retrospectives late in life lack the freshness and authenticity of diaries or letters composed at the time of crucial events. Age also creates a tendency to forget, to paper over cracks, and to apologize, making the author appear in a better light. Moreover, autobiographies are shaped by intervening debates both in the family and in wider society that tend to influence the narrative. But, coming toward the end of a lifetime, many such accounts are surprisingly candid about previous errors and failings. In quite a few cases, they are also based upon consultation of earlier documents, including letters or diary entries, in order to refresh later memory. And they tend to be self-reflexive, contrasting a prior self with the later persona and thereby providing clues to individual and collective learning processes. Since such self-representations seek to seduce the reader, they must be used with critical discrimination.[19]

The value of autobiographies lies precisely in their combination of event narrative and memory construction, missing in other sources such as letters or diaries. In the ruptures of the twentieth century, "biography and contemporary history are interwoven in a complex fashion, and at the same time both are actually produced through autobiographical narration." Such attempts at self-historicization are simultaneously "a retrospective interpretation of one's own life" and "a search for a socially acceptable form" of conveying experience. They possess a strongly diachronic character, representing earlier events and emotions through the lens of later reflection and evaluation. Moreover, personal narratives are products of social interaction and cultural debate. What they lack in accuracy of fact, they gain in textual presentation and reflection. Making sense of the evolution of an individual identity requires explaining the larger developments that have shaped and disrupted its existence.[20] Especially when compared with each other, autobiographies reveal the peculiar ways in which different Germans narrate the twentieth century.

The subsequent analysis of ordinary ego-documents builds upon but also seeks to transcend the tradition of everyday history. Instead of looking down from grand politics, this reverse perspective attempts to reconstruct the relations of ordinary people from below. Rather than focusing on key decisions, it tries to ascertain changes in their daily lives, the transformations of their *Alltag* existence. In contrast to government documents, it consults the memories of "eyewitnesses" who experienced developments, in order to get at their impact on the population at large.[21] But instead of using oral interviews, the current study analyzes written testimonies, generally a result of prior storytelling among families and friends.[22] Moreover, it goes beyond a few prominent *Zeitzeugen* and searches for transpersonal patterns by comparing more than six dozen accounts with each other. This method makes it possible to reconstruct changes in ordinary lives and to recover the agency of little people when confronted with big events.

An intermedial look at the many photographs included in the autobiographies reinforces and amplifies this narrative perspective from below. About half of the memoirs, like Ruth Bulwin's account, are richly illustrated with pictures of their protagonists, making them come alive as individuals. Family photos constitute a visual archive of images of significant life events such as births, confirmations, marriages, retirements, and deaths. In these private photos, politics only gradually makes an appearance through teenagers or men in Hitler Youth (HJ) or Nazi uniforms or portraits of Wehrmacht soldiers. During the war, shots of victorious troops proliferate; defeat and destruction are pictured much less because their photographers were busy with survival. In the postwar period, Western images focus on signs of success such as cars, houses, and vacations, while Eastern pictures show party activities as well. This pictorial record adds another dimension of rather unselfconscious self-representation to the written texts.[23]

A collective biography focused on an age cohort like the Weimar children makes it possible to look at the sequence of German regimes through the eyes of successive life stages. The Wilhelmine Empire appears as a nostalgic evocation transmitted by grandparents, while World War I and its chaotic aftermath show up in the struggles of the parents. A benign Weimar Republic comes into view through the childhood experiences of the authors themselves, whereas National Socialism is seen from the perspective of adolescents in the Hitler Youth. The Second World War appears in youthful reports of harrowing experiences in the military or the home front, reaching a climax in descriptions of suffering in the Holocaust. Germany's defeat and occupation surface as the decisive period in which different trajectories toward maturity opened up, only to diverge into Western democracy and Eastern dictatorship during the Cold War.[24] This linkage between life stages and regime changes opens fresh interpretative perspectives.

One key issue in working with a plurality of autobiographies is the distinction between their individual trajectories and the broader patterns to which they relate. While each life story is unique, consisting of a personal fate different from others, if taken together, such narratives also reveal regularities that illuminate broader social processes. Grouping them according to criteria such as the subject's relationship to National Socialism allows the identification of typical patterns. Moreover, many lives have in common not only a progression of stages but, in a turbulent century, were subject to similar experiences—fighting at the front, sitting in air-raid shelters—which suggest similar reactions. Although the idiosyncrasies of such individual stories are fascinating, their points of intersection reveal *shared experiences* that shed light on collective responses. As in a mosaic where individual stones form a broader pattern, the comparison of over eighty such cases allows the identification of common tendencies that combine into a more general picture.

Another analytical challenge in dealing with individual life histories is the tension between their claim to represent actual experiences and their character as memory narratives. Ostensibly authors write in order to convey actual events from their lives, claiming a truthful rendition of their actions. But, due to the lapse of time, the veracity of presentation remains unclear, requiring corroboration through comparison with other sources. Moreover, autobiographies consist of stories centered on individual actors, who are able to choose what to include, what to leave out, and how to present it. The resulting narratives vary widely, from military adventure accounts to tales of suffering or heroic survival in concentration camps and to success stories of resilient recovery and postwar prosperity. But the repetition of certain stories creates *tropes of memory*, which suggest shared ways of telling and assigning meaning. A critical use of these ego-narratives therefore demands factual confirmation as well as narrative deconstruction.[25]

A final problem is the controversial emphasis of personal narratives on German suffering, which seems insensitive to the pain of their victims. Foreign observers and domestic intellectuals have therefore insisted on fashioning a history that memorializes the millionfold anguish of Jews, Slavs, and other targets of Nazi persecution. But Günter Grass rightly pointed out in his novella *Crabwalk* that this shift of empathy ignored the memories of German sorrow, pushing them underground and leaving them to be exploited by a resentful Right.[26] Making only passing reference to the pain of Nazi victims, these autobiographical retrospectives indeed center on the German sense of victimization. But a critical reading need not accept their stories at face value. Instead, it can interpret the exculpatory tales of suffering as another impetus for postwar learning, which made many chastened Germans vow never again to commit such crimes, lest their dire consequences be once more visited upon their authors.[27]

Examining such an ensemble of life stories requires an almost novelistic technique of blending individual fates with collective narrations. Instead of creating "composite interviews" combining different people, this analysis focuses on a core of seventeen exemplary individuals, whose memoirs represent typical reactions and cover a lengthy period of time.[28] In order to provide additional depth on general subjects such as horrific war experiences, another twenty-one secondary characters are included. Finally, more than forty minor figures are used to illustrate specific points, such as motives for joining the Nazi Party. The repetition of stories, such as those of dramatic escapes from POW camps, makes it possible to discern patterns of shared experiences, while the manner in which they are told shows retrospective tropes of memory. Though more focused than Sabine Friedrich's more than two-thousand-page novel on the German resistance, this multi level approach yields a rich tapestry of collective fates.[29] Such a life-history perspective reveals how much ordinary Germans not only suffered from, but also contributed to their own catastrophes.

Precisely because they are not elite memoirs, these untutored accounts provide a more vivid and personal picture of what it meant to live through the twentieth century. Instead of just recounting the differences between the successive systems of the Second Empire, Weimar Republic, Third Reich, and East and West Germany, they reveal the involvement of individual life decisions in dictatorship or democracy.[30] These narrations show the radicalizing effect of economic crises such as the Great Depression and demonstrate the enthusiasm of youths for the Third Reich. More importantly they reveal the disruptions of lives at the front, in the bomb shelters, and in the KZ, as well as the difficult postwar efforts to resume normal existences. Finally, the accounts cast light on the Cold War decisions between the competing ideologies and the chagrin over the ultimate collapse of Communism.[31] In contrast to fictional media portrayals, these amateur narratives recount actual life events, revealing how ordinary Germans were shaped by outside forces and how they brought trials and tribulations upon themselves.[32]

EXPERIENCES AND MEMORIES

These narratives suggest that Germans overwhelmingly experienced a sense of broken lives in the twentieth century, disrupted often beyond repair. While the first decade inspired hope for continued progress, World War I triggered a catastrophic chain of events that ruptured life plans in many social strata. The political conflicts of Weimar pulled families apart by forcing them to choose ideological sides. Economic instability created a pervasive feeling of insecurity that made all too many believe in the promise of a racist dictatorship. Mass murder and death during the world wars cut short millions of lives, leaving sorrow and despair. The flight and expulsion from the East uprooted countless individuals, taking away their homes and forcing them to start over elsewhere. Many of the responses during the second half of the century can only be understood if they are considered as desperate efforts to avoid a recurrence of such catastrophes.[33] Hence the postwar stress on success seems like a conjuring act, seeking to keep dangers at bay.

These stories are, in effect, narrative efforts to mend fractured memories, alternating between exculpatory claims of victimization and self-critical admissions of responsibility for crimes. Rarely describing their authors' own misdeeds, the autobiographies are full of shocking tales of German suffering, long ignored by academic histories. The reports of terror at the front, huddling in bomb shelters, mass rape, and flight and expulsion are credible enough, but they often fail to mention that their causes lay in earlier German aggression. Obdurate nationalists still present relativizing explanations that "we [were] only doing our job" or "we were all misled by the Nazis" and "betrayed by the *Führer*." More introspective writers try to examine their own conscience, admitting to at least partial involvement in war and repression. A few self-critical spirits even confront their guilt and show a subsequent desire to atone.[34] It is this effort to wrestle with complicity and show contrition that makes German memory culture an exemplary case of attempted rehabilitation in general.[35]

In these autobiographies, experiences and memories blend in a unique fashion that can make it difficult to tell them apart. Their content relates personal occurrences, ranging from humdrum daily life to exceptionally exciting moments, based on a core of actual events. But because these experiences were recollected decades later, their veracity is questionable unless cross-checked by comparison with other accounts, documents, and scholarly analyses. Written down on the basis of memory and seldom supported by actual records, these memoirs are selective, biased, and exculpatory, offering an incomplete picture. But they are also a compelling source showing how earlier experiences are remembered, often following collective scripts that have been constructed by social retelling, cultural reflection, and political discussion. Since such personal stories express memories of experiences, their narrative form needs to be deconstructed in order to get at their multiple levels of meaning. It is the horrible pain inflicted and suffered by Germans that sets their struggle to remember and forget apart.[36]

With their untutored presentation, these recollections reflect the human drama of the twentieth century more directly than many academic analyses. Instead of relating only major events, they present a myriad of individual experiences that interacted with broader changes. More than that of other countries, Germany's development was shattered by surprising ruptures, territorial shifts, and regime changes that destabilized the very notion of a national state. Across these upheavals, ordinary people struggled to pursue normal lives, trying to progress from childhood to adulthood in a predictable fashion irrespective of grand politics. But transpersonal forces kept unsettling peaceful existences, threatening death and destruction.[37]

"Time has passed over us like a wild and turbulent wave of the sea, devastating everything," mused the refugee Jakobine Witolla. Faced with such dangers, people sought to survive somehow by collaborating with dictatorships, ignoring their commands, or even opposing them. Their stories offer a unique window into popular lives and should finally receive their due.[38]

PART I

PREWAR CHILDHOOD

1

IMPERIAL ANCESTORS

Ancestral traditions, even if only dimly remembered, have a powerful impact on the lives of families. While youths may try to escape from familial constraints, their choices are limited by preexisting structures over which they have no control. Ancient legacies establish patterns of belonging such as national affiliations, social settings, religious customs, and regional ties. More directly, grandparents whose lives overlap with those of their grandchildren transmit occupational preferences, material circumstances, and codes of behavior via a mixture of discipline and love. Most immediately parents shape their children's life chances and value choices through their examples and personalities, professional successes and failures. It is this invisible baggage, which pastor Erich Helmer likened to "a backpack, in which we have put everything that life has brought us," that forms subsequent lives, even if most people are hardly aware of it.[1]

Forebears largely shaped the life chances of post–World War I German children by their actions during "the Kaiser's era," also known in retrospect as "the good old days."[2] Seen from the perspective of subsequent upheavals, these "were pleasant, peaceful years." Berlin salesgirl Edith Schöffski recalled that in the countryside "people were contented and often happier than today." Life seemed well ordered and predictable. "Unless something absolutely had to be done in the fields, only essential tasks were completed on Sunday. In the afternoon, women sat on the bench in front of the house with their neighbors or passersby, talking or musing" about their affairs. "That was the reward for the hard work during the week."[3] In the more affluent cities, bourgeois families enjoyed a noon dinner with a roast, promenaded in their finery in a nearby park, and refreshed themselves with coffee and cake. This was a stable world in which everything seemed to have its place.

While living conditions were generally improving, the autobiographies also show that the lower classes experienced the prewar decades of the Second Reich as a "period of poverty and need." Although many businessmen were pleased about rising receipts that allowed them to prosper and professionals enjoyed the social esteem of an academic title, small shopkeepers and artisans just scraped by.[4] According to Edith Schöffski, rural life remained hard for maids and farmhands: "The meager food sufficed just for living and working. [Laborers] had to toil twelve to fourteen hours a day. There was no free time."[5] In the cities, proletarian families lived in damp one-room tenements rife with disease, and their children were regularly beaten in school to enforce discipline. Engineer Karl Härtel recalled that his father, a worker in a power plant, "incessantly tossed coal with an oversized shovel into the insatiable mouth of a boiler for over fifty hours a week."[6] The shining image of growing imperial power and prosperity had a darker underside characterized by hard labor and a basic lack of rights.

The character of Imperial Germany has therefore sparked endless arguments among historians about whether it was basically oppressive or benign. West German apologists initially tried to defend its positive character, while East German Marxists attacked Prussia as repressive, justifying the demolition of the royal castles in Potsdam and Berlin. Inspired by the generational revolt of the 1960s, critical Federal Republic of Germany (FRG, West Germany) historians such as Hans-Ulrich Wehler developed the theory of a "special path," charging that Wilhelmine Germany's partial modernization deviated from Western notions of democracy, following a policy of "social imperialism." But moderate scholars pointed to advances in the rule of law and progress in science and culture, while their British colleagues emphasized that the middle class had more power than it was given credit for.[7] This *Sonderweg* debate has remained somewhat inconclusive, for there is much evidence to support both contending views.

The colorful reminiscences of the children born during the 1920s provide an alternate perspective on German experiences in the Second Reich, because they report on how it was remembered by ordinary people. Shaped by accounts of their grandparents, the image of the Empire created a baseline of expectations according to which later experiences were judged. Forester Horst Andrée recalled that "at family get-togethers talk always turned to our ancestors: who they were, where they came from, where they lived and what occupations they had." While written records such as "deeds, old letters, or photos" and objects of material culture helped establish a family memory to explain who they were, "many questions remained open." More permanent than oral stories, autobiographies are therefore a conscious attempt to commit traditions to paper so as to "provide better insights than those that we had" to one's own offspring.[8] Such personal narratives convey highly ambivalent legacies of the Empire to the children born after World War I.

ANCESTRAL TRADITIONS

The impact of prior generations on subsequent lives is difficult to determine, because most autobiographical narratives are reticent about their distant ancestors. Although the telling of family stories was an essential part of entertainment in the past, references to forebears tend to be vague and sparse.[9] Many autobiographies are full of old photographs of forefathers, carefully posed portraits like that of the grandfather and father of Ruth Weigelt that capture self-important-looking men in uniform (image 2). Other snapshots commemorate significant life events such as weddings, births, or confirmations, but later descendants are often unsure about who the people in the pictures actually are unless the names and occasions are marked on the back. A few writers actually turned to genealogical research in order to construct elaborate family trees, which often contain nothing more than a name, a date, and a place.[10] Hence, references to an earlier family background tend to be shrouded in mystery, allowing later descendants a wide field for the play of imagination.

2. Imperial grandfather and father. *Source*: Winfried Weigelt.

The harmless question of ancestry only turned into a dangerous problem when the Nazis demanded proof of Aryan descent for marriage and public employment. The 1933 law for the restoration of the professional civil service defined as non-Aryan anyone "who is descended from non-Aryan, especially Jewish parents or grandparents." Since it was impossible to prove race with biological measurements, this anti-Semitic provision triggered frantic searches in civil registers and "church books" for documentary evidence. Due to conversion, intermarriage, and secularization, the blurring of religious boundaries had created many individuals of mixed ancestry. Because the discovery of a Jewish grandmother might imperil their lives, many affected families, such as the Helmers, used expedients such as the discovery of a relation to a prominent Nazi to remove such presumed stains from their background. In the racist world of the Third Reich, proving Aryan descent became a matter of survival.[11]

Without such prompting, it took unusual pride in a particular lineage for families to remember earlier generations of ancestry. Working-class memoirs rarely recall their grandparents' names, for the struggle for existence prevented the keeping of records. But middle-class families with uncommon backgrounds, such as descent from Huguenot refugees—like that of forester Andrée from Pomerania—were more likely to preserve that memory.[12] Members of religious minorities struggling for social acceptance, such as the Gompertz family of Jewish merchants in the Ruhr Basin, cultivated a sense of ancestry, especially if their present success contrasted favorably with their humble beginnings.[13] Similarly, authors such as Benno Schöffski who were displaced made an effort to transmit a nostalgic picture of a lost homeland to their offspring.[14] Finally, representatives of the elite like the Scholz-Eule clan, prior owners of an estate in Silesia, maintained memory as a basis for potential claims for restitution.[15]

One basic tradition that these various ancestors bequeathed to their descendants was their cultural identity as Germans. Except for Joachim Fest's quasi-aristocratic grandparents, who conversed in French, and Gerhardt Thamm's Silesian forbears, who also spoke Polish, the men and women in this study all shared the same written language. Moreover, their offspring inherited a series of social customs such as Sunday conviviality in beergardens or gathering around candlelit Christmas trees, which distinguished them from their western and eastern neighbors. The package also included the later-maligned "secondary virtues" of hard work, discipline, punctuality, and respect for authority that rendered the stamp "made in Germany" a commercial success. Finally, the legacy included socialization into a high culture of literary giants such as Goethe and Schiller, philosophers such as Kant and Hegel, and composers such as Bach and Beethoven.[16] These shared customs and cultural referents forged a sense of community, even if their specific interpretation remained highly contested.

Another legacy was a national liberalism that advocated constitutional government and the unification of the fragmented territories into a nation-state. Most of the great-grandparents who were born during the 1830s were disappointed in the failure of the 1848 revolution and the slow process of gaining political rights, which made some emigrate to the United States. But the unexpected success of the drive for unification made the Prussian king into German emperor Wilhelm I and Chancellor Otto von Bismarck into a folk hero who was celebrated in popular culture. Moreover, the battlefield triumphs in three successive wars against Denmark (1864), Austria (1866), and France (1870–1871) also endowed the military with enormous prestige. The building of a common state required a fundamental redirection of loyalties from the local *Heimat* toward a larger national sense of belonging. Bismarck's subsequent struggle with the Catholics, the promulgation of anti-Socialist laws, and the rise of postemancipation anti-Semitism revealed that the Protestant Prussian attempt to reshape Germany in its own image remained contested and incomplete.[17]

Yet another bequest was the memory of the industrial transformation of the environment in the Ruhr, Silesia, and the Saar, which turned a pastoral land of villages into booming coal and steel country. While industry arrived, largely as an import from Britain and Belgium, its support through technical innovation and government sponsorship created rapid progress, catching up with and surpassing the earlier leaders on the eve of the First World War. The introduction of fertilizer and machines into agriculture freed many farm workers, who then streamed into the industrial cities, turning sleepy country towns in the Ruhr and Silesia into bustling cities. In order to improve housing conditions in the national capital, Berlin, Joachim Fest's maternal grandfather helped develop an entire new suburb in Karlshorst. Though factory labor was strenuous and living conditions remained deplorable, this urbanization eventually changed living habits and literacy standards, allowing even some of the proletariat to claim political participation.[18]

A final inheritance was a sense of social mobility that lifted enterprising individuals and entire regions to higher levels of prosperity. For instance, one of Hans Queiser's grandfathers was a beltmaker in the small town of

Idar-Oberstein in the Moselle area. Entering an apprenticeship at a local bank, the son ascended to a position on the board of the institute, lived in a company apartment, and had so much "success in his occupation" that he was able to marry and to employ several servants. The other grandfather, from Cottbus in Brandenburg, had started as a boiler stoker but, with hard work, advanced to become director of a worsted yarn–spinning mill. Similarly, Benno Schöffski's father began as a simple postman, having to carry the mails through all sorts of weather in East Prussia, but ended up as a superior clerk in the regional postal center at Königsberg. Repeated in countless Wilhelmine families, this individual advancement created a collective sense of pride that fueled an optimistic expectation of further progress in the future.[19]

The deep memory transmitted from ancestors through oral stories was therefore somewhat paradoxical. On the one hand, there was much nostalgia for a picturesque past of medieval "home towns" like Rothenburg in Bavaria, whose thick walled castles, gothic churches, half timbered houses, and cobblestoned streets seemed to have remained unchanged throughout the centuries.[20] On the other hand, there was a growing sense of German identity beyond the local loyalty to one's dynasty, a liberating feeling of a larger scope for business and scholarship that would enable the nation to compete with already-established states such as France and Britain. At the same time, the dynamism of the industrial transformation, symbolized by the coming of the railroad and the ocean liner, suggested the acceleration of changes that would destroy the accustomed hierarchy and security.[21] It was this tension between local origin and national belonging, as well as agrarian nostalgia and industrial urbanism, that would challenge a future generation.

GRANDPARENTS' INFLUENCE

In contrast to distant ancestors, grandparents were a living memory; their partly strict, partly loving authority overshadowed many a childhood. Due to the generational difference in age, they commanded respect for their life experience and achievement, whether in managing a farm, running a store, or pursuing a profession. Though a few continued to work in spite of declining strength, most grandparents were retired, now having time for hobbies

3. Wilhelmine grandmothers. *Source*: Benno Schöffski, "Meine Familiengeschichte."

such as cultivating a garden, keeping bees, or just smoking a pipe. For Christmas, Edith Schöffski's grandfather carved "a pretty doll house with furniture, oven and outhouse," while her grandmother "sewed linen and everything else for the tiny beds and of course also baked spice cake [*Lebkuchen*]."[22] Another grandfather told funny stories about his own exploits as a youth and led the children in silly games. While their parents resented the harsh discipline these same men and women had inflicted on them, the grandchildren usually remembered *Opa* or *Oma* fondly once a disease such as tuberculosis took them away.

In their eyes, the grandparents' lives were strictly divided along gendered lines, with grandfather the head and grandmother the soul of the family. The former ruled his flock with paternalistic authority, making all the important decisions, controlling finances, and meting out strict discipline. Grandfather was responsible for his family's material well-being, putting the daily bread on the table and providing a bit of ease beyond. In the countryside, it was the farmer who controlled the servants and the animals, deciding when and where to plow. In the cities, the master lorded over his business, keeping apprentices and clerks in line. The family head was also in charge of relations with the outside world, safeguarding his family's reputation and participating in public tasks. Even if he was only a goldsmith, Hans Queiser's grandfather, a "taciturn man," radiated respectability in his dark Sunday suit.[23]

By contrast, grandmothers were remembered as being in charge of the household and of relationships within large families. Because most dishes had to be cooked from scratch, feeding numerous people each day was an onerous task. Similarly, providing clothing was complicated, for much of what was worn needed to be cut and sewn by hand. Middle-class families employed maids to help with cleaning and child-rearing, but servants had to be supervised. Older women also kept an eye on their daughters and daughters-in-law to make sure that they were behaving appropriately, lest scandal taint the family honor. Grandmothers were also often more religious than their spouses and insisted on taking their grandchildren to church. If grandfathers were authoritarian, their wives had little choice but to knuckle under, seeking to get their way by gentle persuasion rather than bluster. But even if an *Oma* was "a gruff person," a granddaughter might often "love her more than anyone." Photos like that of the Schöffski matrons (image 3) often represent them as formidable personalities, nevertheless smiling and kindly.[24]

For the children, grandparents were a welcome resource who allowed them to escape parental control and routine duties, especially during visits and vacations. If the family had moved to town to engage in factory work, they could return to the farm in the country during holidays, where the children could play with animals and learn the agricultural chores. When grandfather was a craftsman, his grandchildren could come and watch his skill, anticipating a later trade. Or, if he had established his own store, the young could start serving customers and begin to learn the secrets of furs or colonial goods. When grandparents were truly wealthy, their children's offspring could sample upper-class life by staying in a villa or riding in a car. Horst Grothus recalled liking to "saunter through the factory, look at the machines, and watch the workers."[25] Similarly, girls could get a taste of fashion and elegance from visits to urban relatives.

The contrast between paternal and maternal grandparents also provided children with interesting choices. One of Gisela Grothus's grandfathers was a well-known Protestant theologian who had been the educator of the Grand-Duke of Baden. (She describes his wife merely as "a petite lady.") Gisela's mother's parents lived in Berlin because the husband was a military surgeon and personal physician to Wilhelm I. This formidable *Opa* "liked to take me along on his walks; but mainly I remember that he sat at his desk and wrote, sometimes with a quill; what exactly I can't recall." His wife tried to please her granddaughter by offering sweets and applesauce with raisins "which did not taste especially good." But she "had toys prepared for me. Especially my 'doll Christa' as big as a one-year-old child with which . . . I loved to play." Such pleasant memories offered contrasting role models and created an intergenerational bond and a sense of family pride.[26]

A typical upper-middle-class family such as the Eycks blended commercial prosperity with academic training and professional pursuits. Grandfather Joseph was a broker at the Berlin stock exchange, who managed a brewery in Berlin but had to economize in order to maintain a representative lifestyle. The grandmother, Helene, who left a journal, sacrificed her own talents for the sake of her family, writing with trenchant insight about the upbringing of her six children. Trained at the *Gymnasium*, the sons became a lawyer, a liberal politician, and a businessman; the daughters married an architect, another lawyer, and a distinguished doctor. They were brought up in the neohumanist spirit of the classics, considering themselves as part of the educated middle class, the *Bildungsbürgertum*. Although the family was only loosely observant, the rise of anti-Semitic agitation in the 1880s made them conscious of their Jewish heritage.[27]

For working-class families like the Härtels, life was more of a struggle just to make ends meet. Getting enough food to eat was a daily chore, especially when there were numerous hungry children needing an increased share. Older boys were therefore often sent away to learn a trade and girls to become servants. There was also much domestic violence when men, especially after drinking too much, asserted their authority by beating their wives and children. This mindset also extended to employers and employees: when one young man tipped over his hay wagon, "the estate overseer simply whipped him then and there," charging that he had loaded incorrectly. As a result, the mistreated youth left for the Ruhr and went to work in a coal mine. Grandfather Schirmer, a lowly concierge in a high school, was such a rigid disciplinarian that his rebellious son became a sailor and a Communist.[28] The authoritarian effort to maintain order exacted a high price.

During the last decades of the Wilhelmine Empire, the older generation encountered more resistance from their progeny, who no longer automatically followed their will. Often generational conflicts revolved around the choice of an occupation, as when Gerhard Baucke's father rejected paternal advice and became a baker rather than a priest. Gertrud Koch's parents insisted on marrying in spite of the fact that the groom was merely a widowed boilersmith with two children, whereas his bride was a middle-class pharmacist. "When my mother fell in love with my father," she recalled, "the world could have come to an end—it would have been no less terrible for my grandmother." Although "a great, heavyset man with white hair and a white moustache," the proletarian father was fifteen years his wife's senior and a Communist to boot. Even before the outbreak of the First World War, patriarchal authority had started to erode, so that their offspring tried to be more loving and supportive to their own children.[29]

Because most grandparents of the Weimar cohort were born during unification in the 1860s, they bequeathed a nationalism that identified itself unquestionably with the newly created Reich. During their youth, these disparate speakers of German gradually overcame their many regional, religious, and class differences and blended into common citizens of a larger community. In part, this reconfiguration of identities was the result of common coinage and legal codes, supported by maps in school textbooks and male military service. The gradual shift of loyalties was also partly a product of ceremonial visits by the Kaiser and the celebration of holidays such as Sedantag, marking the victory over France in 1870. The Second Empire also propagated the Prussian standard in administration and education as a blueprint for the entire country.[30] Having grown up with the Bismarckian Reich, many of these grandparents were therefore proud of its growing power and international respect.

In spite of much poverty during rapid industrialization, the *Kaiserreich* was later remembered as an era of prosperity and stability in which lives were predictable. The rural hierarchy of noble estate owner, independent farmer, and landless laborer was replicated in the city by business owner, craftsman, and industrial worker. These authoritarian structures were somewhat mitigated by an elite paternalism which felt responsible for its inferiors by providing housing and holiday presents. Though industrialization exploited human labor, increasing sectors of the middle class experienced a sense of progress marked by gradual advancement beyond basic necessities. Moreover, technological discoveries, such as the development of cars by inventors such as Gottfried Daimler, reinforced the feeling that things were getting better.[31] The grandparents' chief legacy was therefore a German nationalism coupled with optimism about the future.

PARENTAL IMPACT

The impact of parents upon their children's lives was even stronger than that of older relatives, since the rise of affective parenting made child-rearing their responsibility. With the reduction in the number of offspring, caring for the remaining children became a more intense task.[32] The autobiographies of the 1920s cohort show how parents' legacy of physical health and emotional stability could favor or impede the lives of their progeny. Similarly, the socioeconomic position of the parents would determine a life of arduous toil or of comfortable leisure for their children. The religious affiliation that marked one as a Protestant, Catholic, or Jew placed one into a majority or minority, subject to approval or discrimination. Moreover, regional residence in the north or south made an enormous difference for identity; boundaries moved as a result of wars, forcing people to relocate. The parents' ideological outlook and political engagement largely governed

4. Weimar family. *Source*: Ruth Bulwin, *Spätes Echo*.

the responses of their offspring. Portraits like that of the Köchy family hint at how strongly such influences shaped the lives of the children (image 4).

In a still-patriarchal world, the role of the father was crucial. He was the authority figure to be obeyed and example to be emulated. Many writers, including Horst Grothus, complain "my father did not pay much attention to me" due to pressures of work or the insistence on discipline.[33] Another father was simply "a gambler and bon-vivant" who neglected his son.[34] But a working-class girl, Erika Taubhorn, remembered her father as "a terrific person" who was able to do anything he set his mind to. In her proletarian world, he was "the chief person" and "he also always played with me."[35] When a prominent man such as Fritz Klein's journalist father died prematurely, the impact upon the children was near-catastrophic, for their material security was threatened and a new caregiver had to be found among relatives or friends such as the family of reform pedagogue Heinrich Deiters in Berlin. Only rarely did a widow remarry. Even then, new stepfathers were seldom as supportive to prior children as the original fathers.[36]

The mother was, nonetheless, remembered as the emotional center of the family, since the rearing of children was her primary prerogative. Due to the large number of births, this was arduous work, even if not all her children survived. Most writers remember their mothers as loving, teaching values and manners by example rather than force. For fortunate households, this effort resulted in "unconditional cohesion within the family [and] in ostensibly complete harmony."[37] But some mothers were rather more "ambivalent." Society women were more interested in their shopping, looks, and entertainments than in taking care of bawling infants, leaving the latter to nannies or unmarried aunts to whom children such as Werner Angress became rather attached.[38] In still-rare cases of divorce and remarriage, mothers often "were more concerned about their new husband than their under-age children." This left their brood with strong emotional ambivalence.[39]

One of the key influences on children's life chances was the social class of their parents. Among the landed elite, fathers often behaved like an "uncrowned king of the village," ruling by tradition and force of personality. One such estate owner, Wilhelm Lehmann, was "a picture of a man, tall and imposing, full of force and power" who drove his carriage standing up, "cracking his whip energetically" and scaring men and animals. His brothers feared and admired him, and "he was the best client of all village pubs." Servant girls hid from him because "he exercised the *jus primae noctis*" on virgins. But even scions of the landed gentry had to be trained in classics at the Gymnasium and study law before they could enter some form of public or military service.[40] These domineering men needed civilizing by a strong-willed spouse from an appropriate elite family. Such a privileged background engendered a lifelong sense of entitlement.

The urban upper middle class had a similar sense of ease due to its prosperous lifestyle. If the father was a successful banker like Angress senior, he worked hard "in full accord with traditional Prussian virtues, the most important of which were honor and a sense of duty." As a result, his family was "quite well off materially; we lived in a comfortable home, wore good clothes, went on trips with our parents, and had a servant girl and a cook who took care of our daily needs." Free of annoying chores, the mother could be a socialite, insisting "on being well dressed and having her hair nicely done" and going on expensive shopping sprees. Her task was to run a hospitable home, often entertaining business associates or relatives during the holidays, and adding a touch of culture and style through her own accomplishments.[41] Growing up in the *Grossbürgertum* class instilled a conviction that merit would be rewarded.

Life in a lower-middle-class family demanded, by contrast, constant efforts to maintain one's social respectability. Because financial means were limited, every expense had to be carefully considered and little luxuries such as an ice-cream cone or a visit to the movies were rare. Urban apartments were cramped and expensive and such closeness often magnified disputes over scarce money. If a father like Ruth Bulwin's was a traveling salesman, he was rarely at home and then insisted on peace and quiet. Since he was "an extraordinary tyrant" and ready to inflict a beating at the smallest provocation, everyone had to tiptoe around him and "there was no family life." Only the grandparents in the country offered a welcome refuge. To improve the family income, Ruth's mother had to go to work herself, designing fancy hats for society ladies.[42] Such a childhood in the *Kleinbürgertum* was often constrained materially and troubled psychologically.

Proletarian families like the Härtels had to struggle even more to make ends meet due to their "miserable economic condition." For the fathers, work consisted of hard physical labor and brought in meager pay, just sufficient to keep the family from starving, while jobs were uncertain, subject to frequent layoffs. Housing was often "a poor cellar apartment" without electricity or a one-room flat without indoor plumbing in the back court of a tenement. Because working-class families tended to be large, space was tight, with parents and children sleeping together in the same room or sharing beds. The mothers would often work as cleaners or in other menial jobs. As a result of poor education and limited sanitation, whole families were often sick from infectious diseases.[43] Survival required ingenuity, such as supplementing food with vegetables from a garden plot or rearing rabbits. The children from such families who survived their infant diseases tended to be tough and street-smart.

Another important cleavage was religious affiliation. The Reformation had split the German lands between Catholics and Protestants. Under Prussian leadership, the latter dominated the new Reich in cultural terms due to their emphasis on biblical learning. The anchor of Protestant influence was the parsonage, a seat of theological learning and social action. Pastor Krapf's son describes his father as "the kindliest and most unassuming person," and notes that he carried himself "with such dignity and propriety that flowed from his faith" that his flock stood "in 'loving awe' of him." Not only did his sermons draw on classical languages and biblical criticism, but he was also busy in social tasks such as Bible hour, youth training, and missionary activities. The wife of a parson had her hands full with both her own household and the social obligations of the women's circle.[44] In this setting, children often had difficulty living up to the high expectations.

By contrast, Catholics felt on the defensive in Imperial Germany because they had lost their protection when the Austrian Habsburgs were defeated by Prussia in 1866. Thereafter they were still strong in some regions, such as the Rhineland and Bavaria, but Bismarck's *Kulturkampf* crusade against their ultramontane adherence to the Roman papacy had made it clear that they were no longer in charge. For a Catholic family such as the Raschdorffs in Hesse, religious observance meant, above all, regular attendance at "holy mass" in order to feel spiritually at peace. Church membership also implied enrollment in a parochial school where Catholic values and outlooks would be taught. Moreover, there were separate youth groups, such as the St. Georg scouts, which made sure that the young would not be misled.[45] For children, Catholicism provided a cohesive subculture punctuated by colorful rituals on frequent church holidays.

Among Jewish families, the question of religious identity was even more central, since it constituted a key element of self-definition as well as ascription from the outside. With emancipation, some barriers to social integration had been removed and the adherence to Judaism had weakened somewhat. But the rise of a racial rather than religious anti-Semitism forced each family to decide whether to maintain a separate identity or to try and blend in with their neighbors. Most chose, in Werner Warmbrunn's words, a classic compromise: "My father wanted very much to be a German citizen of Jewish faith." That meant actively belonging to a synagogue, observing the High Holidays, and respecting the prohibitions of certain foods such as pork. While some Jewish families were rather strict, others converted and intermarried with Christians.[46] Most Jews who joined the Central Association of German Citizens of Jewish Faith (CV) hoped that they would eventually be fully accepted as Germans.

The impact of parental religion on growing children ranged all the way from enthusiastic commitment to total disinterest. Members of Adventist sects such as the New Apostolic Church "were very active in their faith," for they expected the imminent return of Jesus Christ. Against outside skeptics, the congregation rallied around their apostles, generating a close community in which parishioners such as the parents of Edith Schöffski married.[47] More frequent by far were the cultural Protestants or Catholics who continued a nominal affiliation, baptized their children, and celebrated church holidays, but no longer attended services. At the other extreme were the totally secular Liberals or Socialists who no longer had any connection to an organized faith. They tended to transmit a humanist morality based on the German classics.

Yet another significant division among Germans was their regional origin. The bond to landscape and dynasty produced different identities. Benno Schöffski's family, for instance, hailed from East Prussia, "the land of the dark forests and crystal clear lakes." Their farm was located in the Samland, famous for its steep cliffs towering above the Baltic beaches. Living at the Reich's Eastern border, the East Prussians were a heavyset people, slow and ponderous, who rolled their r's and used Slavic terms. The seashore was a tourist magnet, with famous resorts such as Cranz, to which steamers came from afar. After Herr Schöffski's promotion to higher rank in the post office, the family moved to the regional capital, Königsberg, the proud trading city of Immanuel Kant. The shock of their 1945 expulsion from East Prussia cast a nostalgic glow on later memories: "The love of one's home becomes powerful and conscious only when one sees and feels what one has lost."[48]

A special East German region was Silesia, located between Poland and Czechoslovakia and contested between Austria and Prussia. Containing important coal mines along the Oder River and providing many immigrants for Berlin, this province had a strong regional identity. Moreover, its Riesengebirge mountain range was a favorite tourist destination for hiking in the summer and skiing in the winter. Ruth Weigelt grew up in one of the mountain huts on top of the Hochstein peak, while Ursula Mahlendorf hailed from the small town of Strehlen and Fritz Stern from the cosmopolitan city of Breslau, in which Catholics, Protestants, and Jews tolerated each other. It was a region of mountain myths around the willful giant Rübezahl, celebrated by the poet Gerhard Hauptmann. Having held out until the bitter end in 1945, Silesia was an important source of postwar refugees and home to a minority of ethnic Germans, even after its incorporation into Poland.[49]

In the West was "a quite marvelous place of home," the university city of Giessen, located in Hesse on the Lahn River. Around 1900, it was still a traditional town with a gothic city hall, a market square, and an urban church towering over half-timbered houses that lined narrow cobblestone streets. The Schultheis family owned a "very cozy old house" on the market street that provided "a rare refuge which comprised the entire scope of life, such as living quarters and kitchen, a fur store and workshop, storerooms, and attic under one roof." Though also predominantly Protestant, the Hessians were a more lively bunch, open to novelties, adept at trade, and interested in scientific discoveries. Heinz Schultheis later recalled, "For us boys the many sheds and storehouses were an El Dorado of mysterious labyrinthine corners, steps, ladders, walls of boards, dark passages, where one could build hiding places and castles from discarded cartons and slats."[50]

Typical of more Catholic regions was the valley of the Rhine, celebrated by the Romantics for its castles and wine but politically embattled with the French. The Debus family lived on a succession of barges, ships about three hundred feet long that were towed by a tug between the Ruhr Basin and the Dutch port of Rotterdam. The usual crew were the captain and his wife, two sailors, and one ship's boy, for whom landing in a foreign city created "an indescribably exciting atmosphere." Several barges were tied onto a tug in order to carry coal to Holland and iron ore to the forges of the Ruhr. Loading was hard physical work, piloting extended to all daylight hours, and accidents were frequent, allowing little time to enjoy the picturesque scenery. On shore, the family made its home in Kaub, known for its medieval midriver custom station. Living on the water left the Debus children little time for formal schooling; their attendance was limited to the winter, when the river was frozen.[51]

By contrast, rural Swabia in the South still had many quaint farming villages, dominated by hidebound traditions. Agnes Moosmann was born into a cooperative cheese-dairy family in Bodnegg, close to Lake Constance. Her parents collected the milk in heavy fifty-liter cans from local farmers who had a handful of cows, separated the fat, and made butter and various kinds of soft and hard cheeses. As long as "the milk was clean and cool," it could be turned into a superior product, which was sold in market towns like Ravensburg. This endless work was governed by the seasons and centered on religious holidays, organized by the local parish priest. Even without elaborate toys, the children played with the farm animals and did their chores from an early age. In the winter, they sledded down hills. In the summer, they swam in the farm ponds. School concentrated on the "three R's." Only singing provided some entertainment.[52] This was a stable world into which machines such as centrifuges, telephones, and cars were only beginning to intrude.

The most exciting place to grow up in was Berlin. The rapidly expanding city had many faces: It was the capital of the Empire, the seat of the Hohenzollern court, an international metropolis, and a hub of manufacturing, all at the same time. Hence, Transylvanian journalist Fritz Klein was happy to move there as editor in chief of the *Deutsche Allgemeine Zeitung*, an industry-subsidized newspaper of Foreign Minister Gustav Stresemann's German People's Party. During the receptions in his "grand apartment," Klein could hobnob with the Weimar establishment and campaign for the overthrow of "the shameful treaty of Versailles." While he welcomed his guests in a tailcoat bedecked with his World War I medals, his wife "wore her long evening dress with quiet and self-assured elegance." But less-fortunate lower-middle-class families also loved the city due to its amusement parks, movie houses, and leading department stores.[53]

Social class, religious affiliation, and regional residence combined to form four distinctive political camps, which propagated competing visions of what Germans should be like. Eberhard Scholz-Eule, a Silesian refugee, characterized the politics of his father's milieu: "In our family a German national outlook prevailed as with most estate owners." In practice, that meant being a Hohenzollern loyalist, belonging to the Protestant church, admiring the military, and coming from east of the Elbe River. Scholz-Eule's grandfather was addressed only as "captain of the cavalry." The boys "played with wooden swords and a black-white-red flag," indicating their loyalty to the Prussian king.[54] This nationalist outlook idolized Prince Bismarck and opposed many aspects of industrialization. The conservatism of the German National People's Party appealed especially to landowners, officers, public officials, traditional Protestants, and even some farmers and artisans.

The party's chief antagonists were the Liberals, drawn largely from the educated and commercial segments of the urban middle class. These professionals and businessmen believed in the necessity of progress through education, self-help, and individual responsibility—traits to which they owed their own success in life. Erich Eyck, for instance, was a lawyer and journalist who spent his energy "on the general defense of the rule of law and of the parliamentary and democratic system" of government. In order to practice these convictions, he joined the left-liberal German Democratic Party, was elected to the Berlin-Charlottenburg city council, and often gave speeches in the Democratic Club. Like other assimilated Jews, he "identified himself with Germany and culturally felt a deep bond to her."[55] These moderate progressives were convinced that they were entitled to a leadership role—but unfortunately they lacked the mass following that was necessary to prevail in elections.

A third camp comprised the Catholic subculture that rallied around the Church in order to defend its faith in an increasingly secular society. Its regional centers were in the Rhineland and Bavaria, but Catholics formed a sizable diaspora in other areas as well. In the Swabian countryside of Agnes Moosmann, life centered around the church and the priest, especially during the many religious holidays. Bismarck's charge of national unreliability in the *Kulturkampf* led to the formation of a Center Party that used shifting parliamentary allegiances to uphold the organizational autonomy of the Church hierarchy, the sanctity of religious marriage, and the educational independence of parochial schools. Through a dense network of civic associations and colorful holiday celebrations, educated Catholics such as Joachim Fest's father created a cohesive identity in a modernizing world. One cultural battleground was Protestant-Catholic intermarriage. The Church refused to give its blessing to such unions, claiming that couples "lived in sin" unless the Protestant partner was willing to convert.[56]

A final grouping was the labor movement, represented by the Social Democratic Party (SPD), which was still considered subversive by the imperial authorities. Many industrial workers found the shift from farm to factory labor and from village to city life quite difficult. They were paid too little and often laid off. Resenting such deplorable conditions, a worker named Hans Schirmer developed "a hope for a better socialist society with more solidarity and transnational" understanding. While the trade unions struggled with employers for better pay and working conditions, the SPD grew into the largest party in the Reichstag in spite of Bismarck's efforts to suppress it with anti-Socialist laws and a social insurance scheme. Due to its persecution, the labor movement also developed an independent subculture, ranging from public lectures to sports clubs and singing societies.[57] But it was internally divided between moderate reformers and radical revolutionaries who split into competing Social Democratic and Communist parties in 1918.

Because most of the parents of this book's subjects were born during the 1890s, they grew up in the Wilhelmine Empire and experienced the prewar years as the high point of German success. In spite of all the social, religious, regional, and political cleavages, the bulk of ordinary citizens were "loyal to the Kaiser," seeing the ostentatious Wilhelm II as an incarnation of the new nation's progress. In their daily lives, they could observe a real improvement of their living conditions through increased pay, more leisure time, and better housing. In spite of rapid urbanization, the Empire stood for "peace, security and order," a world of fixed hierarchies challenged only by the disadvantaged from below.[58] While they might argue vociferously about politics, most people were proud of Germany's growing reputation abroad and ready to support its imperialist efforts to secure a "place in the sun." As a result, most of the Wilhelmine cohort adopted a cheerful optimism, even if workers such as Gertrud Koch's father continued to struggle "for a better world."[59]

In spite of initial enthusiasm, the First World War turned into an awful nightmare when the magnitude of suffering at the front and at home became clear. Regardless of class or creed, young men volunteered for military service, feeling somehow left out if not accepted. At the tender age of seventeen, Edith Schöffski's father "went to war out of a spirit of adventure. He was a courageous, brave, and companionable soldier, was promoted to sergeant, and received the Iron Cross first class." But when "seeking to help a severely wounded comrade, he was buried in a trench." Though eventually found and dug out, he was never quite the same afterward. In millions of families, sons were killed, while survivors were maimed or disease-ridden. During the British "hunger blockade," many women desperately sought to keep the home fires burning, trying to avert starvation by eating sugar beets and making do with roasted grain as coffee.[60] Due to military censorship, the loss of the long struggle came as a profound shock.

Defeat and revolution hardly brought the kind of peace for which Germans had so intensely longed during four years of fighting. In November 1918 a naval revolt chased away the Kaiser and installed the democratic Weimar Republic rather than a more radical Communist regime. But "even after the war was long over, there was hunger and need." According to Karl Härtel, the economic conditions were "so miserable" that they could hardly have been worse. "Germany was on course to become ungovernable and moved inexorably toward chaos." Moreover, the Allied peace conditions seemed inspired by hatred and revenge. "Newspapers of all political stripes wrote about the dictated [peace] of Versailles which was bound to lead to the total collapse of the largest economic power in Europe."[61] Moreover, the occupation of the Rhineland by French troops triggered widespread resentment. The transition to a peaceful life was therefore a difficult struggle for young parents under conditions of hyperinflation and intermittent civil war.

Gradually the effort to "revive the good old days" and get back to normal took hold, even if the circumstances were more difficult than before. All the talk about "the lost war" and the harsh peace only "reinforced the defiance of middle-class Germans." But life went on. People made do with fewer resources, inventing ingenious survival strategies. They grew vegetables in every available plot of land, even raising tobacco plants on balconies and windowsills. Women also went to work to add a bit of extra income, either sewing things at home or accepting menial jobs outside the home. Even if they had to work hard, most people "still got by." Looking for romance, young couples tried to make up for the lost years of their youth by enjoying life in dancehalls. Ignoring the advice of their elders, many also married. Birth-control devices were rarely used, so babies also began to appear with some regularity.[62] In spite of the postwar chaos, life went on in the hope that better days were bound to come.

AMBIVALENT LEGACIES

Though their family legacies often "lay deeply buried in memory," they constrained the lives of the children born in the 1920s for decades to come. Most people had only vague recollections of their distant ancestors and were aware, at best, of a general frame of reference within which they had developed as their descendants. But those who got to know them recalled the impact of their grandparents more directly, having "highly admired them" for their loving interest and frequent presents. Most obvious was the memory of their parents' efforts to guide their educational development by offering support and advice. Partly by persuasion and partly by compulsion, fathers and mothers sought to instill essential lessons in their children as rules to follow. The sons' and daughters' autobiographies reveal that they viewed this effort at intergenerational socialization with fundamental ambivalence.[63]

In retrospect, the legacies bequeathed by the imperial ancestors to the post–World War I children in Germany were a rather mixed lot, consisting of positive potentials and negative impediments. The list of indubitable advantages was long and impressive. During the Empire, the health of the population had improved dramatically due to sanitation and social medicine, lengthening life expectancy considerably. At the same time, scientific discoveries and technical inventions had developed entire new fields such as electricity and chemistry, not to mention machines such as automobiles, all of which improved the quality of life. In literacy and education, Prussia was also in the forefront. In urban reform and the development of the welfare state, the Germans were considered leaders among the civilized world. Even American visitors such as Mark Twain praised Imperial Germany as a country at the cutting edge of modernity.[64]

But the memoirs of the 1920s cohort also reveal considerable problems that would trouble their young lives. The surprising loss of the First World War and the hyperinflation of 1923 impoverished wide circles of the middle class and threatened the survival of much of the proletariat. The draconian conditions of the peace treaty of Versailles had generated great resentment against the victors from which nationalist parties could draw in order to justify a revanchist foreign policy. The suspension of partisan politics with the "truce within the castle" during the military struggle had only papered over the many ideological divisions of German society, which broke out again with a vengeance during the collapse and revolution of November 1918. The ensuing near–civil war between the leftist Red Brigades and rightist *Freikorps* postponed consolidation for almost half a decade. Caught between nationalist, liberal, Social Democratic, and Communist fathers, the postwar children faced a bleak future that would test their resolve.[65]

Weimar children hence became a key battleground for the allegiance of competing ideological visions of modernity. The military defeat discredited the Imperial German versions of scientific advance, economic growth, bureaucratic order, military power, and welfare state. From the East beckoned the Soviet blueprint of an egalitarian social revolution that promised international peace, social welfare, and technical progress to the working class. From the West came a more moderate US message of liberal democracy that suggested prosperity and freedom to the middle classes. Initially, the majority of Germans gravitated to President Woodrow Wilson rather than to Bolshevik leader Vladimir I. Lenin. But in the early 1920s large segments of the disgruntled Right began to look to the South and the talented journalist Benito Mussolini in Italy, who was concocting a new brew of radical nationalism called Fascism.[66]

The very diversity of their family backgrounds and social networks created a wide range of potential choices for the members of the 1920s cohort. On the one hand, the liberal and Social Democratic strains of their legacy offered them considerable chances for free development; on the other, the decisions of their ancestors had produced an authoritarian and nationalist background that severely constrained actions in the present. Already within single families like the Schirmers, the children reacted differently: one son followed the parental example and turned into a nationalist bureaucrat, while the other rejected fatherly authority and became a rebellious Communist.[67] In wider society, schools, friendship circles, youth groups, churches, and other civil society organizations also offered contending views, encouraging individuals to follow conflicting paths. Unfortunately, many of the Weimar children later had to admit that they ended up making choices that turned out disastrously.

2

WEIMAR CHILDREN

During the 1920s the birth of a new child was usually a joyous event, a reaffirmation of life after the carnage of the Great War—especially when it was a boy. Parents were proud to have a son and heir, even if a demoted female sibling might resent the little newcomer. Middle-class families sent out printed announcements to inform friends and acquaintances of the name of the new member and hired a photographer to record the happy occasion. In order to make the infant a legal member of the community, a registry clerk would fill out a birth certificate in precise Germanic script with information on the child's parents, birthplace, date, and religion. Thereafter, relatives would gather for a formal church baptism, where the baby would sometimes cry when sprinkled with cold water. A loyal official might even succeed in persuading President Paul von Hindenburg to serve as an honorary godfather.[1]

Such descriptions of birth mark the start of most autobiographies, even if the protagonist cannot remember the exact circumstances. "My zero hour was on a sunny morning in early summer of the inflation year 1923, i.e., on June 18 at 12:15 noon," engineer Karl Härtel recalled on the basis of family stories that filled in the details. "I had a relatively easy time, because before me numerous siblings had gone the same way and my mother had survived eight births virtually without a problem."[2] Gerhard Krapf's first "dim and hazy, quite isolated and single-image memories" began at age three, when he remembered looking from a window at a dancing bear in the courtyard. In her novel *Patterns of Childhood*, Christa Wolf, born in 1929, marveled about the magical onset of consciousness through the first crucial enunciation of the word "I."[3] Subsequent narratives then present the unfolding of this incipient personality through an entire life course.

Inspired by the groundbreaking work of Philippe Ariès, historians have begun to explore how this universal pattern, repeated millions of time, has differed in time and place.[4] Their work has demonstrated that childhood is culturally constructed by the ideas and values assigned to it, which run the gamut from treating children as little adults to caring for them as vulnerable infants. Moreover, demographers argue that the population transition in the late nineteenth century from having a large number of offspring, since many died in infancy, to only a few also fundamentally transformed the emotional attitudes of parents from indifference to intense involvement. At the same time, scholars have painstakingly searched the fragmentary record for clues to children's actual experiences in their efforts to wrest control of their lives from adults.[5] The result has been a more complex understanding of childhood as a period of struggle to discover one's self.

Most memories of growing up in the Weimar Republic are surprisingly positive and claim that "my childhood was very happy." Contrasting with the political image of incessant crises, these personal recollections generally emphasize that parents managed to provide "a good sense of comfort and security" that allowed children to flourish.[6] No doubt, ideals of child-rearing remained contested between authoritarian paternalism and permissive liberalism, while family size continued to vary, with poorer parents often having multiple babies due to lack of birth control and bourgeois mothers restricting their number. But this contradictory mixture confronted children with different expectations, providing a combination of support and challenge that encouraged the formation of resilient personalities. Only at the beginning and especially toward the end of the Republic did economic difficulties and political forebodings actively threaten children's futures.[7]

Such "happy, carefree" childhoods had a lasting impact on life trajectories—they created an expectation of security and normalcy that individuals struggled thereafter to regain. In contrast to the privations of World War I, the mass unemployment of the Great Depression, and the suffering at the front and at home in World War II, the Republic's middle years were a time of relative peace. For many workers and socialists, the first German democracy was a time of hope, when rising prosperity and social reform promised a better life.[8] But for defenders of authoritarian traditions and for radical anti-Semites, Weimar's modernist experiments endangered an entire worldview and lifestyle. In order to resolve the paradox between memories of "a golden childhood" and descriptions of Weimar's many problems, it is necessary to take a closer look at the actual experiences in home, school, and neighborhood that governed children's lives.[9]

THE SHELTER OF HOME

In spite of rather "unhygienic conditions," most Weimar children were born at home. Birth was considered a natural act rather than a medical problem. Karl Härtel remembered that when another sibling was about to be born, "a neighbor boiled water in several pots on the small stove, prepared clean towels, and sent my twelve-year-old sister . . . to the midwife so that she could begin her blessed work." The worried father and the nervous children were sent out of the room, listening for the woman's screams during contractions that might signal progress. "Racked by pain, the mother lay in her bed in the tiny cellar room," hoping to hear the "first cry of a new life" that would signal the end of the ordeal. After a cursory cleanup of mother and baby, the midwife called the husband and siblings back in and announced to the latter, "a little sister has arrived for you." They were now supposed to admire the infant: "Look here in the bed, that's where she lies and sleeps."[10] Typical baby pictures such as Ruth Bulwin's celebrate the maternal bond (image 5).

Especially in poor families, birth and infancy remained hazardous, and many children did not survive into adulthood. If their siblings had died as infants, the loss was noted with little emotion: "I never got to know the other five children, since these had already passed away and turned their back on the world," one author stated as a matter of fact. But when a somewhat older brother or cousin suddenly perished, for instance, from a tetanus infection, it was "a human tragedy," for fate seemed to have played a cruel trick on a helpless child. Childhood diseases such as whooping cough,

5. Mother and child. *Source*: Ruth Bulwin, *Spätes Echo*.

scarlet fever, measles, and diphtheria were therefore major trials that upset an entire household, requiring a physician's costly diagnosis, the purchase of medicine from an apothecary, and a lengthy bed rest. After a particularly difficult double pneumonia, one relieved mother told her convalescent son, "It is a miracle that you are still alive."[11]

Usually mother was the center of the childhood universe, as in most families she was "fully responsible for the children and the household." Chemist Heinz Schultheis remembered that, without modern appliances, women had to make virtually everything themselves; therefore the "work-worn mother's hands" could never rest. Laundry was done on the "great wash day" once a month, with every item boiled, wrung out, and hung up to dry before being folded and locked away. Moreover, "pieces of clothing were made within one's four walls," requiring elaborate sewing and mending. At the same time, shopping in little specialty stores and at the weekly farmer's market involved time-consuming haggling over price and bagging by hand. Food was mostly prepared from scratch with recipes guarded or shared like secrets. Toddlers would often tag along when older girls were recruited to do menial household tasks.[12]

Most fathers, by contrast, appeared distant because they had little contact with infants. Their "authority was unquestioned," even if no longer draconian. Due to the gendered division of labor, men were the breadwinners of the family, bestowing their titles upon their wives, who liked to be called *Frau Doktor*, even if they were not themselves physicians. Because fathers were away at work all day, they saw their offspring only in the evening or on weekends, therefore projecting merely a shadowy presence. In most families, the paterfamilias was responsible for maintaining authoritarian discipline, often meting out physical punishment in order to instill social rules and toughen children up for life. But there were also increasing instances of loving concern when fathers helped their children "to learn swimming and biking," which created an affective bond.[13] With increasing maturity, many children began to admire their father's professional achievements as well as their moral authority in times of crisis.

Siblings, the first playmates from whom infants could learn or whom they could boss around, were also crucial influences on early childhood. In large families such as the Krapfs, who had five children, the order of birth determined the role within the group, the specialization of talents, and the assignment of household tasks. While single children were often lonely and spoiled, in bigger households there was much competition for attention from parents, but also considerable freedom, since the adults could not keep track of each infant.[14] A boy's older brother might serve as a role model to be emulated in scholastic success, sports attainment, and the like. If a girl had a little sister, she could mother, protect, and amuse her, learning those female skills that might help in later life.[15] Although a large age gap or gender difference often estranged siblings, early childhood closeness created emotional bonds that lasted for a lifetime.

If a mother was working or busy in society, a nanny would take her place. Named Anni, Emmi, or Kathi, these nurserymaids were usually poor girls from the countryside, sent into the city in order to stretch their parents' budget and learn bourgeois manners. Even middle-class families could afford a girl to take care of feeding, washing, and supervising their small children, thereby relieving the mistress of routine tasks. Nurserymaids played with their charges, read stories to them, and took them for walks to playgrounds and parks. But, by talking about their privation, nannies also taught them what it was like to live in less-favored homes. Engineer Paul Frenzel recalled that "everything that a boy of six or seven years needs in love and education . . . I did not receive from my parents, but from a nurserymaid from Upper Bavaria." Children were often more attached to their maids than to their distant mothers. Only a few children, such as Edith Schöffski or Ursula Mahlendorf, were sent to a *Kindergarten*.[16]

When neither mothers nor nannies were available, networks of relatives and friends had to care for neglected infants, often replacing the parents in every respect. Not just a destination for summer vacations, grandparents were recruited as temporary or sometimes longer-range substitutes, especially if they lived in the countryside in their own houses with gardens. Single children such as Ruth Bulwin felt welcome and protected, because *Oma* and *Opa* spoiled them and patiently explained the rudiments of gardening, home repairs, and other tasks. Other favorites were unmarried aunts, like distant relative Didi who "took over" little Tom Angress, "telling me stories, singing me songs . . . and teaching me very early not to be a crybaby." In rural or artisan families, children were expected to contribute by doing whatever chores they were capable of completing.[17] Generally, there was a host of cousins and friends who could serve as an informal support structure in helping children to come to terms with the demands of the adult world.

The formative environment was the family home, whose size and location depended upon the father's earning power. Upper-class families like the Kleins could afford "a splendid apartment" in Berlin where there were numerous rooms for social representation and daily living. The ample space for a separate "children's room" afforded their offspring "a well-cared for childhood as a son 'from a good family.' "[18] Other middle-class families owned their own abodes: "the cozy old house" of a fur dealer, the sprawling parsonage of a pastor, or the sturdy farmhouse of a Prussian peasant. Individual homes such as the Andrées' forester's house in the East provided a sense of security, allowing children both "care and protection" and "endless freedom" to explore the woods. Building one's own house was therefore an aspiration of many *Bürger*, since one's own four walls provided social recognition and shelter for the children.[19]

In poorer families, the cramped abode was a constant source of irritation as lack of space pitted members against each other. Lower-middle-class households tended to live in apartment buildings, Wilhelmine monstrosities with medieval-style fronts, turrets, and balconies. But children could turn the dank interior courts into adventure spaces with their ingenious games. Proletarian families like the Härtels were condemned to miniscule apartments, often in the cellar, or to a single room in a garret, in which eating, sleeping, and plain living had to take place all at the same time. The lack of privacy in enforced closeness frayed people's nerves. Children and adults had to share beds and use communal toilets in the stairwell. Moreover, everyone had to tiptoe when a tired father returned from his shift, while mothers often had to take in washing or mending to supplement a meager income. This was a tough environment for children who had to struggle to have their most elementary needs fulfilled.[20]

Gardens were a refuge from city life, a source of supplemental food, and a place of wondrous discovery for the fortunate children who had access to them. While upper-class families often had the use of green space behind their impressive city apartments, middle-class homeowners tended to possess sufficient land for aesthetic and practical uses. Lower-middle-class and proletarian families like the Schöffskis therefore strove to rent a garden plot with a bower as a form of recreation and sociability. Daughter Edith later wrote, "This plot was the dream of my parents." In these "allotment gardens," people would grow a mixture of flowers, fruits, and vegetables, such as roses, strawberries, and potatoes. The children were able to play in the area as long as they did not damage crops or fruit trees such as cherries, apples, or pears, from which they could eat their fill. Especially during hard times such as war and depression, these gardens were an essential source of food.[21]

Bringing together all members of the household, meals such as noonday dinner "were veritable fora of daily happenings and concerns." After the family said grace, eating would begin, with father receiving the best cut of meat and mother sometimes sacrificing part of her own portion to make sure that her favorites would get enough. Children had to learn to behave, for "decent table manners [were] subject to special parental scrutiny," with infractions often punished by a quick box on the ears. As long as they showed sufficient respect, the young were allowed to participate in adult conversation, which provided much "formative and invaluable substance." While upper-class children such as Horst Grothus were sometimes fed so much that they gained too much weight, earning him the nickname "fatman," many lower-class children went hungry, dreaming of what it would be like to eat "a banana or grapes."[22]

Whenever possible, children would play, showing much creativity in making up competitions and rules. These games could be as simple as hopscotch on the sidewalk or as elaborate as board games such as checkers. Boys preferred playing with technical toys such as "Märklin erector sets or wind up trains" and tested their skill by spinning tops, flying kites, or shooting marbles. Girls were expected to play with dolls in elaborate houses. Erika Taubhorn recalled, "I liked to play mother and child alone. My seven large dolls were the children. I also really cooked on my small stove. In the closets hung clothes for dressing; the stool was the table. There was also a little bed and a stroller for dolls." While girls recited poems, put on charades, and wrote in their albums, boys roughhoused by playing "cowboys and Indians" or kicking a soccer ball.[23] Even if the number of toys was limited, these elaborate games showed a great capacity for creating happiness without much expense.

The high points of the year were religious holidays such as Christmas, which evoked "the warmest feelings" even in secular families. The sense of anticipation began with an advent calendar with windows for each day, as well as with the construction of the advent wreath with four red candles to be lit on successive Sundays. On December 6, St. Nicholas arrived to determine whether "kids were good or kids were bad," rewarding or punishing them accordingly. Excitement grew with the church service on Christmas Eve, often livened up by a nativity play with children as angels and shepherds. After dinner, the parlor door would finally be opened to display a dazzling spruce tree with colorful ornaments, tinsel, and burning candles. Only after singing "Silent Night" were the children allowed to open their presents—usually a mixture of wished-for items such as a new sled and practical things like woolen stockings, a "cap or gloves."[24] Christmas customs were so pervasive that even some Jewish families began to adopt them.

Vacations were another favorite time, because they interrupted the daily routines by offering new experiences. Even poor children, such as Karl Härtel, could play in an allotment garden, learn to swim in a local river, or go hiking. The somewhat better-off children, such as Ruth Bulwin, were able to take the train from Berlin to the Thuringian Forest, visiting their grandparents and sampling life in the countryside with its healthy air, fresh food, and interesting farm animals. Even wealthier sons, such as Paul Frenzel, would actually go to the Baltic Sea and live in a fancy spa hotel, build elaborate sand castles, splash in the surf with friends, or hide from the wind in a wicker beach chair. Their mothers would show off their finery at teatime and their fathers would join them on the weekend. Children of the elite, such as the Eycks, "often traveled as a family, frequently abroad, to the Netherlands or Switzerland" and so gained a cosmopolitan flair.[25]

The "golden middle years" of the Weimar Republic, between hyperinflation and depression, are therefore remembered as allowing most children to have "a happy, sheltered childhood." The chaotic beginning of civil war was safely past. The economic and political disasters were yet to come. No doubt, widespread poverty, religious prejudice, and nationalist hatred were rather aggravating and made politics contentious for their parents. But compared with the later suffering, this period permitted a relatively stable life, focused on personal concerns that made childhood "idyllic" in retrospect. With "loving and stimulating parents" as well as compatible siblings, even Jewish Germans could "form a closely knit family" that looked with confidence into the future.[26] This upbringing created strong bonds with other family members, durable ties to one's hometown, and lasting identification with German culture that would be severely tested in the years ahead.

THE CHALLENGE OF SCHOOL

Entry into primary school was "a deep caesura" that marked "a new and very important stage of life" for a child. Due to the heritage of the Reformation, German states had already in the eighteenth century developed a sys-

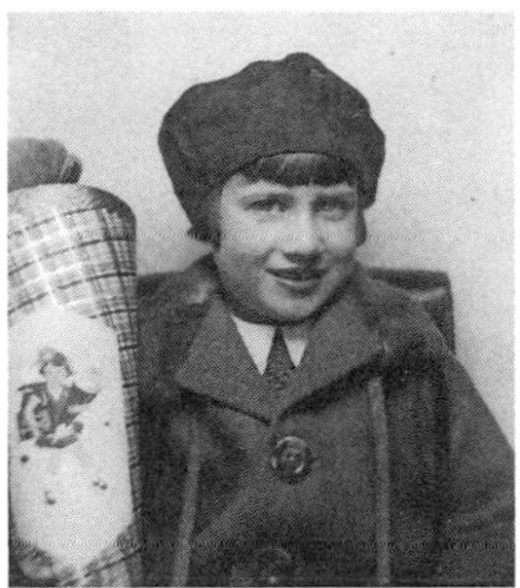

6. Shy first-grader. *Source*: Ruth Bulwin, *Spätes Echo*.

tem of compulsory primary education for the sake of enabling the faithful to read the Bible in the vernacular. In order not to overburden their mental capacity, pupils were required to attend instruction only during the morning, returning home for dinner at noon and enjoying ample time to play during the rest of the day.[27] Due to the cautionary stories of older siblings and friends, the children looked forward with a mixture of eagerness and fear to their first day in an institution that would mark them for life. In order to ease the transition, parents customarily gave anxious sons and daughters such as Ruth Bulwin a surprise cone, filled with sweets and school supplies (image 6). Thus mollified, the beginners would trudge off to the forbidding schoolhouse, carrying leather satchels on their small backs.

Pupils experienced the whole gamut of primary teachers, ranging from kind and helpful pedagogues to rigid and authoritarian disciplinarians. During the Empire, most instructors were men, but during the Weimar Republic, women made inroads, especially in the lower grades. Most teachers focused their efforts on developing skills such as the multiplication tables, imparting information such as the names of the Prussian kings, or stimulating the mind by, for example, discussing poetry.[28] By and large, the teaching methods were still frontal, stressing rote memory and repetition, but there were also "young and modern" instructors who experimented with more informal techniques of progressive education. If a child was lucky, he or she could have a nice teacher who was interested in developing "love of learning," but there were also many nasty classroom tyrants who enjoyed their power. In contrast to some pupils' claims of suffering in school, many others "actually liked it pretty well the entire time."[29]

Classes were large, with forty to fifty children, often segregated by gender, making discipline hard to maintain for so many wandering minds and restless bodies. Some inspired teachers managed to hold their pupils' attention by using novel methods such as impersonations of historical figures in order to hold their interest and inspire their imaginations. But the majority used corporal punishment at every occasion, believing the Greek adage "A man who is not beaten, is not being educated." Erika Taubhorn remembered that "the boys had to bend over and got two or three strokes with the cane on their bottom. The girls had to stretch out the arms and hands, and the teacher hit them two to three times on the hands and fingertips." Nonetheless, most of the institutions were "not barbaric beating-schools" and children expected to be chastised for misbehavior, since "discipline and order were emphasized." In fact, many pupils became successful "doctors, lawyers, or scientists" without being permanently traumatized.[30]

The key instructional medium was a black slate with a wooden edge, a stylus for writing, and a sponge or rag for erasing mistakes. "On one side there were lines for lettering, and on the other boxes for computation," Erika Taubhorn recalled. Children carried their slates to and from school carefully, because they would break if dropped. Learning penmanship was preceded by pictorial examples, such as drawing a big Easter egg on the slate to indicate the letter "O," the start of the German word *Osterei*. Figuring required rote memorization of multiplication tables, which were then recited collectively forward and backward.[31] The teacher would stand in front of the class, drawing on a big blackboard. However, turning his back invited pranks such as spitballs. If he had a sense of humor, the pedagogue could retaliate by squeezing a wet sponge over a pupil's head. Teachers also worked with maps and charts, and enlivened their instruction with stories.

Until the late 1920s "school still seemed to be a space free of politics." Hans Queiser, who grew up in the Palatinate, remembered that "whatever remotely had to do with politics remained outside; hidden or open religious or political indoctrination did not appear during instruction." The only image on the wall was of the ancient President Hindenburg, while local studies concerned merely the history and geography of the broader region. Most of the teachers in Protestant areas were liberal or democratic; in Catholic regions, they supported the Center Party. But this apolitical approach "had unintended consequences: Outside of school the children were vulnerable to the increasing nationalist influences" because they lacked "any preparation or personal judgment" in dealing with controversial issues. When the first political slogans entered the world of the children during the Depression, "they were apparently normal national tones" such as pride in "high achievements in athletics and technology."[32] Ironically, the neutrality of the teachers who defended the Republic left the door open to nationalist agitation.

Finding a place within the class community was not always easy, especially if a child had transferred from out of town or stood out otherwise. One problem was "the social dividing line" between well-to-do and poor pupils, who tended to congregate according to their status rather than crossing class barriers. Ursula Mahlendorf recalled that wealthy children had fancy clothes and spending money, while their poorer classmates were often dirty and lice-infested. Boys, especially, could be quite cruel and make school "almost an ordeal" by picking on spoiled brats for their superior speech and better clothes. Only when Paul Frenzel plucked up his courage and hit a bigger bully back, knocking him over, did "no boy any longer dare to taunt or beat me."[33] Girls, by contrast, tended to be more cliquish, making it important to find a friend to sit next to in order to belong. Classmates also inspired pranks, as when boys threw a folding ladder from a woodpile or girls slid on their satchels down a hill, which resulted in a stern reprimand.[34]

With shared interests, school acquaintances could develop into lifelong friendships that weathered dictatorships and war. Girls tended to share their thoughts and feelings with each other. In her private school, Gisela Grothus met the daughter of a Protestant family of Jewish extraction: "In this manner I gained my first close school-friendship with 'Marthchen' and often played with her." The later bond with another girl as "friends of the heart" lasted an entire lifetime as well. Boys looked more for "buddyship" to do things together or for role models whom they could idolize. The young Jew Werner Warmbrunn first befriended a "blond, athletic . . . leader of the neighborhood gang" and then later admired a "free-spirit" who, as the scion of a noble Nazi family, "cared little of what others thought of him and his actions." Crossing social boundaries, such youthful friendships expanded horizons and proved essential help in growing up.[35]

During the Weimar Republic, most boys and girls were still sent to single-sex institutions, reinforcing the creation of separate gender roles at an early age. While for little children this separation hardly made a difference, for adolescents it was supposed to keep the problems of awakening sexuality out of the classroom. On the one hand, males were supposed to be toughened up in order to become men, ignoring the pain of cuts or bruises according to the adage "A German boy does not cry." On the other, girls had a less demanding academic curriculum, learning instead their roles as future homemakers with classes in sewing, cooking, and the like. Ironically, the sexual segregation created homoerotic friendships, especially evident in boys who were physically attracted to each other in sports or other settings. As a result of being separated, both sexes had some difficulty understanding the other when school segregation could no longer keep them apart and first crushes developed.[36]

At the age of ten, children were faced with a crucial decision—which type of education to pursue beyond the fourth grade. In spite of some minor reforms, parents had to choose from among the three-tiered school system inherited from the Empire. For their child to gain access to the higher professions, he or she had to attend the rather selective *Gymnasium*, a Latin-, modern language–, or science-based high school. If the parents wanted to prepare their children for commercial white-collar pursuits, they tended to pick the less prestigious *Realschule*, a modern-language secondary school. If they aimed only for blue-collar work, their sons and daughters would continue in the *Volksschule*, a modest but free primary school. The choice depended not just upon the feared report card, but also on the family's social aspirations and financial resources. Karl Härtel recalled, "As child of impoverished parents, the possibility of entering a Gymnasium was blocked for me because the monthly tuition of 25 Reichsmark was just not available."[37]

The few pupils fortunate enough to enter a Gymnasium approached the venerable institution with "some palpitations." First, they had to pass a strict entrance examination consisting of an essay and math problems. Then they confronted a demanding curriculum based on Latin, Greek, or modern languages and complemented by natural science classes. Though the teaching methods were often as antiquated as the buildings, the content followed the neohumanist approach to the classics that created a peculiar blend of enthusiasm for antiquity and individual cultivation, called *Bildung*. Somewhat overwhelmed, many boys dropped out because they were unable or unwilling to cope with these challenges. But those like Hans Tausch who had "a good memory and could listen well" were able "to cope surprisingly well."[38] Since the Gymnasium was the gateway to an upper-class future, most pupils endured, even if they resented its demands. Girls usually enrolled in easier high schools that did not prepare them for study at a university.

Less ambitious children tended to choose the Realschule, which had a more modern curriculum but still offered access to middle-class careers. Instead of nine years as in the Gymnasium, this school required only six years of instruction, usually followed by some white-collar training. Because its teaching was oriented toward English and French plus mathematics, many bourgeois parents considered it more practical and pupils understood its occupational relevance more directly. As a result, they met academic requirements more easily, even if performance might vary from a "blue letter" warning of impending failure to the "pleasant surprise" of a more positive report card. When Paul Frenzel turned out to be the second-best in the class, his father immediately suggested additional training in hotel management, which his son stoutly rejected. Attendance at the Realschule was therefore usually "without problems."[39]

The majority of children remained in the Volksschule, a primary school that focused on basic instruction. In contrast to the higher schools, this institution offered only four additional grades until the age of fourteen. Its curriculum centered on learning high German, writing a neat hand, learning about the region, and doing simple math problems. After graduation, most children entered an apprenticeship for a trade, complemented by occupational instruction one day a week in a vocational *Berufsschule*. During the Weimar Republic, reforms opened the door a small crack to further instruction via "accelerated classes" for exceptional individuals. Often, families chose not to send girls to a Gymnasium because of its fees, making Ursula Baehrenburg cry when her dream of further learning was denied. More resilient characters such as Karl Härtel nonetheless profited sufficiently from primary schooling to train in engineering by showing practical aptitude in their craft.[40]

The values that these schools inculcated in their students were fundamentally ambivalent, blending a humanist sensibility with a nationalist orientation. The teaching of German often centered on the classics, memorizing epic poems such as Schiller's *Die Glocke* or discussing plays such as Goethe's *Faust*, even if many pupils hardly understood their messages. Moreover, religious instruction was part of the regular curriculum, transmitting Protestant, Catholic, or Jewish moral imperatives, depending upon the orientation of the school. At the same time, the foreign language teaching of the high schools did open windows onto not only classical antiquity, but also different contemporary cultures through the reading of Shakespeare or Molière. Nonetheless, there was a strong patriotic strain that emphasized the superiority of German *Kultur* when reciting romantic poetry or singing patriotic songs such as "Die Wacht am Rhein" on national holidays.[41]

The poisonous legacy of the lost First World War turned such pride into a noxious nationalism that made children vulnerable to extremist messages. Eva Sternheim-Peters recalled that the young encountered the debris of the Great War even in their homes, where picture postcards of foreign places, "letters from the front," photos of uniformed family members, medals for exceptional valor, and even pieces of uniform recalled a heroic struggle. In geography class, the wall maps still contained "the lost territories" and former colonies of the Reich after the "shameful peace of Versailles," instilling resentment. In history, the "stab-in-the-back legend" claimed that the German Army had not been defeated on the battlefield but betrayed by "November criminals" at home and then subjected to a "war guilt lie" from abroad. Even if moderate Social Democrats pleaded for peaceful understanding, many children developed a "sense of offended innocence" in their patriotic commitment.[42]

The transition to schooling therefore proved to be a mixed blessing for those born in the Weimar Republic. Contradicting the literary cliché of suffering in school, there were quite a few kind teachers who made the experience more positive, inducing many memoirists to confess that "I enjoyed school and was quite good at it." The three-tiered institutions provided children with the basic skills for life, allowing many of them to progress into successful careers. But in spite of reform efforts by progressive pedagogues, Weimar schools were still largely authoritarian institutions that instilled obedience, which hindered the free development of even those who "tried to be a good pupil."[43] In many institutions, the legacy of the lost war transformed love of country into a dangerous nationalism, warping young minds. Because they provided all too few ethical grounds for a cosmopolitan humanism, the schools left most of their pupils at the mercy of National Socialist appeals.

THE LURE OF NEIGHBORHOOD

As they grow older, children gradually began to leave the safety of their own homes and explore their immediate environment. Because at this time primary school was rarely nearby, even small pupils had to walk there, often dawdling, looking into shop windows, or gawking at dogs and birds that caught their attention. When they were late, they were inevitably reprimanded to teach them the importance of punctuality. In the countryside, Horst Andrée found walking to school a real adventure when a "mean gander" or a "beast" of a dog from a neighboring farm terrorized him. When their high school was in a neighboring town, older *Fahrschüler* such as Erich Helmer had to take the train, which allowed them to chat, play games, or do belated homework on the way.[44] While getting to school could be a real nuisance in pouring rain or deep snow, these pupils began to develop a sense of independence by commuting on their own.

During the afternoon when homework was done or parents were busy, children ventured into the neighborhood to discover its many secrets for

7. Vacation at the Baltic Sea. *Source*: Gisela Grothus, "Mein Leben."

themselves. On the farm, there were animals, implements, and crops to be investigated, or fields, meadows, and woods to be roamed unless one was assigned an important chore. In the towns, first the adjacent buildings and eventually entire quarters could be explored. For instance, the old center of Giessen had an "almost medieval warren" of half-timbered buildings lining cobblestone streets. Heinz Schultheis was endlessly fascinated by the small shops with their enticing smells and colorful sights. He loved to wander around the market, marvel at the medieval city hall, and climb the tower of the cathedral to have a look from above. This "small world of childhood" provided a sense of safety and stimulated the imagination when technical marvels such as an airplane or a zeppelin paid a visit.[45]

In a big city such as Breslau or a metropolis like Berlin, there were more fascinating distractions but also real dangers for children testing their independence. Organ grinders with their monkeys would regularly visit the dank courts of tenements, playing doleful tunes to collect a few coins. Or impudent urchins would ring apartment doorbells so that the concierges would chase them. There were parks to be visited, playgrounds to be explored, and open-air concerts to be attended on Sunday. In December Christmas markets with spice cake and mulled wine beckoned. New Year's Eve was punctuated by fireworks. With art museums and technical exhibitions providing special child rates, there was always something to be visited. But concerned mothers warned their daughters "not to go to the door if someone rang or knocked," since beggars might be criminals.[46] When on their own, children had to learn not to trust strangers and to keep out of harm's way.

Growing up also involved meeting other adults who could help their development when they showed real sympathy for children. Some encounters were pleasant, such as "a great friendship with a neighbor family," which provided sociability on long winter evenings of roasting apples or playing cards. Others were scarier, such as errands to fetch a missing spice for mother in a grocery store, which involved overcoming shyness and dealing with money. For Gerhard Krapf, even dreaded music lessons could turn into the opposite: a kind teacher did an "excellent job of initiating [him] into the business of music making" so that he enjoyed it tremendously. When Erich Helmer met a neighbor who was a skilled shoemaker, he was inspired by the man's "respect for his craft and regard for ordinary men."[47] While authoritarian adults could strike fear into children's hearts, more positive contacts inspired deep friendships that created trust in the outside world.

Through comparisons of their own situation with those of their friends, children gradually became aware of the social class that set their family apart. Especially in poor circles, life was a daily struggle to make meager pay stretch enough to cover necessities until the end of the month. Whenever a child craved a treat, the first question was "Do we have any money" to pay for it? Even in middle-class families, financial limits were a constant bone of contention, when a husband drank his pay away or a wife "went on a buying spree" before a vacation, acquiring "a whole collection of summer dresses." Upper-class sons like Tom Angress realized social distinctions when he tried to invite a classmate to his home who was not listed in the phone book; the boy's parents "were poor and couldn't afford a telephone."[48] While he was willing to ignore class lines, the awkwardness of the ensuing birthday party made it clear to him that such barriers were all too real.

Growing children also made contacts with their peers, gradually shifting their attention from their siblings to their own age group. Often inspired by acquaintances in school, such encounters ranged from playing impromptu street games to close friendships that might last an entire lifetime. Chatting about clothes or giggling at jokes, girls tended to express emotions in elaborate diaries (*Poesiealben*) in which they wrote verses to assure each other of undying amity. More inclined to roughhouse, boys often engaged in pranks that created bonds between them or shared technical interests such as experimenting with chemistry sets. Being invited to the homes of friends for parties also opened the door to lifestyles of different social strata. Children's horizons expanded even further if they were taken along during holidays to the mountains or the shore as documented in Gisela Grothus's vacation picture (image 7). Such "almost symbiotic friendships" provided boys and girls with diversion from schoolwork and support when picked on by bullies.[49]

Weimar children were especially impressed by technological innovations such as railroad trains, wireless radios, and movie theaters, which embodied the future. Young Erich Helmer was quite excited to ride the streetcar with his father across town to the train station, where "from afar, I saw the locomotive coming closer with much steam," seeming like an unstoppable monster. Benno Schöffski was excited by the purchase of a radio, which required stringing an antenna and assembling the "small receiver set." Hoping to hear "the first music from the headphones was a tremendous anticipation and joy." As a reward for his improving grades, Karl Härtel was pleased to "be allowed to go to the movies with his mother on a rainy summer day" to see a film about skiing called *The White Dream*.[50] Such amazing experiences left a deep imprint on growing minds, suggesting that technology had an unlimited potential to improve living conditions.

Sports also played an increasing role in older children's lives, promoting both individual pride and group cohesion. Educators promoted team sports to develop the body and teach sportsmanship. For some children, physical education in school was a real trial; only a few, such as Tom Angress, were able to master difficult gymnastic exercises. More popular were swimming lessons, since they led to summer fun in pools or rivers or at the shore, even if not everyone became a club champion like Paul Frenzel. Upper-class children were expected to ride horseback, play tennis, or sail, although some, like Horst Grothus, "found riding not nice at all."[51] Lower-class boys would kick a soccer ball around on informal playgrounds without joining a sports club. Most families took their offspring hiking on weekends in the surrounding countryside or in the mountains during vacations because such outings cost little, if anything.

For older children, membership in a youth group became a way to organize their ample free time and meet with their peers. During the Empire, conservative circles who were worried about the radicalization of working-class youths had created organizations to reinforce a patriotic outlook. During the Weimar Republic, some middle-class girls such as Eva Peters joined the "German national" Queen Louise League, while her brothers became members of the militaristic nationalist "Scharnhorst Youth." Gerhard Krapf and other religious youths instead chose the Christian Association of Young Men, a Protestant counterpart of the YMCA. Heinz Schultheis was interested in the Catholic branch of the Boy Scouts, imported from Great Britain. The key weakness of these religious or political organizations was that they were "not a 'real' youth group" because "they were not led by young leaders," but rather controlled by adults.[52]

By contrast, the Youth Movement prided itself on creating autonomous spaces with "youth being led by youth." Founded by progressive teachers in Berlin around the turn of the twentieth century, this *Jugendbewegung* was a diffuse expression of rebellion against adults that rejected the Wilhelmine lifestyle of smoking and drinking as decadent. During the 1920s, this self-organization was called *Die Freischar* and included a loose conglomeration of youth leagues of the *Bündische Jugend.* Attracted by the weekly meetings and especially by the weekend trips, Paul Frenzel joined the group because it promised a self-determined life. With the uniform of a "blue-grey shirt with a black bandana and grey shorts," the Freischar was attractive because of its members' belief in comradeship and claim to be a self-chosen elite. This Youth Movement embodied a romantic quest for adventure with its nature hikes, folk songs, and campfire conviviality. Many youths, such as Will Seelmann-Eggebert, were "decisively shaped" by it.[53]

These happy childhood years began to peter out with the Great Depression of October 1929, which threatened the survival of many families. With some delay, the Wall Street crash also came to Central Europe when short-term US loans were recalled. This bankrupted many a German business, such as the plumbing shop of the Mahlendorf family. Children felt its effect as the tightening of the family budget created disputes between their parents and forced them to spend vacations with their relatives. If one's father was one of the six million unemployed, even food became scarce, for "conditions were bad [and] regular work was impossible to get." To compensate, one's mother might seek a job in a clothing store or hire herself out for housecleaning or washing of clothes. When the enormous out-of-work numbers overwhelmed the unemployment insurance system, jobless men were forced to go begging or "fall back on crisis and welfare charity." For the unemployed, the result was "hunger and cold, growing pauperization and hopeless, dull despair."[54]

The "economic problems and human distress" radicalized politics, heightening hostile emotions and triggering physical violence. Due to the "atmosphere of embittered passion," some children began to notice heated discussions in their families between adherents of President Paul von Hindenburg, Nazi leader Adolf Hitler, and Communist stalwart Teddy Thälmann. Others overheard "martial speech fragments" on the radio or the street, as well as "rhythmic chants and songs, the thudding of running feet, wild shouts and sometimes even the sirens of the police." During the many "parades and torchlight processions of the NS stormtroopers (SA) and the Communists," children "were encouraged to shout 'Heil Hitler' or 'Heil Moskau.'" Moreover, in bloody "beer hall battles" or street fights, Leftist militias such as the Reichsbanner and Rote Frontkämpferbund clashed with paramilitary groups of the Right such as the Stahlhelm and the Nazis. Though rarely understanding what the struggles were all about, many of the young were impressed by the songs and actions of the Nazi SA and SS because they were "the loudest and most militant."[55]

This polarization also triggered an ugly wave of anti-Semitism, which blamed the Jews for the nation's general misery. During the nineteenth century, right-wing agitators had turned religious prejudice into a quasi-scientific form of racism from which there was no escape by conversion.

Even in assimilated Jewish households such as the Eycks', children became aware of being somehow "different" from others without quite knowing why. When Tom Angress changed schools in Berlin, he had to register his religious affiliation as the "mosaic" confession, marking him as a member of a minority. Although decent classmates maintained their friendships, others began to pick on him: "This was, for me, the beginning of four years of gradual isolation, occasional hostilities, and almost daily small (and sometimes not so small) humiliations."[56] These radical racists were seeking to undo a century of Jewish acculturation to secular German culture.

The chaotic final years of the Weimar Republic politicized children who had been born in the early 1920s by forcing them to take an ideological stand. Catholic and Social Democratic youths could cling to their prior beliefs, but sons or daughters of liberal families, such as Fritz Klein, found themselves adrift due to the crumbling of middle-class democratic parties. Protestant nationalists such as Gerhard Krapf were able to rally behind the imposing figure of President Hindenburg as a guarantor of order and respectability. But if a father was an unemployed worker such as Hans Schirmer, whom "despair and anger" had made a Communist activist, his son might fail to understand the reasons for such radicalism. Ruth Bulwin was even more surprised when "one day father was wearing a brown uniform and was called party comrade which I could not comprehend."[57] The collapse of the Republic drew children into political struggles before they were ready to cope with them.

A HAPPY CHILDHOOD

The overthrow of the Weimar Republic largely dispelled "the carefree atmosphere of childhood." Over seventy years later, Frank Eyck recalled that his "happy, sheltered childhood ended abruptly on the 30th January 1933 with Adolf Hitler's and the Nazis' ascent to power." Twelve-year-old Tom Angress at first thought, "Wow, this will be interesting!" But cracking jokes about Hitler running around the chancellery in search of a "government program" failed to do justice to the gravity of the change. "The next day when I entered the classroom, I immediately felt the tension in the air."[58]

Now Jews, Communists, and intellectuals could be persecuted with impunity, for the radical Right controlled the police and the courts. While life for the smaller children continued largely as before, the older ones now had to decide how to react. Not surprisingly, the vast majority were swept up in the propaganda-fed enthusiasm of the "national revolution."

The autobiographies claim that, compared with World War I suffering and the subsequent dictatorial repression, "those years, just before Hitler came to power, were happy for us children." In spite of the initial chaos and the final economic downturn, they remembered the Weimar Republic as having offered a civil space in which most families could provide a sheltered childhood for their offspring. Even if the working poor were struggling to obtain a minimum of food and shelter, they described their homes as stable places in which affectionate relationships flourished and infants could play with each other in peace. While corporal punishment was used to maintain discipline, schools did teach the classics and sciences in a competent fashion, giving children the tools to succeed. Moreover, streets and neighborhoods were still safe enough to let youths explore the world around them. Ruth Weigelt confirmed such positive recollections: "Hitherto I had a beautiful early childhood with neither sorrows nor cares."[59] All of this ended when the Nazis, in the name of saving the nation, imposed their radical ideology.

Only a minority of the children regretted the passing of the first German democracy, and even these failed to grasp its deadly implications. Though she was "politically disinterested," the rebellious Gisela Grothus proudly "considered [her]self a Republican in [her]family." Few of the boys were as politically aware as Tom Angress, whose Catholic friend Lorenz "snapped to attention, raised his hand in the Hitler salute and called out, 'Wake up Germany, Hitler is making coffee!' " During the 1930 campaign, both youths went around "to remove NSDAP stickers from the house walls" that supported Hitler's election. Around the same time, they called the editor of the Nazi newspaper *Der Angriff* and shouted obscenities into the telephone. At the other political extreme, Fritz Klein "hung the black-white-red flag out of the window" to demonstrate his imperial sympathies. Of course, those sporadic juvenile protests failed to stop the Nazi tide.[60]

In retrospect, the vast majority of the Weimar children hardly noticed the Nazi seizure of power, because they were too young to be interested in politics. Karl Härtel recalled that "we ordinary people only found out from the newspaper that a certain Adolf Hitler, the leader of the National Socialist German Workers Party (NSDAP), was named the twenty-first Chancellor by our aged, popularly elected President Paul von Hindenburg." Somewhat apologetically, he explained: "In 1932 I was only in my tenth year and knew about politics almost as much as a fish about flying." Similarly, Hellmut Raschdorff remembered that "in 1933 we experienced the so-called seizure of power, which was to bring untold changes that were only feared by a few. In our daily routine at school hardly anything changed" except for having to memorize a few new dates and collect money for NS charity. Only gradually did most youths begin to realize that "a terrible time [had begun] when the Nazis gained power."[61]

Many of the memoirists still struggle to explain their own response to the beginning of the Third Reich. Some apologists such as Karl Härtel resented "the accusations of especially younger people" born after World War II that "it was their generation that was responsible for Hitler having been able to precipitate half of the world into misfortune." Instead, they blamed the victors of World War I for the lack of peace that enabled political dilettantes such as the Nazis to seize power. More self-critical spirits such as Heinz Schultheis cited insufficient age as a reason for their complicity: "For us children these circumstances were an unchangeable condition whose importance we completely failed to recognize; and especially because of that our generation automatically grew into the damned 'Third Reich.' "[62] Ironically, it was therefore their sunny Weimar childhoods that left most of these young Germans unprepared to resist the Nazis' siren calls.

3

NAZI ADOLESCENTS

Many nationalists were elated when President Hindenburg appointed Hitler as chancellor on January 30, 1933. But leftists already had a dark sense of foreboding about the Nazi seizure of power. On hearing the news, six-year-old Eka Assmus shouted excitedly, "Now it's the turn of uncle Hans' *Führer*." As an SS member, her relative was already preparing for a torchlight parade to celebrate the victory, while a neighbor woman hurried to fly the swastika flag. Another "old fighter" was so overjoyed that his "enthusiasm brought tears to his eyes. Was this the new savior?" But in Leipzig, two young Communists "were surprised to see countless Nazis march by in endless columns." Although they expected a call for violent resistance, "nobody came, nothing happened." The young Jew Frank Eyck felt instinctively that from that day onward "my parents could no longer protect me. The carefree atmosphere of childhood had gone. Nothing could be taken for granted" any more.[1]

The subsequent Nazification of most German youths was no accident, but the result of a deliberate policy of the NSDAP. Proclaiming "whoever has the youth, has the future," Hitler himself placed a high value on the younger generation as the vanguard of the Third Reich, since many adults were too set in their ways to embrace National Socialism completely. The party youth organization, called the *Hitlerjugend* (HJ or Hitler Youth), was therefore an essential tool for indoctrinating the young and forging the next generation of Nazi leaders, who would be even more committed to implementing the murky ideological aims of the movement. The HJ's martial hymn appealed to youthful idealism by suggesting that it was the task of the young to restore the country's unity and greatness: "Forward! Forward! Blare the bright fanfares / Forward! Forward! Youth knows no fear / Germany shall stand radiant / Even if we fall."[2]

Nazism appealed especially to adolescents during their complicated passage from childhood into adulthood. In earlier centuries the transition, marked by religious rites such as confirmation, had been abrupt: as soon as a teenager entered the working world, he was considered grown up. But around the turn of the twentieth century, psychologists such as G. Stanley Hall and playwrights such as Frank Wedekind "discovered adolescence" as an extended life stage between childhood and adulthood.[3] In this transformation, young people were supposed to construct an independent self, separate from their parents, and reorient themselves toward their peers. The Hitler Youth addressed all of these needs, giving the young a mission of their own, setting them apart from the home, and offering them companionship in their own age group. A psychohistorical analysis of the postwar cohort suggests that the Weimar children were quite vulnerable to this appeal.[4]

The sizable Hitler Youth literature written by former members therefore reflects a fundamental ambivalence about the Nazi experience. On the one hand, there are quite a few apologetic descriptions of the fun and games in the HJ. Former League of German Girls leader Eva Peters admitted, "I, too, was meant, spoken to and called upon to put my life into the service of a great and overpowering [ideal] called Germany." On the other hand, the deadly consequences of this misplaced idealism later forced her to "seek an explanation of what actually caused for [me] and many other youths of the HJ generation that 'great deception'" of believing in the Nazi message. Due to this ambivalence, the memory texts are paradoxical and unstable, drifting from evocative description of enjoyable activities to retrospective condemnation of their catastrophic effect. This mixture of emotions was particularly intense for Jewish victims such as Lucy Mandelstam, who wrote, "I feel nostalgia and sadness at the same time" for a youth cut short by ideology.[5]

The effect of the Nazification of German youth was neither as great as NS leaders claimed nor as slight as later apologists maintain. Due to the Hitler

Youth's increasing organizational monopoly, its membership was almost all-inclusive by the late 1930s. The pressure of home, school and public propaganda compelled most youths to join, unless they were excluded as leftists, Jews, or other "misfits." Their peer group also exerted such a powerful pull through friends, leisure activities, and rebellion against adults that many adolescents insisted on becoming members, studiously ignoring the reservations of their parents. But the constant repetition of slogans, paramilitary training, and endless marching also generated revulsion among some of the young, who only conformed outwardly while ignoring the ideological messages. Though capturing the majority, such compulsion and repression also galvanized opposition, undercutting the very aims the HJ sought to achieve. No matter what the response, Ruth Weigelt recalled, "The Nazis threw everything and really everything into confusion."[6]

YOUTH NAZIFICATION

The indoctrination of German youth had already begun before Hitler's seizure of power with the rapid growth of the Nazi movement. As long as the party was considered to be on the fringe, only fanatic nationalists or racists were ready to join it, and public servants were widely forbidden to become members. But unemployed men such as Ursula Mahlendorf's father increasingly became members of the SA or SS because of their camaraderie and toughness in street battles. In their uniforms, they "cut quite a dashing figure," thereby receiving the respect that they craved. After the election victories of 1930 and 1932 that made the NSDAP the strongest party, white-collar opportunists also began to enter it in droves and soon numerically overtook the hard core of the "old fighters." Moreover, firms exerted pressure on their staff members to join a Nazi organization. Hence, adolescents were increasingly confronted by a dynamic movement that promised to end the Depression, "bring order and stability," and create a better future.[7]

In many families, the rise of the Nazis created conflict. Not only Communists and Jews were horrified by its nationalist message. At holiday get-togethers, intense quarrels broke out between leftists who favored Thälmann, moderates who supported Hindenburg, and rightists who preferred

Hitler. Even if Hellmut Raschdorff did not quite understand the implications, his Catholic father predicted clairvoyantly, "When Hitler takes over, there will be war." Among the Bauckes, the revelation that the father was a NSDAP member created "a great family row." When Mrs. Baucke found the anti-Semitic journal *Der Stürmer* in the family's coffee shop, "she stormed into the study, thumped the paper on the desk and hissed 'Hugo, I won't have this trash in my house,'" reminding him how much they owed to their Jewish customers.[8] Confronted with such emotional scenes, the older children became politicized by having to choose sides.

After the actual seizure of power, the Nazis immediately displaced the Weimar elite and claimed the spoils of victory. Using the Reichstag fire on February 27, 1933 as pretext, they jailed Communists such as Ingrid Bork's great-uncle, who was rounded up while collecting money for indigent leftists and "put into a concentration camp" for a year. On April 1, 1933, NS thugs boycotted Jewish businesses, forcing them to close and turn their clients away. Although fur merchant Albert Gompertz proposed "that all Jews be granted passports to leave the country," the timid leadership of the Centralverein vetoed the idea, lest it rouse more ire. The Nazis did not even respect their nationalist allies such as the journalist Fritz Klein, who "endorsed the change of government in principle." But because he added "numerous question marks" about excessive enthusiasm, they forced him to resign as editor of the *Deutsche Allgemeine Zeitung*.[9] These actions left little doubt that the "national revolution" was creating a dictatorship.

By insisting on a series of shared rituals, the Nazis enforced an appearance of unanimous support for the Third Reich. In daily usage, "*Heil Hitler*" was supposed to replace innocuous greetings such as "good day," to show one's support for the new regime. Critics merely mumbled, joined both hellos together, or waved their arm instead of extending it. On special days, each family was also compelled to hang a swastika banner from the window to make their political approval public. Reluctant folks such as the Schöffskis, who could not completely avoid the hated ritual, showed only the smallest possible flag. Similarly, neighborhood wardens checked to be sure that every household subscribed to the party paper *Völkischer Beboachter* so as to get the official line. But they could not keep old copies from serving as toilet paper.[10] While some adolescents resented their parents' reluctance, others learned to how to appear to obey.

Known political opponents such as Social Democrats or Communists faced intimidation and violence. As long as critics were keeping their opinions to themselves, they were only passed over for promotions or transferred to less-attractive locations. But if they openly "cursed and combated the Nazis," they were "taken into 'protective custody' by notorious SA men," where they were beaten and pressed to divulge names without a court order. Early one summer morning in 1933, Hans-Harald Schirmer's father was awakened by SA thugs shouting, "Get dressed, follow us." Confused, he complied, only to be taken to the police. "In the cellar of an office building [he] was forced by torture, lack of sleep, and starvation to incriminate himself" as having plotted a coup. After a few days, he came home "with bruises, distraught and mentally absent."[11] Caught up in propaganda, many adolescents such as Benno Schöffski failed to understand why their parents resisted Nazi appeals.

In the schools, NS teachers, often wearing an SA uniform, sought to indoctrinate their pupils in nationalist and racist ideas. "Even for us children they were recognizable by their [demeanor], ranging from servile dullness to brutal fanaticism," wrote Hans Schirmer, who was appalled that "the ridiculously bragging Nazi teacher of stenography became rector in 1934 as a dedicated old fighter and party member [in spite of] his rather limited abilities." Tom Angress suffered with a history teacher who had lost a leg in the war: "Now and then he made an anti-Semitic remark that had nothing to do with what he was lecturing on at the moment." Albert Gompertz cringed when "our music teacher, who wore a Swastika button in his lapel . . . led our class in the presence of Jewish students . . . in the singing of Nazi songs, one of which had the refrain, 'When Jewish blood runs from our knives.' "[12] Such verbal abuse made Jewish pupils feel increasingly insecure.

One important part of the Nazification of the school system was the transformation of the traditional curriculum. According to Schirmer, "seen in retrospect, the teaching of history became partisan by introducing Nazi ideology almost imperceptibly." Instead of the usual recital of kings and battles, the national-political instruction tried to be cool and interesting: "The key points of the NSDAP program were the restructuring of Germany and ethnic German states into a Greater German Reich, Hitler's struggle against Bolshevik ideology, and the system of international Jewish-Zionist world capital for the sake of destabilizing and dominating Europe." In Hermann Debus's experience, "the concepts of *Führer*, *Volk* and fatherland were daily presented to us" so as to affirm "an image of Hitler's and his helpers' infallibility."[13] Confronted with such slanted instruction, most pupils could not help but absorb some of its ideological biases.

Another element of indoctrination was the introduction of new subjects such as "racial science," which taught a hierarchy of races with the Aryans on top. When an anti-Semitic chemistry teacher sought to illustrate the differences in phenotypes, he pointed to Tom Angress and announced, "This boy has a well-formed Dinaric head, just like Reich Propaganda Minister Dr. Goebbels." Since he had called the only Jewish pupil in the class an exemplary member of the Aryan race, "a burst of laughter broke out." When he was writing on the blackboard a few days later, the pupils pelted him with dried peas and chased him out of the room. Their homeroom teacher, a Nazi dandy, stormed in, foaming with rage and accusing Angress, "You of all people, YOU have to do something like that." But because the entire class owned up to the prank, he could do nothing but condemn it to three hours of detention.[14] While the claims of racial science seemed hard to believe, its slogans reinforced prejudice.

In spite of their Nazification, schools had to compete with the Hitler Youth for time and importance in training the young. Initially the introduction of the Reich Youth Day made Wednesday afternoons and Saturdays free of classes and turned them over to HJ exercises. Due to countless marches, hikes, sports events, and collection campaigns, Gerhard Krapf remembered later that pupils had little time "to learn how to read and count correctly." In 1936, the HJ Law that required all children to become members stipulated, "All of German youth must be educated beyond home and school in the Hitler Youth physically, intellectually and ethically in the spirit of National Socialism so as to serve the Volk and the national community."[15] Even if it

8. League of German Girls. *Source*: Ruth Bulwin, *Spätes Echo*.

reduced the required time, this legislation set the HJ up as coequal authority with family and school. No wonder that teachers had a hard time coping with arrogant leaders who disrupted instruction. Typical outing photos like that of Ruth Bulwin's League of German Girls group show happy youths roaming the countryside (image 8).

Confronted with propaganda demands, it was risky for administrators and teachers to defend educational standards. In Erich Helmer's Gymnasium in Braunschweig, "the majority of the teachers were politically neutral; one of them was even apparently an opponent of the new regime." Ignoring the obligatory German salutation, he demonstratively greeted the class with "good day" and captivated his pupils with imaginative role-play. At his high school in Lichterfelde, Tom Angress was fortunate to have "a straight German nationalist" as principal, because he "was fair, approachable and had a sense of humor." Other teachers who were proud professionals continued to instruct in their subject matter, although they made occasional rhetorical concessions to the reigning ideology. Even Angress's physical education teacher, a convinced SA man, was so impressed by the teenager's skill in gymnastics that he nominated him for interschool competition.[16] But to speed rearmament, the high-school curriculum was shortened by one year.

Outright opposition in the Third Reich was generally impossible, because open dissent was rigorously repressed by party zealots and servile opportunists. Already in the spring of 1933 Jews, leftists, and Republicans such as Joachim Fest's father were purged from the high-school faculty by the law misleadingly titled "for the restoration of professional public service." Only much later did Gerhard Krapf understand that in his own school, "Herr Scheuermann had been removed because he was Jewish." Other unorthodox teachers were spied upon, censored, demoted, or fired as well. Courageous instructors who dared "fulfill their pedagogical duties wisely" had to dissimulate in order "to offer other perspectives beyond the official version neutrally but interestingly" so as to inspire critical approaches. Since the great majority of the teachers conformed to Nazi ideology, "instruction in school did not offer the pupils any criteria for the distinction between humane and inhumane" actions for their later life.[17]

Increasing Nazi influence in schools isolated Jewish pupils and made them targets of abuse and discrimination. Gisela Grothus became aware of "how many Jewish students there were" in her girls' high school only when half of her classmates failed to observe the Christian holidays. German patriots like Tom Angress felt more and more awkward when having to celebrate national holidays and attend Nazi rallies in which Jews were not wanted. One older Hitler Youth named Arndte, who had already repeated two grades, began to bully him with verbal attacks such as "Wake Up Germany! Death to the Jews!" But he lost much influence when Tom beat him in a rope-climbing contest in gym. Many classmates withdrew from contact with Frank Eyck, but some decent adolescents such as Wolfgang Schmidt continued to befriend him in spite "of the political situation and the division of the German people into Aryan and non-Aryan."[18]

Faced with such ideological hostility, Jewish youths had a difficult time figuring out how to respond. If they were in a liberal institution with kind teachers and other Jewish classmates, they might hope that the entire Nazi storm would eventually blow over. But many of the excluded children "asked their parents, when seeing the marching [Hitler Youth], why they were not allowed to belong" to it. If they were physically assaulted by Nazi sympathizers, they could pluck up their courage like Tom Angress and fight back against the attacker in order to gain the respect of their classmates. When a friendship was strong enough, such as one with a squad leader of the Hitler Youth, it might continue on the basis of mutual respect. But in the long run, Jewish adolescents felt increasingly isolated at the onset of puberty. Many "preferred to deal with instances of malice and humiliation" by themselves.[19]

The rise of anti-Semitism in the schools, punctuated by insults such as "Jewish pig," triggered a partly voluntary, partly compulsory withdrawal of Jewish pupils. When a class project led to the discovery that Erich Helmer had a Jewish grandmother, Pastor Helmer shielded his son by also finding a distant relationship to Joachim von Ribbentrop, the Nazi foreign minister. Tired of the "very depressing" situation in public schools, some Jewish adolescents who were proud of their origin transferred to separate Jewish institutions. Others, such as Frank Eyck, who were fortunate enough to have the means and connections, resolved to continue their schooling abroad: "The anti-Jewish measures affecting my life at school strengthened my willingness to emigrate." Beginning in 1936, most Jewish pupils were expelled from public schools, with the last completing their graduation examinations, or *Abitur*, in 1938.[20]

The indoctrination of gentile adolescents in school was complemented by a stream of general Nazi propaganda that celebrated the "German rising" as a step toward the "rejuvenation" of the country. On "the day of Potsdam," Hitler, dressed in a tailcoat, "bowed in the garrison church to the Reich president in uniform" in a gesture signaling "that the rowdy NS regime had made peace with the Prussian past." Gerhard Baucke experienced the ceremony as a belated form of "inner national exaltation." Similarly, the proclamation of "the day of German labor" on the first of May covered up the destruction of the unions. In "one long procession, not only uniformed party members marched but the different crafts-guilds also showed their skill in great floats." Moreover, in impressive newsreels the Führer and some followers "took the shovel" in order "to break the ground for the building of the [superhighways of the] *Reichsautobahnen*." This message suggested, "things are getting better, soon there will no longer be any unemployed."[21]

The high point of publicity was the staging of the 1936 Olympic Games in Berlin, which appealed especially to the young. Welcoming international youth to the new Olympiastadion, the Nazi regime temporarily suspended its repression and racism in order to show a benign side of the "new Germany." With thousands of schoolchildren like Ruth Bulwin forming the Olympic rings and the flag, "the jubilation and enthusiasm knew no bounds" during the opening ceremony. The "whole world was overjoyed" because it wanted to believe in peace and recovery. While Americans recall the triumphs of Jesse Owens, Germans instead celebrated winning the medal count. Many of the attending foreign journalists and athletes "carried the good news of a vibrant Germany, disciplined and orderly, peace-minded and industrious, into their homelands." Moreover, the talented director Leni Riefenstahl, renowned for her 1934 depiction of the Nazi Party rally in Nuremberg, captured the Nordic beauty of athletic bodies in an impressive documentary film.[22]

More practically useful was the Nazi policy of sending underweight city children to the countryside so as to make them healthier. Even without prodding, families with rural relatives began to ship their offspring to grandparents or other relations on a farm to profit from better air and more copious food during the summer vacations. Moreover, once a year "a public health officer came to school in order to examine all children" for problems that could be corrected by receiving a daily bottle of milk. For the needier he would "propose relocating the children" to a group home in the countryside. There they would spend several weeks with minimal instruction and plenty of fun, while being fed more abundantly than at home. Although a few were initially homesick and had trouble dealing with the regimentation, most enjoyed the change of scenery and gained weight while away. Even if he did not really need it, Hellmut Raschdorff "gratefully accepted this possibility as a present."[23]

The Nazification of adolescents therefore involved a contradictory blend of compulsion and consent. On the one hand, the silencing of critics, persecution of political enemies, and exclusion of Jews from the community showed the dictatorial face of the Third Reich. On the other hand, the real enthusiasm, revived pride, and returned hope reinforced the improvement of the public mood, making the Nazi regime genuinely popular among most of those whose lives were getting better. Especially among the young, these paradoxical impressions generated "an impenetrable mixture of strongly opposing emotions, which ran the whole gamut from childlike or childish enthusiasm [to] revulsion [and] alienation." Heinz Schultheis remembered the "almost schizophrenic feeling" of the initial Nazi years, when the majority of people "could hardly distinguish clearly between the evident successes and the evil compulsion of these new potentates."[24]

PEER PRESSURE

German adolescents were complicit in their own Nazification by assisting in the reappropriation of the Youth Movement's legacy. The original impulse of this high-school-student rebellion at the turn of the twentieth century had been part of an adult life-reform campaign against alcohol and nicotine. At a 1913 meeting at the Hohe Meissner mountain, the Free German Youth vowed that "On their own initiative, under their own responsibility, and with deep sincerity" they were "determined to independently shape their own lives. For the sake of this inner freedom, they [would] take united action under any and all circumstances." This stress on youthful independence revealed resentment against adult Wilhelmine decadence, even if it was accompanied by a strong dose of nationalism. By taking over attractive activities such as hiking, singing, and gathering around campfires, the Nazi youth perverted the movement's original meaning into youthful support for a racist dictatorship.[25]

The Hitler Youth organization was founded in 1922 as a youthful auxiliary of the adult party and a source for future party leaders. After some rival groups were consolidated in 1926, it grew rapidly to over one hundred thousand adherents by 1932, only to explode into several millions after the Nazi

9. Hitler Youth rally. *Source*: Ruth Bulwin, *Spätes Echo.*

seizure of power. It was subdivided into two age groups, with the Jungvolk comprising boys aged ten to fourteen and the Hitlerjugend proper the fourteen-to-eighteen-year-olds. The initially male group was also complemented by a League of German Girls (BdM), which remained strictly separate from the boys. With the appointment of the suave Baldur von Schirach as national leader in 1933, the HJ became more visible, offering a mixture of paramilitary training and leisure activities. Though it eventually became compulsory for all teenagers, the Hitler Youth considered itself the future elite.[26] A snapshot of Rolf Bulwin's Fanfare Corps shows Nazi indoctrination through participation in rallies of party youth (image 9).

The Hitler Youth gradually assumed a monopoly over all youth activities by absorbing its rivals and forbidding all independent associations. One of the first to be swallowed up was the loose Youth Movement confederation Die Freischar. At Pentecost 1933 Paul Frenzel met with about forty thousand of his comrades on the Lüneburg Heath for a national jamboree. When they heard that all different groups had to merge into a new national league [*Großdeutscher Bund*], "the older youths shouted in protest" and tore down the Swastika flag. Even the arrival of ten police units could not persuade the angry adolescents to accept the dissolution of their group. But when SA and SS units surrounded the camp, "even the boldest boys had to capitulate to the armed encirclement." The promise of maintaining some cohesion within the HJ then induced most Freischar members to join. One by one, Boy Scouts, religious groups, and other clubs had to furl their flags and surrender their autonomy.[27]

A whole host of reasons persuaded adolescents to join the HJ. Agnes Moosmann simply considered the patriotic recitations, singing of folk songs, and marching "fun." For Eva Peters, it gave her "a rousing feeling" of independence from home and school to fill out the BdM membership form, because "she wanted to help in the building of the new, third, thousand-year Reich and to carry responsibility." When he watched "endless Jungvolk columns marching in step" with flags flying and drums thudding, Karl Härtel "felt somehow attracted" and wished "perhaps to become part" of such a dynamic group. Because virtually all of his classmates had already joined, Horst Johannsen "wanted to take part in the Jungvolk" and intended to override his parents' veto. For Paul Frenzel, the decision was, rather, a way to demonstrate a minimum of conformity, showing that his family was not opposed to the new regime, even if "my enthusiasm was quite limited."[28] But the HJ cared little about motives as long as it could indoctrinate its members.

In anti-Nazi families, the desire of children to join the Hitler Youth created much generational tension. When a favorite aunt sent Benno Schöffski an HJ uniform with brown shirt, shoulder belt, and black bandana, "my mother got very angry about it and hid the box with its contents." Even after he was compelled to become a member in 1937, his leftist parents allowed him only a minimum of participation, barring him from any trips. Similarly, when Hans Schirmer spotted his son in uniform he exploded angrily: "He forbade me to go to the Hitler Youth. I could not be a member [because] he as father had not permitted it. And that was that!" Young Hans-Harald "did not understand that. The other boys were also wearing these duds" without any problems. Although he sensed that his Communist father considered "Hitler a criminal," the youth failed to comprehend the gravity of the offense. All he wanted was to be like his peers.[29]

Led by a *Führer* barely older than their charges, the Hitler Youth offered a raft of attractive activities that strongly appealed to the ten-to-fourteen-year-olds, making the Jungvolk "an especially important instrument of indoctrination." One fixture was the weekly *Heimabend* or meeting at a clubhouse that "provided variety and fascinating propaganda of war and victory." Usually the group leader would present ideological discussions about "heroes of the [NS] movement," "Germans abroad," or "the national struggle on the ethnic frontiers." But more interesting were the many different games, such as cops and robbers, which often led to roughhousing. The boys especially enjoyed war games (*Geländespiele*) in which two groups would try to capture the flag of their opponents, because that allowed them to run around outside and fight with each other. The evening would conclude with a rousing rendition of propaganda songs such as "The young rise up, prepared to storm! / Let's hoist the flags higher, comrades!"[30]

Even more fun were hiking trips through the countryside or the larger organized camps, pioneered by the Youth Movement. On weekends or vacations, group members would gather in uniform, carrying heavy backpacks full of food, clothes, blankets, and mess kits, in order to hike to a pretty lake, mountain, or forest. There, they would pitch their tents and gather around the fire to hear horror stories, sing folk songs, or sneak up to a rival group to steal its pennant. Rambling gave them a sense of freedom from adult control. In the organized camps, many individual groups would meet to compete with each other in sports, march with bugles, drums, and flags, or listen to speeches by party leaders, extolling the Nazi cause. Karl Härtel was not alone in remembering that hiking through different regions of his fatherland and singing at campfires bonded youth and created "a feeling of true communion with the long-dead generations of our Volk."[31]

Another source of NS popularity was the control of leisure activities through membership in HJ or NSDAP auxiliaries. For all of his Protestant reluctance, Gerhard Krapf was impressed by a show-jumping competition of the NS Rider Corps because he loved horses. Though he was bored by politics, Heinz Schultheis was attracted to the "air-HJ, because here I succeeded in making the jump to flying" actual planes. This was a complicated process, involving learning the physics of flight, weather patterns, and so on. The youths started by building models and then graduated to "'real' soaring" in gliders which were pulled by rope down a hill so that they would eventually become airborne. This was an exciting challenge for an adolescent boy, even if the "flight" lasted only two or three minutes. Similarly, Horst Grothus was quite eager to join the "Flying HJ" since he wanted to design airplanes. By gaining a monopoly over activities such as riding, flying, and boating, the Hitler Youth managed to attract even youths who were otherwise opposed.[32]

Less popular were the service tasks "for the German Volk and fatherland," which Hitler Youths had to perform in order to show their engagement in the national community. In general, the young agreed with the egalitarian aspiration of Nazi ideology that required treating all members of the *Volksgemeinschaft*, the "workers of the fist and the head," as equals. But most adolescents did not really look forward to standing at street corners in uniform, rattling their tin cans in order to collect money for causes such as the Winter Aid to indigent families according to the Nazi slogan "Nobody shall go hungry or freeze." Similarly the idea of eating merely a vegetable stew instead of sumptuous dinner each Sunday and donating the money saved to the Nazi People's Welfare was appealing only in the abstract when one had to swallow "a lukewarm, fatty broth from a big vat" on the market square.[33]

Since the HJ was a favorite audience for party rituals or visiting dignitaries, its members were always compelled to attend and show their enthusiasm. Hours before such an event, the squads would gather, march in formation, stand in rows on the streets, raise their right arms, and shout "Sieg Heil!" The high point of such demonstrations were Hitler's speeches, transmitted live via radio and broadcast through loudspeakers. Gerhard Krapf recalled that the Führer would begin "in a low pitch, weighing each word" to sketch the history of the Nazi movement; gradually he would raise his tone and intensity "to recount the injustices of Versailles, building his crescendo up to fortissimo and the audience to a frenzy." With his voice cracking, he would reach the climax by vowing to return Germany to greatness and sweep the young into "endless jubilation." Though some resented compulsory attendance, many "went away misty-eyed like after a holiday sermon.[34]

The appeal of the HJ also stemmed from its chance to offer leadership posts, giving adolescents unusual scope for action. The 7.7 million members in 1938 needed tens of thousands of leaders to organize their activities. Hence the organization recruited good-looking, ideologically convinced, or personally popular adolescents to lead squads of a dozen members only a few years younger. This commitment to the self-leadership of youth often created strong emotional ties, since these little Führers served as adolescent role models. Once chosen, prospects were trained in special courses how to conduct weekly meetings as well as prepare trips. Eva Peters still marvels "about what the then 14, 15, or 16 year olds all organized, were responsible for and got done." As Wilhelm Kolesnyk remembered, this leadership role reinforced his resolve: "I only committed to National Socialism when I became a *Führer* in the German Jungvolk."[35]

The justification for giving the young such latitude was the "deification of youth" as guarantors for Germany's future. On the positive side, Eva Peters lists "the overcoming of class barriers" in a national community as well as "the realization of the longing for simplicity, authenticity and naturalness" through the "blood and soil" mythology. But in the negative column, she lists far more numerous and disastrous consequences of the HJ-ideology: "The antiliberal and antidemocratic 'cult of leaders and followers'" denounced respect for human rights. "The living-space ideology and ethnic-racist conception of history" rejected a rational and scientific world view. Moreover, "the break with humanist traditions of the enlightenment" fed a barbarous romanticization of the right of the stronger. Finally "the nationalist exaggeration of the feelings for Volk and fatherland" led to a murderous contempt for so-called lesser peoples and races.[36]

The HJ handbook explicated the ideological beliefs members were supposed to internalize in propaganda discussions. It started by emphasizing the "unlikeness of men" that made the Nordic race superior to all others and made dilution dangerous: "The first opposition measures of the National

Socialists must, therefore, aim to remove the Jews from the cultural and economic life of our folk." The second concern was a reversal of the population decline and a return to healthy contact with the soil. The third was the reconquest of territories once inhabited by Germanic tribes and subject to German cultural influences. "This fact justifies the German people's claim to these regions." To remedy overpopulation, reach agricultural self-sufficiency, and gain industrial autarchy, the territory of the Reich had to be expanded.[37] Though still somewhat in veiled language, this was a blueprint for future war.

The core of this murky ideology was "a romanticized notion of the *Führer*" to which the HJ pledge vowed eternal obedience. One propaganda painting showed him "astride a steed, in knightly armor, his mailed fist holding a Nazi banner." According to Gerhard Krapf, this widely distributed image signified "a supernatural hero whom to follow as a faithful vassal . . . was 'the holy duty' of each German." Visualized by Hitler's photographer Heinrich Hoffmann, this conception of leadership sought to meet a popular longing for a strong man, based on the misunderstanding that Bismarck had pursued a power policy of a "mailed fist."[38] Though one infatuated BdM girl gushed, "German youth, Adolf Hitler is your greatest teacher," when Horst Grothus saw the Führer in person, he "was somewhat disappointed," since the leader did not look like a Nordic hero. Nonetheless, the cult seemed like a practical application of Max Weber's conception of charisma, which stressed an irrational emotional bond between leader and followers that required blind obedience."[39]

The ideal type of German youth whom the HJ attempted to produce was a male Aryan fighter or a female mother of the race. Induction into the Hitler Youth was accompanied by the claim, "from now on you belong to the Führer!" Leaders like Hans Queiser understood the "leadership principle" as a mixture of "command and responsibility on the one, obedience on the other side." In practice, this meant carrying out orders from above without question. Hitler himself had demanded that male youths ought to be "quick as greyhounds, tough as shoeleather, and hard as Krupp steel." This image propagated strength of character and physical fitness over intelligence and imagination. Hence the HJ hunting knife carried proudly by boys had the slogan "blood and honor" etched into it. Excluded from this male bonding, girls were supposed to develop a different conception of "faith and beauty."[40] While reality fell often short of this ideal, the constant repetition of such slogans prepared youths for service in the coming war.

Some youths who were just glad to be included were completely swept away by the propaganda and activities of the Hitler Youth. Even mandatory collections and Sunday stew did not discourage Horst Grothus, because "they are talking much better and with pride about our Germany." Hitler's successes, such as the conquest of Austria through the 1938 *Anschluss*, proved to him that "the Nazi policy is correct, unemployment is being rapidly overcome and 'the national community' is better than class warfare." Unlike his skeptical mother, young Horst found it "good that the Nazis hold power. They help Germany regain the greatness which it deserves. They are the leaders of my state." Even when he heard that a friend and his father were incarcerated in the KZ, he considered it right, commenting, "They are enemies of the Reich and must be rendered harmless." Though somewhat ambivalent about anti-Semitic violence, he retained his "unconditional enthusiasm" even during the war.[41] This was the kind of member the HJ wanted.

In contrast to reminiscences of "happy times" in the HJ, most memoirs are curiously reticent about anti-Semitism, suggesting that this was a touchy subject. According to Eva Peters, explicit "anti-Semitism played hardly any role in the League of Younger Girls, perhaps only because it seemed self-evident." Hans Queiser also claimed that he received little Judeophobic material as HJ leader. Many adolescents already had internalized religious or social prejudices against Jews as part of their nationalist upbringing. Even if some Jewish youths wanted to join, they were barred from becoming HJ members for being "un-German." Time and again, the Hitler Youth participated in anti-Jewish actions such as the boycott of stores, the burning of leftist books, or the destruction of synagogues, even if some members were embarrassed by such violence. Ingrid Bork recalled, "Propaganda in school and during the first year in the Jungmädelbund had already reached me and I found it completely correct that Jews were expelled from Germany."[42]

Feeling excluded, many Jewish youths founded organizations of their own in order to create solidarity against persecution by their peers. Considering themselves "first and foremost Germans whose religious faith happened to be 'Jewish,'" Tom Angress and Werner Warmbrunn joined the Black Pennant. Derived from the Youth Movement, "its ideology was clear[ly] *bündisch*, a love of nature, Nietzschean ("be yourself"), adventure ("journey"), romanticism,—campfires, and the belief that the [Nazis] could eventually go away." Being with a group of boys their own age made it easier for young Jews to cope with the daily harassment at school. The comradeship of adventure trips all over the countryside and hostile encounters with the Hitler Youth forged lifelong friendships. But in December 1934 this assimilationist group was forbidden. The Nazis preferred the Zionist group Blue-White, which advocated making *aliyah* to Eretz Israel, thereby removing Jews from Germany.[43]

Ultimately even some gentile adolescents began to rebel against compulsory participation in the Hitler Youth, because they did not want to be regimented. Due to the increasing militarization of HJ duty, Gerhard Krapf "[n]ever developed a positive attitude towards the Jungvolkdienst." He would rather practice the organ than march at the command of a "not too smart and academically very lazy" HJ leader. Having never joined, Joachim Fest did not mind being punished with "mindless exercises in the schoolyard," since being forced to crawl around in the dirt could not dampen his rebellious spirit. Youths like Paul Frenzel who were already apprentices starting their careers simply considered the HJ duty, made mandatory before the war, as a waste of time. Heinz Schultheis confessed that "the entire Nazi stuff got on my nerves" because he disliked "this constant regimentation and control."[44] Some of the older youths, in particular, began to grow sick and tired of Nazi tutelage.

To escape such pressure, reluctant adolescents developed a repertoire of avoidance strategies, especially if supported by their parents. While the HJ claimed millions of members, a minority managed not to sign up at all or to escape active participation. Some, like Gisela Grothus, never quite managed to join or simply got lost when their own groups were absorbed into the HJ. Others, like Heinz Raschdorff, substituted membership in less-political groups such as the youth branch of the Reich Colonial League. Still others showed up only sporadically at the weekly meetings or simply faded away from obligatory parades, never to return. When obnoxious HJ leaders came to question Benno Schöffski's absence, his angry mother threw them out, making excuses about his ill health, lack of money, or insufficient time. Gerhard Krapf was proud that, after a dispute, "I was kicked *out of* the Hitlerjugend," ending his duty.[45]

Ultimately the Hitler Youth exploited the adolescent need for belonging with great virtuosity. As a stateless Ukrainian in Prague, Wilhelm Kolesnyk decided to become German, because he wanted neither to be Czech nor Jewish. He joined the young gymnasts and was absorbed into the Hitler Youth where "I liked it pretty well as a *Pimpf* [cub]." But "it was almost pathological ambition, triggered by the advancement of a hated classmate, which drove me into the arms of the Nazis," since he wanted to be a better HJ leader than his rival. Ruth Bulwin still recalls her BdM squad fondly as "a companionable group." Like many former members, she remembers the "always laughing, joyous faces" of "enthusiastic youths, athletically fit, disciplined and dashing, completely convinced of the cause, uncritical and full of good faith in the future and the *Führer*." Such positive memories suggest that most youths, on balance, liked being members of the HJ.[46]

PRIVATE SPACES

Many youths, nonetheless, managed to retain "private lives" unless they were racial or ideological victims of the NS regime. Beneath the ubiquitous Nazification pressure and compulsory HJ activism, "many things continued unaffected by current events," allowing the pursuit of leisure, completion of schooling, entry into a job, or experience of first love. For instance, by doing small jobs, Gerhard Krapf saved up enough money to purchase his own Stricker bicycle, which permitted him to explore neighborhoods further from home. Considering "hunting in father's district more important" than school, Horst Andrée was proud of "having shot my first buck." Horst Grothus "paddled the whole length of the [Baldeney] lake" in his brother's kayak and learned how to sail in a small dinghy during the summer.[47] Escaping into apolitical pursuits made it easier for teenagers to put up with the ideological demands of the Nazi dictatorship.

Even in the Third Reich, the religious ritual of confirmation or bar mitzvah signaled the end of childhood and the beginning of youth as a new life stage. In all faiths, this rite of passage followed a course of religious instruction that culminated in admission to the congregation of believers. Ruth Bulwin's confirmation photo shows a lanky girl "in a long black dress with a collar of white ruffles, white gloves and a bouquet of lilies of the valley." Boys like Gerhard Krapf would wear "spanking new blue suits with long pants and ties" and "carry a new leather-bound hymnal." In Catholic homes, the celebration followed a similar pattern, also culminating in a family feast. Albert Gompertz recalled his 1934 bar mitzvah as a service in his synagogue and a private get-together among family and friends, complete with gifts.[48] For most adolescents, this ceremony also meant the conclusion of elementary education and the entrance into an apprenticeship.

Those youths who continued with schooling constantly worried about academic failure, which in the three-tier German system cut off access to professional careers. For a successful pupil such as Gerhard Krapf, the curriculum into which he was pressed "was one of the best things to have happened to me" since it laid a firm basis in the classics and exposed him to "anti-Nazi thinking" through some courageous teachers. By contrast, when Gerhard Baucke failed to apply himself sufficiently, he had to be sent to a private school, where he did much better. Horst Andrée flunked all his classes because he was bored and frustrated: "School made me puke and even hunting was no longer any fun." But once again, being dispatched to a friendly but disciplined boarding school on the Baltic shore helped him recover. However, Karl Härtel gave up on advanced classes and decided to stay in primary school so as to enter an apprenticeship.[49]

The attainment of *Mittlere Reife* at the end of junior high school was the educational goal for many pupils who were not able or resolute enough to continue further. In the German "entitlement system," this was the midpoint between grade and high school, which still allowed access to white-collar occupations. Less ambitious or wealthy families with practical aims often sent their offspring to *Realschulen* or *Mittelschulen*, whose graduates only obtained the ninth-grade certificate. Because "something in the [previous] school upset" her, Gisela Grothus "decided to leave the Gertraudenschule with the Mittlere Reife in 1936" and transfer to a less challenging girls' high school. Because he "saw no sense in continuing" due to anti-Semitic discrimination, Tom Angress similarly decided to leave high school with this intermediary certificate and enter practical training to prepare himself for emigration.[50]

For more gifted and ambitious pupils, the goal was the coveted *Abitur* or academic high-school diploma, which opened the door to the professions and higher careers. Instituted by Prussian officials in the late eighteenth century, this graduation examination struck fear into the hearts of youths because failure was a real possibility. Robert Neumaier "later often regretted his refusal" to pursue it, since "I had to acquire with much dedication and perseverance what I had missed in my youth." Heinz Schultheis was more fortunate: his interest in "technical innovations" such as airplanes, gramophones, and radios motivated him to study. In the end, "everything went pretty well" and he passed the exam, which he "celebrated in a dignified and joyous manner." He was lucky, as his "Abitur was the last one during peacetime." For later candidates such as Fritz Klein, the exam was watered down and graduates were immediately sent to the battlefront.[51]

After the end of school, youths faced the difficult task of finding an occupation that would suit their preferences and in which training was available. Although the economy was improving, getting a starting position required a hard struggle. Due to his sister's secretarial job at a vacuum pump builder, Robert Neumaier was able to begin an apprenticeship as a metalworker. Intent on preparing his son for emigration from Germany, Albert Gompertz's father "decided the best way to go was to sign me on as an apprentice in the textile industry" in a Jewish company where he could learn the business from the ground up. Hearing about an opening through his father's work at the local power plant, Karl Härtel managed to pass an entrance examination and start training in the novel occupation of "electrical worker" in 1937.

"This was one of the happiest moments in my not even 14 year old life," for it assured his material future.[52]

With less formal training, young women flocked to white-collar pursuits in stores or offices where they could deal with people rather than doing manual labor. In June 1935 Anneliese Huber "began a mercantile apprenticeship in the office" of a women's fashion store, owned by a "strict but correct" Jewish businessman. There, she learned to keep accounts and take shorthand under the vigilant eyes of her superiors. Needed in the family restaurant, Ruth Weigelt was only allowed to learn a few more useful skills in home economics. Because she had only finished grade school, Ruth Bulwin had to enter a "private commercial school" in 1938, where she learned the basics of accounting, bookkeeping, stenography, typing, and business correspondence: "Surprisingly I even enjoyed learning." Though Gisela Grothus had completed high school, she "did not have the courage to study medicine" and contented herself with training to become a "medical technical assistant."[53] The young women liked their first career steps, which gave them independence and pocket money to spend.

Completing an apprenticeship during the 1930s was not easy: the training took three years and was strictly regimented by a signed contract. Many young people had to board with another family or at a home for apprentices wherever their job was. In their workplaces, trainees had to do all sorts of menial tasks, following the whims of their superiors. Moreover, in crafts they had to start with the simplest of chores. Robert Neumaier, for instance, had to file pieces of different metals to learn their properties, while Paul Frenzel had "to sort coffee beans, stand at the sieve machine, roast coffee . . . and combine the different brands into coffee mixtures."[54] One day a week, apprentices also had to attend a vocational school to acquire systematic knowledge in their field. The workweek lasted forty-eight hours and the wages were meager. If trainees were slack, offended the boss, or ran afoul of Nazi politics, they were summarily fired.

The formal end of apprenticeship was an examination that promoted the candidate to journeyman or commercial assistant. To prepare for this test, eager employees such as Anneliese Huber would take evening courses at trade academies to add a theoretical component to their practical knowledge. Highly motivated apprentices like Robert Neumaier could even try to take the final exam half a year early, if they had gained sufficient skill, finished their vocational schooling, and had "the party or HJ [testify] that I was a good National Socialist." Especially skilled apprentices such as Karl Härtel might even become proud winners of the Reich occupational contest organized by the German Labor Front by completing difficult metalworking and electrical tasks. In contrast to later wartime, Paul Frenzel would recall, "The years of my apprenticeship in Leipzig were on the whole quite happy. I hardly paid any attention to politics."[55]

Passing the trade examination opened the door to a career in the blue- or white-collar occupations. Some youths were, like Karl Härtel, able to continue in the same company, at least for a while. Others, like Anneliese Huber, had to search a new job, for which they had to prove that they were of Aryan descent. Her position in public health insurance "was interesting and wide-ranging." With the first real job came a change in title such as "craftsman" and elevation in status, making the former trainee a regular member of the firm. More important was the raise in pay from ten to fifty pfennigs per hour, which allowed them to buy fancier clothes such as dresses or suits so that they would look more adult. The increase in spending money also made it possible to go to the movies, enjoy concerts, or take weekend trips. But the dream of an easy life soon ran into the obstacle of required Nazi duties such as the men's Reich Labor Service or the women's year in the countryside.[56]

The onset of puberty complicated the launching of careers because it led to a distancing from the family and to a general revolt against authority. According to Heinz Schultheis, the establishment of the Nazi dictatorship "ran parallel to the changes that nature imposes on adolescents independently of any political system." Therefore, it "made life in home, school and HJ not really easier." For Anneliese Huber, the "storm and stress" of growing up meant becoming aware of the disintegration of her parents' marriage, which caused intolerable scenes: "It was the most terrible time of my life." Hellmut Raschdorff provoked a conflict with a superior during boring work in a munitions factory. When he was criticized for taking an unscheduled lunch break, he was incensed about "this impertinence" and talked back to the boss. While Anneliese only had to move away from home, Hellmut was forced to volunteer for the military.[57]

The teenage years in the mid-1930s were also the time when the older members of the Weimar cohort felt the first stirrings of interest in the opposite sex. Much of this was harmless, such as Frank Eyck's helping his friend's sister Rosemarie Schmidt push a bike up a hill in the Grunewald forest in Berlin. (After the war she would become his bride.) Similarly, Robert Neumaier was excited when a new girl named Johanna came into his eighth-grade class: she was "tall, slender, had blue eyes and long blonde braids—a [true] Germanic type." While she was unapproachable and "did not pay any attention to us boys," she always knew the answers without being overeager. "I began to idolize Johanna. It was the first time that I was interested in a girl," he later recalled: "It was my first great love and was destined to remain so, but I did not know it at the time."[58] Though still rather innocent, some such crushes were to have lasting effects.

More serious affairs developed for those youths who were a bit older and ready to stand on their own feet. For middle-class families, the first contact between the sexes, segregated in school, took place during dancing lessons. Gisela Grothus' cotillion photograph (image 10) shows girls in dresses, some still with their hair in braids, sitting in front of a group of boys in dark suits and ties who smile uneasily. When Paul Frenzel practiced these skills in the Palmengarten dance-hall in Leipzig, he asked one young women to dance. "I liked her so much that I called on her the whole evening" and walked her to the train at midnight. Thereby "I got to know my present wife," though he had to overcome his father's resistance to a working-class bride. Ruth Weigelt's childhood friendship with Gerhard simply turned into a more serious attachment. Ruth Bulwin met her later husband during an HJ hike when he saw her photograph and decided to beat out a rival. "Yes, that's the way it was, Rolf was a daredevil; all members of my girl's group had a crush on him."[59]

Yet relationships had a difficult time maturing due to the dictatorial control of the party and the disruption of the coming war. In the Third Reich,

10. Dancing lessons. *Source*: Gisela Grothus, "Mein Leben."

youths were always organized in groups, stressing the ideal of comradeship. Eva Peters recalled that "service in the HJ hardly offered opportunities for contact with the other sex." Hans Schirmer remembered that teenagers were ignorant about the facts of life: "No one of us had a 'glimmer of an idea' of what to do or how to behave." Anneliese Huber recollected that her mother summarily slapped her first suitor in the face. When a young officer later asked to see her with a bouquet in hand, her parents told him to come back in a year and to write letters in the meantime. "Unfortunately he died during the first months of the war. I was very sad about him even if this was not yet 'the great love.'"[60] One of the Nazi regime's casualties was therefore the deepening of contacts to sexual intimacy.

The relative normalcy of youthful lives actually strengthened the Third Reich, since in spite of all the propaganda pressure it allowed a range of responses. Underrepresented among the retrospectives are accounts of genuine enthusiasm for the regime, especially among men. But Eva Peters admits that she was smitten by her new BdM leader, Frieda, in the fall of 1936. The newcomer "was a pretty girl, eighteen years old, with radiant blue eyes." Her call for dedication to Germany "also set the heart of the eleven-year-old on fire. Hence she went along—at least for the next five years." Similarly, Ruth Bulwin reports being a happy BdM member, though she does not touch on its politics. By contrast, Robert Neumaier initially had to be forced to join the HJ in 1938. But eventually "I liked this new life pretty well." Playing games, camping, singing songs, "all of that was great fun for me. I was inspired by being part of a group of comrades, as equal among equals. Finally, I also belonged."[61]

The great majority of apolitical youths were impressed by Hitler's surprising successes and willing to go along as long as the regime did not disturb their personal lives. According to Heinz Schultheis, "the decisive positive aspect . . . was the fact, visible to all 'national comrades,' that things were *now* actually getting better." In retrospect, he called this "the time period in which the NS regime experienced the greatest acceptance in the German population and was not exactly loved, but respected abroad." At the same time, Paul Frenzel had the distinct impression "that the majority of the population was fairly content with the Third Reich after the elimination of mass unemployment, the introduction of some social measures, and the lifting of the discriminatory clauses of the Versailles Treaty." When the Saar was returned to Germany by plebiscite in 1935 and Austria joined the Reich in 1938, Ursula Mahlendorf "was swept away by the nationalist fervor of the jubilant crowds."[62]

But a growing minority only went through the motions and engaged in passive noncompliance, finding ever new ways to avoid Nazi demands. After her youth group the Association of Germans Abroad had been merged with the BdM, Gisela Grothus never quite got around to joining and escaped without facing any punishment. Other members, such as Fritz Klein, were increasingly bored with the irksome demands for marching in demonstrations or applauding Hitler triumphs, so "As much as possible [I] escaped the service with some kind of excuse." As a result, HJ leaders were frustrated by "the number of no-shows" for obligatory service whom they had to track down. Youths who had teachers with integrity or came from nonconformist homes were able to construct "the image of a humane, rational, and peaceful counter-world" to the Nazi dictatorship. In such circles, it went without saying that "one was opposed" to the NS regime.[63]

Some adolescents also found support for a critical attitude in the "Confessing Church," which rejected the Nazification of Protestantism by the German Christians with the Barmen Declaration of 1934. On hearing of the killing of the SA leadership in the so-called Röhm Putsch, Gerhard Krapf's father said, "what has happened here was murder" and joined the Protestant opposition by creating a network of critical pastors. His son, who hated HJ drills, hoped in vain that the Wehrmacht would become a barrier against the Nazi dictatorship. Shocked by reports about the euthanasia of the handicapped, Erich Helmer's father began preaching critical sermons, ignoring Gestapo surveillance in church. To make a point, he even named his brown hens after leading Nazis: "Adolfine, Hermine, Goebbelinchen" and the like. After an HJ leader died accidentally, the son was "not shaken by the death, but by the emptiness of the Nazi cult" that imitated religion. As a result, he left the Hitlerjugend. Similarly the Catholic Joachim Fest followed the maxim "even if all others do—I do not."[64]

Only rarely did "unruly youth behavior" metamorphose into active political resistance; the Gestapo rigorously suppressed any hint of dissidence. In Cologne, Gertrud Kühlem, a teenager from a Communist home, helped gather a group of young rebels who identified themselves by wearing an edelweiss pin, an Alpine flower that symbolized freedom to them. They camouflaged themselves as members of the "Friends of Nature," hiked, camped, and sang to assert their independence. Convinced that "something needed to be done" against the "unjust dictatorship," they scrawled slogans on house walls and freight cars, such as "Aren't you tired yet of the brown shit?" Their actions culminated in dropping hundreds of leaflets from a ladder at the main train station. When the Gestapo finally caught up with them, the women were brutally beaten to extract confessions, while the men were sent to punitive companies at the front.[65]

The elemental desire for freedom among the young also inspired other forms of cultural opposition that became politicized through Nazi repression. In some bigger cities, middle-class youths who liked to listen to jazz or dance to swing music formed a lifestyle rebellion against the clean-cut Nordic standard, turning against the Third Reich when forbidden. In Berlin, a group of young Jews and Communists, led by Herbert Baum, dared to burn down part of a Nazi exhibition on the "Soviet Paradise" in an act of protest against anti-Bolshevik propaganda. In Munich, a small group of students around Sophie Scholl similarly distributed leaflets at the university auditorium, denouncing the murderous war and violations of human rights, for which most of them were executed. Though highly admirable, these acts of exceptional courage in resisting a murderous regime remained isolated efforts and never really endangered Nazi rule. Fanatical HJ members loathed these dissidents as "criminals, notorious shirkers and moral degenerates."[66]

Excluded from the national community, young Jews faced increasing displacement from public areas into segregated spaces that made their lives miserable. As a result of anti-Semitic propaganda, Gerhard Krapf "began to realize that there were 'Jews' as distinct from what the Nazis called Aryans," even if he did not want to respect the difference. Similarly, Tom Angress noticed in school "that I was different from my non-Jewish classmates," but, having been brought up in an assimilated household, "didn't know what difference that made since no one had explained to me what it meant to be Jewish." Increasing discrimination in daily life, ranging from being forbidden to use public transportation to being prohibited to have pets, made it clear that Jews could no longer be Germans and should emigrate. Fifteen-year-old Tom put his distress about this expulsion from Germany into poetic words: "We know no more justice, only repression. / Our homeland doesn't love us anymore."[67]

The Nazi dictatorship could afford to persecute a racial and ideological minority as long as it was sure of the support of most adults and the enthusiasm of the young. "The overwhelming majority of German citizens," explained Karl Härtel, "had evidently the strong feeling that now in our country a government set out to end the exploitation and humiliation that had lasted far too long." Due to the improvement of living conditions, "the brown[-shirted] comrades could count upon the unreserved approval of all those who had been forced to pay the reparation bills with a reduction of their living standard to the poverty limit." And, if approval was not forthcoming, there was always the Gestapo. The son of Edith Schöffski's neighbor reported "that father is being watched by the Nazis since he does not participate in political discussions and does not greet with 'Heil Hitler!'"[68] Such an intimidating rumor was enough to keep most skeptics in line.

A SENSE OF BETRAYAL

When writing about their former embrace of National Socialism, most authors, like Hans Queiser, show strong resentment against "the seduction of our generation" that deprived them of a normal youth. Angry at being figuratively blinded by the Nazis, Ruth Weigelt also complains that "we were robbed of our carefree youth." Seeking to downplay her own responsibility, Ruth Bulwin claimed, "Often we were moved like marionettes, in part by older and accepted traditions, in part by political influences or the drive to survive." Karl Härtel explained that "most survivors, be they perpetrators or victims, initially wanted to repress" the shocking memories of "the cruelties and crimes against humanity" that warped their lives. Seeking to make sense of her engagement in the BdM, Eva Peters mused, "When I think about it, [I am amazed by] how much idealism we had then, and for such a bad cause!"[69] In retrospect, most authors saw themselves as misguided victims in order to minimize their own contribution to the Third Reich.

The collective sense of betrayal is not entirely mistaken, for many their parents and adult role models had also failed to resist the siren call of the Führer. Gerhard Krapf argued that "the Nazis succeeded in stimulating the very best of the Germans, making them truly believe in the high ethical mission of contributing to that new stature of becoming again a Volk, strong, honest, loyal, industrious and proud." This *Volksgemeinschaft* rhetoric promised to create an egalitarian community, while the economic recovery seemed to prove Hitler right. Endless parades and rallies demonstrated unity and strength, since "the Nazis were masters" in "applied mass psychology." But it was even "more humiliating that people like [doctor Ferdinand] Sauerbruch, [composer] Richard Strauss, [writer] Ina Seidel, even [the Catholic] Cardinal Faulhaber . . . engaged in unsolicited support, thereby swaying quite a number of their respective followers."[70] How could the young resist such an atmosphere?

The recollections, however, underplay that there was also a strong tendency toward "self-Nazification" among youths, which is embarrassing for the authors. The indoctrination of the young was so effective, because it was offered not only by adults but by Hitler Youth leaders only slightly older than their charges. Many who were not even very political were impressed by the dynamism of the HJ and, like Robert Neumaier, simply wanted to belong with their peers. Convinced that they represented the future, quite a few adolescents, like Hans-Harald Schirmer, rebelled against the skepticism of their parents and became members of the Hitler Youth. For social outsiders, like the "foreign, homeless, and illegitimate" Wilhelm Kolesnyk, the appeal was even stronger: "Above all [the Nazis] offered everyone upward mobility. . . . That was probably the point which touched me most." Finally, "the overwhelming victories on all fronts" suggested "that we Germans were the chosen people, the greatest in every regard, that ours was the leading role in the world and that we would win it."[71]

The memoirs show that it took exceptional insight and courage to remain aloof, refuse to comply, or actively resist the twisted universe of the Third Reich, since the sanctions were lethal. Among the nationalist elite, such as the Kleins, there was much "distance" from the plebeian Nazis, but "there was also closeness," as many political goals overlapped. In democratic families, opposition was clearer, especially if they were Jewish like the Eycks or prominent-enough liberals to fear for their lives. In homes close to the Confessing Church such as the Helmers, the father was even forced to enter a psychiatric clinic in order to escape Nazi persecution. In Communist and Social Democratic circles, the brutality of the Gestapo was so malicious that resistance was the only possible recourse. But parental skepticism did not automatically inspire adolescents to oppose the regime; even critical youths like Gerhard Krapf felt "torn between sweeping enthusiasm and nagging doubt."[72]

Ultimately the Nazi youths were to suffer dearly for the blindness with which they followed the Führer into a war of annihilation and racial genocide. The combination of nationalist home, Nazified school, and Hitler

Youth indoctrination made the majority obedient tools of Nazi repression and aggression. Agnes Moosmann blames "the deference to authority and lack of critical thinking" for the disaster. There were all too few democrats, Social Democrats, and Communists to stem the brown tide. Some opponents withdrew into inner emigration, others fled abroad, and still others were incarcerated, often in the KZ. Approximately half of the graduating classes of young men were killed in the fighting. The young women had to endure bombing raids, flight and expulsion, or mass rapes by the Red Army. It took these horrifying experiences of their own suffering to show the majority that they had worshiped a false idol. Only a minority of authors, such as Horst Grothus and Eva Peters, have been willing to confront their personal responsibility and commit themselves to doing active penance.[75]

PART II

WARTIME YOUTH

4

MALE VIOLENCE

Early in the morning on September 1, 1939, Gerhard Baucke's father stormed into his bakery to report, "It is war, we have marched into Poland!" Even if this depressing news was not wholly unexpected, "the brutal truth hit us like a crushing blow." All illusions about Hitler's protestations of peace disappeared with one stroke. The foreman of the baking crew could only sigh, "If that ain't a black Friday?!" Soon it became clear that this was an ominous day, indeed. "On Sunday England and France entered the struggle on the side of the Poles. That was the dreaded two-front war." In contrast to the patriotic elation of the August days in 1914, "no flags were flying, there was no approval, no enthusiasm" the second time around, even if most people accepted the renewed struggle as a "just war" for the future of "Germany, our dearly beloved home and our splendid and great fatherland." But the prior conflict had cost too many lives to be repeated lightheartedly. Some people worried, "will the western [defensive] wall hold?"[1]

Actual experiences of World War II varied drastically depending on age, gender, and race. None of the Weimar youths "knew or could know what war means." While indoctrination in school and Hitler Youth portrayed the earlier war as a heroic struggle, their parents' stories of suffering during the interminable years from 1914 to 1918 had tempered such enthusiasm. For the young men, war signified military service, interruptions to their careers and romantic relationships, a trial by fire given patriotic meaning by skillful Nazi propaganda. For the young women, "all of our lives were to change drastically," with blackouts, air-raid exercises, ration cards, and labor in fields or munition factories to make up for the missing men. For political and racial victims of the Third Reich, the restraints of international opinion dropped away, allowing the Nazis to reveal their full brutality. These interwoven but distinctive recollections require a separate analysis.[2]

Many young men experienced the war as a paroxysm of gendered violence against enemies, foreign women, and racial inferiors. A mixture of militaristic propaganda and ruthless basic training stripped them of humanistic scruples and transformed them into efficient cogs in a military machine that executed orders without questioning them. Hans Queiser recalled, "In order to be a useful soldier, a man must overcome his natural aversion against the killing of a member of his own species." The Wehrmacht achieved this aim by dehumanizing antagonists in order to eliminate compassion and create an "us versus them" mentality. "Secondly [the soldier] must suppress his equally inborn drive for security . . . which pushes him to flee from danger in a hopeless situation." The military accomplished this task by systematically breaking a recruit's will and instilling "iron discipline." Both attitudes combined in a murderous concept of "martial masculinity" that displaced civilian versions of manhood and unleashed an unprecedented degree of violence.[3]

By loosening moral restraints, the ensuing ideological war of annihilation drew the Wehrmacht into participation in war crimes and crimes against humanity. After the postwar trials of high officers, the Western Allies abandoned the punishment of military complicity in the early 1950s due to the need for German rearmament during the Cold War. Only half a century later did the left-leaning Institute for Social Research in Hamburg once again indict the German Army through an exhibition of incriminating private photographs that evoked protests from veteran officers such as ex-chancellor Helmut Schmidt.[4] Critical researchers were discovering an appalling record of military involvement in the Holocaust through aid to the notorious SS and police killer squads of the *Einsatzgruppen*. But some moderate historians pointed out that most army units were busy fighting and it was more the security forces in the rear who were generally responsible for antipartisan measures.[5] On balance, the autobiographical accounts tend to support the version of considerable military participation in atrocities and mass murder.

Written half a century or more after the dramatic events, these narratives present a mixture of exciting reportage and grudging reflection. Having witnessed many dramatic situations, the authors feel a need to share their often-improbable experiences. But the ultimate loss of the war and the rise of Holocaust sensibility forced them to question their prior actions. Hence, heroic narrations are rare, reduced to celebrating minor victories within an overriding framework of defeat. Similarly, adventure tales of military tourism to Paris or fighting against overwhelming odds in the East have lost their luster, since the entire purpose of the war seems rather pointless in retrospect. Due to their "aversion to the 'derring-do' of braggarts," most authors instead recount survival stories in which protagonists managed to stay alive due to superior ingenuity or sheer luck. Their accounts, therefore, present the experiences of young soldiers, tempered by subsequent rumination about the consequences of their actions.[6]

PREPARATION FOR WAR

From the first days of his rule, Adolf Hitler prepared Germany systematically for war. In a dinner with army leaders in early February 1933, the new chancellor promised rearmament for the overthrow of the restrictions of the Treaty of Versailles and "the conquest of new living space in the east and its ruthless Germanization." Publicly, the Nazi government promised peace as long as Germany was treated as an equal partner. But clandestinely, Hitler poured enormous resources into developing new weapons systems such as dive bombers, stockpiling the necessary ammunition, and building border defenses. In 1935, Berlin also announced the return of conscription to train additional manpower. A year later it sent troops into the demilitarized zone in the Rhineland after the departure of the French occupiers. While the credulous still believed that "Germany had to be armed for all contingencies," regime opponents concluded that these steps meant another war.[7]

As the actual fighters in the next conflict, young men were subjected to a ceaseless glorification of war so as to militarize their mentality. Heinz

11. Reich Labor Service. *Source*: Ruth Bulwin, *Spätes Echo*.

Schultheis recalled several themes that dominated Nazi propaganda for male adolescents. First, there were the World War I accounts by former soldiers, which celebrated the bravery of German heroes such as "red baron" Manfred von Richthofen, who had shot down eighty Entente planes, or submarine captain Otto von Weddingen, who had sunk three British cruisers. Second, gripping tales of adventure by explorers such as Swedish geographer Sven Hedin and Norwegian discoverer Roald Amundsen, who won the race to the South Pole, fired the imagination of boys. Third, exhibitions of technological wonders such as the Messerschmitt or Heinkel fighter planes fascinated youths interested in new machines. And finally, overt propaganda films such as *Hitler Youth Quex* celebrated the martyrdom of young fighters for the Nazi cause.[8]

The harmless-sounding activities of the Hitler Youth were also a form of paramilitary training to accustom boys to their future role as warriors. In his autobiographical novella *I Was There*, Hans Peter Richter describes an HJ meeting where a new group leader admits, "I regard it as the mission of the HJ to prepare you for your forthcoming military service." In contrast to the free association in the Youth Movement, the HJ insisted on wearing uniforms, marching in step, saluting the swastika flag, and swearing undying allegiance to the Führer. Foreshadowing military discipline, Richter's fictional functionary commanded, "I demand obedience, obedience, unconditional obedience." Hikes in the countryside trained boys in orienteering, camping toughened them up, and popular *Geländespiele* were, in effect, simulated war games of one band against another. No wonder that one skeptical boy in the novel blurts out, "You only seek power! You are driving us into war!"[9]

A wave of air-raid exercises in the spring of 1939 made it clear that "there would soon be war unless a miracle happened." Hans Queiser mused, "One unmistakable sign was the display of mock-up airplane bombs in all big cities as propaganda for the protective measures that had been ordered." The schools and Hitler Youth groups started to sponsor "countless information sessions" about types of airplanes and bombs in order to make it possible to identify the dangers from the sky. Heinz Schultheis remembered that as members "of various HJ Youth organizations we were used to transport away the flammable junk from the attic of apartment buildings that had been deposited at curbside." Designed to signal to the population that the government was solicitous of its safety, these preparations made war seem more likely. But most people reassured themselves by reasoning, "Even if the Führer is running considerable risks in order to increase Germany's greatness, *it has always worked out without war*."[10]

Obligatory service in the Reich Labor Service (RAD) was another step in the militarization of youths. Originally, doing physical labor for minimal pay on community improvement projects was an international idea that was supposed to get unemployed young men off the streets. But from 1935 on, the Nazi labor leader Konstantin Hierl made this voluntary commitment mandatory for men in order to circumvent the disarmament restrictions on preparatory "paramilitary training." Mostly led by retired sergeants, the RAD draftees wore uniforms, exercised in formation, lived in barracks, and were subject to tight discipline, anticipating their induction into the army. This service requirement was extended to women in 1939. These young people's backbreaking work consisted of felling trees, building roads, and constructing defense positions, a mixture of useful and superfluous projects designed to toughen their bodies and militarize their spirits. Although they exercised with spades instead of rifles, photos such as the one of Rolf Bulwin (image 11) document that the RAD "more and more turned into a pre-military training for the subsequent military service."[11]

For the "perverted Nazi leaders" in charge, the Labor Service provided a golden opportunity to haze soft adolescents from bourgeois families. When especially dirty jobs had to be done, sergeants would bellow: "Students, graduates, and criminals step forward!" As the son of a pastor, Gerhard Krapf was always "automatically 'first choice'" for such tasks as cleaning the latrines. Subject to a stream of criticism for not making his bed correctly, "Sunday after Sunday [he was assigned] kitchen duty," denying him the privilege of a free pass around town. In pointless "'service' consisting of stupid formal drilling," Hans Tausch recalled that "our idealism received a strong damper." Ignoring the "unique charm of the [Alpine] landscape," the bookish Joachim Fest also "soon hated everything to do with the labor service." For one sensitive boy named Helmut, the chicanery became so intolerable that he deserted, was caught, and tried to commit suicide, but finally escaped and made it to safety with his uncle in Switzerland.[12]

The next stage after completing RAD duty was conscription into the regular army. An ominous draft notice, or *Gestellungsbefehl*, ordered recruits to report to a military district office on a certain date in order to register. "There were no excuses or possibilities of refusal," recalled Karl Härtel; because this was a legal obligation "everyone had to obey this command." Without any provision for conscientious objection, even youths who were opposed to war were forced to serve in the military. Fritz Klein noted that noncompliance was severely punished, that "compulsion was all powerful." During the last week of August 1939, Paul Frenzel's RAD group was officially transformed into a "construction battalion" of the army and shipped out to the Polish frontier. Similarly, Heinz Schultheis's labor camp was "moved to the West Wall and there attached to the Wehrmacht."[13] While the younger adolescents received a reprieve, for those born in 1920 or earlier, labor service and conscription led directly into the war.

Because they could not imagine the horrors that would await them, a surprising number of young men, such as Joachim Fest, ignored their fathers' insistent warning and volunteered for military service. Nazi propaganda played a considerable role by stressing the expectation that all young men should serve. Peer pressure also motivated skeptics such as Fritz Klein, who "did not want to lag behind the endless numbers of contemporaries, especially those one knew and who were friends." Later on victory announcements made soldiering sound like a heroic adventure, creating concern among recruits that the war would be over before they could participate. For Erich Helmer, who liked to fly, "that was unthinkable." Appeals to masculinity were powerful arguments for overcoming hesitations. Robert Neumaier worried that "after the war I would be called a shirker and [people] would point fingers at me and say 'that is a coward.' "[14] Even most Nazi opponents were therefore ready to do their patriotic duty.

Practical reasons also impelled many young men to come forth on their own without waiting to be drafted, in order to "make the inescapable somewhat less unpleasant." Some, like Hellmut Raschdorff, volunteered so as to escape a conflict at home or at work. Others, such as Hans Queiser, signed up so that they could escape the mindless preliminary grind of the Reich Labor Service. Also quite persuasive was the prospect of being able to choose one's branch of military service. Few youths wanted to slog through the mud as foot soldiers in the army. "At that time volunteers only signed up with the air force or navy because of the pretty uniforms or since flying was attractive." As combat in the air retained some of the earlier allure of chivalry, former members of the air Hitler Youth such as Horst Grothus and Erich Helmer were rather eager to take flight in the new shiny planes.[15] Because the physical requirements for pilot training were quite high, however, most were disappointed to end up in ground support.

The real Nazi fanatics volunteered directly for the Waffen SS, the most dedicated and toughest form of the military. Compared with the plebeian brawlers of the SA, the black-shirted SS projected a more elitist image as the best fighting arm of the regime. It was only logical for gung-ho HJ leaders such as Rolf Bulwin to want to join that select group. But because he was not yet old enough, he had "to forge the signature of his mother" in order to be accepted. Similarly, for the Ukrainian Wilhelm Kolesnyk, "volunteering meant, of course, enlisting in the Waffen SS." Although he was an HJ leader, he could not join the Wehrmacht, as he was not a German citizen. But "the Waffen SS accepted everyone"; in fact, seventeen of its twenty-five divisions consisted of volunteers from foreign countries. Kolesnyk "went there especially because it was the elite-guard of our Führer." Though an SS veteran acquaintance's loss of eyesight ought to have given him pause, Kolesnyk decided that if he was going to do it, he might as well go all the way.[16]

The letdown began with the army physical, a demeaning and arbitrary procedure that decided the life and death of a hapless recruit. "Get undressed! Drop your pants!—Here is a bottle to pee into," wrote Erich Helmer of an inspection process that treated youths as if they were slaughter animals. "Listening [to the lung], checking eyes and ears" were the next steps. Then, "Bend down and pull your buttocks apart!" A medic grumbled, "This man has not only flat feet but also hemorrhoids, with that we can't win a war! Where shall he be assigned?" The answer was "to the air force, sir." The chief doctor agreed: "For that [purpose] this is enough, [he is] ready to serve." The "kv" (*kriegsverwendungsfähig*) classification indicating that a young man was capable of doing his military duty was a crucial decision about his future.[17] In the early years, the standards were high, giving preference to healthy and athletic youths, but with mounting losses later in the war, more and more marginal recruits were selected and convalescents sent back to the front.

More fortunate youths could hope to be spared by being judged physically unfit or indispensable for the war effort. Although girls might sneer at boys who had a medical condition such as tuberculosis, the afflicted could stay at home and serve in nonlethal or civilian capacities. As a result, faking a disease such as asthma or getting a certificate from a sympathetic physician became a way to avoid the draft. Götz Fehr's polio handicap worked to his advantage and kept him out of combat. However, military doctors chose to ignore such conditions when the army was in desperate need of fresh manpower. Another escape route was the classification "uk" (*unabkömmlich*), indicating that a candidate was essential for winning the war at home. Since he was preparing to be an electrical engineer, Karl Härtel was allowed to continue his studies longer than his friends who had already been sent to the front. Similarly Friedrich Flessa was requisitioned as essential by his Nuremberg factory, since he was involved in developing a new kind of cold steel that proved superior to traditional methods of weapons production.[18]

The reality of induction into the military soon disillusioned even the most eager volunteers and recruits. For Hans Queiser, the terrible condition of his Labor Service barracks raised a first doubt. ("This is how we want to win the war?") Then came the shedding of regular clothes, cutting of hair, and donning of uniforms that transformed self-willed civilians into docile soldiers who had to follow their superiors' commands. The rite of passage culminated in a solemn swearing-in ceremony. Gerhardt Thamm describes how "six soldiers grasped the saber's cold steel" while "the flag bearer respectfully lowered his staff." Then "all recruits raised their right arms high" and deep voices intoned: "I swear by God this holy oath, that I will render unconditional obedience to Adolf Hitler, leader of the German nation and people [as well as] supreme Commander of the Armed Forces, and that I am ready as a brave soldier to risk my life at any time for this oath." Even if they had sworn allegiance under duress, the majority of German soldiers considered this oath morally binding.[19]

The first weeks of basic training were tough. Inductees were mercilessly "ground to the bone." Horst Johannsen recalled that his nasty noncom, called *Spieß* in German, did not act like "the mother of the company" but rather as a sadist who enjoyed his absolute power over his charges. Officially the purpose of the exercise was to get the recruits ready for the front as quickly as possible, but often hazing went far beyond that. One method of breaking the will and instilling discipline was to issue difficult orders and punish offenders for not executing them properly. Part of the training also aimed to submerge the individual into the collective, allowing the group to pick on its weakest members with pranks. Barking their commands, sergeants used incentives such as weekend passes to motivate compliance. But if someone like Fritz Klein fell asleep during his watch, all hope of being recommended for officer training vanished. The hated basic training was therefore an amalgam of Prussian militarism and Nazi torture.[20]

In practice, the "severe military drill" consisted of an endless amount of "stupid busy work" to inculcate obedience. Robert Neumaier remembered the harassment of "sweeping barracks, checking uniforms, and scrutinizing the rooms." When a bedsheet was out of line, the noncom would shout, "What a pigsty!" and order latrine cleaning. In the barracks yard, there were hours of monotonous marching, standing to attention, presenting arms, and running with gas masks. Little better were actual field exercises such as crawling through the mud, hiking long distances, orienteering with compass and maps, and playing war games. After instruction in cleaning weapons, there was actual target practice in which a good shot could get extra time off. In the rare leisure moments, Gerhard Krapf remembered, "old front hands" shared a few tricks of the trade to facilitate survival.[21] Largely common to all armies, such basic training was particularly tough in the Wehrmacht, since its soldiers were drilled not for defense but for attack.

Inductees found the training more bearable as soon as they were instructed in special skills that made them feel like real soldiers rather than automatons. Fritz Klein was pleased to be trained as a radio operator for communication duty. Gerhard Baucke was glad to learn how to drive big trucks and half-tracks for the transport corps, because "not [having] to move on foot was very good." Similarly, Hermann Debus had to get a license for all sorts of motor vehicles, finding motorcycle training that required driving off-road up and down the walls of a former gravel pit the most exciting. To toughen up future parachutists, Rudolf Harbig, a world champion middle-distance runner, drove recruits like Robert Neumaier until they collapsed. In contrast to "mostly humdrum training," Gerhard Krapf "really liked the riding lessons" for his future artillery assignment, becoming "a pretty good horseman" after being thrown the first time.[22] Anything that broke the routine of drilling and offered actual combat skills was welcome.

The most popular branch of service was the air force due to its technical novelty and the romantic aura of gentlemanly duels in the sky. Believing "it must be wonderful to rise up into the air," Horst Grothus had joined the air HJ and then the Nazi Flyer corps, learning how to soar with glider planes. When he was finally old enough to join the air force, he graduated to regular motorcraft, passing all of his flying tests in the hope "of becoming a fighter pilot." But just as he completed the elaborate training, the vaunted Luftwaffe ran out of fuel and lost the command of the skies so that he could no longer realize his dream. Other volunteers for the air force who failed to meet the physical requirements, such as Karl Härtel, or who possessed special skills as engineers, were assigned to ground personnel. This "most probably saved [them] from a hero's death," since the mortality rate of pilots was extraordinarily high. Starting as a radio operator, Hans Queiser actually flew a few times as a tail-gunner when he became a war reporter. And the pacifist Erich Helmer became a night interceptor pilot.[23]

Most new soldiers just accepted the inevitable military service and tried to survive it as best as they could. The demanding basic training quickly dispelled "the unconditional enthusiasm" for the war inspired by initial victories. According to Hans Queiser, the cynical effort to turn civilians into real fighting men led to "the rapid dissipation of the idealist fervor which many young soldiers brought into the barracks from the HJ." As Gerhard Joachim was to find out, open criticism of the war, attempts at sabotage, or desertion were ruthlessly suppressed by disciplinary measures ranging from a few days of detention to long imprisonment or assignment to punitive battalions for especially dangerous missions. As a result, most soldiers developed a passive attitude of "accepting the inescapable—if there is no way around it." They learned "never to draw the attention of superiors—not even positively." The lucky ones found a desk job as Paul Frenzel did or were wounded like Rolf Bulwin, after which they were consigned to garrison duty.[24]

The young recruits who "did not relish the notion of killing" assuaged their consciences with a mixture of patriotic and pragmatic arguments. For instance, Gerhard Krapf reasoned that "shielding my family and my homeland, the country of Bach and Goethe, from the Bolshevik horror" outweighed Hitler's responsibility for starting the war. Once in combat, the survival instinct took over, with the alternative of "the simple 'either him or me.'" Pacifist passivity would quickly get one shot. Moreover, industrial warfare made gunning down any attacking enemies, "even from as short a distance as 30 meters . . . more impersonal, hence less revolting than, say, shooting one at close range or bayonetting him." Finally, comradeship demanded resolute action because "any hesitation and/or failure to act in this business of infantry warfare not only endangered yourself but every one of your outfit." While some soldiers also fought for Nazi living space, most believed they were defending their fatherland against mortal danger.[25]

During the initial stages of the war, this mental and physical preparation of youths provided an important advantage to the Wehrmacht. Touched by the verses of the British war poets or the antiwar propaganda of the French popular front, many young men in the West were pacifists or at least civilians who did not want to die in another war. By contrast, many young Germans were indoctrinated by the Hitler Youth in a romantic militarism that prized a hero's death as a necessary sacrifice for the fatherland. Moreover, Joseph Goebbels' propaganda efforts to celebrate the Führer's diplomatic breakthroughs and military successes justified the war as a necessary means to restore Germany's greatness, trampled at Versailles. At the same time, the constant physical exercises in schools and HJ had toughened up youths through paramilitary training that facilitated their transition to the military. "Trusting in the Führer and the victory of our just cause," most young Germans were therefore able and willing to fight.[26]

WEHRMACHT VICTORIES

Initially a stream of victory announcements helped dispel any remaining doubts about the necessity of the war. Introduced by a martial fanfare, special news bulletins would interrupt the regular broadcasts of the national radio network: "Attention, attention, the Supreme Command of the Wehr-

12. Triumphant SS trainees. *Source*: Ruth Bulwin, *Spätes Echo*.

macht announces" that German troops had conquered yet another enemy position. Even critical adults were amazed by "the newsreels [showing] the overwhelming victories on all fronts. What was happening no longer had anything to do with what our fathers had told us about the First World War," observed Wilhelm Kolesnyk. "Everything went incredibly smoothly and precisely as if it were a maneuver or a marching exercise." Teenage boys were glued to the radio at home and marked the progress of German forces on the map with pins in school. Even many soldiers could not quite believe that they were part of what friend and foe considered "the world's best and most powerful fighting machine."[27]

The speed and extent of the triumph over Poland strengthened the Nazi sense of superiority. Since the media had claimed for weeks "that the German minorities living in Poland were being mistreated, beaten, even killed," Gerhardt Thamm believed that "Germany had to act to save fellow Germans." While many people expected a victory "in three-quarters of a year or so," Wilhelm Kolesnyk remembered "how impressive it was when this occurred in eighteen days." In biblical language, Joseph Goebbels crowed, "In eighteen days the Lord has vanquished them." Public opinion failed to notice the part played by the Soviet attack from the rear thanks to the Nazi-Soviet pact of August 1939. Gerhard Baucke recalled the rubble of Warsaw: "Poland—Poland no longer existed. Stalin and Hitler had divided it between them." Most people were convinced that "we Germans were in truth the chosen people, the greatest in every respect, that we were destined to play the leading role in the world and would actually achieve it."[28] Impromptu pictures show SS trainees like Rolf Bulwin having a good time (image 12).

The victories in the West during the spring and summer of 1940 "reinforced this delusion even more strongly." While the invasion of Denmark and Norway seemed "a foolish thing," it was explained as an effort "to beat the *Britishers* to the punch by mere hours." The triumph over France was even more spectacular: it went far beyond the gains of the First World War. Wilhelm Kolesnyk marveled, "Holland conquered in five days, Belgium in twelve and the hereditary enemy France in 49 days in spite of its Maginot line." Gerhardt Thamm's father was part of the assault on the impregnable French defensive system, where "the Führer wanted to demonstrate to the world that 'for a German soldier nothing is impossible.'" Moving in behind the front, Hans Queiser found "a country in defeat," with some buildings destroyed, long columns of POWs, and panic-stricken civilians in full flight. Horst Grothus noted, "We are enthused by our victories and proud of our soldiers who are the best in the world."[29]

By contrast, the importance of losing the air battle over Britain was hardly understood. Grandiloquently Hermann Göring had promised that his Luftwaffe "would beat England into submission." Technically the Messerschmitt 109 fighter was the superior plane, but the Spitfires proved more agile, making the Heinkel 111 bomber a sitting duck. Though German tactics of "free hunt" claimed many British planes, in the long run the use of radar, the rescue of downed pilots, and the location of airfields in the north proved more important. While the initial Luftwaffe attacks on air bases, industrial sites, and supply lines caused considerable damage, the later shift to targeting cities such as Coventry and London in retaliation for British raids proved disastrous. The collateral "killing of 'civilians' by their bombs only troubled a few" airmen, who told themselves "that they were just paying like with like." In spite of relentless attacks, the Germans lost even more planes and failed to achieve the control of airspace that was necessary for an invasion.[30]

The chief reason for the Wehrmacht's initial success on land was its adaptation to the possibilities of a new kind of warfare. As only small cogs in a murderous machine, the memoirists rarely use the word *Blitzkrieg* in order to describe the novel combination of lethal force that made the German Army superior. As first suggested by theoreticians such as B. H. Liddell Hart and Charles de Gaulle, it was the combination of massed tanks, dive bombers, and mobile artillery that breached enemy lines and surrounded entire armies, cutting their communication and supply links in order to force them to surrender. Hitler's massive rearmament had developed weapons systems such as the Stukas, which struck fear into their enemies' hearts, while the systematic militarization of youths had produced crews ready to use them without compunction. But once the victories no longer continued, some soldiers, such as Hans Queiser, began to realize that this was turning into "a war of conquest and annihilation" that might drag on and on.[31]

During the first years of the war, soldiers coped with German losses by considering them necessary costs of ultimate victory. To the young men caught up in the struggle, there was no denying that even military success demanded an increasing death toll. Gerhardt Thamm remembered that in "May, June, and July of 1940, our hometown newspaper was filled with death notices. Silesia had lost the cream of its youth." His father survived a shrapnel fragment that ripped into his chest only because he was carrying "a pocket-sized version of the New Testament." Soldiers tended to pass over the death of a comrade by attributing their own survival to blind luck or better training. In midst of a staff conversation, Heinz Schultheis heard the *hhhssssscht* of an approaching grenade and threw himself down. "A thunderclap" later and the master sergeant was wounded by a splinter in his thigh and the first lieutenant "had turned into a corpse with a smashed head." Although nothing happened to Schultheis, "the uncanny randomness of the hit shocked [him] for a long time."[32]

The actual combat experience was a mixture of excitement, fear, and tedium. Raw recruits tended to look forward eagerly to their "baptism of fire," hoping to prove their mettle. But when they witnessed comrades being wounded or passed disfigured corpses, many soldiers feared they might be next. "Up to this point I had not seen a dead man, was shocked and mortally afraid," Horst Andrée recalled. The survival instinct made them want to be anywhere else. "More than once I said to myself, if I could only be at home." Similarly, flying as a tail-gunner into massive antiaircraft fire, Hans Queiser "got to know a whole new quality of fear." To suppress such fright, commanders often issued extra rations of schnapps or methamphetamine drugs. While noncommissioned officers showed green recruits how to survive combat, lieutenants led the charge in order to inspire the men to follow their example.[33] This system worked fairly well as long as orders seemed reasonable and objectives were gained so that attacks made sense to the men. Between bursts of action, there were also long stretches of boredom, which the soldiers filled by playing cards or writing letters home.

Robert Neumaier reports that "all were enthusiastic to be finally used as real soldiers, defending the fatherland, and participating in the 'ultimate victory.'" But first, they had to be trained for their actual tasks and assembled at their military bases. Then they "were loaded onto a freight train, whose wagons were only furnished with a stove and some straw." Wehrmacht troop transports often took days to reach their distant destinations because they had to wait on sidings to let civilian, supply, or hospital trains pass. Upon arrival, units had to disembark and march on to reach staging areas from which they would be deployed to the front, known as "the main fighting line," in order to reinforce positions, prepare for an attack, or fend off enemy offensives. Since enlisted men had little information about the course of battle, all they could do was to grin and bear the orders that they seldom understood.[34]

An infantry attack created an explosion of violence that heightened perception and released the men's animal instincts. Usually it began with "withering artillery fire opposed by an equally heavy barrage of enemy artillery." Gerhard Krapf describes that in this "suddenly unleashed fury, one mechanically moved forward, sprinting from crater to crater." Due to the shelling "the ground heaved, the air was filled with the deadly and destructive products of man's hatred, the atmosphere shivered with the uproar of murderous machinery." Ignoring "a lovely blue flower," he "moved on, alternately sprinting and firing." Time seemed to stand still. "Hunger, thirst, and sensation no longer registered, on and on we stumbled." At last, coming to a trench, he "was checked by a ghastly obstacle" of intertwined German and enemy bodies. On reaching yet another trench, he made out "Germans, fellows from various units," whom he gathered in order to hold the objective. "Now we had regained [the assigned position], but at what cost!"[35]

Whenever the movement stopped, classic trench warfare developed in intricate fortified positions that shielded combatants from enemy fire. Often prepared by slave laborers of the Organisation Todt, German trenches were narrow, about six feet deep, and ran in zig-zag patterns so as to avoid cross fire. Sections were anchored by machine gun positions and every five yards there were rifle stands with overlapping firing ranges. Forward observation posts were connected to infantry trenches, which were backed up by supply and staging positions. For protection, crews built elaborate bunkers with double bunks, tables, and woodstoves, giving "the impression of comfort and warmth." Gerhard Krapf's dugout was "a model of trench life style," being quite roomy and "covered with a double layer of logs, on top of which had been placed a thick blanket of twigs and dirt."[36] These shelters were the places where soldiers huddled in inclement weather, wolfed down the food of the field kitchens, and killed time between active engagements.

One important key to survival was the comradeship by which soldiers supported each other in life-and-death situations. Living and fighting in close quarters created a male bond that women had a hard time understanding. In the squad, led by noncoms, everyone depended upon the competence of everyone else. Lone fighters did not survive long. In the platoon, headed by lieutenants, the covering of flanks was essential in order to avoid being attacked from the rear. In the company, higher officers set the tone of the outfit by interpreting orders creatively, thereby engendering trust in their troops. Because shirking duty, cowardice before the enemy, and quarreling with one's fellows had lethal consequences, these inclinations were suppressed by the soldiers themselves. The chief reason why wounded men, once recovered, volunteered to go back to their primary group, was this sense of fellowship. Robert Neumaier returned to the front because "there was true existential comradeship; everyone stood up for everyone else."[37]

Wehrmacht superiors also selected exceptionally valorous and battle-proven soldiers for officer training. Many privates, such as Paul Frenzel, were happy to keep their heads down, because not being noticed increased chances of survival considerably. But other patriotic youths such as Hans Tausch, Heinz Schultheis, and Gerhard Krapf were delighted to be promoted and sent to officer school. Due to having been wounded, the latter was exempted from marching drill, "but the greater portion of activities consisted of weapons theory and practice and of classroom instruction in disciplines such as military law . . . tactics . . . troop leadership and such things." Moreover, there was additional specialist training for each respective army branch. For his artillery assignment, he had "to brush up and/or take the trouble to acquaint [him]self with logarithms and a lot of math" for calculating the flight path of shells. When he was on furlough, his "mother was very proud of her officer son who looked so dashing in his new uniform."[38]

A large part of the German forces was not engaged in mortal combat but rather served in relative comfort in the occupied territories. Ethnic Germans, in particular, welcomed Wehrmacht soldiers, as they were grateful to be freed from hostile control. According to Gerhardt Thamm, "after their liberation mother's uncles and aunts confirmed Herr Goebbels' story of atrocities against Germans committed by Poles," which made them glad to be included in the expanded boundaries of the Reich. Other nationalities, such as Hungarians, who looked for German help against their Slavic neighbors were also pleased to be allied with the Wehrmacht and hoped for a return of ethnic diasporas to their national state. Because the fighting had been less acrimonious there and Nazis respected their populations more, the occupation regimes in Western and Northern Europe were generally less oppressive than in the East, which was to be Germanized.[39] In the occupied countries, soldiers who were no longer battle-fit guarded prisoner-of-war camps, supply routes, and military bases.

France was an especially popular billet. Many Germans loved or at least respected the country. According to Hans Queiser, the victors "did not hate the French," having often learned the language in high school and visited its attractive tourist destinations. Most occupiers regretted that Paris had entered the war because of the Polish Corridor and simply reasoned that "it had to be defeated so that Britain can be eliminated." Moreover, the troops lived in relative comfort by settling in to the military installations of the defeated and enjoying the wines and cuisine of their involuntary hosts. While they found that the majority of the French "avoided any contact with the Germans," some young locals who were impressed with the Wehrmacht were interested in talking about "a united Europe under German leadership." A few young women were also willing to flirt with the dashing victors. The collaboration of the conservative Vichy regime made it easy to overlook the first instances of national resistance.[40]

Even better was an assignment to the Channel Islands. Compared with other duties, "living on the island was . . . the purest vacation." Paul Frenzel recalled that "the British did not think of bombing their own island" in order to protect its inhabitants. Hellmut Raschdorff marveled about "the lodgings, dining halls, and lounges—I did not live this well at home." Since the Royal Navy was not about to attack, the main challenge for the occupation forces was not to get too bored. With reading books, watching films, listening to piano recitals, and savoring the food such as the abundant lobsters, the troops tried to idle the time away. While the fortification of the islands by slave laborers required supervision, there was still plenty of time for making anti-Hitler jokes or holding chess tournaments. Even the arrival of a "gold pheasant," a Nazi political officer, who ordered Raschdorff to stand watch in the harbor, could not spoil the mood.[41] Such idyllic duties were exceptional, but they made soldiers temporarily forget the deadly reality of war.

Similarly, being sent to Norway seemed like winning the lottery. After the initial conquest there was no longer any major fighting. Nazi propaganda made it appear to Hans Queiser "that the German Wehrmacht was almost in a friendly country" and that it would not be difficult to convince these "Nordic people" to accept "the necessity of a German Europe." A minority of Norwegians embraced this optimistic offer and the local fascist leader, Vidkun Quisling, was ready to accept his subservient role. Moreover, the long occupation also led to a number of liaisons between Norwegian women and German soldiers which resulted in over nine thousand children. But the majority of the population reacted "with icy disregard" to enemy soldiers when they dared to show up in a theater.[42] In spite of the official rhetoric of friendship, the arrogant behavior of the Germans eventually inspired the formation of a vigorous resistance movement that made the country a rather dangerous place for the occupiers.

By contrast, wherever the Wehrmacht had plundered and supported rigorous Germanization policies, the young soldiers met with open hatred. For instance, in the prewar conquest of the protectorate of Bohemia and Moravia, the ethnic struggle between Germans and Czechs had left deep-seated hostility. The Sudeten German Hans Tausch recalled, "My homeland could no longer be Austrian, it did not want to be Czech, and it would have liked to become Reich-German." The economic exploitation and political repression of the Czechs fueled a fundamental revulsion that equated everything German with National Socialism. Similarly, in the general government of Poland, the brutality of the Nazi conquest, the murder of part of the elite during the combat, and the merciless mistreatment of the defeated population engendered an aversion that made collaboration unpopular. One Polish nurse confided to the wounded Paul Frenzel, "as suppressed [people] we must be quiet. But things will change again someday."[43]

Surprisingly enough, the autobiographies also contain sporadic references to local supporters who eased the burden of warfare for young soldiers. Most Germans looked down upon their allies, such as the Italians, who "just could not do anything right," since they proved unable to defeat even the Albanians. Nonetheless, the Wehrmacht used numerous local assistants, collected in units of HIWIS, an abbreviation for the word *Hilfswillige* (volunteers). Gerhard Baucke commanded thirty POWs as assistants to man a field bakery that produced bread for an entire company. In some instances, a close relationship developed between individual soldiers and their local helpers, since the latter knew the lay of the land. Robert Neumaier baldly states that during the winter retreat in the East, "I owed my life to my Russian comrade." Sometimes it was just an unexpectedly warm reception by a farmer who provided food and shelter or a supportive smile by a young woman that restored a tired soldier's spirit.[44]

The Wehrmacht used a whole range of measures to maintain the morale of its fighting troops. Surprisingly enough, direct political indoctrination is only rarely mentioned in the recollections, if at all. During basic training, soldiers had to attend formal lectures on the purpose of the war, the nature of the enemy, and the like. When it was Gerhard Krapf's turn to hold forth on the adage that "war is the father of all things," he used the opportunity to argue "that war most certainly could not be seen as productive of anything but destruction"—and he actually got away with this critical view. Nazi political officers were generally disliked because they were not considered to be real fighting men. Most soldiers were not in the war to advance National Socialist goals, but rather for the sake of "defending the 'good' Germany from an army of brutal Bolsheviks threatening to bring the war home to Germany." Even while it was serving the Führer's cause, the army "to a degree still represented pre-Hitlerian ideals" of patriotism.[45]

More effective was the slanted reporting from the front by journalists in special propaganda companies. As a war reporter, Hans Queiser recalled that " 'ideological conformity' was a matter of course" because his stories had to pass censorship. "Naturally, top priority was a 'positive' portrayal of German victories and successes—as long as these existed." It also went without saying "that our own losses, failures, and catastrophes were not allowed to be reported." Soldiers only laughed about "invented hurrah-reports," since such whitewashing lacked credibility. With the increasing length of the war, "it was to a certain degree 'desired' for reports to reflect something of 'the toughness of the struggle' " as long as these were not too realistic. Because troops only knew about "the events which took place in their immediate vicinity," the more thoughtful ones were desperate for any news that allowed them to get an overall impression of how the war was going.[46] As a result, many soldiers developed a talent of reading between the propaganda lines.

Another method of reinforcing the fighting spirit was promotion and decoration as a result of exceptional valor. Due to the limitation of the Reichswehr to one hundred thousand men by the Treaty of Versailles, the Wehrmacht had a constant need for officers, especially since junior ranks were most at risk. When a private such as Hans Tausch showed unusual bravery in serving as a tank gunner, his commander promoted him to sergeant on the battlefield "by handshake" in order to take over for personnel killed in action. But as an officer candidate he still had to complete formal training. Soldiers with wounds often received special badges to indicate that they had been hurt in combat. More coveted was the *Eisernes Kreuz* (Iron Cross), a decoration invented during the Wars of Liberation against Napoleon. Though Tausch was immediately decorated with the EKII, Gerhard Krapf never received this honor because a superior blocked the award. The converse was a "death command"—a lethal assignment by an officer who wanted to get rid of a disliked soldier for presumed dereliction of duty.[47]

Regular mail service of letters and packages maintained emotional ties between the front and the home and was essential for shoring up morale. Based on the experience of World War I, the Wehrmacht devoted considerable resources to assuring steady deliveries, since mail served as a sign of life that reduced anxieties about the fate of loved ones. To reassure young soldiers who did not yet have girlfriends, the BdM asked its members to start corresponding with an unknown soldier. One day Erich Helmer received a letter that began: "Dear anonymous recipient, I have no idea what is hiding behind the field-post number except that you must be in the air force." More important was correspondence between newlyweds, such as Kurt and Anneliese Huber: "And yet it is a painful joy to offer consolation to you while I myself need it because of the separation from you which is so hard to bear."[48] Although censorship suppressed military information and political commentary, the letters were an emotional lifeline for both partners.

When the front was stable enough, entertainment was an important means to distract soldiers from the murderousness of fighting. One means of diversion was the showing of films like the fabulous adventures of Baron von Münchhausen starring Hans Albers, "which let one forget the war." The radio was also essential for troops stationed far away from home. Sentimental hits such as "Lili Marlene" by singers such as Lale Andersen touched the heart by promising a reunion: "Underneath the Lantern / by the barrack gate / darling, I remember / how you used to wait." Few soldiers were as lucky as the noncom pilot Rudi Müller, who beat out his officers in attracting the favor of the touring popular singer Evelyn Künneke, best known for the song "Have You Kissed in the Dark?" For troops stationed in the rear, there were also occasional church services, in which the chaplains prayed patriotically for Germany's victory.[49] During short leaves, small-town soldiers often engaged in military tourism, marveling at the cultural wonders of Vienna, Paris, or Rome.

The Wehrmacht also made arrangements for the sexual urges of the soldiers, which intensified in a male company facing potential death. Many young men were still inexperienced and channeled their fantasies into ribald jokes. When Erich Helmer wanted to meet a girlfriend, his noncom bellowed, "without a condom, no liberty," forcing him to beg one from his comrades, much to his embarrassment. In France, Hans Queiser was ordered to make use of a "plush bordello" populated by local prostitutes. "In spite of service in five minute intervals, queues formed in the street." His own experience was not exactly appealing. "To be sure the little French woman who took me to her room was friendly, but rapidly 'took care of business.'" Erich Helmer was shocked to encounter Jewish women who had been forced to choose between a "KZ or bordello . . . ! What kind of human beings are these who order something like that?"[50] Such facilities were supposed to decrease venereal disease and rape at the price of reducing lovemaking to a biological act.

Another measure to restore the spirit was the granting of furloughs in order to get away from the violence of combat and see loved ones. Before being shipped out to the front, Gerhard Krapf enjoyed a couple of precious weeks at home, getting ready for the challenges to come. By contrast, Erich Helmer risked disciplinary action by sneaking away from his unit on weekends to spend time with his girlfriend, fortunately escaping the censure of a couple of zealous party members. When Karl Härtel received "five days of furlough," he traveled home to Breslau in overcrowded trains, "coming completely unexpectedly" for Christmas. "Nonetheless, or perhaps because of the surprise, the joy of our reunion was especially great." Such breaks from military discipline allowed soldiers to savor free time in a peaceful setting that reminded them what they were fighting for. Mothers, especially, used the opportunity to lavish love on their sons by feeding and caring for them because they might never see them again.[51]

A more painful way to escape combat was to be wounded seriously enough to be shipped home, but not so gravely as to die. Scouting an enemy artillery position, Gerhard Krapf "felt a sharp rap at my left elbow and—somehow I seemed to have sprained my ankle [and] fell backwards" because he was being "shot at with an automatic pistol." Playing dead face-down in the mud, he used a shell explosion nearby to scramble back to his unit, where a medic cut open his boot and diagnosed a bullet in his ankle. "Moaning and thrashing about" at night, he was then wheeled on a cart to an assembly point and from there taken by motorized ambulance to a triage station that sent him on to a field hospital. After making sure that he was not faking, a fanatical Nazi doctor had him loaded on "a hospital train" to the rear where more extensive examination revealed that the elbow had been grazed but the bullet that had gone through the right foot had smashed his heel bone.[52] This was a classic *Heimatschuss*, requiring therapy at home.

In contrast to the improvised first-aid behind the lines, soldiers experienced the treatment in military hospitals in Germany as a real relief. "Spanking clean, beautiful white linen, fresh smelling blankets, good mattress . . . what luxuries!" Gerhard Krapf remembered. He found the nurses solicitous, and the doctors competent. "What a wonderful feeling it was to be home in Germany, and in such a lovely place, as yet totally untouched by the war." Though Hans Tausch was wounded in the left heel as well, he was delighted not to have been killed: "I had gotten away with it again." Due to an accident that required three operations on his left foot, Paul Frenzel was hospitalized for several months, but eventually discharged as no longer fit for military duty. Krapf's and Tausch's rehabilitation also took time, requiring lengthy physical therapy and a stint of duty in the reserves, but eventually they recovered sufficiently to be sent back to the front.[53] A moderately severe wound was therefore a ticket home—at least for a time.

Being at home also allowed young men to renew their romantic relationships. The uncertainty of war often led to a more rapid consummation than during peacetime. After another affair, Erich Helmer discovered the love of his life in Gretel and persuaded her on the spot to become his bride. Even if it had not been infatuation at first sight, but "a deepening affection," Karl Härtel and Erna Katterwe also decided to become engaged due to "the confrontation with this miserable war." Against the opposition of his status-conscious father, Paul Frenzel resolved to get married to a spirited working-class girl, "his Martel," since he was making enough money in war production to support a young family. "Happy to have found one another," BdM leader Ruth Kolb and Waffen SS soldier Rolf Bulwin tied the knot in a secular Nazi wedding ceremony called "marriage consecration." They vowed to enter "a union of fidelity to each other and our Führer." The registrar enjoined them "to become a family, blessed by many children."[54]

When the war dragged on and on, the young soldiers gradually gave up hope for a quick ending and became cynical about Nazi propaganda. Gradually the victory announcements of the Wehrmacht on the radio, popularly known as "Goebbels' snout," lost their impact as the fighting continued. Also, party slogans such as "the Führer commands—we'll follow" sounded more and more hollow, because it was not clear where the voyage would lead. Instead anti-Nazi jokes circulated in the barracks. One favorite was: "A real German is blond like Hitler, athletic like Göring, clear-eyed like Himmler, with physical prowess like Goebbels." (This was funny because the Führer had dark hair, the air force head was fat, the SS leader wore glasses, and the propaganda chief had a club foot.) And another, after Hitler's deputy surprisingly flew to England: "Churchill asks Hess, 'Are you the crazy one?' 'No sir,' Hess replies, 'I am his deputy.' "[55] While the mood at the front turned sour, the less-informed public still believed in the Führer and final victory.

In spite of the continually increasing death toll of their comrades, the young soldiers continued to fight. Karl Härtel described his shock upon receiving a letter with the news that his older brother had just died. "Every day one could read about the heroic death of unknown people, but when it concerned my own brother, I had to recognize that behind every one of the many little notices towered an immense mountain of pain and suffering." Mothers usually took bereavement harder than fathers, who tended to rationalize the need for military sacrifices. Even if other siblings had already passed away in peacetime, the pain was intense, since Hans "was an outstanding member of our family and its whole pride [was] due to his achievements" as an officer. Similarly, Erich Helmer was inconsolable when in April 1945 he received the telegram "Your brother Justus has been killed in action."[56] While this traumatic scene was repeated in thousands of families, memorial ceremonies heroicized such deaths as service to the fatherland.

INEXORABLE DEFEATS

Hitler's invasion of Russia on June 22, 1941 once again changed the character of the war, this time from lightning strikes to plodding attrition. The Balkan detour to bail out Mussolini in the spring was the last Blitzkrieg, though it cost time, materiel, and manpower that could not be replaced. Skeptics who believed that "those Italians can't carry water in a bucket" were reassured by the daring exploits of Rommel's Africa Corps. But the attack on Russia was another matter. The Soviet Union was a vast country with a large population and immense natural resources. All leaves were cancelled, new recruits like Heinz Schultheis were called up, and war production was raised to a higher level. One morning during training, Schultheis's sergeant woke up the troops to convey the shocking news: "War with the Soviet Union!" Since the mutually beneficial neutrality had seemed "like quite a stroke of genius of our great Führer," the announcement caught soldiers unawares. But "now everyone knew: This war will last a long, long time!"[57]

The initial months of the Russian campaign belied such forebodings. The Wehrmacht advanced with dazzling speed. In spite of intelligence warnings, Stalin was surprised and Russian defenses in Eastern Poland were overrun relatively quickly. In forced marches, lugging heavy gear, German soldiers then poured into Ukraine and Belarus. "Almost daily huge victories were announced," Gerhard Baucke remembered. "In great encirclement battles thousands upon thousands of prisoners and big amounts of war materiel fell into German hands." Ethnic Germans, Ukrainians, and Tartars "greeted us as liberators from Bolshevism, asked us into their clean, pretty houses and entertained us with what little they had left." According to Horst Grothus, the pictures of "emaciated POWs" shown in newsreels "confirm[ed] everything we had expected from the Russian subhumans."[58] When the Wehrmacht reached the gates of Moscow, Nazi leaders and followers succumbed to the illusion that the war had already been won.

The Soviet counteroffensive quickly proved that Russia was not about to collapse; it halted the German advance and made the invaders defend their gains. Hellmut Raschdorff remembered the wet fall "in which we almost drowned in the mud," because the rain rendered the dirt roads impassable. "Then inexorably a winter approached whose rigors we could not imagine." The Wehrmacht troops were unprepared for the severity of the cold, which reached −50C°, forcing them to stuff their boots with newspaper and wear "two undershirts, two briefs, overalls, and on top the uniform and coat." These incredibly low temperatures halted supplies, stopped tanks in their tracks, shattered metal gun barrels, and froze the food. Attacking with fresh troops transferred from the Far East of Russia, the Red Army used its devastating rocket launchers and the unstoppable T-34 tanks.[59] The astounded Germans were forced to retreat from the outskirts of Moscow, stabilizing their lines only by desperate efforts further west.

Though the Wehrmacht and its Finnish allies were able to encircle Leningrad, they proved unable to conquer it. Heinz Schultheis was sent to reinforce the stranglehold of German forces around the city with his motorized antiaircraft battery. The troops were shocked by the cold, which even a special decoration, colloquially called the "frozen flesh medal," could not alleviate. "This winter has saved the Soviet Union." Shooting down fighter planes like the Ilyushin 2 from fortified bunkers soon became routine. But even continual German dive-bomber attacks failed to cut the last remaining supply line into the city, which was always repaired overnight. Hitler then made a "decidedly criminal" decision, condemning the besieged city to starvation. "The 'success' of this unsoldierly, deeply dishonorable and rather characterless order were 750,000 mostly civilian victims." After stopping the first assault, the Russian defenders rallied and counterattacked and finally broke the encirclement after two bloody years.[60]

While the Wehrmacht was bogging down in Russia, "the news of the Japanese attack on Pearl Harbor broke," further complicating the strategic situation. "A few days later Hitler declared war on the United States," expanding the "war in Europe [into] a new world war, which now got the ordinal number two." The belittling claim "many enemies—much honor" struck Gerhard Baucke as "a stupid propaganda phrase!" Due to Washington's manpower and industrial production, Gerhardt Thamm's father thought that "this time [Hitler] overstepped himself" and that "he had no idea how strong and big America really was." Hitler's error was compounded by a signal lack of military coordination between the Axis allies. Bent on conquering raw materials from Western colonies, Japan missed the opportunity of attacking Russia from the rear. While it took time before the military consequences of that fateful decision became clear, critical minds instinctively understood that the entry of the United States meant "that Germany would lose the war for sure."[61]

The Russian stalemate and the US entry forced Nazi Germany to make a more systematic effort to mobilize its manpower and materiel reserves to make up for its structural inferiority. One effect was extending the draft to younger age cohorts, those born in the mid-1920s. Gerhard Krapf's high-school instruction was broken off and his classmates received their graduation diplomas one year early. Moreover, wounded soldiers such as Paul Frenzel who had been dismissed were called up and shipped back to the front lines in the East. The military physicians steadily lowered their requirements for combat duty in order to fill the thinning ranks. At the same time, the output of war production was increased so as to provide the necessary tanks and airplanes for a prolonged struggle. Finally, Goebbels' propaganda began to predict "the total enslavement of the German people" in case of defeat. Instead of confidence in victory, the soldiers' mood deteriorated to "resignation and fatalism—soon it was only a matter of survival."[62]

During the summer of 1942, the Wehrmacht launched another strike to regain the initiative in the East by moving toward the oilfields of the Caucasus. "We attacked Soviet units marching toward the front and rolled over the Russian artillery positions," Hans Tausch remembered. "As quickly as we showed up, we disappeared in wide steppe. Thereby we struck the enemy, but were no longer able to mount large operations with far-flung objectives as in the year before." Nonetheless, Benno Schöffski's outfit "could see in the distance the 5,600-meter-high Mount Elbrus," on which some intrepid alpinists had managed to plant the German flag. In early fall, these advances carried the German troops into the outskirts of Stalingrad, a large industrial city that commanded the crossing over the Volga River. Its strategic position as the hinge of the entire Southeastern front meant that the Wehrmacht absolutely wanted to conquer it, while the Soviet defenders were willing to fight to the last man in order to hold it.[63]

The decisive battle that shook the Wehrmacht's confidence and turned the tide of the war in the East therefore took place at Stalingrad. The close house-to-house fighting negated its advantages in tank mobility and artillery firepower, favoring the Red Army's desperate resistance with small arms and willingness to die for the motherland. The attackers managed to clear most of the western part of city except for a small enclave, but failed to get to the eastern side of the river. Arriving in January 1942 at the outskirts, Robert Neumaier found the conditions terrible. Already a large number of his comrades had been killed at the train station with a grenade. He then had to dig into the icy soil to create a foxhole for protection, was forced to warm his frozen food in his pocket before he could eat it, and developed scabies from not being able to wash. "At the dawn the Russians stormed down from the hills upon our positions" shouting a terrible "Urrrray, Urrrray." Although machine gun fire stopped their attacks, "we grew more and more afraid that would no longer get out alive."[64]

The outcome of the struggle was decided by a Russian counterattack at the periphery. North of the city, the Soviet forces "had punched a wide hole into the front composed of weak German and allied units," turning west and then southward, thereby trapping the entire Sixth Army at Stalingrad. Though

Hitler had vowed "nobody else will get to where a German soldier has gone," his command to Field Marshal Paulus not to retreat sealed the invaders' fate when Field Marshal von Manstein's effort to break the encirclement failed. A courageous battalion commander nonetheless "ordered a breakout in the direction of Millerowo." The Russians let the soldiers pass, then killed nine hundred of the 1,200 men by running over fleeing Germans, Italians, and Romanians with tanks. Suddenly Neumaier faced a Soviet soldier with his rifle drawn. "We looked at each other, neither of us shot, we nodded and separated." Unlike the 150,000 dead and ninety-one thousand captured Germans, by joining the desperate flight he "escaped the Hell of Stalingrad.!!!"[65]

Gradually soldiers and civilians realized that this defeat "marked the turning point of the war which, from then on, was no longer winnable." Gerhardt Thamm remembered that "the whole country was in mourning, yet we were also proud of our soldiers." The problem was that "other devastating news" followed this tragedy. "In May 1943 some 250,000 Germans and Italians were captured in North Africa" when the Anglo-American forces surrounded the vaunted Africa Corps. In late July, the Fascist Grand Council voted 16 to 9 to depose Mussolini, and in early September Italy switched to the Allied side. Retrained as a parachutist, Robert Neumaier reported, "The Italian barracks close to us were stormed during the night." In the battle for Rome "we met strong resistance," but his small force actually succeeded in capturing the city. More important was the failure of the Wehrmacht attack at Kursk in the largest tank battle in history, in which the Germans squandered their new Panthers and Tigers without regaining the initiative.[66]

One of the chief reasons for the turning of the military tide was the seemingly inexhaustible manpower of the Red Army and its willingness to take casualties. Still new at the front, Gerhard Krapf had to face a Russian infantry charge in which "all hell broke loose." The attack began with an artillery barrage with hundreds of guns shelling furiously for over two hours, making "horrendous noise" and heaving the earth. Krapf's "stomach was registering all this with 'knotting together,'" and he "cowered down at the floor of the trench, seeking protection." One of his men "had been hit, his left eye was hanging out of its socket." And then the Russians came: "In one huge line they advanced, running in short spurts . . . shouting a piercing 'Urrrrray.'" The German defenders "responded with calmly aimed machine gun and carbine fire. But on and on they came, a second, a third line." Fortunately, Krapf got his jammed machine gun working again. "The Russian attack had faltered, they had sustained tremendous losses. Ours were relatively small."[67]

Another cause of the growing number of Wehrmacht defeats was the superiority of the Allied weapons used against it. Initially German systems such as the Stuka dive bombers and the tanks connected by voice radio had proven effective, but, misled by the victories, Hitler stopped further development. Trying to catch up, the Western Allies constructed entire new technologies such as radar, which wreaked havoc on enemy airplanes and submarines. In the East, the simpler Russian weapons proved better adapted to the climate than complicated German machines. The infantry especially feared the "Stalin organs," mobile rocket launchers that were inaccurate but nonetheless deadly by "widely scattering shrapnel." Similarly, the T-34 tanks had "two ingenious advantages." Their "track-drives were twice as wide" as the German ones, making them superior in mud and ice, and "they were built with steel plates of oblique angles" that proved difficult to pierce. Frantic German efforts to catch up were too little and too late.[68]

Even more important in a prolonged struggle was the inferiority of Nazi Germany in war production in spite of the resources of the occupied countries and allies. Simply put, in all essential categories such as manufacturing airplanes, artillery pieces, or tanks, not to mention ammunition and gas for jeeps and trucks, the equipment of the Grand Alliance of Britain, the United States, and the Soviet Union was vastly superior. Horst Grothus noted, "Our armaments are generally poor, rather uneven" due to the diversity of captured weapons. "Our losses in men and materiel rose frightfully," Hans Tausch reported about bottlenecks: "We had no more tanks, replacements were not supplied." Similarly, according to Hans Queiser, experienced fighter pilots were unable to cope with masses of often-neophyte enemies. Lacking sufficient fuel, their aircraft could no longer fly or be repaired or replaced. Since "there were no longer enough interceptors available for an effective defense," the consequence became "crystal clear: the Amis and Brits had air superiority over the 'Greater Reich,' but we did not."[69]

Sporadic comments in the autobiographies suggest that the war was also being lost politically: the Wehrmacht setbacks raised doubts about a German victory. Trying to mobilize for "total war," Goebbels' propaganda machine talked euphemistically about "shortening the front lines." Even if some still believed the Nazi lies, others who followed the news on the map realized that German territory was shrinking drastically. Because "the political climate was no longer as strongly characterized by fear, open criticism began to be voiced." Similarly, it was difficult to understand that "Germany occupied Hungary and Romania while Hungarian and Romanian army units were still fighting bravely alongside their comrades." In the occupied countries, collaborators began to distance themselves noticeably from the Wehrmacht, worried about what would happen to them should the Germans lose.[70] Finally, the defeats encouraged local resistance attacks on Wehrmacht supply lines, which led to savage retribution.

During the interminable retreats, death became an ever more-threatening presence for the young soldiers. It was no longer just an occasional misfortune that one could write off as a necessary evil in a great enterprise, but rather an ubiquitous danger. In a letter from home, Hermann Debus heard that both sons of a neighbor had "been killed in action. Hans drowned with a submarine and Willi perished in Russia. Within a fortnight the family lost both sons." Moreover, "I had to read that my friend—Hermann Hehner—also died in Russia." Similarly, Joachim Fest lost his much-admired older brother to a miserable "lung infection" contracted in a military hospital in the East because there were no antibiotics. His mother considered the death "an unspeakable misfortune for our family" and was in no mood to forgive Hitler. More and more youths became convinced that "this war cannot be won any longer." And yet military discipline held and the soldiers continued to fight.[71]

On the battlefield, the transformation of the character of the war from rapid conquest to prolonged struggle unleashed an explosion of violence that surpassed all accepted bounds. Due to technical developments, weapons had already become deadlier than during the First World War, wreaking more physical havoc and costing more human lives than before. During the initial Blitzkrieg, the ferocity of the attack remained focused on breaking through enemy lines and encircling whole armies. This limited the carnage to largely military targets, even if the Polish campaign already showed the potential for indiscriminate use of force. But with the shift to attrition, the violence intensified. More soldiers and increasingly also civilians were killed. In addition, the ideologization of warfare dehumanized enemies, leading to large-scale mass murder when the aim became not just victory, but the annihilation of entire populations. As a result of increasing brutality, troops experienced "the terrible, cruel soldierly life [as a] dirty, stinking, bloody reality."[72]

One aspect of the increasing violence was the "scorched earth" tactic, favored during withdrawal in order to deny the advancing enemy potential resources. Initiated by the Red Army, this policy was adopted by the Wehrmacht when they lost control of occupied territory so as to delay pursuit and leave a gruesome reminder of its power. Gerhard Baucke describes the retreat from the Crimea: "For the population the withdrawal was a catastrophe. I do not want to go into the details and only say that the pioneers were the rear-guard, doing a real job of scorched earth. Nothing, absolutely nothing was left for the cautiously following foe." This devastating method not only destroyed military supplies and ammunition that could not be carried along, but demolished infrastructural targets such as bridges, train tracks, and roads.[73] The orgy of destruction engulfed raw material and factories as well as power plants and food depots, leaving the civilians without means of survival. Due to its brutality, this tactic sowed hatred and inspired revenge.

Another dimension of the protracted struggle was a successive dehumanization of the troops. This led to increased cruelty against enemies, even when they had surrendered. In the beginning, the Wehrmacht somewhat respected the rules of the Hague Convention, for it did not want its own soldiers subjected to inhumane treatment if captured. But with the prolonging of the war, respect for such limits vanished. Robert Neumaier reported that a wounded Russian prisoner who was walking directly in front of his tank "was caught by a tread and smashed under it. We drove over him, making me sick." Hellmut Raschdorff recalled that "a comrade next to me raised his gun and fired into a group of civilians." When challenged about the criminality of his action, "he merely replied 'what of it, they are only Russians.'" Similarly, when "a Russian appeared with his hands raised . . . a soldier standing next to us took his rifle and just shot him."[74] These were no longer isolated incidents, but rather typical signs of the escalation of violence.

The so-called antipartisan actions, in particular, erased the distinction between soldiers and civilians and contributed to the increase in the brutality of warfare. When Gerhard Baucke was crossing the Bug River, he "suddenly heard rifle fire," but military police told him to move on: "Go away, there is nothing to be seen, only partisans have been shot!" The next morning, he was gripped by "sheer horror" to see the corpses of "old men, young men, women and children—they were supposed to have been partisans?" An NCO calmed the troops by claiming, "during the conquest of Nikolaev, civilians had participated in the street fighting. Jews were involved as well and in revenge a number were herded together and shot." Similarly, during a Czech school trip, Wilhelm Kolesnyk saw "smoke mushrooming over a village and heard detonations of explosions." While he still "considered the massacre of Lidice a singular case," his father and a Waffen SS veteran testified that "such atrocities happened regularly in Ukraine and in Russia."[75]

The memoirists only hint at the full extent of the violence because its graphic description would be too unsettling. One former soldier described the process of mutual dehumanization in an oral interview. When partisans massacred a hospital train, they had dragged the wounded soldiers out, "cut off their penis, stuck it into their mouths, blinded their eyes and nailed the soldiers to barn doors with their bayonets." He was horrified by the corpses of "two Red Cross nurses whose breasts were cut off and genitalia mutilated." In retaliation, he said, his unit "surrounded a village and started to shoot with tracer and incendiary bullets." When the houses caught fire and people came out, "we mowed them down." As a result of his anger, "this was one of the few times that I shot with determination and conviction" until nothing stirred any longer. "Old men, women, children, partisans." Justified as retaliation for enemy atrocities, such confessions of indiscriminate killing are all too rare, although the actions were repeated countless times.[76]

Ethnic cleansing and racial genocide also involved Wehrmacht soldiers in atrocities that had no military purpose whatsoever. None of the memoirists admits to having been personally involved, but their texts do reveal a widespread knowledge of the Nazi project of annihilation. When Gerhard Baucke was trying to get food, he had "an unforgettable, terrible encounter" with cattle cars on another track: "The doors were locked, and through the small hatches people wailed for water: *Woda pan*, water . . . !" When he tried to help them, a black-uniformed SS guard threatened, "*Nix* water, you comprehend? . . . Get lost or you shall go along as well!" Similarly, Erich Helmer saw the "barracks camp in which Jewish women and girls were housed" who had to work at his airfield: "Here we witnessed the hollowed out bodies with faces larger than life and oversized eyes which begged us 'hunger-hunger!'" Unable to help, he was shocked to hear that, during the subsequent withdrawal, "they were all murdered, just shot."[77]

Increasing violence could only postpone the German defeat after the Western Allies finally landed in Normandy on June 6, 1944. "Three thousand planes were in action in our sector and dropped their bombs," Robert Neumaier recalled the fierce assault on the bunkers of the Atlantic Wall. "We had horrible losses; some of my comrades were buried [alive]." The defenders desperately fired on parachutists, creating "a terrible sight: Dead Americans hung from their chutes in the trees." But Karl Härtel noted, "ever more often we had to witness that our bombers were shot down by enemy fighters or antiaircraft guns," and air cover was lost. Hitler's refusal to commit his reserves against the initial attack proved a decisive mistake. Hans Tausch wondered why "one of the best equipped tank divisions in the West remained inactive" until it was too late. Toward the end of July, the invaders broke through to the South, pulverizing German defenders at Avranches.[78] Within a couple of months, all of France lay open. Photos by the victorious

13. Surrendering SS soldier. *Source*: Stiftung Preussischer Kulturbesitz.

Allies document the surrender of defeated SS troops on the Western front (image 13).

The strategic impact of the Allied landing was shattering: it caught Nazi Germany in an ever-tightening vise from which there was no longer any escape. Robert Neumaier remembered, "With our high casualties, the superior weapons of the enemy and the manpower pressure of the Americans, it was clear that we would not be able to hold out for long." He noted that, among the troops, discipline began to break down when some infantry soldiers "preferred to be taken prisoner. Thereby the war was over for them." Those who, like himself, did not want to give up, continued an adventurous retreat in the direction of the fatherland, traveling on bicycles at night to escape the advancing American tanks and the vengeful resistance fighters. But they failed to construct a new defensive line, and Paris surrendered without a fight. City commander General Dietrich von Choltitz disobeyed orders because he "wanted to avoid the destruction of precious cultural artifacts." Even SS fanatics were unable to stop the dissolution of the front until the retreating troops reached the border of Germany.[79]

The surprising assassination attempt of July 20, 1944 increased the confusion among the soldiers further, for it violated a deep-seated Prussian taboo. Shortly after midnight, Gerhard Krapf "heard Hitler over the radio saying (with a rather hoarse voice) that a 'small clique of ambitious and irresponsible and, at the same time, senseless and stupid officers' had plotted to eliminate him, but that he was unhurt and well." Disappointed regime critics such as Erich Helmer wondered, "why did this not work?," and began to believe that "the war is lost." By contrast, Nazi supporters such as Gerhardt Thamm felt "shock, pure shock," because soldiers had sworn personal oaths to Hitler. "People were confused, they wondered, '*Why would they try to kill the Führer?*'" Instead of praising the heroic resistance effort, most Germans were horrified by it. "With every failed attempt on his life, Hitler's mystique grew." He seemed immortal. Only much later did Gerhard Krapf realize "that on that day Germany's fate had been sealed."[80]

In the East, the Wehrmacht found no effective defense against the relentless Red Army advance, celebrated as "the ten great blows." The Russians amassed superior firepower and personnel in one limited part of the front, broke through the German lines, and stopped after a gain of many miles, only to begin again somewhere else. According to Krapf, the "fearsome T-34s" made the difference due to "the devastating psychological effect of those agile monsters moving toward you, belching deadly-aimed direct cannon fire." The German officers could only entreat their troops not to be caught in the open, "to stay put and not climb out of the trench and run." Instead, they were to fire with their machine guns "at the infantry behind the tanks." The T-34s "indeed rolled over our trench and toward the rear," where artillery annihilated them and the infantry charge was beaten off.[81] While Krapf could breathe a sigh of relief, in the long run the repetition of such attacks broke the Germans' spirit.

Although it "contained a kernel of truth," the popular hope that "miracle weapons" would bring victory turned out to be another propaganda lie. At the end of 1944, even the regular fighter squad to which Hans Queiser was attached had to be "closed down for lack of airplane fuel." The new Messerschmitt 163 rocket fighter, the fastest airplane in the world, reaching speeds of 965 kmh, was still being field-tested, emitting an "incomparable roar." But it could only fly for a few minutes and was produced in too-small numbers to regain control of the skies. The fuselages of the Messerschmitt 162 fighter-bomber, the first jet plane, were built by slave laborers in an underground factory in the north and the engines were manufactured in the south. "But the machines [could] not be put together. Transport ha[d] stopped." Instead of producing antiaircraft missiles, Hitler put priority on the construction of "revenge weapons," the V1 and V2 rockets, which did frightful damage in London, but failed to turn the tide of the war.[82]

The discouraging news of continued "victorious retreats" gradually eroded the morale of the Wehrmacht, even if many soldiers continued to cling to hope. "It was true that the constant retreating, both regarding the large picture [of the] various fronts and the small perspective from within one's regimental sector, produced a general awareness of the war no longer being winnable." It was also discouraging that Finland, Romania, and Hungary followed the Italian example and dropped out of the war or switched sides. Warning of the terrible consequences of defeat, the Reich radio therefore broadcast "endless appeals to persevere." Moreover, the Gestapo, SS, and military police severely punished defeatist commentary with imprisonment or sent the authors of innocuous Hitler jokes on "suicide missions" at the front. When Joachim Fest voiced his "disgust about the death of [his] brother," only the good luck of a sympathetic officer who beat down a denunciation with a "final warning" saved him from a court martial.[83]

Considering the war lost, some discouraged soldiers even attempted to desert to the enemy. Erich Helmer rejected the surprise offer of a French resistance member to convey him to safety in Switzerland out of a sense of patriotic responsibility. But, "preferring to stay alive," Wolfgang Hubbe used a reconnaissance assignment to "jump into freedom" by going over to the British in September 1944. Similarly, pacifist Gerhard Joachim was willing to "desert in order to escape to Sweden and wait for the end of the war there." With a comrade, he left his unit and hid in his parents' apartment, but was awakened on the third night by banging and shouts of "Gestapo, open the door!" Caught, he was condemned to nine months in an army prison for "totally unmilitary behavior." Undiscouraged, he tried again, this time marching in the direction of the Red Army in January 1945. While sheltered at a Polish farm, he watched the SS shoot another soldier, but finally reached the Russian lines, where he was received with a friendly "*stoi*" (stop) and "*Gitler kaput!*" (Hitler is busted).[84]

In spite of ever grimmer prospects, most soldiers believed themselves to be defending Germany's very existence and continued to fight until the bitter end. The Wehrmacht's draconian discipline made malingering into a life-and-death matter: the infamous MPs called *Kettenhunde* tended to shoot without asking questions. The misguided fanaticism of increasingly younger recruits also played a part. When a sergeant told a unit of anti-aircraft boys in too-large uniforms to "go home, war is no playground for kids," they answered glibly: "Grandpa, now *we* will show you how to defeat an enemy." Moreover, horror stories of Russian atrocities did not have to be fabricated, since what Goebbels "said would happen to German men and women, particularly women, should the Red Army be allowed to enter Germany, did happen" at Nemmersdorf in East Prussia. Hence, Gerhard Krapf felt a "genuine determination to keep the Russians from entering Germany." Finally there was also "the feeling for solidarity and comradeship" toward one's survival unit.[85]

The final effort to defend the Reich in 1945 nonetheless fell far short because the Wehrmacht was collapsing from within. Goebbels still "promised ultimate victory, now that President Roosevelt had died," and claimed that miracle weapons would save Germany. But on many fronts, the army was running out of supplies, for Allied air attacks had ruptured the transportation grid. In terms of manpower, "the Wehrmacht was scraping the bottom of the barrel," drafting the hitherto-exempt, Hitler Youths, and older men and throwing them into battle without training. Devoid of planes to fly, air force pilots such as Horst Grothus were converted into infantrymen and used to plug holes in the front despite a lack of appropriate instruction, leadership, and equipment. Due to unrealistic orders, discipline was also breaking down. When commanded to “waste” his unit, Gerhard Krapf dared to contradict a general. Fortunately, he was backed up by a major who revoked the order.[86] Because losses could no longer be made up, the high command moved armies around that existed only on paper.

Even the last-ditch attempt to stop the Allied advance with a people’s militia, called *Volkssturm* in propaganda terms, proved ineffective. As commander of the Reserve Army, SS leader Heinrich Himmler instituted a draft of all sixteen-to-sixty-year-old males and ordered them to fight “until the last man” to defend Germany. But in practice, the militia looked pathetic and had little military value. The Volkssturm lacked weapons other than antiquated rifles and a few antitank bazookas. It did not have uniforms other than armbands to indicate its combatant status. Moreover, it was commanded by veterans who were no longer fit for combat and hardly trained for its tasks. To stop enemy armor, they dug antitank ditches, erected cobblestone barriers, and placed explosives under bridges. But in actual fighting, these inexperienced boys and grandfathers accomplished little: the fanatics among them were killed and the skeptics sneaked home.[87] If they resisted, they only hastened the destruction of their home towns.

During the apocalypse of the Reich, many soldiers began to distance themselves from the fighting and think of their own survival in defeat. Horst Johannsen remembered, “In many cases order, obedience, and authority began to dissolve, allowing more and more scope for individual survival measures.” After Erich Helmer’s brother died, a humane superior ordered him “to go home on furlough, since the war is lost anyway.” When a nineteen-year-old turned up with “a self-inflicted rifle wound in his left hand,” a kind officer merely dressed him down and assigned him to rear-line duty rather than having him shot. A few days later, Krapf stumbled upon a captain who held a pistol in his hand, “about to shoot himself” and take the honorable way out in defeat. Though he stopped the suicide, he was unable to prevent the disintegration of his own unit. With discipline rapidly eroding and Russians attackers on their heels, soldiers fled frantically. “Now it was everyone for himself!”[88]

On the Western Front, some still-intact Wehrmacht forces put up tough resistance, while other crumbling units were ready to surrender. In stopping the "Operation Market Garden" fighting in the Hürtgen Forest or attacking in the Battle of the Bulge, the German Army fiercely sought to defend its fatherland. When Robert Neumaier led an inexperienced group of boys aged fifteen to seventeen in Holland, ten of the dozen were immediately killed. Once US advance units had managed to cross the half-destroyed bridge at Remagen and British forces had gotten across the Rhine River further north, the western defenses were breached. On April 1, 1945, Eva Peters witnessed how "two American armies . . . closed the ring around Army Group B in the Ruhr Basin." Once the industrial heart had fallen, its commander, Field Marshal Walter Model, committed suicide. More and more towns ignored Himmler's order and hung white sheets in their windows as a sign of surrender.[89] As a result, the Western Allies advanced to the Elbe River more rapidly than expected.

In the East, combat was even more ferocious, for the Red Army was paying back with interest the atrocities the Wehrmacht had committed in Russia. Due to Hitler's refusal to withdraw, large German forces remained stranded in shrinking bridgeheads in Courland and East Prussia along the Baltic coast. In Silesia, Gerhardt Thamm was drafted to unload ambulance trains carrying "young men with horrible wounds, with holes ripped into their bodies, with limbs shot away," while the roads were clogged by endless columns of refugees. Bypassing the "fortress cities" and overrunning the "walking encirclements" behind the Vistula, the Red Army rapidly advanced to the Oder River. "Now all hope for the fatherland was lost!" Ragtag defenders were able neither to stop the crossing in April nor the encirclement of Berlin in the battle of the Seelow Heights. On April 30, the radio announced that the Führer "has fallen in his command post in the chancellery." Herrmann Debus noted, "I cannot recall that this news triggered any special grief or dismay."[90]

In a scribbled note, Wilhelm Homeyer vividly described "the final hours" of the attempt to defend East Prussia. Worried about the looming battle, he pondered the absurdity of fighting against Russians who had "done nothing to him." At 6:00 a.m. the German artillery roars. The earth shakes. The air burns. Rushing forward, Homeyer reaches "a trench, the enemy line is already broken." A small "farm *must* become ours, that is the order." All at once, "there is intense MG fire" and a Russian soldier pops up, but is killed. Now an enemy rocket launcher homes in, first shooting long, then short, and finally hitting his group: "Bursting grenades, cries . . . four men are an unrecognizable pool of blood." Survivors now run back, propelled by "fear of the end . . . Everyone wants to live." Suddenly, there is "a warm feeling on his leg. Hit. 'Damn.'" Homeyer sprints for his life, but his limbs give out. Playing dead, he begs Russian scavengers to treat him as "comrade." Shouting "*dawai*," they order him to move, and he thinks "it is all over"—but he is only captured.[91]

During April the Eastern Front collapsed and the Wehrmacht turned into a mass flight westward to escape captivity by the Red Army. Because "he had come to the sad conclusion that all was lost," one sergeant demanded an immediate withdrawal "to reach Germany before the Russians did." Gerhard Krapf noted rumors that "Grand Admiral Doenitz . . . had issued orders for all troops at the Eastern Front to retreat" in order to create "a common front [with the Americans] against the Soviets." After Hitler's death, one commander offered his troops "the personal option to request a discharge" or to go on fighting. "Thus began our race with fate, the outcome of which had already been decided, though we did not know it." Some fanatical SS officers still tried to form new "fighting groups," while MPs threatened "to shoot any bastards running away." But nothing could stop the "huge, motley column" of desperate soldiers who had "thrown away their weapons and ripped off their insignia." It was "a rout of truly Napoleonic dimensions."[92]

The ensuing surrender was somewhat anticlimactic because it happened successively at different fronts. In Italy, one battalion commander assembled his troops on the morning of May 7 to announce, "Our Führer Adolf Hitler is dead and the Italian front has capitulated. Every soldier is relieved of his duty." In the West, the fighting fizzled out when individual units were overrun and the formal capitulation took place a day later. Joachim Fest remembered encountering a surprised American GI who pointed a submachine gun at him and commanded him to raise his hands in surrender. In the East, news that "the German Wehrmacht has capitulated to overwhelming forces" took a day or two longer to get to the dispirited troops. In most cases, retreating soldiers such as Gerhard Krapf or Horst Grothus simply ran into a Russian patrol, which yelled "*Voina kaput! Urr yest?*" (War is over. Do you have a watch?). Their superiors explained, "that means capitulation; we can do nothing more than wait."[93]

The end of the war triggered confused emotions, ranging from dejection at defeat all the way to joy over survival. Unable to bear the shame of the loss, some officers committed suicide rather than be captured. Many ordinary soldiers, such as Karl Härtel, were depressed, because "at the bitter end we lost the war and everything such as home, property, and the claim to justice before history." By contrast, Hans Queiser "was neither dejected nor desperate," because "no 'Germany' and certainly no Führer remained in his head. Only the will to get through what would now follow and then to go home." Skeptical spirits such as Erich Helmer "were almost stunned" by the capitulation, wondering what sense all the previous sacrifices made now. "At the same time we felt the total vacuum which had opened before us. What will happen? What shall we do?" But a barmaid in a Western pub reassured the dejected youths, "Boys, the war is over, finished for all of us!" She urged the worried soldiers to drink to that. "Cheers, boys! You have survived!"[94]

A fatal alliance between fanatical Nazis and patriotic Germans had allowed the war to continue, causing more deaths in the last six months than in the entire time before. In spite of the approaching end, fervent Hitler Youths and BdM girls were still willing to sacrifice themselves for the cause. Ignoring his own doubts, Horst Grothus wrote in his diary in March 1945, "We believe in our victory, believe our Führer who only a few days ago predicted a decisive turnabout for this year." Others, such as Gerhardt Thamm, "had already lost all illusions of glamour and heroics depicted so cleverly in magazines and newsreels. There was nothing beautiful, nor was there anything good about war, only gut-tearing sorrow, seeing young men and women each in his or her private hell."[95] The willingness of most young soldiers to carry on the fight regardless of their beliefs trapped them in an existential struggle from which there was no escape. In the end, all too many paid for this misguided dedication to their country with their lives.

WAR MEMORIES

Written half a century or more after 1945, these German accounts of the Second World War have a particular narrative shape. The totality of the defeat generally prevents the heroic tone characteristic of victorious renditions of war experience. There is still pride in the recollections of the exciting initial victories, but they are overshadowed by the inexorability of the ultimate loss. Many renditions of the middle period of the war treat combat as an exciting adventure, a dirty and dangerous world demanding male toughness and daring exploits. The final phase of the struggle is usually described as a survival story, full of references to defensive bravery, fallen friends, and miraculous escapes. Typical of this perspective is Hans Queiser's report of "New Year in the Realm of White Death." In this gripping story of a downed airplane in Norway, two crewmen struggle in deep snow, realizing that they "have to fight for their lives." Six days after the crash, the wounded sergeant is rescued by his comrade, who has gone for help.[96]

These recollections picture war as a pervasive domain of male violence that centers on mass murder and mass death. They describe basic training as systematic initiation that provides the necessary weapon skills and silences moral qualms by instilling rigid discipline. Erich Helmer therefore calls the Iron Cross a cross of iron: "What is a basic taboo in peace—not to be allowed to kill—is made into a duty in war." Many authors relate how this pent-up tension was released through a ferocious assault on "the enemy," which made the Wehrmacht troops especially lethal during the first half of the war. They brush aside potential ethical worries according to the situational logic of "us or them" that required beating a foe to the draw. Finally, they admit that this destructive force would turn against its German initiators during the second half of the war with saturation bombing and tank attacks. In such an ideological war of annihilation, the initially focused violence eventually escaped all legal and instrumental bounds.[97]

The authors of the autobiographies attribute their survival to a number of factors, ranging from "a lot of luck" to experience in staying out of harm's way. With most fighting taking place at a distance, random chance played a large role; many people to the right or left were killed, while the writers escaped somehow. Unlike his comrades who were fresh recruits, Robert Neumaier considered familiarity with combat conditions important, since making smart use of available cover and not taking unnecessary risks would reduce the likelihood of death to some degree. Moreover, getting an assignment behind the front as assistant to a motor pool supervisor, as Paul Frenzel did, clearly improved the odds of coming out alive unless one was shot by partisans. Ironically, receiving a moderate wound as Fritz Klein did was also desirable: healing required a lengthy rehabilitation at home or exempted one from combat altogether. Nonetheless, surprisingly, many convalescents volunteered to go right back to the front.[98]

These retrospectives make it clear that the impending defeat and the realization of German crimes gradually made soldiers question the purpose of Hitler's war. When the fighting reached the Reich, Nazi propaganda lost the last shreds of credibility and "total fear and great desperation spread, halting daily life and activity." Disturbing impressions of the exploitation of slave laborers, the bloody suppression of partisans, and the racist persecution of Jews could no longer be ignored and raised moral questions about the justification of German actions. Fritz Klein recalled that patriotic youths slowly realized that they were "willingly or reluctantly participating in a criminal war of incredible dimensions." Hermann Debus remembered how "it gradually dawned upon me, that 'our Führer' had abused us. At any rate, we were no longer convinced of his infallibility." While some fanatics continued to cling to their nationalist faith, many soldiers began to disassociate themselves from the "damned hoax" of a bankrupt regime.[99]

Even before the carnage had ended, the abiding lesson that war was reprehensible was emerging in the minds of the soldiers who had caused and suffered so much grief. "Why are we still all going along?" Erich Helmer remembered asking himself. "Would it not be necessary to articulate the feeling of senselessness and cry out: 'Stop this War!?'" Across political affiliations, thoughtful Germans drew the same conclusion from disastrous defeat and destruction. The terrible end to hostilities reinforced for Gerhard Krapf the "hard-won conviction that the notion of a 'good war' in the sense of St. Augustine [or] Thomas Aquinas is just as absurd as is Nietzsche's" philosophical heroization of warfare. "War and the wages of war are evil, period." It was therefore the shocking experience of the murderous and criminal war that turned most Germans into postwar pacifists. The Thousand-Year Reich "had been an exercise in arrogance, mediocrity and brutality. It was a welcome reprieve for mankind that it foundered."[100]

5

FEMALE STRUGGLES

On March 27, 1945, sirens wailed to warn the city of Paderborn that Allied bombing squadrons were approaching. Huddled in her air-raid shelter, twenty-year-old Eva Peters experienced "the eardrum-shattering roar and crash of exploding bombs . . . , the impenetrable darkness" after the lights went out, "the asphyxiating chalk dust in nose and lungs" and the "stone chunks falling on heads and shoulders." The "entire cellar danced and shook like a ship in a hurricane." She was less afraid of being buried alive than angry "at those pilots who from high above dropped their bombs in order to murder women and children who posed no military threat." After the attack was over, her three-year-old brother asked, "Are we now all dead?" On the surface, a firestorm raged whose sky-high flames quickly consumed her home and most of the city. "Many hundreds of people, principally women and children, found a horrible death."[1] Shared thousands of times, this frightening exposure to bombing raids was typical of female experiences in the war.

As a result of such horrors, many commentators initially considered women only as victims of the belligerent Third Reich. From antiquity on, women have been forced to endure male depredations during war, support fighters in combat, or serve as prizes of victory. Moreover, the Nazi movement itself was a product of male bonding in the trenches of World War I, as well as of the uniformed militias of the Weimar Republic, which gave the entire leadership from the Führer on down a misogynist tinge. Bristling at the cliché of women's limitation to "children-kitchen-church," feminists such as Kate

Millett, Betty Friedan, and Alice Schwarzer therefore denounced the Nazi cult of motherhood as a patriarchal plot designed to keep them in an inferior place. According to historian Gisela Bock, "German women were the subjects of Nazi policy, not its agents."[2] This view conveniently conflates maternalism and natalism with National Socialism as chief enemies of emancipation, ironically absolving women of most of their responsibility.

More recent research has rejected this image of female passivity and stressed that women played a rather more active role in the Nazi dictatorship. While they were underrepresented among the NSDAP members, they provided almost half the votes for the party. In some auxiliaries such as the People's Welfare Organization, women took the lead as an extension of mothering from their homes to society at large. Nostalgic descriptions of "how much fun we had in the BdM" also demonstrate that the Hitler Youth was quite popular among adolescent girls, and service duties such as helping farmers during the *Landjahr* in the countryside were considered exciting because they allowed young women to escape from the controls of home.[3] In an odd form of subaltern emancipation, considerable numbers of adult women helped maintain the regime with their professional work. A hard core of female perpetrators among the military auxiliaries, concentration camp guards, and SS brides also committed shocking atrocities while participating in Nazi crimes.[4]

Perhaps a gender perspective will help to resolve this ideological debate about women's paradoxical role in the Third Reich. The new work on military violence has suggested the notion of "martial masculinity" to describe the image of an ideal male soldier forced upon men by the Nazi Party and the Wehrmacht. Research on female experiences as army auxiliaries or laborers in munitions factories suggests the need for a comparable concept such as "volkish feminity" that would reconcile maternalist rhetoric with female agency in the Third Reich.[5] Since the total war blurred the lines between civilians and combatants, women were the backbone of the home front and actively contributed through their completion of traditional domestic tasks and their involvement in economic mobilization.[6] Therefore, they faced an increasing disparity between their role expectations as wives and mothers who were supposed to keep the home fires burning and their actual wartime duties in the service of their nation.

The testimonies of ordinary women demonstrate how collaboration with the Nazi dictatorship eventually turned them into its victims. During the prewar years, women struggled with the contradiction between the regime's restrictive misogynism and the chances for career advancement by joining the cause. Somewhat shielded by Hitler's effort to maintain domestic morale, in the first part of the war when the Wehrmacht victories opened up grand vistas of domination, German women overwhelmingly supported the struggle. But during the second phase of approaching defeat, they were caught up in the suffering through the horror of bombing raids, flight and expulsion from the East, and mass rape by Red Army soldiers. Not only the objects of sterilization, members of the resistance, Jewish women, and Slavic slave laborers, but also ordinary German women suffered the dreadful consequences of NS bellicosity and racism.[7] Their later recollections therefore show a distinctive experience that parallels the disillusionment of men.

A MISOGYNIST SYSTEM

During peacetime, Nazi attitudes toward women were an odd blend of racist phobias and volkish ideals. Due to the Social Darwinist view that national strength rested on a growing population, a concerned Hitler sought to reverse the decline of the German birthrate by encouraging women to bear more children. At the same time, the NSDAP's virulent racism suggested that "asocial" and "genetically defective females" should be sterilized and members of "inferior races" be kept from polluting the Aryan stock.[8] In cultural terms, the NS leadership loathed the decadent urban lifestyle of the "new women" during the Weimar Republic as a betrayal of their biological duties. Instead, they preferred elements of the turn-of-the-century life reform movement, which promoted a "natural" and "healthy" look without the use of cosmetics.[9] As mothers of the next generation, women were also supposed to be the guardians of the vaunted *Volksgemeinschaft* who would produce a genuine national community.

A campaign of fulsome praise that enlisted popular poetry sought to reshape the image of German womanhood in a maternalist direction. In his ode to an unborn child, Theo Scheller celebrated the "eternal mother, called Germany" as the future destination of a growing life. A presumably female poet who used the Nordic pseudonym Frigga praised the miracle of birth in a nationalist fashion: "We need mothers who carry in their womb / a hard race as if forged by iron ore / without servility and fearful doubt / that boldly scales new heights not reached before." Such kitschy rhymes used religious language to celebrate Hitler as deliverer from material want and foreign servitude. Similarly, a child's verse claimed, "Hail to you Hitler / You are and will be my best friend." Anne Marie Koeppen celebrated women even more pompously, writing, "You carry honor, purity and light. / Your virtue has made Germany great. / You are the face of the people. / The future sleeps in your womb." Many young women therefore wished "fulfillment [in] the life of a wife and mother."[10]

In actual practice, the new Nazi regime promoted the redomestication of women in order to reduce the unemployment of male heads of households during the Great Depression. Concretely that meant reversing some of the occupational gains of the Weimar Republic, when young women embarked upon white-collar careers as salesgirls or secretaries. During decisions about secondary schooling, girls such as Renate Finckh were shunted into non-academic tracks to prepare them for their role as homemakers. In the universities, a new regulation supposedly to reduce academic overcrowding reserved space for young men who aspired to become professionals and set a quota of 10 percent female students. In public service, a law already prepared before 1933 prohibited the employment of a married woman if her husband already held a government job, even a high-school teaching position.[11] While these restrictions were gradually abandoned when full employment was reached in the later thirties, initially they had a deterrent effect on women's ability to work.

The same contradiction between subordination and assertiveness animated the NS *Frauenschaft*, the women's auxiliary of the Nazi Party. As "Adolf Hitler's guard," the NSF's "chief charge is and remains the National Socialist indoctrination of the German women." While rejecting the "erroneous paths of the democratic-liberalist-international women's movement," the principles of the Frauenschaft praised "the physical and spiritual task of mothering the entire people" on the one hand and endorsed "the training and occupational integration" of unmarried women on the other. Without challenging the misogynist character of the party, the NSF saw to it that "females in large numbers were to be socialized in Nazi ideology and included in public life." The NSF therefore assumed control of a broad range of welfare services that opened up career possibilities for women considered to be Aryan.[12] At the same time it policed society by making sure that "asocial" women would not reproduce and Jewish men would not sire children with gentile German women.

For adolescent girls, the Third Reich offered a surprising range of activities. The *Bund deutscher Mädel* was an attractive organization where they could spread their wings. "In their earlier years as Jungmädel, girls could enjoy a freer and less restricted modern life outside the boundaries of their families than had previous generations." Ursula Mahlendorf fondly recalled that they "could travel with their groups to rallies, in their 'separate sphere' compete in sports and in fact relish most of the activities boys enjoyed." Especially for lower middle and lower class girls, the BdM provided chances for leadership training and advancement that gave them unprecedented responsibilities. The somewhat older adolescents were trained "in health, child care, domestic skills, and self-improvement in preparation for motherhood, domesticity, and comradeship in marriage."[13] In spite of this maternalist twist, participation in the Hitler Youth gave many girls a new sense of independence and empowerment.

The price of membership in the Nazi youth group was nationalist and racist indoctrination and preparation for war. Often feeling alone in her home and picked on at school, Renate Finckh was delighted to be able to join the

Jungmädel of the BdM when she turned ten: "In the new community I felt secure." She enjoyed the weekly meetings and activities and had a crush on her female group leader, who inspired her with principles such as "German girl, be good, loyal, and true." The festive swearing-in ceremony at which they pledged, "we want to have clear eyes and active hands" went "straight to [her] heart." But the ideological training discredited humane values and the wearing of uniforms, marching in ranks, listening to speeches, and waving of flags followed the militarization of male adolescents. While Renate applauded the Anschluss and "liberation" of the Sudetenland, seeing the wanton destruction of the November pogrom in 1938 made her doubt the anti-Semitic justification, especially when a girlfriend argued that, after all, "Jews are also human beings."[14]

The BdM nonetheless had difficulty in dealing with the awakening sexuality of its members. Because middle-class mothers did not like to enlighten their daughters about biological changes, Ursula Mahlendorf was distressed by the onset of her period. The kitchen maid from the farm only laughed at her naiveté, warning, "when your boyfriend fucks you, you might get pregnant." As a result, "the feeling of being dirty, of not being acceptable poisoned [her] adolescence and young adulthood." Her BdM leader was no help when providing "factual information" on "intercourse and impregnation Nazi style." She began by pointing out, "you will enjoy having many children for the Führer, and that is why you must keep yourself pure." The explanation of the physical act was rather gruesome: "When your future husband makes you a mother, he will put his member into you like a sword thrusts itself into its sheath, and his seed will impregnate the ovum in your belly." Teenage Ursula was shocked by such "a violent, obscene metaphor."[15]

For many female adolescents, the "new ideal of femininity" nonetheless "appeared enormously progressive at the time." Nazi leaders appealed to youthful idealism, the wish to overcome class barriers, and the search for authentic experience. Eva Peters "was caught up in body and soul" when using magic words as a leader such as "honor, loyalty, bravery comradery, freedom, community, home, struggle, death, flag, heroism, blood, soil, faith, duty, people, fatherland, Führer, and follower." As special "carriers of culture," women were tasked with preserving folk songs and ethnic customs, traditional crafts and peasant dress, while transmitting them to their children. For older adolescents, the BdM founded an advanced group called "Faith and Beauty" that was supposed to help teenagers to mature into full womanhood through music and gymnastics. While the organization ultimately prepared girls for motherhood, these activities tried to carve out an intermediary female sphere that left "preponderantly happy feelings" in retrospect.[16]

Girls looking for spiritual moorings did not see religion as an alternative, for BdM propaganda disparaged traditional faiths. The most radical Nazis subscribed to a neopaganism that hearkened back to Nordic mythology and substituted secular rites of passage for the Church rituals of marriage and baptism. Brought up without contact with religion, Renate Finckh was delighted to hear about the German Christians, a Protestant group that saw it as "a sacred duty to cleanse Christian faith from Jewish influences." To her this creed was acceptable, since it was "a Christianity without Jews." By contrast, the party claimed that the Confessing Church of Protestants who rejected the Third Reich for reasons of faith was "a bunch of biased, arrogant, and straitlaced people." While her friends went to confirmation, Renate participated in a Nazi "youth consecration" and vowed, "I believe in Germany and fight for it." Among young women from religious families, those who belonged to a Protestant sect, such as Edith Schöffski, proved impervious to such irreligious appeals.[17]

At home and in school, girls had less freedom than boys of the same age. Their mothers watched over them more closely. In families without servants, it went without saying that they were responsible for taking care of their younger siblings, even if they were barely old enough to look after themselves. Also, in most modest households, adolescent girls had to help their mothers in preparing food, shopping, gardening, and the like. While parents were willing to invest in their sons' educations, they considered schooling for their daughters less important. In spite of her good grades and intellectual ambition, Ursula Mahlendorf was forced to remain in primary school because "it is not right that you should be better educated than your brother," who preferred an apprenticeship. Similarly, the parents of Ursula

Baehrenburg did not keep their promise to send her to a commercial academy. Decades later she remarked wistfully about female limitations: "From early on, I learned to do without."[18]

One diversion for poorer girls was the *Kinderlandverschickung* program that sent urban children into the countryside in order to render them healthier. Welfare organizations such as the NSV selected needy city boys and girls to be shipped either to private families or camps for four to six weeks of fresh country air, physical activity, and more copious food. Some of the girls who had never been away from home battled with homesickness, but friendly host families and new friends quickly dispelled their shyness. As a working-class girl, Erika Taubhorn was sent away twice, first to a private home and then to a camp with over a dozen other comrades. Another Berlin girl, Edith Schöffski, had the good fortune to be shipped to the Baltic coast, where she "ran around the beach and searched for amber." The ample food and vacation atmosphere usually had their desired effect. "The recreation was good for all of us," Taubhorn recalled, adding, "I gained ten pounds."[19]

For graduates of primary schools, the BdM invented the *Landjahr*, a year of volunteer work helping shorthanded farmers in ethnically disputed areas. With eighty other girls, Ruth Bulwin went to a camp at the Dutch border where she did chores "for the home, garden, and stable, for laundry . . . kitchen and field." She did not mind the indoctrination and enjoyed working with plants and animals, even if the "iron discipline" was a pain. Other young women, such as Lore Walb, also worked on farms, where they "got to know and appreciate the difficulty and importance of agricultural work." In 1938 this duty became mandatory, a female form of Labor Service, in order to help rural families or urban households with many children. Gisela Grothus lived with the family of a medical officer and learned how to take care of infants. Ruth Bulwin was sent to a Bavarian farm where she had to learn how to dump manure without falling on the pile. While the work was difficult, she grew to like it because it earned her respect.[20] Her private snapshots show that it was not easy for urban girls to cope with rural tasks (image 14).

These Nazi obligations complicated occupational training for those girls who had finished their education by graduating from primary school. Some

14. Female Farm Service. *Source*: Ruth Bulwin, *Spätes Echo.*

parents tried to guide their daughters into white-collar jobs, but when Ursula Mahlendorf's mother suggested she become a beautician, she balked. Ruth Bulwin had more luck: she was allowed training in a private academy in Berlin where she actually "liked learning" stenography, typing, and other commercial skills. Anneliese Huber was even better off: she started with bookkeeping in a Jewish firm that was eventually Aryanized. To have a more secure future, she then applied for a position as a "head secretary" at the public health insurance office in Pforzheim. After proving her Aryan birth, she got the job and found out that it "was interesting and many sided." Erika Taubhorn was less fortunate; an uncooperative labor official only allowed her to train as a seamstress. Dictated by inclination and expediency, such decisions showed the limitation of female career options.[21]

Occupational training and first jobs allowed teenagers to leave the home, gave them independence, and gradually transformed them into young adults. Ten-hour workdays, including Saturdays, offered little leisure time, but they provided a bit of income that could be used for diversion. To escape her mother's temper tantrums, Anneliese Huber usually went hiking with her girlfriends on Sundays, enjoying nature and "singing joyous songs." If there was any money left after contributing to the household expenses, they would occasionally go to the movies. Their aspirations grew gradually to include opera productions or stage plays. Later on, they took their first vacations at the Bavarian Chiemsee with the Nazi "Strength through Joy" organization. This introduced Anneliese to the Alpine mountains, which "became [her] great love." Ruth Bulwin preferred the metropolitan excitement of Berlin, sauntering every day from the zoo station to the Tauentzienstrasse, "right through the pulsating life, just what a teenager loves."[22]

Inevitably, becoming more independent also led to their first romantic contacts with the other sex, most of them harmless for the time being. The HJ propagated an ideal of "clear and clean comradeship" while keeping its members busy enough to prevent emotional entanglements. As a result, Lore Walb's stirring of interest in boys during cotillion did not lead to anything. For Renate Finckh, dancing lessons created a conflict between her dedication to BdM duty and her interest in a boy who was critical toward the Third Reich. When a young man walked Anneliese Huber home, her vigilant mother met him with a slap on the face, nipping the relationship in the bud. But Anneliese was none too upset, since "it was nothing serious on [her] part" yet. Drafted into auxiliary duty in Königsberg, Ruth Weigelt could only communicate with her Gerhard in the military by letter. When one good-looking HJ leader saw Ruth Bulwin's picture, he insisted on a double date and started a long-term relationship that eventually turned into a wartime marriage.[23]

Many young women transferred their adulation to Hitler, responding to his charisma with "hysterical rapture." The BdM leader Lore Walb gushed in her diary in October 1933, "I have seen our Führer!" During a rally "he stood in his car with his right arm raised, so serious, so strong and so great." Swept away by happiness, the Nazified girl confided that "this was the most beautiful, moving and powerful moment of my fourteen-year-old life." Some years later, a skeptical Anneliese Huber reported a similar response: When Hitler came down the street in a roadster, "all hands stretched out toward him." To her surprise, the Führer suddenly reached out to her over the heads of the others: "His eyes exerted a demonic power over me and involuntarily I gave him my hand." When a young officer reported the same magnetism, Ursula Mahlendorf "was fascinated by the idea that Hitler's eyes could have such a powerful effect."[24] Many girls' diaries reveal a fervent adulation of a figure who was father, lover, and savior all at the same time.

This intoxication with National Socialism was strong enough to override any scruples about the violence against German Jews. Ursula Mahlendorf, then nine years old, was shocked by "the screaming, crashing, splintering of glass" during the anti-Semitic pogrom of the "night of crystal" in November 1938. "I saw and heard what happened in our [Silesian] town and was terrified by it, though I failed to understand its full significance." When she inquired about the destruction of stores and the violence against neighbors, her mother replied "Don't you ever dare to ask that again." As she viewed the burning synagogue in her home town of Paderborn, BdM leader Eva Peters "felt no outrage at all about the desecration and destruction of a holy site." Instead, public resentment focused more on the anarchic process than on the persecution of Jews. When questioned by his girlfriend about the pogrom, HJ leader Rolf Bulwin admitted that he had been ordered to participate in a raid on a Jewish orphanage. But he was so moved by the children's terror that he "just decamped."[25]

The eugenic program of Nazi biopolitics seemed sensible to many women as long as it did not involve their own families. One typical BdM leader liked to harp on the need for "national and racial hygiene" that sought to keep the body politic healthy through preventive measures. According to the 1933 law on hereditary disease, "if mental illness or physical deformity is frequent in their family" people "should be sterilized or not marry." Such individuals "are a burden to themselves, to their families, and to the state." Nazi doctors therefore argued that it would be a kindness to end their suffering. "That is what euthanasia, mercy killing is all about." Only when the actual practice of mass sterilization and euthanasia involved someone they knew did unaffected people realize its dehumanizing implications. While Renate Finckh was shocked that her sister-in-law was confined to a wheelchair due to polio, she understood that she nonetheless radiated an inner light. Yet Eva Peters was fanatical enough to reject Bishop Clemens von Galen's warning against murdering helpless human beings.[26]

During the prewar years, even apolitical women became convinced that things were finally improving for gentile Germans. Influenced by her SA father and Women's League mother, Renate Finckh summarized the change in public sentiment: "Since the Führer is here, there is 'work and bread,'" ending the crisis of the Great Depression. "Since the Führer is here, 'peace and order' have returned," overcoming the chaos of the Weimar Republic. "Since the Führer is here, 'a firm bond links head and heart, city and countryside,'" creating a true people's community. "Since the Führer is here, mothers with many children are no longer despised but honored," receiving a mother's cross instead of child support. "Since the Führer is here, we are someone again!," with Germany respected by other countries. BdM members such as Lore Walb, in particular, believed in the promise of a better future under the Führer. Ursula Mahlendorf recalled, "I was intoxicated by the jubilation of the 'freed populations,' by the adulation of the crowds at party rallies."[27]

The nine essays that Lore Walb wrote as high-school assignments demonstrate that the Nazis had surprising success in preparing young women for a coming war. They start harmlessly enough with a plea for understanding between the city and countryside, but already her discussion of Jeanne d'Arc turns into a glorification of the Führer's quest to restore national honor. Her treatment of the role of art completely follows the volkish line; in writing about air-raid protection she uncannily anticipates the terrors of mass bombing. Considering airplanes "the most dangerous weapon of war," she predicts that "women, children, the old and those incapable of fighting" will be annihilated at home. In the conflict between humanity and honor, exemplified by the dark figure of Hagen in the Nibelungen saga, she even justifies his murder of Siegfried. She concludes, "The will and power of the German people are incorporated in the person of the Führer."[28] It was precisely the heroization of war and blind belief in Hitler's leadership that would lead to disaster.

HOME FRONT CHALLENGES

The outbreak of the war fundamentally separated the experiences of young men from those of young women. While the former were drafted by the

Wehrmacht and sent to the front, the latter stayed behind and worried about their loved ones in harm's way. Because they "knew almost nothing of what is happening" in combat, they could only follow the shifting military fortunes vicariously through "intoxicating special news bulletins." Their patriotic fervor found little outlet, for the military had no use for adolescent girls. Because they were initially far from actual fighting, "the events of the war still remained remote and abstract." Nonetheless, "all of our lives were about to change fundamentally," Ruth Bulwin recalled. "Nobody had understood it yet, but circumstances took care of making us every day more aware of what that really meant."[29] Though Hitler tried to protect the home front, it soon enough became obvious that in a prolonged war of annihilation, women would have to bear an essential part of the burden.

Compared with the male adventure of combat, continuing a domestic routine seemed disappointing to patriotic young women. Eva Peters found what remained for girls to do "during a war much more boring, monotonous, and unclear." Completing homework for school appeared less interesting than the variety of BdM service projects. Also, "having to help a lot at home," doing chores for their working mothers, or watching over their younger siblings seemed mundane by comparison with actual fighting. Initially, accustomed rituals such as religious confirmation and middle-class dancing lessons continued unchanged from peacetime. But primary school graduates now had to find jobs in the war economy, while other young women had mixed feelings about the privilege of studying at a university during such a heroic time. And then there was the challenge of finding a suitable young man, preferably in uniform, in order to go to the movies or to enjoy dancing. Step by step, young women were drawn further into the Nazi war.[30]

For many young women, following wartime events became "more interesting and exciting than the monotony of everyday duties." The defense of the fatherland revived "the comradeship of the trenches," even rallying people to the national cause who had been skeptical of the Nazi Party before. "After three weeks school resumed and Poland was defeated," Renate Finckh remembered. "The jubilation about this rapid victory, the reconquest of the corridor and the liberation of the Germans was great." According to Eva

Peters, the succession of special victory bulletins on the radio and impressive shots of advancing Wehrmacht units in newsreels soon turned her initial skepticism into "habituation, confidence and the calming reassurance: 'German soldiers are invincible.'" It was fun for schoolgirls to trace the movement of the front lines on a map at home. "For three years there were lightning wars and lightning victories." Intoxicated by the triumphs, many girls were "proud to be German and to be living in such a great time."[31]

This "continual sense of exhilaration" was, however, dampened by preparations for defense against air raids, which suggested that the actual fighting might also involve civilians. Although the Führer had promised that no enemy airplane would be able to drop its bombs on a German city, Britain's Royal Air Force soon demonstrated that this was a futile boast. In the cities, huge concrete bunkers were built as shelters, while in private homes, cellars were reinforced to withstand the impact. "The entire population was compelled to participate in air-defense exercises where we learned to fight against fires and incendiary bombs" by using sand, Ruth Bulwin recalled. "The owners of apartments had to make sure that all windows were equipped with black blinds," for after twilight, "not a single ray of light was supposed to get outside." Moreover, "black caps were put onto automobile headlights, leaving only a small slit." Even if such preparations were only a nuisance, they made it clear that women would not be spared.[32]

Another irksome consequence of war was the imposition of rationing, which complicated shopping for housewives and caused exasperating lines. In order to guarantee equal access to scarce goods, coupons were introduced in 1939 that governed how much nutrition, clothing, or gasoline a person could obtain. Ruth Bulwin remembered, "Initially some foods were rationed, such as butter, meat, and bread; later on everything else." These restrictions led to shortages in the cities, forcing people to rely on their rural relatives or turn their flower gardens into potato or vegetable plots. Moreover, clothing was sold on the basis of cards as well, since most of the cloth production went into uniforms. As a result, people began to mend their apparel and clever seamstresses turned old dresses into new fashions. BdM girls such as Ursula Mahlendorf were also busy with "collecting herbs and recyclables—scrap iron, rags, bones, paper—with which to make guns, uniforms, medical supplies for [the] troops."[33] Lacking sufficient raw materials, Nazi Germany had to reuse what it had.

When the attack on Russia bogged down during the winter of 1941, women faced a new task: providing military men with warmer clothing. "Everybody donated, whether she was devoted to the Führer or not," Renate Finckh remembered. "Everyone wanted to help the freezing soldiers." Ursula Mahlendorf went from house to house to collect "wool clothing for our soldiers in Russia from our families, neighbors, or friends." In the weekly squad meetings, "we knitted mountains of gloves" and socks. During holidays, the *Mädchen* also baked cookies and sent hundreds of packages "to an unknown German soldier" to cheer up the lonely young men. The intensification of Allied bombing attacks created another chore closer to home as well. Now the teenagers engaged "in rounding up children's clothing and household utensils for bombing victims." Although it was not clear whether the material "ever reached the troops or the air-raid targets," the effort had a positive effect on the collectors, one of whom reported, "I felt we were helping the war effort."[34]

Because most field hands were at the front, the BdM also expected its members "to help in bringing in the harvest." Ursula Mahlendorf's offer to work in the fields on her uncle's estate was therefore "accepted as a matter of course." Little did she know that she would have to do hard physical labor during long days together with adult women. While teenage boys were allowed to drive tractors, she had "to bind the sheaves of wheat and pile them upright against each other to dry out." Unused to such exertions, she "was so exhausted that [she] began to sob involuntarily." She resented "the coarse sexual jokes and rough bantering of the German women." But "all of the field hands hated the foreman," who drove his laborers mercilessly, yelling, "Come toil and slave, you damned bitches!" This challenging experience was a far cry from Hitler Youth propaganda about a healthy rural life, close to the soil. Only the taste of self-baked bread and the "hefty sum" of money at the end of the summer made the entire exercise seem worthwhile.[35]

German women were also helped by foreign laborers who, partly by contract and partly by coercion, assisted them in the households and the fields. Not even sixteen years old, a Ukrainian farm girl named Sonja Kolesnyk was brutally abducted in the spring of 1942 by men with machine-pistols, put into a cattle car, and first shipped to the outskirts of Vienna. Helpless because she spoke no German, she was stripped, deloused, and had her possessions stolen. Upon arriving in Bavaria, she was requisitioned by a farmer's wife whose husband was at the front. Unused to German food, Sonja "cried a lot" while peeling mounds of potatoes and helping around the farm. Falsely accused of miscegenation with a German farm laborer, she was almost killed, like a young Polish man who was hanged for sleeping with a German woman. Fortunately, the farm woman "stood up for" her, fed her decently, and treated her almost as a member of the family. Because the news about mass murders in the Ukraine was discouraging, Sonja ultimately decided to stay in Germany.[36]

Some BdM leaders also volunteered for "service in the East," the *Osteinsatz* that supported settlers while Germanizing the western Polish region of the Warthegau. According to one Nazi tenet, an overcrowded "Germany needs living space. The Führer has now won it for us. The East beckons!" In the summer of 1943, Renate Finckh participated in this "noble mission" of transforming conquered territory into German land. The local Polish farmers had been expelled to make room for German resettlers from Bessarabia and Volhynia. When the farm woman to whom she was assigned "lay sick in bed," thirteen-year-old Renate had to run the household, even having to "kill, pluck and carve a duck." Shocked by the dirt of the settlers, who had "medieval notions of hygiene," she started to clean up the farmstead. Only by ramming her knee into the groin of the local Nazi peasant leader did she escape being raped. But she did beat a Polish boy for not minding the cows.[37] Ashamed, she became aware that she had sown hatred.

Older teenagers who had finished school often had to take over jobs for which men were no longer available. "We poor women must replace the entire male society. That creates a bunch of additional work," Christel Beilmann wrote to her brother at the front. Ruth Bulwin was fortunate enough to find a position at an important firm that made "generators for producing gas from wood as a replacement for petrol." After passing a difficult entrance test, Edith Schöffski managed to get a bookkeeping job at the home office of a postal bank in Berlin because she was good with figures. When almost the entire office complex was destroyed by bombs and she had barely escaped alive in the air-raid shelter, she changed over to the central telephone office. There she manned a switchboard for long-distance calls as "an operator girl." Toward the end of the war, Eva Peters stopped her studies and became a streetcar conductor, proud of her uniform and status. "Eva loved her 'occupation' for technical, athletic and personal reasons."[38]

Nursing wounded soldiers was another wartime women's occupation that became more important with the greater the number of German casualties. After her training as a "medical technical assistant," Gisela Grothus was assigned to a "military hospital for the brain impaired" in Berlin, where she "encountered the bloody traces of the war every day." Ursula Mahlendorf responded to a Red Cross call for trainee nurses' aides in Silesia, where she learned about "putting bandages on every conceivable body part . . . how to take temperatures . . . [and] how to give hypodermic shots." The reality of coping with wounded soldiers smelling of "shit, urine, and acrid sweat" was more gruesome than she had imagined because "they are just like the boys [she went] to school with." She got used to seeing "flesh wounds to arms and legs laced with pus." But watching men die without being able to help was hard, even if some bragged of committing atrocities. Overwhelmed by the suffering, she at least believed to be doing something meaningful.[39] A typical photo shows a Red Cross nurse bandaging a wounded soldier (image 15).

Party authorities also encouraged teenage girls to correspond with unattached soldiers in order to foster romantic relationships. Ursula Baehrenburg developed a "pen friendship during the war. Joachim and I wrote to each other regularly. We had gotten close as if we had known each other for a long time and yet had never seen each other." Toward the chaotic end, she received a letter with the vow, "Our Führer will not leave us in the lurch," but never heard from Joachim again. Through a friend, Anneliese Huber met Kurt, a young soldier who loved playing the piano and had a good

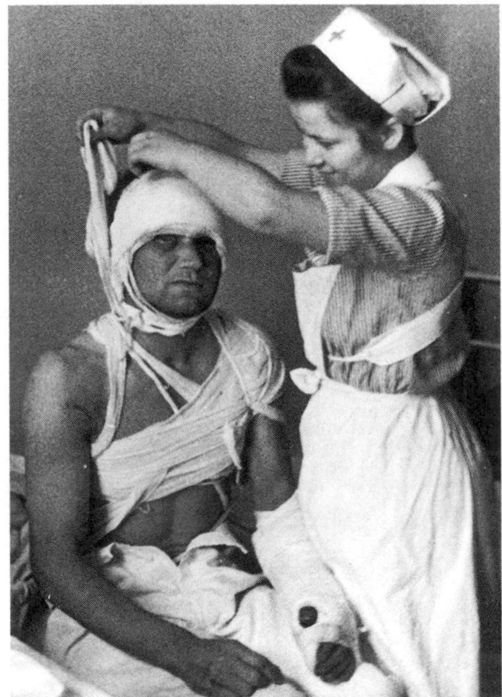

15. A nurse bandages a wounded soldier.
Source: Stiftung Preussischer Kulturbesitz.

voice. This acquaintance grew into an intimate correspondence, admired even by the military censor. "I don't know how it was possible for him to write almost daily, sometimes in the worst situations. But I believe that gave him the power to persevere," she recalled. Since both were "romantically inclined," they fell in love with each other, which sustained Kurt when he was imprisoned for defeatism.[40] Such epistolary bonds were crucial for maintaining the morale of both sides.

Young women's social life with men was limited to the precious days of furlough when the boys came home to enjoy their company. Even in timid Ursula Baehrenburg, "the first tender feelings toward the other sex awakened." She developed a crush on a friend of her brother, a "dashing air force soldier," with whom she went on walks and was happy when he put his arm around her shoulders. Similarly, Anneliese Huber was delighted when

Kurt asked to see her again, for she found him a kindred spirit, interested in music and literature. When he received a convalescence leave after being wounded, they spent many hours enjoying the sights of medieval Strasbourg together, and at Christmas he sent a poem with the suggestive line "Love me, as I do you." Ruth Bulwin was more forward when her Rolf came to visit, ignoring the warning: "Don't do anything stupid!"[41] Though in general premarital sex was still frowned upon, the uncertainty of survival accelerated the consummation of relationships.

Inevitably, such involvements also led to marriages, which were somewhat constrained by the circumstances of the war. Rolf and Ruth Bulwin were lucky: he was assigned to garrison duty in Prague after being wounded and her father allowed her to marry although she was underage. On January 4, 1943, their civil wedding took place in an "impressive ceremony" with a speech by the corps commander, but without any family present. Similarly, Anneliese and Kurt Huber got engaged in Vienna a few months later, accompanied by relatives from both sides. "It was a wonderful, happy time which we crowned with our marriage on July 24th, 1943." The bride even managed to have her dress sewn from Brussels lace. The couple drove to the church in a carriage, and the ceremony was "framed by beautiful music." But by August the new husband was once again sent to the front, reducing their relationship to long and passionate letters. Having procured a necessary white dress, Ruth Weigelt married her Gerhard on January 4, 1944, in spite of his typhoid fever.[42]

In due course these unions produced babies, whose birth affirmed the continuation of life in murderous circumstances. Anneliese Huber's pregnancy was complicated by the shocking news that her husband was missing in action. But in May 1944 she gave birth and was "happy to hold a healthy boy in [her] arms." Two days later an alive Kurt suddenly stood at her bedside: he had finally gotten parental leave. The family celebrated the baptism and the new parents "spent a few blissful days" before the father once again had to leave the young mother to cope on her own. The Bulwins were more fortunate. Ruth was pampered by both grandmothers. She delivered a little girl, named Brigitte, in November of 1944. Her husband was not disappointed that it was not a boy, since she was "such a sweet thing." The proud parents could then parade with the baby carriage through the streets of Prague, until Rolf was also returned to combat duty in the final futile struggle of the Reich. During the collapse of July 1945, Ruth Weigelt gave birth to her oldest son, Reiner.[43]

Many war marriages were, however, cut short by untimely death, causing "endless suffering and grief." In the newspapers, death notices multiplied as more and more soldiers were killed at the front. Increasingly, women wore black mourning dresses and suddenly broke into tears for no discernable reason. "Everywhere it is now dark, because the times are cruel and full of danger," Kurt described his forebodings to his wife Anneliese in September 1944. Then a dry form letter destroyed her happiness: "Unfortunately I have to convey to you the sad news that your dear husband, the infantryman Kurt Huber, fell on September 17 for Führer, Volk, and fatherland. An enemy grenade prematurely ended his life." The young mother reeled from "the heavy blow of fate." She had now joined hundreds of thousands of bereaved wives as a "war widow" and would have to bring up her son alone. Echoing a Nazi cliché, Lore Walb commented on the loss of many classmates, "It is always the most courageous, bold, and valiant—the best who have to die."[44]

More fortunate young women might actually profit from the war if they participated in the occupation of enemy territories. Early in the conflict, Lore Walb was sent to the "protectorate" of Bohemia and Moravia to serve with a German farm family. She found it interesting "to encounter a foreign people" for the first time and to become aware of their resentment against the victorious colonizers. Later on, Ruth Bulwin moved to Prague to be close to her SS husband. With housing scarce, she joined the police force and was delighted to be assigned the "first apartment of her own, completely furnished," even if it was only a student dorm. Eventually she moved to a better place and was pleased that "many things could still be gotten here, if one knew the right people," though contact with Czechs could have bad consequences. "In general, the Nemeckys (the Germans) were better off in the protectorate than in the Reich." Gradually she also realized that the local population "curses the occupiers, hates them and wishes them to the devil."[45]

The need for manpower could even help young women to overcome class barriers and advance their careers by assuming responsibilities otherwise reserved for men. Liselotte S. was born into a rather poor family, denied education, though she wanted to learn, and not even allowed to join the BdM. When her father died of tuberculosis, she had to enter domestic service with a farmer who raped and exploited her. But when she saw a job announcement at a train station, she applied to the stationmaster, who initially hired her only to clean. After a few weeks, he realized that she was "an intelligent woman" and assigned her various white-collar tasks. Thus she learned how to sell tickets, send baggage, and even dispatch freight trains. She gradually worked her way up to become a "railroad aide" with a uniform and growing responsibility. Only "through the war did I get out and was able to learn something." Otherwise she would have had no chance. But with bombing raids and political repression, it was nonetheless a terrible time: "I lived like in a dream."[46]

The mounting losses of the Wehrmacht drew an increasing number of young women into the military, overriding the sexist role division. About 1.4 million females served in administration, communication, air-raid defense, or nursing, and some even in combat with antiaircraft guns. Twenty-three-year-old Catholic Rita H. was conscripted in January 1945 in order to free men for front line service. Since she was rather small, she was fitted out with oversized uniform pieces and served as a telephone operator, helping to convey military messages. In spite of her only quasi-military status as part of the Wehrmacht, she had to march, stand to attention, and train with sidearms for self-defense. A friend related that one girl who abandoned her station during a bombing raid was court-martialed and summarily shot. But Rita was pleased with her final task of burning incriminating files, since it signaled "the downfall of a godless government." Fortunately the military aides merely needed to take off their uniforms to become civilians again.[47]

Another form of Nazi service was the wish "to give a child to the Führer" in the "fountain of life" (*Lebensborn*) program, organized by the SS. To counteract the falling birthrate, Heinrich Himmler had initiated a eugenic experiment of having Aryan males impregnate racially pure women to produce superior infants. The prospective mothers, many of them unmarried, were allowed to deliver anonymously in special homes where their offspring were cared for until adopted, preferably by an SS family. This program also extended to the occupied areas, where Wehrmacht soldiers would father children with local consorts; presumably Aryan children were also taken away from their mothers in the East. In practice, this elaborate effort was largely a failure, as it produced only about eight thousand babies in Germany and about twelve thousand in Norway, a preferred site because of its Nordic population. Toward the end of the war, Ursula Mahlendorf was shocked at the mothers' and nurses' neglect of these infants "that nobody wanted anymore."[48]

An even more popular way to support the Nazi regime was the denunciation of dissidents to the secret police. Since the Gestapo had only about fifteen thousand members by 1941, it had to rely on information about NS opponents, volunteered by block wardens or envious neighbors. As a known leftist, Ursula Baehrenburg's father was first forbidden to sell the bread he had baked. When that did not silence him, he was denounced as being Jewish. His mother, who had hitherto refused to name the source of her illegitimate twins, cleverly named a deceased sailor as an Aryan father in order to save him. Similarly, Renate Finckh heard a rumor that some young people of her town had been detained. "Students who had protested. They had distributed flyers and defaced house walls" with lies about the Führer and calls for peace. One of them had already been in prison. "A female classmate had turned him in" following her political convictions. With her "soul frozen" in zealotry, Renate could not help but admire this denouncer.[49]

A select group of female fanatics even served in the machinery of death as infamous guards in the concentration camps. Though shrouded somewhat in mystery, the KZ were reputed to be corrective institutions for "work-shy elements." Nazi families approved of them because the inmates were "supposed to be Communists. The men were picked up because they were against the Führer." Some Nazi professionals, such as Marianne Busch, were sent as support personnel to teach the children of the German staff at Auschwitz. About 3,700 women guards who were attached to the SS worked directly in the camps as supervisors, targeted on female inmates. Survivor Ruth Elias recalled, "Especially evil were the SS-women" who were "young and sadistic," beating and stealing from the prisoners. Their cruelty seemed more shocking than the bestiality of men because it contradicted the image of feminine gentleness. One of the most notorious of these was Ilse Koch, the so-called "witch of Buchenwald," who was married to the camp commander, abused the prisoners, and had extramarital affairs with other officers.[50]

Fanatical women were an integral part of the machinery of death, often failing to respect the simplest dictates of humanity. In 1941, for instance, an Austrian resistance member, Antonia Bruha, was interrogated by the Gestapo after having been betrayed by a spy. During the interview the young mother held her baby. But when her interrogators were ready for her to sign a confession, a female social worker "tore the child from my hand! She ran to the door, I wanted to follow, but two SS men with revolvers beat me back. And the child cried." Bruha was devastated. Once they had moved her to solitary confinement, she knew that the baby would die. After a year, she was sent to the women's KZ Ravensbrück, where she experienced some solidarity from other prisoners. She befriended a small Dutch girl named Hella who "was pretty" as a ward and helped her survive—until their guards sent her to Bergen-Belsen to be murdered. Antonia "could never understand what the purpose of killing children was, but [she] recognized thereby that the Nazis did not stop at anything, not even the murder of infants."[51]

Though numerous clues demonstrated the repressive nature of the Nazi dictatorship, most young women ignored this evidence and kept supporting the murderous regime. Ursula Mahlendorf recalled that the father of a friend had been sent to a KZ after "someone had reported him to the Gestapo" for defeatism. He had "gone around claiming that after Stalingrad defeat was inevitable." While "the adults said that he had been beaten up, [they] would not talk about it." Similarly, Ursula Baehrenburg's father reported from an old-age home "that new people who were dead after a few days arrived continually." It was obvious that something sinister was going on, but nobody stood up against it. "Jewish stores no longer existed" because the "Jewish owners had all been transported away. Nobody knows where to." But when Renate Finckh saw a long line of pitiful figures wearing yellow stars, a friend told her that "they are now going to Poland. There all of them will be killed." In her mind, pity struggled with guilt.[52]

As a result of their lack of interest in politics, few young women resisted the Third Reich. In general, "there were two different minorities" of critics and supporters of the regime. "The majority of the people were in the middle, apolitical and pretty well conformist. At most these folks shook their heads." Some families simply retreated into silence in order not to make their dislike for the regime noticeable in public. Others told jokes that made fun of leading Nazis, camouflaging their distaste for the crudeness of the SA by irony, even though such criticism could land them in jail if the wrong person was listening. The inane demands and rigid party discipline of the BdM even triggered some noncompliance among its adolescent members. But it was rare for a fanatic such as Renate Finckh to meet a young man who used his "entire energy in order to work against National Socialism."[53] A few young women, such as Gertrud Koch, were courageous enough to join the rebellious Edelweiß pirates in open opposition.

The stream of victory bulletins reinforced faith among women that Germany was bound to win the war in the end. Following the fighting closely in her diary, Lore Walb noted "an incredible jubilation and enthusiasm" after the triumph over Poland and added, "It is wonderful to be a German." While she was longing for a male friend to whom she could bare her soul, she was convinced that "we . . . can only win this war!" All her adulation was focused on the greatness of the Führer: "He had already proven his political genius, but he is no less militarily brilliant." Although she was an intellectual, she accepted the Nazi ideal of marriage and motherhood. Only the rising toll of young men and the heavy bombing attacks gradually revealed the "cruelty of the war" to her. Nonetheless she "still believe[d] in victory, which will and must be ours, since we want to live!"[54] Even if the consequences of war became more real, during its first three years most young women continued to believe that Germany would ultimately prevail.

HORRORS OF DEFEAT

With the turn in fortunes after the defeats in Stalingrad and North Africa, the mood of women at the home front gradually turned pessimistic in early 1943. The special army bulletins that talked about "straighten[ing] out extended front lines" or "strategic retreats" could no longer hide the shrinking of the area that the Wehrmacht occupied, and soldiers on leave reported desperate defensive battles against superior enemy forces. Ursula Mahlendorf recalled that "we stopped keeping our war diaries on the fate of our troops." Moreover, "after a while the map of Europe disappeared from our classroom" in order to hide the reverses and the teacher "concentrated his efforts on earlier historical heroics" so as to bolster morale. As a result, she "soon lost interest altogether and [her] world grew ever narrower." Similarly, Lore Walb noted: "It is best not to talk about the war at all. One no longer sees any path that seems to lead to an end." For her the war had changed from an exciting adventure into "a punishment from heaven."[55]

Young women began to feel the increasing pressure of total war by a gradual deterioration of their daily lives. In spite of the use of foreign slave laborers on farms, rationing led to scarcity, which made for long shopping lines and bartering of consumer goods for food. Real coffee was replaced by a roasted grain substitute called *Muckefuck*, which tasted horrible, and regular dark bread was turned into indigestible square loaves of *Kommissbrot*, stretched with the addition of ground tree bark. Due to the priority of military movement, trains became irregular and overcrowded, making travel exasperating and requiring special priority passes for long-distance trips. In the fall of 1944 Renate Finckh "was dismissed from school from one day to the next" because "manpower was needed." For Bettina Fehr, early graduation meant a constant lowering of intellectual standards for the sake of additional labor in the munitions factories.[56] No wonder that grumbling increased among the populace and Nazi critics who had hitherto been silent began to speak up more openly.

When the hope for victory faded and war became "a permanent condition," the Nazi leadership redoubled its efforts to shore up the home front.

Propaganda chief Joseph Goebbels shrieked into the radio, "Hitler and our scientists will prevail, if our nation will but hold out bravely!" Calling for energy conservation for the war effort, posters "in schools, municipal offices, banks and other public places warned of *Kohlenklau* (coal theft)." To make sure that all members of the Volksgemeinschaft suffered equally, another campaign pilloried war profiteers: "Hoarding food supplies or obtaining rationing cards by some pretext or other counted as felonies." A similar effort sought to suppress rumors and to keep news of defeats from spreading. "Another sign in railroad cars, streetcars and buses proclaimed 'Caution: Enemy listening in.'" Anyone caught tuning in to foreign radio such as the BBC was threatened with jail. And the "worst offense was to defame Hitler."[57] This punitive approach showed that the Nazis were starting to lose control.

By early 1943 the "total mobilization" of manpower reserves also conscripted women to war duty. Head of the labor service Fritz Sauckel called on all not-yet-employed "men and women to report for duty to defend the Reich." His order, directed at women between the ages of seventeen and forty-five who had no children, created "an enormous uproar." Else W. recalled that she "had to work hard" in a munitions factory without sufficient food. Side by side with slave laborers, she made "detonating fuses for tank grenades. We had to work in blue overalls and wear wooden clogs," Renate Finckh was ordered to do labor service in the Bavarian countryside. The conditions were miserable, her uniform did not fit, and the food was terrible, but she "felt free as never before" because she had escaped from her quarreling parents. She was doing "a man's job" and glad to be contributing to the war effort. With the men gone, the remaining women "shouldered the entire burden in war production, railroad, post-office, administration or agriculture."[58]

The frantic nature of women's efforts to distract themselves from the grim reality of the war was another clue that in spite of all protestations of "perseverance," doubt was beginning to grow. One favorite form of entertainment was going to movies and admiring stars such as Paula Wessely or Emil Jannings. In response to public wishes, Goebbels shifted motion-picture production from propaganda films such as *Jud Süss* to romantic comedies in order to make female viewers forget their wartime struggles through fantasy lives. Though she resented the sexism of the few available men, Lore Walb went to student parties to enjoy "dancing, kissing, laughing, eating, and talking" and to flirt a little. Still a teenager, Ursula Mahlendorf disliked her mother's raucous celebrations with officers: "They played cards, sometimes danced; they always drank heavily." Growing cynicism made the jokes crude and the mood sentimental: "Children, enjoy this war, the peace will be terrible."[59]

By 1943 the increase in Allied bombing attacks brought the war to the women at the home front by putting their lives directly at risk. After the radio announced that enemy airplanes were on their way, the wailing of sirens and booming of flak (antiaircraft) guns confirmed their imminent arrival, making people dash for the flimsy protection of shelters. Initially, it seemed like a game for neighbors to huddle in a private cellar, but when the bombs got closer it turned deadly in a hurry. In a public bunker in Krefeld, Rita H. saw men drinking schnapps and smoking while women knitted to combat their fear. Everywhere children and old people were lying on the ground, trying to sleep. She reported, "I had the feeling of having gotten into an underworld of dirt and chaos." In Berlin, Liselotte G. noted in her diary thirty bombing alarms within the span of two and a half months. Interrupting sleep and spreading terror among civilians, these air raids made life miserable.[60] But, contrary to Allied expectations of eroding morale, the attacks only reinforced the Germans' will to persevere.

When neither antiaircraft guns nor Luftwaffe interceptors could stop the bombing, people sought to escape the inferno by evacuating themselves to safe areas. Many families, such as the Jarauschs, moved mothers and infants from industrial target cities such as Magdeburg to friends in the Bavarian countryside, where they would get better food and more likely be secure. The NSV also organized an extended version of the *Kinderlandverschickung* in which entire school classes were sent to remote areas with their teachers. Edith Schöffski was moved with her sister to Upper Silesia, far from bombing range. Her host family took good care of them. There was even a loose form of instruction, but the two girls still enjoyed their freedom from maternal supervision. In spite of the marginal food, lack of privacy, and some homesickness, Ingrid Bork quite fondly remembered being sent to Bohemia, as well as to the Baltic coast.[61] While urban areas lost much non-essential population, this mass evacuation minimized the human losses.

One typical attack on May 31, 1943 destroyed the industrial city of Wuppertal, located in a river valley in western Germany. Erika Taubhorn remembered how her father showed her what looked like Christmas trees in the night sky—flares that marked the bombers' targets. "Now we grabbed clothes from the wardrobe and rushed into the cellar" while the first bombs dropped. The lights failed and the neighbors arrived, "almost all in pajamas." Taubhorn huddled under her father's coat in a corner. "The bombs continued falling, and the cellar door broke open from the impact. A giant cloud of dust came in. Mother suffered a heart attack, so that father had to take care of her in the dark." Then the frightened housemates broke down the door to the adjoining cellar to open an emergency exit. "We were lucky, no bomb fell on our house"; only the courtyard had been hit by incendiaries, which they doused with water. But in the entire building "windows were smashed by the air pressure and the curtains set on fire."[62] Fortunately enough, these people all escaped with their lives.

As a result of the deliberate strategy of creating firestorms with phosphate bombs to kill civilians, the entire center of Wuppertal soon went up in flames. Erika Taubhorn had to run from her house when the blaze from neighboring buildings threatened to engulf her home. Next door, "a paralyzed woman cried out. She was being burned alive because the entire house was aflame." Her mother led the frightened child—who had snatched up "the Sunday roast and [her] puppet"—to an open square where they spent a harried night. But her aunt's house was burned down. The Red Cross tried to help the victims by providing sandwiches. In the street where her uncle had lived, she "saw only rubble to the right and left." On a big sign with the names of the inhabitants, someone had scrawled the question: "Where are you?" But in these narrow lanes, nobody could have escaped alive. She almost stumbled over a corpse that "looked like a charred piece of wood in the form of a human being." Older BdM girls then had to rescue what possessions might yet be saved.[63]

After a saturation bombing, major cities looked like a wasteland in which no one could continue to live. Worried about her home town, Ulm, Renate Finckh was glad when a telegram announced: "Parents healthy. Business destroyed." During leave, she saw that "the parental house at the edge of town was still standing" and her father was trying to fix the holes in the roof. "We were nailing the shattered windows shut with boards and cardboard," happy to be alive. But the next morning they "struggled through the smoking ruins of the city center. The streets are completely impassable." It remained dark "since smoke and dust clouds block the light." But "most horrible is the stench. It smells a thousandfold like burned flesh." Because there might be survivors under the rubble, "everywhere hooded figures shovel with dull faces." In the destroyed family store, they found "a small white coffee pot" with a broken spout. The BdM leader "registered the horror with rare clarity," but still did not want to abandon her Nazi beliefs. Private pictures of endless ruins graphically show the extent of Berlin's destruction (image 16).[64]

The air raids created a new group of bombing victims who had lost everything in contrast to their more fortunate neighbors who had escaped somehow. Wherever possible, stunned survivors of the inferno gathered their family members and few rescued possessions in order to walk into the safer countryside, hoping to be received by friends or relatives. "Please come to us, even if you have nothing left. We shall share everything with you," wrote a former servant who invited Eva Peters to her home. Those who stayed behind in damaged buildings had to bury the many dead, clear away the rubble from the streets, and repair their own apartments so as to have shelter from the elements. If their house was destroyed, they were billeted with strangers who had enough space but resented the newcomers. Even Nazi supporters such as Lore Walb noted that the war was coming home. "The terror attacks have become unexpectedly horrible. . . . Countless people perish in every attack; irreplaceable cultural values are being destroyed."[65]

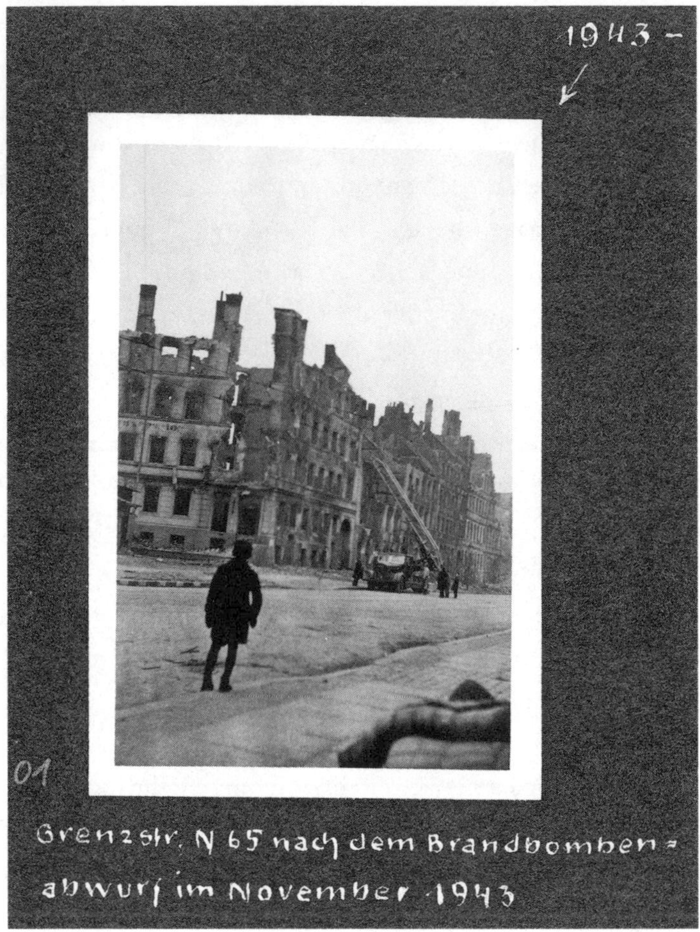

16. Destroyed Berlin. *Source*: Kempowski photo collection.

The continual pounding from the air also gradually made it clear to young women that the war economy was grinding to a halt, for new damage could no longer be repaired. The destruction of railway tracks, switches, and bridges made transportation haphazard, especially when the ubiquitous "low level strafers" (*Tiefflieger*) were hitting trains. Since raw materials could no longer be delivered, war production plateaued and the new miracle weapons did not get to the front. Ursula Baehrenburg noted that "letters from Berlin complained that the supply of food no longer sufficed and our relatives suffered from hunger." With rations continually shrinking, only those folks with friends in the countryside could count on having enough to eat. Moreover, during the cold winter of 1944–1945, city-dwellers froze because mining output decreased and coal was no longer distributed equitably. Eva Peters noticed that the initial "enthusiastic support of broad circles of the population" was "replaced by a no less stable, fatalist, desperate resolve."[66]

Among Nazified girls, the surprising news of the July 20, 1944 attempt to kill Hitler triggered a "mixture of feelings" ranging from fear to relief. "Evil officers, despicable traitors have tried to assassinate our Führer," noted Renate Finckh. "But nothing happened to 'HIM,' the greatest German. The criminals have already been caught." During the BdM flag-raising, she spoke to her charges from her heart about "loyalty and the unbroken faith in victory." Similarly, Eva Peters felt relieved at "having escaped from a terrible danger": at no other moment her "beloved and adored Führer appeared to be more irreplaceable than at this point in time." Instead of reinforcing resentment against a pointless war, the resistance plot often had the opposite effect, for to some people, Hitler symbolized hope. "There was another final wave of great solidarity with a man to whom the German people had abandoned themselves." Peters recalled a renewed resolve "for the defense of people, home and fatherland, for the ultimate struggle over being or nothingness, life or death."[67]

In spite of military retreats and "terrible air attacks," committed young women clung to their faith in the National Socialist cause. "The misfortune began with Stalingrad," Lore Walb wrote, acknowledging a succession of defeats including the "irresistible advance of the Russians" in the East and the gains of the Anglo-American invaders. "We all ask, what will the future bring??? Germany *cannot* perish—and yet one sees no way out. The [Allied] superiority is overwhelming." As a result of continued reverses, "my eternal optimism and faith are now almost completely gone." Despite irrefutable evidence that defeat was inevitable, these Nazified young women rejected the obvious conclusion that they had served a false cause. Eva Peters was disgusted that the initial opportunists were now "carefully distancing themselves."

Believing in "duty and loyalty" until the end, Renate Finckh even enrolled in a Nazi leadership academy. When her distraught father asked, "don't you see that everything is over?," she could only stutter, "I—do—not know it."[68]

The hardening of the struggle at the front and at home also suppressed any sympathy for the real victims of the Third Reich. When Renate Finckh observed "a young woman tied to a pillory, her hair shorn and spit at" because she had had an affair with a French POW, her mother argued, "This is war, and tough measures are necessary. The enemy is ruthlessly trying to destroy us." Finckh was uncomfortable sitting at the same table with slave laborers or prisoners at a farm, even after she realized that they were just people like herself. She was shocked when her brother Werner returned "shaken and upset" from the East, relating that the train tracks "were beleaguered by starving women and children," crying out, "please bread, please bread! [*sic*]." She could not forget having earlier seen the haunting eyes of a Jewish classmate in a column of deportees, since "thereafter [she] *knew*." She wondered why another friend who "had a terrible experience" in the East was sent to a mental hospital.[69] But concern with her own survival tended to trump human compassion.

During the winter of 1944–1945 it became "scary, how the war [was] approaching the borders" of the German Reich. "Combat became ever more brutal. The front retreated," Ursula Baehrenburg remembered. "The cities were bombed. In our village we saw the glow of fires from Stettin." While the Red Army was overrunning East Prussia and rushing to the Oder River, the Americans were capturing Aachen and trying to cross the Rhine. Though fleeing soldiers signaled the impending defeat, there were neither "official warnings" nor any "evacuation plans for the civilian population." The Mahlendorfs and other families had to decide on their own when "to pack our belongings" because it was "no longer safe" in Silesia due to the advance of the enemy. The key question became "When would it be our turn to flee?" If one left too early, one risked losing all possessions, but if one stayed put, one might no longer get out. While the military withdrew some personnel to the rear, many civilians waited until it was too late.[70]

Especially behind the Eastern Front, rumors of Russian atrocities spread like wildfire, fanned by a Nazi propaganda that tried to rally troops for a desperate defense through fear of revenge. When the Wehrmacht recaptured the village of Nemmersdorf in East Prussia, "our soldiers found the raped and mutilated bodies of women, children, and old men." They had been slaughtered indiscriminately. According to Ursula Mahlendorf, Goebbels made the most of the massacre, screaming in a radio address, "This, my fellow countrymen, is what awaits you if you surrender! We will never surrender. You must fight to the last drop of blood!" Wounded soldiers in a field hospital knew that the Red Army was retaliating for the atrocities previously committed by the Wehrmacht: "We must have shot the entire village when one of ours got a bullet from a partisan—old men, women, and even the kids" and particularly Jews.[71] Because Germans could expect no mercy from the approaching conquerors, they could only hope to escape retribution by fleeing to the West.

The cowardly flight of the local party leaders in the final weeks of the war disillusioned young women who were trying to cling to their Nazi faith. "When the Russians break through," one soldier explained to volunteer nurses, "you will have to know how to defend yourself" by using rifles and antitank guns. On another morning, a high BdM leader exhorted them to fight: "You may die bravely . . . you might be taken prisoner . . . they'll take you to Siberia, but remember you are proud German girls. Keep your purity." But the next day this Nazi functionary was gone, leaving her distraught charges behind. While her girlfriend fumed, "the big wheels are leaving for the West and letting us kids take the shit," Ursula Mahlendorf finally understood "that our 'leaders' are forsaking us." Enraged over this adult betrayal, she "was utterly bewildered and confused" when Hitler ended his life by his own hand. Out of desperation, she even joined a suicide pact with other BdM leaders, but was fortunately saved by realizing "I want to live!"[72]

With the approach of the front, panic spread among the deserted civilians. The first to flee were the Baltic Germans and East Prussians, who were forced to leave their homes, animals, and possessions behind. Led by noblewomen such as Countess Isa von der Goltz or by resolute farmers, entire villages set out westward to reach safety in the core of the Reich. From late 1944 on, Ursula Mahlendorf began to witness such treks with "horse drawn wagons, piled high with suitcases, bedding, bales of hay, old people, children. People fleeing, people bedraggled, stone faced, silent, wheels crunching on snow." The roads were overcrowded with wagons driving next to each other, while the center was kept open for military vehicles. Initially marshals, the NSV, or the Red Cross tried to provide shelter and food at night from the bitter winter cold. But what started out as a semiorganized stream soon dissolved into utter chaos. Soldiers and civilians were desperate to escape a trap that was closing further by the hour. Ruth Weigelt recalled, "I only wanted to hide, see nothing, hear nothing, feel nothing."[73]

In the eastern cities, women with friends or families increasingly ignored the "prohibition of wild flight," leaving on the last trains, army trucks, or anything that could get them away from the approaching Red Army. On February 1, 1945, a despondent Jakobine Witolla "started the trek across the ice of the Frische Haff," walking thirty kilometers in the cold to reach a refugee camp in Danzig. Many farmers driving wagons with horses broke through the ice and drowned; some refugees were shot by Soviet airplanes, while infants and the old "died of cold or exhaustion." But Jakobine and a friend were lucky enough to meet a couple of sailors who invited them onto their ship. After carousing all night, the captain actually allowed them to stay on the small military vessel and got them to Kiel unharmed. Though sad about losing her home, she took a train to Hameln, where her parents were overjoyed to see her alive. By contrast, many other ships, such as the army transport *Wilhelm Gustloff*, overcrowded with refugees, were sunk by Russian submarines, resulting in the loss of as many as nine thousand lives in a single stroke.[74]

The Silesians had more warning; they had already been able to observe the mass flight from further east. When the Russian offensive stalled temporarily, some chose to stay. Others retreated to the safety of the mountains. With her husband fighting nearby, Ruth Weigelt did not know where to go: "Just leave? Abandon home?" Inge Lindauer's family decided to flee in

February 1945 on a Red Cross train via Thuringia to the Austro-Bavarian border. By March the first bombing raids on Prague made it clear to Ruth Bulwin that she had to flee with baby Brigitte. "Our house was not hit, but we finally woke up!" Sending some of her possessions ahead via the still-functioning mails, she obtained a travel permit. But the few trains that were still running were so overcrowded that she had to fight through people hanging from doors in order to get on. Separated from her child, she heard her cry, but was lifted in through a window, managed to recover her, and did reach her aunt in Rudolstadt.[75] During their flight, the frightened refugees witnessed indescribable scenes of both ruthless egotism and selfless help.

Rampant fear even spread to the western areas of Germany, forcing young women to decide how to deal with the arrival of the Americans. In Alzey, Lore Walb helped feverishly to pack up the military dental clinic where she worked without knowing where the facility would be relocated. In late March she confided to her diary, "The enemy has entered our dear homeland and I have fled." A concerned druggist warned her against staying because "the Americans are perhaps a little less brutal, but you should not expect anything good." Though she "did not know what to do," Lore placed her belongings into a backpack and left her distraught mother in order to bike to a village further in the rear where a girlfriend lived. Encountering the sad refugees from Mannheim, she cycled for 230 kilometers in spite of flat tires and strafing planes until she finally reached Ebingen, where she "was received so nicely and warmly that she felt almost at home."[76] Toward the end of the war, it seemed that half of Germany was on the move, trying to find someplace safe.

Those young women who left East Prussia, Pomerania, or Silesia too late were ultimately overrun by the advancing Red Army. Ursula Baehrenburg never forgot that the local Nazi leader threatened her father with a pistol to leave the horses when he had loaded his wagon. "We were all desperate." But suddenly Ukrainian slave laborers turned up with a team and they all were able to drive into the forest to hide. They clung together under the tarp because the night was so cold. "Terrible fear made us all unable to move. I cried for many hours." On the second day the foreign men signaled, "the front has passed": they had survived and could return to the village. Similarly, Ursula Mahlendorf fled with other nurses in a maelstrom of soldiers and civilians with "everybody running for their lives." During one chaotic night "the Russians overtook us" in the Sudeten mountains, but she remained unharmed and set out on the dangerous path of returning home.[77] Up to one million other women and children were not so lucky and perished during the mass flight from the East.

Amplified by rumor and propaganda, one set of female fears of the Red Army centered on the fate of German soldiers due to the violence of the final struggle. Having not heard anything from her son who was missing in action, one worried mother kept hoping that he might somehow still be alive. Jakobine Witolla was greatly relieved when she finally got a postcard in 1946, proving that her husband was living in a Soviet POW camp. Loved ones worried that soldiers who had managed to shed their uniforms on their way home would be discovered and sent to Siberia. Ursula Baehrenburg recalled how civilians like her father were rounded up as well: "The Russians are taking the men away. Dad was grabbed from the bakery without shoes." Her mother was overwhelmed by the loss: "Papa is gone, now I also have to die. I cannot live without my husband." She refused to eat, lay in bed, and was dead a few days later.[78] Going beyond legitimate security concerns, the brutality of the Red Army left abiding resentment in German memory.

Another area of women's concern was what would happen to their possessions. Since "our enemies had always been pictured as barbarians," Ingrid Bork remembered, "we buried our most precious things in the ground." Of course, Hitler pictures, Nazi emblems, and anything else that could implicate people in the Third Reich were thrown away. Ursula Baehrenburg recalled that Russian soldiers on horseback "looked awe inspiring" when they threatened to shoot German women. "Wardrobes and drawers were ripped open, banknotes and papers torn apart, valuables taken along." Ursula Mahlendorf similarly described that during her flight "now and then . . . a Russian soldier broke rank, either to ask for a watch or some jewelry from a refugee." Once she even laughed "as he pushed the tenth or eleventh watch up his arm. He grinned back at us."[79] Beyond the age-old military desire for plunder, there was also much gratuitous destruction, perhaps inspired by resentment against the superior living standard of most German homes.

The greatest female anxiety concerned the inviolability of their own bodies when sex-starved and drunken Russian troops sought revenge for what the Wehrmacht had done to their women. It was essential to avoid the dreaded command "*Frau* come!" in order not to be dragged screaming into the woods. German women developed desperate strategies to escape the inevitable. Some teenagers who were young enough "dressed as a boy." Other women wore rags, dirtied their faces with ashes, and smeared themselves with blood to make themselves unattractive, or held onto crying children. Ursula Baehrenburg hid in the attic of her house after being saved by a Ukrainian slave laborer from the first rape attempt. Still acting as nurses in a stationary hospital train in Silesia, Ursula Mahlendorf and a girlfriend "crawled into a space below the cabinets," with wounded soldiers lying in front of them. "All through the night, we heard women crying out, men cursing, children screaming, wagon doors rolling open and shut."[80] Using such tricks, she escaped unharmed.

For less fortunate girls, the experience of being raped was so terrible that the shock remained etched into their psyche "for an entire lifetime." After the death of her mother, Ursula Baehrenburg no longer tried to hide. A few days later a "Mongol came into the room," grabbed her and dragged her along. When she tried to run to the cemetery, he pushed her into a garage full of refuse and oil. "Pointing a machine pistol to my head, he tore the clothes from my body. With pain, revulsion and fear I experienced the brutality of my first encounter with a man. I menstruated strongly and blood flowed down my legs." After it was over, she "lay there alone, with only one thought and wish, to be able to die." But even through this unbearable anguish, "resistance grew in me. I began to live again." This horrible experience was shared by up to two million women, including Edith Schöffski, who sacrificed herself to save other mothers and children. "The psychological pain which had been inflicted upon me was irreparable." The shame attached to this violation was so great as to create a taboo that rendered exact counts impossible.[81]

Young women coped with this painful experience in different ways, ranging from suicide to indifference. Due to widespread ignorance of "this sexual act," the most difficult part was the "sense of defenselessness" against strange soldiers' whims and the loss of control over one's own body. When resistance was impossible, one victim recounted, "I just let it happen to me." One way to survive was to distance oneself from what could not be stopped: "This is not you yourself, this is only the body, the miserable body! You are far, far away." Those mostly upper-class women who had developed an idealized version of their own purity experienced rape as a profound desecration, a profanation of their honor that would taint them forever. Lower-class women were more matter-of-fact in dealing with the inevitable, considering their violation merely "a war wound." Often female solidarity helped, whether protecting one another or sharing dreadful experiences. While some women ended their lives, the great majority found the courage to live on by feeling needed by their children or parents.[82]

As a collective gender fate, the mass rapes by the Red Army in the spring and summer of 1945 were a systematic product of a Stalinist dictatorship bent on avenging "what [Germans] had done in their lands." While victorious Western soldiers also raped defeated women, in the Soviet case such behavior was apparently so frequent as to be largely condoned from above.[83] Only some decent officers such as Lev Kopelev tried to stop the practice out of compassion. Diaries such as Marta Hillers' gripping account *A Woman in Berlin* show the peculiarity of this frenzy of sexual violence. Due to the breakdown of discipline, the soldiers raped indiscriminately across the entire age range, from prepubescent girls to aged grandmothers. Incited by liberal doses of vodka, they not only abused women once but repeatedly and in groups. Often they used physical force or even killed their helpless victims. If the violated women survived, they had to worry about pregnancy and sought out folk remedies or doctors willing to provide abortions. Powerless to stop the outrage, many German men compounded the humiliation by blaming their own women.[84]

The Third Reich dissolved in general chaos even before the end of the fighting because the Nazis lost control over their own population. Initially the arrival of refugees from the East and the cleaning up after bombing attacks had been "well organized" by trek marshals or NSV women. But when party functionaries fled to save their own skins, public order disappeared from the cities even before these were conquered. Similarly, the senseless command "to hang whoever shows a white flag" could not stop courageous mayors or individual homeowners from showing their readiness to surrender. Even the military police's practice of "stringing up all men and boys who try to run" failed to keep individual soldiers or whole units from fleeing toward the West in order to be captured by the Americans. At the same time, some starving slave laborers rebelled and rampaged to repay their prior suffering. Even German civilians started "to rob and plunder" food stores and military depots. It was "madness and futility wherever one looks." With Silesia occupied by the Poles, Ruth Weigelt sighed, "I believe we are lost."[85]

The collapse of the Nazi order made survival an individual challenge that helped liberate young women from social constraints. When public authorities crumbled, they had to take charge themselves, either falling back on family ties or relying on friendships, however temporary, in order to help one another. Girls and young women began a frantic search for ways to assure food and shelter as well as safety from marauding enemies. Ignoring the prohibition of desertion, Reich Labor Service worker Agnes Moosmann simply ran home. In spite of her protests, Lore Walb left her mother to seek safety with a girlfriend in a remote village of the Swabian Alps. Angered by her mother's unwillingness to leave, Ursula Mahlendorf followed her military hospital westward into Bohemia, relying on the safety of serving wounded soldiers. Refusing to accept that the Nazi Reich was falling apart, Renate Finckh ran away from her family to a BdM leader who counseled her to "go home" to take care of her mother. "You have to live. Already too many have died."[86]

For the Nazified youths, the failure of their ideals was rather shattering, for it required admitting that they had followed a false idol. Most moderates, such as Christel Beilmann, were simply relieved: "We did not cheer. We cried. The bombing had ceased. The war was over for us." But nationalists such as Lore Walb found it "hard to believe that the countless sacrifices of this war should have been in vain" and considered the surrender, though necessary, "deeply shameful and humiliating." Nazi true believers like Eva Peters were appalled at how the opportunists "tried to jump from the train which was ever more quickly speeding toward catastrophe." Having to cope with the death of her brothers, she added bitterly, "Liberation?—yes from everything which I loved and held dear." Similarly, the BdM leader Renate Finckh stubbornly clung to her faith: "I saw that the end had come and that it would be terrible and unimaginable. But I wanted to stand up for everything I had said. I belonged to the Führer even now."[87]

The "immense national catastrophe" nonetheless raised troubling questions about female support for National Socialism, and initiated a prolonged self-examination. Ursula Mahlendorf admitted that "much of what I had learned in the HJ leadership group began to evaporate in the heat of my disillusionment with the Nazi bosses in the last days of the war." Still resenting efforts at reeducation, Eva Peters deplored the "boundless stupidity and cynical hypocrisy of 'political enlightenment.'" But the totality of the defeat and the immensity of Nazi crimes made Lore Walb realize that "all faith, all sacrifices were in vain." Time and again, she heard "that we must have accumulated great guilt, especially the SS must have committed shameful deeds, we don't even know what atrocities." Such uncensored information inspired Renate Finckh to "a terrible recognition: Whatever I had loyally tried to keep in my heart had changed into remorse and shame." When the Third Reich collapsed, a painful self-questioning began.[88]

COSTS OF COMPLICITY

Female authors write ambivalently about their role in the Third Reich because they are trying to reconcile their earlier Nazi enthusiasm with their later disillusionment. Nostalgia for an innocent youth before Auschwitz suggests many positive memories. But presenting an honest account also compels them to admit that "most of us, boys and girls alike, participated with 'heart and soul'" in the Nazi regime. Only "under the pressure of war experiences did a process of disenchantment and rethinking begin," which accelerated when the full extent of German crimes became known. This "confrontation with [their] collaboration" precipitated a rather painful self-examination that compared the earlier naïve self to a later critical one. Each in her own way, Christel Beilmann, Renate Finckh, Ursula Mahlendorf, Eva Peters, and Lore Walb were haunted by "anger, grief, shame, and remorse" that inspired their autobiographical search.[89] Hence they wrote fractured texts in which positive memories were inextricably linked to negative results.

Taken together, these autobiographies suggest that women had quite a different war experience from men that was trying in its own right. As long as the Wehrmacht was winning, many followed a traditional pattern of caring for their families, dealing with shortages, and keeping up the home front. At the same time, they coped with the separation from the men by writing letters to soldiers and sending packages in order to keep up their morale. But when the struggle escalated into a total war and losses mounted, they supported the effort more actively by working hard in munitions factories, growing food with slave laborers on the farms, and serving in military support roles as Wehrmacht aides, flak gun helpers, or hospital nurses. Agnes Moosmann justified her service at an antiaircraft battery simply as "self-defense." Especially for the half-million women in the military, the half a million in air-defense, and the four hundred thousand in nursing, the war mobilization offered paths of advancement and escape from home. In a subaltern emancipation, women made an essential contribution to the war effort that kept the conflict going.[90]

These personal reminiscences also show that National Socialism had more support than was acknowledged during the postwar years. Some religious youths such as Edith Schöffski or working-class teenagers such as Erika Taubhorn kept their distance from the Nazis and noted "occasional opposition to Hitler." But the apolitical majority of women such as Ingrid Bork inadvertently stabilized the regime by their effort to carry on normal lives by going to school, training for jobs, or laboring in war production. More openly nationalist individuals such as Gisela Grothus were ready to serve the embattled fatherland as nurses, considering patriotic engagement their wartime duty. Most enthusiastic were the BdM leaders such as Eva Peters, who applauded German victories, considered the persecution of Jews justified, and bought into the Nazis' imperialism in the East. Even if such fanatics whose "belief in Hitler and the greater German Reich was unshakable" remained a minority, it was their enthusiastic embrace of volkish femininity that coerced their lukewarm peers into maintaining the war effort.[91]

For this complicity, the young women of the Weimar cohort paid a terrible price that destroyed their own lives, families, towns, and country. In the beginning only the Jewish, Communist, and other targets of persecution suffered. The increasing deaths in the Wehrmacht were limited to men such as these women's fathers, brothers, or lovers, who had themselves killed enemies. But with the shift toward total war, women themselves became targets of saturation bombing, which claimed between six hundred thousand and eight hundred thousand civilian lives, most of them female. Similarly, the desperate flight of about twelve million from Nazi-held areas and German provinces in the East, triggered by the panic that "the Russians are coming," killed perhaps another million people, the majority once again being women. The up to two million rapes by the victorious soldiers, mostly of the Red Army, were directed only against women.[92] Though the total number of female deaths was lower than that of men, these sacrifices were nonetheless horrifyingly large and left a bloody trail in collective memory.

After such terrifying experiences, it was not surprising that many young women constructed victimization narratives to explain their suffering. Preoccupied with their own pain about "flight, hunger, expulsion, rape, loss of home [and] separation of families," most just "complained, groaned, cursed and felt sorry for themselves." Some simple souls such as Liselotte S. claimed that the horror "came over us like a fate, at least for girls like myself." More sophisticated observers such as Lore Walb blamed the cruelty of the Russians and other enemies for "robbery and probably also murder" while railing against the "bombing terror" of the Anglo-Americans. Disappointed Nazi supporters such as Ruth Bulwin also held the party leaders responsible for their misery: "We were betrayed . . . left alone in our misfortune."

Only a few clear-eyed observers "recognized that [they] had been loyal to evil." Shocked by the totality of the defeat, Renate Finckh acknowledged her own contribution to the disaster, writing, "Searching for comfort, I let myself be captured by a great lie."[93] It would take decades to spread this insight to others.

6

VICTIMS' SUFFERING

For endless hours the train rolled eastward. The prisoners in the crowded cattle car clung to each other, choked by nauseating stench. When the motion stopped, SS men ripped the doors open and barked orders to "get out" and "hurry up." Stumbling down the ramp, the Ukrainian Jew Anna Fränkel realized that she had been taken to Auschwitz, "a death camp" in which "only one in ten thousand remained alive!" Marching between electric fences and passing a "pile of charred corpses," she resolved to do everything in her power to live. "My horror about what I saw was so great that I no longer had the energy to be shocked." An older prisoner explained that the smoke billowing from crematoria indicated that "all Jews who arrived today have been taken there immediately." Then Fränkel was stripped naked and had her hair shorn and a number tattooed on her arm. But because she was young and healthy, she survived the selection process. Repeated thousands of times, this arrival in hell in April 1944 was a scenario of ultimate victimization.[1]

Originally such concentration camps (KZ) were not directed against Jews, but rather potential opponents of the Third Reich. According to Fritz Stern, "it is all too often forgotten that the first victims of National Socialism were its domestic political enemies, the brave people who had fought and in previous elections sometimes bested the Nazis." After the seizure of power in 1933 the SA arrested thousands of anti-Fascists, vastly exceeding the holding capacity of ordinary prisons. Hence the storm-troopers improvised detention centers in factories or fields close to towns such as Dachau and

Oranienburg in order to eliminate leftists from public life and intimidate them through brutality to make them acquiesce to Nazi rule. In public, concentration camps were justified as reeducation facilities that would teach their inmates to respect the new order through discipline and hard labor.[2] Eventually the SS took control and widened the circle of victims to asocials, homosexuals, Sinti, and Roma, as well as others excluded from the national community. Yet ultimately the lawless terror of the Nazi system focused most on Jews.

The persecution of Jews was complicated process, because it involved a complex linguistic and legal separation from gentile Germans and a reconfiguration of their hybrid identities as solely Jewish. Even when persecuted, Communists always remained Germans, but when Jews were stripped of their Germanness they were thrown back upon religious or ethnic identifications. Exclusion from the national community was a shocking insult, especially for successful secular and assimilated families such as the Fröhlichs and Sterns, who felt German in every sense of the word. Moreover, the deprivation of their livelihoods by successive decrees and the revocation of their citizenship left the older generation at a loss. Suddenly they were forced to recover Jewish roots about which many knew little or hardly cared, to assume a new self-image in order to function in a segregated society. For the younger generation, this rediscovery often led to an exciting process of Zionist commitment, but for their parents it threatened lifelong emotional ties.[3]

The politics of memory have created an odd competition between the various groups claiming victimhood. In East Germany, mostly anti-Fascist opponents of the Third Reich were considered "Victims of Fascism" in order to make them into Communist heroes. In neighboring countries, slave laborers, refugees of ethnic cleansing, and war dead were exemplars of a narrative of national martyrdom. With the rise of a broader Holocaust sensibility, Jews assumed primacy among the persecuted groups, since only they were targeted for complete annihilation, ignoring even the twisted logic of serving the war effort.[4] Surprisingly enough, German soldiers and civilians also began to stress their own suffering at the front and at home and claim to have been victimized by the Nazi leadership. Because critical memory insists on the priority of those persecuted by the Nazis, the emphasis on victimhood in popular German recollections has created a troubling rivalry that effaces the causal difference.[5]

One way of countering such obfuscation is to look more closely at the stories told by political opponents or racial victims, which deal with unspeakable horrors and intense agony. Survivors chronicle the disintegration of their lives under Nazi pressure and the endless debates about emigration until it became too late to escape. Those caught in the SS prisons or concentration camps relate their desperate struggle for survival, contrasting many acts of vile brutality with a few instances of kindness. Their accounts stand for untold voices that were silenced by the oppressors, but offer only an indirect and partial understanding of those who perished. These autobiographies also tell of courageous efforts at resistance by the anti-Fascist underground, captives, and the Allied forces that finally defeated the Third Reich. Due to their emotional charge, Ruth Klüger counsels that these testimonies need to be read with critical sympathy: "neither traditional forgiveness nor martyr worship" will do their terrifying experience justice.[6]

NAZI PERSECUTION

For Hitler, "fighting Marxism" was both an ideological aim of reinvigorating culture and a practical necessity of solidifying his hold on power. From the beginning, the Nazi movement had denounced the corrosive effects of Marxism on cultural traditions and deplored the Bolshevik seizure of power in Russia. Moreover, he considered the radical Communist Party (KPD) a political rival when unemployed workers during the Great Depression saw a social revolution as their only hope for a better life. In the streets and beer halls, the Hitler Youth and SA brawled with the Communist Youth and Red Brigades for control of public space, hailing Hitler or Stalin while beating or even killing their enemies. Accusing a Dutch Communist of having set the Reichstag on fire on February 27, 1933, the Nazi leadership seized upon the opportunity to incarcerate most KPD and some Social Democratic (SPD) leaders and bourgeois democrats on the pretext of preserving order. Only by suppressing the Left could the Nazi rule be secure.[7]

Thereafter rebellious working-class youths and intellectuals who opposed Hitler had no choice but to continue their struggle underground. In order to carry on, they began to adopt "conspiratorial forms of class struggle," forming small cells and adopting code names. In secret meetings, anti-Fascist youths studied the Marxist classics and heatedly debated the "predictions of revolution." Camouflaged as ordinary members of the Youth Movement, they hiked in the countryside, discussed the irresistible extension of Nazi control over public life, coped with their disappointment in the party leadership, and reinforced their faith in the Soviet Union as a beacon of a better future. The more daring ones, such as Heinz Zöger, printed leaflets on hidden presses and scrawled anti-Nazi slogans such as "Hitler Means War" and "Communism Lives" on factory walls. Seeking to maintain their courage, they channeled their anger at repression into "a firm resolution to resist with all means."[8]

The amateurish nature of such "illegal work" made it easy for the Gestapo to arrest the Socialist youths involved. Zöger, who had just turned eighteen, was roused by his mother with the shout "The police are here." Like dozens of his friends, he was taken to the Leipzig police prison, interrogated, beaten, and cursed as "red pig . . . We'll crack you yet." He almost failed to recognize his group's leader, Kurt Lenge, due to his "broken teeth, swollen eyes, blue and yellow-green face." In his few contacts with other prisoners, "we supported each other in holding out and not giving in." Months later, a kangaroo court in Zwickau sentenced the seventy or so young Communists to lengthy prison terms. Because of his youth, Zöger received only nine months in the infamous "yellow misery" prison in Bautzen, having to pull threads out of cloth. As a "hard case," he was given no privileges, but was proud to have held on to his convictions. Thousands of other young Socialists, including youth leader Erich Honecker, experienced the same fate.[9]

For domestic opponents, the Nazis built infamous concentration camps—a euphemism for mass prisons—such as Buchenwald, outside the cultural city of Weimar. Established in the late 1930s, this was run by death's-head SS guards under the cynical motto "right or wrong, my country." According to the Socialist Moritz Zahnwetzer, the camp housed "political prisoners, criminals, and Seventh Day Adventists," to whom asocials and eventually Jews were later added. "The first general impression is that here in the heart of Germany a city is being erected, in which the inmates have to do slave labor." In order to build barracks for the SS, the prisoners worked in quarries: "The labor is hard, the food is inadequate, hunger is a steady companion." At the slightest pretext, the guards killed inmates for working too slowly, for trying to flee, or just for fun. One prominent victim was Protestant pastor Paul Schneider, who spent sixteen months in solitary confinement for his religious convictions. While claiming to "reeducate" the inmates, the SS, in effect, sought "to eradicate the opponents of the Nazi system" by sadistic cruelty.[10]

Hitler was even more passionate about anti-Semitism, but had to be more circumspect in persuading the population to adopt radical measures. True enough, a hard core shared Julius Streicher's fanaticism, expressed in the "political pornography" of the sexual caricatures in *Der Stürmer*. But even if they shared some social prejudice against Jews, most people were more preoccupied with overcoming the consequences of the Great Depression or reversing the military defeat than with the "racial purification" of the German Volk. Moreover, many Germans knew their own "decent Jews" whom they considered exceptions and appreciated as competent doctors, lawyers, bankers, and the like. While propaganda pressure gradually persuaded the gentile majority to cut their personal ties to Jewish friends, a minority of courageous anti-Fascists maintained their relationships.[11] Compared to widespread approval of suppressing Communism, it took more time to convince most Germans of the need to persecute Jews.

Part of the difficulty stemmed from the considerable success in integration that made many Jews indistinguishable from their gentile neighbors. Only the new arrivals from Eastern Europe who worked in Berlin's Scheunenviertel neighborhood approximated anti-Semitic stereotypes, with their kaftans, earlocks, and Yiddish dialect. Many established families, such as the Gompertz clan, were "Germans of Jewish confession," observant of their orthodox religion but proud of their military service during World War I. Other less religious people, such as the Angress family, occasionally went to reform synagogues, mixed German and Jewish holiday customs, and sometimes married non-Jewish spouses without paying any particular attention to cultural borders between themselves and their now-"Aryan" friends. Even more secularized folks, such as the Sterns, lived entirely German lives with only a vague recollection of ethnic difference. By profession, identity, behavior and intermarriage, in Peter Gay's words, "they were Germans."[12]

Until 1933 the defensive strategies of Jewish Germans had worked well enough to suggest that lingering prejudices would be overcome in the future. On the local level, their involvement in public charities created much goodwill in the gentile community. On the national plane, the majority of Germany's half-million Jews voted for the Liberal and Social Democratic Parties, which had supported emancipation and legal equality. Jewish veterans, often decorated with Iron Crosses, gathered in the National League of Jewish Front Soldiers, a nationalist organization that stressed their disproportionate sacrifices in World War I. More moderate Jews belonged to the Central Association of German Citizens of Jewish Faith, whose very title suggested that its sixty thousand members saw themselves as both Jewish and German. Finally, a growing minority of the younger generation followed the clarion call of Zionism without actually going to Palestine. This formidable array of organizations implied that their future in Germany was secure.[13]

The Nazi boycott of Jewish businesses, the purge of the civil service, and the restriction of higher education therefore came as horrible surprises. On April 1, 1933, the government announced that "all businesses owned by Jews had to close for the day." Photos show uniformed SA men trying to discourage shoppers by asking, "Don't you know that this is a Jewish store?" (image 17). A week later, the Nazi regime purged public employment of leftists and Jews under the pretext of "restoring the civil service," excepting solely veterans of the First World War. Extended even to lawyers in private practice, this prohibition destroyed professional livelihoods and signaled that Germans should no longer do business with Jews. At the same time the government claimed to reduce overcrowding of universities by limiting Jewish access to academic training to less than 1 percent, the proportion of Jews in the population,

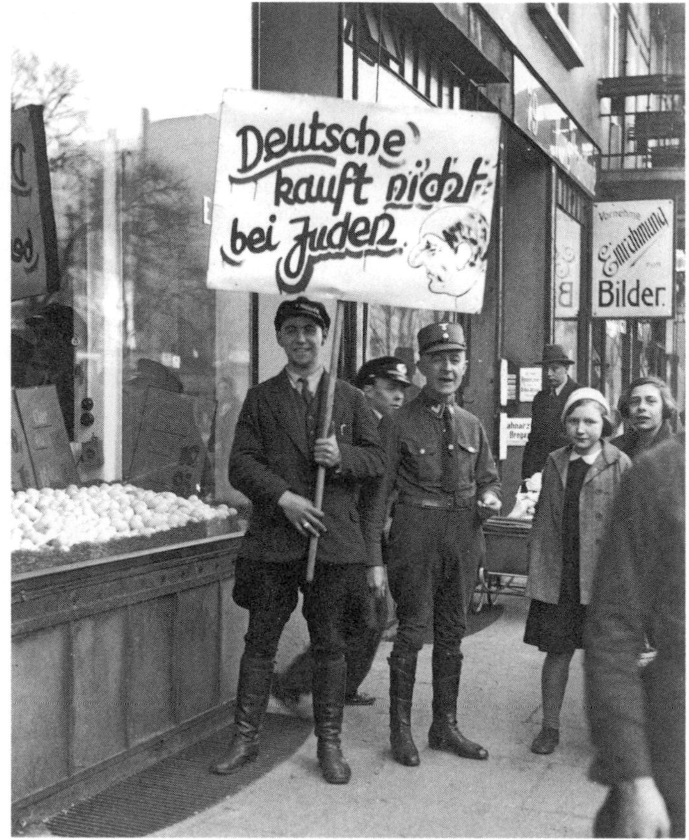

17. SA boycott of a Jewish store. *Source*: Stiftung Preussischer Kulturbesitz.

thereby denying them higher education. Though shocked by the harshness of these measures, the leaders of the Centralverein decided merely to hope that the storm would blow over as it had often done in the past.[14]

The brutality of the SA and the lawlessness of the state triggered a first wave of flight into Austria and other neighboring countries where German-speakers might be welcome. Prominent Nazi opponents, especially if they were both Jewish and leftist, had no choice but to escape across the borders if they did not want to end up in "protective custody" like the Social Democrat Kurt Schumacher. But even ordinary Jews such as Samuel Keil decided to flee to Vienna, for the police no longer guaranteed his security in Germany. One day a horde of brownshirts stormed into his warehouse "and started to knock crates of eggs off their storage platforms," finding the mess hilarious. When a war veteran employee with an Iron Cross protested, they tore "the medal from around his neck" and forced him to wipe the floor. Jack Keil recalled his father's humiliation: "I had never seen a man cry before." Better-off families such as the Sterns, feeling "apprehensive, became determined to emigrate" as well. But after finding job prospects in France uncertain, they decided to stay.[15]

While their parents were wrestling with grave decisions, teenagers sought refuge in Jewish youth groups, largely patterned on the German Youth Movement. The Aryan-looking Ingeborg Hecht joined the "German-Jewish Hiking Group Comrades" to roam through the North German heath until "our beautiful League was prohibited in 1936." Diminutive Tom Angress became a gung-ho member of the boys' club "Black Platoon," which considered itself patriotically German and religiously Jewish at the same time. "Finally I belonged to a group of boys my age and thus could cope much better with the daily unpleasantness of school." More dedicated Jews such as Lucy Mandelstam "became interested in Zionist youth movements and joined Blue White." There, she sang "Hebrew songs, danced the Hora and learned about Israel." Imbued by "national Jewish agrarian romanticism," Georg Iggers idolized the kibbutz.[16] In an increasingly hostile environment, these youth groups provided comfort and companionship.

The Nuremberg Laws of 1935, which "excluded Jews and non-Aryans from German citizenship," were "a further shock," as they reduced Jews to the status of "state subjects." In racist terms, they prohibited marriages and extramarital sex between Jews and gentiles and forbade the employment of female Aryan servants under the age of forty-five in Jewish households. Moreover, the "Reich citizen law" robbed Jews of their rights as citizens and made them helpless against bureaucratic chicanery, "casting them out of the German national community." Thereafter, any official act such as getting a passport or government job required proof of Aryan ancestry back to one's grandparents. (This resulted in a new industry of checking church records.) The new distinctions also produced a class of "mixed race" persons who were three-quarters, half, or one-quarter Jewish, like Ingeborg Hecht or Bettina Fehr, whose survival became increasingly precarious.[17] With one stroke, Jews had lost a century of progress toward emancipation.

As a result of such brutal exclusions, German Jews had to reaffirm their sense of Jewishness and began a difficult search for the submerged side of their heritage. Peter Gay asserted unequivocally that, without their own doing, "we had suddenly become Jews." In the same vein, Fritz Stern reported, "I began to feel that I was not German" without really understanding what he now needed to become. Georg Iggers similarly alluded to his transformation of identity, "I saw myself more and more as a Jew than as a German." Ruth Klüger stated that after the Anschluss, "when my shaky belief in Austria began to waver, I became Jewish in self-defense." She even changed her nickname from the sweet "Susi" to "an appropriate Jewish name" and adopted the biblical "Ruth." Unsure what Jewishness could mean beyond religious affiliation, Tom Angress put his pain over the loss into verse: "Once we were sons of this land / And now? Woe to us, such woe. / We know only hate, know only distress / and still love Germany so much."[18]

In order not to succumb to self-loathing, most Jewish youths developed coping strategies that made it easier to survive the mounting pressure of the Third Reich. Isolated by decree and behavior from their Aryan peers, they were forced to construct segregated lives in the shrinking spaces that remained available. One important stratagem was focus on one's own family. According to Peter Gay, "my parents were a refuge, an island of order and reason, just by being there." Another mechanism of retaining sanity was the development of hobbies that could be pursued in one's own home, such as listening to foreign radio stations, voracious reading, or stamp collecting. Watching spectator sports was yet another outlet, since one could cheer for the American sprinter Jesse Owens to triumph over Nazi athletes or boxer "Jersey Joe" Walcott to defeat the German heavyweight champion Max Schmeling. Adolescents who were still young enough to go to school, such as Georg Iggers, could also attend separate Jewish institutions or, like Tom Angress, prepare for later emigration by learning how to do practical farm work.[19]

After the Nuremberg Laws made future prospects bleak, the main topic of discussion in Jewish families "wasn't religion—it was emigration." Leaving Germany seemed to be full of risks, since Nazi regulations required that by going to a foreign country, one give up one's economic security, social position, and cultural capital. Tom Angress remembered, "We waited, tried to adjust, hoped the Nazis would change their mind about the Jews and otherwise went about our daily activities." As long as business remained acceptable, it did not seem necessary to leave everything behind. "Papa was reluctant to take his wife and children to a foreign country, where his future would have been uncertain." But once the "deteriorating situation of the Jews in Germany" made emigration a necessity, families "were encouraged to explore all possible avenues." As intermediate strategies, the Warmbrunns shifted their business to neighboring Holland, while the Eycks sent their son to boarding school in England.[20]

Even after a decision to emigrate had been made, many obstacles stood in the way of its timely implementation. The contradictory nature of Nazi policies wanted to push Jews out, but at the same time profit from their leaving. This complicated obtaining exit papers. Legal emigrants had to sell their businesses at a discount, leave behind virtually all their possessions, and pay an exorbitant Reich Flight Tax on their assets while being allowed only ten Reichsmark in foreign currency per capita. At the same time, the reluctance of potential receiving countries to add more indigents to an overcrowded labor market still reeling from the effects of the Great Depression made it difficult to gain entrance to safe havens. In many countries, consular officers were themselves anti-Semites who were reluctant to let Jews in. Obtaining an entrance visa required financial sponsors and a place within a country's restricted quota.[21] As a result, it took much time and determination to complete the necessary paperwork.

While frantically searching for a way out, Jewish families tried to carry on in reduced circumstances that made escape ever more imperative. Assimilated folks such as the Fröhlichs thought, "we were Germans; the gangsters who had taken control of the country were not Germany—we were." Occasionally this identification with the "better Germany" was reinforced by contacts with courageous gentiles such as helpful teacher Elisabeth Flügge, attesting "to surviving pockets of decency in Nazi Germany, even of quiet resistance." Peter Gay recalled, "For many thousands of German Jews like my parents, however alert they had to be to the hostile atmosphere that bore down on them, a certain separation of spheres seemed plausible, even appropriate." While revolted by Nazi brutality, many Jews considered Hitler's threats "so utterly implausible" as to be "unreliable guides to future conduct. They were literally incredible."[22] As a result they tried to continue somewhat normal lives while at the same time preparing to leave.

Once they were expelled from regular schools, youths sought to acquire practical skills that might help them in their new lives outside of Nazi Germany. One essential strategy was to learn English or French so as to be able to communicate abroad. Teenagers like Irmgard Mueller took up typing, stenography, sewing, or cooking, combining commercial and homemaking abilities. In order to acquire a trade, Albert Gompertz became an apprentice to a textile business, which proved quite useful in the United States. The training farm for Jewish emigrants at Gross Breesen in Silesia, led by a charismatic war veteran, Professor Kurt Bondy, tried to provide knowledge for settling in Palestine. After moving there in 1936 Tom Angress learned skills like carpentry and fieldwork, while at the same time experiencing an intense "sense of community" and imbibing "ethical and cultural values" for a lifetime. Another extended family from Bohemia, which included Wilma Abeles-Iggers, managed to get a Canadian visa by applying for agricultural settlement.[23]

The increasing plunder of businesses under the euphemism of "Aryanization" speeded preparations for emigration by destroying the material basis of Jewish life. Lawyers were forced to dissolve their partnerships with gentiles and allowed only to act as legal consultants for Jewish clients. Similarly, doctors lost their insurance privileges and were restricted to practicing for Jewish patients, even if some gentiles were loath to give up their trusted medical authorities. From 1938 on businessmen were also compelled to turn over legal control of their enterprises to gentile partners, often selling their shares much below market value. When the prosperous Breslau industrialist

Ernst Schwerin was warned by a loyal accountant that the Gestapo was about to arrest him, he fled the country overnight although the Finance Ministry had found no irregularities. Tired of constant SA harassment, prosperous Gelsenkirchen furrier Leo Gompertz also decided to cut his losses and liquidate his business in order to leave the Third Reich.[24]

By the late thirties the ever more massive NS repression turned the trickle of Jewish emigrants into a veritable flood. Tom Angress did not want to abandon Gross Breesen when told "that Papa had decided to leave Germany with the family." But his resourceful father smuggled one hundred thousand Reichsmark, his entire property, out of the country, while his son escaped Gestapo scrutiny at the Dutch border in spite of his Jewish passport. In September 1938 Major Edgar von Zerbony, the husband of a patient, knocked on the door of Fritz Stern's father. "He urged us to depart at once," since his comrades "had told him that Hitler was determined to destroy Czechoslo vakia" and that would make escape impossible. Because they had also finally found a sponsor who put up the $3,500 to obtain a US visa, the terrified Sterns immediately flew to Amsterdam and took a boat to New York. A few weeks later the Iggers family similarly escaped by train to Holland.[25] Seeing the handwriting on the wall, all Jews who could do so now fled in haste.

In March 1938 the Anschluss extended the persecution of Jews to Austria, adding more than two hundred thousand new victims. When "trucks of brown-shirted Nazi SA toured the streets" to celebrate the reunion with Germany," Lucy Mandelstam recalled, her "whole world fell apart and everything changed" and "my beautiful Vienna suddenly became a menacing and frightening place." Jack Keil remembered "the eerie feeling" of sitting with his parents in their darkened apartment and listening "to the screaming, yelling, hoarse but strangely fascinating voice of Adolf Hitler." The shouts of "Sieg Heil" and "Jews out" by men in Nazi uniform made it clear that "what took a while in Germany, came about literally overnight" in Austria. The quick extension of the Reich's anti-Semitic measures implemented by Adolf Eichmann signaled unmistakably that Jews had become "once again the object of violence and fury." Due to widespread racism, "the Austrian Nazis were even more virulent than their German counterparts in 1933."[26]

A yet greater shock was the *Kristallnacht* on November 9, 1938, called the "night of broken glass" due to the smashing of shop windows. Leo Gompertz experienced the pogrom in Gelsenkirchen. It "supposedly was caused by the 'boiling soul of the German people' " against the murder of a minor diplomat in Paris, "but in reality it was organized by Goebbels and Goering and carried out by the storm-troopers." First the riled-up crowd set the synagogue on fire. Fire trucks arrived, but "only to protect the neighboring buildings." Then the mob broke into stores, looted valuable merchandise, and destroyed the interior. Finally, "came the dreaded knock at the door" and the SA burst into the apartment: "They first searched for hidden weapons and took me away" to police headquarters while the police refused to stop the rioting. Lucy Mandelstam's father was sent to a KZ where he was "beaten and starved and many died." Gompertz was only ordered to sell his house for a pittance and "to emigrate as soon as possible." The purpose of such intimidation and brutality was to frighten the Jews into leaving the country immediately.[27]

The "night of broken glass" created a panic in the Jewish community and turned emigration from a matter of choice into a necessity for survival. Even patriots such as Peter Fröhlich's father became determined "to do anything, no matter how illegal, to get the three of us away from the German nightmare." Families frantically searched for sponsors, wrote letters, and besieged consulates to obtain entrance visas for a safe haven. The Fröhlichs finally obtained an exit certificate and left two weeks earlier than planned on a steamer to Cuba. This saved their lives, for their original ship, the *St. Louis*, was tragically turned back and many passengers perished. After completing the formalities, Gompertz sent his children ahead to Holland, eventually managed to join them, and they sailed to the United States. Less well prepared, Hanna Marlens and her family used her father's Czech citizenship to leave Vienna "in secrecy" with "no goodbyes to anyone." In such life-and-death situations it took a combination of luck, persistence, and daring in order to manage a family escape.[28]

In this rush to leave, neighboring countries played a crucial role as stopping places from which safety might eventually be reached. Lacking sympathy for Jews, Switzerland only served as a transit route, while Czechoslovakia no longer offered escape after falling under Nazi control. Even Poland refused to renew the passports of Jews living in Germany, rendering the stateless Keils' escape through Belgium more difficult. In spite of its own unemployment problem, France was more hospitable, but forced refugees such as the Marlens to make a living by starting an "independent business enterprise." Britain remained restrictive, preferring children and potential domestic servants. Holland was more open: it sheltered Werner Warmbrunn until his US papers came through and allowed Tom Angress to organize the transit of the Gross Breesen group and made it possible for his mother and brother to survive underground. Cuba became a favorite refugee asylum because from there people such as the Fröhlichs could hope eventually to reach the not-very-welcoming United States.[29]

The occasional help of gentile friends or officials in assisting Jews to escape was all the more impressive because it required courage to ignore Nazi decrees. When Lucy Mandelstam's father was incarcerated in the KZ, a former classmate turned SS officer brought him food and news. Emil Busse, a close family friend, hid the Fröhlichs during the Night of Broken Glass and found ways to smuggle their jewels, silver, and stamp collection out of the country on their departure. Similarly, a group of loyal acquaintances helped veteran Erich Alenfeld avoid imprisonment, and a postal worker did not betray Ingeborg Hecht's identity when she was hiding in the Swabian countryside. It took a Luxembourg border guard to look the other way, a friendly Belgian to provide refuge, and aid from another surprising SS man to permit the Keils to escape. A daring airline official helped get Werner Warmbrunn a seat on one of the last planes out of Berlin, a "good German who took some (probably minor—this was 1941) risk to help a young Jew to safety."[30]

Unfortunately, about a third of the German Jews either did not want to or were unable to leave and therefore became trapped in the Holocaust. Older men who had fought in the Great War, in particular, were reluctant to go away because they were emotionally invested in Germany. Many Jews "belonged to that naïve majority who believed that [the Nazis] would not last and that everything would be back to normal again." Those living in a "privileged mixed marriage" with Aryan partners who "thought Christian, but felt Jewish" also wanted "to defend their position as Germans for the sake of the children." Others, such as Ruth Klüger's family, had the means to send only her father to safety; her mother "could not get the money" needed for the exit tax as "her property had been sequestered and the bank accounts blocked." Similarly the Mandelstams were unable to leave because the father's visa to Shanghai turned out to be a fraud and he was once more put into a KZ.[31] For each heart-warming story of close escape, there are many others of tragic failure.

The farewells from Europe for those fortunate enough to leave were "short but emotional," with different feelings contending with each other. While experiences of persecution had instilled an "indiscriminate hatred" of Germans in Peter Fröhlich, his arrival in Cuba nonetheless triggered a "profound depression"; the "sinister shadow" of Nazi Berlin followed him into exile. In contrast to his father, who "was saying goodbye to all he had once held dear," Fritz Stern "had no regrets. I felt nothing but joy" at having escaped from a repressive system that had taken away his air to breathe. Because "Hitler and the Nazis weren't letting us be Germans," Tom Angress' father argued that "Germany was no longer our homeland." But his son wanted "to hang on to [his] blind German patriotism" and felt "incredibly sad."[32] Though escape offered a path to survival, refugees realized that mastering a future without resources in a new country with a different language and culture would involve a difficult struggle.

MASS MURDER

The unleashing of World War II sharply worsened the situation for Nazi victims: it removed international inhibitions and confronted opponents with a charge of treason. After the attack on the Soviet Union, Germany's surviving Communists intensified their clandestine agitation. But the "Nazis had institutionalized terror. Torturers, judges, executioners, and wardens only fulfilled different functions within the same terrorist system." The resistance faced brutal repression, arbitrary incarceration, and death by sham trial. In March 1942 the Gestapo arrested about fifty Leipzig Communists in order to try the charismatic leader Herbert Bochow for "forming a group for high treason."

During the show trial, the defendant predicted that the Fascists would be one day accused of "barbarism, imperialist wars of conquest and enslavement of whole peoples." But this courage only speeded his execution. His accomplice Heinz Zöger was condemned to several years in the penitentiary, where he was treated sadistically and had to work in war production.[33]

For partly Jewish Germans, the war brought new uncertainty, for the progressive radicalization of the Third Reich threatened their ambiguous racial status. Due to his half-Jewish wife, Bettina Fehr's father, a medical doctor, experienced "a chain of private and public humiliations" in spite of his selfless effort to help sick patients.The Wehrmacht, needing manpower, generally let sons of such marriages serve in its ranks. However, the application of decorated veteran Erich Alenfeld was rejected because he was completely Jewish. Even when such husbands lived in a "privileged marriage" with an Aryan wife, they lost their jobs and had to pay a property contribution as Jews. Moreover, with the beginning of deportations into Poland, they faced being included in ghettoization. At the same time, Ingeborg Hecht's divorced parents were accused of "miscegenation" because they had still maintained sexual contact after formal separation. Even after she married a gentile soldier, Mrs. Hecht and her little girl faced continual uncertainty. To extend the sweep, Nazi bureaucrats invented a new concept of *Geltungsjuden*, mixed-race people identifying with Judaism, who were to be treated as regular Jews.[34]

By blocking escape routes through hostile countries, the fighting also closed the door to further emigration, although Himmler prohibited it only in October 1941. When the Central Office for Jewish Emigration assumed control, Nazis imposed a new emigration tax, putting asylum destinations such as Honduras and Shanghai out of reach for impecunious refugees. Meanwhile, the Wehrmacht victories trapped those Jews who had only relocated to neighboring countries such as France or Holland, because their governments protected long-time resident Jewish citizens from deportation by the SS and its local helpers better than newly arrived refugees. In the east, the advance of the Red Army with the Nazi-Soviet Pact allowed some fortunate individuals such as Lucy Mandelstam's father to escape from Poland into the Soviet

Union, where they would be safe if they moved far enough to stay out of the reach of German soldiers. In the west, only a trickle of refugees managed to cross into Spain or Portugal and catch a boat to safety.[35] While some desperate escapes continued, on the whole, the mass exodus stopped.

For those Jews remaining in Nazi-controlled Europe, the war also imposed the required wearing of a yellow star as a "sign of shame." The conquest of Poland allowed SS leader Richard Heydrich to insist that all the country's Jews wear this mark in public, a practice extended in 1941 to the conquered Russian territories. After passports were stamped with a "J" as Jewish, the star of David was also introduced into the Reich, with severe penalties threatened for anyone who refused to comply. This requirement further isolated Jews from gentile neighbors who might have been willing to maintain their ties, since if caught, they would be accused of being "Jew-lovers." Ingeborg Hecht remembered the fear of denunciation. "When a 'wearer of the star' visited us, he tried to cover up and hide the thing, because such a visit was one of the forbidden practices." Ruth Klüger recalled how public appearances changed in Vienna: "Everywhere we met people who also wore the star." One passing Jewish woman ironically complimented her mother by saying, "it fits your blouse."[36]

The Polish campaign of the fall of 1939 was the first step toward systematic mass murder. The Nazi leadership not only wanted to defeat the neighboring country, but also to acquire living space. The rapid conquest unleashed a wave of violence as retribution for real or imagined Polish reprisals against ethnic Germans during September's "bloody Sunday" in Bromberg. But the shootings of civilians were also motivated by plans for ethnic cleansing, to change the balance in the nationalities' struggle and re-Germanize territories in West Prussia and Upper Silesia lost in the Versailles treaty. In its "intelligentsia action," mobile SS Einsatzgruppen and regular Wehrmacht soldiers murdered about sixty thousand civilians in order to snuff out any possibility of future Polish resistance. Jews were caught up in this bloodbath as well, beginning an extermination policy that has come to be called "the Holocaust by bullets." Back in the Reich, Lucy Mandelstam and her family kept picking up "unreliable rumors. We had heard about ghettos and camps, but we did not know how bad the situation really was, at least we did not want to know."[37]

For the Jews still remaining in Germany, living conditions deteriorated with every Wehrmacht victory. The Nazi leadership lost all restraint. Irene Alenfeld remembered, "The noose grew tighter from month to month, the plunder more and more open." With fanatic ingenuity, party bureaucrats dreamt up a succession of petty regulations to make Jewish life miserable: Jews were forbidden to use public transportation or go to the movies. Their telephones and pets were taken away. Their shopping was restricted to one hour in special stores and they could no longer purchase meat, eggs, or milk. Even after they had lost their regular jobs, they had to pay growing sums to the government under a variety of pretexts that took away their property and made them destitute. Eventually they were even evicted from their apartments and homes, and forced to live together in segregated Jewish houses. Going on required a passive kind of heroism. "There are things in life which you cannot change, but only bear."[38]

One way to postpone the looming deportation was to be indispensable to the war effort or the Jewish community. In the spring of 1941 Austrian Lucy Mandelstam "was one of fifty girls who were called up to work in Germany." They were sent to harvest asparagus, backbreaking labor because the stalks had to be cut by hand in the soil. Similarly, Irmgard Mueller, the daughter of a prominent lawyer from Halle, was shipped east to help with agricultural work, replacing soldiers who had been sent to the front. Working "in a cigarette paper factory" or a munitions plant was boring, but a paycheck came in handy for buying on the black market "as our food rations became smaller and smaller." Lucy Mandelstam's mother worked at an institute for the blind. Ruth Klüger's mother "got a position as a nurses' aide and physiotherapist" in a Jewish hospital where there was food and heat. But "eventually things became hopeless." In spite of all such efforts, the Klügers "were deported from Vienna with about the last Jews in the 'hospital transport' of September 1942."[39]

More daring was the attempt to go underground and to beat the Nazis at their own game. When her aunt told Anna Fränkel that she had barely escaped murder in Belzec, the sixteen-year-old girl decided to use her "'Aryan' face," blue eyes, blonde braids, and peasant dress and scarf to turn into a Ukrainian. A local priest gave her the birth certificate of a dead Christian and she took the identity of Anna Osimok. Her family hit upon the ingenious idea of her "volunteering for work in Germany" in order to escape death in the ghetto. Protected by a cross pendant, she embarked with a friend on the long train ride to the Reich with much trepidation. "I felt that I was going into a war in which I needed fortitude, circumspection, flexibility and iron nerves as weapons." Eventually "Osimok" was assigned to the Steinkeller estate in Austria where the mistress liked her due to her good manners and ability to speak German. But "I had a hard time while getting used to the idea that I had to take care of the children of an SS officer" who was her mortal enemy.[40]

In the end, Fränkel was unable to keep up the charade. She was sustained by her friendship with Nadja, another Jewish girl from her region who also posed as a Christian Ukrainian. But when she finally tried to get away from the SS estate to another employer, she attracted the attention of the secret police, who secured information about her true identity from Lemberg, her home town. In late 1943 she was arrested by the Gestapo and brutally interrogated to make her admit her real name. But in spite of the terrible conditions in jail and threats of being beaten, she stuck to her Ukrainian disguise, telling herself, "don't give in, your head is still on your shoulders, everything is not yet lost." After sixty-three harrowing days in the penitentiary, she was released and the policeman admitted, "If you are not Ukrainian, you are a great actress." But her relief did not last, because in April 1944, she was rounded up again on the basis of new evidence and sent to a so-called work camp, which turned out to be the KZ Auschwitz.[41]

By contrast, with a mixture of daring and luck Marie Jalowicz Simon actually succeeded in surviving illegally in Berlin as one of about 1,700 "U-boats" who had gone underground. As a bold and beautiful twenty-one-year-old, she was determined to escape deportation and resolved, "I am going to do everything imaginable to survive." When the Gestapo came to pick her up, she ran away, ripped off her yellow star, and sought shelter with anti-Nazi friends who provided a fake identity card. But she paid dearly for her daring when the husband of her protector demanded to sleep with her during the absence of his wife, as a result of which she was forced to have an abortion. Dodging the constant threat of denunciation, she became the mistress of a rabid Nazi businessman. Then she took up with a Dutchman with whom she lived for two years, half-protected by a pro-Nazi woman who became a hated and loved substitute mother. When the desperately hoped-for German defeat finally came, she was raped by a Russian soldier. Simon therefore paid a high price just to stay alive.[42]

One somewhat unusual KZ was Theresienstadt, which the Nazis used as a showcase for foreigners to prove that conditions were acceptable. It "was a strange and confusing place," a former Austrian garrison town "meant for a few thousand people" but numbering "at least ten times as many." Looking like a normal ghetto, the camp was designed for older Jews who could move around in relative freedom. There were "shops that sold items stolen from our luggage, a coffeehouse where an orchestra played every afternoon, a library." Moreover, Rabbi Leo Baeck could explain the Jewish heritage to spellbound youths. But "behind the façade there was unbelievable misery." The inmates had no money. There was widespread hunger. Diseases such as dysentery or typhus ran rampant. While Lucy Mandelstam could fall in love there with a Czech man, her marriage was cut short by his being transported to the gas chambers of Auschwitz. Ruth Klüger both loved the chance for Jewish self-assertion and hated the transit function of the camp as a "holding-pen for slaughter."[43]

The sinister KZ at Oświęcim, known by its German name of Auschwitz and built around a former Austrian military compound, was an even more deadly place. It actually consisted of three different camps: the Stammlager holding Poles, political prisoners, homosexuals, and criminals; the adjoining Birkenau, dedicated to murdering Jews; and a series of satellite camps of forced labor for German companies. SS man Joachim Bässmann, sent there to handle foreign currency, found the ensemble of electric fences, wooden barracks, and the gate's misleading promise "work will set you free" rather depressing. "Tired, wearing blue-white striped sack-cloth, groups of prisoners shambled by on their way to work." He had "no doubt that those Jews who were not fit to work, were killed," according to the simple logic, "the Jew was the enemy who was responsible for the first and second world war." Similarly teacher Marianne Busch, dispatched to instruct the guards' and ethnic Germans' children, was told, "Every week more inmates are added, but the number always stays the same."[44]

Already the sheer horror of their arrival at Auschwitz had seared itself into the survivors' memories. While costing some lives, the hunger, thirst, and stench of the transport in cattle cars were only preparatory steps toward dehumanization. "When the train stopped and the doors were opened all hell broke loose," with blinding lights, shouting guards, and barking dogs creating "terror and confusion." Separated from her mother, Lucy Mandelstam remembered only fragmented images such as "standing naked in a shower," then being "clothed in a striped dress with wooden clogs on my feet" and "getting a number tattooed on my arm" and finally ending up in a big barrack. Though "I was hungry, I was afraid," she tried to push her threatening surroundings out of her mind. "How I did that I don't know, it was impossible to ignore the smell of burning and the red sky, but I did not want to think of death." Twelve-year-old Ruth Klüger similarly clung to her will to live: "I would not perish here, certainly not I."[45]

The process that decided over life and death was called "selection." An SS guard described the routine: When a transport arrived at the ramp, translators reassured "the people that they were coming into a work camp but would have to be inspected and cleaned up." Separated by sex, the Jews were then "divided into those who could walk and those who would be driven to the camp." Actually, "the first column really went into the camp for labor while the others came to extermination." Though some people understood that they would be gassed, "there was never an attempt to break out or a rebellion. The deception was very good." Those who passed the first test were later scrutinized again. Lucy Mandelstam remembered that "it was the most humiliating experience parading naked in front of everybody" and being separated from her mother. The sick and feeble, children under fourteen,

18. German soldier killing a mother and child.
Source: Stiftung Preussischer Kulturbesitz.

and adults over forty continued to be weeded out. Ruth Klüger was lucky enough to have an inmate tell her to lie about her age before the examiner. The bald claim "I am fifteen" saved her life.[46]

Because mass shooting of helpless civilians was hard even on the executioners (image 18), the SS developed a semiautomatic procedure for killing in Auschwitz. The testimony of SS man Joachim Bässmann describes the truth of mass murder beyond a shadow of a doubt. During a night alarm, he witnessed that numerous Jews had been forced into a bunker-like structure. "A sergeant put on a gas mask" and went to an air vent. He "opened a can in his hand and poured the content into the opening." Immediately the cries inside got louder, "because the powder in the can turned into a deadly gas through the oxygen in the bunker." After a short while the shouts diminished and then ceased altogether. Then the noncom looked through a peephole to ascertain the effect of the gas. "The Jews in the bunker were all dead." On his way home, Bässmann passed burning pits for reexhumed corpses, which seemed to come alive again in the heat. The teacher Marianne Busch was "deeply shocked and horrified" when she realized that the white-grey flakes she saw in the air were "human ash" from the crematoria.[47]

For inmates who had passed selection, the "real horror that was Auschwitz" was only beginning, for the camp itself constituted a slow but certain death. Lucy Mandelstam had difficulty in sleeping in the overcrowded bunks crawling with lice. "Once a day the food consisted of watery soup with some rotten vegetable leaves floating around," inducing theft and starvation. Ruth Klüger found her thirst almost worse, and her body became covered with sores, since there was no water to wash. The unsanitary toilets also produced mass diarrhea, forcing people to stand in lines to take their turn to relieve themselves. Especially tiring were the endless roll calls in the morning, the evening, or the middle of the night to count the number of inmates. Moreover, the capos, prisoner police, were often cruel criminals who beat strangers and played favorites with their supporters. Hence many prisoners deteriorated into so-called Muselmänner, "people who had lost the drive to survive in the KZ." On this "hostile planet," only gratuitous acts of mutual help could keep the prisoners' spirits up.[48]

Survival in these terrible conditions was possible through an exceptional combination of luck and fortitude. A prisoner had to be young and strong to begin with, and spend only a limited time in the KZ because health deteriorated quickly within the camp. Getting a special assignment helped to keep one alive. Irmgard Mueller was sent to the laundry, where she could stay clean, then moved to the kitchen, where food was a bit better, and finally dispatched to the camp administration, where she kept prisoner records in relative comfort. Lucy Mandelstam was dispatched to work on a farm and dig antitank ditches. Ruth Klüger was forced to do backbreaking labor in a satellite camp in the forest. Finding caring nurses in the sick bay could speed a recovery and help one avoid another round of selections. Fraternizing with other prisoners and shows of kindness such as sharing food or talking about the approaching defeat of the Wehrmacht restored hope.[49] While most inmates rapidly succumbed, a fortunate few managed to cling to life by instinctively making the right decisions.

The inhumanity culminated in the medical experiments on helpless inmates, which violated the Hippocratic Oath. Their author Dr. Josef Mengele, known as the "angel of death," was "a monster in human form." One of his functions was "selection" in the family camp, where he decided on the fate of naked prisoners "with a frozen face." Auschwitz was rife with rumors about his altitude, cold, twin, medicine, and other experiments, which resulted in unimaginable pain, disfigurement, and death to their hapless victims. Ruth Elias was terrified when she was highly pregnant and sent to the sick bay, "his domain." After a midwife helped her give birth, Mengele forbade her to nurse the baby in order to find out how long it would live without food. The new mother was feverish from her blocked milk and desperate because she was unable to help her wailing infant. Finally, a Czech doctor took pity on her, slipped a morphine syringe into her hand, and entreated her, "Ruth you are young, you must live." Distraught, she "committed the deed. Yes I killed my own child. Yes, Dr. Mengele made me a child murderer."[50] But thereby she saved her own life.

Attempts at active resistance also revived the spirit of prisoners; their heroism suggested that one did not have to give in. Ruth Elias participated in an "intellectual resistance" that kept the mind alive through discussions, music, and the like. Ruth Klüger even carried out small acts of sabotage that hindered the German war effort. Anna Fränkel hoped that a Belgian woman named Malah, who had herself smuggled out of the camp in an empty lime barrel, would get away and "everywhere spread the terrible truth about Auschwitz." But when the escapee was caught at the Czech border, and about to be hanged, she cut her veins and hit the commandant with her bloody hand, crying, "You murderer! The day of judgment is approaching! Then you will have to pay for every drop of blood!" Some weeks later there was suddenly a loud detonation and the inmates thought, "now the crematorium itself is being burned." A courageous Jewish work detail had blown a hole in the fence so that fifteen youths could escape. Unfortunately, thirteen of them were caught and executed, leaving only the hope that the Red Army would liberate the camp soon.[51]

For the German guards, serving in Auschwitz was incomparably more tolerable than for the inmates but still so strenuous that some had to drown their qualms in liberal doses of alcohol. According to Bässmann, "camp life was a quite ordinary existence like in a small bourgeois town in Germany." The well-to-do factory personnel of IG Farben were a society of their own, as were the civil administrators. The SS men "lived only in the camp, a few kilometers away from the town." They had their quarters outside the fences, with their own store and "a big cafeteria where [they] would eat dinner and were able to shop." To keep up morale, there was a stage where shows were put on and movies were shown. The sauna was also popular, as were the sports fields. Every Sunday a camp band played marches and operetta tunes. Theoretically the SS guards were supposed "to act correctly and non-violently," but the apologetic claim "there were no transgressions in the area of the Stammlager" was bound to be a face-saving exaggeration.[52]

Because he was trained as a bank employee, the SS man Joachim Bässmann participated in the despoliation of the Jews, which proceeded with frightening efficiency. Whenever a transport arrived, "great amounts of Jewish property were piled up in the open: clothes, watches, jewels, shoes, glasses and so on." Anna Fränkel was ordered to sort these and "make packages with clothes" to be sent to Germany. The valuables were checked by SS jewelers and put into sealed boxes. Scrupulously registering the pilfered dollars, pounds, and marks, Bässmann was astounded that the collected money "contained all conceivable currencies of the world. And that in big amounts!" When enough coins and bills had been gathered, a special armed transport was organized to take them and the valuables to the Chief Economic and Administrative Office of the SS in Berlin, from which they were forwarded to the Reichsbank.[53] With this plunder, the Nazis rewarded their own elite, forcing the Jews to pay for their destruction themselves.

As a schoolteacher, Marianne Busch had only an indirect contact with the machinery of death. In September 1943 the young instructor was assigned to the Gymnasium in Auschwitz and she accepted from a sense of adventure. There she had to instruct the children of the SS, the industrialists, and the ethnic Germans in high-school subjects such as English and history. She was shocked to hear from her charges on the first day, "This morning so many people arrived in cattle cars and were unloaded at the ramp." Her sixth-graders knew about "this cruel process, called selection" and she was at a loss as to how to comfort them. Though she had access to the Stammlager library, the death camp Birkenau remained off-limits. But she refused to share her growing knowledge of mass murder with others so as neither "to besmirch the image of the leadership nor to weaken the fighting spirit." Busch wrote that having "to live so close to proven inhumane crimes was a constant strain on my conscience."[54] But she admitted that she sympathized more with the SS than with its victims.

The perpetrators developed elaborate justifications for "accepting the incredible as a fact at that time." In contrast to a colleague who pleaded, "I have to get away. I am a social democrat and hate this town," Marianne Busch "knew that hardness was the price which had to be paid for our security." Hence she considered her time in Auschwitz a "trial of perseverance under most difficult circumstances of physical as well as mental duress." Similarly, "the SS men lived in the belief that they were the 'most loyal of the loyal ones,'" who alone could be assigned "this terribly dirty job." Joachim Bässmann silenced his conscience with the rationale that "world Jewry" was the chief enemy and was even willing to use Communism "in order to gain domination over the globe." The current war was "a struggle which this time involves the very existence of the German people." The Mauthausen SS guard F. W. claimed to his granddaughter that he "was forced to serve."[55] Such perpetrators and accomplices had a hard time explaining how a sense of duty and virulent nationalism could have misled them into participating in racist atrocities.

With the approach of the front, German control of conquered territory and order in the camps began to break down. Every day prisoners looked up into the sky for Allied planes and shared rumors of Wehrmacht defeats, only to be disappointed by how long liberation was taking. When the SS shut down a satellite camp, Lucy Mandelstam jumped off the truck taking her to Stutthof. This saved her life: the rest of the group was never seen again. "The situation in the camp was now completely different than before," since it was less crowded and brutal, even if there was little food. "During the last days the Germans had become very nervous, not paying much attention to us." Even fanatical Nazis began to realize "that the war could no longer be won and the situation was becoming more and more threatening." When Marianne Busch's school was closed, she volunteered as a nurses' aide and returned to Auschwitz from a break to save her children. The desperate prisoners "only hoped that [their captors] would not kill us at the last moment."[56]

The unspeakable suffering of the KZ inmates culminated in "death marches" in the bitter cold, which sought to hide the evidence of mass murder from the advancing Red Army. On January 18, 1945, columns of prisoners left Auschwitz, closing "the door to a hell which was conceived, built and administered by the Germans." Even Marianne Busch was shocked to see "the poor wretches sway and stumble forward" so as to "drag themselves along with their last energy, bent over, weak, emaciated, deathly pale, with hollow eyes and cheeks." They appeared to the German teacher "as grey ghosts, transparent like spirits, even their worn clothes had turned as dreary as their collapsed faces." In the back, she heard the shots with which SS guards killed those who could no longer keep up or tried to escape. Even years later Busch admitted, "Never have I seen such a picture of suffering and merciless cruelty." The prisoners were trudging toward the train station, from which those who survived the horrendous march were sent to other concentration camps such as Ravensbrück in the Reich.[57]

The dissolution of the Third Reich provided daring Jewish youths with opportunities to escape by turning into German refugees, fleeing from the Russians. In early February Ruth Klüger persuaded her mother and sister to leave their death march by hiding in a stable. "Freedom meant [getting] away from" SS guards and enjoying their "bare life, because for the first time it really belonged to us." They merged into the great trek westward, begging for food from farmers and shelter from the NSV, passing a checkpoint with the help of a friendly policeman—even persuading a pastor to issue them false papers. Lucy Mandelstam, meanwhile, spontaneously hid behind a tree and joined a group of Italian slave laborers, whom she helped to escape using her fluent German. "It is difficult to explain, but I felt like two different people, one the Jewish girl who had to hide her identity in order to survive, the other a German refugee." She endured a bout with typhus in a hospital and made it onto a boat to safety in Flensburg.[58]

If they were unwilling to leave the death marches, other Jewish youths were freed by Allied forces. Ilse Polak refused to desert her column, arguing "No, I don't want to be shot. I'll go where I am supposed to." One evening her group from Stutthof was penned into a barn and were "mortally afraid" that they all would be burned. But after the door opened, "Russian tanks stood in front of the shed" instead, and when the SS guards came out, it was they who were all shot. Stunned and relieved, Polak lost her speech for several months. Anna Fränkel was forced to leave Ravensbrück and moved to another camp where "the hunger tortured us terribly." Finally, on May 5, there was no morning roll call and a strange silence. "Then the women began to push against the bars of the windows" and break open the doors. Excited, everyone shouted, "We are liberated—free—get out!" But the British soldiers would not enter the camp for fear of contracting typhus from the inmates. Ruth Elias remained behind at her camp and led a group to the American lines, where an officer received her with "Shalom aleichem, I am also a Yid."[59]

The long wished-for liberation turned out to be both exhilarating and disappointing. Lucy Mandelstam "was the happiest person in the world, but I had to hide it—all around me the Germans were crying and wondering what would happen to them now." Anna Fränkel "did not hold back [the] tears" flowing in streams down her face. She realized that this moment was "not like how I had pictured it thousands of times." Being freed "left a feeling of emptiness which is difficult to describe." Starving prisoners first stormed the food depot, gorging themselves with what had been denied them and often getting sick. Many of the survivors had to cope with diseases such as typhus and needed diligent nursing care to recover. Adding insult to injury, many of the young women who were liberated by Russian soldiers were then violated by them. And beyond all the practical problems loomed the psychological issue of their postwar identity: Who were they, what was their home, and how did they want to live?[60]

The ghastly evidence of piles of corpses and living skeletons in the liberated camps made it difficult for Germans to deny their participation in mass murder. When Marianne Busch told her father about "the misery and horror of KZ Auschwitz," he cried out, "that is not true, that cannot be right!" and asked her to tell no one since "that could cost your life." Ruth Klüger caught most Germans looking away when "a column of KZ-prisoners marched" through a Bavarian town at the end of the war, not wanting to see what they did not wish to admit. In an ironic role reversal, panic-stricken perpetrators and accomplices were now themselves preoccupied with surviving the defeat of the Third Reich: "So that is the collapse! That is what it looks like when there is no more hope." Stunned by the extent of the Nazi atrocities, Allied commanders forced the local populace to visit camps such as Buchenwald and recorded their reactions on film. In retrospect, Bässmann admitted that he "repressed everything which I find hard to explain today."[61]

The autobiographies suggest that more ordinary Germans were involved in the Holocaust than apologists admit, but at the same time fewer participated than some critics claim. At the core of the mass murder were the direct killers in the SS, Einsatzgruppen, Wehrmacht, and ethnic auxiliaries who were helped by merciless bureaucratic organizers and cheered on by racial ideologues. Clustered around them were the indirect enablers in the police and railroad personnel who rounded up victims and shipped them to the East, supported by Nazi Party fanatics who justified the genocide and unscrupulous opportunists who were all too ready to profit from the removal of the Jews. The largest group was nonetheless composed of ordinary Germans who witnessed the persecution without intervening and did their duty while aiding the war effort. The only exceptions were a small number of people impervious to NS appeals or anti-fascist convictions, some of whom were active in the resistance. Almost all Germans were therefore in some way implicated, though many continued to claim not to have harmed anyone directly.[62]

FIGHTING FASCISM

While the majority of the Reich's victims submitted dejectedly to their fate, courageous minorities actively fought against Hitler and contributed to the defeat of the Nazis. Political opponents and prominent Weimar politicians such as Ernst Reuter went into exile in Prague, Paris, or London to continue the struggle from the outside. Inside the Third Reich, members of the Left such as Erich Honecker carried on a campaign of subversion, while some officers and members of the elite, such as Claus Schenk von Stauffenberg, sought to topple the NS dictatorship in July 1944. For Jews such as Heinz Meyerstein, the key aim was to survive in the underground and escape to Palestine in order to foil Himmler's extermination plans. While some of those who managed to emigrate in time then participated in anti-Fascist propaganda, others, such as Tom Angress, actually joined the Allied forces and put their lives on the line.[63] Since Nazi opponents were the exceptions rather than the rule, traces of their resistance are harder to find in the autobiographies of ordinary Germans.

One important element of the struggle against the Nazis was the critical publicity by exiled authors that contradicted the positive image of the Third Reich spread abroad by its defenders. The German-language programs of the BBC provided news untainted by Goebbels' propaganda apparatus and were eagerly listened to by people who were critical of the Nazis. One source of such information was the gentile lawyer and journalist Raimund Pretzel, who was forced to emigrate to Great Britain in 1939 because his Jewish wife was expecting a child. (This constituted "race defilement" according to the Nuremberg Laws.) Having learned English and adopted the pseudonym Sebastian Haffner, he published a scathing attack in 1941 called

Germany—Jekyll and Hyde, based on his own negative experiences. His call "to mount all possible forms of resistance against Hitler without condemning the country as a whole" resonated with many skeptical Germans, even if such exposés largely ignored the fate of the Jews.[64]

The political émigrés had greater difficulties in spreading their oppositional message to the German population due to the Gestapo's rigorous suppression of any hint of communication and resistance. Communists such as Heinz Zöger were surprised by the swiftness of the Nazi assault, which disrupted their underground organization time and again so that messages from the Comintern in Moscow rarely reached the party members. The Social Democratic leadership fled to Prague, where it set up a Social Democratic Party in Exile (SOPADE) that tried to establish a network of correspondents to report on the mood of the working class. But the cooperation between both leftist parties in a popular front came too late and their hope for a proletarian uprising continued to be disappointed due to Hitler's apparent successes. Activist youths such as Willy Brandt were therefore forced to flee the country lest they be arrested and carry on the fight from exile in Norway. Lacking such organization, bourgeois politicians could only go into "inner emigration" and wait for a better day.[65]

As a result, attempts at internal resistance against the dictatorship by Communist and Jewish youths were doomed to failure. As the daughter of a persecuted Communist, Gertrud Koch "could not just watch [war and injustice] without doing something." In Cologne, she found a like-minded group of "Edelweiß pirates" who believed "a worse misfortune than Hitler cannot happen." Hiking together, they decided to produce anti-Nazi flyers with slogans such as "Let's finally get rid of the brown horde." When caught distributing leaflets at the train station, they were brutally punished. In Berlin, the young Jew Herbert Baum, a forced laborer in a Siemens plant, gathered a circle of Jewish and Communist friends who also criticized the Nazi repression and debated how to bring about a socialist future. In May 1942, the group set fire to an anti-Communist and anti-Semitic propaganda exhibition about the Soviet Union prepared by Joseph Goebbels. But the

Gestapo quickly caught the dissidents and stamped out any opposition before it could develop.[66]

The actual political and military resistance was an elite affair, considered treasonous by most Germans during a life-and-death struggle. Even while Hitler was successful, conservative circles disliked the crudeness of his style, and some generals, such as chief of staff Ludwig Beck, worried about the coming war. When military fortunes turned in 1942, it was no longer enough to make Nazi jokes or to criticize obnoxious policies. Action was called for. A circle of officials, diplomats, soldiers, pastors, and trade union leaders coalesced around Leipzig's mayor, Carl Goerdeler, determined to overthrow the Nazi dictatorship. These men were motivated by the looming defeat and reports of anti-Semitic and anti-Slavic atrocities in the East and sought to restore Germany's honor. Unfortunately, the officers' July 20, 1944 plot failed as had several previous attempts; the bomb placed in Hitler's Eastern headquarters did not kill him. Even if the political ideas of the resistance were somewhat authoritarian, the willingness of these men and women to risk their lives to restore humane values still commands respect.[67]

Sure of popular support for harsh penalties, the Nazis unleashed an unprecedented burst of violence in retribution for the putsch. Its military leaders, including Claus von Stauffenberg, Henning von Treskow, and Hans Oster, were summarily shot in the army headquarters at the Bendlerstrasse in Berlin. The Gestapo then hunted down the supporting political network, ranging from the members of the shadow cabinet to mere sympathizers of the conspirators. The persecution extended to these people's family members and others who were barely involved, such as the father of later television journalist Wibke Bruhns. As chief prosecutor of the People's Court, the Nazi fanatic Roland Freisler had a field day accusing the resistors of treasonous betrayal of their oath to the Führer. The killing spree continued into April 1945, costing the lives of such upright men as Protestant theologian Dietrich Bonhöffer.[68] With the murder of hundreds of regime opponents and the incarceration of thousands of others, this purge severely damaged the Prusso-German elite and impaired postwar rebuilding.

More successful were some individuals' efforts to escape Nazi murder through illegal flight into countries where they would be safe. It took exceptional courage, acting ability, and a support network to get away. Born in Göttingen in 1920, mechanic's apprentice Heinz Jehuda Meyerstein was imprisoned in Dachau in 1938. After his release a few months later, he fled to Holland where he worked in a Jewish Werkdorp, an agricultural labor camp, in preparation for emigration. But when Nazi raids got too dangerous in 1942, he volunteered for war production with fake papers as a Dutch laborer in the Ruhr Basin. When the Gestapo found out, he returned illegally to occupied Holland and then began to work with false Wehrmacht documents in France for the Organisation Todt, hoping to get to Spain. After a failed first attempt and a brief stint with the French resistance, Meyerstein and a group of comrades finally succeeded with immense effort in crossing the snow-covered Pyrenees in early March 1944. "Before him lay freedom and the way to Eretz Israel."[69]

For those Jews fortunate enough to escape the Nazis' clutches, the next challenge was to complete their odyssey by finding a place where they could remain more or less permanently. If they had, like the Marlens family, merely fled to a neighboring country such as France, they had to get a visa to someplace beyond the reach of the SS. A favorite transition point was Cuba, where the Fröhlichs waited in anxious suspense for a couple of years until they were admitted to the United States. Another safe haven was Great Britain, which increased its refugee quota to fifty-five thousand individuals in the hope that they would, like Gerhard Weinberg's family, merely pass through on their way to North America. By interning all people with a German passport, whether Jewish, like the Eycks, or not, the UK made it clear that it preferred to be only a temporary destination. Some refugees had to travel as far as Shanghai in order to reach a safe haven from which they could move to Israel. Forced "to flee from the terrifying Jewish fate to a faraway foreign world," families were "dispersed over vast distances."[70]

As an act of symbolic rejection of the German past, many refugees also changed their names in order to facilitate integration into their new homes. A distant relative who took in Georg Igersheimer and his eight-year-old sister anglicized their last name to Iggers in order to make it sound less German and Jewish. Although he was at first angry at this change of identity, he eventually accepted the transformation, since it made dealing with US authorities easier. Similarly, a cousin of Peter Fröhlich had translated the family name to Gay, because the former was "hard to spell and impossible to pronounce." Moreover, "he wanted to say farewell, as categorically as he could, to the country of his birth in behalf of the country of his future." He thereby became Peter Gay, since his "overriding desire was to become a good American." When confronted by an immigration official, Werner Karl Angress, after some rumination, decided merely to drop his middle name and become "Tom," which "sounded much more like my new self."[71]

But shedding a German origin was not so easy. The expulsion continued to haunt especially those secular Jews who had been fully integrated before. While children adjusted quickly, adults found that their accents, clothing style, and behavior gave them away. Many refugees to the United States who wished to maintain their lifestyle congregated in immigrant quarters such as Washington Heights in Manhattan, known colloquially as "the Fourth Reich." In contrast to native-born Americans, the new arrivals remained focused on events in Europe, eagerly following the news and sending letters until replies ceased to come. While some teenagers saw emigration as an exciting adventure, others more socialized in German culture, such as Peter Gay, suffered from rejection, picking fragments of Berlin "from my skin as though I had wallowed among shards of broken glass." At best, they assumed, like Fritz Stern, "a double life: the German past, ever present, ever ominous, and the American present, immediate, uncertain, but ever promising."[72]

The key difficulty for all refugees was building new lives in constrained circumstances without the resources they had been forced to leave behind. Albert Gompertz recalled, "Naturally, all of us were happy to have arrived in this wonderful country where we immediately felt what it meant to be a free person." In order not to depend upon charity or relatives, "we all had to find work immediately to support ourselves." But for middle-class professionals or businessmen who had once employed assistants or servants, obtaining jobs in a strange environment was difficult. Moreover, not being fluent in English made the search for gainful employment frustrating. Penniless refugees were often reduced to accepting menial tasks in the immigrant community for low wages, starting once again from the bottom. The only consolation was having survived, since, as in Gompertz's case, "mother's parents and many of their brothers and sisters were later deported by the Nazis and killed in the extermination camps."[73]

For most Jewish families, emigration meant social demotion, and fathers were rarely able to maintain their prior social status. Only established scholars such as Albert Einstein could gain positions in an overcrowded academic job market with the help of aid committees. By contrast, doctors like Fritz Stern's father had to study hard and retake the medical boards, even if they had already practiced successfully for decades. Lawyers had to learn a whole new legal code and financial system and until then were reduced to lesser jobs like Gerhard Weinberg's father, an assistant to an accountant, or switched careers entirely like Erich Eyck, who became a popular historian. If they arrived without capital, businessmen such as Leo Gompertz or Gay's father had to begin as traveling salesmen or accept a lower position such as the metalworks job taken by Iggers senior. Faced with such difficulties, Werner Warmbrunn's father "committed suicide with lab cyanide—ostensibly over despair over [his] work situation, his inability to perform work that he felt was expected of him."[74]

Surprisingly enough, women turned out to be better able to deal with the status loss and keep their families afloat, even if they had never worked before. Still in Nazi Germany, Lucy Mandelstam's "mother became the head of the family; without her we would have starved." In New York, Fritz Stern's "more robust and cheerful" mother "sought and gradually found work tutoring children and introducing her method for teaching arithmetic at a few private schools." Erich Eyck's wife "took over and ran a boarding house"; Georg Iggers' mother "catered to new arrivals with meals and rooms" as well. Albert Gompertz remembered that "my mother managed to find work right away by sewing evening bags at home (although she had really never done such work) and was paid by the piece." Other former society ladies resorted to cleaning and washing in order to put food on the table.[75] The refugee women cultivated social relationships with other exiles, immigrant friends, and new American acquaintances.

It went without saying that older teenagers also had to work in order to contribute to their families' meager budgets. Since he had crossed the Atlantic with Gross Breesen friends, Tom Angress found himself doing agricultural labor in Hyde Farmlands, Virginia, which was "pleasant, interesting and sometimes even exciting" in the beginning. Werner Warmbrunn had to pitch in on his sister's farm in upstate New York before beginning college on a scholarship. Starting out as errand boy in a delicatessen, Albert Gompertz was eventually fortunate enough to get a job in his occupational field, a millinery supply house, for $12 a week. "Everything I earned went towards our support and I was happy to be of help." Peter Gay had to drop out of high school in Denver and started as a shipping clerk at the Imperial Cap Company before moving up to office work and becoming "a clerk in a wholesale distributor of magazines." By contrast, his struggling father never quite made it. "Hitler had broken him."[76]

If they wanted to go to college, younger teenagers first had to complete their schooling which had often been broken off in Germany. Few were as fortunate as Franz (renamed Frank) Eyck, who received a scholarship to St. Paul's School, an elite secondary institution in the United Kingdom, in 1936. Against the wishes of his family, who preferred vocational training for him, Georg Iggers chose the academic track at his high school in Virginia. His superior performance earned him an interest-free loan by a Jewish organization to attend the University of Richmond. Due to his superior German training, Fritz Stern was able to skip his sophomore year in a private New York high school and enter "the small, male undergraduate division of Columbia University" led by Nicholas Murray Butler. In spite of his interrupted schooling, Peter Gay completed his studies at East High School and in 1943 received "a full scholarship to the University of Denver."[77] By opening new cultural doors, this training speeded the Americanization of the young refugees.

In these institutions, the young Jewish men took a strong stand against Nazi Germany, cheering the Allied war effort. Peter Gay recalled that "all through the war my hatred of Germany and Germans retained this high fever pitch," and that he justified the bombings from an "imperious hankering for revenge." Frank Eyck pleaded in a letter to the London *Times* for understanding for the refugees' plight: "We shall sacrifice our lives if necessary in the struggle to uphold Western Civilization, remembering the inhuman suffering of those who are so dear to us." Nonetheless, the "panic, fear, suspicion, and general mistrust of foreigners" plus "a certain amount of anti-Semitism" induced the British to intern thirty thousand people on the Isle of Man. The attack on Pearl Harbor turned Fritz Stern into an "enemy alien," although he "continued writing or speaking about current affairs" in order to warn Americans of "the lessons of failed democracies." Like Georg Iggers, he heard rumors about the persecution of Jews, but at the time found mass murder hard to believe.[78]

Faced with choosing between "deplorable and senseless" internment or military service, Frank Eyck volunteered for the Royal Army. But the shadow of suspicion allowed him only to serve in the Pioneer Corps, doing heavy physical labor in Britain from 1940 to 1942. After strenuous lobbying, he graduated to the Education Corps for the following two years, where he tried to build morale by explaining "The British Way and Purpose" of the struggle to skeptical troops. These propaganda lectures triggered intense discussions about the meaning of democracy, the appeal of Communism, the truth of stories about Nazi atrocities, and the like. It took until the summer of 1944 for Eyck to use his language and culture skills for psychological warfare through radio monitoring, POW interrogation, and BBC broadcasts, as well as German programs in the *Soldatensender* Calais intended to "undermine German morale." He also helped to produce leaflets that persuaded Wehrmacht soldiers to surrender and end the war.

In the US Army, Albert Gompertz had a more typical military career, although he was fortunate enough to be spared lengthy combat. The young volunteer was inducted in December 1942 and classified as "an interpreter because of my knowledge of the German language." For the first time, "living with American-born men from all walks of life, I felt like a real American." Impressed by the enormous resources of the United States, he became a naturalized citizen in May 1943, with full citizenship delayed until his honorable discharge. Trained by interrogating Wehrmacht captives at Fort

Hood in Texas, he was shipped to Britain in March 1944 and participated in the D-Day invasion. ("Luckily for us, our troops and our allies had established a solid beachhead by then.") Thereafter, he was moved from one POW camp to the next, where he was annoyed at the soft treatment of the German prisoners. Though offering to do front-line duty at the Battle of the Bulge, he was sent to Paris instead in order to prepare for the establishment of the occupation government.[79]

Military service was even more difficult for Tom Angress because the isolation of his farm meant that he spoke little English. Sworn in in May 1941, he went through basic training at Fort Meade, where he felt rather lonely, but was taken under the wing of some comrades. Though fairly small in stature, he remained in the infantry, where he was harassed as a Jew until he was called up to Fort Ritchie for training as prisoner interrogator. He later recalled, "I quickly learned that my military intelligence training wouldn't be nearly so secret, or so intelligent as I had expected." Nonetheless, he met some impressive intellectuals, including Stefan Heym and Ernst Cramer, and learned the organizational structure of both the German ground troops and the Waffen SS so that POWs could not disguise their unit or rank. Naturalized as a citizen and promoted to sergeant, Tom was shipped to Britain in January 1944. Together with three other German Jews, he formed an interrogation team for the 82nd Airborne Division, getting ready for the invasion.[80] One striking photo (image 19) shows Angress in his new identity as tough American paratrooper.

During the Normandy landing, Angress jumped out of a C-47 that had just been hit and was taking evasive action away from its intended target. Floating through the night sky, he avoided the tracer bullets and touched down in an apple tree. But where were his comrades? For nine days he helped gather dispersed paratroopers, hiding by day in the fields and begging for food at night in broken French. After several close calls, a farmer betrayed the fifty US troops to the Germans, who surrounded them and forced them to surrender. Wounded by shrapnel, Tom was taken to a military hospital. During debriefing, the intelligence officer noted that his first name was Werner and asked whether he was of German descent. Not letting

19. Victorious Jewish GI. *Source*: Tom Angress, *Witness to the Storm*.

on that he spoke German and was Jewish, he claimed that his grandfather had emigrated in the nineteenth century. On the whole, he was treated decently, since, as his captors told him, "Today you our prisoners, tomorrow, we your prisoners! [*sic*]."[81] After twelve interminable days, he was freed and put in charge of his former captors.

At the end of the war, Angress even helped to liberate a concentration camp—a profoundly shocking experience. Battle-hardened in Market Garden and the Ardennes, he saw the Wehrmacht disintegrate, obtaining information by pitying rather than bullying German captives. But he felt "perfectly helpless" when he discovered Camp Wöbbelin, a satellite camp of Neuengamme, in early May 1945. The SS guards had already fled, "leaving the half-starved prisoners to their own devices." Still unaware of the extent of Nazi mass murder, Tom was revolted by the stench of rotting corpses and could hardly believe what he saw: "In the washhouse dead bodies had been stacked like firewood," some already in a state of putrefaction. He now made German soldiers clean up the mess, gave the dead a decent burial, and helped the captives who were still living to recover. To counter the obdurate denial of the local populace, he compelled "the entire adult population" of a neighboring town and "a number of captured German officers" to witness the burial ceremony.[82]

The feelings of young Jewish men returning to their erstwhile homes in Allied uniforms ranged all the way from triumphant revenge to humane sympathy. On one hand, Albert Gompertz recalled, "It gave me great satisfaction to be at the wheel of an American Army Jeep" and to "see some of the once-beautiful towns and villages destroyed" and many Germans "suffering and miserable." On the other, Frank Eyck was shocked by the "total chaos" of the destruction of Hamburg: "One could not feel any Schadenfreude" given that "millions of innocent people suffered in the process." But he was glad that "divine justice had caught up with those who had perpetrated massive crimes against humanity." Much of their response depended upon whether relatives and friends were still alive. Tom Angress was overjoyed upon realizing that his mother and two brothers had survived underground in Holland. "When we found my mother, she sobbed like a child." But all too many survivors, like Lucy Mandelstam, could only mourn their dead.[83]

Due to their knowledge of the language and culture, Jewish refugees from Germany played an important role in setting up the initial occupation. After "having been forced to flee Germany as a 'racially inferior subhuman,'" Angress enjoyed the reversal of power as "kind of a symbolic triumph." His last task in a POW camp was to sort the "sheep" from the "goats" by finding out "whether the individuals had joined the Waffen SS voluntarily . . . or whether they had simply been assigned" to it. Together with a dozen officers and enlisted men, Albert Gompertz was ordered "to administer the Zehlendorf district" of Berlin, requisitioning the comfortable villa of Admiral Canaris, chief of counter-intelligence. As part of Information Control,

Frank Eyck helped set up the initial postwar Hamburg radio station and put out "the first news-sheet produced there by the British Army for the German civilians." To counter rumors, he had the important task of finding journalists to reestablish democratic media in northern Germany.[84]

Since the racial victims of the Nazis identified with their newfound refuges, only the political exiles were willing to return to their former homes after the war. In spite of his sympathy for the defeated, Frank Eyck declared, "I could never call myself a German again." Angrier spirits like Tom Angress were "more than ever convinced that the German nation stinks" because of their "dog-like submission" to the victorious allies. Wanting to get on with their civilian lives, many GIs merely waited, like Albert Gompertz, to accumulate sufficient service points in order to be sent back to the States. Similarly, the few survivors of the KZ wanted to get as far away as possible from their torturers, going to Israel as Anne Fränkel did or waiting for a visa to the United States like Ruth Klüger. Only political refugees such as Willy Brandt and Sebastian Haffner risked coming back to build a better Germany. But in spite of their integration into a new country, emotional ties to their former home remained in exile: "As for so many refugees, you could get us out of Germany, but you couldn't get Germany out of us."[85]

Far from being just passive targets, the Nazis' victims made underrated contributions to the defeat of the Third Reich. Within the country, the very existence of circles who did not subscribe to Goebbels' propaganda kept a flickering hope alive for an alternative, while for an international public renowned figures such as Thomas Mann or Albert Einstein proved the existence of an anti-Fascist Germany. Among the younger generation, dissident groups provided some encouragement to those who did not want to go along with the regime, while youthful exiles informed their new peers abroad of the dangers of Nazi aggression and the criminal nature of the racist dictatorship. Outside of Germany, some of the educated teenagers participated in public debate and attacked apologists for the Reich in public forums. Finally, some Communists joined the Red Army and many Jewish exiles fought in Anglo-American uniforms, serving in combat and helping military intelligence with their cultural expertise and commitment.

VARIETIES OF VICTIMHOOD

The autobiographical recollections of the Second World War were profoundly shaped by the shift from heroization to victimhood triggered by Holocaust memory. Initially, the unquestioned heroes were the intrepid members of the resistance who risked their lives in the struggle against Fascism. After all, they had fought against barbarism and idealistically sought to create a better democratic or socialist world after the war. Moreover, they had been systematically pursued and suffered fearfully from Gestapo torture or SS execution when caught. They made both a symbolic statement through their steadfast example and a practical contribution by disrupting Wehrmacht supply lines. Though admirable for their courage, the resistance fighters lost much of their moral luster when they participated in postwar purges or supported nationalist politics on the Right. Moreover, some were discredited when their resolute anti-Fascism served as justification for the establishment of a Communist dictatorship that denied human rights.[86] As a result, their heroism gradually became less venerable.

Somewhat surprisingly, German soldiers who had assumed the role of villains in public memory also claimed to have been victimized by the Third Reich. To begin with, they believed they were fighting a heroic struggle for the fatherland to reverse the defeat and shameful peace of the First World War. Official condolence letters for "having fallen at the front" and newspaper praise of noble sacrifice for the national cause worked within a traditional paradigm of male duty to Volk and fatherland. While the loss might be painful for parents, wives, or friends, it possessed a transcendent meaning that consoled them. But this conventional appreciation foundered on the immensity of the number of sacrifices, the turn of military fortunes toward defeat, and the increasing awareness of atrocities in the East. Instead of being heroes, German soldiers came to see themselves as betrayed victims of a megalomaniac Führer and Nazi dictatorship.[87] Because their heroism had become meaningless, they were left only with claims of victimization.

In contrast to male perpetrators, German women have appeared to be better candidates for the status of victimhood. Their recollections are replete with suffering. Such claims also fit a feminist perspective that considers women the victims of male brutality in general, independent of particular circumstances. Moreover, during war it was females who were caught in the bomb shelters, raped by victorious enemies, or forced to flee in subzero temperatures. Even during postwar rebuilding came "the hour of the women" in holding together the remnants of their families and assuring their survival through hunger and cold. Though appealing, this stereotype ignores the widespread enthusiasm for the Nazis among young women, which misled many to volunteer for munitions factories or service in Germanization in the East. As a result of their own complicity, self-critical women eventually began to question their role in the Third Reich and admit that they had brought much of their suffering on themselves.[88]

Jewish narratives, however, remain the most convincing renditions of victimization, since their authors were the key targets of mass murder in the Holocaust. While Nazi ethnic cleansing brutalized Slavs and the machinery of death also swallowed Polish intellectuals, homosexuals, Sinti, and Roma, Hitler targeted only the Jews for complete annihilation. Their autobiographies tell different, yet related tales of suffering. One fortunate version relates the increasing discrimination and persecution in the Third Reich, which compelled emigration and required the adoption of a new identity in a safe haven. Another presents a story of survival by luck or instinct against all odds in the murderous maelstrom of the KZ, offering irrefutable testimony to Nazi inhumanity. Yet another variant relates the adventures of resistance, with its author going underground, joining anti-Fascist groups, or escaping from German-occupied Europe in spite of incredible difficulties. The emotional impact of such narratives is so strong that they have rendered victimhood the prime prism through which to remember Nazi atrocities.[89]

The memory competition for acknowledgment of victimization as a basis for restitution is nonetheless problematic for several reasons. The attempt to compare degrees of suffering by rival groups tends largely to obliterate its underlying causes. Treating the recollections of resistance fighters, Wehrmacht soldiers, Nazified women, and targets of mass murder as separate developments also ignores their essential interconnectedness. While both suffered, the difference between perpetrators caught in their own trap and victims of their repression remains essential for historical understanding. This is why Helmut Kohl's amalgamation in the dedication of the Neue Wache Memorial in Berlin with the phrase "To the Victims of War and Tyranny" has provoked such public protest. Yet the singularity of Jewish suffering also remains problematic when it downplays the pain of other groups subjected to persecution and war. The universal lesson of ethnic cleansing and mass murder is therefore that only a general prohibition of genocide and reaffirmation of human rights can ultimately do justice to their victims.[90]

PART III

POSTWAR ADULTHOOD

7

DEFEAT AS NEW BEGINNING

During his prerelease interrogation in the summer of 1945, Martin Sieg anxiously faced a British major who introduced himself as a Polish Jew. For a moment, the German POW hesitated, but then confessed that he was an officer candidate of the air force from Rastenburg in East Prussia. After asking, "Was Adolf Hitler not there?" the major demanded, "Were you not also a leader in the Hitler Youth?" Overcoming his rising panic, Sieg claimed that "anyone who was relatively intelligent and athletic automatically became an HJ leader without being asked." To his surprise, the officer jumped up and saluted him, showing his respect. "You are the first of almost a hundred of your comrades who has admitted to having been an HJ leader." More generally the questioner went on: "If Germany wants to start over again, the Germans have to confront their past, no matter how they acted during that time." Sieg was overwhelmed by the humanity of the officer: "This Polish Jew had shown me a way to a new beginning—without hatred, accusations or threats."[1]

Only gradually did former soldiers realize the full implications of having "really lost the war." Seeking to return to his father's house, Erich Helmer walked through a veritable desert: "Indeed, as far as one could see, rubble, rubble and rubble as well as ruins which jutted ghostlike into the sky." On the cellar wall of a destroyed house, he found a message: "Willy, we are still alive and living with Else." Looking for the main road, Helmer encountered a distressed woman, pitifully querying whether her son had survived: "Have you seen Paul?" Counseling her to be patient, he wondered "how many Pauls will never come back?" Seeing trucks filled with debris made him wonder: "Will it ever be possible to get rid of all the ruins, the rubble?" And "how long will it take, until new life will grow out of the ruins?"[2] The utter devastation of most cities threatened the survival of those who had gotten through the war. The Germans now confronted the hunger, cold, and suffering that they had earlier brought upon others.

Almost worse than the physical challenges were the psychological difficulties caused by the political disorientation due to the loss of the war. For everyone the future seemed without hope. "We youths were especially badly off, because we had no training and no occupation." Martin Sieg wondered, "What prospects existed for us in a shattered Germany? To me the past which had only left emptiness seemed like an apparition" that nobody wanted to talk about. Nationalists like Karl Härtel complained bitterly that, after winning for years, "we lost the war and everything, home, property and the claim to historical justice." In the prison camps, captives struggled to understand the reasons for the defeat, with unregenerate Nazis who tried to hang on to their misguided faith coming to blows with budding democrats who were willing to admit Germany's crimes. Captivity "was the end of high-flying plans and dreams," Hermann Debus recalled. "At least we now knew that we had been betrayed and sold out by Hitler and his minions."[3]

The totality of defeat ruptured biographical trajectories and reoriented life patterns, creating a major break in virtually all postwar narratives. This does not mean that 1945 constituted a "zero hour," because that apologetic claim signals the illusion of shedding a negative past in order to make a new beginning. Nor does it imply the contrary, more recent contention of substantial Nazi continuities, since that underestimates the massive disruption of individual lives. Rather, to survive in a world dominated by victors' punitive policies the defeated had to develop new, obsequious strategies to get what they wanted. Under the occupation powers, the hegemonic Volksgemeinschaft transformed into a community of defeat, held together by shared guilt and suffering. Moreover, the collapse of the Third Reich reversed social hierarchies, with former Nazis losing their privileges and their erstwhile victims having the power to decide on their fates.[4] The German collapse and postwar chaos between 1944 and 1948 therefore fundamentally changed social positions and altered many life plans.

For the Weimar children, the "great upheaval" of 1945 finally provided "an opportunity to become a full-fledged adult." The fighting at the front, the huddling in bomb shelters, and the suffering in concentration camps had created a warped maturity through exposure to mass murder and mass death, aging adolescents before their time. But the Nazi war had also postponed the completion of schooling, entry into occupations, and foundation of families, all of which are considered part of normal development. By supporting Hitler's conquests and atrocities, most of the parents had also lost their authority as guides: the fathers were tainted by Nazism and the mothers overwrought by their daily cares. When the fighting ended, the skeptical youths therefore had a lot of catching up to do as they took charge of the rebuilding themselves. Martin Sieg remembered the impact of this experience: "At eighteen I was completely grown up, responsible for my life alone. All plans, decisions, and attempts of shaping the future now lay in my hand."[5]

TASTE OF DEFEAT

After the German surrender, "the population began to feel what it meant to lose a war," Agnes Moosmann remembered. "Hardship and misery only increased." Ideological propaganda and military orders had loosened the constraints of civilization—only now the Germans found themselves at the receiving end of brutality. According to the motto of not taking any prisoners, the hatred and revenge caused by Wehrmacht crimes and civilian atrocities led to spontaneous killings of soldiers trying to surrender. At the same time, the conflation between Nazi perpetrators and all Germans encouraged violent behavior against noncombatants. Martin Sieg's mother "was raped and hanged herself after her apartment had been looted." Joachim Fest's dejected grandfather simply gave up: "Cause of death should be given as: No interest [in living] any longer."[6] While the end of the official fighting came as a relief, the transition into peacetime was fraught with danger to soldiers and civilians alike.

Номер / Nummer 194

Для фотокарточки / Raum für Lichtbild

Фамилия / Name: Bulwin — БУЛВИН

Имя / Vorname: Rolf — РУДОЛФ.

Год рождения / Geburtsdatum: 27.5.20 — 27.5.20.

Место рождения / Geburtsort: Berlin — БЕРЛИН

Профессия / Beruf: Maschinen-u.Motorenschlosser — МАШ.СЛЕСАР

Местожительство / Wohnort: Königsee — КЕНИГЗЕЕ.ТЮР.

Округ / Kreis: Rudolstadt — РУДОЛЬСТАДТ

Выдано / Ausgestellt am: 31.10.45 — 31.10.45г

Бургомистр / Der Bürgermeister

Подпись владельца / Eigenhändige Unterschrift des Inhabers

20. German POW in Russia. *Source*: Ruth Bulwin, *Spätes Echo*.

During the dissolution of the Wehrmacht, young soldiers desperately tried to avoid being killed in the final battles or being taken into captivity by the victors. If they were stationed close to home, they could hope to escape the military police who shot deserters, as well as the advancing enemy forces, which were focused more on military targets than on taking prisoners. When sixteen-year-old flak gunner Martin Greiffenhagen heard officers plot their withdrawal into private life, he "decided to end the war" too, by shedding his uniform. Putting on shorts and a colorful shirt made it possible for the harmless-looking teenager to simply walk home. Joachim Fest's brother Winfried managed "a small escape" of his own by going into hiding when he received his call-up papers. Caught by the Gestapo and marched toward a safer prison, he suddenly threw himself down a slope, ran away, and hid from the search party.[7] Other, older soldiers also shed their uniforms, dropped their weapons, and shredded their service records in order to reemerge as civilians.

Even after having been officially captured, some Wehrmacht troops managed to escape from the chaos of improvised POW camps. Fearing retribution, SS officer Rolf Bulwin ignored the order "to go voluntarily to a collection point" in northern Bohemia. Stopped during a patrol by the lights of a Russian truck, he leapt into the shadows and hid in a succession of barns. Bulwin walked at night and eluded all checkpoints for ten days. He barely escaped renewed capture several times while struggling toward Rudolstadt in Thuringia. With exceptional luck and daring, he actually made it back to his wife by hiding his Soviet POW identification card (image 20). When baker Gerhard Baucke realized that he was destined to become a slave laborer in Russia, he likewise decided that, although he liked his Soviet captors, "I must get away from here." He used a drive to the black market during a torrential thunderstorm to jump out of their truck in Berlin, duck into the subway, and walk freely to his home. After hiding for a while with a friend of his father's, he hired on with the US Army, thereby getting the papers necessary for receiving food and housing.[8]

The great majority of the Wehrmacht soldiers, however, became prisoners of war during the final battles or as a result of surrender. Defending the Remagen bridge across the Rhine, Joachim Fest "almost bumped into an American GI who was holding his submachine gun at the ready and instantly started shouting, 'Hands up! Come on! Hands up, boy!'" Utterly surprised, Fest obeyed, dropped his weapons, and went into captivity. Similarly, Karl Härtel "suddenly ran into about ten Amis [US soldiers] who held their machine-pistols ready in their hands." Using the surprise, he quickly shouted "Don't shut we surrender" [*sic*] as instructed by American leaflets and thereby remained unharmed. By contrast, on May 7 Horst Andrée's commander announced the capitulation of the Wehrmacht in Italy to his troops and explained: "Every soldier is relieved of his duty and can try to get home. But those who stay have to go into American captivity with all the others." Far from home and attached to their comrades, they had no choice but to risk becoming POWs.[9]

Most German soldiers wanted to go into American custody in the hope that treatment would be better and release would come more quickly. On the Eastern Front, a mass migration developed trying to reach the Elbe River, which marked the border of the US zone. Seeking to cross the icy water, Martin Sieg built a small raft. It capsized, but several black GIs dragged him to shore and their campfire and revived him—a surprising gesture of humanity. Others, such as Karl Härtel, fared less well in US captivity, losing their watches, sleeping in tents on muddy soil, and receiving only minimal food. An American lieutenant with a Palatinate accent shouted at Fest, "You Nazi louts will have to get used to the fact that you'll have no say about anything now." Horst Andrée experienced the whole gamut from a relaxed imprisonment to a merciless captivity, commanded by a Jewish officer bent on revenge.[10] Some of the appalling conditions in the Rhine meadows camps were simply the result of the US Army's being unprepared for handling up to two million POWs.

According to many testimonies, imprisonment by the Americans was nonetheless the best of the lot. Treatment there was less brutal. The fresh captives were debriefed by US intelligence officers like Tom Angress—often themselves refugees—and then checked for SS membership. (Himmler's guards were subjected to more punitive handling.) Wehrmacht prisoners such as Karl Härtel were astounded by the informality, loose discipline, good health, and ample supplies of their captors. Finding it hard to understand how such soft "Yanks" could have defeated the battle-hardened Wehrmacht soldiers, he attributed their victory to superior resources. After the POWs were transferred to established camps, most were happy to be well-fed, decently housed, and allowed to compete in sports. When reeducation lectures and camp journals promoted a critical view of the Third Reich, some irreconcilables defended "Hitler's greatness," while others denounced the "idiotic war."[11] When Joachim Fest was recaptured in France after an escape attempt, his punishment of six weeks in a cage was relatively light.

A British camp was also acceptable, for the treatment was correct, even if the resources were less abundant. Horst Andrée reported a happy camp life in Italy in which "all institutions like kitchen, clothing supply and shoemaking were run by German prisoners." To escape boredom, the lightly guarded prisoners played cards, chess, and soccer. POWs were even allowed to go to the beach and fraternize with Italian farmers. Though living in tents, they had "all the conveniences, a theater and movie house." There was even "a kind of university in which captive German professors gave lectures." By contrast, in North Germany "terrible hunger arrived with the British." Because escaping POWs were shot, Martin Sieg volunteered for agricultural labor, for which he would be released. Erich Helmer faked being a chemist to get his walking papers, while Horst Andrée aggravated an irregular heartbeat so as to be discharged for medical reasons. Robert Neumaier got out of a miserable British camp by altering his military record and jumping from a POW train.[12]

French imprisonment was tougher yet, for the destroyed country was poorer and hostility toward Germans consequently greater. "As putative chief victim of the war, which it had declared, France needed cheap slave laborers for the rebuilding of the thinly settled country." As one of about two million soldiers imprisoned there for several years after the war, Karl Härtel loathed the camp in Poitiers. He wrote, "We suffer much from the unacceptable hygienic conditions, the complete lack of drinking water and a starvation diet, which is far below the minimum for existence, in a totally overcrowded tent city in almost subtropical temperatures." To counteract depression, he filled out forms in the camp administration and attended lectures by a professional mathematician. Later on, in Le Pallice, he seized the chance to volunteer as technical draftsman and helped to "draw a series of wiring diagrams" of the German U-510 submarine, restored by the French Navy. Though this job improved his condition and his engineering skill, he remained bitter about being cooped up for so long.[13]

Wehrmacht soldiers captured by the Russians expected brutal treatment, which inspired them to flee if they could. Frisked and forced to bury corpses, eye doctor Günter Gros had to watch women being "dragged in a beastly manner into the woods and raped. We hear[d] their cries and calls for aid, unable to help." When he was about to be transported to the Soviet Union, he stayed behind in an abandoned factory building and walked for three weeks on aching feet, crossed several rivers, and evaded patrols until he finally reached his home in Giessen. Similarly, while en route to Russia, truck driver Paul Frenzel used a knife and cramp iron to pry away a rotten board of the cattle car, open the door, and jump out of the train. Landing in Transylvania, he begged for food, clothing, and advice from Hungarian farmers and managed to walk over two thousand kilometers. He was able to fool Russian patrols by posing as a shepherd, escaped renewed capture by the United States, and finally reached his East German hometown.[14]

Captivity in the Soviet Union was even more lethal because the living standard was lower and resentment against Nazi atrocities stronger. The lives of POWs were cheap due to the destruction, poverty and corruption of a Stalinist system with its own internal gulag where millions of prisoners were incarcerated. Captured in Bohemia, Gerhard Krapf was initially taken to Auschwitz, where, in an irony of history, Wehrmacht soldiers were collected. He found "that being bereft of the most basic freedom of movement was the single most wearying aspect of imprisonment." As a wounded officer, he was initially better off, but soon he was put to work digging coal in a mine, working at a breakneck Stakhanovite pace on inadequate food. Shipped to a series of different camps, Krapf experienced "a distressing existential pattern of hunger, boredom, hunger, exhaustion, hunger, fading hope of repatriation," and so on. Only his Christian faith and dedication to music kept him alive, until by chance he was selected to fill a homebound quota for a rejected SS man after three years of imprisonment, weighing only ninety pounds.[15]

In spite of much "unrestrained hatred," a few prisoners were so fortunate as to experience exceptional moments of humanity. Air force trainee Horst Grothus was captured in the East and transported to Gorkij in the Soviet Union. Tormented by lack of food and water, he was horrified by the "general neglect" that reduced Russians to spiritless automatons. After unloading barges, he had to lay electrical cables and sort scrap metal in a tank factory. The Soviet commander raked off profits and resold food meant for the prisoners. The condition of the POWs deteriorated rapidly so that many succumbed to starvation. While unpacking a freight train, Grothus' shoes caught under a rail and a freight car rolled over his ankles. After stopping the hemorrhage, a Soviet doctor who had himself lost a leg amputated both of the young man's feet, reassuring him, "you should not be sad. You will be able to walk again." Only through the subsequent care of several nurses did he survive a series of other diseases and begin to grow ashamed of seeing "the vestiges of the German atrocities."[16]

One lifeline during extended captivity was correspondence with home, which reassured POWs as well as families that their loved ones were alive. The collapse of the civilian postal system, the changes of address due to bombing and flight, and the prohibitions against prisoners writing letters had kept husbands and wives in the dark about each other's fate at the end of the war. Even if its content was rather banal, Karl Härtel was all the more overjoyed when "after a year full of uncertainty he received the first sign of life from Germany"; it renewed his flagging hopes of an eventual return. In March 1946 Horst Andrée similarly experienced "the day which I won't ever forget in my entire life." He had received mail that reassured him that his parents and siblings had "survived the flight from Pomerania." Desperate for a sign of life, Jakobine Witolla was also overjoyed when the first preprinted prisoner postcard arrived from her fiancée, Wilhelm Homeyer, whom she would later marry: "I could have cried and danced."[17]

As a result of the terrible conditions in the camps, Soviet efforts at anti-Fascist indoctrination generally had little success. Many prisoners were impressed by the size of Russia and its capacity for suffering, and even willing to listen to agitators explain the Marxist-Leninist classics or read leftist writers such as Friedrich Wolf. Happy that "the war was over for us" and Germany liberated from Fascism, deserter Gerhard Joachim "felt the breath of a new and different world, which also inspired our reorientation" toward "the dream of a just society." But the vast majority of the homesick prisoners rejected the lectures of the National Committee for a Free Germany, focusing instead on their lack of food and day-to-day survival while hoping against hope for a rapid release. Cut off from reliable news about the world and hearing only rumors about the fate of Germany, most POWs rejected "the seemingly neutral anti-Fascism." Hans Queiser recalled that Soviet efforts "to win us openly for Communism" generally failed.[18]

The longer captivity lasted, the stronger the urge grew to escape somehow, even if failure threatened massive punishment. Fleeing from a Russian

POW camp was virtually impossible due to the size of the country, difference of language, and controls on travel. Getting away from a French POW facility seemed easier, but required extensive logistical preparation. When he failed to win release, Karl Härtel decided that "the last way out of this misery was flight." By selling submarine models and purchasing food for the cafeteria in town, he had accumulated sixteen thousand French francs, bought civilian clothes, and obtained tickets as well as a Michelin map through the girlfriend of a comrade. Firmly resolved "to risk everything," he absconded on December 17, 1947, took the night-train to Paris, and bought a ticket to the Saar border. Secretly he crossed the frontier on foot and reached a friend's family, who supplied him with discharge papers. Using this fake release form, he traveled on, reaching his wife in the Soviet zone at Christmas.[19]

Trying to speed legal release, every POW thought up ways to hasten the end of his captivity. The victors used positive criteria for letting prisoners go (such as the need for reconstruction skills) and negative standards (such as involvement in atrocities) for delaying discharge. The Russians used a fitness test in which the camp doctor pinched the buttocks of a naked POW to classify him in one of four levels according to the remaining muscle mass. Those close to death were retained as being unable to stand the transport; those too weak for heavy labor were the first to be sent home. Hellmut Raschdorff used his asthma brought on by shaking straw pallets in order to obtain a medical release. But the stronger and younger men were kept "to bring in the harvest, repair streets and railroads," or work in the mines. While Wilhelm Homeyer tried to ingratiate himself with the Communist camp authorities to be released, Dieter Schoenhals used fake Yugoslav papers to escape imprisonment under the Americans.[20]

Among the last prisoners to be discharged were civilians and soldiers who had been locked up for being leading Nazis or members of the SS. In internment camps in the West and so-called *Spezlager* in the East, several hundred thousand men were intensively scrutinized for their actions. Gerhard Baucke's father was arrested when "the renters of mother's apartment denounced him." Because he had joined the party early on, served in the city council for the NSDAP, and led the local chapter of HAGO (the Nazi Craft, Commerce, and Business Organization), he was thrown into a British military prison and only freed in 1948. Similarly, SS member Rolf Bulwin barely escaped a routine screening when he switched from the "to be examined" to the "finished" line during a moment of inattention by British officers. But his wife's father was arrested for being a party and SS member and having commanded a resettlement camp in Poland. Though his family could visit him, it took a long time to get him released when "there was no one to accuse him."[21]

After so many years of war and captivity, the returning POWs experienced tearful reunions, with families crying for joy to see each other alive. In order to cushion the positive shock, Krapf called his incredulous father from the station, asking, "Pastor, do you know who is speaking to you . . . ? It is Gerhard, your son." Rolf Bulwin stunned his young wife Ruth when he walked in unannounced: "I sat as if frozen and hardly wanted to believe it." As a result, "happiness overwhelmed us, and everyone in the small kitchen had tears in their eyes." Hellmut Raschdorff remembered, "I cannot express in words how great the joy of reunion was on this Sunday, since my parents had not heard from me for over a year and had long feared that they had lost me like my brother Ernst." Horst Andrée's parents were utterly astounded to see him in a tattered parachutist's uniform; his "mother cried for joy" to have him back, while "I could also hardly say anything myself." Only Joachim Fest noted how much his parents had aged.[22]

Though they were glad to have survived, returning prisoners were in for a shock, for the country had changed fundamentally during their absence. "Berlin took my breath away," Fest remembered, for "there was nothing to be seen but a grey-brown desert of ruins, stretching to the horizon." Even after their release, former soldiers had to accept the domination of the occupation forces whose controls complicated their lives and whose edicts, tacked onto walls, had to be obeyed no matter what one thought of them. Moreover, the division into occupation zones forced Erich Helmer to undertake hundreds of anxiety-evoking border crossings in order to visit his parents in the East while finishing his schooling and theological studies in the West. Many former POWs such as Horst Andrée no longer had a home to go to, with East Prussia now under Russian and Polish administration. He was shocked to find the six members of his refugee family crammed into a single small room on a West German estate.[23]

While coming home was "a wonderful thing," the reintegration of physically shattered and "psychologically broken" POWs was a lengthy process. Bathing extensively and burning all clothes to get rid of lice and bedbugs was a pleasant first step. More complicated was eating the right amount of food to restore health, for the craving of hunger often led to overindulgence that made people sick. Gerhard Krapf even found the "comfortable luxury" of sleeping in a bed difficult and instead lay down on the floor. "True enough, I had difficulties at first getting used again to the niceties of civilized society." Overcoming the recurring nightmares of war or imprisonment took even longer. Admitting to fear was not considered "manly" and often went untreated. Then there was talking to catch up on missed experiences, with civilians showing only limited interest in POW suffering and many things remaining unsaid. Finally, disappointments had to be gotten over, when a girlfriend had decided to move on in the meantime.[24]

Obtaining the right kind of papers was the next challenge. Living in an occupied land under rationing required a series of officially stamped permits. For Erich Helmer, "the first day of 'freedom' was really a day of unfreedom, since it consisted of running from one office to another." The most important certificate was one's proof of orderly discharge. Rolf Bulwin created his own with a fake stamp, made from a potato; others used blank forms stolen by students. With this document, a former POW then had to go to the local mayor's office for a "residence permit" entitling him or her to stay in a certain town. This permission enabled him to get a coveted rationing card, an essential requirement for buying food from stores and without which one could not survive. He also needed to get a housing assignment, since so many dwellings had been destroyed. When a bureaucrat questioned Karl Härtel about why he was living with two unrelated females, he simply decided to marry his girlfriend immediately.[25]

After getting his documents in order, the returned POWs might experience a few days of fleeting liberty without immediate responsibilities. At last "we felt free" from the years of Nazi pressure, while the end of imprisonment allowed "us gradually to find ourselves," Horst Johannsen recalled. "But what a great error!" While trying to resume his earlier job, he was requisitioned by the Soviet-installed authorities for "slave labor" although he was neither a war criminal nor a political detainee. "Now a former farm worker, made mayor by the caprice of the Communists, dictated compulsion and repression again." First Johannsen was ordered to take down "all overhead wires" for the second train track at Weissenfels; then he was assigned to disassemble the huge excavator of an open-pit lignite mine. While it was understandable that manpower was needed for reconstruction tasks, the dismantling of East German industries for shipping to the Soviet Union hardly endeared the Russians to those workers who were trying to rebuild them.[26]

In order to put food on the table, the returned soldiers had to find temporary jobs without insisting on resuming their prior careers. "Through dismantling and lack of raw materials the economy was in bad shape," and many firms where they had worked had been forced out of business. Hence Paul Frenzel had no choice but to work as a waiter in his father's railroad-station restaurant, acting more as a "house servant and errand boy" than a trained merchant. Younger men who had gone to war without finishing their educations had an even harder time. Glad to find employment at all, Erich Helmer decided to "go to the railroad," doing physical labor as a maintenance worker. His rationale was that "If we want to survive, we have to help rebuild" the country. Hermann Debus was fortunate enough to be rehired on a tugboat on the Rhine, but this work was now dangerous because the river was clogged with sunken ships and pieces of broken bridges. Even returnees who wanted to study at a university, such as Heinz Schultheis, had to do "work which helped the reconstruction of Germany" as a condition of admission.[27]

Sometimes a Nazi past would catch up with a jobseeker and ruin the best-laid plans. In order to hide his SS membership, Rolf Bulwin cut the incriminating blood tattoo from his arm, leaving a scar. On the advice of a friend, he hired on with the local police force in the small town of Königsee in Thuringia while hiding his prior activities. Everything seemed to be going well when he was suddenly ordered to report to the mayor. This official had just gotten the news that Rolf had been an HJ leader and SS member and could no longer tolerate him in the force in the Russian sector. He told Bulwin, "To be true, I am a Communist, but first of all a German," and warned him, "you have three days' time" to leave for the West. Frantically, the Bulwins and their daughter crossed the zonal border on foot, registered at the transit camp Friedland, and made their way to Celle, where Ruth's father was. With their dreams of security shattered, they had to live at one end of a horse stable while Bulwin started over as tractor driver for a tree nursery.[28]

Both remaining civilians and returning soldiers had to face scrutiny of their political involvement in the Third Reich. During his homecoming, Erich Helmer had to fill out a lengthy questionnaire about his affiliations, which he had no difficulty completing due to his anti-Fascist attitude. With the help of denunciations "about the brutal Nazi behavior and machinations of the Gestapo and Hitler's Bodyguard," the Americans "even went after old Nazis in their former offices, schools, and the bureaucracy." In the Russian zone, "old Communists suddenly appeared who thought their hour had come," Horst Johannsen recalled. "Now it was their turn to catalogue people from the Nazi period as accomplices or perpetrators. Hence a new wave of arrests and secret detentions began" with the help of the Soviet secret service. As a result, the death sentences of the Nuremberg Trials remained rather controversial: "Who gave the victors the right, to judge like gods, although they themselves had killed and murdered without scruples?"[29]

Already in the POW camps and then at home, a process of collective soul-searching began that tried to find explanations for the Nazi catastrophe. Unregenerate nationalists tended to blame the allies and members of the resistance, reviving "old enemy images" such as "the capitalists, world Jewry or the Communists." Many military officers held Hitler's arrogance and incompetence responsible for strategic errors, attributing the defeat to his "loss of realism" in taking on the entire globe. Gradually a minority, like Martin Sieg, "realized that one man together with his minions had engulfed half a world in flames, destruction, and death by unleashing a global catastrophe with his belief in ideology and enormous power." But taking the next step and admitting their own participation in Nazi crimes was psychologically difficult for most defeated Germans, even if ultimately "there was no escape from it." It was easier to assuage one's conscience, as Hans-Harald Schirmer did, by claiming "We knew nothing about the special annihilation camps with their gas chambers and crematoria for the murder of the 4.5 or 6 million Jews."[30]

The war ended for Germans at rather different times depending on their age and gender, and sheer luck. The first civilians to be liberated in October 1944 were the inhabitants of Aachen. It took half a year longer for the rest to escape the final struggle through the capitulation in May 1945. The Wehrmacht's surrender created about ten million POWs who were only gradually released, with the last survivors leaving Russia in 1955. During his lengthy period of captivity, Karl Härtel complained bitterly, "Whenever I hear that many young men are already home or were never away, anger grips me and something rises up within me, I feel resentment against a fate that knows no justice." Speaking for many desperate POWs, he continued. "We have risked our lives and have the pleasure of being imprisoned, while others strut about at home, enjoy themselves, and perhaps laugh at us." Though the prolonged captivity was necessary to atone for Nazi crimes and rebuild destroyed countries, it broke bodies and minds and made it difficult for many Germans to face their own responsibility.[31]

HOUR OF THE WOMEN

The collapse of the Third Reich into postwar chaos was the "hour of the women" because they had to tidy up the mess their menfolk had created. Not only had several million young men died in the Wehrmacht, but millions of others were absent as POWs. Therefore the challenge of assuring daily survival amid the ruins or on the refugee treks fell largely on female shoulders. This new responsibility sometimes made women stronger. Joachim Fest's sister related, "In the one and a half years of my father's absence our sensitive mother had turned into a robust person," completely shedding her gentility. "Without any ceremony she had taken charge of the building, issued instructions to the occupants, conducted tough negotiations on the black market and traveled into the countryside on roofs of the suburban trains to get hold of a handful of potatoes, a cabbage or a paper bag of wrinkled winter apples."[32] This surprising strength, enshrined in the popular image of the "rubble women," showed a female capacity for action that had been suppressed by the heavy hand of patriarchy.

In dealing with the occupying armies in 1945, women had both advantages and disadvantages. The Allies feared male Werewolf guerilla resistance, but females were assumed not to pose any security threat. Because they were largely focused on the private domain, they also did not protest against the victors' policies such as the dismantling of industries. As their networks of solidarity remained personal, they escaped Allied control of public life. But the many stories of rape were not just mere revanchist fabrication, especially because they also mention sexual depredations by French and American soldiers. Moreover, females were helpless when victorious troops burst into their homes to plunder valuables or to wreck the furniture just for the fun of it. Especially galling was the quartering of occupation troops in their houses. In coping with Russian soldiers, Ursula Baehrenburg found that "joy and suffering were always distributed equally."[33] Everything therefore depended upon how the gendered relations between victors and vanquished were managed.

In the Western zones, the initial ban on fraternization between soldiers and German *Fräuleins* quickly broke down, for both sides longed for company. To maintain distance from the defeated enemy, the US Army had forbidden relations with German women, portraying them as a source of venereal disease with a caricature called "Veronika Dankeschön." But with thousands of youths of both sexes looking for diversion, GIs and girls quickly found ways to circumvent the ban. These attachments developed partly for material reasons—the victors offered access to coffee, chocolate, and cigarettes—and partly out of genuine feeling for each other. As a result of a wave of petitions, the army lifted the ban on "German brides" in December 1946 and allowed GIs to marry and bring their spouses back to the United States. Because of segregation, unions between black soldiers and white girls required the permission of an American officer, which was often denied for racist reasons. Returning POWs also resented fraternizing females and referred to them as "Ami whores."[34]

By contrast, in the Soviet zone relations between the victors and the defeated remained tense. Especially in areas initially occupied by the Americans, the arrival of the Red Army was greeted with "great resentment and continual fear of depredations," hardly conducive to cordial interaction. Beyond the expected plunder of jewelry, watches, cameras, and bicycles, "the population continued to be held in fear and terror by the brutal assaults upon women and girls by members of the Red Army." Horst Johannsen remembered that when "they had gotten hold of alcohol for their always thirsty throats, one was well advised to get away in time." Individual Russian soldiers could be kind and sentimental, as Ursula Baehrenburg found out when she befriended amiable youths called Sascha or Nikolai. But as a collective they were unpredictable, with moods swinging widely between generosity and cruelty. In some instances, liberated Poles or Czechs behaved even more brutally, so that, ironically, harassed women sometimes asked Russian authorities for protection.[35]

In the Eastern territories assigned to Russian and Polish administration, the power relations were suddenly reversed: former servants became the new masters and sought to obliterate all signs of prior German ownership. Returning refugees became "strangers in their own land." Glad to be alive at all, Silesians such as Erika Scholz-Eule and her sister Traudel "did not want to leave, not only for themselves but also for Germany." But when they were evicted from their homes, expelled from their jobs, and deprived of their citizenship, they could only stay on as a new underclass. With more and more displaced Poles from the East arriving daily, Ursula Baehrenburg noted that "the German farmers now had to work as laborers and servants on the farms which they had inherited for generations." The former inhabitants tried desperately to hang on by slaving in the fields, laboring as masons, and so on. They now found out what it meant to live under foreign rule in "a state of complete lawlessness."[36]

Try as they might, in the long run the defeated Germans could not prevent their systematic expulsion from their former homes. When a drunken Pole started to undo her clothes to rape her, seventeen-year-old Ursula Baehrenburg "resolved to get away from this hour on." She sewed backpacks from sacks and persuaded her reluctant father to get the required exit permit. Since they "could hardly take anything along" beyond food, "irreplaceable valuables remained behind. Everything that my parents had built in laborious work was gone." On the way to the station, her father put a bag over his head in order to be spared the sight of what he was losing. In the next town, they joined a "transport for Germans leaving" East Prussia, only to be crammed into cattle cars. "Full of fear," they huddled during the long journey in the unheated wagons, hearing cries for help when another car was ransacked during a halt. In Stettin, the expellees rushed the train to the West; all had only one thought: "to depart, to be saved."[37] One such photo shows expellees emerging from the same kind of cattle cars that had shipped Jews before (image 21).

Similarly, the "shadow existence" of Germans under Polish authority in Silesia could not last; the occupiers wanted the land cleared for their own citizens who had been expelled by Stalin further East. With no news but rumors, the remaining Germans had no idea that they were to be transferred in an "orderly and humane manner" to the West according to the Potsdam Agreement. But they did notice that "revenge was the order of the day" through constant humiliation and hunger. Still dressed as a boy and recovering from typhoid fever, sixteen-year-old Ursula Mahlendorf had the good fortune to be able to work as an assistant nurse; this provided her with official papers allowing her to remain. In long hikes in the countryside she helped to distribute medical supplies to needy Germans hidden from the Polish militia. Though she had learned some of the language, she could not avoid expulsion in the summer of 1946. All the Germans of Strehlen were loaded into an otherwise empty freight train and sent to the West. Even then, Mahlendorf "knew with amazing clarity: We would never return."[38]

Polish policy toward the remaining Germans was contradictory: Warsaw wanted to clear Silesia to make room for settlers from the East, but

21. Expulsion from Silesia. © Gerhard Gronefeld / Deutsches Historisches Museum.

forbade competent specialists to leave. In the chaotic transition, the Germans, identified by white armbands, lost their possessions, houses, food, and work. "Systematically we were deprived of any possibility to live." In May of 1946 Ruth Weigelt's family finally managed to join the deportees in cattle cars to the West in order "to live as Germans in Germany." They were first processed in the Friedland transition camp, then temporarily settled in Lower Saxony. Ruth herself remained behind because, as coal miners, her in-laws and returned POW husband were considered essential workers and were forbidden to leave. Because "we were stuck," they decided "to arrange themselves with the new occupiers" by learning Polish and making friends through music. Things gradually improved. Then, in 1957, they obtained permission to depart as *Spätaussiedler*, or repatriates. Weigelt wrote of that time, "On the one hand, we were happy finally to be able to leave; on the other, it was clear that we had lost our home and would never get it back."[39]

Germans in the Sudetenland faced discrimination by the Czechs and eventual ejection as well. As long as their labor was needed, farmers were allowed to bring in the harvest, but thereafter "mass evictions began in the villages." Twenty-three-year-old former POW Hans Tausch was arrested, imprisoned, beaten, and accused of being "a Nazi pig" without discernable cause. Because of such nationalist reprisals, "it was clear to my relatives and me that under the present circumstances remaining in our home was not only unimaginable but dangerous." Not waiting for their formal expulsion, the Tauschs moved some of their possessions over the lightly patrolled border to Franconia. With an official permit, they drove their remaining property minus two confiscated violins to Bavaria on December 8, 1945. Tausch's parents were distraught and "looked back, tears in their eves; they never saw their homeland again." Crossing the frontier "meant a caesura in my life, which initiated developments of decisive importance for my future."[40] Although the Czechs had suffered less than the Poles, their vindictiveness was even greater.

Even after arriving in Germany, the trials of the expellees were far from over. Their receiving communities resented them as a drain on scarce resources. Upon disembarking from the trains, they were processed in relocation facilities such as Friedland, deloused, registered, and fed. If they had relatives, they were encouraged to go immediately to join them; if not, they were put into refugee camps, where they could barely survive. Christel Groschek had to move from employer to employer in order to escape unwanted sexual advances. Ursula Mahlendorf found herself in an abandoned airfield outside Delmenhorst with insufficient food and lack of heat. Only by appealing to the liberal minister of education, Marie Elisabeth Lüders, was she finally accepted by a high school in Bremen. More galling yet was the "distrust" of the local population, who treated the newcomers as "homeless beggars and vagrants." Feeling resented, belonging to a different denomination, and being "poor as church-mice" did not exactly help the refugees to come to terms with their displacement. But their resolute determination to pitch in gradually earned them respect.[41]

In the devastated cities, the rebuilding began with removal of the rubble. This was accomplished largely by female labor without machinery. Male Nazis who were classified as collaborators (*Mitläufer*) by denazification courts were often sentenced to clear the streets as a form of community service. According to Ingrid Bork, every person or "pupil who wanted to work or go to school in Bremen" had to show "a certificate of voluntary labor" in order to be able to enroll. "We all complied without grumbling, since we were glad that the war was over." But postwar photographs show that it was mostly women wearing pants, rough shirts, boots, and headscarves who shoveled the debris onto trucks. Erika Taubhorn remembered, "Many women chipped mortar from the bricks so that these could again be used for rebuilding."[42] Responding to the shortage of workers, women at this time also took over other jobs once held mainly by men, such as baking bread and running streetcars.

Due to the inadequate food supply, many urban Germans starved during the immediate postwar years. During the final struggle, production had plummeted while the loss of agricultural territories and lack of transportation inhibited distribution. Robert Neumaier recalled that "hunger was our daily companion; all our thinking only revolved around eating." Inefficient and gendered by favoring physical labor, the rationing system offered only about half of the daily minimum of nutrition. This endangered everyone, but especially the old and infants. Mothers, who were doing most of the cooking, stretched traditional recipes and ordered their older children to collect wild berries, mushrooms, fruit from roadside trees, dandelion greens—anything that might be edible. Horst Johannsen recalled gleaning fields for leftover kernels of wheat that could be milled into flour. Other families used their garden plots to grow potatoes, greens, and beets to supplement their meager rations. Nonetheless, Ursula Baehrenburg remembered, "Often hunger tormented me at night so that I could not sleep."[43]

One way to acquire more food than with ration cards was to trade valuables in rural areas for supplies from friendly farmers. This foraging was called *hamstern* after the rodent's habit of collecting and hoarding supplies. Erich Helmer remembered that "trains that ran out of the cities were often hopelessly overcrowded; people with their backpacks hung on to the cars like grapes," all in order "to trade for or buy something in the countryside to improve their nutrition." Starving urbanites offered money or prized possessions such as family silver, jewelry, and china to farmers who would be willing to part with some hams, sausages, eggs, or potatoes. Another strategy was to discover a long-lost uncle on a farm who could be talked into sharing his surplus. Fortunate families such as the Fehrs with American relatives or friends also received CARE packages as human relief, which stilled their hunger temporarily.[44] Because this unequal trade was often akin to begging, girls and women were especially skilled at evoking sympathy and evading the law on the way home.

Starving urbanites also used other, less-legal methods for obtaining something to eat by plundering stores or trading on the black market. When Wehrmacht depots were opened during the chaotic collapse, local people hastened to pillage supplies, no matter whether they were shoes or canned goods. Often they bartered these stolen wares on the black markets that had sprung up close to train stations in order to circumvent the restrictions of rationing. Primarily interested in such spoils as cameras or Nazi mementos, occupation soldiers were willing to offer PX goods such as coffee, nylons, or tobacco in return. Erich Helmer traded lumps of coal for butter or chocolate. In such whispered transactions, cigarettes became a substitute for the depreciated Reichsmark, allowing nonsmokers to turn Lucky Strikes or homegrown tobacco into foodstuffs. But the black market was dangerous; "getting caught with cigarettes" during an Allied raid netted prison sentences.[45] Nonetheless, the trading continued unabated.

Coping with the cold was another trial, for the fuel supply was inadequate and the winter of 1946–1947 was one of the most severe of the entire century. With miners starving, the coal output declined and the destruction of the rails hindered deliveries. Moreover, many houses' windows and heating stoves were broken. "When I opened my eyes in the morning, the entire wall and ceiling were covered in ice crystals," Ingrid Bork remembered of that heatless winter. "We could not wash, since the water in the pitchers and buckets was frozen solid." Some people, including Ursula Baehrenburg, went to parks and forests and cut down trees or dug out stumps that might be burned. Even older women such as Edith Schöffski's mother climbed up on the slowly moving coal trains and threw lumps down to the side of the track. Even Catholic Cardinal Frings absolved such "organizing" if people were trying "to get something in need." Tired of chattering teeth, blue hands, and aching bones, Ursula Mahlendorf loved the "hot noon meal" provided by Americans to all school pupils.[46]

Obtaining clothes for braving the elements provided another challenge, for there was nothing to buy with worthless money. Even if they had not been pillaged by occupation troops, the prewar items had become threadbare and "shoes had either grown too small or were worn out." Women such as Ingrid Bork once again became champion improvisers by "sewing a dress out of our flag." Moreover, "the old horse blanket became a coat," while curtains salvaged from a bombed house were transformed into another dress. "The uniforms of the men were dyed so that one could no longer recognize their field grey." This need gave Erika Taubhorn a new vocation: "Since clothing was scarce, I went to a sewing school where I remained for seven years." There she "learned for instance to make a new dress from two old ones which were either too tight or no longer nice enough." Ursula Mahlendorf's mother also struggled to get by as a seamstress, although her customers often had to pay with victuals rather than money.[47]

Living conditions were crowded due to the destruction of about half the housing stock and the arrival of refugees. This hit women especially hard. Gertrud Koch's apartment had been destroyed and she was glad to find shelter from the elements in an abandoned cellar. Other women made do with garden sheds, garrets, and the like. Expellees such as Ursula Baehrenburg had to share one unheated room under a leaky roof with five people, trying "to live peacefully together." Ruth Bulwin was happy to graduate from a horse stable to a larger room with a stove in a Labor Service barracks, even if they owned only a table, chairs, and a bed as furniture. While the constant struggle against lice and bedbugs was annoying, they were able to cultivate a small garden plot with tobacco, while other neighbors kept chickens or rabbits to supplement their food.[48] Because the scarce housing was administered bureaucratically, strangers were often assigned to share the space, leaving little privacy for one's own affairs.

Women also took the lead in reassembling family members dispersed during the war and the Third Reich's collapse. The breakdown of the postal service meant that letters had to be carried by friends, who had to struggle through a disrupted transportation system with irregular trains and impassable roads. For Edith Schöffski, "the day on which Anneliese came" remained unforgettable. Her younger sister had been left in the countryside, where she was raped multiple times by Russian soldiers. Ingrid Bork recalled that a friend went to the train station every day hoping to find her missing brother, since "Munsterlager was the release point for British POWs." When he turned up years later, the twenty-year-old "had white hair and hardly spoke a word." For the untold racial victims of the Nazis, such as Ruth Elias, it was essential to find out which family members might still somehow be living, even if "we no longer had a home." The Alenfelds treasured the news from relatives that "we are alive, we escaped the Nazi terror," although they also referred to "new grief" from the Red Army.[49]

All these tribulations combined for war widows with little children who were displaced from their prior homes. In moving letters to a female friend, the desperate Lotte Wriedt described her seemingly impossible challenges: having had no clear confirmation of her husband's death, she hoped that he would still turn up some day, but failing that, she needed legal proof that he was deceased in order to qualify for a meager widow's assistance. With four small children to take care of, she had little time to find gainful employment and was thrown back upon the private charity of friends and relatives. Often the mother and children starved, having to eat only beets or scrounge for mushrooms, gleanings from fields, or wild apples. "Why have we not all died? Why are we destined to be alone without our father? No, I don't know if I can cope with this problem. My nerves are shot." Often she was depressed: "Nobody can help me. I want to cry like an animal but it does not help."[50] Only for the sake of the children did she struggle on.

The first Christmas after the war was an emotional roller-coaster, relief about the return of peace mixing with pain about the losses of the war and fear of an uncertain future. Still under Polish rule in East Prussia, Ursula Baehrenburg considered it "a sad holiday" that left no memories. Though Irene Alenfeld's mother "felt no Christmas spirit at all," the family read the nativity story at home "in many languages in the hope for a coming Europe."

Martin Sieg had an even more touching Christmas, for a female teacher had invited a group of "homeless and single soldiers" who did not want "to be alone with their depressing thoughts" on that evening. "A small spruce tree decorated the room. Candles burned and a few cookies lay on small plates," since nobody had any riches to offer. "Nonetheless the table was set for us in cordial fashion like in Bethlehem of old." Even if Sieg did not yet appreciate the religious message of the Christmas story, such female efforts to share a bit of human warmth encouraged people to go on.[51]

Maintaining good family relations was difficult for women, since many of the surviving men were damaged by the war and unsuitable as partners. Even after they had returned from POW camps, veterans tended to be uncommunicative, sharing their stories only with their former comrades. If they had seen tensions beforehand, unions like that of Ruth Bulwin's parents tended to fail, while prolonged separation such as the Johannsens' made it likely "that the marriage would break up some day." But finding mates during the postwar chaos was difficult when one's almost-adult children, such as Ursula Baehrenburg, spoke up against a new connection by saying, "We do not want any half-siblings." She found living under a stepmother trying because the newcomer tended to favor her own offspring. Some war widows such as Erika Taubhorn's mother even advertised in the newspaper, only to be disappointed by the suitors who turned up. More successful was the slow growth of a relationship, as between Anneliese and Paul Huber, who married in 1953.[52]

Trying to make up for what they had missed, young adults jumped into those pleasures they could afford. During the summer, swimming and hiking in informal groups offered a welcome change of pace. Ingrid Bork was willing to stand in line for hours to catch a movie, even if the power might go out in the middle of the action. Her friends tried to distill their own alcohol because the spirits sold in stores were exorbitantly expensive. Horst Johannsen was so good with his harmonica that the Communist youth group asked him to play for dances, providing him with entertainment, company, and some money. When he finally overcame his shyness and went to a dance, Hermann Debus was astounded that "the women and girls almost threw themselves at the few men present" due to the gender imbalance of about two females to every male of marriageable age. When she was offered twenty marks for quick sex, Erika Taubhorn took the money and ran: "I have never understood the women and girls who surrendered themselves for one night."[53]

Even if many youths only wanted diversion, the longing for companionship often turned such encounters into love. A movie date with the attractive actress Christel grew serious when Gerhard Baucke dared to kiss her: "It was the beginning of a great love, a love which had to weather many trials." Only out for pleasure, Erika Taubhorn rejected so many suitors that her mother was convinced she would never marry. But when leaving yet another show, she "looked a young man directly in the face. He stared at me and smiled, and I returned the smile." This was love at first sight with Alfred, whom she married soon thereafter, since they "understood each other well." Similarly, during one of the dances, Hermann Debus met a vivacious blonde named Ilse with whom he got on well. In spite of the lack of most basic necessities on board his tugboat, "we were very happy. We had each other—and were content with that." Introduced more conventionally at a tea, Gisela and Horst Grothus discovered that they shared basic values and married as well.[54]

Marriages during the postwar chaos were wagers on a better future, a sign of optimism that lives would improve if faced together rather than alone. When Erich Helmer declared his intention to wed Gretel, his future mother-in-law warned, "Children, you don't have anything, no job prospects, not to mention an apartment, furniture, or china." But they were undismayed: "Indeed, we believed that everything would turn out well, even if the world around us was still full of shards and rubble." The ensuing ceremony was an ironic mixture of wishes for a "good socialist marriage" and Christian vows to the power of love. Even the Russian guards who caught them as they crossed the border celebrated their marriage with lots of vodka over several days! Similarly, Robert Neumaier was "the happiest man" alive when his adored schoolmate Johanna accepted his proposal. After the fighting and imprisonment had forced Karl and Erna Härtel to wait for five years, they were finally able to tie the knot in an impressive ceremony in 1948.[55]

Having children was an even stronger affirmation of life during the late war and postwar period. Anneliese Huber gave birth to her son Wolfgang in May 1944, but struggled hard in order to provide enough food and medicine during the inevitable childhood diseases. As a war widow, she had to work and care for him at the same time. But "the happy child gave me much joy and created a purpose for my life." Ruth Bulwin had her daughter Brigitte in November 1944, but in the chaos of flight to the West the baby refused to eat. Only when she sweetened the oatmeal did the infant begin to feed again and get strong enough to resist infections. Although Ruth was depressed when she became pregnant again, she encouraged herself by reasoning, "whoever was alive had already won the lottery and we were young." When her son Manfred was born in July 1946, they somehow managed to feed another mouth. Even worse off were the many children who had lost their parents and had to live in Red Cross or church orphanages.[56]

In spite of their search for romantic relationships, young women continued to work outside the home in order to earn a livelihood and to gain greater independence. For those with little education but practical skills like Erika Taubhorn, being a seamstress was sufficient as long as she was paid enough. Others who were more ambitious, such as Ursula Baehrenburg, went back to school; she did so in order to advance from exploited help to a regular position as a nursery-school teacher. Still others, such as Erna Katterwe, had the good fortune to be drafted as a "new teacher" by the local mayor, who had fired the Nazi instructors and now needed personnel to staff the schools even if they lacked formal training. Gisela Grothus had already obtained her degree and found herself much in demand as a medical technical assistant. She moved away from her home town since she "wanted to be independent and self-reliant." Because clinics desperately needed fully trained staff, she worked long hours and "my job completely occupied me."[57]

Due to their resoluteness in dealing with chaos, German women earned much public acclaim, even if their subsequent retreat into family life denied them full legal equality. When likened to "the strong woman from the Bible," Joachim Fest's mother indignantly rejected the description, protesting, "I would still rather . . . sit down in front of the piano." By contrast, during a feminist lecture in the Bremen America House, Ursula Mahlendorf insisted, “My mother works too—as a matter of fact so do I. And I don’t intend to ever stop doing so. I want to have some profession.” She continued, “I cannot imagine ever being dependent on a husband for earning the family income.” If men like her father could die, it was important to be self-sufficient. As a result of women’s impressive strength, the constitutions of both German states promised equality between the genders. But because many women wanted to return to the traditional homemaker role after mastering the postwar chaos and male politicians dragged their feet during the revision, it took several decades in East and West Germany to reform family law toward this ideal.[58]

REBUILDING LIVES

With every passing year German lives inched further toward normalcy—albeit under the new circumstances of a four-power occupation regime that lasted until 1949. Without defining the connotations of what seemed normal, the autobiographies describe this process by referring to a return of the stability and predictability of a civilian life. For struggling people, “finding a way back to peace, to the normalization of existence” meant having enough food to eat, housing to shelter from the elements, and jobs to earn a living. But with the suspension of sovereignty in June 1945, the Germans had become wards of the Allied Control Council. They lost authority over their own affairs and were forced to obey the occupiers’ orders. The slow reversal of the occupation policies from prevention of World War III and punishment for Nazi crimes to “starting the reconstruction and restoration of democracy” offered the defeated space for a new beginning. “At any rate, times gradually normalized,” Ruth Bulwin recalled, “and it slowly grew light again at the end of a long tunnel.”[59] Hence her family photo shows a renewed optimism (image 22).

One irritating consequence of the occupation rule was the division of German territory into four zones, with each victorious power controlling its own territory. Though the Potsdam Agreement had created a common policy of “demilitarization, denazification and decartelization,” the imple-

22. Living in barracks. *Source*: Ruth Bulwin, *Spätes Echo*.

mentation of these aims diverged so that every zone gradually assumed the character of its controlling power. Moreover, the division created new borders, policed by each of the victors, which required an official pass to be crossed. For refugees from the east such as the Krohmer family, the controls were a vexing obstacle; the permits were difficult to get, necessitating the hiring of a smuggler to help them get across. With his wife and parents on different sides of the "Iron Curtain," Erich Helmer "ended up crossing the border more than three hundred times."[60] Because the barriers hindered recovery, the United States finally pushed for their abolition in the West.

Another hurdle was the process of denazification, which sought to weed out leading Nazis and punish them for their misdeeds. In the Soviet zone, a collective purge of discredited elites attempted "to eliminate the old capitalist influences," while in the West an individual effort tried to ascertain personal culpability with the help of a 131-item questionnaire. Reliable anti-Fascists such as Joachim Fest's father and Nazi victims such as the

Communist mother of Gertrud Koch were put in charge of denazification courts, which investigated membership in various NS organization and assessed actual behavior. Suddenly the few surviving Jews, such as lawyer Erich Alenfeld, were overrun by petitioners asking them to provide an affidavit, called *Persilschein* after a laundry detergent, that would prove their innocence. Though he approved of the Nuremberg judgments, Fest senior found "the tribunalization of the Hitler years . . . extremely dubious" and declared that life was too complex to be judged. Only the highest Nazis were sentenced, while most accomplices merely had to pay a fine.[61]

Though rather imperfect, the ouster of Nazis allowed dedicated anti-Fascists and bourgeois democrats to be appointed to lead the reconstruction. Due to the connections of the Communist underground, Hans-Harald Schirmer's father was put on the city council of the sleepy town of Wolfenbüttel. For a few weeks Gertrud Koch's mother served as mayor of a small village in the Swabian Alps before returning to Cologne. The Americans had actually prepared a "whitelist" of reliable anti-Nazis and non-Nazi specialists to whom they entrusted such offices. Working for the British military government, Frank Eyck was happy to find that the father of his friends the Schmidts had survived, a man of "wide and varied industrial experience as director of the Deutsche Bank, and yet with an ethical outlook on life deeply rooted in Christianity." While the Soviets did not entrust Dr. Schmidt with any important task, he became close to the circle of Konrad Adenauer, the first postwar chancellor of West Germany. Similarly, Bettina Fehr's father was appointed public health official for the city of Essen at the Ruhr, because he had been discriminated against by the Nazis due to his half-Jewish wife.[62]

This reversal of power relationships triggered a wave of opportunism in which Nazi collaborators changed sides and embraced the ideology of the occupying powers. Cultivating good relations with the victors could prevent the loss of a job and make it possible to take over the property of denounced neighbors. Joachim Fest's father was astounded "that suddenly the country was full of people who had always been 'against them.' He did not want any part of it." Horst Johannsen was appalled by "the Nazis who speedily no longer want to be any." When listening in on conversations, he was disgusted with previously fanatical supporters of the Führer who "regretfully claimed never to have wanted the war and its consequences, to have been forced into the party and not to have hurt anybody." Hans Tausch was likewise "astonished with what nonchalance the mass of captive officers now abhorred a system and repudiated an ideology that had motivated them to the greatest sacrifices and achievements during the war years."[63]

The rebuilding of a largely destroyed country was an enormous task, requiring an endless succession of small steps that gradually restored a semblance of order. Local governments organized the removal of the rubble; debris piled up in veritable mountains at the edge of cities such as Berlin. Urban authorities also sought to repair water mains and restore power lines for washing, cooking, and heating. Even before the fighting ended, private citizens had begun to fix the bombing damage to their roofs and nail windows shut until they could get new panes. With horses dead and farm machinery out of fuel, hungry urbanities had to volunteer to dig up crops such as potatoes in return for a small share for their own consumption. Workmen scoured destroyed factories for any tools or raw materials that might be used to resume production, while railroad and road crews repaired tracks and highways in order to get transportation going again. Out of innumerable individual and collective initiatives, a miraculous reconstruction (*Wiederaufbau*) eventually emerged.[64]

Often forgotten in the depictions of "mountains of reconstruction work" is the concurrent process of the "intellectual rebuilding of Germany" through a revitalization of its values and institutions. Minorities in both Christian churches had resisted Nazi pressure. Their spokesmen, such as Bishop Hanns Lilje, provided spiritual orientation for disillusioned veterans who were in search of a moral compass by distinguishing between positive patriotism and destructive nationalism. Though even more tarnished by collaboration, the nation's universities also offered intellectual guidance by uncompromised professors, such as Friedrich Meinecke in Berlin and Alfred Weber in Heidelberg, who sought to nourish the "spiritual hunger" of former soldiers. Helped by émigrés such as Frank Eyck, the occupation authorities also reconstructed the licensed media as a democratic public sphere, free of Nazi lies and distortions. Erich Helmer was delighted by the appearance of the newspaper *Braunschweiger Nachrichten* as a reliable news source and "first step towards normalcy."[65]

For the younger members of the Weimar cohort, another part of normalization was their ability to complete the schooling that had been interrupted by Nazi anti-intellectualism and wartime manpower needs. Now the authorities created special remedial courses for veterans that tried to cram the missing academic content into a year or two. Sitting at a school desk and memorizing Latin verbs was not easy for youths such as Erich Helmer who had been Wehrmacht officers. Students of technology and the natural sciences had to relearn the basics of mathematics, physics, and chemistry even if they, like Karl Härtel, had already practiced such skills in the military. But in spite of destroyed classrooms, lack of textbooks, and untrained teachers, the resumption of schooling generally proved "a happy time." Ursula Baehrenburg and other youths "went to school with enthusiasm: nothing was more fun than to be allowed to learn."[66]

After passing the difficult *Abitur* college preparatory examination, many youths were finally able to throw themselves into studying at the university. For the first postwar cohort, this was not the romantic student life of carousing in fraternities, but rather a bitter struggle against hunger, cold, and inadequate facilities. Older veterans such as purser Hanns Stekeler had "to study pretty hard" in order to learn the complicated regulations to obtain a law degree. Robert Neumaier remembered that only "a determined will to persevere and good comradeship helped us get through." In spite of the harsh conditions, these students were animated by "a sense of new departure" into a better future. They resolved not to repeat the disastrous mistakes of their elders. Budding theologians such as Erich Helmer wanted "to champion the truth and freedom of the Gospel." Even engineers such as Heinz Schultheis hoped to help society to "build a future democratic state out of the useless materials of intellectual rubble."[67]

The completion of their training finally allowed the Weimar children to advance from temporary jobs into permanent careers. Even without the appropriate school certificate, some resourceful and energetic youths managed to become journalists, as Gerhard Baucke did, or traveling salesmen, like Rolf Bulwin. Those who had completed an apprenticeship and passed the required tests could become secretaries, like Anneliese Huber, seamstresses, like Ingrid Bork, or technicians, like Horst Johannsen. If they had received additional specialized training, they might enter an occupation such as forester (Horst Andrée), schoolteacher (Ursula Baehrenburg), ship's captain (Hermann Debus), or bank employee (Paul Frenzel). Only if they had finished their university studies could Erich Helmer and Martin Sieg become theologians or Horst Grothus, Robert Neumaier, or Heinz Schultheis engineers.[68] Although their professional development was long delayed, these young men and women showed an impressive will to catch up.

Another dimension of normalization was encounters with modern culture that offered impulses for self-reflection and coming to terms with terrible experiences. "I have never again in my life been so starved for cultural events as I was then," Ursula Mahlendorf recalled. She loved the paintings of abstract expressionism that had been denounced by the Nazis as "degenerate art," finding Franz Marc's blue horses simply "glorious." Joachim Fest thought the "first concert for which I obtained a ticket" rather memorable: Wilhelm Backhaus played Beethoven's fifth piano concerto, offering consolation amid the ruins. Friends introduced him to the authors of the "inner emigration" and later expanded his horizons to philosophers such as Jean-Paul Sartre in other languages. Erich Helmer was "swept away by the weekly Bach cantatas" because "they let us forget" the rubble and hunger for a while.[69] With these encounters, the skeptical youths recovered older traditions that were less corrupted by the Nazis and got to know the forbidden works of international modernism.

Disillusioned due to their betrayal by Hitler, the young adults of the postwar period tried to find political and moral orientation that might give their lives a new and better direction. Erich Helmer remembered that they "all searched for an answer to the unmastered past, looked for something to hold onto in a chaotic world." In the resulting discussions between veterans and civilian students, "nobody was offended," because "they got at the core of things." Saving "every penny and sacrificing every free minute in order to escape the black hole of ignorance," Martin Sieg found sympathetic company in the Protestant student circle at the Technical University of Hanover, where they wrestled "about a future in which the past would never be allowed to repeat itself." By contrast, the younger Ursula Mahlendorf gained support at the Bremen America House, which "became for me more than a library to study in." Such self-reflection drew upon the works of critical authors such as Carl Zuckmayer, Wolfgang Borchert, and Heinrich Böll.[70]

The postwar reorientation of these young adults, sometimes also called "forty-fivers," was a laborious process that led to a range of competing outcomes. While the failure of the Nazi policies was self-evident, admitting the enormity of the regime's crimes was another matter. Many young adults were unwilling to trust the shocking pictures of piles of corpses or walking skeletons shown in the newsreels by the occupying powers. Some self-critical Germans such as Martin Sieg still claimed that these atrocities "had largely happened without the knowledge of the mass of the population." But "when the entire scope of the bestial state criminality became known and documented so it could be checked, I was deeply ashamed" of the "official and systematic murder" in a country claiming to be highly cultured. Even if confronting Nazi complicity remained painful, the Allies also took a more positive approach by providing young "Germans with an opportunity to educate themselves in democracy." Ursula Baehrenburg explained what ultimately made the difference: "We experienced a lived freedom."[71]

Discouraged by the extent of the destruction, some of the young Germans chose to leave their country in search of better lives elsewhere. They were part of the last great wave of emigration that propelled over one and a half million former perpetrators, bystanders, and victims of the Third Reich abroad. Some, like engineer Fred Flessa, tried to escape the material privation of Nuremberg. Others, such as Bavarian farmer Walter Lichti, sought to get a fresh start in distant places without any of their Nazi baggage. Some intellectuals, such as Irene Alenfeld, sought psychological distance from their tarnished home by idealizing another culture: she found a "second home" in France through study abroad and work as an au pair. Organist and composer Gerhard Krapf so enjoyed the warmth of his reception during his fellowship year at Redlands University that he decided to stay permanently in the United States. Because she felt "unwanted in Germany," Ursula Mahlendorf wished to emigrate "anywhere" and accepted a teaching assistantship in German at Brown University.[72]

Former slave laborers and other uprooted people, called displaced persons or DPs, wanted to leave the country of their oppressors, but had difficulty deciding where to go. Overjoyed by their liberation, many of them "wanted to avenge themselves for everything that had been done to them before" and broke into houses, assaulted women, and plundered goods. In the chaotic transition, a few also helped other surviving victims, such as Lucy Mandelstam, with shelter and food. The Allied assumption that all of the more than six million DPs should be shipped back to their homes as soon as possible turned out to be mistaken: many East Europeans no longer had a country to return to because the borders had shifted, and they did not want to be under Soviet control. Moreover, former Nazi collaborators among them had ample reason to fear the retribution of the Red Army. Sonja Kolesnyk, for example, remained in Bavaria and married a fellow Ukrainian. Most of the rest waited instead until they could get an immigration visa to Australia, Canada, or the United States.[73]

Jewish survivors had ample reason to emigrate. However, a few of them stayed on in their former country even if all too many ordinary Germans had become accomplices to Nazi crimes. When there was no home to return to and their beloved family members had been murdered, the emotional ties ruptured. But, although her Jewish father had been killed, Ingeborg Hecht remained, for she had a son by a gentile soldier who had died in the war and she realized that "the invisible walls which had been erected between us and 'the others' could gradually be removed again. But it was not easy." Living in a mixed marriage, Erich Alenfeld also stayed on with his wife and children, tackling the frustrating task of filing restitution cases. Similarly,

Marie Jalowicz Simon decided not to leave, because she "had already emigrated from Hitler's Germany to the Germany of Goethe and Schiller," representing a cosmopolitan humanism. As "a German Jewish woman," she continued to be attached to her home—for, among the murderers, "many Germans risking their lives, made great sacrifices to help me."[74]

Most survivors of the KZ were, however, glad to accomplish that emigration for which they had wished so dearly. Unless they were as fortunate as Judith Magyar, who became engaged to an American captain, they had to find a way through "a maze of regulations and quotas" that was insensitive to their suffering. In spite of the positive reception in her hometown of Papenburg, Ilse Polak thought "it better for me, if I left the past behind me and emigrated to America." This time around it was easier to find a sponsor, and in the fall of 1949 she finally arrived in New York Harbor. "It was a very emotional moment. I cried. It was as if I saw a new future before me." Also impatient to leave, Ruth Klüger resented her mother's decision to move to the United States rather than to Israel. The process took several years, making it necessary to complete her high school studies and start at a university in Bavaria. During this time she befriended a refugee and grew to understand that "memory connects us, memory separates us."[75] Unable to escape her cultural imprinting, she eventually taught German literature in America.

The "most secret of wishes" was, however, getting to Eretz Israel, the homeland that, according to Zionists, promised to "end the suffering in diaspora." After recovering from typhoid, Niza Ganor (née Anna Fränkel) made her way to southern France and registered with the Jewish Agency. As early as September 1945 she boarded a ship, arrived in Haifa, and sneaked on shore illegally. Also convinced that she "wanted nothing to do with" Germans, Lucy Mandelstam first lived in a series of UN relief camps in order to recover sufficient strength to travel. Joining a group of Jewish emigrants, she then started her voyage in a kibbutz in Germany and moved on to Italy. Only in 1947 was she able to get a space with 1,400 others on a rickety ship named *Ghetto Fighters*. But, trying not to offend the Palestinians, the British authorities sent the would-be émigrés back to Cyprus. After another trying year in a refugee camp, Mandelstam was overjoyed to enter the state of Israel in 1948, ready to "start a new life." Similarly Ruth Elias was relieved when she at last got to Palestine: "For the first time after 2,000 years we finally have our home. Our land! Eretz Israel."[76]

Those Jewish émigrés who had already arrived in the United States before the Holocaust integrated themselves further into their adopted country while drawing on the cultural capital that they had brought with them. If, like Fritz Stern or Georg Iggers, they had been too young to enlist, they went to college and obtained graduate degrees, involving themselves in liberal causes. Those who had fought in Allied uniform, such as Albert Gompertz, returned to their new homes, entered business, and became citizens as a reward for their military service. Some, like Tom Angress, also profited from the GI bill in order to get their college and graduate degrees. While quickly Americanizing themselves by learning the language and participating in US youth culture, they retained rather ambivalent feelings about their background. Having lived "through a small part of the German horror, but enough to feel and recognize its centrality," quite a few studied European history and became a "second generation" of Euro-American scholars.[77]

While young adults in Germany were busy getting back on their feet, politics gradually intruded once again upon their lives by forcing them to take sides in the Cold War. Feeling betrayed by the Nazis and controlled by the occupation powers, many withdrew into a private realm, creating what sociologist Helmut Schelsky called a widespread "without me" syndrome. But because the victors needed local personnel to help them administer the defeated country and restore basic services, they appointed mayors and recruited technical administrators. To legitimize their decisions, they held the first elections as soon as 1946, allowing anti-Fascist parties to compete on the local and then increasingly the state level. The return of politics triggered endless debates between partisans of the "great hopes for Communism" in the East or defenders of the chances for "freedom" of the West. When Paul Frenzel consulted his two uncles about what to do, one advised him to join the KPD, while the other insisted that he become a member of the SPD.[78]

In the competition for the allegiance of young adults, the Communists—the more resolute enemies of the Nazi dictatorship—had a head start. In the East, they counted on the presence of the Red Army and the return of the "Ulbricht group," KPD functionaries who had survived the purges in Moscow. In June 1945, the Communist Party issued its first public proclamation, promising to rebuild the country in a democratic and socialist fashion. To veterans such as Fritz Klein, this "appeared to be a grand vision, suitable as guidepost for a decided change of direction, demanded by history for Germany." For critical spirits, the Marxist notion of the class struggle offered a coherent "theory which was able to provide orientation for future thought and action." Other young intellectuals, Eka Assmus and Christa Wolf among them, also embraced this blueprint for building a better Germany. Only skeptics such as Erich Helmer saw that the compulsory fusion of the KPD and SPD into the "Socialist Unity Party" (SED) in the spring of 1946 would create "a 'democracy' under Russian rule."[79]

The difference between occupation styles and political parties made it more difficult for the Western zones to articulate a coherent version of the future. Contrasting with French control, the prosperity and openness of the Anglo-Americans and the return of democratic emigrants such as Willy Brandt were attractive. The diversity of the religious and ideological offerings of the Western zones also appealed to youths such as Ursula Mahlendorf who were tired of Nazi regimentation. But the individualized denazification procedure in the West overlooked too many Nazis. This resulted in a succession of scandals, such as when Adenauer picked a chief of staff, Hans Globke, who had written a commentary on the racist Nuremberg Laws. The establishment of competing parties such as the bourgeois Christian Democratic Union (CDU), the working-class Social Democratic Party (SPD), and the business-based Free Democratic Party (FDP) also proved confusing. Only once widespread disillusionment with the establishment of a proletarian dictatorship in the East had set in, did the excitement about the freedom of choice help legitimize the democracy of the West.[80]

This ideological competition was decided by the currency reform of June 1948, which accelerated the recovery of the West and left the East behind.

According to the liberal vision of economist Ludwig Erhard, the old Reichsmarks were devalued at the rate of 10:1 and each person received forty new Deutschmarks as start-up capital. A shocked population saw its savings, stocks, and bonds wiped out. Profitable black market dealings with cigarettes also dried up, since the new money had actual buying power. "Suddenly as if by magic many things could be bought," Ruth Bulwin recalled. "The shop windows displayed unanticipated and long forgotten goods; much of what had been sold secretly under the counter at exorbitant prices now became officially" available. As a result, "people bought and intoxicated themselves with things they had long done without and spent the new money liberally."[81] Although it forced everyone to begin again with very little, the return to a competitive market helped jump-start the Western zones' economies.

Yet the currency reform also deepened the division between the Eastern and Western occupation zones. First, the Soviets introduced their own money. The increasing tensions between the erstwhile allies had already stalemated the Allied Control Council and kept the prime ministers of the German states from preserving unity in their final meeting in 1948. Now "the barriers at the border crossings to West Germany descended, the Russians no longer delivered potatoes to West Berlin from their zone and switched off the power." Due to the blockade, institutions such as Ursula Bachrenburg's Berlin school were split into Eastern and Western parts. Moreover, Communist propaganda beckoned with offers of food and warmth, if the citizens of Berlin joined its side. But the Russians had not counted on the steadfastness of SPD mayor Ernst Reuter, who argued, "it is better to hunger than to give in." US general Lucius Clay came up with the brilliant strategy of an "airlift" of Western airplanes regularly flying "provisions to supply the city." As a result of this joint eleven-month resistance, "occupiers became helpers, and helpers turned into friends."[82]

Still struggling with the aftermath of the war, young adults, above all, strove to have their lives "gradually return . . . to [their] familiar pattern." In the first postwar years, Eka Assmus believed that "it was no longer a matter of politics. It was about survival" among the ruins. Joachim Fest remembered that "basically I had spent the past twenty years outside the sphere of normal life" due to Nazi pressure at home, in school, or the army, or as a prisoner of war. "We children never complained about the difficulties the Hitler years had imposed on us." Nonetheless, the new "initiatives after the end of the war were quite fruitful," according to Ursula Baehrenburg. "We were a young generation which after the difficult experiences was full of ideals and goodwill to build a better future." After managing to survive the end of the war and the postwar chaos, the young adults had to start over again, coping no longer with extreme situations but with peacetime challenges. As Ruth Weigelt remembered her arrival in the West, "In the coming years a quite normal life awaited us with its highs and lows."[83]

NARRATING NIGHTMARES

The individual memories described in these German autobiographies demonstrate that the impact of defeat fundamentally disrupted their lives and set them in new directions. Millions of soldiers, civilians, and NS victims had been killed. Hundreds of thousands of grieving widows, such as Anneliese Huber, had to bring up their children alone and hope to find a new partner. Millions of surviving POWs, such as Horst Grothus, returned from the camps physically or psychologically damaged, making it difficult for them to resume their civilian lives. Untold numbers of women who, like Edith Schöffski's sister Anneliese, were raped, had to hide their shame and needed abortions, even if they were still in their early teens. Many millions of refugees who lost their homes in the East struggled to build a new life in the West, as Ursula Mahlendorf did. Finally, tens of thousands of Nazi victims, like Ruth Klüger, or gentile veterans, such as Gerhard Krapf, left the destroyed country.[84] These biographical upheavals were the biggest rupture of lives in recent German history.

To describe such tribulations, many authors of recollections adopted the perspective of heroic victimization and described a struggle against an overwhelming fate. Their accounts reinforce the impression that the most intense period of German suffering lasted from the final stage of the war well into the postwar years.[85] Testimonies by soldiers such as Wilhelm Homeyer or civilians like Ursula Baehrenburg stress the challenge of sheer survival in the final battles, the firebombing of cities, and the flight and expulsion from the East, during which they needed luck, cleverness, or help just to stay alive. During occupation, narratives like Edith Schöffski's shift to dealing with the victorious soldiers and to coping with hunger, cold, and poverty on a daily basis. Further on, memoirs such as Erich Helmer's engage the makeshift efforts to complete an education, find an occupation, and marry to start families, a tale of gradual normalization. Accounts such as Ruth Bulwin's exude pride in having been able to overcome such extraordinary challenges, coalescing into a founding myth of postwar recovery.[86]

Many of these memoirists write with a stance of "diachronic disbelief," contrasting the Nazi convictions of their youth with the democratic understanding that came with maturity. One such self-reflective author is Dieter Schoenhals, a former enthusiastic Wehrmacht soldier who later emigrated to Sweden to teach German Studies. He admitted, "Only after my return from prison camp did I become really aware how criminal the regime was that murdered and gassed millions of Jews for which I had been ready to sacrifice my life." In writing, he forced himself "not to leave out anything" in order to warn his students against another war. Catholic youth activist Christel Beilmann also wrote a self-critical memoir, in which she stated, "1945 was for me the beginning of a liberation." Only when she understood "what we did not know in God's [realm] and the Third Reich" did she gradually realize the enormity of German guilt. This diachronic self-dialogue is typical of many memoirs and shows that the rupture of these lives initiated an astounding learning process.[87]

The memoirs also demonstrate that the younger generation grew impatient with their elders' reluctance to admit personal culpability for the crimes of the Third Reich. Joachim Fest reported that incorrigible Nazis "continued to deny any involvement [of Hitler] in contributing to this collapse." Horrified "by the details of the acts of inhumanity in the camps," Ursula Mahlendorf "despised the many adults [she] encountered, including my mother, who claimed they had known nothing, or who denied the charges at Nuremberg as enemy propaganda, as victor's justice." When her teacher wanted her to reaffirm her belief in Nazi ideals, she blurted out, "No! You still don't understand, do you? Loyalty to them? They were criminals, all of them." Stunned by the personal report of Auschwitz survivor Jesse Rosenberg, Hans Tausch sought "an appropriate reaction to the horrible truth about National Socialism." He wondered, "how would the directly guilty, how would our entire nation be able to deal with this guilt?"[88]

Most of the autobiographies also show an almost desperate attempt to draw a positive meaning from the terrible experiences of their youth. In spite of the hunger and cold, these authors describe the postwar years as an exciting time of new departures in which they reached full adulthood, finally becoming responsible for their own lives. For many, such as Joachim Fest or Ursula Baehrenburg, this meant rejecting the advice of their parents: the older generation had discredited itself by its collaboration with National Socialism. Their coming of age involved providing the material basis for reconstruction with long hours of labor, a lack of food, and life in crowded, unheated quarters. Overcoming the Nazi heritage also involved, in Ursula Mahlendorf's words, "personal regeneration through . . . reflection" and "taking responsibility for what we have done." But the occupying powers presented diametrically opposed blueprints—Communism or democracy. While they were constrained by circumstances, the "Sunday children who had survived the war" once again had to choose.[89]

8

DEMOCRATIC MATURITY

During the summer of 1950 the Bulwins decided to build their own house in order "to escape their miserable quarters" in a former Labor Service barracks. For 500 DM in cash, they bought half an acre of forest land from a local farmer and then set out to cut down the trees. They dug the cellar with the help of neighbors, and filled half of it in again to stop the groundwater. When the building inspectors asked, "what are you doing there?," they managed to pay the required fee and get an appropriate construction permit. Then they labored to pour cement for the foundation and erect the cellar ceiling as well as the exterior and interior walls. Only when things got too complicated did they hire craftsmen to build the roof and do the plumbing and electrical work. Saving every penny, they got a loan from a local bank, stretching their meager finances to about 35,000 DM altogether On June 1, 1953, "we moved into our own home. What a day, what a proud feeling!" Such "personal initiative" and "mutual help" were typical of the years of reconstruction.[1]

It was a resolute and energetic spirit that inspired the rebuilding, since nobody else would "help the Germans out of the chaos into which we had gotten ourselves." Those young adults who had been fortunate enough to survive the war understood that they could rely merely on their own efforts. Ruth Bulwin remembered the mood: "We had to get it done, we would force it to happen. Now more than ever!" Similarly, the newly married Hellmut Raschdorff recalled asking his pregnant wife who had awakened in the middle of the night whether she was in pain. She answered "no, but I am starving." Living in a cramped room without running water, the couple looked forward to having their first child, even if the expectant mother had to quit her job and her husband's manual labor in the forest hardly provided enough money to make ends meet. "It was not an easy time, but we faced the future with optimism." Only after the currency reform "did things slowly improve." Every purchase had to be considered twice, "but we were used to doing without."[2]

By mastering such daily challenges, the Weimar cohort gradually gained a sense of maturity and independence. Though he admired his father's Catholic convictions and his mother's ability to deal with shortages, Joachim Fest's "doubts as to the principles of existence coincided with the long-overdue process of detaching myself from my parents." Still in high school, Ursula Mahlendorf "shared with my classmates a fundamental distrust of all adults" who were responsible for the German catastrophe. In heated exchanges with her favorite teacher, "I accused his whole generation. I articulated my age group's feeling of having been shortchanged by our elders and of being berated for what they had failed to teach us." Similarly, theology student Erich Helmer voiced his cohort's "search for answers to the questions: What can still be believed? What is solid after the ground of reality has and is continuing to cave in everywhere?"[3] By succeeding in finding their own way, these young adults gradually completed their maturation.

In contrast to academic self-congratulations for the successful development of the Federal Republic, the largely apolitical memoirs barely mention the founding of the West German state. The fusion of the Western zones, the restoration of federal states, the constitutional convention at the Herrenchiemsee, and finally the creation of the Bonn Republic between 1946 and 1949 were elite events that hardly touched the daily lives of ordinary Germans. This "skeptical generation" wanted nothing to do with the parties reconstituted from Weimar, which seemed to be "old boys' clubs and has-beens." To Ursula Mahlendorf's friends, "politics was a dirty word and any form of group association suspect. Politics meant the Nazi Party, Nazi politics." Only gradually did such constructive measures as financial aid to refugees and restitution to Jewish victims demonstrate that politics could also accomplish something constructive. Due to the widespread "count me out" reaction, it took the FRG's superior performance in providing space for normal lives to make it accepted as the postwar framework in the West.[4]

The "internal democratization" of ordinary Germans was therefore a lengthy process that took several decades to accomplish. It helped that the prior alternatives of the Second and Third Reichs had failed disastrously, and that the establishment of a "dictatorship of the proletariat" behind the Iron Curtain did not look inviting either. As a government system, the Federal Republic was "a donated democracy," imposed from the outside after the defeat of Hitler. Only a minority of German democrats who had hidden in "inner emigration" or returned from "outer emigration" after the war actively fought for its establishment. Overcoming the poisonous legacy of authoritarianism required winning countless psychological contests and institutional battles. According to Martin Sieg, "a whole state had to learn how to implement the idea of democracy convincingly."[5] Only with positive experiences such as rising prosperity did the instrumental acceptance of the parliamentary system turn into an affective bonding to self-government.

PROFESSIONAL SUCCESS

The political framework for reconstruction was the Federal Republic of Germany, founded as a merger of the American, British, and French occupation zones in 1949. This second German democracy sought to resume the prior tradition of decentralized self-government while avoiding the defects that had undermined the Weimar Republic. Restored via citizens' participation from below and cast into federal form, it contained strong constitutional safeguards against the resurgence of dictatorship through the civil rights provisions of the Basic Law. Konrad Adenauer, Kurt Schumacher, and Theodor Heuss, the fathers of this Bonn Republic (named after its capital in a sleepy university town on the Rhine River), were acutely aware that they were but a minority in the population and had to win over a skeptical majority of citizens through a better performance than in the past. They sought to stabilize democracy by restoring the rule of law, alleviating social suffering, providing economic prosperity, responding to citizens' wishes, and accepting millions of refugees.[6]

The West Germans were fortunate to have constructive occupation powers that used just the right mixture of coercion and assistance to reestablish democracy. Though the discovery of the Holocaust made their initial policies punitive, the Western victors shifted toward reconstruction in the fall of 1946, easing restrictions on industrial production and eventually ending the dismantling of factories. While the French had to be coerced to go along, the occupiers ultimately realized that they had to cooperate in order to restore a semblance of trade and communication between their zones and gradually worked toward their merger in a Western state. One psychologically important signal was the inclusion of western Germany into the Marshall Plan aid that helped to reignite the West European economies. Moreover, their efforts at ideological reorientation also offered intellectual access to fascinating innovations of modernist culture.[7] When the Federal Republic wanted to become part of the West, most of its neighbors were willing to reintegrate it gradually into the international community.

The surprisingly rapid rebuilding after the war required much hard labor, which eventually became a source of collective pride. In the early postwar years, the removal of the rubble, the gathering of crops, the reconstruction of transportation, and the rebuilding of housing involved great physical effort in order to reassemble an infrastructure for normal existence. In factories, many people worked under "appalling conditions" for ten to twelve hours per day, six days a week, with bosses quite intolerant of slackers, since there were enough unemployed willing to take their place. While young adults were mercilessly exploited at work, they also slaved at home to improve their living situation and grow vegetables, fruit, or tobacco in their gardens. There was little gender difference: young women were also expected to supplement the family's income before they had children.[8] In retrospect, the visible achievements of this enormous effort gradually restored German self-confidence.

Finding the right career in the postwar chaos was difficult because it required guessing about an uncertain future. Some young adults were able to follow family tradition, like Horst Andrée, who became a forester, or Hermann Debus, who became a skipper on the Rhine River. But other paths were blocked by the allies. Horst Grothus, for example, was prohibited from designing airplanes. While some young women such as Anneliese Huber were able to follow their inclinations and work in a pleasant business office, others were, like Edith Schöffski, compelled to accept boring employment as a saleswoman in a store rather than following their dreams. Erich Helmer wrestled long with his conscience before resolving "to become a theologian," whereas Joachim Fest gave up his Renaissance interests and turned into a historical journalist. Often the choice was a matter of persistence and luck in getting a transatlantic fellowship, as happened to Ursula Mahlendorf.[9] Though the decisions were nerve-racking, virtually all of the memoirists considered them correct in retrospect.

Many higher pursuits required additional training, which was complicated by the restoration of traditional standards. Wanting to finish as soon as possible, the postwar student cohort threw itself into academic work with much enthusiasm. "We were all engrossed in our studies and expected to complete our degrees in two or three semesters." Ursula Mahlendorf recalled, "Everyone knew exactly what he or she wanted to accomplish in life." Because his future marriage depended upon a rapid graduation, Horst Grothus surprised his professor at the technical university in Karlsruhe by finishing the coveted engineering diploma in a record time of only six semesters. Other students, such as Joachim Fest, rejected the parental wish to study law and instead took advantage of their academic freedom to listen to prominent lecturers such as historian Gerhard Ritter or sampling creative works of modern culture. "Overall," he wrote, "the university was something of an Arcadia." Still others, such as Erich Helmer, chafed at the antiquated discipline of theological training.[10]

At the end of the "wonderful time" of studying, however, loomed the difficult state examination that would decide the admission to a profession. Having worked hard, talented biochemist Heinz Schultheis was rewarded with excellent grades. By contrast, Horst Andrée, who would rather hunt than do paperwork, just barely got passing marks on his forestry examination. Horst Grothus managed to bluff his way to an engineering degree by concentrating on one subject at a time and taking the exams sequentially, even impressing a professor of economics with his reading. Although she considered pedagogical theory fairly useless in the classroom, the diligent Ursula Baehrenburg received a good grade on her teachers' exam. But Erich Helmer managed to anger his church examiner, a former Nazi, so much in a discussion about the moral legitimacy of joining a plot to assassinate Hitler that he received only a bare pass and had to repeat the ethics exam.[11] On the whole, the candidates nonetheless succeeded in gaining the necessary professional degrees.

Because so many older people had been killed, these young adults quickly made the "transition into professional life," though some encountered unforeseen difficulties. Having already trained as auxiliary forester, Horst Andrée was glad to be "able to work independently" when his superior fell ill. After a study tour to the United States, Horst Grothus accepted the invitation of his uncle to join his factory producing motorcycle chains and was told, "You are beginning with me on January 1," 1952. After repeated rejections, Robert Neumaier was "offered a position in the technical office" by his apprenticeship firm, where he started to design circular pumps. By contrast, teacher Ursula Baehrenburg was shocked by having to cope with twenty handicapped children without appropriate toys and material. "A hard time began. Often I helplessly confronted the mountain of difficulties in despair." Similarly, Erich Helmer felt as if he had been thrown into the water without knowing how to swim when he was asked to replace his father as pastor of a rural parish.[12]

For sons, the easiest decision was to follow in their father's footsteps. Hermann Debus, for example, used his family's occupational know-how to become a Rhine River captain. Debus was born in the Ruhr Basin in 1926 and grew up on a tugboat when not in school, becoming an apprentice sailor as a matter of course. Persuaded by a fanatical teacher, he turned Nazi and was trained as a Navy SEAL, but survived unharmed. After the war he had no choice but to hire on to another tug, navigating the dangerous river around destroyed bridges and sunken ships. He survived a false accusation of negligence by a "hard and unjust" boss, got married, and became a captain in 1954. With a better salary—he was even able to build a house on shore—he was gratified that his life was slowly "becoming normal again." But when oil replaced coal as fuel, Debus had to make the transition to a diesel tanker and ran great risks due to time pressure from petroleum companies. He considered the increased pace of these trips rather irresponsible.[13]

In the postwar uncertainty, working for the government promised a more secure future. After fleeing from East Prussia, Horst Andrée managed to get admitted to forestry training in the Palatinate, where he earned a small salary while continuing the family tradition. Moving from one office to another, he passed his examination—although a massive oak that he was supposed to cut down fell on another tree, to the hilarity of the examiner. Once accepted into public service, his life improved with the purchase of a motorcycle and his 1956 marriage to Metchthild, which produced two children. In 1961 he was finally appointed Chief Forester of his own district, a promotion that provided him with a restored forester's lodge and allowed him to pursue his passion for the hunt. During the following years he coped with emergencies such as "snow-breaks, forest fires, and storms" while supervising workers in managing tree harvesting and planting. Similarly, both Benno Schöffski and Anneliese Huber's second husband, Paul, joined the police force in order to support their families.[14] While the pay was limited, the security and respect of being an official made up for it

Teaching, which combined the safety of tenure with intellectual stimulation, was another popular profession after the war. The Bohemian refugee Hans Tausch had always wanted to study at a university, but had to sell his stamp collection in order to raise the funds to do so. When his teacher advised, "you should become a philologist," he chose Greek, Latin, and history as his subjects, having to work hard to master the ancient languages. While he passed his examinations with flying colors, he resented the authoritarianism of his superiors even after he obtained a regular position in upper Franconia. Another memoirist who fled from the East, Ursula Baehrenburg, was inspired by her love for children to train as a kindergarten teacher. But the reality of working in difficult circumstances soon "dampened her idealism" and made her try to get additional education. After several personal crises, she became a special education teacher. She was frustrated by the disinterest of the authorities but gratified by the love of her charges.[15]

More difficult was the decision to become a Protestant pastor, which raised issues of Christian faith in a secular world. Taking his father's resistance against the Nazis as an example, Erich Helmer nonetheless overcame his personal doubts and resolved to study theology. Impressed by the answers of Bishop Lilje to his burning questions about the Holocaust, Martin Sieg abandoned his technical studies and chose the church as well. Religious training turned out to be quite difficult: it required fluency in the ancient languages and mastery of the different positions of Karl Barth's dialectical theology, Rudolf Bultmann's biblical demythologizing, and Friedrich Gogarten's lived Christendom. Though helped by their spouses, the young theologians often felt inadequate when having to console, reassure, and comfort their flock: Helmer was overwhelmed to be asked moral questions by a Nazi perpetrator, while Sieg had to hear the confession of a murderous SS leader.[16] Both young men favored a reformist opening of the church to social issues.

Attracted more by chance than design, budding journalists also had to wrestle with the questions of German guilt and the Cold War division. Baker Gerhard Baucke was delighted when the SED paper *Neues Deutschland* printed some of his poems, one of which began, "Youth let the flag fly high / and give the wind your song. / Call those who stand aloof / and remain an idle throng." Hired by the Free German Youth to write about the young, he nonetheless refused to work for East Berlin Radio during the blockade, for he resented the "miserable blackmail" of the Communists. Hoping to become "a private scholar," Joachim Fest fell in love with Italy's "warmth, lightness, naïve animality and theatrical sparkle." But when he wrote a few essays on Romanticism, the director of Berlin Radio in the American Sector noticed his literary talent and insisted "that I edit or preferably write a series of broadcasts on German history."[17] Even if this was not his favorite topic of study, the Renaissance, Fest thereby found his calling.

Engineers, who were needed for the manifold tasks of reconstruction and economic growth, had a more direct career path. Some who started out as technicians had, like Karl Härtel, to go to special evening classes to obtain the coveted diploma. Others like Robert Neumaier quickly rose up the ranks after his first pump design and the subsequent public lecture were successful. This encouraged him to write a book about "modern pumps" and he moved to another company that constructed urban waterworks. Eventually he returned to his first firm with another pay raise, wrote several more books on circular pumps, and became an international authority through foreign lecture tours. Chemist Heinz Schultheis did so well in his examinations that his professors opened the door for academic and business advancement. He only had to decide which branch of chemical research he wanted to pursue.[18] Such technical careers both propelled the Economic Miracle and profited from it.

Constrained by maternalist ideals, many women struggled between the full-time task of managing a household and caring for children or working outside the home. The teacher Ursula Baehrenburg wanted to be independent and held on to her job. But Erica Taubhorn reported laconically that her husband believed "that a woman belongs in the home and for that reason I stopped working after half a year." Widow Anneliese Huber, who brought up her older son alone, similarly confessed that "it was not easy for me to give up my employment because I liked the recognition I received there." After her remarriage and the birth of her second son, Kurti, she was glad to have done so: "It was a very happy time!" But as soon as her own children were beyond infancy, Ruth Bulwin allowed her mother to take care of them and the household and resumed her job as a judicial employee to bring in additional money. After Gisela Grothus' offspring were old enough, she similarly worked as an executive assistant in her husband's firm.[19]

As a result of manpower losses, many young professionals ascended rapidly to positions of responsibility after the war. In his uncle's factory Horst Grothus became an informal general manager in charge of about five hundred employees. When he had to fire almost half of them due to a business downturn, he began to rationalize production, modernize technology with small robots, and diversify the products beyond motorcycle chains. Often undertaken "against the intentions" of his traditionalist uncle, these reforms allowed "the firm finally to begin making money again." He received "a general power of attorney and took over practically all functions of a technical director but was never formally appointed." After his auspicious start Robert Neumaier was similarly offered a permanent position with a good salary and "put in charge of the technical office" of his pump company. There, he changed "almost the total production program of our circular pumps to more efficient and cheaper models."[20]

Those individuals who could not get into an established firm had to use ingenuity and perseverance to build their own businesses from scratch. When the unemployed Hellmut Raschdorff no longer saw any chance "to get a job," he decided "to try to make it on his own." With credit from a wholesaler, he started to hawk textile products from door to door in the villages around Kassel. When he helped an elderly lady with her suitcases, she was kind enough to order 100 DM worth of goods from him. This revived his courage. After securing the necessary permits, Raschdorff hired a small storeroom, working eighteen to twenty hours a day (while suffering from a severe type of hepatitis). Gradually he built up "a firm list of clients in the villages . . . who were regularly visited by me," first by bicycle, then on a moped, and finally in a small car. It was this "personal service" that led to the typical business pattern of expansion, construction of a regular store, and the acquisition of a competitor's business. Such success stories, repeated by Gerhard Baucke in establishing his printing business, were typical of the Economic Miracle of the 1950s.[21]

For many enterprising young men in the postwar era, self-exploitation opened doors to social advancement. Initially the former SS member Rolf Bulwin could work only at unpleasant tasks such as disposing of animal cadavers for a slaughterhouse. But when that concern went bankrupt, his wife's cousin got him a job as traveling salesman for a machine firm. This was "a complete turn-around. Had he needed physical strength before . . . now he had to become a well-dressed dandy." For five days a week, Bulwin had to drive all over the Ruhr Basin to reach his clients, putting in long hours on the road and dealing with big sums of money. But when it became clear that his boss had cheated him out of his commission, he sued him for back pay. After getting the appropriate "commercial permit," he then made himself independent as a "free commercial agent." Due to his energy and persuasiveness, the business grew so well that he needed his wife for bookkeeping and could employ his older son as well. From the social margins, he had ascended into the middle class.[22]

Some engineers opted for independence because working alone corresponded better to their individualistic personalities. By the late 1950s Horst Grothus decided to quit his uncle's company, and therefore felt "relieved of the psychological pressure." Using his management experience, he then focused on the problem of "preventive maintenance" of machines, which cost factories a great deal of money when these were stopped for repair. With the help of a research fellowship from the Association of German Engineers, he explored the literature and practice of this crucial field. After obtaining his first consulting job in a cable factory in Nuremberg, he disassembled the machines, consulted the skilled workers, and drew up maintenance plans to avoid downtime in the future. Once he had received orders from a broad cross-section of enterprises, he developed a series of seminars and became an authority on "zero failure management." Though always somewhat precarious, this career as consultant proved largely satisfying to him.[23]

For some professionals, the increasing pace of performance got to be too much and forced them to seek a less hectic alternative. When the oil companies demanded that tankers travel for at least sixteen hours a day, "the occupation which I had loved grew more and more repugnant" to Hermann Debus. In 1969 he decided to change jobs, for "it could not be the purpose of life to work day and night in order to earn a pile of money." But finding a new career proved rather difficult at the age of forty-three, forcing him to work shifts at a chemical factory. He did not want to remain an hourly laborer for the rest of his life, so Debus applied for a job in the financial services of local government. This paid only one-third of his former salary, but he was nevertheless happy about the reduced stress and quickly advanced to a higher pay grade in the tax division. Though risky, this change of occupation saved him from a three-hour commute and left him more time to pursue such hobbies as master's swimming and amateur theatricals.[24]

Due to the war-induced maturity of the entering professionals, generational conflicts were inevitable with superiors who wanted to restore the authoritarian patterns of the prewar period. Hans Tausch had to sue the Bavarian government for summer pay, which he was legally owed as a teacher trainee. Erich Helmer had a series of run-ins with the conservative administration of the Protestant church, since as a married veteran he wanted to live with his wife and child rather than in an ecclesiastical seminary. Accused by the bishop of being "a stubborn man and troublemaker," he threatened to resign from the cloth unless his parishioners were taken care of and he received more flexible accommodations. Rejecting the complaints of the shipping companies that "loading and anchoring were taking too long," Hermann Debus as union representative claimed that the fault lay with unrealistic management. But when his underpaid workers demanded increased wages, patriarchal businessman Hellmut Raschdorff rejected their demands as excessive.[25]

One secret of the postwar recovery was the close connection between academic research and practical application of its results in industry. The results of Heinz Schultheis' chemical experiments were so promising that after he completed his dissertation, two professors of chemistry competed for his services. After working several years as research assistant in Marburg, he joined the chemical giant Bayer. In his own dissertation, Horst Grothus introduced American "expert systems for management consulting in machine industry" in a German context. His subsequent career as a consultant not only built on practical problem-solving, but also on the systematization of knowledge for improving management decisions through publications and seminars. Robert Neumaier sought to spread his expertise on centrifugal pumps "by writing a real reference book which takes into account the wishes of our clients." The publication of four handbooks and numerous articles made him a respected authority in his field.[26]

Another element of successful rebuilding was the promotion of German business approaches and products through international contacts. In the early 1950s the United States was the example from which engineers such as Horst Grothus wanted to learn innovative production methods (and a more relaxed lifestyle). By the mid-1970s the relationship had largely reversed, and he began offering seminars on management topics to a US audience. Now speaking in English, Grothus widened his travels from neighboring countries like Switzerland to the Balkans, the Near East, and Japan. Robert Neumaier reasoned similarly, "Being responsible for selling our products, I recognized the necessity of directing our activities mainly toward export" after the domestic demand had dried up. Hence he visited trade fairs in Russia, Eastern and Western Europe, and the Balkans "as a kind of traveling preacher" for German machines. This tireless promotion, the high quality of the products, and reliable maintenance were the secrets behind the FRG's astounding export surplus.[27]

The recovery of "the global reputation" of firms such as the electrical giant Siemens was largely the result of the ability and dedication of their employees. For instance, a teenager named Hans-Gerd Neglein started an apprenticeship at Siemens in 1946, convinced "he had to succeed" on his own because his officer father had died in the war. In the early years of rebuilding he had to "work, work, work" for ten hours a day and on the weekends. When his superiors noticed his talent for making semilegal exchanges of electric motors for food, they had him trained as an accountant, believing "everything has to be correct." He wanted "to get out into the world" and so served the company for fifteen years in Brazil, until he was ordered back to Germany in order to oversee the Latin American business. Known as "a tough guy," he nonetheless took care of the employees below him. Due to his intense devotion and personal modesty, he eventually became a top manager of Siemens, in charge of worldwide sales, through which he met political leaders Mikhail Gorbachev and Helmut Kohl.[28] In many ways, this stellar individual career was typical of German business success.

A final reason for German prosperity was the backbreaking labor of foreigners, recruited as so-called "guest workers." To provide needed manpower for its factories, the FRG signed treaties with Italy, Spain, Greece, and Turkey to recruit temporary help, which relieved unemployment at home. One such newcomer was the welder Mehmet Ünaldi, who decided to seek his fortune in *Alemanya* in order to get away from an unresponsive wife. After an interminable train trip, he arrived in Munich in the summer of 1962, only to be shunted to a bridge-building factory in Düsseldorf. Although respected for his skill and dedication by his colleagues, he also encountered prejudice and discrimination. But he took courses to overcome the language barrier and gradually became used to the strange culture of his new country. Falling in love with a German woman and having a son made him decide to stay in his new home, visiting Turkey only during vacations. As was typical of many *Gastarbeiter*, he realized that "two souls live in my breast": he felt homesick for Turkey when in Germany and for Germany when in Turkey.[29]

With some delay, the postwar boom also led to an increase in prosperity through rises in wages and salaries. While the initial expansion was driven by self-exploitation through long working hours and deferred compensation, from the mid-1950s on pay began to increase as well. Hermann Debus remembered, "Of course, we earned much money through our countless overtime hours." Gerhard Baucke, now the owner of a growing printing company, also reported profiting from the general business expansion, which yielded "a comfortable prosperity." But the pump engineer Robert Neumaier had to change to another firm in order to double his income, and to receive another raise before he ultimately returned to his original company. Convinced that he "earned too little," freelancer Horst Grothus "lost much money" when his colleagues in a joint consulting firm were unwilling to follow his advice. Even if some refugees, such as Christel Groschek, were forced to work at marginal jobs, on the whole public salaries for teachers and policemen also rose gradually along with labor pay.[30]

A particularly memorable benchmark of prosperity was the acquisition of the first car, partly for business and partly for pleasure. When Hellmut Raschdorff fell ill while selling his textiles door to door, he finally "realized that the growing tasks" required a small automobile. Hence he purchased a little plastic Borgward Lloyd car with a 13 HP motorcycle engine and a hatchback for loading the wares. Expending 2,000 DM seemed like a big

23. Pride in a first car. *Source*: Kempowski photo collection.

risk, but the greater ability to reach his clients paid off handsomely. Hoping to sell his machines all over the Ruhr Basin, Rolf Bulwin also needed an automobile. In order to get around with his samples, he bought a used Opel and was very proud to be able to take his family on trips during the weekend. When he first decided to become an independent consultant, Horst Grothus purchased a used VW Beetle and had it repainted.[31] In many postwar recollections this motorization is an important caesura documented by proud photos (image 23). It signaled growing affluence.

Astounding even the participants, the continual business expansion until the mid-1970s became known as the Economic Miracle. One such success story was Gerhard Baucke's printing company, started in 1955 when he purchased his first Rotaprint machine. With much determination, he printed children's books and Christian literature, buying a bigger machine every few years. Eventually he got an order for pamphlets from the electrical giant AEG, which allowed the firm to stabilize. While happy about such success, his mother warned him that "the firm is beginning to own you." In a similar fashion, "the Economic Miracle also made itself felt in our company,"

Robert Neumaier recalled. When the city of Freiburg blocked the necessary expansion of its production capacities, Lederle and Co. moved to a neighboring town and split into three separate divisions. As key engineer behind the success, Robert Neumaier was promoted to manager in two of them—but at the price of a gallstone operation and permanent diabetes.[32] The strains of war and reconstruction made the Weimar children particularly vulnerable.

Even if the reality was somewhat less spectacular than the memory, these "miracle years" restored West German self-confidence. The tone of later anniversary celebrations in Baucke's and Raschdorff's firms was rather self-congratulatory, since nobody could quarrel with the evidence of amazing progress. Almost three decades of economic growth had not only rebuilt a ruined country, but also propelled its citizens into an affluent consumer society far beyond Weimar or the Third Reich. Critical intellectuals such as Ursula Mahlendorf correctly pointed out that all the "calls for spiritual values and moral regeneration faded like ghosts in the glare of the new material consumption." Moreover, the expellees, refugees, returned POWs, and war widows were slower to reap the benefits than the newly rich businessmen driving shiny Mercedes sedans.[33] But by overshadowing historical guilt, the postwar boom generated a new pride in the deutschmark as hard currency and made it possible for Germans to regain some control over their own destiny.

PRIVATE REWARDS

The rise of prosperity also supported a more satisfying private life as a reward for all the strenuous labors. While some critics observed "the collapse of the bourgeois world," the postwar ideal still remained the nuclear family, no longer as a defensive survival community, but rather the center of a rewarding personal existence. Increasingly, the now-adult children of the 1920s ignored the advice of their parents and struck out on their own through university studies or making headway in their professional careers. That meant also moving out of the home and making new friends who provided different perspectives. It also made it possible to explore leisure

24. Postwar wedding. *Source:* Gisela Grothus, "Mein Leben."

activities such as camping vacations in the summer and skiing in the winter. Moreover, it implied widening one's horizons by attending lectures, concerts, plays, and other cultural events.[34] While many autobiographies report this emancipation from parental tutelage, they also show that the authors' core aspirations centered on having a meaningful family life.

After the postwar chaos, the young adults had a veritable hunger for companionship, not only as sexual attraction, but also as mutual understanding and support. Anneliese Huber needed long talks and many letters to be sure of "the good character of a man" with whom she wanted to spend her life. Similarly, Anne Raschdorff had to get over her negative impression of Hellmut by watching him during church service to "gain assurance that I could entrust myself to you." Though Erika Taubhorn and her Alfred "got along well with each other," she had to overcome her mother's skepticism and the hostility of her future mother-in-law (who had already picked out another bride) in order to get engaged to him. For Gisela Grothus "it was not love at first sight" but rather similar conservative expectations for life that made her inclined to wait until Horst had finished his engineering studies. "We imagined our future from then on as my parents had lived it: Children, living for them and with them. All together and for each other in love."[35]

The result of these romantic relationships was a series of festive weddings that returned to traditional customs and displayed increasing prosperity. Gisela and Horst Grothus tied the knot on April 1, 1952 in an elaborate ceremony. The wedding-eve party "was an enjoyable meeting" of families and friends who played out funny skits and offered "welcome practical things for our future home." The next morning Horst had to wait until "his wife was poured into the white dress" previously worn by her sister and her hair fixed with a veil: "When I was allowed to enter the preparation room, I was stunned by the beauty of my bride." Then followed a carriage ride to the Dahlem village church in Berlin, where Gisela's uncle preached a personal sermon. Back in the new wife's home, "a tasty and festive wedding dinner was served" and then the newlyweds departed on their wedding trip to Lake Constance. A striking photograph of the pair preserved the memory of this happy occasion (image 24). Other couples followed this pattern, though some of the partners, such as Bettina Fehr, had to convert to Catholicism to satisfy the Church.[36]

Not everyone was fortunate enough to find a partner for life, because now for each available man there were 1.6 women of marriageable age. Ursula Baehrenburg was one such "young woman, who longed for love and wanted to share a common goal in life with a husband." She liked her childhood friend Heinz well enough, but he was merely a "good comrade" who failed to understand her "female desires." Then she met a married man named Willi, with whom she fell in love, "experiencing hours of happiness and complete abandon." But because he grew "morbidly jealous" and rampaged about drunkenly, she sent him back to his wife. "Willi belonged to the men who only feel sorry for themselves." Other attempts also failed to produce a lasting bond. But then she met an Indian family and befriended their son and daughter, while similarly becoming godmother to the son of a friend. These emotional bonds compensated for her not having children of her own. In retirement she finally renewed her relationship with Heinz and moved with him into a rebuilt house.[37]

Some hastily entered relationships did not survive the postwar struggle for existence. Having lost her family during flight, eighteen-year-old Christel Groschek accepted a marriage proposal from a shoemaker sixteen years her senior while working on a farm in a North German village. Unfortunately, her husband turned out to be an alcoholic who squandered his earnings, abused her and the children, and even antagonized his neighbors. Moreover, as a strict Catholic he opposed birth control and fathered four children, which strained the family's meager resources. When Christel could no longer take the mistreatment and sought a divorce, her husband managed to prevent it by claiming that the tension was her fault. After more than a decade, she finally escaped his clutches by taking the children and secretly moving away to another city. There she established a new life, gratified by the successful growth of her children, and even moved to the Spanish coast in retirement. Other relationships, like Hans-Gerd Neglein's first two marriages, foundered under the strain of work and travel during the return of prosperity.[38]

Getting a decent place to live was an essential precondition for a happy family life. However, this goal was difficult to reach due to the postwar housing shortage. Hanne and Robert Neumaier initially had to make do with a single student room without running water. Anne and Hellmut Raschdorff were happy to have two chambers in separate houses without a bath of their own. Anneliese Huber was overjoyed when her second husband, Paul, managed to find a small two-room apartment that required only 3,000 DM as a construction cost subsidy: "Finally we had a home of our own and were together!" With help from his uncle, Horst Grothus managed to obtain a small apartment for Gisela and himself with two rooms, kitchen and bath: "We are very glad about it." When Edith Schöffski heard about a newly remodeled penthouse apartment, she "was enthusiastic" about the tiled bath, big living room, and modest price.[39] With increasing prosperity, these young couples gradually moved up into better living quarters.

Families were still expected to have babies during the 1950s, so in short order these marriages produced sons and daughters. With so many men having died in the war, Gisela Grothus was particularly happy to become "a mother" because "I had for a long time wished to have children." Between 1952 and 1957 she had one boy and two girls. Anneliese Huber added another boy to her son from her first marriage, and then had twins, which almost cost her life because of heavy bleeding that required a transfusion.

When he arrived at the hospital from a business trip, Robert Neumaier was also surprised to be confronted with twins, whose arrival doubled the number of his children. Although she had not wanted to give up her job, Gisela Grothus remembered, "I felt completely fulfilled by feeding, caring and supporting this delicate being." Her husband Horst also recalled, "The children were the center around which we organized our lives." Like many other postwar families in Germany, "we played, sang, and did crafts with them."[40]

By contrast, the death of one's parents was a "painful caesura in family life," for the bond between the generations had been especially close during the German catastrophe. Many Weimar children owed their own survival in war and postwar chaos to the extraordinary efforts of their fathers and mothers. This created a lasting sense of indebtedness, even after they went their own ways and differed politically. While many of the fathers had been killed, their mothers helped selflessly in the household and with their grandchildren. Because they had suffered great privations for the sake of their children, the surviving older Germans often had health problems. Nonetheless it was a shock when Anneliese Huber's father "lay dead in his bed as if asleep" shortly before his seventieth birthday. Seven years later, her mother "suffered a stroke" and quickly passed away without regaining speech. Even if she had alienated him by constant meddling, Horst Grothus felt distraught when his mother died unreconciled in an old-age home.[41]

Increasing prosperity provided the means to progress, from purchasing basic necessities to fulfilling long-held desires. With a combined salary of 300 DM, Benno and Edith Schöffski initially had to weigh every penny when deciding what they could afford to buy. But after the currency reform, Ursula Mahlendorf recalled that "consumption went in waves." At first, people "bought huge quantities of food that had been rationed" and rapidly regained their prewar body weight. Then came "clothes and shoes," such as a warm coat or winter boots. After that, they turned to replacing worn-out furniture with new beds, couches, or wardrobes in order to be more comfortable in their homes. Benno Schöffski was delighted to receive a Grundig radio, bought by his mother on a layaway plan, "since he could now listen to sports broadcasts." Anneliese Huber was overjoyed "to finally get a washing machine!" And the Weigelts crowded around their new TV set in 1961 to watch a British crime series. While not all West Germans shared the bounty equally, this buying spree showed that "prosperity has broken out."[42]

Business success also made it possible for an enterprising minority to build their own houses and become proud homeowners. Robert Neumaier obtained a lot from a developer when he designed a water pump system for a subdivision. But he had to scramble to raise 15,000 DM as down payment toward the total cost of 50,000 DM. His wife was shocked at his plan, "assuming I had a fever because we had not a single mark in the bank." But with the help of his father, his company, and a Swiss friend, he put together the required sum. Then came the question of design, to which Neumaier added another apartment for his sister in case she returned from her husband's job in England. Hellmut Raschdorff insisted on a central fireplace and separate bedrooms for each of his children. During the actual construction, a future owner like Hermann Debus had to supervise the contractors and pitch in with painting, laying floors, and other simple tasks. "But we were happy and content, finally to be able to stay and live on our own property."[43]

The hard work required for advancement left little time for the kind of relaxation that would regenerate body and soul. Homeowners such as the Raschdorffs liked to garden, advancing from supplementing nutrition with potatoes or strawberries to the more decorative planting and landscaping of their properties. Gerhard Baucke and other individuals with good voices sang in choirs, which provided musical pleasure and personal sociability. Families with cars also visited the countryside on weekends, exploring natural sights and quaint villages or going on hikes in nearby forests. Hermann Debus took up swimming to help him cope with a health problem and brought home a series of trophies in masters competition. He also discovered a hidden talent for acting when his home town Kaub on the Rhine River put on historic plays to entertain tourists.[44] But on the whole, leisure activities were exceptions because men were stressed out by work and women were busy keeping the household running.

Annual vacations were therefore one of the high points of the year: they interrupted the work rhythm, offered relaxation, and generated family memories.

People with modest means such as the Hubers "went on many hikes in the summer [and] made it possible for the children to learn to ski" and explore destinations further away. But even well-to-do couples like the Raschdorffs were content to go "hiking in the Röhn" mountains at the border to East Germany, marveling at dramatic rock formations. "Thus we undertook many tours with the children over the years, but they gradually grew into their own friendship circles." Including cultural highlights and religious services, such excursions provided the family with funny anecdotes—as, for instance, when a waiter in a restaurant mistook Hellmut Raschdorff for an adolescent and warned him, "Boys, behave, or you will be kicked out." Gradually the range of their explorations extended to the Austrian Alps where their hiking group scaled many famous mountains such as the glacier-capped Großvenediger in the fog.[45]

The "improvement of the financial situation" in the 1950s inspired a widespread desire among West Germans to travel further afield, most notably to the South where the climate was warmer. The first such trip took the Neumaiers to the Lago Maggiore in Italy, where they rented a vacation apartment: "The kids had much fun and learned to swim in the lake." In subsequent years they took interesting holiday "boat trips to Greece, Morocco, Italy, Yugoslavia and Lanzarote." A few days after the Six-Day War they went to Israel with Jewish emigrants and the beautiful Hanne won a bottle of champagne in a "Miss Ship" pageant. On another trip, "the children wanted to buy a donkey in Tangiers" and could only barely be persuaded to give up the idea. Other voyages took them to Crete and Egypt, where a river cruise was "an unforgettable experience." They even went to China and by airplane around the world.[46] Such international journeys became coveted items of conspicuous consumption, with highlights shown to friends in slide shows or home movies.

With advancing age, the cohort's health problems multiplied, some a direct result of the war and others due to excess work. After returning from his Russian POW camp Horst Grothus had to have several operations to stabilize his leg stumps. Experiencing "excruciating pain around her hips," Erika Taubhorn was diagnosed with a severe kidney disease that required the removal of one damaged organ and months of difficult convalescence. Similarly, Hellmut Raschdorff contracted a serious case of jaundice that changed his skin to "a brown color like an overripe banana." It almost ended his life until he used the home remedy of swallowing sixty live sheep-lice, which stopped the liver infection. While her tonsils were taken out, Anneliese Huber suffered a collapse of her vegetative nervous system that took months to cure; her husband Paul had a stroke due to a clogged artery that left him permanently impaired.[47] While many postwar illnesses stemmed from lack of nutrition, the prosperity diseases often resulted from excessive indulgence in sweets, alcohol, or cigarettes.

Declining physical and mental powers inspired the older members of the cohort born in the early 1920s to retire from their jobs beginning in the mid-1980s. Suffering from hip ailments due to his many hours of standing on the bridge of a tugboat, Hermann Debus "went into early retirement at 57 due to disability." Tired of her conflicts with unresponsive colleagues and in deteriorating health, Ursula Baehrenburg accepted an early pension from her special education school. Hellmut Raschdorff was happy to turn over the direction of his firm to his son when he was sixty-three, for he was confident of the competence of his successor and thereby gained time for hobbies such as singing in a church choir. Following social custom, Robert Neumaier "ceased his activity as sales director when reaching the age of 65," but he kept writing and lecturing about his pumps for another fourteen years. Horst Grothus continued to work into his eighties as a freelancer, finishing his last consulting job in 2008.[48]

In eastern Germany "reaching retirement age" had a special significance: it opened the door to travel or resettlement in the West. Regime critics such as Paul Frenzel, who had dared to publish a negative treatise in the FRG on the deficits of the GDR's planned economy, were not only fired from their jobs, but stripped of their academic degrees. In 1982 the state encouraged him to apply for a passport by drastically cutting his pension, forcing him to move to West Germany, where he was still hounded by the Stasi. Regular citizens such as Günter Krause were so "astonished by the variety of the western economy" on their first visit to West Berlin that they "wanted to stay immediately in the West." When his wife asked, "Do you still want to resettle?," he spontaneously agreed. The GDR "wanted to get rid of retirees cheaply," so the couple was allowed to leave in February 1988. When they set foot in West Berlin, "they were greatly relieved, finally [to be] free."[49]

On both sides of the German border the loss of a spouse was a "devastating blow," especially when the partners depended upon each other in practical and psychological ways. In 1983 Hellmut Raschdorff's wife Anne was diagnosed with cancer, but the treatment seemed promising. During an emergency stop at a local hospital, she said: "Hellmut, I really did not know how much you loved me." When he was told that his wife had passed away due to a ruptured aorta, he only gradually "realized the full implications and merely recalled that [he] cried like one possessed." But he was consoled by his Catholic faith that her life was fulfilled in Christ. Similarly, Hermann Debus watched the irreversible deterioration of his spouse's health, and when she died, he was stunned and wept uncontrollably. Ruth Weigelt was also shattered by the early death of her husband due to a stroke. Gerhard Baucke experienced the loss of his wife as if the sun had ceased shining: his "heart was caught in darkness." A psychologist counseled him, "What you cannot let go you have to conquer by remembering," inspiring the writing of his memoirs.[50]

Life after bereavement "was not easy"; it required a drastic adjustment to take over daily chores and deal with loneliness. Gerhard Baucke's wife had "trained him to be a widower," so he was able to cope. The irrepressible Hermann Debus even found a new partner in Margrit, a seamstress from Berlin who had lost her husband to cancer. Not wanting to live alone, Ruth Weigelt similarly moved together with the widowed half-brother of her deceased husband. Forced to develop into a "houseman," Hellmut Raschdorff had to learn everyday chores such as cooking, cleaning, and doing laundry. Seeking a "new start" for the last third of his life, he moved into the Collegium Augustinum close to Freiburg, an academic retirement home at the edge of the Black Forest. Through singing and hiking he met Margot, a widow who became his partner. Courageous enough to enter a new relationship, they merely married in church without registering so as not to lose their individual pension benefits. "Our togetherness has developed interestingly and well, we are grateful to experience much with one another."[51]

Even in advancing age, the retirees could enjoy their children and grandchildren and participate in their lives vicariously. The autobiographies are full of pictures of happy mothers and laughing infants, showing satisfaction in their schooling and careers. Anneliese Huber was proud "that we had healthy children" and "that they have become honest, industrious and considerate human beings." The Raschdorffs and Bulwins were gratified when their sons took over the firm, while Horst Andrée was pleased that his daughter followed his calling. But when children like the Bauckes' had problems with their jobs or relationships, they could also create constant worries. Watching grandchildren grow up was more of a pleasure because grandparents did not have to discipline them; when they were small, they could be played with and encouraged in their development and when they were older they could be taken along on holiday travels. Ruth Weigelt was delighted to have become a five-time great-grandmother. An increasing sense of mortality could therefore be balanced by the reassurance of family continuity.[52]

The prevalent sense of satisfaction of the Weimar cohort's memoirs was a product of both professional advancement and private happiness. In contrast to the "cruel war time" and postwar chaos, the gradual return to a normalcy of peace and the rule of law provided the room in which an "interesting and successful professional life" could unfold. This was complemented by the recovery of a private space that allowed personal development from childhood to maturity without interruption by political demands. No doubt, the first years of the Federal Republic were still difficult due to material shortages and ideological disorientation. But in contrast to the Nazi and Communist dictatorships, West Germany offered considerable freedom for individual growth that allowed a plurality of life plans to unfold into maturity and old age. Moreover, the Economic Miracle created an expectation of continual material improvement. Ironically, it was this apolitical private realm that ultimately helped produce a new appreciation of public liberty.[53]

PUBLIC ENGAGEMENT

Though most West Germans were leery of politics, they did learn some basic lessons from the disaster that facilitated their reorientation toward democracy. The consequences of the Nazi dictatorship were so drastic that they reinforced the pacifist Weimar slogan "never again war!" Moreover, the military verdict was so definitive as to preclude the emergence of a large-scale movement of revanchism, forcing even most expellees to embrace peaceful means for regaining their homes. The incontrovertible evidence of mass murder through survivors' testimonies, documentary films, and literary representations also discredited anti-Semitism in public. Finally, the negative experiences with the SED rule in the East made West Germans reject Communist despotism as well, which they recognized as a new form of repression. Martin Sieg summarized his cohort's view: "As the most important lesson of the cruel past I have taken away that the spiral of hatred and retribution and new hatred pulls all of life into the abyss and can therefore never be the solution to conflicts."[54]

The search for new moral moorings on which to build a post-fascist community led many young Germans back to religion. Though the Protestant and Catholic Churches had lost much credibility from their collaboration with the Third Reich, the core of the Christian message offered consolation through contrition for guilt and hope for forgiveness. "Indelibly ashamed of belonging to this nation, of speaking the language of the KZ guards and having sung the songs of the Hitler Youth," Dorothee Sölle was "quite fascinated by a radical Christianity independent of the Church" and eventually became a leader of leftist "liberation theology" in Germany. By contrast, Hellmut Raschdorff sought solace in the silent contemplation of a Catholic monastery as an antidote to the hectic materialism of the Economic Miracle. Yet in retrospect, pastor Erich Helmer concluded that "our Church has missed a unique chance" by not responding sufficiently to "the hunger for spiritual nourishment," which offered an opportunity for a more lasting regeneration.[55]

Others who were more politically inclined saw the United States as a model of the future. Ursula Mahlendorf devoured the classics of English literature in the Bremen America House and engaged in heated discussions about democracy. Horst Grothus was also fascinated by the magazines, books, and films offered by a US Information and Education center. To prepare for his profession, he took the boat to New York in 1951, where he visited an uncle and inspected the car factories of Detroit, which impressed him with their "mechanized and partly automatic production processes." In order to get to know the economy better, he worked at the Schwinn bicycle factory for seventy-five cents an hour—and suggested a new welding technique. Although he felt at ease in this country, he declined an offer to stay and returned home. On a more academic level, Martin Greiffenhagen loved his year in England, which culminated in studying at Oxford, "the El Dorado of academic life."[56] Such positive exchange experiences hastened the Westernization of postwar Germany.

Yet another foundational consensus of the Federal Republic was anti-Communism, partly fed by stereotypes and partly reinforced by negative experiences. In the West, remnants of Goebbels' wartime propaganda that played on deep-seated anti-Slavic prejudices fueled an aversion to the Soviet system. Such resentment was reinforced by oral reports of Red Army cruelty during flight, expulsion, and occupation. While the surviving German Communists were excited about building a socialist future, many people were upset when "men were deported and women raped." Though some occupiers were also friendly, Eka Assmus summed up popular hostility to "*the* Russians" as "a collective characterization that was laced with fear and hatred." The horror stories told by unfortunate victims such as Günter Krause, whom the Soviet secret service imprisoned in a work camp for half a decade, confirmed such negative impressions.[57] Anti-Communism therefore became an ideological bridge that allowed former Nazis to cooperate with budding democrats.

The postwar search for "intellectual orientation" fastened upon anti-Fascist role models of convincing moral integrity or intellectual acuity.

It usually took mentors such as Bishop Hanns Lilje or scholar Karl Löwith to point out individuals or ideas not tarnished by the brown plague. Members of the resistance who had survived Nazi imprisonment such as Kurt Schumacher or Bruno Apitz had the highest credibility, since they had put their lives on the line. Moral critics such as philosopher Karl Jaspers offered guidance for addressing the issue of German guilt, while the posthumous writings of theologian Dietrich Bonhöffer suggested ethical grounds for resistance. German-language authors such as Carl Zuckmayer, Wolfgang Borchert, and Heinrich Böll exposed the murderousness of the NS regime, while writers from other countries, such as Jean-Paul Sartre and Ernest Hemingway, opened up new worlds of existentialist thinking.[58] Though largely prepolitical, these various strands prepared the ground for a new beginning.

Busy with their survival, most Germans paid little attention to the formulation of the Basic Law that would govern their subsequent lives. This provisional constitution of the Federal Republic sought explicitly to learn from the mistakes of the Weimar Republic in order to prevent their repetition. The limitation of the authority of the president was intended to avoid presidential rule by decree, the inviolability of civil rights was supposed to be a barrier against any return of dictatorship, and the revival of federalism was aimed at keeping power from being too centralized. Moreover, the introduction in 1953 of a 5 percent hurdle for representation in parliament was designed to prevent political fragmentation by splinter parties. The reestablishment of parliamentary government also served as a counterpoint to the creation of a dictatorship of the proletariat in the East. "The bill of rights' provision of a citizen's right to free development of the personality,'" Ursula Mahlendorf remembered, "won me over to the [civics] lessons as well as to the Basic Law of the emerging Federal Republic."[59]

The political party that most put its stamp on the West German state was the Christian Democratic Union (CDU), founded by Cologne mayor Konrad Adenauer in 1946. This new group appealed to bourgeois moderates looking for a moral grounding of conservative politics. Drawing upon Catholic voters, it also sought a broader base by including traditional

Protestants under the comprehensive umbrella of a *Volkspartei*. As soon as he reemerged from captivity, Catholic high-school teacher Johannes Fest started to go to CDU committee meetings and gave public lectures on the collapse of the Weimar Republic and the "debasement of law" in the Nazi dictatorship: "What had just happened to our country must not happen again. Once was shameful enough." The Jewish lawyer Erich Alenfeld also pledged "to participate in the rebuilding of a democratic Germany" by joining the CDU. His daughter recalled that in "questions of conscience he was rigorous, but he advocated compromise and mutual understanding" in practical issues and restitution cases.[60]

The CDU's chief rival was the Social Democratic Party of Germany (SPD), founded in 1869 and led by the intense World War I veteran and KZ survivor Kurt Schumacher. As a representative of moderate workers, it fought for the rights of the underprivileged and was a resolute opponent of the Nazis. Hailing from an anti-Fascist working-class family, Günter Hagemann became a leader of the Socialist Workers' Youth when he returned from British captivity in 1948. He joined the SPD and went into politics, declaring that he "wanted to help assure that what had happened before would never occur again." Elected to the Hamburg city government in 1966, he focused on youth issues in order to build a viable democracy based on human rights and social justice, where "one can speak one's mind, not be afraid of state power, and freely engage in politics."[61] Ultimately the SPD lost the close competition with the CDU for power, because Schumacher's nationalist neutralism seemed riskier than Adenauer's patriarchic support of reconciliation with the West.

The remnants of various brands of liberalism came together in 1948 in the Free Democratic Party (FDP), which remained small but became essential for creating government coalitions. Strong in the Southwest, the liberals were led by aesthete Theodor Heuss, who became the first president of the Federal Republic. When looking back at his life, Horst Grothus had difficulty deciding where his own beliefs fit in: they had changed over time from nationalism to pacifism. He wrote, "For many years my empathy has been inspiring me to become a champion of the weak and underprivileged." But to him, the expansion of the welfare state also seemed to have negative consequences: "I observe how many people become more dependent and less self-reliant. Therefore they move away from my ideal of an independent human being and are discontented on top of it." More and more, he believed that "every man is the architect of his own fortune. Hence I am a liberal."[62] Due to its narrow social base and occasional relapses into nationalism, the FDP remained a minor party.

The political spectrum of the Federal Republic was truncated by the prohibition of both neo-Nazi and Communist extremes. The Potsdam Agreement dissolved all NS organizations and the occupation powers also prohibited the rise of any successor groups. But in 1949 former Nazi military and political leaders founded the Socialist Reich Party, an only thinly disguised neo-Nazi group. In 1952 the Constitutional Court declared this party illegal, which pushed its propaganda underground and forced other rightist efforts such as the National Democratic Party of Germany (NPD) to pretend to be democratic. Though the Communists were initially permitted in the West as part of the anti-Fascist renewal, their opposition to Adenauer's rearmament and their dictatorial behavior in the GDR rendered them suspect. After years of deliberation, in 1956 the Constitutional Court also declared the KPD illegal; this initiated thousands of prosecutions and dismissals, which gave West Germany a bad name. Only with the SPD-FDP coalition in the 1970s was the party relegalized under a changed name as German Communist Party (DKP).[63]

Most ordinary folks were content with this "chancellor democracy," which reconciled political stability with parliamentary government. As a septuagenarian remnant of the Kaiserreich, the Catholic Rhinelander Konrad Adenauer led West Germany for almost fourteen years. His grandfatherly and authoritarian style suggested continuity, and he regained international respect for the nation with his policy of Western integration. He was supported by the popular economics minister Ludwig Erhard, an avuncular Protestant Franconian and father of the Economic Miracle, whose "social market economy" promised continued prosperity in the future. The tenor of these postwar decades was therefore a paradoxical blend of conservative modernization that sought to restore available religious and bourgeois traditions while supporting technological innovation, mass consumption, and popular culture. Like the rest of the apolitical majority of the population, Hermann Debus noted with satisfaction "that except for a few restrictions, life in the Federal Republic had almost become normal again."[64]

As many people were skeptical of democracy due to its Weimar failure, its acceptance depended upon the FRG's performance in overcoming the postwar chaos. Initially the victor powers, helped by the United Nations Relief and Reconstruction Agency and the Red Cross, tried to deal with the masses of DPs, KZ survivors, and German refugees. But after 1949 coping with the many victims of the war on top of the rebuilding became a challenge for the fledgling FRG. The government had to take care of tens of thousands of late-returning POWs (*Spätheimkehrer*) who needed medical help and assistance with reintegration into civilian lives. Similarly, millions of expellees from the East had to be distributed equitably between the federal states, while hundreds of thousands of refugees from the GDR needed to be absorbed as well. With a system of transit camps including Friedland and Marienfelde, the government sought to register and process the needy, offering housing, food, and job assistance.[65]

In wise foresight, the Federal Republic set up special programs such as the Equalization of Burdens Law to help those people who had had an especially hard time in the war. "Immediate help grants" in 1949 mitigated the worst suffering of veterans and orphans "to tide them over." As part of a wider integration strategy, resettlement assistance was a "generous and farsighted government policy which largely resolved the postwar expellee and refugee problem." Even more important was the permanent burden-sharing program instituted in 1952, which compensated expellees "sufficiently to equip their households, start new businesses and receive loans for purchasing property." Its funds were raised by taxing those Germans whose wealth had survived the war unscathed. While Ursula Mahlendorf got only a small scholarship, Karl Härtel eventually received several thousand DM as compensation. Because it succeeded in helping those in special need, "the Equalization of Burdens Law was one of the eminent social achievements of the West German state."[66]

The restitution payment to Holocaust victims was another effort that showed that the FRG had accepted moral responsibility for the suffering caused in Germany's name. In 1952 the Adenauer government decided to pay three billion DM to the state of Israel and additional millions to survivors as a symbolic gesture and practical help. Individuals had to file claims in person for their lost properties, ruined businesses, and broken careers, a humiliating bureaucratic process that sought to ascertain the amount of damage. Ruth Klüger's mother was too proud or afraid to travel to the FRG in order to apply. But Peter Gay's parents did not "object to these payments. For them, they were not blood money but funds owed." While some victims, such as Lucy Mandelstam, got a one-time sum, others like the Gompertz parents, "received a monthly check as pension and German Social Security, which, of course, made their life in the US easier but in no way compensated for what they had lost in fleeing Germany."[67]

Such acts of symbolic contrition also helped many émigrés to deal with the ambivalent memories of their German background. Some Jewish victims, such as Albert Gompertz, so successfully reinvented themselves as Americans that they shed virtually all traces of their prior existence. But other ethnic German emigrants kept in contact through letters and visits. Composer Gerhard Krapf even persuaded nurse Gertrud Lichti in a touching transatlantic courtship to become his future wife. The specialists in German language, literature and history (for example, Ruth Klüger and her sometime-husband Tom Angress) returned intermittently to Central Europe for their academic research. Even more prominent intellectuals such as George L. Mosse and Fritz Stern, involved themselves actively in the construction of a critical memory culture and the democratization of the Federal Republic.[68] While public efforts at atonement could never undo the suffering caused by the Nazi crimes, they could begin a difficult process of reconciliation.

Proud of their success in rebuilding a devastated country, the adults born in the 1920s were surprised by the generational revolt of the late sixties, which seemed to call all of their achievements into question. Many of them were already too old to participate in a movement driven by their own children.

Only some leftist intellectuals such as Dorothee Sölle—who was deeply ashamed of the Nazi past and opposed to West German rearmament—sympathized with the youth revolt. Blaming the conflict on US neocolonialism, she recalled that "an important part of my development from a liberal to a radical-democratic socialist took place in the context of the Vietnam war." While she admired the Quakers, the US intervention in Southeast Asia "made me realize for the first time, what kind of country it was under whose domination we lived." Considering the student movement a wonderful mobilization of many like-minded protesters, she organized a series of "extra-parliamentary, interconfessional" evening prayers that gradually evolved into a fundamental opposition of the FRG.[69]

Most of the Weimar cohort viewed the youth rebellion skeptically as a loss of order and discipline. Though rather apolitical, Ursula Baehrenburg noticed a "spirit of aggression and destruction" in her school, in which the older pupils terrorized the younger ones. "Free love began in the faculty. Most marriages broke up. Young teachers who came from the universities wanted to change society through the education of the children." She despised the smoking, beer drinking, and pot parties of the teachers and pupils. Even "among some of the little ones an unchildlike arrogance and obscene expressions appeared" that she had never noticed before. On her daily trips to and from school in a Frankfurt suburb she worried about being caught in clashes between the police and demonstrators. "Young colleagues saw my generation suddenly as Nazis and cursed us" without understanding its postwar achievements. She therefore concluded "that from this time on the FRG has changed for the worse" due to a new "egotism, elbow mentality, and irresponsibility."[70]

More liberal spirits were more sympathetic toward the sixty-eighters' reform demands, even if they were the prime targets of the rebellion. The Weimar children who were already in their forties experienced the youth revolt as a midlife crisis in which their marriages foundered. Political science professor Martin Greiffenhagen encountered student radicalism as, above all, an intolerant call for using Marxist approaches, emphasizing "economic or class dependencies" in analysis. The entire language was changing, for "radical feminists demanded an emancipatory grammar." He experienced the change to a looser style of academic discourse as liberating, but the assumption of equality between professors and students struck him as silly. Some aspects of the "value change," such as the emphasis on "self-realization," were overdue, but the habitual "violations of bourgeois discipline" rather irksome. Although one of his student opponents became Greiffenhagen's second wife in a partnership marriage, he "did not long for the decade of departure and upheaval."[71]

One positive result of the youth revolt was the formation of a set of "new social movements" that ultimately coalesced into the Green Party. "During the 1970s more and more people realized how important it was to preserve the resources of the soil and of nature and to save the environment," Gisela Grothus recalled. "We participated from the beginning. We thought that much in our immediate surroundings could be improved." She and her husband got involved because "the Greens want to be 'ecological, grass roots democratic, nonviolent [and] social,'" things that appealed to them. Horst "was a member from the first day on," while Gisela worked for the cause without joining. "During the first years, when all members were still guided by their ideals, we discussed 'the state of the world' harmoniously and formulated solutions to its many problems." But once some Green representatives were elected, the city councilors no longer listened to grass-roots demands. When the party later decided to send German soldiers as peacekeepers to Kosovo in the Balkans, Horst resigned.[72]

Propelled by memories of World War II, the preservation of peace during the nuclear arms race of the Cold War was another key issue of civic mobilization. Dorothee Sölle experienced the 1979 NATO decision to station intermediate-range missiles in West Germany "as one of the blackest days of German postwar history," for "I could no longer live in a country with bombs." She therefore tried "to organize resistance" through a "broad, comprehensive, center-to-left movement against militarism." The slogan "if you don't fight back, you make a mistake!" was designed to overcome citizens' feeling of impotence. Inspired by her theological understanding of the Bible, Sölle called for "radical forms of civil disobedience against the militarist state" through "nonviolent illegality." Though the protest was able to rouse over three hundred thousand concerned citizens to demonstrate in Bonn, the peace movement failed to prevent the stationing of missiles in the FRG. But it did articulate a widespread pacifism that later on inspired the German reluctance to join in the Gulf Wars.[73]

Another important cause was the campaign for women's equality, which sought to end the domination of an often-violent patriarchy. Instead of submitting to male control, many young women shared Ursula Baehrenburg's desire "to be a loving wife, but to maintain my independence and freedom." Realizing "how much women were disadvantaged in almost all societal areas compared to men," Gisela Grothus made feminist causes "the center of her future social engagement." With other activists, she founded a women's shelter in her home town of Dorsten in 1983 in order "to protect battered women and their children from further violence. And then their independence should be strengthened, so that they can make their own decisions." Starting with a small apartment, her group gradually expanded the shelter into a real house, hired social workers, gained municipal support, and became a refuge for about two thousand abused women and 2,800 children during its first twenty-five years. The approach of offering "help for self-help" proved amazingly successful.[74]

Other feminist activities set out to change social consciousness and make "women's equality a matter of course in daily life." For instance, Gisela Grothus inspired the foundation of a women's forum as a pressure group that would allow those "interested in the situation of women to meet, articulate problems, and initiate measures of improvement." This discussion circle tried to make discrimination publicly visible, strengthen "female solidarity," and launch other activities to help women. One method was to raise awareness of the subtle gender discrimination in children's books (image 25). Another was the creation of a "women's café" as a meeting place that would provide a "public space in which we can exchange our daily experiences, stimulate and inform each other." The flyer announced: "We don't want to be the silent losers of this society, but rather develop confidence and trust in our achievements and abilities." The agitation of the group succeeded in

25. Feminist activism. *Source*: Gisela Grothus, "Mein Leben."

getting the city to appoint an "equal opportunity officer" as watchdog and initiator of further activities such as "women's culture days."[75]

The third dimension of civil society engagement was environmental activism, both in fighting pollution and in providing nature protection. Shocked by the exploitation of resources in Brazil, Hans-Gerd Neglein moved to Andalusia after coordinating the German participation in the 1992 Seville Expo and bought a *finca* of about seven hundred acres in order to conduct biologically based agriculture, animal husbandry, and forestry. His biggest challenge was the recurring drought, which he fought by creating several impoundments. The local populace was convinced that "this German is *loco*." But torrential rains finally came and quickly filled his ponds, allowing him to irrigate his land without depleting the groundwater. In order to address the problem beyond his own farm, he created the foundation Monte Mediterraneo to promote the reforestation of the entire region, which also benefited local wildlife. After decades of merciless managerial competition, which had ruined his first two marriages, this ecological commitment and a new partnership finally brought him peace. He wrote in his memoir, "Never in my life have I been as contented and happy as today."[76]

These new social movements also strengthened civil society engagement in other areas where reforms were needed, but to which the political authorities were paying too little attention. From the late 1960s on Gisela and Horst Grothus sponsored numerous "projects in which we are not only spectators or visitors but rather become actively involved." They started with traditional charity initiatives such as looking after a couple of truant working-class youths in order to keep them out of jail and organizing a Christmas Eve party for the homeless. In the wake of the youth rebellion, the couple also pleaded for strengthening school self-government and for creating a center that would improve apprentice training. In order to increase the literacy of underprivileged children, Horst initiated a twice-weekly reading program in which volunteers read stories aloud. He also helped found a playgroup for Turkish toddlers to help them learn the German language. Such initiatives sought to address specific problem areas in a piecemeal fashion.[77]

Over several decades, the growth of public involvement created a civil society infrastructure that helped to solidify the second German democracy. In contrast to the Nazi and SED repression, people were initially happy if "politics played no role at all" so they could pursue their careers and private lives. Hence they were willing to put up with Adenauer's authoritarian style and the paternalism of the bureaucracy. Only the trade unions and the

SPD protested for higher wages and against rearmament. But during the 1960s a critical public sphere developed that encouraged youths to rebel with mass demonstrations and to demand more substantial changes. The social-liberal coalition under Willy Brandt responded to this challenge with the call "to dare more democracy," which promised internal reform. When welfare state expansion failed to address problems such as the environment, critical spirits founded a series of new social movements during the 1970s.[78] Propelled by the postwar cohort, these successive pressures managed to reform and broaden a reluctant FRG.

The surprising overthrow of the SED dictatorship in 1989 seemed to confirm the West German choice of liberal democracy and market economy. Most Westerners had little interest in the GDR, unless they had fled from there or still had relatives on the other side of the Iron Curtain. The Ministry of All-German Affairs continued to sponsor school trips to Berlin, while the June 17 holiday commemoration of the GDR uprising reminded the FRG citizens rhetorically of their less-fortunate "brothers and sisters in the East." But the gap between the two successor states had grown so wide that Westerners could merely observe the mass exodus, growth of demonstrations, and fall of the Wall with sympathetic interest. Only when Eastern relatives in their unfashionable clothes and funny cars arrived on their doorsteps did they have to confront the enormous task of reunification. Pondering the GDR's lack of success, Horst Grothus concluded, "Socialism has always failed, since it contradicts more important needs of human beings, which appear to be better satisfied in other social systems."[79]

SUCCESS STORIES

When reflecting on their adult lives, most memoirists have represented their experiences as a successful mastery of difficult challenges. Some ceased reporting with the postwar years, when their life lost its drama and normalized, "which is the reason why it is not worth writing about." Those who continued their story through the subsequent decades emphasized the contrast between their war-induced struggles for survival and their increasing postwar success. "When I looked back on the years that went by since the end of the war," Hans Tausch reminisced, "I had to admit that many things turned out to be better than I had dared to expect." Due to the division of labor, the narratives are once again gendered, with men emphasizing their professional advancement and increasing prosperity and women their families and personal happiness. While most of the accounts ignore politics, they implicitly concede that West Germany's "free democratic order" created a supportive framework for their professional achievements and private satisfaction.[80]

Male writers have portrayed their career success as a product of hard work, intellectual acuity, and ability to seize an opportunity. The autobiographies are full of outward indicators that signal professional achievement. Some authors, such as Horst Andrée, stressed their advancement through the ranks to positions of influence. Others, like Gerhard Baucke, emphasized increasing prosperity, commenting that "it was almost scary how fortune was spoiling me." Still others, including Robert Neumaier, reported on the positive reception of their books and articles. Consultants such as Horst Grothus described their international travels so as to demonstrate the popularity of their work. Almost all of them, like Hellmut Raschdorff, wrote about building houses, buying cars, and taking exciting vacations. Reaffirming the credo of the Economic Miracle, these narratives follow a plotline of great effort and intense struggle that rewarded the authors with their subsequent prosperity. The common tenor of these retrospectives is gratitude for "the great richness of my life to this point."[81]

Accounts by female authors follow a different pattern that is centered on family and personal relationships. Some writers, including Edith Schöffski, described work outside the home with pride in their competence. Others reported resenting being confined to the domestic sphere and then engaging in charitable work, like Gisela Grothus. But all wrote extensively about their parents and siblings, first describing how they emancipated themselves from their tutelage and later also reflecting on how they took care of their failing health. Most of these narratives focus on the task of finding the right partner, which was not at all easy, as Ursula Baehrenburg found out, for she wanted more than a physical relationship. The narrators described their marriages in great detail and reported with much satisfaction on the growth of their children. Of course, men also mentioned their personal relations and gratitude for the appropriate spouses. But it was women such as Anneliese Huber who articulated the maternalist message: "My happiness was solely the joy of a love fulfilled."[82]

This private perspective portrays the democratization of West Germany as an inadvertent process that grew only gradually out of positive personal experiences. At first, the surviving democrats had to battle widespread skepticism, withdrawal from politics, and remnants of Nazi ideology. The often-clumsy efforts at Allied reorientation produced a backlash among some of the defeated, making them unwilling to admit their responsibility. But a consensus that the Third Reich had been an abject failure, that war was to be avoided in the future, and that the Communist alternative remained inacceptable helped the new beginning. Only a minority were, like Günther Hagemann, willing to join political parties, even if most behaved like model democrats. The decisive factor in the long run was rather the stable space the FRG offered for professional development and private growth. In contrast to the dictatorships, the Bonn Republic provided a supportive environment. As Ruth Weigelt explained, "We were free, could make our own decisions, lived in a democracy, everything was well ordered and nobody (hardly anyone) was disadvantaged."[83]

Reaching maturity also involved a constant effort to come to terms with the disturbing memories of an unmasterable German past. "What we did to each other as members of our nations and as soldiers, is unbelievable for normal people under regular circumstances," Hans-Harald Schirmer summarized: "Both undemocratic and inhumane, German and Soviet dictatorships have created the preconditions for this human degeneracy with their ideological suppression of the individual." Haunted by the Nazi crimes of their youth, many Germans could no longer develop "an unselfconscious relationship to the notions of patriotism and nation." Carola Stern reflected on the continued irritation by the past that her generation has "become skeptical of promises of salvation." Because so many people had lost their lives through politics, she believed "the only yardstick for political action . . . is the respect for human life." Günter Krause concluded similarly, "I have experienced both highs and lows, the Nazi dictatorship, the terrible war and Communism, but the freedom of a democracy is the best, even if it is also a difficult time."[84]

9

COMMUNIST DISAPPOINTMENT

On July 5, 1945, Germany's surviving Communists held their first public meeting in Leipzig after the arrival of the Red Army. It was an "unforgettable reunion." People who were thought missing or dead hugged each other and could not believe "you are alive, comrade!" Many had aged by decades in the Nazi prisons, their hollow faces deeply lined and their eyes protruding. Some still wore their striped KZ garb and caps, which hung from their emaciated bodies. "There was nobody who did not have tears in his eyes." Even those who had survived torture were moved when recalling friends who could not be saved. Writer Bruno Apitz recited the Buchenwald poem: "They have driven us through mud and death / they have stomped and spit upon us / they have ground us down and crushed us / in winter's ice and summer's heat." Elated survivors marveled, "What a triumph it is to be alive at this hour!"[1] With the help of the Soviet Union, this so-called "founding generation" (*Aufbaugeneration*) of young adults set out to shape a better future with equality and justice for all.

Forty-five years later, this socialist dream lay shattered. Its incarnation, the German Democratic Republic, was foundering because it had disappointed too many of its citizens. The ex-dictator Erich Honecker was hospitalized in the Charite, the prestigious East Berlin clinic. For the visiting pastor Werner Braune, "it was a unique experience to see the once most powerful man of the GDR old and in pajamas. His health was bad. For the second time, he had been operated on for a malign tumor." Yet Honecker still believed "socialism was an excellent idea in principle . . . only the new comrades in power who had gotten rid of him were bad people." His physician, Professor Althaus, commented, "He has not yet understood that he has lost." Evicted from his Wandlitz villa, Honecker was repudiated by his former followers who were trying to save their own skins. Ironically, he had to ask for asylum from the very institution against which he had fought—the Protestant Church.[2] As a humanitarian gesture, Pastor Uwe Holmer took him in until he left for the Soviet Union.

People's opinions of the GDR's character are deeply divided according to their differing ideologies, experiences, and legacies. For supporters of the socialist experiment, such as Fritz Klein, the world wars and Nazi crimes were so heinous as to make it necessary "to choose that model of society which offered the prospect of overcoming the old order with its program and implementation." But for Günter Krause and other victims of the SED regime, East Germany was an "illegitimate state" (*Unrechtsstaat*) without human rights, in which the Communist Party and its secret service, the notorious Stasi, suppressed its citizens arbitrarily and illegally. Most East Germans, like physician Klaus Hübschmann, tried to live a "normal life" between these extremes, for they appreciated the anti-Fascist commitment and social benefits of the regime, but they were frustrated by the narrow-mindedness of the party bureaucrats and resented the lower standard of living compared to the West.[3] As a result of contrasting experiences, interpretations of the GDR remain bitterly contested to this day.

At the core of the dispute about the SED system are contradictory notions of "democracy," toward which all victors at the Potsdam Conference had agreed to work. For Communist supporters such as Werner Feigel, the "dictatorship of the proletariat" was necessary since it "was directed against the exploiters," acting in a Rousseauian sense "for the people." Concretely that view legitimized the rule of the SED as "vanguard party," which one had to approach submissively with petitions so as to "participate in the formation of the socialist order." For Western-style democrats such as Paul Frenzel, democracy meant observing civil rights such as freedom of speech, constituting legal safeguards according to Montesquieu's notion of a division of power. Frenzel was utterly shocked when a Stasi member told him how to supervise an election by voting in public and falsifying the result in private with extra ballots in order to approve "the anti-Fascist-democratic order."[4] Though both sides used the same term, they meant quite different things by it.

The asymmetrical effect of division on East Germany has politicized GDR life stories more strongly than narratives of the West. During the Cold War, the Germans found themselves on the fault line between the two opposing blocs of NATO and the Warsaw Pact, in which "armed military formations of immense size confronted each other in a terrible reality." While "the West clothed its ideology in the exercise of rights, the East saw its role as proclaiming slogans of peace." Horst Johannsen recalled the ensuing process of alienation between the sides: "Due to the differing social and living conditions, there were no longer similar forms of action and concepts in the East and West," which resulted in even the common language being divided. "Though people struggled in many ways against this development, they could not escape their dependence on the state."[5] Whereas FRG memoirists enjoyed the luxury of focusing on their private lives, the memoirists of the smaller and less legitimate GDR continually had to confront intrusive SED policies.

SOCIALIST HOPES

Idealist supporters considered the German Democratic Republic "the better Germany" because its socialism tried to realize "the dream of a just society" and of living in peace. The East German leadership drew upon the long-held Marxist traditions of the radical wing of the labor movement in striving for greater equality. At the same time, the Communists claimed the mantle of anti-Fascism because they had resisted the Nazi tyranny more consistently than any other party. As junior partner of the mighty Soviet Union, they vicariously adopted the Bolshevik Revolution and shared in the victory of the Red Army according to the slogan "To learn from the Soviet Union is to learn how to be victorious." By contrast, the Federal Republic's claim to be the successor state of the Third Reich and the considerable continuity of personnel laid the Bonn government open to charges of neo-Nazism. Searching for "a just, harmonious, as well as peaceful society" Gerhard Joachim therefore "quite consciously chose Socialism . . . and logically joined the party."[6]

The appeal of this "grand vision" for the Weimar cohort was, however, somewhat undercut by the nature of the Soviet occupation, which hindered its implementation. The "brutal encroachments of members of the Red Army" so alienated German civilians that the Russian soldiers had to be segregated in their own bases. Though economic exploitation through dismantling factories and exacting reparations was understandable as compensation for Wehrmacht destruction, it shocked even workers who were fascinated by the Soviet experiment. Moreover, the Soviet secret service (NKVD) frightened the populace by engaging in "a new wave of arrests and secret incarceration" in special camps without legal recourse. At the same time, the Stalinist political style according to Walter Ulbricht's motto "it must look democratic, but we have to control everything" disillusioned bourgeois collaborators.[7] Even the Soviet officers' impressive support of a cultural rebirth and their occasional personal conviviality could not make up for such negative impressions.

To obtain a pliant tool for the social revolution, the German Communist Party (KPD) pressured the more moderate Social Democrats (SPD) to join them in a common workers' party in the spring of 1946. Many workers welcomed this effort, which promised to overcome the split of the labor movement that had opened the door for Hitler's seizure of power. Some SPD members were therefore willing to follow this invitation in order to create a "common anti-Fascist front" that would be strong enough to prevent a revival of Nazism and create a better socialist society. But the veteran West German leader Kurt Schumacher resolutely opposed the merger: he considered the KPD undemocratic. This inspired most of the SPD members to reject the offer in the West, while the Communists often used force in order to squelch resistance in the East. Apologists such as Günter Manz still claim that "the concept of compulsory merger does not dovetail with the facts." But for critics such as Albert Leithold, "the dictatorship of the proletariat turned out to be the oligarchy of a bloody-minded clique of functionaries."[8]

The social transformation of East Germany began with the structural approach to denazification that punished whole strata in order to establish the rule of "the working people." Not really interested in individual guilt as in the West, the SED used plebiscites "to dispossess the monopolies, big capitalists and nobles which had always started, financed and profited from wars, creating a peoples' property for the first time in Germany." Concretely that meant taking factories, banks, and large businesses away from their owners and turning them into "people's-owned enterprises" called VEB. In the countryside, a land reform "confiscated holdings of over 100 hectares" according to the slogan "Junkers' land into peasants' hand," creating many small farms. All teachers who had been Nazi members were summarily dismissed, "fueling an enormous demand for instructors," who often arrived without any training. While many dispossessed elites fled to West Germany, this upheaval opened new career doors for young socialists.[9]

The gradual establishment of state socialism required a complicated planning system to "control the commanding heights of the economy." Proud of the achievements of the successive Five Year Plans, the Soviet Military Administration in Germany (SMAD) officers insisted upon the practical adoption of their own ideological model. Its key point was the substitution of economic planning for market competition by ignoring cost and price relationships and giving political allocation decisions priority. During the initial rebuilding after the war, this system of policy decisions worked fairly well, since reconstruction of infrastructure, factories, and housing was labor-intensive and raw material–dependent. But in the long run, bypassing supply and demand fostered the establishment of a "bureaucratic apparatus which developed a certain life of its own remote from the realities." When "planning goals and numerical indicators alone governed the whole economy," the result was inefficiency and scarcity, disillusioning even engaged supporters of socialism.[10]

The increasing ideological and social division of Germany led eventually to the founding of an independent Eastern state called the German Democratic Republic. In the fall of 1949 pressure by German Communists finally overcame Stalin's hesitation over whether to prefer a united and neutralized Germany or a Soviet client state. With a "people's congress movement" that even gathered some support among workers in the Federal Republic, the Socialist Unity Party created a country of its own, still in the hope that the larger West would eventually follow its lead. To "young anti-Fascists" such as Gerhard Joachim, the returned resistance fighters served "as a moral legitimation for the new state against the old Germany, the FRG, so to speak the successor of the Third Reich." While "a large number of people were taken in by the new development," skeptics like Horst Johannsen understood that thereby "the SED took over unlimited power and opened the fatal path to that centralism" that established a new leftist dictatorship.[11]

The party's youth organization, the Free German Youth (FDJ), used many of the same methods as the HJ, albeit to instill a diametrically opposed ideology. While the uniforms and parades were similar, the emphasis on Marx, Lenin, Stalin, and the construction of "a new social order and future economic organization" were not. Many apolitical youths tried to ignore the ideological "red light radiation" in order to enjoy the FDJ hikes and dances. Policeman Werner Feigel just "felt good among the young friends." When belonging became compulsory for admission to higher education, Klaus Hübschmann and other 1920s children "eventually just became FDJ members." Gerhard Baucke was especially "interested in joining in" because the FDJ organ *Neues Leben* gave him a chance to publish some of his first poems and essays on the situation of the young, written "by me and about me." For Fritz Klein, membership was a deeply held intellectual conviction: "I wanted to join in what now had to be done."[12]

With many older men dead or incapacitated, collaboration with the SED opened unusual career opportunities for the Weimar cohort. If they were reliable "cadres," they could advance quickly by enrolling in correspondence courses or attending a party school. For instance, the working-class lad Werner Feigel joined the people's police to have a secure job and defend socialism against the class enemy. Having been trained in business, Paul Frenzel rapidly became head of a local bank and advanced to the central financial administration in East Berlin. Making just enough political compromises, Klaus Hübschmann used his intellectual ability to train as a pediatric physician and headed a children's clinic at a young age. After being sent to a party school, Gerhard Joachim became a cultural functionary in order "to participate in the democratic renewal of our culture." As one of the first German students to learn a Marxist interpretation of history, Fritz Klein was entrusted with the editorship of the leading professional journal while still in his thirties.[13]

During the initial years of the GDR, memoirs mention considerable resistance among those people who did "not want to become an accomplice of a despised political system." Paul Frenzel reported that old SPD members who vowed to prevent "the merger with the KPD" had to be forced to join or purged from the SED. Agitators, such as Horst Sindermann, the head of the party paper *Neues Deutschland*, were shouted down when they tried to explain the loss of the Eastern territories to an audience of refugees. When public protest became too dangerous, many people resorted to private grumbling among friends or making fun of Walter Ulbricht's Saxon accent. Quite harmless jokes about scarcity (such as "if you introduce socialism to Africa, the Sahara is going to run out of sand") already carried the risk of imprisonment. After the bourgeois parties had been cowed, specialists such as Klaus Hübschmann could only invoke professional competence or withdraw into private life. When all these stratagems failed, one might, like Karl Härtel and about three million others, flee to the West through the still-open border in Berlin.[14]

A central conflict involved the Protestant Church, the only quasi-public organization in the GDR that remained independent. While a militant minority of SED atheists hoped to get rid of religion entirely, many Protestants were conservative nationalists who wanted to maintain ties to the West, whose financial support they needed. The key battleground was youth. The party tried to convert the young to socialism through "youth consecration," a secular coming-of-age ceremony intended to replace religious confirmation. When the Church Youth fought back, the party forced the young to submit to its *Jugendweihe* as prerequisite of education. Pastor Werner Braune reported an endless stream of harassment, discrimination, and outright violence, insisting, "At no time did GDR leaders and the SED view the Church and Deaconry as partners." Since Lutheranism insisted on obeying the state, a sort of accommodation as "a church in socialism" was eventually reached, but on the ground, the battle remained unresolved.[15]

To win the class struggle, the SED launched a combination of repression and propaganda in order to convince its reluctant population. With printed media and radio, the party indoctrinated its own cadres so that they could "reeducate" the populace and "keep down" the overthrown capitalists. The key instrument of this reorientation program was the "people's police." Gerhard Joachim explained, "We were, so to speak, the eye that was watching everywhere." Werner Feigel saw the policemen (*Vopos*) as "working-class children who are responsible for the safety of the people." In practice, this meant fighting against the economic sabotage of the dispossessed owners as well as against efforts of subversion from their putative allies in the West. The people's police were tasked with "the complete control of all activities" and securing the "implementation of all legal orders." That meant a constant surveillance of public space and oftentimes even private homes.[16] Instituting a Stalinist dictatorship of the proletariat, the SED tried to convince the workers of Socialist superiority by building showy streets like the Stalinallee in Berlin (image 26).

Autobiographies also show that the unfortunate individuals who were considered a serious threat faced massive retribution with methods reminiscent of Nazi brutality. While vigilance against Cold War enemies was understandable, the NKVD and Stasi operated unpredictably and without legal restraint. In April 1946 Günter Krause was arrested by the Soviet police for having distributed a flyer that promised that Germans would one day return to Silesia from where his family had been expelled. After escaping, he was caught again and was told, "Why you flee, we now shoot you!? [*sic*]" Krause was accused of spying and beaten with clubs until he finally signed a confession—in Russian. In a sham trial without defense he was condemned to ten years of hard labor for spreading "anti-Soviet propaganda." Thereafter he was sent to the *Spezlager* in Sachsenhausen on the grounds of the former

26. East Berlin Stalinallee. *Source*: Kempowski photo collection.

Nazi concentration camp. Starving, freezing, and working hard, he fell ill several times. After five years he was released, weighing only eighty pounds and sworn to silence.[17] Fear was a constant companion in the early GDR.

To counter the influence of the "decadent, capitalist entertainment industry," the SED attempted to offer an attractive "cultural life" that combined "amusement with cultivation." In the first postwar years the FDJ revived dances and shows in villages and towns. In the cities, intellectuals such as Fritz Klein participated in "anti-Fascist democratic" lectures and discussions of leading authors and cultural critics, organized by the League of Culture (Kulturbund). But the core of the party's effort was to bring culture to the toiling masses in the factories through "the Bitterfeld way," which encouraged workers to take up writing and acting themselves. In the clubhouse of the Warnow shipyard in Rostock, Gerhard Joachim sponsored a diverse set of entertainers' shows, proletarian plays, writing circles, dancing groups, and even dialect discussions. While some of these productions were stylistically innovative, they were ultimately constrained by the petit-bourgeois taste of "socialist realism" emanating from a Stalinist Soviet Union.[18]

Another SED effort to strengthen links to Russia was the Society for German-Soviet Friendship (DSF), which brought Red Army officers together with German civilians. In part, this initiative tried to overcome negative stereotypes by demonstrating the "deep humanity" of the Russians; in part it also tried to show "gratitude to the Soviet Union for having liberated us from the Hitler gang and ended the war." Beyond cultural lectures, there were banquets to celebrate various Soviet holidays such as the anniversary of the October Revolution with copious food and endless toasts with vodka. Delegation voyages and holiday trips to the Soviet Union were special rewards that let awed visitors admire the shining Moscow subway or enjoy the beaches at the Crimea. For Werner Feigel's daughter, the encounter was so impressive that she ended up marrying a Tartar from the south of Russia. While some scientists were willing to work with the Soviets, many citizens remained skeptical, viewing a DSF membership as merely a lesser evil.[19]

In the GDR, education was a potent weapon in the class struggle. The old elite were excluded and those who advanced were the children of workers and peasants. The SED tried to reach the labor movement aim of "breaking the privilege of cultivation" through polytechnical training combining school and work. On the one hand, the party discriminated against the offspring of professionals, only allowing them advanced training in cases of exceptional talent. On the other, it pushed children from uneducated families into continued education, offering them upward mobility through additional qualification. Energetic youths such as Werner Feigel and Karl Härtel were encouraged to embark on correspondence courses, with the former earning a law diploma and the latter an engineering degree. Feigel complained, "These four and one half years of distance learning were a tough time, because all of that came on top of the hard work and overtime hours." By earning advanced degrees, Gerhard Joachim and Fritz Klein became grateful members of the new socialist elite.[20]

Professional advancement into higher echelons was strictly controlled by a "cadre system" that followed the Soviet pattern of personnel management.

Every prospect for an important job had a personal file in which evaluations of technical competence and political reliability decided upon the course of his or her career. Gerhard Joachim recalled that cadres were not only the party functionaries who "were recorded as SED-*nomenklatura*," but also occupants of "key positions in all social areas," which gave the SED complete control. Candidates for advancement like Paul Frenzel had to undergo "cadre conversations" with party managers that covered everything from their ability to meet the demands of their new jobs to their "ideological weaknesses," which they had to remedy through Marxist study. Only in areas like medicine or engineering where performance really mattered would competence be allowed to prevail. Werner Feigel and other conformists were rewarded with prizes, premiums, vacations, and cars—allowing them to enjoy a good life GDR style.[21]

According to many recollections, the massive politicization of the GDR as a "thoroughly ruled society" made private life even more important than in the West. Surprisingly enough, the bourgeois family pattern continued with only minor modifications. When his girlfriend told Klaus Hübschmann that she was pregnant, he immediately married her: "That was the custom even among students, there was no flinching or hesitation." Because Communists were supposed to obey the dictates of "socialist morality," established by Walter Ulbricht, those offenders "caught in sex adventures with female students" were subject "to discipline and party punishment." Due to meager pay it went without saying that wives would continue to work, whether as teachers, like Erna Härtel, or party functionaries, like Feigel's spouse. When children arrived, the household and work burden on women usually doubled. Nonetheless, the memoirs describe the family as an almost sacred space of retreat from politics. Dissident Vera Lengsfeld's betrayal by her husband, who was a Stasi informer, was therefore especially shattering.[22]

Living in East Germany was also complicated by the comparison to the larger and more prosperous West; in fact, remaining there required constant justification. Officially West Germany was "NATO, imperialists, exploiters, enemies of workers, warmongers, speculators—in principle only evil things." Privately those East Germans like Horst Johannsen who traveled West before the building of the Wall were amazed: "At first blush the appearance of the western economy was akin to a fairy paradise compared to the conditions in the GDR." But on closer inspection, "the financial situation of some strata of the population was not so rosy." Most of the East Germans who were directly persecuted by the SED chose to leave for as long as they could. But others who had family, friends, possessions, and careers in the GDR, such as Paul Frenzel, were more reluctant to start over in the competitive West. While continually tempted to go, they nonetheless decided to stay, as Klaus Hübschmann did, and devoted their energies to making a meaningful life in the East.[23]

Aware of widespread resentment against it, the SED made strenuous efforts to establish political uniformity in order to impose its will on a reluctant populace. Merging Communists and Social Democrats into a single working class party had been complicated enough, for the former understood itself as a revolutionary vanguard while the latter emphasized intraparty democracy. Using the cadre system as an instrument and unleashing repeated purges of the membership, the Communists pushed most of the Social Democrats like Paul Frenzel aside in order to assert their own control. Moreover, Stalin's rejection of Anton Ackermann's proposal of "a German path toward socialism" created deep cleavages within the SED by compelling the party to follow the Soviet lead. Time and again moderates such as agronomist Heinrich Buschmann lost leading positions, accused of "a lack of partisanship and objectivism." Even socialist idealists admitted in retrospect that as a result of the suppression of "free exchange of opinions," the party became progressively Stalinized.[24]

The popular uprising on June 17, 1953 came as a rude surprise because the SED had lost touch with the actual lives of the working masses. When the party raised production targets by 10 to 20 percent, angered construction workers in Berlin went out on strike, calling for their revocation. When the news was spread by Western radio stations, popular resentment exploded all over the GDR, with demands escalating from economic reforms to the overthrow of the dictatorship and German reunification: "The goatee [Walter Ulbricht] must go!" Incensed demonstrators ripped off Paul Frenzel's party badge and demanded, "the mismanagement in the East must cease." Shocked functionaries like Karl Mewis blamed "the putsch on counterrevolutionary forces, in part directed by the West," who had misled "honest workers." More thoughtful commentators such as Günter Manz were willing to admit that it was the Politburo's fault. But after Russian tanks quickly restored order, the party leadership had to make only minimal concessions to remain in control. Leithold recalled that "gradually quiet returned. The people knuckled under."[25]

Instead of democratizing East German socialism, the 1956 upheavals further cemented the dictatorial course of the SED. When Russian premier Nikita Khrushchev accused his predecessor of atrocities and corruption during the twentieth congress of the Communist Party of the Soviet Union, Ulbricht was willing only to denounce excesses of Stalin's "cult of personality" without really liberalizing the system. The Polish disturbances that brought Władysław Gomułka into power and the Hungarian Uprising in the fall that was put down with Russian tanks had the opposite effect in the GDR, inspiring the party to tighten political controls. Gerhard Joachim was disappointed that his wish for "a somewhat more liberal course of cultural policy" was largely ignored. Feeling doubly insecure, the SED leaders launched a massive campaign against all kinds of "revisionism" by Communist intellectuals such as Wolfgang Harich and Walter Janka, eliminating any potential rivals. As a result, historian Fritz Klein lost the editorship of the *Zeitschrift für Geschichtswissenschaft*.[26]

In the late fifties the SED leaders used a combination of repression and incentives to retain their hold on power. Under Erich Mielke's guidance, the secret police expanded surveillance, while the people's police added a new kind of "community policeman" to keep better tabs on popular opinion. Independent socialist intellectuals such as Gerhard Joachim were "relegated to production for a couple of years" so that they would rehabilitate themselves through physical labor, and Fritz Klein was removed to the Academy of Sciences to do academic research. Mortally afraid of autonomous social initiatives, the SED "handed over practically all of public life to the mass organizations" to which citizens had to belong in order to prove their reliability. Horst Johannsen explained, "Through dependence on job, position, and rank, through wishes for career, advancement, training and entitlement, everything was directed according to the official views." This process established "an arrogant, undemocratic rule by functionaries" of the SED.[27]

For many East Germans, "the growth of such an unlimited dictatorship and its consequences were no longer tolerable." Horst Johannsen recalled that the departure of dispossessed business owners, independent professionals, collectivized farmers, church members, and union activists "resembled a mass flight" to the West. Many a valued colleague disappeared overnight only to resurface in the Federal Republic. Karl and Erna Härtel waited until he had finished his studies and then systematically prepared for their escape. First Erna went to her sister-in-law in the Rhineland to scout the terrain. Then they mailed their possessions in sixteen boxes across the Iron Curtain. Caught during an attempt to go to a Catholic convention in West Berlin, Karl managed to obtain another identity card needed for travel. After he received his degree in 1959, the Härtels finally used the Pentecost holidays to take separate trains to Berlin. She was detained for twelve hours, but in the end was released. Both were happy to be free in the West at last.[28]

East German memoirs show that the imposition of Communism was accompanied by a considerable degree of compulsory Sovietization that did not really fit the country. Some intellectuals genuinely admired the creativity of Russian writers and composers and joined the Society for German-Soviet Friendship. Many World War II veterans were impressed by the inexhaustible manpower of the Red Army that had defeated them and were happy to have such a powerful protector. Party functionaries also looked to the Soviet version of Marxism/Leninism for inspiration in their own effort to create a "workers' and peasants' state." The SED leaders in particular paid eager attention to Moscow so as to follow the correct party line for their own survival. But other East Germans resented the military occupation, the loss of the Eastern provinces, and the economic exploitation. Students who were supposed to learn Russian in school showed “open distaste for the language.”[29] Hence the relationship with their so-called friends remained quite equivocal.

ABNORMAL NORMALITY

In time, the “real existing socialism” that had initially seemed abnormal became the new normality of the Weimar cohort’s adult lives. Once established, the state factories, collective farms, polytechnic schools, and prefabricated housing developments became the framework for daily existence. Although they had to deal with Soviet domination, SED dictatorship, and annoying scarcity, residents could nonetheless take pride in the GDR’s social equality, anti-Fascist commitment, and Marxist ideology. SED propaganda hammered at the expropriation of capitalists, heroism of the resistance, and certainty of progress. But even despite such heavy-handed politicization, it was possible for those who succeeded in coping with the system to “live a wonderful life” within it. Horst Johannsen explained that “in view of the unstoppable progress of socialism, one was well advised to go along, since any negative attitude was inevitably tracked down.” Many tasks that seemed easy in the West required a real struggle. Klaus Hübschmann was proud of his small triumphs: “Again we had succeeded in something even if it was only [making] marmalade.”[30]

Still, the GDR remained precarious as long as the exit door was open. Soviet leader Nikita Khrushchev tried to close it by turning Berlin into “a free city” without Allied troops in 1958. For ordinary East Germans, the Western sectors exerted a strange fascination, with their glitzy Kudamm shopping windows, subsidized movie theaters, and raucous rock concerts. For the party, “Westberlin” was the seat of capitalist corruption and decadence as well as of “numerous centers of espionage and terror”—in short, of promoting counterrevolution. As a result, the SED began a propaganda campaign to convince West Berliners to accept the Soviet ultimatum and neutralize their city. When he was sent to agitate from door to door and distribute flyers, Paul Frenzel had no luck at all. In spite of all disclaimers, Russian threats “spread the fear that ‘the free city’ would only be the beginning of the complete annexation of the West by the East.” This popular refusal

27. Building of the Wall. *Source*: Stiftung Preussischer Kulturbesitz.

opened his eyes to "how far the GDR fell short of the goal" of "overtaking the Western standard of living."[91]

The Berlin ultimatum and SED repression heightened popular worries about being trapped, prompting an increasing number of people to flee to the West. Part of the reason was the compulsory collectivization that converted farms into larger, machine-supported, and more efficient Agricultural Production Cooperatives (LPGs). Heinrich Buschmann described how many farmers left their family properties behind rather than be reduced to agricultural laborers. Another part was the blatant discrimination against churchgoers; Youth Consecration was made mandatory to indoctrinate teenagers in the "methods of class struggle." Yet another was the unremittent pressure on the independence of professionals that prompted "over 3,300 doctors, about 16,700 teachers and ca. 17,000 engineers" to leave for the West. According to Horst Johannsen, "hardly a day passed in which a position did not go empty overnight." When more than two thousand East Germans fled each day, the mass exodus threatened to depopulate the GDR.[32]

A panic-stricken SED leadership therefore finally persuaded Khrushchev to authorize the "preposterous operation" of building a wall that would cut off West Berlin from the eastern part of the city. Ulbricht's logic was quite simple: "We must immediately plug the escape routes to West Berlin—with guards of the border police, perhaps with barbed wire." On Sunday night, August 13, 1961, four NVA divisions moved into Berlin, twenty Red Army divisions stood in readiness, and twenty-five thousand factory militiamen supported the sealing of the border. News photos show eager border guards supervising its construction (image 27). Asleep in a Brandenburg FDJ camp, student Gabriel Berger suddenly woke up to "a roaring in the air" that could only come from tanks. Someone turned on a Western RIAS radio, on which an announcer reported "with an excited voice, that GDR troops had closed all border crossing points from East to West. . . . The purpose of the GDR leadership was evidently to prevent the mass flight of the Easterners to the West by force." To a shocked FDJ eyewitness, the border closing was "a scenario of total military dictatorship."[33]

The SED had a difficult time explaining the building of the Wall as an "anti-Fascist protection barrier" for self-defense. The official version stressed, "To interdict enemy actions of the revanchist and militarist forces in West Germany and West Berlin such a control of the GDR borders has been introduced as is customary at the frontier of every sovereign state." Convinced Communists such as Gabriel Berger sought to justify the action: "We may not like what is going on in Berlin, but it is happening out of necessity. Or do you think that any state in the world would passively look on as it bled white without fighting back?" Some ordinary people away on summer holiday realized only gradually that they had, in fact, been imprisoned by their own government. Many intellectuals "voiced a certain degree of understanding that a situation had been ended which could not continue in that manner" without resulting in bloodshed. Unwilling to abandon the socialist experiment, Fritz Klein, an SED member, justified the Wall "as the lesser evil."[34]

Many memoirs indicate that the political effect of shutting the last escape route to the West was quite paradoxical. In the short run, the Wall helped stabilize the GDR by forcing its citizens and the international community to accept the permanence of the German division. Now the East German state was here to stay. Though initially somewhat successful, people's efforts to escape by jumping out of windows, digging tunnels, hiding in hollowed-out car seats, and swimming through canals only led to the state's perfection of the Wall by raising its height, creating a "death strip," and emptying out a restricted zone behind it. The party quickly suppressed spontaneous shouts of protests such as "SED, no way!" with the persecution of hundreds of culprits and countless propaganda sessions. But in the long run, the Wall was a public relations disaster for the GDR. Approximately 138 East Germans died while trying to cross it in Berlin. Harrowing news pictures were sent around the world, such as when would-be escapee Peter Fechter bled to death without help.[35] Ultimately the Wall became a symbol of Communist repression that invited incessant criticism from abroad.

Protected by the Wall, Walter Ulbricht could experiment with the transition to socialism by tightening control in some areas and relaxing pressure in others. Gerhard Joachim considered the SED general secretary a "labor functionary steeled in revolutionary struggle" and an "ice-cold dictator" who had survived the Stalinist purges in Moscow. Personally modest, Ulbricht proclaimed a "socialist human community" to indicate "a historically new political-moral and intellectual-cultural quality of living and working together in GDR socialism." In practice, that meant introducing elements of competition and cost pricing in a New Economic System of Economic Planning and Direction (NÖSPL) in 1964 in order to galvanize a stagnant economy. Fascinated by the potential of cybernetics to direct planning, Ulbricht promoted the "scientific-technical revolution," initiated by the transition to computers. But his campaign of "overtaking the West without catching up to it" failed due to the low productivity of the economy.[36]

In order to make the GDR a full-fledged member of the Warsaw Pact, Ulbricht also initiated an open militarization of East German society. Erich Hasemann described how special units of the "people's police" were transformed into a National People's Army (NVA) "tactically integrated into the fraternal alliance of the Eastern armies." After the building of the Wall, the SED could dare to impose military conscription on a reluctant population who did not really want to wear a uniform again. Although they were supported by some Protestant pastors, young men who refused service were punished by imprisonment until a compromise was worked out that allowed them to become "construction soldiers" without weapons. Fearing another counterrevolutionary putsch, the party also instituted "factory militias" in which able-bodied men were forced to serve. At the same time, it geared up military instruction in schools under the slogan "fighting for peace." As a result, the militarized GDR was honeycombed with "countless installations" of the Red Army and NVA.[37]

By contrast, cultural life behind the Wall was somewhat less constrained. The party allowed creative spirits more latitude to push the limits of what was permitted. In spite of the firm Stalinist limits set by doctrinaire apparatchiks, the Kulturbund continued to be a place to meet "interesting people" for "anti-Fascist democratic" intellectuals such as Fritz Klein. "Here we could really discuss pro and contra in the true sense of the word," because all participants were in agreement about striving for a better socialism. While independent spirits such as Gerhard Joachim loved to provoke audiences with shocking plays, these time and again ran into censorship by narrow-minded functionaries who imposed a restrictive party line. Much of the factory-level cultural production consisted of shallow popular entertainment and was stultifying. Horst Johannsen resented the compulsory "integration of the private sphere into the social puppet show," since "personal freedom gradually collapsed entirely under the rule of the dogmatists."[38]

In spite of its difficult starting conditions, the GDR economy made gradual progress in achieving a smaller but nevertheless impressive miracle of its own. Wits in neighboring countries quipped that if anyone could make socialism work, it would be the Germans. After the rebuilding, the planned economy targeted priorities such as "the extension of chemical industry . . . metallurgy, electronics, machine building," and so on. The Five-Year Plans created a series "of economically important industrial sites" such as the chemical complex at Leuna, the Wismut uranium mines, the Lübbenau power station, Brandenburg's metal industry, and car production in Eisenach. In such "socialist model cities" as Eisenhüttenstadt, Marxist planners created new kinds of communities that combined industrial work with improved housing and socialized public space. Working in Leuna, Horst Johannsen was impressed that "the capacity and effectiveness of the GDR developed astonishingly well in spite of many counterproductive practices." Yet, the Eastern economy never quite overcame its "scientific-technological backwardness."[39]

For consumers, East Germany nonetheless remained a "scarcity economy," characterized by bottlenecks and standing in line to acquire coveted goods. When she was reassigned to work in an industrial plant, Werner Feigel's wife was shocked: "The discussions among the workers, but also in the party meetings, revolved solely around deficits in production and provision." When Pastor Braune wanted to improve facilities for the handicapped, he first had to search far and wide until he found the right electrical water pump; moreover, his church had to patch together a transformer station, which the town then shared. While trying to repair his house, Klaus Hübschmann time and again had to trade one rare item for another in order to get hold of a third. Compared to the West, durables such as refrigerators, TV sets, and cars arrived years later, were of inferior quality, and often looked ugly. Neither dryers nor dishwashers existed, and home computers were years behind. The difference between a plastic Trabi and a shiny VW Rabbit was startling. Because the economy was unable to provide the right kinds of consumer goods, individuals constantly had to improvise.[40]

Those East Germans who agreed with the socialist vision but were frustrated by its practice experienced the failure of the Czech attempt at liberalization in the summer of 1968 as a major disappointment. To reform the economy by reintroducing market incentives, Slovak party chief Alexander Dubček lifted censorship and allowed free speech, hoping to create "socialism with a human face." After the Prague Spring inspired "great hopes," its crushing was all the more devastating. On a visit to the Czech capital, Günter Manz witnessed "trucks with demonstrators driving through the streets, women crying in front of shops, closed gas stations and an explosive mood." The brutal "suppression by Soviet tanks and the public suicide of the student Jan Palach" made it all too clear that orthodox Communists would not allow the system to be democratized from within. Mortally afraid that something similar would happen in the GDR, the SED vigorously suppressed all protests among intellectuals and students. Though it retained power, the regime thereby proved to be unreformable.[41]

To forestall unrest in East Germany, its new leader, Erich Honecker, offered a paradoxical mixture of Communist orthodoxy and consumer economy. With Soviet help, he had pushed aside the aging Ulbricht in 1971 by accusing him of economic and diplomatic deviation from the party line. In contrast to the Great Depression, Honecker claimed that the GDR had become "a developed socialist society" in order to indicate that it had reached a new and higher stage of development. As a kind of socialist Keynesianism, "the unity of economic and social policy" would improve economic productivity through the provision of more attractive consumer goods. In a grand bargain, the SED would provide an improved standard of living in exchange for the political acquiescence of the population. Gerhard Joachim was glad to use the greater freedom for "a happy synthesis of entertainment, cultivation, and sociability." But all too soon he found out that "real existing socialism" set clear limits on the public discussion of its shortcomings.[42]

West German *Ostpolitik*, switching from confrontation to accommodation to improve relations with its eastern neighbors, provided new opportunities and threats to the GDR in the early 1970s. As mayor of Berlin, foreign minister, and then chancellor, Willy Brandt had pursued a "policy of small steps" of limited negotiation with the SED in order to obtain "humanitarian relief" for the divided city. In exchange for hard-currency fees, a series of "crossing permit agreements" allowed West Berliners to visit their relatives in the East during the holidays, thereby providing a temporary passage through the Wall. More substantial was the Basic Treaty of 1972, which de facto recognized the GDR, although a supplementary letter stressed that the FRG retained its right to pursue German unification. As a result, both Germanys joined the United Nations and the Helsinki Declaration of 1975 reaffirmed the sanctity of the postwar borders in Europe.[43] While such recognition was a great short-term success for the SED, in the long run it also allowed the magnetism of the West to undermine its rule.

For ordinary folks, the turn to détente meant an increasing SED effort to stop such "aggression in slippers" by painting the West as class enemy in a policy of demarcation. East Germans' letters were consistently opened and packages rifled, with forbidden goods then sold in shops for the secret service. Though about half a dozen cross-border telephone lines were switched on, East-West calls were monitored and taped in order to gather evidence of subversion. Once TV sets became available to the general public, FDJ groups tried to tear down antennas that could receive Western programs—only to be foiled by the passive resistance of viewers "who started to mount replacements under the roof." Travel to the West was allowed only for the retired ("*erst vergreisen, dann verreisen*") or for especially trustworthy members of the party, the so-called travel cadres (*Reisekader*). Allowing coveted Western goods such as coffee, chocolate, and alcohol to be sold in hard-currency Intershops ultimately reinforced the popular conviction that Western wares were superior.[44]

Fear of Western subversion also inspired a rapid expansion of the Ministry of State Security (MfS), known colloquially as the Stasi. Established as a separate ministry in 1957, this "sword and shield of the party" was led for decades by Red Front fighter Erich Mielke. In order to have complete control over the population, the Stasi created a vast network of formal spies and informal informants (IM) in all parts of society. Even the well-known historian Fritz Klein was persuaded to write reports about his foreign travels and contacts with Westerners. He admitted, "I agreed—without feeling pressured." Moreover, the MfS insisted on keeping GDR problems secret. When Paul Frenzel called the exchange of banknotes in 1957 a "complete fiasco" he got into trouble, for "divulging of secrets" was punishable by up to fifteen years' imprisonment. It was "clear that we were under permanent observation and had to take that into account in our political statements." But Klaus Hübschmann shrugged off this surveillance, believing that "the outsized apparatus" choked on its own information.[45]

Academic autobiographies reveal that even scholarship was supposed to participate in the class struggle against the capitalist West. Not only was there no academic freedom, but research materials such as computers were inferior and access to Western literature restricted. For natural scientists and physicians such as Klaus Hübschmann, "politics played no role"; lip service to Marxism sufficed and ideology did not touch upon their cognitive core. But according to Fritz Klein, "historians were exposed to an incomparably greater pressure to conform to the party line than in earlier periods" due to the SED's monopoly of interpretation. Economists such as Paul Frenzel faced ever-stronger demands "to support the demarcation policy of the party" by demonstrating to students "the inevitability of the 'defeat of imperialism' and the 'global victory of socialism'" with concrete examples. In disciplines such as philosophy, where Marxism/Leninism itself was supposed to provide the answers, research was severely compromised by having to follow ideological dictates.[46]

The enormous pressure to exhibit conformity led to the widespread practice of "split thinking" and doubletalk in the populace. Because access to education or career advancement depended upon public declarations of loyalty, it was necessary to mouth the shifting ideological vocabulary. But one's personal integrity also required keeping a critical distance from the regime, which could be voiced only in one's own family or with close friends. Paul Frenzel noticed the clash between "expressions of thought that conformed with the party or state on the one hand and maintaining a personal, independent way of thinking as 'private individual'" on the other. The critical loyalist Fritz Klein concluded that "this way of reasoning led into a trap, which I did not see clearly enough for a long time." Supporting the basis of the regime while trying to reform its imperfections "created an inner contradiction," because in case of doubt it required defending the SED in spite of "the reform-resistant pursuit of power and violence of its rulers."[47]

Proof of the improvement of living standards was the easing of the housing shortage with prefabricated buildings that created satellite cities such as Halle-Neustadt and Marzahn in East Berlin. During the postwar chaos, people were happy just to have roofs over their heads, even if they lived in close quarters without hot water, central heating, or toilets. But reconstruction efforts slowly allowed the Weimar cohort to move into more comfortable surroundings. Horst Johannsen was glad to "receive a company apartment at the edge of town, about which we were enthusiastic due to its quiet location in nature." In order to provide attractive housing, Honecker launched a massive construction program of prefabricated concrete flats (*Plattenbauten*) that were easy to assemble and cheap to build. Though their space was still limited to about seventy square meters, these apartments were popular due to their modern kitchens, new bathrooms, and central heating.[48] Only in the 1980s did attention shift to the rehabilitation of historic quarters in the city center and rescuing more interesting older buildings from deterioration.

The public pressure of politics made a retreat into the private world of leisure all the more important in the GDR. Its primary symbol was the weekend home, called *Datsche* according to its Russian model. It took little money to rent a space in a permanent campground along the shore of one of Brandenburg's or Mecklenburg's many lakes. More fortunate folks might have access to a set of company-sponsored cabins at the water's edge. But everyone really wanted to own a simple cottage in the woods in order to get away during weekends and holidays. Considering that supplies were scarce and state-controlled, it was amazing to see that "tens of thousands [of units] were built annually" from the beginning of the 1970s on with materials diverted from somewhere else. Klaus Hübschmann was fortunate enough to buy a derelict farmhouse on the island of Rügen for a pittance, turning it into "a comfortable home" with years of labor. "Each time it was a terrific feeling when we said: we are going to Polchow."[49]

Because motorization came late to the GDR, it was a special pleasure to get a car of one's own at last. The heavily subsidized public transit system made it unnecessary to have an automobile except when one's profession, such as as country doctor or pastor, required it. Developed out of the prewar designs of Auto Union, two types of car were produced in the GDR, the somewhat large Wartburg sedans and the smaller Trabants, encased in a plastic body. Using two-stroke engines in which gas and oil were mixed, these cars provided basic transportation but no luxury. For this purpose, the party nomenklatura imported Volvos from Sweden. Horst Johannsen and other private citizens without connections had to wait an average of ten years between placing an order and delivery. This created a booming used car and parts market. The only way to circumvent this bottleneck was to receive an automobile as a gift from Western relatives, as Klaus Hübschmann did. "One day a VW actually stood in front of my door!"[50]

Another prized goal was the assignment of a coveted vacation space by the trade union secretary. The Free German Trade Union (FDGB) controlled all public holiday facilities from the Baltic shores to the mountains of Thuringia and used them as rewards for its activists. Because "the prices were quite cheap, this was a popular achievement, which benefited its members." The only problem was that demand vastly exceeded supply. As a result, Horst Johannsen chose the less-popular winter vacations for years before daring to ask for a summer space at the Baltic. "Quite impressed by the view of the sea, we quickly forgot our tiredness and from the first hour on got into the mood for a beautiful holiday." Higher party cadres such as Werner Feigel were rewarded with trips to the warm beaches of Bulgaria or the cooler coast of the Baltic outside of Leningrad, where they admired the rebuilding and the cultural heritage "of the Venice of the North." Only people with more resources or better connections managed to vacation in private quarters.[51]

Contrary to Communist egalitarianism, "a socialist class society" with a pronounced hierarchy of its own gradually developed. On top was the nomenklatura in the party, military, and secret police, which "arrogated to itself the capacity of alone deciding about the correct interpretation of the 'holy' writs of Marx, Engels, and Lenin." Below them ranked the holders of Western currency, because they could buy scarce goods in the Intershops or have them sent from abroad through a special company for buying presents with foreign currency (GENEX). Then came the skilled craftsmen such as electricians, plumbers, and carpenters, whose services were so sought after that they commanded a high price. In the working-class society of the GDR, laborers also earned as much money as the intelligentsia, which was only compensated for by higher retirement pay. Irrespective of socialist promises, there was also a large bottom layer of people left out of East German prosperity such as the retired, handicapped, asocial, or imprisoned.[52]

In spite of its leveling efforts, the GDR also retained some bourgeois remnants who presented a quandary for the SED. The "workers' and farmers' state" could not completely do away with the services of some groups that managed to maintain a degree of independence. One profession was the doctors, such as Klaus Hübschmann, for even Communists got sick and wanted the best treatment, irrespective of ideology. Engineers such as Karl Härtel also had some latitude, since in designing a bridge, safety considerations were more important than partisanship. Similarly, clergymen such as Werner Braune represented an alternative set of Christian values, while the Church claimed a public role irrespective of party directives. Though more easily influenced, writers, artists, and musicians such as Christa Wolf also had their own standards of creative excellence. Finally scholars such as Fritz Klein, who were dedicated to finding the truth, tended to conflict with assertions of the party line.[53] So, despite its public claims, SED control was never complete.

POPULAR DISENCHANTMENT

Just when the GDR seemed to be there to stay, the autobiographies report a widespread disillusionment that would eventually topple the SED from within. In his annual conversations with Leonid Brezhnev, Honecker proudly pointed to East Germany's international recognition as a separate state, to its athletic success, and to its economic progress. Even among senior members of the Communist Party, discontent began to grow when true believers such as Werner Feigel were put out to pasture for not following the latest shift in the SED line. Moreover, efforts to discipline intellectuals such as Gerhard Joachim for their sexual affairs or cultural experiments left deep scars. Sympathetic scholars such as Fritz Klein also began to long for "freer, less dogmatic thinking" that would allow greater scope in their research. Economic specialists such as Paul Frenzel who just wanted to do their jobs resented "being continually subjected to ideological conformity." Tired of future promises, the population at large simply wanted to gain a Western standard of living immediately.[54]

One social policy of which the SED was particularly proud was the greater equality of women in the GDR than in the Federal Republic. Seeking to realize this traditional aim of the labor movement, the GDR supported female education and employment to compensate for the labor shortage due to the mass exodus. A whole series of measures—state-run nurseries, after-school care, maternal leave, a monthly household day—tried to make it easier for women such as Dorle Klein to work outside of the home while at the same time having children. In spite of natalist concerns to keep up the birthrate and the objection of the churches, GDR women gained the right to abortion in the early 1970s. Moreover, divorce according to the no-fault principle made it easier to leave unsatisfactory relationships. While the SED opened traditionally male workplaces to women, patriarchal prejudices remained strong enough to retain a double burden and a socialist glass ceiling.[55]

All accounts agree that the Achilles' heel of the GDR proved to be the economy: the SED could not keep Marxist promises to outperform the decadent capitalist West. No doubt its starting conditions were more difficult due to Soviet exploitation and lack of raw materials. But the failure also had much to do with the dominance of an "oppressive party and state bureaucracy which considered itself the final authority." Ulbricht's effort to ignite greater growth through the introduction of some market elements was abandoned in 1971, as "allowing temporary disproportions" violated ideological purity. Horst Johannsen was appalled that no serious attempts were made "to counter the economic collapse that became ever more evident." Instead, "the rulers continued to brag about the successes of the first socialist state of workers and farmers on German soil."[56] Most people cared little for the theoretical debates about managing a planned economy. They were only interested in changing the result—a continual shortage of consumer goods.

The Soviet reduction of oil deliveries in the early 1980s as a result of OPEC's drastic price increase proved to be a fatal blow to the planned economy. The cut of two million tons annually was devastating for the GDR, which in the past had sold the surplus refined derivatives to the West so as to earn hard currency. As an alternate energy source, the SED shifted to lignite, which contained more sulfate and was obtained by strip-mining, thereby ruining the environment. The economic tsar Günter Mittag therefore decided to merge the 3,500 or so industrial enterprises of East Germany into 250 giant companies, called *Kombinate*, according to the Soviet model. "The consequences were disastrous," Horst Johannsen recalled, "Productive small and mid-size companies were absorbed and one-sided production monopolies formed" without price competition. As a result, "Honecker sought help from the class enemy," asking for credits from West German banks. To pay the interest, the Stasi economics tsar Alexander Schalck-Golodkowski surreptitiously started to sell anything movable to the West.[57]

Increasing East–West travel during the 1980s reinforced the GDR image of material inferiority through personal inspection. It was no longer just the colorful world of TV series such as *Dallas*, the Christmas packages with Western coffee and cigarettes, or the FRG visitors with their obligatory presents. Now retired East Germans could travel and people like Horst Johannsen who claimed "pressing family matters" such as the death of a father might get to see the at once fascinating and repulsive West with their own eyes. Visitors were awed by the variety and quality of goods, yet nervous about Western speed and competitiveness. Some "carefully selected, reliable travel cadres, schooled in agitation of western partners," such as Paul Frenzel, were permitted to visit the West for professional reasons such as attending a conference. While not all encounters were positive due to Cold War anti-Communism, these personal experiences created an image of Western superiority for most visitors.[58] It took true ideological commitment to socialism or deep attachment to family and home town for travelers such as philosopher Alfred Kosing to return to the GDR.

Among those who could no longer bear the SED dictatorship, "the wishes, desires and requests to leave the GDR became everyday matters in the mid-1980s." Pastor Braune recalled some of the manifold reasons: "The methods of the state, party, government, and Stasi prepared the ground so that many did not want to remain any longer." With no right to travel, the arbitrariness of decisions about whether one was allowed to go created a feeling of being penned up, that increased the impulse to get out. "The GDR provided a special treatment for [such] 'applicants,'" whom it considered misled citizens who needed to be won back by agitation or threatened with loss of jobs, long waiting periods, or imprisonment, if they spoke up in public. "The GDR made a good profit from letting people leave": the Federal Republic paid about eight billion DM as ransom to the GDR via the Protestant Church for the release of about thirty-four thousand prisoners and 250,000 refugees. Even a one-time discharge of thirty thousand people in the early 1980s could not stop the flow, for it encouraged more to apply.[59]

Some of the children of the Weimar cohort who were "searching for justice and new moral values" grew especially critical of the GDR when they noticed "the growing contradiction between theory and practice in everyday life." Exposed to an informal American lifestyle of rock music, jeans, and chewing gum that contrasted with the boring orderliness of the FDJ, some nonconformists established a "regime critical scene" in East Berlin and other cities. Gerhard Joachim's son Waiko, who worked in a gas power plant, joined his countercultural friends in "illegally occupying an empty apartment in the Prenzlauer Berg area." Caught while trying to escape, he was imprisoned and sentenced to one year and three months for "attempting to cross the border without authorization." After eight months he was released to the West through the mediation of lawyer Wolfgang Vogel. Although his brothers were also harassed by the GDR police, Waiko apparently shot himself out of loneliness after his arrival in the West. His father was devastated. "Never in my whole life was I as shaken as by this news."[60]

The systematic militarization of East German society also inspired the formation of an independent peace movement that took the SED at its word. Recollections stress that one bone of contention was the introduction of "military education" in the schools, and another the obligation of military service as prerequisite for a future career. Critics assembled behind the banner of "swords into plowshares" under the protection of some Protestant pastors who were willing to organize prayers and vigils for peace that also condemned the nuclear arms race. One youthful dissident was Horst Johannsen's son Berndt, who wanted to be a painter, but was rejected by the Association of Visual Artists for his avant-garde techniques. When he refused to "defend the GDR ideology with a weapon in his hand," this "attitude netted him a prison sentence of six months." Though he had to do hard labor in a steel factory in Thale, he stubbornly clung to his beliefs. A frustrated Stasi denounced the emergence of this civic peace movement as "a collection of hostile negative forces."[61]

Another public irritant was the terrible degradation of the environment, which the SED seemed unable to remedy. On the one hand, strip-mining erased whole villages from the map; on the other, burning lignite poisoned the air, making it hard to breathe in the so-called chemical triangle of Halle, Merseburg, and Bitterfeld. Pastor Braune noted that "the high smokestacks of the Lauta power plant belched much dirt into the sky. Keeping our kids clean was a continual struggle." Horst Johannsen recalled that in the winter, the "fumes and exhaust gases crystallized and covered the region with so-called Leuna snow." This inspired him to write a critical poem about the pollution in "the cauldron of chemistry": "The air— / one can almost see and feel it. / One's breath wants to stand still. / Air exhales unnoticed / from inside without being seen." When the noxious atmosphere, foul drinking water, toxic fields, and wild garbage dumps were not addressed, local activists tried to stop the abuse and finally began to oppose the SED system as such.[62]

Numerous stories show how the regime's heavy-handed repression of public criticism turned objection to specific policies into a more fundamental campaign for human rights. One woman's attempt to join her husband who had failed to return from a trip to the West landed her in prison without naming "an official reason." She had to sell half of her possessions to get permission to leave. A sixteen-year-old pupil was arrested for "distributing flyers for freedom of expression." Though free speech was a constitutional right, he was condemned to over three years of imprisonment before he was finally released. In 1985 the arbitrary nature of the system inspired the foundation of an opposition group called "Initiative for Peace and Human Rights." When Freya Klier and Stephan Krawczyk unfurled a banner quoting Rosa Luxemburg that "freedom is always the freedom of those who think differently," Pastor Braune had to drive the dissidents to the West during their expulsion from the GDR. After the terrible prison conditions, "the discovery of freedom could begin."[63]

The resolute efforts of the Stasi to curb the emergence of a domestic opposition failed because it found no effective way to deal with the dissidents. One strategy was to increase the number of MfS officials to ninety-one thousand and informal informants to about 190,000. Another was the assiduous collection of data, archived in endless paper records on individuals, designated as "operative case files." Yet another was to switch from physical intimidation to softer methods of disinformation and incentives such as rewards for loyalty. The key problem was the simplistic definition of class enemies as subversives from the outside rather than as inside critics who believed in socialist ideals but hated the repressive practices of the GDR. As a result, the state's final option was expulsion to the West. Regime opponents such as Günter Krause were either allowed to leave when they finally reached their pension age or were expelled, as Paul Frenzel was after years of surveillance for publishing a critical manuscript in the West.[64]

Even more important than youth disaffection and intellectual criticism was the growing disenchantment of the working class with the SED regime. The party's proclamation of the impending victory of socialism in weekly indoctrination sessions was losing conviction due to actual comparisons with the West. The endless socialist competitions between brigades for prizes were no longer effective enough to motivate workers to increase their productivity, when they had to contend with antiquated machinery and lack of raw materials. The military exercises of factory militias and the mandatory attendance of SED demonstrations felt like onerous duties that kept laborers from enjoying their leisure time. The disappointed socialist idealist Gerhard Joachim wrote a bitter poem after the death of his son that accused the ruling elite: "They did not just build a Wall in Berlin / but an even thicker cordon around themselves / And the greater their fear of the workers grew / the more these reactionaries dug their own grave."[65]

Many writers reported that a pervasive sense of stagnation engulfed the GDR during the 1980s, when the economy stalled while the West moved ahead. Some of the problems resulted from the Stalinist priority of coal and steel production over consumer goods. Others had to do with the meddling of party bureaucrats; to Horst Johannsen, "it was never completely clear who had the final say." Yet other stumbling blocks derived from the socialization of the remaining private businesses and artisan shops, which decreased innovation. Karl Härtel was appalled that in his power plant, machines "were ruthlessly run down and only minimal investments made in the renewal and maintenance of equipment." Campaigns such as the building of a Megabit computer chip devoured huge resources but failed to produce a competitive product. The Politburo lived in a fantasy world; the state even prettied up houses on their daily route to work. While the senescent leadership celebrated the GDR as the tenth-largest industrial nation, the actual economy was falling apart. Contrary to incessant self-praise, "the facts were depressing."[66]

Hope for a reform of socialism ultimately came from an unexpected quarter—the charismatic leader of the Soviet Union, Mikhail Gorbachev. Unlike his conservative predecessors, he no longer prevented change, but rather demanded a thorough reform of the system. Because the Soviet economy was in disarray, Gorbachev proposed a policy of restructuring (*perestroika*) and of open discussion to correct mistakes (*glasnost'*). Fritz Klein recalled that "people like me, engaged socialists like myself, observed the process as if electrified." The formerly frustrated Gerhard Joachim was overjoyed: "Like a phoenix from the ashes, he carried the hopes for a better, more humane socialism, for the renewal of all of its aspects." The reform proposals of the new Soviet leader "had such an echo in the GDR" because they promised "a fundamental change of political and economic conditions."[67] Opponents could even hope to get rid of the repression altogether. While the leaders of Poland and Hungary responded positively, chief ideologist Kurt Hager warned that the SED was not about to redecorate because someone else changed the wallpaper.

In the GDR, the Soviet reform impulse triggered a generational struggle over the future course of the SED. Feeling threatened, the "old and grey, sclerotic leadership" who had been born in the Empire refused to budge, claiming that things were going so well that they did not need any reforms. Socialists of the Weimar cohort who had been shunted aside, such as Gerhard Joachim and Fritz Klein, wanted to seize the opportunity for reform by citing Gorbachev: "Briefly said, we need a comprehensive democratization of all dimensions of society." Their postwar children were especially attracted to the "new thinking," because it offered a chance to overcome the stagnation of the GDR. Other skeptics wanted a yet more "radical change in the direction of privatization, market economy, and true democracy." But the Politburo was unwilling to change its course, forbidding the distribution of the Soviet journal *Sputnik* because it disseminated reformist texts. The older members of the Weimar cohort could no longer spearhead this transformation themselves because they were already going into retirement.[68]

While party members still debated, ordinary East Germans took advantage of détente and left the GDR in ever-increasing numbers for the "golden West." From May 1989 on Hungary no longer sent fleeing refugees back to East Berlin and formally opened its border to Austria on September 11. This was "in the true sense of the word an earth shaking action" because it lifted the Iron Curtain. During the summer "more and more young GDR citizens tried to flee to the West via Hungary or by occupying embassies" in Prague and Warsaw. The hardliner Werner Feigel reasoned that "they let themselves be deceived by appearances" because "they saw the difference in the popular standard of living and did not hear any plausible explanation for the deficits in the supply of some goods." When a surprised Gorbachev refrained from interfering, the SED leadership failed to find a way to stop the flow. Once "the dam was broken," Western TV showed tens of thousands of happy East Germans tearfully enjoying the first days of "their new freedom" in the West.[69]

An even bigger challenge to the regime was the spread of demonstrations demanding a fundamental reform of the GDR. In spite of Stasi subversion, human rights, peace, and ecology groups formed a dissident network that challenged the falsification of the May 1989 vote results. From September on, the Monday evening vigils at the Nikolai Church in Leipzig grew bolder, with attendees claiming, "we are *the* people." Though initially the SED used force against the protests, in a crucial confrontation in Leipzig on October 9, the authorities restrained the police, Stasi, and militia, conceding control over public space. Week by week the protests became louder, demanding "fundamental reform and democratization of the GDR, the dismantling of party rule, freedom of travel, opinion and assembly, true elections and an end of the ubiquitous system of spying by the Stasi." Finally losing their fear, protesters "drummed for true justice," shouted slogans, held placards, and founded public opposition groups such as the New Forum, which denounced the SED.[70] News shots documented the protesters' claim that they, not the party, were the people (image 28).

Unprepared for such a wave of peaceful protests, the SED crumbled because the unrest contradicted its ideological claim of serving the people. Intent on celebrating the fortieth anniversary of the GDR's founding, the leadership was divided between hardliners who wanted to suppress the "counterrevolution" and reformers who were willing to initiate a public dialogue. Officers of the security apparatus, such as Werner Feigel, were distressed that the party "had made no preparations" for such a challenge. In mid-October 1989 more flexible Politburo members overthrew the ailing Honecker and put in power his deputy Egon Krenz, who had been tarnished by supporting the Tiananmen Square massacre in China. Horst Johannsen observed that "comrades and entire party collectives began to lose their trust in hierarchy and to follow its alienating cynicism ever less." When opposition groups like the New Forum collected thousands of signatures, the "peaceful popular demands gained an unstoppable ascendancy."[71] SED concessions were too little and too late.

The "true turning point" was the fall of the Wall, which had divided Berlin for almost three decades. In "a grandiose illusion," half a million citizens

28. East German protests. *Source*: Stiftung Preussischer Kulturbesitz.

had demonstrated on November 4 at the Alexanderplatz for the reform of an independent GDR. But five days later the SED gave in to public pressure and promised a new travel policy, allowing freedom of movement without prior restriction. When Günter Schabowski announced this change to the press, he triggered an unintended tidal wave: "During the same night thousands of East Berliners massed at the Wall and pressured the few crossing points. The border guards faced a human avalanche which overpowered all control mechanisms." Once the floodgates were opened, Horst Johannsen recalled, "during this night the entire area of West Berlin resembled a real festival: people hugged each other, bakers presented their wares on the street, drinks and fruit were offered, everywhere there were heartwarming encounters." Unable to believe what they were seeing, jubilant crowds kept repeating, "This is incredible."[72]

The contest therefore shifted to a struggle between those who wanted to reform an independent GDR and those who pleaded for a reunification with the FRG. Hoping for a "third way," many intellectuals appealed "for our country" by promising to "develop a society with solidarity, peace and social justice, individual freedom, free travel, and protection of the environment" that would be "an alternative to the Federal Republic." But, tired of further socialist experiments, the majority of the populace began to demand a merger with the more prosperous and free West Germany, following Chancellor Helmut Kohl's suggestion of a federation in his surprising Ten-Point Plan of November 28, 1989. When the slogan shifted to "we are *one* people," Horst Johannsen observed that "in early December demands for reunification began to dominate the Monday demonstrations more and more."[73] Even the repudiation of Stalinism and the renaming of the SED as the Party of Democratic Socialism (PDS) could no longer stop the trend toward ending the division of Germany.

The first free election on March 18, 1990, decided the issue: a clear majority of East Germans endorsed reunification. Following the Polish example, a roundtable of SED functionaries and opposition members managed the transition. The party now had power but no legitimacy, while the civic movement had legitimacy but no power. The key compromise was the agreement to hold free elections in order to decide the future. The campaign turned into a three-cornered contest in which defenders of the regime confronted activists of the civic opposition movement and members of the pro-Western parties. With well-orchestrated appearances, West German chancellor Kohl supported the centrist CDU and ex-chancellor Brandt campaigned for the leftist SPD, while the FDP and the Greens played only minor roles. "In the end the majority of the voters chose the governing party of the FRG" and rejected the Third Way. As a result of the verdict for unification, Gerhard Joachim recalled that "all my dreams [of reforming socialism] blew away like spring blossoms."[74]

The currency and social union of July 1, 1990 took a crucial step toward the merger of both economies. Most East Germans had been looking forward to gaining the DM, which they regarded as a kind of "magic currency" since it offered access to coveted goods. While several thousand marks of savings were exchanged 1:1, most of the East German money was converted at a rate of 1:2, which was still higher than GDR productivity. On the day of the exchange, "people were happy and exuberant," standing in long lines to receive their Western bills. Almost overnight "real Western goods" filled the store shelves, displacing the drab but utilitarian Eastern products. At the same time "prices in fact tripled" for most transactions. "Ignorance and insecurity in dealing with the DM were shamelessly abused," initiating a kind of criminal capitalism that plundered the naïve. While the DM made consumption dreams come true, its excessive conversion rate made goods too expensive and threatened Eastern jobs. Easterners expected prosperity to follow automatically, whereas Westerners underestimated the transformation cost.[75]

The memoirs suggest that the legal process of reunification took place over the heads of the people in complex negotiations that nonetheless had major consequences for ordinary lives. Instead of a merger of equal partners, it was the accession of a failing state to a flourishing neighbor, according to paragraph twenty-three of the Basic Law of the FRG. The GDR revived its five original states in order to fit into the federal structure of West Germany. A lengthy and complex unification treaty regulated the legal process for such controversial issues as property rights, allowing exceptions for a transition period for abortion rights, but in principle transferring Western patterns to the East. At the same time a complicated negotiation between the two Germanys and the four victors of World War II determined the international dimensions of the new state. Over the protests of the expellee organizations, the enlarged Federal Republic had to accept the loss of its

Eastern territories as permanent. A muted and civil celebration marked the restoration of unity on October 3, 1990.[76]

Retrospective feelings about reunification were rather mixed, with some former East Germans lamenting the failure of socialism and others welcoming the return to freedom. Of course, members of the SED regime such as Werner Feigel complained about the loss of their free medical care, higher pensions, and other privileges: "This balance sheet demonstrates that the so-called unification could not make me happy." Also, supporters of the Third Way, such as Gerhard Joachim, regretted that "our peaceful revolution for a better GDR remained a footnote of world history" and failed to reform all of Germany. But many other GDR citizens, such as Klaus Hübschmann, were relieved: "Of course, we were jubilant when with the Wall, the entire Stasi, and SED corruption were removed," even if "we came from the rain into the shower" by having to face unexpected transition challenges. Regime opponents such as Werner Braune, who had suffered under persecution, were particularly delighted with the recovery of the rule of law: "We were all moved and grateful for the unification which had taken place."[77]

FAILURE NARRATIVES

East German autobiographies have a peculiarly defensive character, since their authors attempt to justify individual lives in spite of having to admit the system's failure. Structured around important political caesuras, all accounts agree on the fiasco of "real existing socialism," because the self-dissolution of the GDR cannot be denied. Though feeling overwhelmed by the experiment in social engineering, most of these authors cling to pride in their personal achievements in adverse circumstances. In contrast to the Western emphasis on success, East German stories stress coping with difficulties, ingenious improvisation, professional accomplishments, and private satisfaction. While party apologists such as Werner Feigel reaffirm the attractiveness of socialist ideals, apolitical specialists such as Klaus Hübschmann tend to downplay the price of conformity for their attainments. Relatively few writers, Günter Krause among them, condemn the SED dictatorship outright. Interestingly enough, even intellectuals such as Gerhard Joachim who were repeatedly disciplined by the party still assert that "socialism is the most exciting blueprint for society."[78]

Many memoirists find it painful to concede that the GDR lost the Cold War competition with the FRG, because their lives there were more closely intertwined with the system than in the West. In order to show that "the GDR was after all more than an insignificant footnote of world history," they cite, like Heinrich Buschmann, a list of its advantages: "Not everything was bad in the GDR, some things were models even for Germany as a whole. . . . Support for families with many children was exemplary in the GDR" due to free nurseries, financial assistance, and the like. "For all talented children education up to the doctorate was free of charge." Moreover, "health care of the citizens did not cost anything." The fees "for the elderly in old age homes were modest." Unwilling to consider their life a failure, many East Germans therefore remember the GDR "not only as an authoritarian dictatorship," but are in general in "agreement with the social and societal measures" of the SED. Only for victims are "the opening of the Wall and German reunification a wonderful, unexpected gift."[79]

When trying to explain the GDR's collapse, the memoirists suggest numerous contradictory reasons. Incorrigible Communists such as Werner Feigel blame a capitalist conspiracy that deceived the naïve East Germans with false promises. More critical spirits such as Günter Manz hold "the Stalinist system of the Soviet Union" responsible and assert that the GDR "was not at all a socialist state." By contrast, economists such as Horst Johannsen point to the difficult starting conditions of the East German regime in which the Soviet occupiers dismantled many factories and exacted heavy reparations. Accomplished professionals such as Klaus Hübschmann complain about the constant interference of "unspeakable party bureaucrats" who overrode rational arguments with political considerations. And wags claim that "the chief enemies of socialism were spring, summer, fall and winter."[80] Ultimately even defenders of its humanistic ideals admit that "real existing socialism" collapsed due to its inability to reform its practice.

Recollections of the defunct GDR are also colored by their authors' difficulties with the transition to what they considered as neoliberal capitalism. Gerhard Joachim's high hopes during the peaceful revolution of bringing about a new synthesis between democracy and socialism were bound to be disappointed. Heinrich Buschmann observed that many rural people had trouble adjusting from SED collectivism to the unbridled individualism of the West. Already retired, Fritz Klein tried to help colleagues in the Academy of Sciences who faced losing their jobs due to the breakup of this large research institution into smaller segments in order to fit it into the decentralized academic structure of the FRG. But what incensed socialist partisans such as Werner Feigel most was the accusation of having served a lawless state, an *Unrechtsstaat*, which justified a drastic cut in their pensions.[81] Missing the familiarity of the GDR, many East Germans resented the Western media attacks on the SED dictatorship as callously disrespectful of their own lives.

But in spite of a widespread (n)ostalgia for the SED regime, hardly any of the memoirists want the GDR back. While they might regret the loss of community in the East or grumble about the "casino capitalism" of unified Germany, they admit that their living standard had noticeably improved. As reluctant citizens of the Federal Republic, they can publicly criticize its institutions, organize lobby groups, and travel freely anywhere in the world. While the socialist philosopher Alfred Kosing still longs for "a socialist society with democratic structures" and an "open intellectual life," he clearly states, "But I do not wish the SED back." Similarly, the long-time collective farm director Heinrich Buschmann admits, "Neither from my brain nor from my heart do I want to return to GDR conditions." Looking back on the succession of regimes, journalist Carola Stern and Socialist Heinz Zöger conclude, "After [our] experiences in the Weimar Republic, the Nazi state, and the GDR [we] consider the Federal Republic of Germany the best German state yet."[82]

CONCLUSION

Memories of Fractured Lives

The autobiographies of the cohort born in the 1920s present an intriguing record of ordinary lives in extraordinary times. With advancing age, their untutored authors looked back upon their trials and tribulations, trying to make sense of their ruptured biographies. The former BdM member Ruth Bulwin confessed that "for a long time I have been driven to record memories of our life for my children and nephews, and last but not least for myself." When reflecting on the progression "from [NS] dictatorship to [SED] dictatorship," the East German engineer Horst Johannsen tried "to reproduce life experiences from the perspective of a simple citizen." In contrast to GDR apologias, he wanted to present "in really objective form a better testimony that attempts to recall the past for descendants of my family and to present answers to questions about the course of contemporary history." This didactic purpose of drawing political lessons from personal experience of "a very turbulent time" is typical of many Weimar children's memoirs.[1]

For readers, such ego narratives are both problematic and promising. Joachim Fest admitted that they have many pitfalls as a source of "what actually happened." Autobiographies are rather selective, eliding embarrassing details; they tend to be laudatory, justify the writer's actions, and present a linear progression that ignores the actual twists and turns of development. Nonetheless, personal accounts also have redeeming merits because they record "how one became who one is." An individual perspective on a particular life course offers more concrete detail than structural generalizations. Moreover, it presents stories of incidents that would be lost with the death of its author. Finally, its diachronic character allows writers to reflect on the discrepancy between their former and present selves. Hence the historian Fritz Klein attempted "a serious self-examination, a resolute questioning of what good or bad, right or wrong one has done, said or written." Such rigorous self-analysis provides insights otherwise not available.[2]

In contrast to recollections from other countries, German autobiographies have to confront a "double burden" of problematic pasts. On the one hand, these life courses tend to have been more dramatically disrupted by war, Nazi repression, the Holocaust, and Communist dictatorship than the peaceful developments among neutral neighbors. On the other hand, the individuals involved in these experiences make up the entire spectrum, from perpetrators through bystanders to victims, within one nation. As a single intellectual couple, Carola Stern and Heinz Zöger "had to come to terms with their past in different ways and not for the same reasons." While she had to deal with her youthful enthusiasm for the Third Reich, he was forced to cope with his prominent role in the GDR. In a similar vein, mechanical engineer Günter Krause concluded, "I have experienced National Socialism and also the GDR. Both dictatorships have only brought disaster for the people."[3] Many of these memoirs are passionate appeals to prevent the recurrence of such events.

Seen from the perspective of ordinary people, German history in the twentieth century reveals a dramatic reversal from catastrophe to civility. Not just the fatal decisions of chauvinistic elites, but also the enthusiastic acclaim of the masses precipitated the country and with it the continent into two wars, depressions, dictatorships, and the Holocaust. These self-inflicted disasters toppled regimes, moved borders, killed millions—in short, caused untold suffering that engulfed the very people who had unleashed them. Family photo albums are full of pictures of proud soldiers celebrating Wehrmacht victories, but also contain images of destroyed cities and the defeated struggling for survival in the rubble. Only after giving up hegemonic dreams in the Cold War stalemate did the divided Germans in East and West prosper and reflect on some of their prior misdeeds. It was not just political leadership and intellectual criticism, but a much broader process of social introspection that finally produced the chastened Germans of today.[4]

RETIREMENT RETROSPECTIVES

For members of the Weimar cohort in the West, retirement from their occupations provided the leisure and motivation to "review their past" for a final time. While for some dissatisfied individuals giving up work came as a welcome relief, for others, such as Robert Neumaier, "who loved [their] profession, saying goodbye was associated with a certain wistfulness." His daughter pressed him to "record his war experiences for posterity as eyewitness of a slowly dying generation" in order to "fill the gap" left by the end of his working life. When reading the resulting text, she was impressed with "his colorful life, marked by highs and lows." Unlike her own peacetime generation, "he experienced extreme situations, was subjected to great physical and psychological stress and nonetheless never lost his courage to live." Having withdrawn to the "second row of the theater," Gerhard Baucke was also happy to learn a spectator role: "I have a good partner on my side. It does not get boring. Fall, too, has beautiful days."[5]

The last pages of their accounts show that many retirees made a smooth transition into old age, which enabled them to reflect dispassionately on their lives. Intellectuals such as Joachim Fest continued to pursue their cultural interests, but in a less formal setting. Businessmen such as Hellmut Raschdorff went on acting as consultants and gathering honors from professional associations. Social activists such as Gisela and Horst Grothus stayed involved in their communities, supporting civil society initiatives to address local or global problems. Other professionals turned to hobbies; Hermann Debus, for example, participated in swimming competitions and theatrical productions. Especially if they came from modest backgrounds, pensioners were proud of their well-appointed houses with big gardens that kept them busy. Those retirees who had been tied down for political or financial reasons, such as Erika Taubhorn and Günter Krause, finally traveled to far-flung places like "Cyprus, Crete, Morocco, Madeira."[6] Photos show that other couples, such as the Andrées, were content to stay closer to home, enjoying each other's company (image 29).

29. Contented retirees. *Source:* Horst Andrée, *Stationen meines Lebens.*

Aware of "the short path which we can still pursue," women were gratified by the growth of their children, since according to traditional gender roles they had played a crucial role in nurturing them. Many autobiographies are full of pictures of smiling infants and playing children, suggesting that "this was a happy time." The texts also report the usual illnesses, problems in school, and disciplinary issues—but always with a positive undertone of difficulties having been overcome. Fathers such as Rolf Bulwin or Hellmut Raschdorff were proud of their offspring's professional advancement, and delighted when their sons could take over the family firm. Mothers were more concerned with the personal relations of their children, hoping that they would find the right partners. Anneliese Huber recalled, "When I look back today, I am grateful to fate that we had healthy children who did not create any worries otherwise."[7] Once grandchildren arrived, the new grandparents were even happier, since they could enjoy their growth without any direct responsibility.

The texts suggest, however, that advancing age also brought increasing health problems to the Weimar cohort. Paul Debus's hip pain got worse, although he strenuously fought it with swimming and exercise. Other setbacks came as shocking surprises, such as Paul Huber's "slight vision problems and temporary paralysis," the result of an almost complete clogging of his throat artery. During the subsequent triple bypass operation, he had a stroke, rendering him "completely helpless, connected to apparatuses and hoses, unable to move arms or legs." It took a concerted rehabilitation effort to get him back on his feet. Even if it was "a hard time," his wife was "glad and grateful that Paul could again lead an almost normal life." Similarly, Günter Krause had a heart attack and was taken to his hospital by ambulance. He also suffered a subsequent stroke due to a blocked artery, but eventually recovered well enough to take extensive trips.[8] Such incidents were early warning signs of mortality.

The awareness of "having to attempt to do less" because of no longer "being as resilient" was a major incentive for authors to write down their life stories as long as they could. If they were at peace with themselves, like Hellmut Raschdorff, they could look back upon "the great richness of my life" and clothe its meaning in the poetic image of a mowed meadow to reassure their children that cut flowers would grow again next year. For the bereaved Gerhard Baucke, "writing [was] a therapy for long sad winter evenings," because it allowed him to create "a history, a lived life," able "to reflect back" its disappearing light. For self-critical spirits such as Horst Grothus, drawing up a balance sheet required admitting errors and defeats that he wanted to pass on to his children as cautionary tales. "I have experienced, done, accomplished, and suffered much." Nonetheless, he ultimately found his life "worthwhile."[9] Committing their own biographies to paper was therefore a way of living beyond death in their intimate family circles as well as a wider public.

Penning an autobiography was, moreover, a method for some Weimar children to cope with the recurring nightmare of mass murder and mass death that left indelible traces in their psyches. During their professional lives, they had been too busy coping with the destructive aftermath of the

Nazi dictatorship to confront the question of what role they had played in it. Only the success of subsequent recovery provided enough psychological distance for them to face memories of the terrible events. In retirement, their thoughts returned to their adolescence, which was dominated by the HJ or BdM, evoking happy images of growing up, first love, and so on. But recollecting a Third Reich youth inevitably raised the troubling question of their individual and collective responsibility for the NS dictatorship, the subsequent war, and its attendant atrocities. Ursula Mahlendorf felt "a special obligation to speak to [her American] students about what we Germans had participated in and what had happened to us."[10] The Nazi terror would never leave her and her peers.

Coming to terms with their own past was even more complicated for East Germans, because it coincided with the peaceful revolution in the GDR. People who were born during the 1920s reached retirement age in the 1980s, so the collapse of Communism complicated their transition into a life after work. Surprised West Germans who were awed by the peaceful protests in the East were gratified when the Wall fell. "The first shot was not fired," Gerhard Baucke marveled. "Once more we had gotten away with it and had little reason to triumph; we could only be grateful." By contrast, the GDR historian Fritz Klein, who had long advocated a reform of Communism, was stunned when "the world of real socialism dissolved with ever increasing speed." Clearly, he "had not wanted the change [*Wende*]," but since "our side had shown itself unable to resolve its problems on its own, I was ready to accept it as undeniable progress."[11] For those who had suffered from the division, reunification also brought political relief.

Older supporters of the SED dictatorship found the collapse of Communism especially galling, for it invalidated their life project. If, like the Union of Cooperative Stores, their employer went under, they were "released into preretirement" like Erich Hasemann. When the Academy of Sciences was dissolved, well-known scholars such as Marxist philosopher Alfred Kosing were forced to accept early pensions. "It started to become clear that great parts of the academic intelligence of the former GDR were to be pushed out of public life in a quite simple manner." Refuting the media accusation that the SED regime had been a "lawless state," the economist Günter Manz railed against the Western "process of colonization." Hard-hit by the reduction of his "intellectual's pension," Werner Feigel zealously campaigned for an increase in retirement pay. Only when they were relieved that the SED was finally gone, as agronomist Heinrich Buschmann was, were they willing to give the new system a chance.[12]

By definition, the autobiographies of the Weimar cohort remain incomplete, since their authors can not report their own passing away. Most hoped, like Robert Neumaier, "to be able to spend a few more years together" in their "home in peace and contentment." But the approach of death cast its shadow in advance. "I live with the idea of mortality," Anneliese Huber noted, "and since then I have begun to consider life as a gift." After her seventy-fifth birthday Ursula Baehrenburg sensed that "memory disappears in fog—everything pales." Even her conflicts with her brother no longer bothered her after he died unmourned: "My heart grows calmer day by day. Thus a slow passing away takes its merciless course." Already ninety-two at the time she began her memoirs, Ruth Weigelt was grateful for having her son to "write down my life." Only religious believers such as Hellmut Raschdorff were more optimistic: "If one day God considers the time right to remove me from this world, I only wish that I can make a grateful departure in anticipation of the meeting with eternity."[13] In different ways, each writer sought consolation for the inevitable end.

BROKEN LIVES

The dominant experience shared in the retirement retrospectives of the Weimar cohort was the disruption of their own life courses by historic forces outside of their control. Their existence was not the expected progression from happy childhood via turbulent adolescence to mature adulthood with professional success and loving family, but rather a constant struggle against the surprising challenges of depression, dictatorship, war, privation, and the like. Engineer Heinz Schultheis called his account "an entirely unheroic history of a boy whose fate decreed to be growing up in a 'great time.'" Looking back, he explained his "recurring astonishment about the often absurd vicissitudes

30a. Wartime destruction. *Source*: Kempowski photo collection.

of life" as the result of "the rather hectic multiplicity of the twentieth century compared to which even great events and transformations of the past generally pale."[14] Many private snapshots, as well as official photos of buildings, illustrate the tension between a depressing record of untold destruction and mass death and a later return to peace and prosperity (image 30).

In most of these ego narratives, the German Empire functions as a positive background foil. Transmitted by stories from grandparents and their

30b. Postwar rebuilding. *Source*: Preussischer Kulturbesitz.

adherence to a code of "secondary virtues" such as discipline, cleanliness, and thrift, the Kaiserreich appears as a period of order and stability, quite in contrast with its rapid population increase, economic growth, and rampant urbanization. The foundation of a national state through a series of military victories, the acquisition of overseas colonies, the rise of prosperity, the renown of scientific research and technical invention all contributed to a sense of continued progress, celebrated even by Thomas Mann. This optimistic self-image stood in startling contrast to the grinding rural poverty, urban plight, economic exploitation, social strife, militarism, and authoritarianism mentioned in many autobiographies. It was the even more negative experience of the Great War and the postwar chaos that made the Second Reich ultimately appear as "the good old days."[15]

Based on their own recollections, virtually all authors describe the Weimar Republic as surprisingly benign; their childhoods appear to have been quite happy in contrast to later suffering. This memory differs from much of the scholarly literature, which emphasizes the chaotic beginning and hyperinflation, the ephemeral stabilization, and the subsequent economic crisis that crippled the Republic from its birth. This widespread nostalgia is a tribute to the efforts of parents to shelter their offspring from economic and political strife and make their early years pleasant. But it is also a reflection of Weimar's positive efforts in school reform and welfare support, which created progressive chances for some children of limited means. Only with the Great Depression did memoirists and writers such as Alfred Döblin mention deprivation from unemployment or the street battles between the SA and the Red Front for control of public space.[16] These positive descriptions indicate that Weimar really did have a chance.

In many ways, representations of Nazi adolescence were the most difficult subject for the writers, since they were forced to reconcile positive memories with their disastrous consequences. Often written by former HJ or BdM leaders, the narratives paint their involvement in rather attractive colors. This ought not to be surprising, for these associations provided young people with leisure activities and freedom from parental contro, and promised them a generational project of making Germany great again. But many authors go on to describe a process of disillusionment due to the gradual realization of Nazi crimes that culminated in the collapse of their worldview and led to a personal breakdown, as with Christa Wolf. The incredible destruction, personal suffering, and enormity of mass murder inspired a bitter soul searching that confronted German guilt. The diachronic self-examinations that contrast youthful errors with mature criticism are fascinating testimonies of that wrestling with conscience that ultimately transformed memory culture.[17]

The memoirs show that the disruption of life plans began in earnest with World War II, when young men were involved in mass murder and mass death. The dirty reality of interrupted schooling, military discipline, and lethal danger was not what HJ leaders had promised during Nazi indoctrination. Initially the recollections still show traces of a spirit of adventure and enthusiasm for victory that could justify death as a heroic sacrifice. But the failure to conquer Britain, the invasion of Russia, the US entry, and rumors about terrible atrocities finally fed nagging doubts about the war's legitimacy. Most of the accounts focus on the inevitability of defeat due to inferior weapons, lack of resources, and resistance by the conquered. The total collapse of the fronts in the East and the West therefore rendered all individual sacrifices and killings of comrades pointless. Young men lost their entire youth on the battlefield, leaving them, as Walter Kempowski recorded, disillusioned and confused about the future.[18]

The autobiographies demonstrate that the lives of young women were similarly disrupted by the war, even if they generally remained at the home front. The absence of men complicated relationships, breaking up families and forcing women to shoulder new responsibilities. While the Nazis initially tried to shield females in order to maintain morale, eventually many had to work in war production alongside slave laborers. From the middle of the war on, the killing started to threaten women themselves: saturation bombing did not differentiate between military and civilian targets. With the collapse of the Eastern Front, many mothers had to organize the precipitous flight from the Red Army and cope with the subsequent expulsion, since men were dead or in captivity. And then there was the crowning indignity of mass rape, with its attendant brutalization, pregnancy, and shame that sexually signaled defeat. Diaries, like the anonymously published notes of Marta Hillers, vividly describe female suffering.[19]

The texts also illustrate that actual Nazi victims were even more at risk. Millions of them lost their lives to the racial terror if they did not manage to flee in time. They describe countless instances in which the SA beat up, incarcerated, and killed political opponents on the Left with little regard for legality. Medical records also reveal the systematic attempt at euthanasia that sought to eliminate the "biologically unfit" from the body politic in spite of religious objections. With the war came the ethnic cleansing of Poles in the areas to be Germanized by settlement, as well as the starvation of Russian POWs and the exploitation of slave labor. All of these horrific crimes culminated in the discrimination, persecution, ghettoization, and mass murder of the Jews, Roma, homosexuals, and others in what is commonly called the "Holocaust." Only a few lucky or resourceful people, such as Victor Klemperer, managed to escape this orgy of killing and create an incontrovertible record of crimes against humanity in their diaries, letters, or memoirs.[20]

During the post–World War II chaos, the ego narratives demonstrate a frantic effort to reassemble the fragments of lives during defeat and under occupation. The liberated concentration camp and prison survivors needed to be nursed back to health in order to have a future. The millions of displaced persons had to be repatriated or allowed to emigrate to more hospitable shores. The Wehrmacht soldiers who had become prisoners of war were to be investigated for war crimes and then either used as reconstruction laborers in Russia and France or sent home. Over ten million German-speaking expellees from the lost Eastern territories needed to be processed and distributed in order to be integrated into new communities. The millions of homeless men, women, and children whose apartments or dwellings had been destroyed by bombs had to be housed. All of this swirling mass of humanity created an unforeseen humanitarian emergency for the victors and a confused search for meaning among the defeated pictured in Heinrich Böll's novels.[21]

Western stories of subsequent rebuilding center on the desire for "normalization," i.e., getting back to a predictable civilian existence. Concretely that meant some distancing from National Socialism, the source of the disastrous defeat. But many ordinary citizens were also reluctant to ask too many questions about their personal involvement in the Third Reich. The first priority was getting enough food and shelter so as to resume studies or land a decent job. Another concern was the reuniting of scattered family members and transforming of romantic relationships into marriages with homes and children. Many young Germans also looked to go abroad and learn what other Western countries had done better in order to rejoin the international community. But only a minority of intellectuals was ready to heed Karl Jaspers' call for confronting German guilt or to follow Günter Grass in criticizing the oblivious success stories of the Economic Miracle.[22]

Autobiographies from the East focus on the exciting experiment of building a new socialist society. In disillusioned youths such as Hans Modrow, the example of anti-Fascist resisters inspired a conversion to a purportedly more humane ideology that would govern their lives. The deaths of older people and the purge of occupations also opened attractive career prospects in the GDR. Unfortunately, the Stalinist implementation of socialist ideals established a new dictatorship that justified itself dialectically as acting for the people. To escape persecution, many businessmen, landowners, and professionals fled to the West, while SED members struggled with their consciences about whether to overlook repression in the service of their cause. In the end, the socialist project failed by not living up to its ideals and not providing a better standard of living. Eastern novelists such as Eugen Ruge wrestled with the disappointment of the failure of a noble ideology.[23] All these accounts show that twentieth-century German lives were fractured in multiple ways.

CONTESTED MEMORIES

Among postwar Germans, these shared experiences created a largely apologetic "communicative memory" that was orally transmitted and differed from public memory culture. At its core were private stories shared at family holidays, gatherings with neighbors, or reunions with friends. In these meetings, people talked about their personal fates, trying to make sense of what had happened to them. Through frequent repetition, their tales of common suffering gradually evolved into group identifications among veterans, expellees, or rape victims, who found solace in hearing that they were not alone. Picked up by pressure groups such as the League of Expellees, these narratives also served to justify claims for political acknowledgment or monetary compensation for past pain. Generally, these memories lived in a semipublic realm of manuscript autobiographies, grey literature, or niche publication. In contrast to the critical stance of the public memory culture, this subterraneous social memory failed to fully describe Nazi crimes and focused mainly on German victimhood.[24]

To a large degree, the thrust of this semipublic memory culture was determined by the truncated spectrum of authors who wrote about the past. Due to public shaming, hard-core Nazi perpetrators hardly dared to present autobiographical accounts, and even accomplices such as Joachim Bässmann felt they should apologize for what they had done. By contrast, SED functionaries such as Alfred Kosing insistently defended socialism as ideal while criticizing its real practice. Most Nazi victims' voices were silenced. If they managed to flee, they wrote in the tongue of their adoptive country, as Lucy Mandelstam did. Supported by sympathetic media and foundations, people persecuted under Communism, such as Günter Krause, were quite vocal about the injustices done to them. Moreover, the Cold War split memories between Communist anti-Fascism celebrated in the GDR and the bourgeois-military resistance lauded in the FRG. Most of the apolitical authors, such as Ursula Baehrenburg, moved between the poles of somewhat apologetic to moderately self-critical narratives.[25]

In trying to explain the Nazi catastrophe to later readers, ordinary memoirists tended to resort to several standard excuses. Martin Sieg argued, "we did not choose the time in which we were born" and "were generally only reacting" to overwhelming outside forces. Will Seelmann-Eggebert claimed "that the majority of Germans did not know anything of the criminal murder of many million human beings." Youthful ex-soldiers like Gerhardt Thamm blamed "the guilty, the Nazi party bosses, the executioners, concentration camp managers" for their misfortune and justified fighting against the Red Army by trying to "delay, to save, to stave off annihilation." Some unregenerate nationalists such as Karl Härtel instead held the Allies responsible: "We were not perpetrators but victims of a pogrom against the German people and Reich, initiated by our opponents with the dictated [peace] of Versailles." Accusing history in general, the Nazi leadership in particular, or even their wartime enemies absolved individuals from taking personal responsibility. Instead, they could claim, "We were cheated out of our youth."[26]

A more complex explanation invokes the argument of betrayal of well intentioned patriotism by the Nazi leadership. Heinrich Buschmann formulated this popular reasoning: "[My] honest national feelings for the defense of the fatherland have been abused." This frequent claim supposes that it is normal for young men to serve in the military in order to defend their country. With this appeal to patriotic duty, even those who did not share the racist ideology of the Nazis could be mobilized for the war effort. Due to fascination with the new technology of flight, Horst Grothus and other youths trained with glider planes to become prestigious Luftwaffe pilots. It took a series of reverses for disillusionment to set in: "After I had recognized that this war, for which I had volunteered, was not a defensive struggle but a war of conquest," Buschmann reported, "my feelings changed during the year 1942 from a volunteer to an opponent of the war and of the Hitler regime."[27] Typical of veterans, this gradual change of mind beginning with Stalingrad informs many memoirs.

An even more critical argumentation often found in the memoirs of HJ or BdM leaders stresses the seduction of youthful idealism. By writing about her life on the basis of her student diaries, a mature Lore Walb sought self-clarification in order to "confront my having been a follower" of the Third Reich. As the daughter of a party member, she was "captivated by the spirit of the Nazi era, swept away by propaganda and slogans, fascinated by the figure of the '*Führer*' and his speeches." To her later chagrin, her banal young girl diaries "are representative of the enthusiasm of the silent majority during the Nazi period." Only "through the pressure of war events alone, a process of disillusionment and change of thinking slowly began" that took years to complete, culminating in a psychological crisis. Later confrontation with the youthful self made it possible "to accept my involvement in the Nazi period and the degree of my share of guilt more clearly and precisely than before."[28] This testimony marks the critical turn of self-reflexive autobiographies.

For decades this semipublic memory culture of victimization persisted, irrespective of official condemnations of the Third Reich. Some memoirists merely wanted to defend their childhood and youth, which contained happy experiences, even if they took place within a criminal system. Others rejected the charge of collective guilt by claiming that they had neither been involved in committing war crimes nor in implementing the Holocaust. Asserting, "I am not conscious of any personal culpability," East German engineer Albert Leithold typically argued "that the existence of concentration camps was known, but never their number and the degree of inhumane cruelty" in them. Though aware of the persecution of Jews, people had looked away so as not to have to oppose it. When confronted by the shocking pictures of the piles of corpses and living skeletons, many postwar Germans denounced them as Allied " brainwashing" and refused to accuse their fellow citizens in order "to maintain the peace of their community."[29] It was therefore quite difficult for the Weimar cohort to confront its own complicity.

Only after a long struggle did public memory culture succeed in turning the private social recollections in a more critical direction. One essential precondition was the total defeat of the Third Reich, which discredited the Nazi Party and set a process of reorientation in motion. At least initially, there was widespread agreement with the need to punish the NS leaders and the SS in the Nuremberg trials for launching a war of aggression and violating human rights. Though internment of perpetrators was a blunt instrument and denazification turned into something of a farce, these punitive measures removed Nazi elites temporarily from office and gave anti-Fascists a head start in rebuilding political institutions. The licensing of media also played a crucial role in providing critical information on the Third Reich. Finally, positive incentives such as America Houses and exchange programs appealed to young people such as Ursula Mahlendorf.[30] The Western Allies used just the right combination of severity and liberality to transform political culture.

The clear anti-Nazi stance of postwar politicians also fostered a new orientation in youths searching for a democratic or socialist future. Many Western leaders such as Chancellor Konrad Adenauer and President Theodor Heuss reemerged from internal emigration, while Kurt Schumacher, Willy Brandt, and other Social Democrats survived imprisonment or came back from exile. Similarly, prominent Communists such as Walter Ulbricht and Erich Honecker returned from emigration to Moscow or incarceration. Although Adenauer appealed to an apologetic center-right electorate, he understood that integration into the West would only succeed if he also expressed contrition for German crimes and offered restitution to the state of Israel and the Jewish community. Similarly, the East German leadership claimed an anti-Fascist mantle for integration into the Soviet Bloc. For young men such as Martin Sieg and Fritz Klein, such authority figures as Bishop Hanns Lilje and pedagogue Heinrich Deiters played a crucial role in deciding their allegiance.[31]

Several well-publicized court cases against prominent perpetrators in the early 1960s also turned the tide from widespread apologetics to a critical stance toward German crimes. Resenting the notion of "collective guilt," many nationalists had been arguing for the reintegration of former Nazis and the release of war criminals, following widespread public sentiment. But the Ulm Einsatzkommando trial in 1959 brought incontrovertible evidence of police involvement in the mass murder of Jews in Memel. Even more spectacular was the Eichmann trial in Jerusalem in 1960, which indicted the organizational mastermind of the Final Solution, who turned out to be a pale bureaucrat and was hanged in 1962. Closer to home, the Frankfurt Auschwitz trial organized by intrepid prosecutor Fritz Bauer in 1963 accused twenty-two concentration-camp guards of mass murder. (It was immortalized in *The Investigation*, a stage play by Peter Weiss.) Though these efforts were far from achieving justice, they made it clear even to perpetrators like Joachim Bässmann that "there cannot be any excuse for the annihilation and murder of an entire people."[32]

In East Germany, "mandated anti-Fascism" was an essential element of legitimation for SED rule, which claimed to be constructing a better Germany. "After removing the material and intellectual rubble," the "young anti-Fascists" such as Gerhard Joachim set out to "liberate the still slowly growing elements of a new society, which had formed in the lap of the hitherto disastrous development for the German people." The Weimar cohort of East German intellectuals such as Fritz Klein bought into this socialist project of the GDR as the sole method of breaking the Nazi spell of the past. Unfortunately, the celebration of the anti-Fascist resistance in camps like Buchenwald or Sachsenhausen soon turned into the legitimation of a new minority dictatorship by the SED. Creative Marxists such as Alfred Kosing began to run afoul of party apparatchiks, were disciplined, and lost faith in "real existing socialism." In the end, it was the opposition who claimed the legacy of Rosa Luxemburg in order to overthrow the SED dictatorship.[33]

The cumulative pressure of public memory criticism gradually also produced some genuine contrition, closing the gap to private recollections. The Weimar children were confronted with literary representations by famous authors such as Günter Grass and Christa Wolf, well-known memoirists such as Ruth Klüger and Victor Klemperer, powerful media messages such as the US *Holocaust* TV series, and local memorialization efforts by everyday historians that dramatized the ubiquity of Nazi crimes. Taken together, these initiatives documented the shocking extent of mass murder, substantiated the truthfulness of the Holocaust allegations, and created an emotional impact that could not be ignored. The result was a heightened tension between nostalgic recollections of youth and mature concern about responsibility that, for Ursula Mahlendorf and Lore Walb, resulted in psychological crises that could only be resolved by conscious admission of guilt. Some intellectuals, such as Gisela and Horst Grothus, Dorothee Sölle, and Werner Braune therefore dedicated their subsequent lives to doing penance through civic engagement.[34]

This critical turn of "communicative memory" also opened the door to a limited German-Jewish reconciliation. For some émigrés such as Albert Gompertz, the negative feelings ran so deep that they prevented meaningful communication during a return to Germany. Similarly, Niza Ganor had an awkward encounter with the family of her former Nazi employer, who had turned her over to the SS. But with her brother still living in her home town, Ilse Polak found her visits heartwarming because they connected her with childhood memories. For Lucy Mandelstam, a late-in-life visit was also liberating: "I felt my life had now come full circle and that I had come to terms with the past." Of course, specialists in German history or literature such as Fritz Stern and Ruth Klüger developed professional ties to the FRG, whose liberalization they supported. But few went as far as Georg Iggers, who returned temporarily to Göttingen, or Tom Angress, who moved permanently back to Berlin in order to teach young Germans about the Holocaust. As Auschwitz survivor Judith Magyar Isaacson wrote, "We cannot forget, but we have to learn to forgive."[35]

NEW GERMANS

The horrific experiences and troubling memories of the twentieth century have transformed the majority of Germans, making them profoundly different from their European neighbors. While British media can still be proud of their imperial past, the French public glory in their cultural achievements, and Polish patriots find solace in their "martyrology," the citizens of the Federal Republic have a more negative history to refer to. In international comparisons of "national pride," the Germans consistently rank at the bottom of the scale, below other developed countries full of robust self-esteem such as the United States. Even if they show some pleasure in their economic prowess, athletic success, or liberal constitution, they remain more willing to identify themselves as "Europeans" than do members of other countries. And, in spite of nativist backlash, Chancellor Angela Merkel has therefore been more inclined to accept refugees from abroad. Surprisingly enough, in a 2016 business survey by *US News & World Report* Germany came in number one among "the world's best countries"—even beating out the United States.[36]

In part, these autobiographies show that this transformation was a response to the negative German experiences of the twentieth century. The initial confidence of the Empire was shattered by the privations of the First World War and the chaotic aftermath of defeat. The Weimar consolidation that provided happy childhoods disappeared in the Great Depression. The temporary improvement during the peaceful years of the Third Reich led into frightful suffering in World War II and the Holocaust. Moreover, the postwar project of creating a more egalitarian society ended up in a Communist dictatorship. Only the somewhat bumbling beginning of the Federal Republic led to peace, prosperity and reunification. Whenever Germans tried to lord it over their neighbors, they ended up suffering the consequences, turning from perpetrators into victims themselves. Even nationalists such as Karl Härtel realized that "in inhumane and cynical disregard such a policy has degraded the people and their fate into an instrument of their striving for power."[37]

Having to deal with oppressive memories has made many postwar Germans more self-critical than their neighbors. Setting out to convey the "subjective feeling about this fatal development" required courageous introspection rather than evasive self-justification. Looking back on their lives, writers such as Heinz Schultheis understood that their individual trials were inextricably linked to the larger disasters of the country. This realization posed the question of personal responsibility: what had they done to support the Nazi genocide or what had they left undone to help the victims? For Renate Finckh, this self-examination led to "a terrible recognition. What I had wanted to keep safely in my heart, had turned into guilt and shame." In this process, she "saw that I had been loyal to evil" and assisted in a "whole big lie." But she found the courage to live on after such a youth. "Since I could grow, everything was not finished."[38] Even if a right-wing fringe continues to deny German responsibility, the critical consensus on the past remains strong.[39]

Heeding the lessons of experience and memory has transformed many Germans into sincere democrats and pacifists who want to prevent a recurrence of earlier horrors. Once a proud soldier who "believed in German victory," Dieter Schoenhals sought to make his Swedish students learn from his own mistakes in order "to prohibit above all the abuse of youthful idealism by irresponsible demagogues" in a racist dictatorship. "Everything possible needs to be done in order to avoid another war, not just a nuclear conflict, but war, period." Toward the end of their lives, Weimar children formulated their conclusion in the triple injunction "never again" to permit a dictatorship, war, or Holocaust. Seeking to come to terms with their broken lives, most of them embraced human rights, pacifism, social solidarity, and ecology.[40] According to British historian Timothy Garton Ash, "it is an irony of history . . . that today it is Germany which is an island of stability and the last hope of liberalism."[41] Even if not all have seen the light, many Germans have changed so much that their imperial ancestors would hardly recognize them.

Acknowledgments

This book is an answer to "Spinoza," a reader of my synthesis *Out of Ashes*, who called for a history "from what you would really experience on the streets of these German cities" on Amazon.com on July 31, 2015. Since books are written conversations, I would like to thank all the many interlocutors, such as Erich Helmer, Johanna Hagenauer, Dorothea Klessmann, Siegfried Mews, Irmgard Mueller, Joachim Petzold, Hellmut Raschdorff, and Gerhard Weinberg, who shared their personal stories with me. Moreover, I am truly grateful to Ulrich Grothus, Karen Hagemann, Katharina Hochmuth, Gerhild Krapf, Helmi Lehmann, Nina Lemmens, and Michael Schoenhals for allowing me to read the manuscript recollections of their parents or grandparents. I am also indebted to the families of Günter Gros, Karl Härtel, Anneliese Huber, Gerhard Joachim, Robert Neumaier, Heinz Schultheis, Erika Taubhorn, and Hans Tausch for permitting me to quote from their autobiographies. Moreover, I am thankful for being able to reproduce images from Horst Andrée, Ursula Baehrenburg, Ruth Bulwin, Horst and Gisela Grothus, Winfried Weigelt, and the Kempowski collection, as well as the photo archive of the Stiftung Preussischer Kulturbesitz.

I would also like to express my gratitude to Maren Horn of the Literaturarchiv of the Akademie der Künste in Berlin, Jutta Jäger-Schenk of the Deutsches Tagebucharchiv in Emmendingen, and Frank Mecklenburg of the Leo Baeck Archive for giving me access to their rich collections of autobiographies. At the same time, I want to give thanks to the Z. Smith-Reynolds Foundation for a senior research and study leave in 2016, as well as to the Georges Lurcy Foundation for supporting the gathering of material and the writing. Moreover, I am grateful to Christiane Lemke and Helga Welsh for commenting on the manuscript and to Caroline Nilsen for pre-editing the text. I am immensely indebted as well to Brigitta van Rheinberg's criticism and encouragement during the revision of the manuscript. Finally, I want to dedicate this book to my many graduate students whose curiosity has inspired me to look at the past through the eyes of ordinary Germans.

Notes

INTRODUCTION: NARRATIVES OF GERMAN EXPERIENCES

1. Johanna Hagenauer, "Bericht über die Nacht vom 16. März 1945, in der ein englischer Großangriff Würzburg vollständig in Schutt und Asche legte" (MS, Munich, 2015). Cf. W. G. Sebald, *Luftkrieg und Literatur* (Munich, 1999). The brief notes only provide source citations and a few suggestions for further reading.
2. Bettina Fehr, "Erinnerungen" (Bonn, 2005), 227. For a general framework, see Konrad H. Jarausch, *Out of Ashes: A New History of Europe in the Twentieth Century* (Princeton, NJ, 2015).
3. Robert Moeller, *War Stories: The Search for a Usable Past in the Federal Republic of Germany* (Berkeley, 2001).
4. Konrad H. Jarausch, *After Hitler: Recivilizing Germans, 1945–1995* (New York, 2008).
5. Peter Fritzsche, *The Turbulent World of Franz Göll: An Ordinary Berliner Writes the Twentieth Century* (Cambridge, MA, 2011) focuses on one extraordinary individual, while Mary Fulbrook, *Dissonant Lives: Generations and Violence through the German Dictatorships* (Oxford, UK, 2011) draws on an unspecified number of testimonies.
6. Dirk Moses, *German Intellectuals and the Nazi Past* (Cambridge, UK, 2007); Bernd Weisbrod, "German Generations: The Anxiety of Belonging in Modern German History," in Kierstin Gerland, ed., *Generation und Erwartung: Konstruktionen zwischen Vergangenheit und Zukunft* (Göttingen, 2013).
7. http://www.biographyonline.net/people/germans-greatest-100.html, checked on February 14, 2016.
8. For the methodology, see Dorothee Wierling, *Geboren im Jahr Eins: Der Jahrgang 1919 in der DDR: Versuch einer Kollektivbiographie* (Berlin, 2002) and Volker Benkert, "Biographien im Umbruch. Die um 1970 in der DDR Geborenen zwischen Geschichte und Erinnerung" (Diss., Potsdam, 2016).
9. Konrad H. Jarausch, *Die Umkehr: Deutsche Wandlungen 1945–1995* (Munich, 2004); Edgar Wolfrum, *Die geglückte Demokratie: Geschichte der Bundesrepublik Deutschland von ihren Anfängen bis zur Gegenwart* (Stuttgart, 2006).
10. Christopher Browning, *Ordinary Men: Police Battalion 101 and the Final Solution in Poland* (New York, 1993).

11. Thomas Kohut, *A German Generation: An Experiential History of the Twentieth Century* (New Haven, CT, 2012); Nicholas Stargardt, *The German War: A Nation under Arms, 1939–1945* (London, 2015).
12. Karen Hagemann and Jean Quaetert, eds., *Gendering Modern German History: Themes, Debates, Revisions* (New York, 2007).
13. Cornelia Siebeck, "'Einzug ins verheißene Land': Richard von Weizsäckers Rede zum 40. Jahrestag des Kriegsendes am 8. Mai 1985," *Zeithistorische Forschungen* 12, no. 1 (2015), online edition, http://www.zeithistorische-forschungen.de/1-2015/id=5177.
14. For instance, Gisela Grothus, née Wagner, "Mein Leben" (Dorsten, n.d.).
15. See the extensive presentation at https://www.lbi.org/.
16. Walter Kempowski, *Das Echolot: Ein kollektives Tagebuch* (Munich, 1993–2005), 12 vols, covering the years from 1941 to 1945. See also the electronic catalogue of the Literaturarchiv in the Akademie der Künste.
17. Deutsches Tagebucharchiv Emmendingen, http://www.tagebucharchiv.de/.
18. Janosch Steuer and Rüdiger Graf, eds., *Selbstreflexionen und Weltdeutungen: Tagebücher in der Geschichte und der Geschichtsschreibung des 20. Jahrhunderts* (Göttingen, 2015), 336–62.
19. Judith Magyar Isaacson, *Befreiung in Leipzig: Erinnerungen einer ungarischen Jüdin* (Witzenhausen, 1991), 228–38. Cf. Jeremy Popkin, *History, Historians and Autobiography* (Chicago, 2005) and Christopher Cowley, *The Philosophy of Autobiography* (Chicago, 2015).
20. Volker Depkat, "Autobiographie und die soziale Konstruktion von Wirklichkeit," *Geschichte und Gesellschaft* 29 (2003): 441–76. Cf. Christiane Lahusen, *Zukunft am Ende: Autobiographische Sinnstiftungen von DDR-Geisteswissenschaftlern nach 1989* (Bielefeld, 2014).
21. Alf Lüdtke, *Alltagsgeschichte: Zur Rekonstruktion historischer Erfahrungen und Lebensweisen* (Frankfurt, 1989); David Crew, "Alltagsgeschichte: A New Social History 'from Below'?," *Central European History* 22 (1989): 394–407.
22. Gerhard Botz, ed., *Schweigen und Reden einer Generation: Erinnerungsgespräche mit Opfern, Tätern und Mitläufern des Nationalsozialismus* (Vienna, 2005).
23. Gerhard Paul, *Visual History: Ein Studienbuch* (Göttingen, 2006); Irina O. Rajewski, "Intermediality, Intertextuality, and Remediation: A Literary Perspective on Intermediality," *Intermédialités* 6 (2005): 43–64.
24. Konrad H. Jarausch and Michael Geyer, *Shattered Past: Reconstructing German Histories* (Princeton, NJ, 2003), 317–41. Cf. Martin Sabrow, ed., *Autobiographische Aufarbeitung: Diktatur und Lebensgeschichte im 20. Jahrhundert* (Göttingen, 2012).
25. Konrad H. Jarausch, "Towards a Social History of Experience: Postmodern Predicaments in Theory and Interdisciplinarity," *Central European History* 22 (1989): 427–43. Cf. Ulrike Jureit, "Autobiographien: Rückfragen an ein gelebtes Leben," in Sabrow, *Autobiographische Aufarbeitung*, 149–57.
26. Günter Grass, *Crabwalk: A Novel* (Orlando, FL, 2003).
27. Bill Niven, ed., *Germans as Victims: Remembering the Past in Contemporary Germany* (Basingstoke, 2006); Helmut Schmitz, ed., *A Nation of Victims: Representations of German Wartime Suffering from 1945 to the Present* (Amsterdam, 2007).
28. Kohut, *A German Generation*, 9–12.

29. Sabine Friedrich, *Wer wir sind: Roman* (Munich, 2002). See also the tighter novel by Regina Scheer, *Machandel. Roman*, 4th ed. (Munich, 2014).
30. Fritz Stern, *Five Germanys I Have Known* (New York, 2007).
31. Eckart Conze, *Suche nach Sicherheit: Eine Geschichte der Bundesrepublik Deutschland von 1949 bis in die Gegenwart* (Berlin, 2009).
32. Ulla Hahn, *Das verborgene Wort: Roman* (Stuttgart, 2001); Uwe Tellkamp, *The Tower: A Novel* (London, 2014).
33. Ruth Klüger, *Weiter leben: Eine Jugend* (Göttingen, 1992). Cf. Tony Judt, *Postwar: A History of Europe since 1945* (New York, 2005).
34. Isaacson, *Befreiung in Leipzig*, 73. Cf. Jeffrey Herf, *Divided Memories: The Nazi Past in the Two Germanys* (Cambridge, UK, 1997); Gilad Margalit, *Guilt, Suffering and Memory: Germany Remembers Its Dead of World War II* (Bloomington, IN, 2010).
35. Konrad H. Jarausch, "Towards a Critical Memory: Some German Reflections," keynote address at conference on comparative East European and East Asian memories, Osaka, Japan, Thanksgiving 2015.
36. Konrad H. Jarausch and Martin Sabrow, eds., *Verletztes Gedächtnis: Erinnerungskultur und Zeitgeschichte im Konflikt* (Frankfurt, 2002).
37. Ulrich Herbert, *Deutsche Geschichte im zwanzigsten Jahrhundert* (Munich, 2015); Helmut Walser Smith, *The Continuities of German History: Nation, Religion, and Race across the Long Nineteenth Century* (Cambridge, UK, 2008).
38. Jakobine Witolla, "Tagebuch, 1923–1990" (Hameln, 1990).

CHAPTER 1. IMPERIAL ANCESTORS

1. Erich Helmer, "'Der Tornister:' Autobiographie 1922–1983," vol. 1, 2.
2. Heinz Schultheis, *Kindheit und Jugend zwischen den Kriegen und Erwachsenwerden danach* (Leverkusen, 2007–2010), 9.
3. Edith Schöffski, "Erinnerungen: Nur in der Rückschau, in der Zusammenfassung alles Erfahrenen, besitzen wir unser Leben ganz" (Berlin, n.d.), 6.
4. Jürgen Kocka, ed., *Bourgeois Society in Nineteenth Century Europe* (Oxford, UK, 1993).
5. Schöffski, "Erinnerungen," 4; Agnes Moosmann, *Barfuß aber nicht arm. Kindheit und Jugend in Bodnegg* (Sigmaringen, 1985).
6. Karl Härtel, "Leben in grosser Zeit: Von den goldenen 20ern bis zum Zusammenbruch des Deutschen Reiches und dem beginnenden Wiederaufbau" (Leopoldshafen, 1996), 15.
7. Thomas Kühne, "Demokratisierung und Parlamentarisierung: Neue Forschungen zur politischen Entwicklungsfähigkeit Deutschlands vor dem Ersten Weltkrieg," *Geschichte und Gesellschaft* 31 (2005): 293–316; Konrad H. Jarausch and Michael Geyer, *Shattered Past: Reconstructing German Histories* (Princeton, NJ, 2003), 1–33.
8. Horst Andrée, *Stationen meines Lebens* (Boxberg, 2000), 3.
9. Benno Schöffski, "Meine Familiengeschichte von 1835 bis 1980" (Berlin, 1980), 3.
10. Härtel, "Leben in grosser Zeit," 1–6.
11. Helmer, "Tornister," vol. 1, 74. Cf. Thomas Pegelow Kaplan, *The Language of Nazi Genocide: Linguistic Violence and the Struggle of Germans of Jewish Ancestry* (New York, 2009).

12. Andrée, *Stationen meines Lebens*, 7–8.
13. Albert Gompertz, "Experiences of Albert Gompertz: From Nazi Germany to America" (Palm Beach, 1998).
14. Schöffski, "Familiengeschichte," 3–14.
15. Eberhard Scholz-Eule, ed., *Wir Scholz-Kinder vom Herrnvorwerk: Aus dem Leben einer schlesischen Familie daheim und in der Zerstreuung*, 4th ed. (St. Georgen, 2008).
16. Joachim Fest, *Not I: Memoirs of a German Childhood* (New York, 2013), 3; and Gerhardt B. Thamm, *Boy Soldier: A German Teenager at the Nazi Twilight* (Jefferson, NC, 2000), 9. Cf. Peter Watson, *The German Genius: Europe's Third Renaissance, the Second Scientific Revolution, and the Twentieth Century* (New York, 2010).
17. Alon Confino, *The Nation as a Local Metaphor: Württemberg, Imperial Germany, and National Memory, 1871–1918* (Chapel Hill, 1997).
18. Fest, *Not I*, 4–5. Cf. Jürgen Osterhammel, *The Transformation of the World: A Global History of the Nineteenth Century* (Princeton, NJ, 2014).
19. Hans Queiser, *"Du gehörst dem Führer!": Vom Hitlerjungen zum Kriegsberichter: Ein autobiographischer Bericht* (Cologne, 1993), 20–22; Schöffski, "Familiengeschichte," 55–57, 61–65.
20. Mack Walker, *German Home Towns: Community, State, and General Estate, 1648–1871* (Ithaca, NY, 1971).
21. Theodore S. Hamerow, *The Birth of a New Europe: State and Society in the Nineteenth Century* (Chapel Hill, NC, 1983).
22. Schöffski, "Erinnerungen," 1–3.
23. Queiser, *"Du gehörst dem Führer!,"* 18–19.
24. Schöffski, "Familiengeschichte," 41; Ursula Mahlendorf, *Shame of Survival: Working Through a Nazi Childhood* (University Park, PA, 2009), 53.
25. Horst Grothus, "Horst in seiner Zeit," 3rd ed. (Dorsten, n.d.), 9–10.
26. Gisela Grothus, "Mein Leben" (Dorsten, n.d.), 9–10
27. Frank Eyck, *A Historian's Pilgrimage: Memoirs and Reflections*, edited by Rosemarie Eyck (Calgary, 2009).
28. Schöffski, "Erinnerungen," 3; Hans-Harald Schirmer, "Erinnerungen an die Familie Hans und Luise Schirmer aus Wolfenbüttel," 9; and Gerhard Baucke, *Das Buch gehört dazu: Gute Seiten—Schlechte Seiten: Spiegelbild erlebter Zeiten 1919–1999* (Berlin, 2002).
29. Gertrud Koch, *Edelweiß: Meine Jugend als Widerstandskämpferin* (Reinbeck, 2006), 26–27; Queiser, *"Du gehörst dem Führer!,"* 23.
30. Siegfried Weichlein, *Nation und Region: Integrationsprozesse im Bismarckreich* (Düsseldorf, 2004).
31. Schirmer, "Erinnerungen." Cf. James Retallack, *Germany in the Age of Kaiser William II* (New York, 1996).
32. Philippe Ariès, *Centuries of Childhood: A Social History of Family Life* (New York, 1962).
33. Grothus, "Horst," 8.
34. Gerhard Joachim, "Wundersame Reise des Odysseus des XX. Jahrhunderts: Von Hitlers Aufstieg bis zum Untergang der Stalinistischen Ära" (Rostock, 1998).
35. Erika Taubhorn, "Mein Leben: Erinnerungen," (Wupperthal, 2000), 4.

36. Fritz Klein, *Drinnen und Draußen: Ein Historiker in der DDR; Erinnerungen* (Frankfurt, 2000), 54–58. Cf. Daniel Fuda, Dagmar Herzog, Stefan-Ludwig Hoffmann, and Till van Rahden, eds., *Demokratie im Schatten von Gewalt: Geschichten des Privaten im deutschen Nachkrieg* (Göttingen, 2010).
37. Grothus, "Mein Leben," 11.
38. Werner T. Angress, *Witness to the Storm: A Jewish Journey from Nazi Berlin to the 82nd Airborne, 1920–1945* (Durham, NC, 2012), 7–11.
39. Härtel, "Leben in grosser Zeit," 10. Cf. Ann Taylor Allen, *Feminism and Motherhood in Germany, 1800–1914* (New Brunswick, NJ, 1991).
40. Helmi Lehmann, "Verwehte Spuren: Aus dem Leben unseres Vaters Friedrich Wilhelm Lehmann" (Schliersee, n.d.).
41. Angress, *Witness to the Storm*, 6–30.
42. Ruth Bulwin, *Spätes Echo: Erzählungen aus Großmutters jungen Jahren* (Wismar, 2014), 6–32.
43. Härtel, "Leben in grosser Zeit," 9–15.
44. Gerhard Krapf, "Recollections" (Edmonton, 1990s), 124–90. Cf. Helmut Walser Smith, *German Nationalism and Religious Conflict: Culture, Ideology, Politics, 1870–1914* (Princeton, NJ, 1995).
45. Hellmut Raschdorff, "Mein Leben von 1922 bis Ende 2003" (Freiburg, 2003). Cf. Also Jonathan Sperber, *Popular Catholicism in Nineteenth Century Germany* (Princeton, NJ, 1984).
46. Werner Warmbrunn, "The Terrace Memoirs," 1ff. Cf. Jehuda Reinharz and Walter Schatzberg, eds., *The Jewish Response to German Culture* (Hanover, NH, 1985).
47. Schöffski, "Erinnerungen," 1–2, 12.
48. Schöffski, "Meine Familiengeschichte," 1–15, 90.
49. Winfried Weigelt, *Mein langes Leben* (Schwerin, 2017), 38–55; Ursula Mahlendorf, *Shame of Survival*; and Fritz Stern, *Five Germanys I Have Known* (New York, 2007), passim.
50. Schultheis, *Kindheit und Jugend*, 1, 15.
51. Hermann Debus, *Ein Leben im Wandel der Zeiten* (Dörscheid, 1998).
52. Moosmann, *Barfuß*, 9–95.
53. Klein, *Drinnen und Draußen*, 22–35; Ingrid Bork, *Jedes Unglück hat ein Glück in sich: Friedrichshainer Lebenserinnerungen* (Berlin, 2010). Cf. Gerhard Masur, *Imperial Berlin* (New York, 1972).
54. Scholz-Eule, *Wir Scholz-Kinder*, 15. Cf. Rainer Lepsius, *Demokratie in Deutschland: Soziologisch-historische Konstellationsanalysen: Ausgewählte Aufsätze* (Göttingen, 1993).
55. Eyck, *Historian's Pilgrimage*, 36–60. Cf. James J. Sheehan, *German Liberalism in the Nineteenth Century* (Chicago, 1978).
56. Moosmann, *Barfuß*, 23, 55; Fest, *Not I*, 17–24; Härtel, "Leben in grosser Zeit," 10–11. Cf. also Michael E. O'Sullivan, "From Catholic Milieu to Lived Religion: The Social and Cultural History of Modern German Catholicism," *History Compass* 7 (2009): 837–61.
57. Schirmer, "Erinnerungen," 9. Cf. Vernon A. Lidtke, *The Alternative Culture: Socialist Labor in Imperial Germany* (New York, 1985).
58. Schirmer, "Erinnerungen," passim. Cf. also John Röhl, *Kaiser Wilhelm II, 1859–1941: A Concise Life* (Cambridge, UK, 2014).

59. Koch, *Edelweiß*, 28–30.
60. Schöffski, "Erinnerungen," 1; Angress, *Witness to the Storm*, 7; Härtel, "Leben in grosser Zeit," 15ff. Cf. Belinda Davis, *Home Fires Burning: Food, Politics and Everyday Life in World War I Berlin* (Chapel Hill, NC, 2000).
61. Schöffski, "Erinnerungen," 1; and Härtel, "Leben in grosser Zeit," 16–17. Cf. Adam Seipp, *The Ordeal of Peace: Demobilization and the Urban Experience in Britain and Germany, 1917–1921* (Farnham, 2009).
62. Schultheis, *Kindheit und Jugend*, 10; and Weigelt, *Mein langes Leben*, 26.
63. Queiser, *"Du gehörst dem Führer!,"* 22. Cf. Barbara Stambolis, *Leben mit und in der Geschichte: Deutsche Historiker Jahrgang 1943* (Essen, 2010).
64. Scott Krause, "Surveying the Reich of the Future: American Observers' Paradoxical Perceptions of Wilhelmine Germany's Relative Modernity, 1888–1914," in *Different Germans*, edited by Konrad H. Jarausch, Karin Goihl, and Harald Wenzel (New York, 2016), 25–52.
65. Eric D. Weitz, *Weimar Germany: Promise and Tragedy* (Princeton, NJ, 2009).
66. Konrad H. Jarausch, *Out of Ashes: A New History of Europe in the 20th Century* (Princeton, NJ, 2015).
67. Schirmer, "Erinnerungen," passim.

CHAPTER 2. WEIMAR CHILDREN

1. Horst Andrée, *Stationen meines Lebens* (Boxberg, 2000), 9–12; Bulwin, *Spätes Echo: Erzählungen aus Großmutters jungen Jahren* (Wismar, 2014), 7.
2. Karl Härtel, "Leben in grosser Zeit: Von den goldenen 20ern bis zum Zusammenbruch des Deutschen Reiches und dem beginnenden Wiederaufbau" (Leopoldshafen, 1996), 9.
3. Gerhard Krapf, "Recollections" (Edmonton, 1990s), 1. Cf. Christa Wolf, *Patterns of Childhood* (New York, 1984), 6.
4. Philippe Ariès, *Centuries of Childhood: A Social History of Family Life* (New York, 1962).
5. Hugh Cunningham, "Histories of Childhood," *American Historical Review* 103 (1998): 1195–208.
6. Härtel, "Leben in grosser Zeit," 14.
7. Rüdiger Graf, "Either—Or: The Narrative of 'Crisis' in Weimar Germany and in Historiography," *Central European History* 43 (2010): 592–615.
8. Krapf, "Recollections," 8. Cf. Karen Hagemann, *Frauenalltag und Männerpolitik: Alltagsleben und gesellschaftliches Handeln von Arbeiterfrauen in der Weimarer Republik* (Bonn, 1990).
9. Doris Bühler-Niederberger, "Sozialisation in der Kindheit," in *Handbuch Sozialisationsforschung*, 8th ed., ed. Klaus Hurrelmann (Weinheim, 2015), 833–49.
10. Härtel, "Leben in grosser Zeit," 9; Heinz Schultheis, *Kindheit und Jugend zwischen den Kriegen und Erwachsenwerden danach* (Leverkusen, 2007-2010), 16.
11. Härtel , "Leben in grosser Zeit," 10; Erich Helmer, "'Der Tornister:' Autobiographie 1922–1983," vol. 1, 4; Andrée, *Stationen*, 15; and Robert Neumaier, "Das war—Das ist mein Leben, 1924–2006," 7.
12. Schultheis, *Kindheit und Jugend*, 20–24.

13. Erika Taubhorn, "Mein Leben: Erinnerungen" (Wuppertal, 2000), 3f; Hans Queiser, *"Du gehörst dem Führer!": Vom Hitlerjungen zum Kriegsberichter: Ein autobiographischer Bericht* (Cologne, 1993), 23.
14. Krapf, "Recollections," passim; Bulwin, *Spätes Echo*, 23.
15. Härtel, "Leben in grosser Zeit," 39; Edith Schöffski, "Erinnerungen: Nur in der Rückschau, in der Zusammenfassung alles Erfahrenen, besitzen wir unser Leben ganz" (Berlin, n.d.), 15ff; and Winfried Weigelt, *Mein langes Leben* (Schwerin, 2017), 13.
16. Paul Frenzel, *40 verlorene Jahre: Erinnerungen an die Diktatur des nationalen und des realen Sozialismus* (Stuttgart, 1994), 25–28. Cf. Fritz Klein, *Drinnen und Draußen: Ein Historiker in der DDR; Erinnerungen* (Frankfurt, 2000), 25; Schöffski, "Erinnerungen," 20; Ursula Mahlendorf, *Shame of Survival: Working Through a Nazi Childhood* (University Park, PA, 2009), 20.
17. Bulwin, *Spätes Echo*, 12–16; Werner T. Angress, *Witness to the Storm: A Jewish Journey from Nazi Berlin to the 82nd Airborne, 1920–1945* (Durham, NC, 2012), 24–26; Moosmann, *Barfuß aber nicht arm: Kindheit und Jugend in Bodnegg* (Sigmaringen, 1985), 91ff.
18. Klein, *Drinnen und Draußen*, 24; Angress, *Witness to the Storm*, 31–34.
19. Schultheis, *Kindheit und Jugend*, 1; Krapf, "Recollections," 10–40; Andrée, *Stationen*, 15; Neumaier, "Das war—Das ist mein Leben," 4.
20. Bulwin, *Spätes Echo*, 8; Härtel, "Leben in grosser Zeit," 11–12.
21. Edith Schöffski, "Erinnerungen," 21–24.
22. Krapf, "Recollections," 16–17; Härtel, "Leben in grosser Zeit," 18; Schöffski, "Erinnerungen," 24; Horst Grothus, "Horst in seiner Zeit," 3rd ed. (Dorsten, n.d.), 8.
23. Schultheis, *Kindheit und Jugend*, 13; Taubhorn, "Mein Leben," 4. Cf. Grothus, "Horst," 10; Bulwin, *Spätes Echo*, 19–22.; and Moosmann, *Barfuß*, 62ff.
24. Krapf, "Recollections," 49–66; Härtel, "Leben in grosser Zeit," 21. Cf. Joe Perry, "Nazifying Christmas: Political Culture and Popular Celebration in the Third Reich," *Central European History* 38 (2005): 572–605.
25. Härtel, "Leben in grosser Zeit," 19ff; Bulwin, *Spätes Echo*, 16ff; Frenzel, *40 Verlorene Jahre*, 28ff; and Frank Eyck, *A Historian's Pilgrimage: Memoirs and Reflections*, edited by Rosemarie Eyck (Calgary, 2009), 66ff.
26. Angress, *Witness to the Storm*, 34; Eyck, *Historian's Pilgrimage*, 57.
27. Schultheis, *Kindheit und Jugend*, 17; Härtel, "Leben in grosser Zeit," 35. Cf. Karen Hagemann and Konrad H. Jarausch, eds., *Children, Families and States: Time Policies of Childcare, Preschool and Early Education in Europe* (New York, 2011).
28. Marjorie Lamberti, *The Politics of Education: Teachers and School Reform in Weimar Germany* (New York, 2002); Krapf, "Recollections," 113.
29. Bulwin, *Spätes Echo*, 28f; Schultheis, *Kindheit und Jugend*, 18f. Cf. Konrad H. Jarausch "Professor Unrat: Schule als kultureller Erinnerungsort," in *Deutsche Erinnerungsorte*, edited by Etienne François and Hagen Schulze, 315–31 (Munich, 2001).
30. Bulwin, *Spätes Echo*, 28 f; Taubhorn, "Mein Leben," 5; Schultheis, *Kindheit und Jugend*, 19; Moosmann, *Barfuß*, 81ff.
31. Taubhorn, "Mein Leben," 4; Schultheis, *Kindheit und Jugend*, 19; Härtel, "Leben in grosser Zeit," 35.

32. Hans Queiser, *"Du gehörst dem Führer!,"* 25–29.
33. Mahlendorf, *Shame of Survival*, 43ff; Klein, *Drinnen und Draußen*, 32; Frenzel, *40 verlorene Jahre*, 26f.
34. Schöffski, "Erinnerungen," 27f; Helmer, "Tornister," vol. 1, 5.
35. Gisela Grothus, "Mein Leben" (Dorsten, n.d.), 13–15; Warmbrunn, "Terrace Memoirs," 3–5. Cf. Schultheis, *Kindheit und Jugend*, 29.
36. Krapf, "Recollections," 113; Schultheis, *Kindheit und Jugend*, 11; Warmbrunn, "Terrace Memoirs," 3–6; Moosmann, *Barfuß*, 88ff. Cf. Ann Taylor Allen, *Feminism and Motherhood in Germany, 1800–1914* (New Brunswick, NJ, 1991).
37. Härtel, "Leben in grosser Zeit," 57. Cf. *Handbuch der deutschen Bildungsgeschichte*, vol. 5: *Die Weimarer Republik und die nationalsozialistische Diktatur*, edited by Dieter Langewiesche and Heinz-Elmar Tenorth (Munich, 1989).
38. Schultheis, *Kindheit und Jugend*, 28ff; Grothus, "Horst," 11; Hans Tausch, "Mein Lebensbericht" (Forchheim, 1984), 9ff. Cf. Margret Kraul, *Das deutsche Gymnasium: 1860–1980* (Frankfurt, 1984).
39. Frenzel, *40 verlorene Jahre*, 49; and Hans-Harald Schirmer, "Erinnerungen an die Familie Hans und Luise Schirmer aus Wolfenbüttel."
40. Ursula Baehrenburg, "Maikäfer flieg: Lebenserinnerungen 1920–2005" (Lautertal, 2005); Moosmann, *Barfuß*, 95ff; and Härtel, "Leben in grosser Zeit," 60–72.
41. Grothus, "Horst," 10; Warmbrunn, "Terrace Memoirs," 2. Cf. Christoph Führ, *Zur Schulpolitik der Weimarer Republik* (Weinheim, 1970).
42. Eva Sternheim-Peters, *Habe ich denn allein gejubelt? Eine Jugend im Nationalsozialismus* (Berlin, 2015), 20–44.
43. Grothus, "Mein Leben," 13; Baehrenburg, "Maikäfer flieg"; Krapf, "Recollections," 114. Cf. Paul Shirley, *The Politics of Progressive Education: The Odenwaldschule in Nazi Germany* (Cambridge, UK, 1992).
44. Andrée, *Stationen*, 15; and Helmer, "Tornister," vol. 1, 47.
45. Schultheis, *Kindheit und Jugend*, 2–15.
46. Bulwin, *Spätes Echo*, 26; Schöffski, "Erinnerungen," 6.
47. Benno Schöffski, "Meine Familiengeschichte von 1835 bis 1980" (Berlin, 1980), 59; Schöffski, "Erinnerungen," 18; Krapf, "Recollections," 122; Helmer, "Tornister," vol. 1, 4.
48. Schöffski, "Erinnerungen," 24; Frenzel, *40 verlorene Jahre*, 29; Angress, *Witness to the Storm*, 38.
49. Bulwin, *Spätes Echo*, 21; Grothus, "Erinnerungen," 15; Schultheis, *Kindheit und Jugend*, 29.
50. Helmer, "Tornister," vol. 1, 6; Schöffski, "Familiengeschichte," 60; Moosmann; *Barfuß*, 90; Härtel, "Leben in grosser Zeit," 36.
51. Angress, *Witness to the Storm*, 56; Frenzel, *40 verlorene Jahre*, 34; Grothus, "Horst," 7, 10.
52. Sternheim-Peters, *Habe ich denn*, 180–86; Krapf, "Recollections," 134–35. Cf. Franz-Josef Krafeld, *Geschichte der Jugendarbeit: Von den Anfängen bis zur Gegenwart* (Weinheim, 1984).
53. Frenzel, *40 verlorene Jahre*, 35–39; Will Seelmann-Eggebert, *Weder Narren noch Täter—der Schock kam erst später* (Ahlhorn, 2004), 33. Cf. Rüdiger Ahrens, *Bündische Jugend: Eine neue Geschichte* (Göttingen, 2015).

54. Mahlendorf, *Shame of Survival*, 12; Frenzel, *40 verlorene Jahre*, 31; Bulwin, *Spätes Echo*, 31; and Sternheim-Peters, *Habe ich denn*, 72–91. Cf. Harold James, *The German Slump: Politics and Economics, 1924–1936* (Oxford, UK, 1986).
55. Joachim Fest, *Not I: Memoirs of a German Childhood* (New York, 2013), 38f; Neumaier, "Mein Leben," 5; and Schultheis, *Kindheit und Jugend*, 26–27. Cf. Dirk Schuman, *Political Violence in the Weimar Republic, 1918–1933: Fight for the Streets and Fear of Civil War* (New York, 2009).
56. Eyck, *Historian's Pilgrimage*, 62ff; Angress, *Witness to the Storm*, 55ff; Warmbrunn, "Terrace Memoirs," 2. Cf. Konrad H. Jarausch, *Students, Society and Politics in Imperial Germany: The Rise of Academic Illiberalism* (Princeton, NJ, 1982), 264ff.
57. Eyck, *Historian's Pilgrimage*, 60; Klein, *Drinnen und Draußen*, 33–38; Schirmer, "Erinnerungen," 25; Bulwin, *Spätes Echo*, 33. Cf. Eric Weitz, *Weimar Germany: Promise and Tragedy* (Princeton, NJ, 2007).
58. Eyck, *Historian's Pilgrimage*, 75–76; Angress, *Witness to the Storm*, 65–66. Cf. Henry Turner, *Hitler's Thirty Days to Power: January 1933* (Reading, MA, 1996).
59. Krapf, "Recollections," 143; Weigelt, *Langes Leben*, 26.
60. Grothus, "Mein Leben," 17; Angress, *Witness to the Storm*, 45–46; Klein, *Drinnen und Draußen*, 33–42.
61. Härtel, "Leben in grosser Zeit," 50; Hellmut Raschdorff, "Mein Leben von 1922 bis Ende 2003" (Freiburg, 2003), 16; and Schöffski, "Erinnerungen," 21.
62. Härtel, "Leben in grosser Zeit," 50–51; Schultheis, *Kindheit und Jugend*, 12. Cf. Lu Seegers and Jürgen Reulecke, eds., *Die "Generation der Kriegskinder": Historische Hintergründe und Deutungen* (Giessen, 2009).

CHAPTER 3. NAZI ADOLESCENTS

1. Carola Stern, *In den Netzen der Erinnerung: Lebensgeschichten zweier Menschen* (Hamburg, 1986), 85f; Gerhard Baucke, *Das Buch gehört dazu: Gute Seiten—Schlechte Seiten: Spiegelbild erlebter Zeiten 1919–1999* (Berlin, 2002), 19; and Frank Eyck, *A Historian's Pilgrimage: Memoirs and Reflections*, edited by Rosemarie Eyck (Calgary, 2009), 75f.
2. Edward J. Kunzer, "The Youth of Nazi Germany," *The Journal of Educational Sociology* 11 (1938): 342–50; Eva Sternheim-Peters, *Habe ich denn allein gejubelt? Eine Jugend im Nationalsozialismus* (Berlin, 2015), 193.
3. John and Virginia Demos, "Adolescence in Historical Perspective," *Journal of Marriage and Family* 31 (1969): 632–38. Cf. Erik Erikson, *Identity, Youth, Crisis* (New York, 1968).
4. Peter Loewenberg, "The Psychohistorical Origins of the Nazi Youth Cohort," *American Historical Review* 76 (1975): 1457–502.
5. Sternheim-Peters, *Habe ich denn*, 193ff; Lucy Mandelstam, "Memoirs" (Netanya, 1998), 1.
6. Hans-Harald Schirmer, "Erinnerungen an die Familie Hans und Luise Schirmer aus Wolfenbüttel," 48; Winfried Weigelt, *Mein langes Leben* (Schwerin, 2017), 56ff; and Michael Kater, *Hitler Youth* (Cambridge, MA, 2004).
7. Ursula Mahlendorf, *Shame of Survival: Working Through a Nazi Childhood* (University Park, PA, 2009), 24, 38; Werner T. Angress, *Witness to the Storm: A Jewish Journey from Nazi Berlin to the 82nd Airborne, 1920–1945* (Durham, NC, 2012), 52; Gerhard Krapf,

"Recollections" (Edmonton, 1990s), 131; Ingebrog Grah, "Die rote Käthe,"; and Weigelt, *Mein langes Leben*, 84. Cf. Michael Kater, *The Nazi Party: A Social Profile of Members and Leaders, 1919–1945* (Cambridge, MA, 1983).

8. Huber, "Das war mein Leben," 9; Hellmut Raschdorff, "Mein Leben von 1922 bis Ende 2003" (Freiburg, 2003), 16; and Baucke, *Das Buch gehört dazu*, 19f.
9. Ingrid Bork, *Jedes Unglück hat ein Glück in sich: Friedrichshainer Lebenserinnerungen* (Berlin, 2010), 50; Albert Gompertz, "Experiences of Albert Gompertz: From Nazi Germany to America" (Palm Beach, 1998), 9–10; Fritz Klein, *Drinnen und Draußen: Ein Historiker in der DDR; Erinnerungen* (Frankfurt, 2000), 37–42.
10. Krapf, "Recollections," 151; Benno Schöffski, "Meine Familiengeschichte von 1835 bis 1980" (Berlin, 1980), 68; Bork, *Jedes Unglück*, 48.
11. Angress, *Witness to the Storm*, 52f; Schirmer, "Erinnerungen," 28. Cf. Eric A. Johnson, *The Gestapo, Nazi Terror, Jews and Ordinary Germans* (New York, 1999).
12. Schirmer, "Erinnerungen," 43; Angress, *Witness to the Storm*, 66; and Gompertz, "Experiences," 23. Cf. Lisa Pine, *Nazi Education* (Oxford, UK, 2010).
13. Schirmer, "Erinnerungen," 48; Hermann Debus, *Ein Leben im Wandel der Zeiten* (Dörscheid, 1998), 40. Cf. Gilmer Blackburn, *Education in the Third Reich: A Study of Race and History in Nazi Textbooks* (Albany, 1985).
14. Angress, *Witness to the Storm*, 60–62. Cf. Änne Bäumer-Schleinkofer, *Nazi Biology and Schools* (New York, 1995).
15. Krapf, "Recollections," 345f. Cf. Daniel Horn, "The Hitler Youth and Educational Decline in Nazi Germany," *History of Education Quarterly* 16 (1976): 425–47.
16. Helmer, "Tornister," vol. 1, 63; Angress, *Witness to the Storm*, 66–73. Cf. Konrad H. Jarausch, "The Perils of Professionalism: Lawyers, Teachers and Engineers in Nazi Germany," *Historical Social Research*, Supplement 24 (2010): 157–83.
17. Joachim Fest, *Not I: Memoirs of a German Childhood* (New York, 2013), 47–51; Krapf, "Recollections," 149–152; Schirmer, "Erinnerungen," 43; Angress, *Witness to the Storm*, 74–75; and Hans Queiser, *"Du gehörst dem Führer!": Vom Hitlerjungen zum Kriegsberichter: Ein autobiographischer Bericht* (Cologne, 1993), 31–33, 66–69.
18. Gisela Grothus, "Mein Leben" (Dorsten, n.d.), 13; Angress, *Witness to the Storm*, 56–77; Eyck, *Historian's Pilgrimage*, 84–89.
19. Heinz Schultheis, *Kindheit und Jugend zwischen den Kriegen und Erwachsenwerden danach* (Leverkusen, 2007–2010), 33, 50; Angress, *Witness to the Storm*, 68–77. Cf. Marion Kaplan, *Between Dignity and Despair: Jewish Life in Nazi Germany* (Oxford, UK, 1998).
20. Raschdorff, "Mein Leben," 32; Helmer, "Tornister," vol. 1, 74; Gompertz, "Experiences," 22; Eyck, *Historian's Pilgrimage*, 92–3.
21. Schultheis, *Kindheit und Jugend*, 32–34; Baucke, *Das Buch gehört dazu*, 21. Cf. Krapf, "Recollections," 164ff.
22. Bulwin, *Spätes Echo: Erzählungen aus Großmutters jungen Jahren* (Wismar, 2014), 36–37; Schultheis, *Kindheit und Jugend*, 41–42; Krapf, "Recollections, 172–173. Cf. David Clay Large, *Nazi Games: The Olympics of 1936* (New York, 2007).
23. Bork, *Jedes Unglück*, 33; Schöffski, "Erinnerungen," 29ff; Raschdorff, "Mein Leben," 18ff.
24. Schultheis, *Kindheit und Jugend*, 25.

25. Peter Stachura, *The German Youth Movement, 1900–1945: An Interpretative and Documentary History* (New York, 1981).
26. H. W. Koch, *The Hitler Youth: Origins and Development, 1922–1945* (New York, 1976).
27. Paul Frenzel, *40 verlorene Jahre: Erinnerungen an die Diktatur des nationalen und des realen Sozialismus* (Stuttgart, 1994), 40–44; Krapf, "Recollections," 153, 156.
28. Moosmann, *Barfuß*, 99ff; Sternheim-Peters, *Habe ich denn*, 192ff; Karl Härtel, "Leben in grosser Zeit: Von den goldenen 20ern bis zum Zusammenbruch des Deutschen Reiches und dem beginnenden Wiederaufbau" (Leopoldshafen, 1996), 68; Horst Johannsen, *Ein Leben von Diktatur zu Diktatur* (Bromskirchen, 2003), 22; Frenzel, *40 verlorene Jahre*, 45.
29. Schöffski, "Familiengeschichte," 65f; Schirmer, "Erinnerungen," 39f; Queiser, *"Du gehörst dem Führer!,"* 38f.
30. Queiser, *"Du gehörst dem Führer!,"* 44; Johanssen, *Ein Leben*, 22; Sternheim-Peters, *Habe ich denn*, 196–203; Krapf, "Recollections," 195.
31. Bulwin, *Spätes Echo*, 35f; Härtel, "Leben in grosser Zeit," 68; Krapf, "Recollections," 171; Qeiser, *"Du gehörst dem Führer!,"* 46–47.
32. Krapf, "Recollections," 166; Schultheis, *Kindheit und Jugend*, 40; Horst Grothus, "Horst in seiner Zeit," 3rd ed. (Dorsten, n.d.), 28–33.
33. Sternheim-Peters, *Habe ich denn*, 123–41; Krapf, "Recollections," 163; Raschdorff, "Mein Leben," 38.
34. Krapf, "Recollections," 166–69, Schultheis, *Kindheit und Jugend*, 45–47, Schöffski, "Familiengeschichte," 66–67.
35. Sternheim-Peters, *Habe ich denn*, 203–12, 224–38; Wilhelm Kolesnyk, "Wie es dazu kam, dass ich Nationalsozialist wurde," 42; Härtel, "Leben in grosser Zeit," 87; and Queiser, *"Du gehörst dem Führer!,"* 57ff.
36. Sternheim-Peters, *Habe ich denn*, 251ff; Schultheis, *Kindheit und Jugend*, 47–48; Queiser, *"Du gehörst dem Führer!,"* 40–41.
37. Harwood Childs, ed., *The Nazi Primer: Official Handbook for Schooling the Hitler Youth* (New York, 1938), 78, 145.
38. Krapf, "Recollections," 190. Cf. Richard E. Frankel, *Bismarck's Shadow: The Cult of Leadership and the Transformation of the German Right, 1890–1945* (Oxford, UK, 2005); and jacket image of George L. Mosse, *The Crisis of German Ideology: Intellectual Origins of the Third Reich* (New York, 1964).
39. Bulwin, *Spätes Echo*, 35; Sternheim-Peters, *Habe ich denn*, 212–24; Grothus, "Horst," 26. Cf. Ian Kershaw, *Hitler* (London, 2008).
40. Queiser, *"Du gehörst dem Führer!,"* 74–76; Sternheim-Peters, *Habe ich denn*, 269ff.
41. Grothus, "Horst," 20, 24–28. For a female equivalent of such Nazi enthusiasm, see Eva Sternheim-Peters.
42. Sternheim-Peters, *Habe ich denn*, 308–57; Queiser, *"Du gehörst dem Führer!,"* 78f; Bork, *Jedes Unglück*, 50; Moosmann, *Barfuß*, 102f.
43. Angress, *Witness to the Storm*, 97–127; Warmbrunn, "Terrace Memoirs," 29, 36–38; Mandelstam, "Memoirs," 5.
44. Krapf, "Recollections," 193–94; Fest, *Not I*, 207f; Frenzel, *40 verlorene Jahre*, 56–57; Schultheis, *Kindheit und Jugend*, 44.

45. Grothus, "Mein Leben," 17; Raschdorff, "Mein Leben," 32; Schöffski, "Familiengeschichte," 66–67; Krapf, "Recollections," 447–50.
46. Koleznyk, "Wie es dazu kam," 20, 39–43; Bulwin, *Spätes Echo*, 34.
47. Fest, *Not I*, 62; Schultheis, *Kindheit und Jugend*, 34; Krapf, "Recollections," 265–69; Horst Andrée, *Stationen meines Lebens* (Boxberg, 2000), 20; and Grothus, "Horst," 13.
48. Bulwin, *Spätes Echo*, 38 f; Krapf, "Recollections," 246, 371; Gompertz, "Experiences," 23–24; Angress, *Witness to the Storm*, 90–92.
49. Krapf, "Recollections," 325ff; Baucke, *Das Buch gehört dazu*, 21f; Andrée, *Stationen*, 22ff; and Härtel, "Leben in grosser Zeit," 70f.
50. Grothus, "Mein Leben," 21; Angress, *Witness to the Storm*, 75–77.
51. Neumaier, "Mein Leben," 11; Schultheis, *Kindheit und Jugend*, 53; Klein, *Drinnen und Draußen*, 85.
52. Neumaier, "Mein Leben," 12; Gompertz, "Experiences," 24; Härtel, "Leben in grosser Zeit," 72–73.
53. Huber, "Das war mein Leben," 11–12; Weigelt, *Mein langes Leben*, 99, 102f; Bulwin, *Spätes Echo*, 49–50; Grothus, "Erinnerungen," 27.
54. Neumaier, "Mein Leben," 14; Frenzel, *40 verlorene Jahre*, 50f; Raschdorff, "Mein Leben," 12f.
55. Huber, "Das war mein Leben," 12; Neumaier, "Mein Leben," 14f; Härtel, "Leben in grosser Zeit," 75–96; Frenzel, *40 verlorene Jahre*, 64.
56. Huber, "Das war mein Leben," 18–19; Härtel, "Leben in grosser Zeit," 103–4; Frenzel, *40 verlorene Jahre*, 59, 66, 69.
57. Schultheis, *Kindheit und Jugend*, 39; Huber, "Das war mein Leben," 14–15; Raschdorff, "Mein Leben," 37–38.
58. Eyck, *Historian's Pilgrimage*, 88–96; Neumaier, "Mein Leben," 10–13.
59. Grothus, "Erinnerungen," 21; Frenzel, *40 verlorene Jahre*, 59–63; Weigelt, *Mein langes Leben*, 112f; Bulwin, *Spätes Echo*, 48–49.
60. Sternheim-Peters, *Habe ich denn*, 242ff; Schirmer, "Erinnerungen," 52; Huber, "Das war mein Leben," 15–16. Cf. Dagmar Herzog, *Sexuality in Europe: A Twentieth Century History* (Cambridge, UK, 2011).
61. Sternheim-Peters, *Habe ich denn*, 201f; Neumaier, "Mein Leben," 6.
62. Schultheis, *Kindheit und Jugend*, 32, 39; Frenzel, *40 verlorene Jahre*, 65; Mahlendorf, *Shame*, 42.
63. Grothus, "Erinnerungen," 17; Klein, *Drinnen und Draußen*, 73–76; Queiser, *"Du gehörst dem Führer!,"* 59f.
64. Krapf, "Recollections," 177–87; Helmer, "Tornister," vol. 1, 46, 66–69; Fest, *Not I*, 76. Cf. John Moses, *The Reluctant Revolutionary: Dietrich Bonnhoefer's Collision with Prussian-German History* (New York, 2009).
65. Gertrud Koch, *Edelweiß: Meine Jugend als Widerstandskämpferin* (Reinbeck, 2006), passim.
66. Gustav Ehrle, "Lebenserinnerungen," Anlage 2. Cf. Michael H. Kater, *Different Drummers: Jazz in the Third Reich* (New York, 2003); John M. Cox, *Circles of Resistance: Jewish, Leftist and Youth Dissidence in Nazi Germany* (New York, 2009); Inge Scholl, *Students*

against Tyranny: The Resistance of the White Rose, Munich, 1942–1943 (Middletown, CT, 1970).

67. Krapf, "Recollections," 161; Angress, *Witness to the Storm*, 75–87; oral communication from Irmgard Mueller, Chapel Hill, 2005.
68. Härtel, "Leben in grosser Zeit," 64; Schöffski, "Erinnerungen," 34. Cf. Robert Gellately, *Backing Hitler: Consent and Coercion in Nazi Germany* (New York, 2001).
69. Queiser, *"Du gehörst dem Führer!,"* 9–10; Weigelt, *Mein langes Leben*, 86, 101; Bulwin, *Spätes Echo*, 5; Härtel, "Leben in grosser Zeit," 1; Sternheim-Peters, *Habe ich denn*, 203.
70. Krapf, "Recollections," 162–73, 181–84. Cf. Sternheim-Peters, *Habe ich denn*, 69–179.
71. Neumaier, "Mein Leben," 6; Schirmer, "Erinnerungen," 39; Kolesnyk, "Wie es dazu kam," 44–46, 53.
72. Klein, *Drinnen und Draußen*, 43–47; Eyck, *Historian's Pilgrimage*, 79; Helmer, "Tornister," vol. 1, 75–76; Koch, *Edelweiß*, 24–67; Krapf, "Recollections," 187.
73. Moosmann, *Barfuß*, 104; Grothus, "Horst," 244; Sternheim-Peters, *Habe ich denn*, 14–18.

CHAPTER 4. MALE VIOLENCE

1. Gerhard Baucke, *Das Buch gehört dazu: Gute Seiten—Schlechte Seiten: Spiegelbild erlebter Zeiten 1919–1999* (Berlin, 2002), 43; Hans Queiser, *"Du gehörst dem Führer!": Vom Hitlerjungen zum Kriegsberichter: Ein autobiographischer Bericht* (Cologne, 1993), 90; and Adolf to Amanda, September 1, 1939, in Pirmin Stekeler-Weidhofer, "Papas Briefe und andere" (Leipzig, 2017).
2. Helmer, "Tornister," vol. 1, 82ff; Ruth Bulwin, *Spätes Echo: Erzählungen aus Großmutters jungen Jahren* (Wismar, 2014), 52. Cf. Nicholas Stargardt, *The German War: A Nation under Arms, 1939–1945* (London, 2015), passim.
3. Queiser, *"Du gehörst dem Führer!,"* 99f. Cf. Frank Werner, "'Hart müssen wir hier draußen sein': Soldatische Männlichkeit im Vernichtungskrieg,1941–1944," *Geschichte und Gesellschaft* 34 (2008): 5–40.
4. *Eine Ausstellung und ihre Folgen: Zur Rezeption der Ausstellung "Vernichtungskrieg. Verbrechen der Wehrmacht 1941 bis 1944,"* by the Hamburg Institut für Sozialforschung (Hamburg, 1999). Cf. Helmuth Schmidt, *Kindheit und Jugend unter Hitler*, with Willi Berkhan et al. (Berlin 1992).
5. Omer Bartov, *Germany's War and the Holocaust: Disputed Histories* (Ithaca, NY, 2003); and Waitman Beorn, *Marching into Darkness: The Wehrmacht and the Holocaust in Belarus* (Cambridge, UK, 2014) versus Christian Hartmann, *Operation Barbarossa: Germany's War in the East 1941–1945* (Oxford, UK, 2013).
6. Hellmut Raschdorff, "Mein Leben von 1922 bis Ende 2003" (Freiburg, 2003), 40. Cf. Konrad H. Jarausch and Michael Geyer, *Shattered Past: Reconstructing German Histories* (Princeton, NJ, 2003), 317–41; and Oliver von Wrochem, "Deutsche Generalsmemoiren nach 1945 als Grundlage nationaler Opfernarrative," in *Autobiographische Aufarbeitung: Diktatur und Lebensgeschichte im 20. Jahrhundert* (Göttingen, 2012), 44–71.
7. Note by Generalleutnant Liebman, February 3, 1933, in Thilo Vogelsang, "Neue Dokumente zur Geschichte der Reichswehr 1930–1933," *Vierteljahrshefte für Zeitgeschichte*

2 (1954): 434–35; Heinz Schultheis, *Kindheit und Jugend zwischen den Kriegen und Erwachsenwerden danach* (Leverkusen, 2007–2010), 79. Cf. Jonas Scherner, "Nazi Germany's Preparation for War: Evidence from Revised Industrial Investment Series," *European Review of Economic History* 14 (2010): 433–68.

8. Schultheis, *Kindheit und Jugend*, 56–63. Cf. Queiser, *"Du gehörst dem Führer!,"* 84–85.
9. Hans Peter Richter, *I Was There* (New York, 1972), 114–24.
10. Queiser, *"Du gehörst dem Führer!,"* 87; Schultheis, *Kindheit und Jugend*, 80; Horst Grothus, "Horst in seiner Zeit," 3rd ed. (Dorsten, n.d.), 38. Italics in original.
11. Schultheis, *Kindheit und Jugend*, 84. Cf. Kiran Klaus Patel, *Soldiers of Labor: Labor Service in Nazi Germany and New Deal America, 1933–1945* (Cambridge, UK, 2005).
12. Schultheis, *Kindheit und Jugend*, 83; Hans Tausch, "Mein Lebensbericht" (Forchheim, 1984), 20; Gerhard Krapf, "Recollections" (Edmonton, 1990s), 492f; Joachim Fest, *Not I: Memoirs of a German Childhood* (New York, 2013), 259; and Paul Frenzel, *40 verlorene Jahre: Erinnerungen an die Diktatur des nationalen und des realen Sozialismus* (Stuttgart, 1994), 71–77.
13. Karl Härtel, "Leben in grosser Zeit: Von den goldenen 20ern bis zum Zusammenbruch des Deutschen Reiches und dem beginnenden Wiederaufbau" (Leopoldshafen, 1996), 133; Fritz Klein, *Drinnen und Draußen: Ein Historiker in der DDR; Erinnerungen* (Frankfurt, 2000), 88; Frenzel, *40 verlorene Jahre*, 78; and Schultheis, *Kindheit und Jugend*, 87f.
14. Fest, *Not I*, 254f; Tausch, "Mein Lebensbericht," 21; Klein, *Drinnen und Draußen*, 86; Helmer, "Tornister," vol. 1, 84; Neumaier, "Mein Leben," 15f.
15. Raschdorff, "Mein Leben," 37f; Queiser, *"Du gehörst dem Führer!,"* 91f; Grothus, "Horst," 28–35.
16. Bulwin, *Spätes Echo*, 59f; Wilhelm Kolesnyk, "Wie es dazu kam, dass ich Nationalsozialist wurde," 51f.
17. Helmer, "Tornister," vol. 1, 84–85; Krapf, "Recollections," 489.
18. Härtel, "Leben in grosser Zeit," 112ff; Bettina Fehr, "Erinnerungen" (Bonn, 2005), 115, 129; oral communication from Fred Flessa, Cheshire, CT, 1967.
19. Queiser, *"Du gehörst dem Führer!,"* 97ff; Gerhardt B. Thamm, *Boy Soldier: A German Teenager at the Nazi Twilight* (Jefferson, NC, 2000), 20; and Krapf, "Recollections," 505f.
20. Horst Johannsen, *Ein Leben von Diktatur zu Diktatur* (Bromskirchen, 2003), 66–67; Krapf, "Recollections," 501ff; and Klein, *Drinnen und Draußen*, 86–90.
21. Neumaier,"Mein Leben," 16–17; Krapf, "Recollections," 501ff; Härtel, "Leben in grosser Zeit," 138ff; and Queiser, *"Du gehörst dem Führer!,"* 99–104.
22. Klein, *Drinnen und Draußen*, 89 f; Baucke, *Das Buch gehört dazu*, 43f; Hermann Debus, *Ein Leben im Wandel der Zeiten* (Dörscheid, 1998), 107; Neumaier, "Mein Leben," 27ff; and Krapf, "Recollections," 508ff.
23. Grothus, "Horst," 20–36; Härtel, "Leben in grosser Zeit," 148; Queiser, *"Du gehörst dem Führer!,"* 141ff; and Erich Helmer, oral communication, June 20, 2017.
24. Grothus, "Horst," 20; Queiser, *"Du gehörst dem Führer!,"* 102; Gerhard Joachim, "Wundersame Reise des Odysseus des XX. Jahrhunderts: Von Hitlers Aufstieg bis zum Untergang der Stalinistischen Ära" (Rostock, 1998), 36f; Frenzel, *40 verlorene Jahre*, 89ff; and Bulwin, *Spätes Echo*, 72.

25. Krapf, "Recollections," 561. Cf. Konrad H. Jarausch, ed., *Reluctant Accomplice: A Wehrmacht Soldier's Letters from the Eastern Front, 1939–1942* (Princeton, NJ, 2011).
26. Richter, *I Was There*, 124ff; Adolf to Amanda, September 1, 1938, in Pirmin Stekeler-Weithofer, "Papas Briefe." Cf. James Franklin Williamson, "Memory with No Clear Answers: Volkstrauertag, Opfer des Faschismus, and the Politics of Publicly Mourning the War Dead in Germany, 1945–1972" (Diss., Chapel Hill, 2013).
27. Thamm, *Boy Soldier*, 21, 59; Kolesnyk, "Wie es dazu kam," 44.
28. Ibid.; Baucke, *Das Buch gehört dazu*, 44.
29. Kolesnyk, "Wie es dazu kam," 44; Thamm, *Boy Soldier*, 26ff; Queiser, *"Du gehörst dem Führer!,"* 107ff; Grothus, "Horst," 40.
30. Thamm, *Boy Soldier*, 29; Queiser, *"Du gehörst dem Führer!,"* 118–22.
31. Ibid. Cf. Robert M. Citino, *Quest for Decisive Victory: From Stalemate to Blitzkrieg in Europe, 1899–1940* (Lawrence, KS, 2002).
32. Thamm, *Boy Soldier*, 26; and Schultheis, *Kindheit und Jugend*, 106f.
33. Horst Andrée, *Stationen meines Lebens* (Boxberg, 2000), 38f; and Queiser, *"Du gehörst dem Führer!,"* 154. There are surprisingly few actual battle descriptions in the autobiographies.
34. Ibid, and Neumaier, "Mein Leben," 20f.
35. Krapf, "Recollections," 578ff.
36. Ibid, 562–66.
37. Neumaier, "Mein Leben," 29. Cf. Thomas Kühne, *Kameradschaft: Die Soldaten des nationalsozialistischen Krieges und das 20. Jahrhundert* (Göttingen, 2006).
38. Frenzel, *40 verlorene Jahre*, 89; Krapf, "Recollections," 610ff and 625; Tausch, "Mein Lebensbericht," 32; and Schultheis, *Kindheit und Jugend*, 103ff.
39. Thamm, *Boy Soldier*, 22. Cf. Jarausch, *Reluctant Accomplice*, 47–137.
40. Queiser, *"Du gehörst dem Führer!,"* 107–126. Cf. Robert Paxton, *Vichy France: Old Guard and New Order, 1940–1944* (New York, 1972).
41. Frenzel, *40 verlorene Jahre*, 90ff; Raschdorff, "Mein Leben," 54–60.
42. Queiser, *"Du gehörst dem Führer!,"* 138ff. Cf. Hans F. Dahl, *Quisling: A Study in Treachery* (Cambridge, UK, 1999) and the forthcoming dissertation on Lebensborn children by Caroline Nilsen.
43. Tausch, "Mein Lebensbericht," 16; and Frenzel, *40 verlorene Jahre*, 81f. Cf. Chad C. Bryant, *Prague in Black: Nazi Rule and Czech Nationalism* (Cambridge, MA, 2007) and Jan T. Gross, *Polish Society under German Occupation: The Generalgouvernement, 1939–1940* (Princeton, NJ, 1979).
44. Thamm, *Boy Soldier*, 33; Baucke, *Das Buch gehört dazu*, 72f; Neumaier, "Mein Leben," 25; and Krapf, "Recollections," 652ff.
45. Krapf, "Recollections," 520f, 552. Cf. Omer Bartov, *Hitler's Army: Soldiers, Nazis, and War in the Third Reich* (New York, 1991).
46. Queiser, *"Du gehörst dem Führer!,"* 126–36.
47. Tausch, "Mein Lebensbericht," 28; Krapf, "Recollections," 601; Neumaier, "Mein Leben," 41.
48. Helmer, "Tornister," vol. 1, 107ff; and Anneliese Huber, "Das war mein Leben," 43f. Cf. Jarausch, *Reluctant Accomplice*, 22ff.

49. Raschdorff, "Mein Leben," 55; Queiser, *"Du gehörst dem Führer!,"* 147f. Cf. Doris L. Bergen, ed., *The Sword of the Lord: Military Chaplains from the First to the Twenty-First Century* (Notre Dame, IN, 2004).
50. Helmer, "Tornister," vol. 1, 98f; Queiser, *"Du gehörst dem Führer!,"* 114f.
51. Krapf, "Recollections," 533ff; Helmer, "Tornister," vol. 1, 118–21; Härtel, "Leben in grosser Zeit," 156f.
52. Krapf, "Recollections," 589–595; Tausch, "Mein Lebensbericht," 32; Hanns to Amanda, September 30, 1942, "Papas Briefe."
53. Krapf, "Recollections," 596–604; Tausch, "Mein Lebensbericht," 32; Frenzel, *40 verlorene Jahre*, 78–82.
54. Helmer, "Tornister," vol. 1, 122; Härtel, "Leben in grosser Zeit," 163f; Frenzel, *40 verlorene Jahre*, 87f; Bulwin, *Spätes Echo*, 74f; and Hanns to Amanda, July 19, 1942, "Papas Briefe."
55. Thamm, *Boy Soldier*, 33f; Helmer, "Tornister," vol. 1, 102.
56. Härtel, "Leben in grosser Zeit," 171f; Helmer, "Tornister," vol. 1, 128. Cf. Jarausch, *Reluctant Accomplice*, 364ff.
57. Thamm, *Boy Soldier*, 37; Schultheis, *Kindheit und Jugend*, 92. Cf. Jarausch, *Reluctant Accomplice*, 237ff.
58. Baucke, *Das Buch gehört dazu*, 60; Schultheis, *Kindheit und Jugend*, 95; Grothus, "Horst," 42.
59. Raschdorff, *Mein Leben*, 41–44; Baucke, *Das Buch gehört dazu*, 60f; Schultheis, *Kindheit und Jugend*, 96. For further details of the Russian campaign, see Hanns to Amanda from June 1941 to March 1945, "Papas Briefe."
60. Schultheis, *Kindheit und Jugend*, 95–103; Raschdorff, "Mein Leben," 42f. Cf. Anna Reid, *Leningrad: The Epic Siege of World War II, 1941–1944* (New York, 2011).
61. Baucke, *Das Buch gehört dazu*, 62; and Thamm, *Boy Soldier*, 38.
62. Krapf, "Recollections," 495; Frenzel, *40 verlorene Jahre*, 88f; Queiser, *"Du gehörst dem Führer!,"* 136; Schultheis, *Kindheit und Jugend*, 103.
63. Tausch, "Mein Lebensbericht," 28; and Schöffski, "Mein Leben," 78. Cf. Jochen Hellbeck, *Stalingrad: A City that Defeated the Third Reich* (New York, 2015).
64. Neumaier, "Mein Leben," 20–25. Cf. David M. Glantz, *Endgame at Stalingrad*, 2 vols. (Lawrence, KS, 2014).
65. Ibid; Tausch, "Mein Lebensbericht," 28. Cf. Robert M. Citino, *Death of the Wehrmacht: The German Campaigns of 1942* (Lawrence, KS, 2007).
66. Krapf, "Recollections," 514; Thamm, *Boy Soldier*, 42f; Neumaier, "Mein Leben," 34–39. Cf. Robert M. Citino, *The Wehrmacht Retreats: Fighting a Lost War, 1943* (Lawrence, KS, 2012).
67. Krapf, "Recollections," 557–60.
68. Krapf, "Recollections," 558; Schultheis, *Kindheit und Jugend*, 97f; Raschdorff, "Mein Leben," 42; and Helmer "Tornister," vol. 1, 117.
69. Grothus, "Horst," 43; Tausch, "Mein Lebensbericht," 28; Queiser, *"Du gehörst dem Führer!,"* 147ff; and Schultheis, *Kindheit und Jugend*, 104.
70. Thamm, *Boy Soldier*, 49–52; Raschdorff, "Mein Leben," 51; Grothus, "Horst," 43.
71. Debus, *Ein Leben*, 119; Fest, *Not I*, 270ff; Krapf, "Recollections," 552ff; Helmer, "Tornister," vol. 1, 125ff; Moosmann, *Barfuß*, 110f.

72. Hans-Harald Schirmer, "Erinnerungen an die Familie Hans und Luise Schirmer aus Wolfenbüttel," 65. Cf. Jörg Barberowski and Anselm Doering-Manteuffel, *Ordnung durch Terror: Gewaltexzesse und Vernichtung im nationalsozialistischen und im stalinistischen Imperium* (Bonn, 2006).
73. Baucke, *Das Buch geört dazu*, 75. Cf. Michael Geyer and Adam Tooze, eds. *War, Economy, Society and Culture*, vol. 3 of the *Cambridge History of the Second World War* (Cambridge, UK, 2015).
74. Neumaier, "Mein Leben," 40; Raschdorff, "Mein Leben," 50f.
75. Baucke, *Das Buch gehört dazu*, 60f; and Kolesnyk, "Wie es dazu kam," 50f. Cf. also Isabel Hull, *A Scrap of Paper: Breaking and Making International Law during the Great War* (Ithaca, NY, 2014).
76. Sandra Paweronschitz, "Damit der Krieg ein anderes Gesicht kriegt!," in *Schweigen und Reden einer Generation: Erinnerungsgespräche mit Opfern, Tätern und Mitläufern des Nationalsozialismus*, edited by Gerhard Botz (Vienna, 2005), 39–46. Cf. Ehrle, "Lebenserinnungen," Anlage 3.
77. Baucke, *Das Buch gehört dazu*, 71; Helmer, "Tornister," vol. 1, 125ff. Cf. Peter Longerich, "*Davon haben wir nichts gewusst!*" *Die Deutschen und die Judenverfolgung 1933–1945* (Munich, 2006).
78. Neumaier, "Mein Leben," 49–53; Härtel, "Leben in grosser Zeit," 187f; and Tausch, "Mein Lebensbericht," 32. Cf. Anthony Beevor, *D-Day: The Battle for Normandy* (London, 2009).
79. Neumaier, "Mein Leben," 52f; Thamm, *Boy Soldier*, 59ff. Cf. Randall Hansen, *Disobeying Hitler: German Resistance after Valkyrie* (Oxford, UK, 2014), 72–120.
80. Krapf, "Recollections," 623f; Thamm, *Boy Soldier*, 60f; Helmer, "Tornister," vol. 1, 125f; Helmut Donner to Walter Kempowski, July 18, 2004, SK. Cf. Peter Hoffmann, *The History of the German Resistance, 1933–1945* (Montreal, 1996).
81. Krapf, "Recollections," 586. This kind of description is repeated in many other accounts.
82. Queiser, "*Du gehörst dem Führer!*," 178–80; Baucke, *Das Buch gehört dazu*, 84; Fest, *Not I*, 283. Cf. Ralf Schabel, *Die Illusion der Wunderwaffen: Die Rolle der Düsenflugzeuge und Flugabwehrraketen in der Rüstungspolitik des Dritten Reiches* (Munich, 1994).
83. Hanns to Amanda, February 21, 1942, "Papas Briefe"; Krapf, "Recollections," 646; Thamm, *Boy Soldier*, 62; and Fest, *Not I*, 275f.
84. Helmer, "Tornister," vol. 1, 116f; Wolfgang Hubbe, "Übernen Graben: Protokoll einer Fahnenflucht," ch. 10, SK; Joachim, "Wundersame Reise," 36–51; Charles Glass, *The Deserters: A Hidden History of World War II* (New York, 2013).
85. Helmer, "Tornister," vol. 1, 128; Krapf, "Recollections," 646ff; Ehrle, "Lebenserinnerungen," Anlage 3. Cf. Stephen G. Fritz, *Endkampf: Soldiers, Civilians, and the Death of the Third Reich* (Lexington, KY, 2004).
86. Krapf, "Recollections," 702–60; Neumaier, "Mein Leben," 60f; Grothus, "Horst," 46ff.
87. Queiser, "*Du gehörst dem Führer!*," 186–94; Grothus, "Horst," 44. Cf. David K. Yelton, *Hitler's Volkssturm: The Nazi Militia and the Fall of Germany, 1944–1945* (Lawrence, KS, 2002).
88. Johannsen, *Ein Leben*, 71; Helmer, "Tornister," vol. 1, 129; Krapf, "Recollections," 738–51; Thamm, *Boy Soldier*, 90f.

89. Neumaier, "Mein Leben," 61f; Eva Sternheim-Peters, *Habe ich denn allein gejubelt? Eine Jugend im Nationalsozialismus* (Berlin, 2015), 769. Cf. Peter Caddick-Steel, *Snow and Steel: The Battle of the Bulge, 1944–1945* (Oxford, UK, 2015). For Italy, see Andrée, *Stationen*, 34–39.
90. Schultheis, *Kindheit und Jugend*, 107; Thamm, *Boy Soldier*, 70–95; Debus, *Ein Leben*, 120. Cf. Anthony Beevor, *The Fall of Berlin, 1945* (New York, 2002).
91. Wilhelm Homeyer, "Die letzten Stunden: Gefangennahme im 2. Weltkrieg, 19. Februar 1945 in Medenau bei Königsberg," handwritten manuscript, SK, 6301/2. Cf. Grothus, "Horst," 45.
92. Krapf, "Recollections," 763–72; Queiser, *"Du gehörst dem Führer!,"* 196f; and Thamm, *Boy Soldier*, 128. Frenzel, *40 verlorene Jahre*, 96–104 describes a dramatic flight by truck.
93. Andrée, *Stationen*, 39f; Fest, *Not I*, 288f; Krapf, "Recollections," 774f; Grothus, "Horst," 49. Cf. Frenzel *40 verlorene Jahre*, 104; Thamm, *Boy Soldier*, 156f.
94. Krapf, "Recollections," 778; Härtel, "Leben in grosser Zeit," 223; Queiser, *"Du gehörst dem Führer!,"* 197; and Helmer, "Tornister," vol. 1, 144.
95. Grothus, "Horst," 101; and Thamm, *Boy Soldier*, 81ff.
96. Thamm, *Boy Soldier*, 111–25; and Queiser, *"Du gehörst dem Führer!,"* 164–70. The story ran into trouble with air force censorship because it was too realistic.
97. Helmer, "Tornister," vol. 1, 132. Cf. Volker Rolf Berghahn, *Europa im Zeitalter der Weltkriege* (Frankfurt am Main, 2002), 132ff.
98. Frenzel, *40 verlorene Jahre*, 89ff; Klein, *Drinnen und Draußen*, 94ff; Krapf, "Recollections," 695.
99. Johannsen, *Ein Leben*, 72f; Klein, *Drinnen und Draußen*, 88ff; Debus, *Ein Leben*, 119; Grothus, "Horst," 101; and Johann to Amanda, "Papas Briefe," July 27, 1942.
100. Helmer, "Tornister," vol. 1, 132; Krapf, "Recollections," 778f. Cf. James J. Sheehan, *Where Have All the Soldiers Gone? The Transformation of Modern Europe* (Boston, 2008).

CHAPTER 5. FEMALE STRUGGLES

1. Eva Sternheim-Peters, *Habe ich denn allein gejubelt? Eine Jugend im Nationalsozialismus* (Berlin, 2015), 760–65.
2. Gisela Bock, "Ganz normale Frauen: Täter, Opfer, Mitläufer und Zuschauer im Nationalsozialismus," in *Zwischen Karriere und Verfolgung: Handlungsräume von Frauen im nationalsozialistischen Deutschland*, edited by Kirsten Heinsohn, Barbara Vogel, and Ulrike Weckel, 245–77 (Frankfurt, 1997).
3. Ruth Bulwin, "Briefe an ihre Eltern, 1937–1945," copied by Brigitte Stark. Cf. Melita Maschmann, *Fazit: Kein Rechtfertigungsversuch* (Stuttgart, 1963).
4. Claudia Koonz, *Mothers in the Fatherland: Women, the Family and Nazi Politics* (New York, 1987); and Wendy Lower, *Hitler's Furies: German Women in the Nazi Killing Fields* (Boston, 2013).
5. Karen Hagemann, "Military, War and the Mainstreams: Gendering Modern German Military History," in *Gendering Modern German History: Rewriting Historiography*, edited by Karen Hagemann and Jean Quataert, 63–85 (New York, 2007).

6. Belinda Davis, *Home Fires Burning: Food, Politics, and Everyday Life in World War I Berlin* (Chapel Hill, NC, 2000).
7. Barbara Bronnen, ed., *Geschichten vom Überleben: Frauentagebücher aus der NS-Zeit* (Munich, 1998); and Margarete Dörr, ed., *"Wer die Zeit nicht miterlebt hat . . ." Frauenerfahrungen im Zweiten Weltkrieg und in den Jahren danach*, 3 vols. (Frankfurt, 1998).
8. Elizabeth Heineman, *What Difference Does a Husband Make?: Women and Marital Status in Nazi and Postwar Germany* (Berkeley, CA, 1999).
9. Renate Bridenthal, Atina Grossman, and Marion Kaplan, eds., *When Biology Became Destiny: Women in Weimar and Nazi Germany* (New York, 1984). Cf. Karen Hagemann, *Frauenalltag und Männerpolitik: Alltagsleben und gesellschaftliches Handeln von Arbeiterfrauen in der Weimarer Republik* (Bonn, 1990), 639–51.
10. Citations from Dorothee Klinsiek, *Die Frau im NS-Staat* (Stuttgart, 1982), 139–50; and Lore Walb, *Ich, die Alte, ich die Junge: Konfrontation mit meinen Tagebüchern 1933–1945* (Berlin, 1998), 181.
11. Renate Finckh, *Sie versprachen uns die Zukunft: Eine Jugend im Nationalsozialismus* (Tübingen, 2002), 98. Cf. Jacques Pauwels, *Women, Nazis, and Universities: Female University Students in the Third Reich, 1933–1945* (Westport, CT, 1984); and Jill Stephenson, *Women in Nazi Germany* (Harlow, UK, 2001).
12. "Grundsatze und organisatorische Richtlinien der NSF," in: Klinksiek, *Die Frau im NS-Staat*, 151ff. Cf. Jill Stephenson, *The Nazi Organisation of Women* (London, 1981).
13. Mahlendorf, *Shame of Survival*, 92–95.
14. Finckh, *Sie versprachen*, 106–27.
15. Mahlendorf, *Shame of Survival*, 122ff.
16. Sternheim-Peters, *Habe ich denn*, 244–79.
17. Finckh, *Sie versprachen*, 92f, 135, 164f; Edith Schöffski, "Erinnerungen: Nur in der Rückschau, in der Zusammenfassung alles Erfahrenen, besitzen wir unser Leben ganz" (Berlin, n.d.), passim.
18. Schöffski, "Erinnerungen," 23; Mahlendorf, *Shame of Survival*, 78f; Ursula Baehrenburg, "Maikäfer flieg: Lebenserinnerungen 1920–2005" (Lautertal, 2005), 64.
19. Erika Taubhorn, "Mein Leben: Erinnerungen" (Wuppertal, 2000), 5–10; and Schöffski, "Erinnerungen," 38.
20. Ruth Bulwin, *Spätes Echo: Erzählungen aus Großmutters jungen Jahren* (Wismar, 2014), 39–46, 51–57; Gisela Grothus, "Mein Leben" (Dorsten, n.d.), 25; Walb, *Ich, die Alte*, 108f, 190–97; Schöffski, "Erinnerungen," 73f; Moosmann, *Barfuß*, 119ff.
21. Mahlendorf, *Shame of Survival*, 78; Bulwin, *Spätes Echo*, 49f; Huber, "Das war mein Leben," 11–19, Taubhorn, "Mein Leben," 31.
22. Huber, "Das war mein Leben," 12–20; Bulwin, *Spätes Echo*, 50.
23. Walb, *Ich, die Alte*, 45ff; Finckh, *Sie versprachen*, 178ff; Huber, "Das war mein Leben," 15–16; Winfried Weigelt, *Mein langes Leben* (Schwerin, 2017), 119ff; and Bulwin, *Spätes Echo*, 48–50.
24. Bella Fromm, *Als Hitler mir die Hand küsste* (Reinbek, 1994), 98–117; Walb, *Ich, die Alte*, 35f, 179; Huber, "Das war mein Leben," 25; and Mahlendorf, *Shame of Survival*, 143f.

25. Mahlendorf, *Shame of Survival*, 61–69; Sternheim-Peters, *Habe ich denn*, 401–13; Bulwin, *Spätes Echo*, 51.
26. Mahlendorf, *Shame of Survival*, 125f; Finckh, *Sie versprachen*, 129ff; Sternheim-Peters, *Habe ich denn*, 432–64; Walb, *Ich, die Alte*, 233f.
27. Finckh, *Sie versprachen*, 94–98; Walb, *Ich die Alte*, 43f; Mahlendorf, *Shame of Survival*, 42.
28. Walb, *Ich, die Alte*, 43f, 47f, 55–57, 61–64, 67ff, 74, 83, 91ff, 97ff. Cf. "Es it nicht nötig, dass ich lebe, wohl aber dass ich meine Pflicht tue . . ." in Dörr, "*Wer die Zeit nicht erlebt hat*," 287–89.
29. Christel Beilmann, *Eine katholische Jugend in Gottes und dem Dritten Reich* (Wuppertal, 1989), 30; Mahlendorf, *Shame of Survival*, 73ff; Finckh, *Sie versprachen*, 167; Bulwin, *Spätes Echo*, 52.
30. Sternheim-Peters, *Habe ich denn*, 730–45; Schöffski, "Erinnerungen," 52ff; Mahlendorf, *Shame of Survival*, 150, 158; Finckh, *Sie versprachen*, 183; Walb, *Ich, die Alte*, 139, 154–65.
31. Finkh, *Sie versprachen*, 147–52; Sternheim-Peters, *Habe ich denn*, 721–25.
32. Bulwin, *Spätes Echo*, 52; Taubhorn, "Mein Leben," 17f; Schöffski, "Erinnerungen," 48f.
33. Bulwin, *Spätes Echo*, 52; Baehrenburg, "Maikäfer flieg," 65; Mahlendorf, *Shame of Survival*, 102; Sternheim-Peters, *Habe ich denn*, 131f.
34. Finckh, *Sie versprachen*, 175f, 198; Mahlendorf, *Shame of Survival*, 117f.
35. Mahlendorf, *Shame of Survival*, 85ff.
36. Sonja Kolesnyk, "Alte Zeiten," 71–132. Cf. Ulrich Herbert, *Hitler's Foreign Workers: Enforced Foreign Labor in Germany under the Third Reich* (Cambridge, UK, 1997).
37. Finckh, *Sie versprachen*, 171, 203–209. Cf. Elizabeth Harvey, *Women and the Nazi East: Agents and Witnesses of Germanization* (New Haven, CT, 2003).
38. Beilmann, *Katholische Jugend*, 15–44; Bulwin, *Spätes Echo*, 63; Schöffski, "Erinnerungen," 82–88; Sternheim-Peters, *Habe ich denn*, 753f. Cf. Leila Rupp, *Mobilizing Women for War: German and American Propaganda, 1939–1945* (Princeton, NJ, 1987).
39. Grothus, "Mein Leben," 27; Mahlendorf, *Shame of Survival*, 193f, 201–7.
40. Baehrenburg, "Maikäfer flieg," 74; Huber, "Das war mein Leben," 26–36; Walb, *Ich, die Alte*, 195.
41. Baehrenburg, "Maikäfer flieg," 71f; Huber, "Das war mein Leben," 27–33; Bulwin, *Spätes Echo*, 58–62; Moosmann, *Barfuß*, 116ff.
42. Bulwin, *Spätes Echo*, 72–76; Huber, "Das war mein Leben," 36–39; Weigelt, *Mein langes Leben*, 140ff.
43. Huber, "Das war mein Leben," 52–67; Bulwin, *Spätes Echo*, 91–94.
44. Bulwin, *Spätes Echo*, 81; Mahlendorf, *Shame of Survival*, 141; Huber, "Das war mein Leben," 64–68; Walb, *Ich, die Alte*, 227–30.
45. Walb, *Ich, die Alte*, 193; Bulwin, *Spätes Echo*, 76–81.
46. "Ich hab gelebt wie im Traum . . . ," in Dörr, "*Wer die Zeit nicht miterlebt hat . . . ,*" 202–22.
47. "Ich möchte mal wieder tanzen!," in Bronnen, *Geschichten vom Überleben*, 182–93; Ingrid Bork, *Jedes Unglück hat ein Glück in sich: Friedrichshainer Lebenserinnerungen* (Berlin, 2010), 77. Cf. Franka Maubach, "Als Helferin in der Wehrmacht: Eine paradigmatische Figur des Kriegsendes," *Osteuropa* 55 (2005): 197–205.

48. Mahlendorf, *Shame of Survival*, 194–98. Cf. Volker Koop, *"Dem Führer ein Kind schenken": Die SS-Organisation Lebensborn e.V.* (Cologne, 2007).
49. Baehrenburg, "Maikäfer flieg," 66f; Finckh, *Sie versprachen*, 215–21. Cf. Robert Gellately, *The Gestapo and German Society: Enforcing Racial Policy 1935–1945* (Oxford, UK, 1990).
50. Finckh, *Sie versprachen*, 96; Sternheim-Peters, *Habe ich denn*, 488ff; and Ruth Elias, *Die Hoffnung hielt mich am Leben: Mein Weg von Theresienstadt und Auschwitz nach Israel* (Munich, 1990), 85. Cf. Lower, *Hitler's Furies*, passim.
51. Regine Fritz, "Und die kommt und reißt mir das Kind aus der Hand!," in *Schweigen und Reden einer Generation: Erinnerungsgespräche mit Opfern, Tätern und Mitläufern des Nationalsozialismus*, edited by Gerhard Botz (Vienna, 2005), 66–71.
52. Mahlendorf, *Shame of Survival*, 168; Baehrenburg, "Maikäfer flieg," 69; Finckh, *Sie versprachen*, 219. Cf. Eric A. Johnson, *What We Knew: Terror, Mass Murder and Everyday Life in Nazi Germany* (Cambridge, UK, 2005).
53. Mahlendorf, *Shame of Survival*, 149, 160; Finckh, *Sie versprachen*, 165, 186f, 213ff.
54. Walb, *Ich, die Alte*, 140, 162, 179, 227, 239; Finckh, *Sie versprachen*, 176.
55. Mahlendorf, *Shame of Survival*, 152; Walb, *Ich, die Alte*, 246ff.
56. Finckh, *Sie versprachen*, 230, 242; Bettina Fehr, "Erinnerungen" (Bonn, 2005), 163f; Mahlendorf, *Shame of Survival*, 153; Taubhorn, "Mein Leben," 34; Moosmann, *Barfuß*, 111f.
57. Finckh, *Sie versprachen*, 217; Walb, *Ich, die Alte*, 261; Mahlendorf, *Shame of Survival*, 154.
58. Walb, *Ich, die Alte*, 257; Finckh, *Sie versprachen*, 243–46; Bork, *Jedes Unglück*, 74; Dörr, *"Wer die Zeit nicht mitgemacht hat,"* vol. 2: *Kriegsalltag*, 112–19. Cf. R. J. Overy, *War and Economy in the Third Reich* (Oxford, UK, 2002).
59. Walb, *Ich die Alte*, 201, 214, 217; Mahlendorf, *Shame of Survival*, 176. Cf. Laura Heins, *Nazi Film Melodrama* (Urbana, IL, 2013).
60. Grothus, "Mein Leben," 29; Lieselotte G., "Rede von Adolf Hitler: Abends Strümpfe gestopft," and Rita H., "Ich möchte mal wieder tanzen!," in Bronnen, *Geschichten vom Überleben*, 166–71; 182–84. Cf. Randall Hansen, *Fire and Fury: The Allied Bombing of Germany, 1942–45* (Toronto, 2008).
61. Schöffski, "Erinnerungen," 58–64; Bork, *Jedes Unglück*, 59–66; Finckh, *Sie versprachen*, 234ff.
62. Taubhorn, "Mein Leben," 36f; Grothus, "Mein Leben," 29. Cf. Jörg Friedrich, *The Fire: The Bombing of Germany, 1940–1945* (New York, 2006).
63. Taubhorn, "Mein Leben," 36f; Schöffski, "Erinnerungen," 65, 71f, 80; Bork, *Jedes Unglück*, 71ff.
64. Finckh, *Sie versprachen*, 248–52; Schöffski, "Erinnerungen," 85f, 88; Beilmann, *Katholische Jugend*, 24ff.
65. Johanna Hagenauer, "Flucht aus Würzburg 1945" (Ms, Munich, 2015); Sternheim-Peters, *Habe ich denn*, 766; Walb, *Ich, die Alte*, 263, 275ff, 294.
66. Baehrenburg, "Maikäfer flieg," 65; Mahlendorf, *Shame of Survival*, 137; Sternheim-Peters, *Habe ich denn*, 551f; "Da musst du durch, das Leben geht weiter . . ." in Dörr, *"Wer die Zeit nicht miterlebt hat,"* 241f.
67. Baehrenburg, "Maikäfer flieg," 74f; Finckh, *Sie versprachen*, 236f; Sternheim-Peters, *Habe ich denn*, 747f; Grah, "Die rote Käthe," 259f.

68. Walb, *Ich, die Alte*, 292ff; Sternheim-Peters, *Habe ich denn*, 749; and Finckh, *Sie versprachen*, 237–41, 257.
69. Finckh, *Sie versprachen*, 219–27. Cf. Baehrenburg, "Maikäfer flieg," 65f; Sternheim-Peters, *Habe ich denn*, 414ff.
70. Baehrenburg, "Maikäfer flieg," 72; Mahlendorf, *Shame of Survival*, 185ff; Grothus, "Mein Leben," 33; Beilmann, *Katholische Jugend*, 40f.
71. Mahlendorf, *Shame of Survival*, 181, 206, 211.
72. Ibid, 196ff, 208ff, 214ff.
73. Ibid, 187; Dörr, "*Wer die Zeit nicht miterlebt hat . . .*," 448–89; Weigelt, *Mein langes Leben*, 146f.
74. Jakobine Homeyer, "Flucht aus Ostpreussen über kurisches Haff (Feb. 1945)," Tagebuch, SK. 6301/1. Cf. R. M. Douglas, *Orderly and Humane: The Expulsion of the Germans after the Second World War* (New Haven, CT, 2012).
75. Inge Lindauer, "Tagebuch 1945," SK 4022; Weigelt, *Mein langes Leben*, 191ff: Bulwin, *Spätes Echo*, 89–102. Cf. Theodor Schieder, ed., *Die Vertreibung der deutschen Bevölkerung aus den Gebieten östlich der Oder-Neisse* (Bonn, 1954–1960).
76. Walb, *Ich die Alte*, 300–19.
77. Baehrenburg, "Maikäfer flieg," 76ff; Mahlendorf, *Shame of Survival*, 213–18.
78. Baehrenburg, "Maikäfer flieg," 61f, 81ff; Witolla, "Tagebuch," April 20, 1945; and Homeyer, dozens of postcards from Russian POW camp, January 9, 1946ff.
79. Bork, *Jedes Unglück*, 78; Baehrenburg, "Maikäfer flieg," 79; Mahlendorf, *Shame of Survival*, 216.
80. Baehrenburg, "Maikäfer flieg," 80ff; Mahlendorf, *Shame of Survival*, 219f. Cf. Dörr, „*Wer die Zeit nicht miterlebt hat . . .*," vol. 2: 419–32.
81. Baehrenburg, "Maikäfer flieg," 85f; Schöffski, "Erinnerungen," 94f, Christel Groschek, *Die totgemachte Seele* (Egelsbach, 1999), 12–15. Cf. Heineman, *What Difference Does a Husband Make?*, 75ff.
82. Gudrun Fischer, "Mein 14. Geburtstag und dann . . . . Eine Allensteinerin berichtet," 24–34, SK; and oral history testimonies in Dörr, "*Wer die Zeit nicht miterlebt hat*," vol. 2, 409–27.
83. Fischer, "Mein 14. Geburtstag," 32ff. Cf. Norman Naimark, *The Russians in Germany: A History of the Soviet Zone of Occupation, 1945–1949* (Cambridge, MA, 1995) versus Miriam Gebhardt, *Als die Soldaten kamen: Die Vergewaltigung deutscher Frauen am Ende des Zweiten Weltkriegs* (Munich, 2015).
84. Weigelt, *Mein langes Leben*, 151ff; Lev Kopelev, *Ease My Sorrows: A Memoir* (New York, 1983); Anonyma, *Eine Frau in Berlin: Tagebuchaufzeichnungen vom 20. April bis 22. Juni 1945* (Munich, 2003).
85. Bork, *Jedes Unglück*, 77; Walb, *Ich, die Alte*, 327–33; Mahlendorf, *Shame of Survival*, 189ff, 211; Weigelt, *Mein langes Leben*, 198ff; Moosmann, *Barfuß*, 127ff.
86. Moosmann, *Barfuß*, 128ff; Walb, *Ich, die Alte*, 315ff; Mahlendorf, *Shame of Survival*, 212ff; and Finckh, *Sie versprachen*, 256–62.
87. Beilmann, *Katholische Jugend*, 47; Walb, *Ich, die Alte*, 320, 334; Sternheim-Peters, *Habe ich denn*, 749, 780; Finckh, *Sie versprachen*, 259ff.

88. Sternheim-Peters, *Habe ich denn*, 772, 782; Mahlendorf, *Shame of Survival*, 183; Walb, *Ich, die Alte*, 339–45; Finckh, *Sie versprachen*, 265–69.
89. Finckh, *Sie versprachen*, 7; Mahlendorf, *Shame of Survival*, 1–11; Sternheim-Peters, *Habe ich denn*, 14–17; Walb, *Ich, die Alte*, 9–28.
90. Moosmann, *Barfuß*, 126ff. Cf. Karen Hagemann, "Mobilizing Women for War: The History, Historiography and Memory of German Women's War Service in the Two World Wars," *Journal of Military History* 75 (2011): 1055–93; and "Good Soldiers? Women and the Military in World War Two," *The Berlin Journal* 28 (2015): 36–41.
91. Schöffski, "Erinnerungen," 74; Taubhorn, "Mein Leben," 8; Grothus, "Mein Leben," 27; Sternheim-Peters, *Habe ich denn*, 16ff; Grah, "Die rote Käthe," 260ff.
92. Walb, *Ich, die Alte*, 346ff; Mahlendorf, *Shame of Survival*, 181ff; Dörr, *"Wer die Zeit nicht miterlebt hat . . . ,"* vol. 2: *Kriegsalltag*, 203–302, 375–489.
93. Weigelt, *Mein langes Leben*, 174: Beilmann, *Katholische Jugend*, 45; Mahlendorf, *Shame of Survival*, 217; "Ich hab gelebt wie im Traum," in Dörr, *"Wer die Zeit nicht miterlebt hat,"* vol. 1, 220; Walb, *Ich, die Alte*, 331ff; and Finckh, *Sie versprachen*, 268f.

CHAPTER 6. VICTIMS' SUFFERING

1. Niza Ganor, *Wer bist du, Annuschka? Die Überlebensgeschichte eines jüdischen Mädchens* (Hamburg, 1996), 97–99. Cf. Lucy Mandelstam, "Memoirs," 16f; Ruth Klüger, *Weiter leben: Eine Jugend* (Göttingen, 1992), 106–117.
2. Eugen Kogon, *Der SS-Staat: Das System der deutschen Konzentrationslager* (Munich, 1946); Fritz Stern, *Five Germanys I Have Known* (New York, 2007), 93f. Cf. Nikolaus Wachsmann, *KL: A History of the Nazi Concentration Camps* (New York, 2015).
3. Peter Gay, *My German Question* (New Haven, CT, 1998), 49ff; Stern, *Five Germanys*, 97ff. Cf. Thomas Pegelow Kaplan, *The Language of Nazi Genocide: Linguistic Violence and the Struggle of Germans of Jewish Ancestry* (New York, 2009), passim.
4. Tadeusz Borowski, *This Way for the Gas, Ladies and Gentlemen and Other Stories* (New York, 1967). Cf. John Cox, *To Kill a People: Genocide in the Twentieth Century* (New York, 2017).
5. Aleida Assmann, *Shadows of Trauma: Memory and the Politics of Postwar Identity* (New York, 2016); and Mary Fulbrook, *Erfahrung, Erinnerung, Geschichtsschreibung: Neue Perspektiven auf die deutschen Diktaturen* (Göttingen, 2016).
6. Klüger, *Weiter leben*, 38. Cf. George C. Rosenwald and Richard L. Ochberg, eds., *Storied Lives: The Cultural Politics of Self-Understanding* (New Haven, CT, 1992).
7. Christian Hartmann et al., eds, *Hitler, Mein Kampf: Eine kritische Edition* (Munich, 2016). Cf. Timothy Scott Brown, *Weimar Radicals: Nazis and Communists between Authenticity and Performance* (New York, 2009).
8. Carola Stern, *In den Netzen der Erinnerung: Lebensgeschichten zweier Menschen* (Hamburg, 1986), 64–85, 88–90. Cf. Eric Weitz, *Creating German Communism, 1890–1990: From Popular Protests to Socialist State* (Princeton, NJ, 1997).
9. Stern, *In den Netzen*, 97–105. Cf. Martin Sabrow, *Erich Honecker: Das Leben davor* (Munich, 2016).
10. Moritz Zahnwetzer, *Konzentrationslager Buchenwald: Erlebnisbericht* (Kassel, 1946).

11. Klüger, *Weiter leben*, 53; Stern, *In den Netzen*, 118f; Georg Iggers, *Zwei Seiten einer Geschichte: Lebensbericht aus unruhigen Zeiten* (Göttingen, 2002), 59. Cf. Philippe Burrin, *Nazi Anti-Semitism: From Prejudice to the Holocaust* (New York, 2005).
12. Gompertz, "Experiences of Albert Gompertz: From Nazi Germany to America" (Palm Beach, 1998), 5ff; Werner T. Angress, *Witness to the Storm: A Jewish Journey from Nazi Berlin to the 82nd Airborne, 1920–1945* (Durham, NC, 2012), 41; Stern, *Five Germanys*, 98ff; Gay, *My German Question*, 49ff. Cf. Steven Aschheim, *Brothers and Strangers: The East European Jew in German and German Jewish Consciousness, 1800–1923* (Madison, WI, 1999).
13. Gompertz, "Experiences," 6f; Frank Eyck, *A Historian's Pilgrimage: Memoirs and Reflections*, edited by Rosemarie Eyck (Calgary, 2009), 57ff. Cf. Ismar Schorsch, *Jewish Reactions to Anti-Semitism 1870–1914* (New York, 1972); and Jehuda Reinharz, *Fatherland or Promised Land: The Dilemma of the German Jew 1893–1914* (Ann Arbor, MI, 1975).
14. Gompertz, "Experiences," 11; Ingeborg Hecht, *Als unsichtbare Mauern wuchsen: Eine deutsche Familie unter den Nürnberger Rassengesetzen* (Hamburg, 2010); Gay, *My German Question*, 59; Angress, *Witness to the Storm*, 82. Cf. Konrad H. Jarausch, *The Unfree Professions: German Lawyers, Teachers, and Engineers, 1900–1950* (New York, 1990), 115ff.
15. Jack Baruch Keil, "Untitled Memoirs," 3; Stern, *Five Germanys*, 101. Cf. Peter Merseburger, *Der schwierige Deutsche: Kurt Schumacher: Eine Biographie* (Stuttgart, 1995).
16. Hecht, *Als unsichtbare Mauern wuchsen*, 41; Angress, *Witness to the Storm*, 97–127; Mandelstam, "Memoirs," 5; Iggers, *Zwei Seiten*, 61ff. Cf. Glenn R. Sharfman, "The Jewish Youth Movement in Germany, 1900–1936: A Study in Ideology and Organization" (Diss., Chapel Hill, 1989).
17. Stern, *Five Germanys*, 113f; Hecht, *Als unsichtbare Mauern wuchsen*, 47ff; Bettina Fehr, "Erinnerungen" (Bonn, 2005), 144f. Cf. Sonya Grabowsky, *"Meine Identität ist die Zerrissenheit": "Halbjüdinnen" und "Halbjuden" im Nationalsozialismus* (Giessen, 2012).
18. Gay, *My German Question*, 47; Stern, *Five Germanys*, 99; Iggers, *Zwei Seiten*, 61; Klüger, *Weiter leben*, 41f; Angress, *Witness to the Storm*, 84f.
19. Warmbrunn, "The Terrace Memoirs," 37; Gay, *My German Question*, 92–110; Klüger, *Weiter leben*, 51ff; Iggers, *Zwei Seiten*, 63f; and Angress, *Witness to the Storm*, 128ff. Cf. Marion Kaplan, *Between Dignity and Despair: Jewish Life in Nazi Germany* (Oxford, UK, 1998).
20. Stern, *Five Germanys*, 111ff; Angress, *Witness to the Storm*, 80; Warmbrunn, "Terrace Memoirs," 43; and Eyck, *Historian's Pilgrimage*, 92ff. Cf. H. A. Strauss, "Jewish Emigration from Germany: Nazi Policies and Jewish Responses," *Leo Baeck Institute Yearbook* 25 (1980): 313–61 and 26 (1981): 34–49.
21. Iggers, *Zwei Seiten*, 65f. Cf. Frank Caesteker and Bob Moore, eds., *Refugees from Nazi Germany and the Liberal European States* (New York, 2010).
22. Gay, *My German Question*, 66, 74, 111ff; Hecht, *Als unsichtbare Mauern wuchsen*, 54ff.
23. Gay, *My German Question*, 115; Irmgard Mueller, oral communication; Gompertz, "Experiences," 24ff; Iggers, *Zwei Seiten*, 31, 65; Angress, *Witness to the Storm*, 128–59.
24. Stern, *Five Germanys*, 121f; Gompertz, "Experiences," 11ff; Keil, "Memoirs," 10f. Cf. Götz Aly, *Hitler's Beneficiaries: Plunder, Racial War, and the Nazi Welfare State* (New York, 2007).

25. Angress, *Witness to the Storm*, 157–164; Stern, *Five Germanys*, 128ff; Iggers, *Zwei Seiten*, 65f. Cf. Walter Laqueur, *Generation Exodus: The Fate of Young Jewish Refugees from Nazi Germany* (Hanover, NH, 2001).
26. Mandelstam, "Memoirs," 6; Keil, "Memoirs," 8ff; Klüger, *Weiter leben*, 23ff. Cf. Evan Burr Bukey, *Hitler's Austria: Popular Sentiment in the Nazi Era, 1938–1945* (Chapel Hill, NC, 2000).
27. Gompertz, "Experiences," 12f; Mandelstam, "Memoirs," 7; Gay, *My German Question*, 131ff; and Zahnwetzer, *KZ Buchenwald*, 23ff. Cf. Alan E. Steinweis, *Kristallnacht 1938* (Cambridge, MA, 2009).
28. Gay, *My German Question*, 134–54; Gompertz, "Experiences," 14–16; Hanna Marlens, "Untitled Memoir," 1.
29. Keil, "Memoir," 10–17; Marlens, "Untitled Memoir," 2; Angress, *Witness to the Storm*, 187–200; Warmbrunn, "Terrace Memoirs," 60ff; Gay, *My German Question*, 155ff.
30. Mandelstam, "Memoirs," 7; Gay, *My German Question*, 133ff; Irene Alenfeld, *Warum seid Ihr nicht ausgewandert? Überleben in Berlin 1933 bis 1945* (Berlin, 2008), 118ff; Hecht, *Als unsichtbare Mauern wuchsen*, 131; Keil "Untitled Memoir," 14–16; Warmbrunn, "Terrace Memoirs," 69.
31. Mandelstam, "Memoirs," 8; Hecht, *Als unsichtbare Mauern wuchsen*, 25; Alenfeld, *Warum seid*, 30–37; Klüger, *Weiter leben*, 31.
32. Gay, *My German Question*, 133, 154; Stern, *Five Germanys*, 129; Angress, *Witness to the Storm*, 168ff. Cf. Marion Berghahn, *Continental Britons: German-Jewish Refugees from Nazi Germany* (Oxford, UK, 1988).
33. Stern, *In den Netzen*, 141ff, 175–189. Cf. Allan Merson, *Communist Resistance in Nazi Germany* (London, 1985).
34. Fehr, "Erinnerungen," 93f; Alenfeld, *Warum seid*, 136ff; Hecht, *Als unsichtbare Mauern wuchsen*, 89, 103, 105. Cf. Beate Meyer, *"Jüdische Mischlinge": Rassenpolitik und Verfolgungserfahrung 1933–1945* (Hamburg, 1999).
35. Keil, "Untitled Memoirs," 11; Mandelstam, "Memoirs," 11; Hecht, *Als unsichtbare Mauern wuchsen*, 94ff. Cf. the dissertation by Laura Brade on networks of emigration from Czechoslovakia (Chapel Hill, 2017).
36. Hecht, *Als unsichtbare Mauern wuchsen*, 105; Klüger, *Weiter leben*, 50ff. Cf. Gerhard Schoenberner, *The Yellow Star: The Persecution of the Jews in Europe, 1933–1945* (New York, 2004).
37. Mandelstam, "Memoirs," 12. Cf. Jürgen Matthäus, Jochen Böhler, and Klaus-Michael Mallmann, *War, Pacification, and Mass Murder, 1939: The Einsatzgruppen in Poland* (Lanham, MD, 2014).
38. Alenfeld, *Warum seid*, 133–56; Hecht, *Als unsichtbare Mauern wuchsen*, 67ff.
39. Mandelstam, "Memoirs," 11f; Irmgard Mueller, oral communication; Krüger, *Weiter leben*, 65f.
40. Niza Ganor, *Wer bist du, Annuschka?*, 5–41.
41. Ibid, 79–96.
42. Marie Simon, *Underground in Berlin: A Young Woman's Extraordinary Tale of Survival in the Heart of Nazi Germany* (New York, 2015).

43. Mandelstam, "Memoirs," 13–15; Klüger, *Weiter leben*, 81–105.
44. Joachim Bässmann, "Bericht eines SS-Mannes über Dienst in Auschwitz," 41–43; Marianne Busch, "1. September 1943 bis 21. Januar 1945," 7–9. Cf. Ernst Klee, ed., *Auschwitz: Täter, Gehilfen, Opfer und was aus ihnen wurde: Ein Personenlexikon* (Frankfurt, 2013).
45. Mandelstam, "Memoirs," 16f; Klüger, *Weiter leben*, 106–17; Ganor, *Wer bist du, Annuschka?*, 97–100.
46. Bässmann, "Bericht eines SS-Mannes," 58f; Mandelstam, "Memoirs," 17; Klüger, *Weiter leben*, 132f; Judith Magyar Isaacson, *Befreiung in Leipzig: Erinnerungen einer ungarischen Jüdin* (Witzenhausen, 1991), 85ff.
47. Bässmann, "Bericht eines SS-Mannes," 61–62; Busch, "1. September 1943," 20.
48. Mandelstam, "Memoirs," 17f; Klüger, *Weiter leben*, 107ff; Ganor, *Wer bist du, Annuschka?*, 100ff; Isaacson, *Befreiung in Leipzig*, 95ff.
49. Mueller, oral communication; Mandelstam, "Memoirs," 18ff; Klüger, *Weiter leben*, 1416ff; and Ganor, *Wer bist du, Annuschka?*, 100ff.
50. Ruth Elias, *Die Hoffnung hielt mich am Leben: Mein Weg von Theresienstadt und Auschwitz nach Israel* (Munich, 1990), 155–91; Isaacson, *Befreiung in Leipzig*, 118ff. Cf. Paul Weindling, *Victims and Survivors of Nazi Human Experiments: Science and Suffering in the Holocaust* (London, 2015).
51. Elias, *Die Hoffnung*, 218, 227; Klüger, *Weiter leben*, 151ff; Ganor, *Wer bist du, Annuschka?*, 106–12.
52. Bässmann, "Bericht eines SS-Mannes," 83ff; Busch, "1. September 1943," 24.
53. Ganor, *Wer bist du, Annuschka?*, 105; Bässmann, "Bericht eines SS-Mannes," 43, 52.
54. Busch, "1. September 1943," 4–30.
55. Busch, "1. September 1943," 30, 35, 39, 43; Bässmann, "Bericht eines SS-Mannes," 42f. Both texts are only fragments. The archives have no further information on the authors beyond what is provided in the reports themselves. Cf. Monika Rammer, "Die Geschichte meines Großvaters," in *Schweigen und Reden einer Generation: Erinnerungsgespräche mit Opfern, Tätern und Mitläufern des Nationalsozialismus*, edited by Gerhard Botz (Vienna, 2005), 72–81.
56. Mandelstam, "Memoirs," 20f; Busch, "1. September 1943," 52–63; Rammer, "Die Geschichte," 78f.
57. Ganor, *Wer bist du, Annuschka?*, 112ff; Busch, "1. September 1943," 66f. Cf. Daniel Blatman, *The Death Marches: The Final Phase of Nazi Genocide* (Cambridge, MA, 2011).
58. Klüger, *Weiter leben*, 166–86; Mandelstam, "Memoirs," 21–24.
59. Ilse Polak, *Meine drei Leben: Die Geschichte einer Papenburger Jüdin* (Papenburg, 2013), 38f; Ganor, *Wer bist du, Annuschka?*, 113ff; and Elias, *Die Hoffnung*, 239–49.
60. Mandelstam, "Memoirs," 25f; Ganor, *Wer bist du, Annuschka?*, 117ff; Polak, *Meine drei Leben*, 39ff.
61. Busch, "1. September 1943," 62–70; Klüger, *Weiter leben*, 184f; and Bässmann, "Bericht eines SS-Mannes," 47, 85. Cf. David A. Hackett, *The Buchenwald Report* (Boulder, CO, 1995).
62. Daniel Jonah Goldhagen, *Hitler's Willing Executioners: Ordinary Germans and the Holocaust* (New York, 1996) versus Christopher Browning, *Nazi Policy, Jewish Workers, German Killers* (Cambridge, UK, 2000).

63. Heinz Jehuda Meyerstein, *Gehetzt, gejagt und entkommen: Von Göttingen über München und das KZ Dachau nach Holland, Deutschland, Holland und durch Frankreich über die Pyrenäen in Spanien gerettet* (Konstanz, 2008). Cf. Patrick Henry, ed., *Jewish Resistance against the Nazis* (Washington, DC, 2014).
64. Uwe Soukup, *Ich bin nun mal Deutscher: Sebastian Haffner: Eine Biographie* (Berlin, 2001), 39–96. Cf. Iggers, *Zwei Seiten*, 77f.; and Konrad Heiden, *Der Fuehrer: Hitler's Rise to Power* (Boston, 1944).
65. Stern, *In den Netzen*, 138ff; Willy Brandt, *My Life in Politics* (New York, 1992). Cf. Sozialdemokratische Partei Deutschlands, ed., *Deutschland Berichte der Sozialdemokratischen Partei Deutschlands* (Frankfurt, 1982).
66. Gertrud Koch, *Edelweiß: Meine Jugend als Widerstandskämpferin* (Reinbeck, 2006), 91–120; Stern, *In den Netzen*, 152ff. Cf. John Cox, *Circles of Resistance: Jewish, Leftist and Youth Dissidence in Nazi Germany, 1933–1945* (New York, 2009).
67. Peter Hoffmann, *The History of the German Resistance, 1933–1945* (Montreal, 1996); Theodore S. Hamerow, *On the Road to the Wolf's Lair: German Resistance to Hitler* (Cambridge, MA, 1997).
68. Wibke Bruhns, *My Father's Country: The Story of a German Family* (New York, 2008). Cf. W. H. Koch, *In the Name of the Volk: Political Justice in Hitler's Germany* (London, 1989), 196ff.
69. Meyerstein, *Gehetzt, gejagt und entkommen*, 13–106.
70. Marlens, "Untitled Memoir," 3; Gay, *My German Question*, 155–69; Eyck, *Historian's Pilgrimage*, 73, 95. Cf. Laqueur, *Generation Exodus*, passim.
71. Iggers, *Zwei Seiten*, 66f; Gay, *My German Question*, 170; Angress, *Witness to the Storm*, 211.
72. Gay, *My German Question*, 154–73; Stern, *Five Germanys*, 133ff; Angress, *Witness to the Storm*, 201ff.
73. Gompertz, "Experiences," 27ff; Stern, *Five Germanys*, 131ff.
74. Stern, *Five Germanys*, 138, oral communication from Gerhard Weinberg, Eyck, *Historian's Pilgrimage*, 117; Gompertz, "Experiences," 29; Gay, *My German Question*, 176; Iggers, *Zwei Seiten*, 68f; Warmbrunn, "Terrace Memoirs," 93.
75. Mandelstam, "Memoirs," 8; Stern, *Five Germanys*, 138; Eyck, *Historian's Pilgrimage*, 117; Iggers, *Zwei Seiten*, 69; Gompertz, "Experiences," 27.
76. Angress, *Witness to the Storm*, 201–26; Warmbrunn, "Terrace Memoirs," 76ff; Gompertz, "Experiences," 217f; Gay, *My German Question*, 175ff.
77. Eyck, *Historian's Pilgrimage*, 109–43; Iggers, *Zwei Seiten*, 73ff; Stern, *Five Germanys*, 162f; Gay, *My German Question*, 171–84. Cf. Andreas Daum, Hartmut Lehmann and James Sheehan, eds., *The Second Generation: Émigrés from Nazi Germany as Historians* (New York, 2016).
78. Gay, *My German Question*, 174f; Eyck, *Historian's Pilgrimage*, 136–55; Stern, *Five Germanys*, 158ff; Iggers, *Zwei Seiten*, 78f.
79. Gompertz, "Experiences," 31–37.
80. Angress, *Witness to the Storm*, 227–58. Cf. Christian Bauer, *The Ritchie Boys* (DVD, New York, 2007).

81. Angress, *Witness to the Storm*, 258–74, and his "Normandy Diary," June 6 to 27, 1944, 335–342. Cf. Cornelius Ryan, *The Longest Day: June 6, 1944* (New York, 1959).
82. Angress, *Witness to the Storm*, 314ff; Gompertz, "Experiences," 38.
83. Gompertz, "Experiences," 37f; Eyck, *A Historian's Pilgrimage*, 288ff; Angress, *Witness to the Storm*, 318–22; Mandelstam, "Memoirs," 27f.
84. Angress, *Witness to the Storm*, 323ff; Gompertz, "Experiences," 38ff; Eyck, *Historian's Pilgrimage*, 286ff.
85. Eyck, *Historian's Pilgrimage*, 289; Angress, *Witness to the Storm*, 309. Cf. Renate Bridenthal, "Out of Germany," in Daum, *Second Generation*, 131. Cf. Marita Krauss, *Heimkehr in ein fremdes Land: Geschichte der Remigration nach 1945* (Munich, 2001).
86. Konrad H. Jarausch, "The Failure of East German Anti-Fascism: Some Ironies of History as Politics," *German Studies Review* 14 (1991): 85–102. Cf. Thomas Lindenberger and Martin Sabrow, eds., *German Zeitgeschichte: Konturen eines Forschungsfeldes* (Göttingen, 2016).
87. James Franklin Williamson, "Memory with No Clear Answers: Volkstrauertag, Opfer des Faschismus, and the Politics of Publicly Mourning the War Dead in Germany, 1945–1972" (Diss., Chapel Hill, 2003).
88. Margarete Dörr, *"Wer die Zeit nicht miterlebt hat . . ." Frauenerfahrungen im Zweiten Weltkrieg und in den Jahren danach*, vol. 3, *Das Verhältnis zu Nationalsozialismus und Krieg* (Frankfurt, 1998); Wendy Lower, *Hitler's Furies: German Women in the Nazi Killing Fields* (Boston, 2013), passim.
89. Gay, *My German Question*, 1318ff; Klüger, *Weiter leben*, 69ff; Meyerstein, *Gehetzt, gejagt und entkommen*, 100ff; and Elias, *Die Hoffnung*, 151f. Cf. Dominick LaCapra, *Writing History, Writing Trauma* (Baltimore, 2014).
90. Zahnwetzer, *KZ Buchenwald*, 26ff. Cf. Bill Niven and Chloe Paver, eds., *Memorialization in Germany since 1945* (Basingstoke, 2010).

CHAPTER 7. DEFEAT AS NEW BEGINNING

1. Martin Sieg, *Im Schatten der Wolfschanze: Hitlerjunge auf der Suche nach Sinn—Autobiographische Skizze eines Zeitzeugen* (Münster, 1997), 91f.
2. Helmer, "Tornister," vol. 2, 2–9. Cf. Tony Judt, *Postwar: A History of Europe since 1945* (New York, 2005), passim.
3. Sieg, *Im Schatten*, 86f; Karl Härtel, "Leben in grosser Zeit: Von den goldenen 20ern bis zum Zusammenbruch des Deutschen Reiches und dem beginnenden Wiederaufbau" (Leopoldshafen, 1996), 223; and Hermann Debus, *Ein Leben im Wandel der Zeiten* (Dörscheid, 1998), 120. Cf. Sönke Neitzel and Harald Welzer, *Soldaten: The Secret World of Transcripts of German POWs* (New York, 2012).
4. Konrad H. Jarausch, "1945 and the Continuities of German History: Reflections on Memory, Historiography and Politics," in *Stunde Null: The End and the Beginning Fifty Years Ago*, edited by Geoffrey Giles, 9–24 (Washington, DC, 1997); and Stefan-Ludwig Hoffmann, Sandrine Kott, Peter Romijn, and Olivier Wieviorka, eds, *Seeking Peace in the Wake of War: Europe, 1943–1947* (Amsterdam, 2015).
5. Bettina Fehr, "Erinnerungen" (Bonn, 2005), 183f; Heinz Schultheis, *Kindheit und Jugend zwischen den Kriegen und Erwachsenwerden danach* (Leverkusen, 2007–2010), 115; Sieg,

Im Schatten, 97. Cf. Fulbrook, "Generationen zwischen zwei deutschen Diktaturen," in idem, *Erfahrung, Erinnerung, Geschichtsschreibung: Neue Perspektiven auf die deutschen Diktaturen* (Göttingen, 2016), 35–61.

6. Moosmann, *Barfuß*, 139ff; Sieg, *Im Schatten*, 93; Joachim Fest, *Not I: Memoirs of a German Childhood* (New York, 2013), 343.
7. Martin Greiffenhagen, *Jahrgang 1928: Aus einem unruhigen Leben* (Munich, 1988), 44; Fest, *Not I*, 336ff.
8. Ruth Bulwin, *Spätes Echo: Erzählungen aus Großmutters jungen Jahren* (Wismar, 2014), 106–15; and Gerhard Baucke, *Das Buch gehört dazu: Gute Seiten—Schlechte Seiten: Spiegelbild erlebter Zeiten 1919–1999* (Berlin, 2002), 93ff.
9. Fest, *Not I*, 288ff; Härtel, "Leben in grosser Zeit," 223; Horst Andrée, *Stationen meines Lebens* (Boxberg, 2000), 39f.
10. Sieg, *Im Schatten*, 80–84; Härtel, "Leben in grosser Zeit," 224–31; Fest, *Not I*, 289; Dieter Schoenhals, "Erinnerungen aus meiner Kriegsgefangenschaft" (Uppsala, 1985), 1ff; Ehrle, "Lebenserinnerungen," Anlage 3.
11. Härtel, "Leben in grosser Zeit," 231ff; Fest, *Not I*, 289–331. Cf. Günter Bischof and Stephen E. Ambrose, *Eisenhower and the German POWs: Facts against Falsehood* (Baton Rouge, 1992).
12. Andrée, *Stationen*, 47–54; Sieg, *Im Schatten*, 89ff; and Helmer, "Tornister," vol. 1, 145–48; Neumaier, "Mein Leben," 64f. Cf. Hellmut Raschdorff, "Mein Leben von 1922 bis Ende 2003" (Freiburg, 2003), 60–69.
13. Härtel, "Leben in grosser Zeit," 231f, 241–74.
14. Günter Gros, "Flucht und Heimkehr aus russischer Kriegsgefangenschaft," 2–46; Paul Frenzel, *40 verlorene Jahre: Erinnerungen an die Diktatur des nationalen und des realen Sozialismus* (Stuttgart, 1994), 113–23; Horst Grothus, "Horst in seiner Zeit," 3rd ed. (Dorsten, n.d.), 103ff.
15. Gerhard Krapf, "Recollections" (Edmonton, 1990s), 780–958; Neumaier, "Mein Leben," 66; Ehrle, "Lebenserinnerungen," Anlage 3. Cf. Andreas Hilger, *Deutsche Kriegsgefangene in der Sowjetunion, 1941–1956: Kriegsgefangenenpolitik, Lageralltag und Erinnerungen* (Essen, 2000).
16. Grothus, "Horst," 103–34. Cf. Huber, "Das war mein Leben," 96f.; Hans R. Queiser, *"Du gehörst dem Führer!": Vom Hitlerjungen zum Kriegsberichter: Ein autobiographischer Bericht* (Cologne, 1993), 201–34; and Schultheis, *Kindheit und Jugend*, 110ff.
17. Härtel, "Leben in grosser Zeit," 259; Andrée, *Stationen*, 49; Jakobine Witolla, "Flucht aus Ostpreussen über kurisches Haff," November 22, 1945; and almost one hundred postcards as well as letters from Wilhelm Homeyer, December 14, 1941 to March 17, 1948, SK. Cf. Hanns to Amanda, February 12, 1946 to September 24, 1948, "Papas Briefe."
18. Gerhard Joachim, "Wundersame Reise des Odysseus des XX. Jahrhunderts: Von Hitlers Aufstieg bis zum Untergang der Stalinistischen Ära" (Rostock, 1998), 51–56; Queiser, *"Du gehörst dem Führer!,"* 217–20.
19. Härtel, "Leben in grosser Zeit," 288–319. Cf. Queiser, *"Du gehörst dem Führer!,"* 221.
20. Alois David to Amanda, December 4, 1945, "Papas Briefe"; Homeyer to Binte, July 15, 1948; Raschdorff, "Mein Leben," 68; Huber, "Das war mein Leben," 97; Schoenhals, "Erinnerungen," 9f.

21. Baucke, *Das Buch gehört dazu*, 19f, 96, 121; Bulwin, *Spätes Echo*, 127, 129, 136. Cf. Kristen Dolan, "Isolating Nazism: Civilian Internment in American Occupied Germany, 1944–1950" (Diss. Chapel Hill, 2013).
22. Krapf, "Recollections," 956; Bulwin, *Spätes Echo*, 115; Raschdorff, "Mein Leben," 69; Andrée, *Stationen*, 55; Fest, *Not I*, 352. Cf. Frank Biess, *Homecomings: Returning POWs and the Legacies of Defeat in Postwar Germany* (Princeton, NJ, 2006).
23. Fest, *Not I*, 353; Helmer, "Tornister," vol. 2, 6ff; Andrée, *Stationen*, 55. Cf. Fritz Krohmer, *Verwischte Spuren: Erinnerungen eines Kriegskindes, 1933–1945* (Erdmannhausen, 1992), 121ff.
24. Amanda to Hanns, June 29, 1949, "Papas Briefe"; Krapf, "Recollections," 957ff; Schultheis, *Kindheit und Jugend*, 114. Cf. Svenija Goltermann, *Die Gesellschaft der Überlebenden: Deutsche Kriegsheimkehrer und ihre Gewalterfahrungen im Zweiten Weltkrieg* (Munich, 2009).
25. Helmer, "Tornister," vol. 2, 3; Bulwin, *Spätes Echo*, 104, 116; Frenzel, *40 verlorene Jahre*, 123; Härtel, "Leben in grosser Zeit," 308, 321ff; Schultheis, *Kindheit und Jugend*, 115. Cf. Birgit Schwelling, *Heimkehr, Erinnerung, Integration: Der Verband der Heimkehrer, die ehemaligen Kriegsgefangenen und die westdeutsche Nachkriegsgesellschaft* (Paderborn, 2010).
26. Horst Johannsen, *Ein Leben von Diktatur zu Diktatur* (Bromskirchen, 2003), 79–107; Irene Alenfeld, *Warum seid Ihr nicht ausgewandert? Überleben in Berlin 1933 bis 1945* (Berlin, 2008), 452. Cf. Rainer Karlsch and Jochen Laufer, eds, *Sowjetische Demontagen in Deutschland 1944–1949: Hintergründe, Ziele und Wirkungen* (Berlin, 2002).
27. Frenzel, *40 verlorene Jahre*, 1245ff; Helmer, "Tornister," vol. 2, 22f; Debus, *Ein Leben*, 136; and Schultheis, *Kindheit und Jugend*, 116.
28. Bulwin, *Spätes Echo*, 118–28. Cf. Derek Holmgren, "'Gateway to Freedom': The Friedland Refugee Transit Camp as Regulating Humanitarianism, 1945–1960" (Diss. Chapel Hill, 2015).
29. Helmer, "Tornister," vol. 2, 58; and Johannsen, *Ein Leben*, 76–85. Cf. Kim C. Primel and Alexa Stiller, eds, *Reassessing the Nuremberg Military Tribunals: Transitional Justice, Trial Narratives, and Historiography* (New York, 2012).
30. Sieg, *Im Schatten*, 88ff; Hans-Harald Schirmer, "Erinnerungen an die Familie Hans und Luise Schirmer aus Wolfenbüttel," 78; Will Seelmann-Eggebert, *Weder Narren noch Täter—der Schock kam erst später* (Ahlhorn, 2004), 107ff; Debus, *Ein Leben*, 119. Cf. Neitzel and Welzer, *Soldaten*, passim.
31. Undated letter in Härtel, "Leben in grosser Zeit," 277.
32. Fest, *Not I*, 356f. Cf. Christian von Krockow, *Die Stunde der Frauen: Bericht aus Pommern 1944 bis 1947* (Stuttgart, 1988); and Heineman, *What Difference Does a Husband Make?*, 75ff.
33. Ursula Baehrenburg, "Maikäfer flieg: Lebenserinnerungen 1920–2005" (Lautertal, 2005), 91–108.
34. "US Army Ends Ban on War Brides," *New York Times*, December 12, 1946; Baehrenburg, "Maikäfer flieg," 113. Cf. Marika Höhn, *GIs and Fräuleins: The German-American Encounter in 1950s West Germany* (Chapel Hill, NC, 2002).

35. Johannsen, *Ein Leben*, 83–86; Baehrenburg, "Maikäfer flieg," 91–107.
36. Gerhardt B. Thamm, *Boy Soldier: A German Teenager at the Nazi Twilight* (Jefferson, NC, 2000), 161; Eberhard Scholz-Eule, ed., *Wir Scholz-Kinder vom Herrnvorwerk: Aus dem Leben einer schlesischen Familie daheim und in der Zerstreuung*, 4th ed. (St. Georgen, 2008), 27; Baehrenburg, "Maikäfer flieg," 98; Ursula Mahlendorf, *Shame of Survival: Working through a Nazi Childhood* (University Park, PA, 2009), 235ff.
37. Baehrenburg, "Maikäfer flieg," 116–22. For other narratives, see the documentation on *Die Vertreibung der deutschen Bevölkerung aus den Gebieten östlich der Oder-Neisse*, edited by Theodor Schieder (Bonn, 1954).
38. Mahlendorf, *Shame of Survival*, 234–68. Cf. Scholz-Eule, *Wir Scholz-Kinder*, 32ff.; and Christel Groschek, *Die totgemachte Seele* (Egelsbach, 1999), 16–21.
39. Winfried Weigelt, *Mein langes Leben* (Schwerin, 2017), 216ff, 300–307. Cf. Andreas Kossert, *Kalte Heimat: Die Geschichte der deutschen Vertriebenen nach 1945* (Munich, 2008).
40. Hans Tausch, "Mein Lebensbericht" (Forchheim, 1984), 42–49. Cf. Chad Bryant, *Prague in Black: Nazi Rule and Czech Nationalism* (Cambridge, MA, 2007).
41. Mahlendorf, *Shame of Survival*, 269–304; Groschek, *Die totgemachte Seele*, 21–25; Weigelt, *Mein langes Leben*, 355ff. Cf. Kossert, *Kalte Heimat*, passim.
42. Ingrid Bork, *Jedes Unglück hat ein Glück in sich: Friedrichshainer Lebenserinnerungen* (Berlin, 2010), 84; Erika Taubhorn, "Mein Leben: Erinnerungen" (Wuppertal, 2000), 41; and Baehrenburg, "Maikäfer flieg," 87. Cf. Leonie Treber, *Mythos Trümmerfrauen: Von der Trümmerbeseitigung in der Kriegs- und Nachkriegszeit und der Entstehung eines deutschen Erinnerungsortes* (Essen, 2014).
43. Neumaier, "Mein Leben," 69; Bork, *Jedes Unglück*, 80f; Johannsen, *Ein Leben*, 85; Baehrenburg, "Maikäfer flieg," 142; Alenfeld, *Warum seid*, 432.
44. Helmer, "Tornister," vol. 2, 38f; Taubhorn, "Mein Leben," 48; Bork, *Jedes Unglück*, 84f; Fehr, "Erinnerungen," 195. Cf. Thomas Abhe and Michael Hofman, eds, *Hungern, Hamstern, Heiligabend: Leipziger erinnern sich an die Nachkriegszeit* (Leipzig, 1996).
45. Johannsen, *Ein Leben*, 78; Helmer "Tornister," vol. 2, 25f; Andrée, *Stationen*, 68; Huber, "Das war mein Leben," 80f; Neumaier, "Mein Leben," 70; Taubhorn, "Mein Leben," 42f. Cf. Paul Steege, *Black Market, Cold War: Everyday Life in Berlin, 1946–1949* (New York, 2007).
46. Bork, *Jedes Unglück*, 80ff; Baehrenburg, "Maikäfer flieg," 141; Helmer, "Tornister," vol. 2, 23; Edith Schöffski, "Erinnerungen: Nur in der Rückschau, in der Zusammenfassung alles Erfahrenen, besitzen wir unser Leben ganz" (Berlin, n.d.), 114f; Mahlendorf, *Shame of Survival*, 301.
47. Bork, *Jedes Unglück*, 83; Taubhorn, "Mein Leben," 44; Mahlendorf, *Shame of Survival*, 292.
48. Gertrud Koch, *Edelweiß: Meine Jugend als Widerstandskämpferin* (Reinbeck, 2006), 250ff; Baehrenburg, "Maikäfer flieg," 140ff; Bulwin, *Spätes Echo*, 131ff; Bork, *Jedes Unglück*, 87. Cf. Clara Oberle, "City in Transit: Ruins, Railways, and the Search for Order in Postwar Berlin, 1945–1948" (Diss., Princeton, NJ, 2006).
49. Schöffski, "Erinnerungen," 100; Bork, *Jedes Unglück*, 85; Ruth Elias, *Die Hoffnung hielt mich am Leben: Mein Weg von Theresienstadt und Auschwitz nach Israel* (Munich, 1990), 263, 280; Alenfeld, *Warum seid*, 428; Baehrenburg, "Maikäfer flieg," 111, 151.

50. Letters of Lotte Wriedt to Amanda Stekeler from December 13, 1945 to June 1, 1949, "Papas Briefe."
51. Baehrenburg, "Maikäfer flieg," 115; Alenfeld, *Warum seid*, 441; Sieg, *Im Schatten*, 98f.
52. Andrée, *Stationen*, 67; Bulwin, *Spätes Echo*, 145f; Johannsen, *Ein Leben*, 89; Baehrenburg, "Maikäfer flieg," 146ff; Taubhorn, "Mein Leben," 59f; and Huber, "Das war mein Leben," 123.
53. Bork, *Jedes Unglück*, 88; Johannsen, *Ein Leben*, 109ff; Debus, *Ein Leben*, 152; Taubhorn, "Mein Leben," 61.
54. Baucke, *Das Buch gehört dazu*, 80; Taubhorn, "Mein Leben," 72; Debus, *Ein Leben*, 160; Gisela Grothus, "Mein Leben" (Dorsten, n.d.), 39f.
55. Helmer, "Tornister," vol. 2, 28–35; Neumaier, "Mein Leben," 71; Härtel, "Leben in grosser Zeit," 322–29; Krapf, "Recollections," 961.
56. Huber, "Das war mein Leben," 53, 74, 83; Bulwin, *Spätes Echo*, 92, 130, 137f; Baehrenburg, "Maikäfer flieg," 137ff.
57. Tauborn, "Mein Leben," 50; Baehrenburg, "Maikäfer flieg," 124–35; Härtel, "Leben in grosser Zeit," 319f; and Grothus, "Mein Leben," 35–37.
58. Fest, *Not I*, 357; and Mahlendorf, *Shame of Survival*, 296. Cf. Alexandria Ruble, "'Equal but not the Same': The Struggle for 'Gleichberechtigung' and the Reform of Marriage and Family Law in East and West Germany, 1945–1968" (Chapel Hill, NC, 2017).
59. Helmer, "Tornister," vol. 3, 8; Frank Eyck, *A Historian's Pilgrimage: Memoirs and Reflections*, edited by Rosemarie Eyck (Calgary, 2009), 298–300, 339; Bulwin, *Spätes Echo*, 148. Cf. Konrad H. Jarausch, *After Hitler: Recivilizing Germans, 1945–1995* (New York, 2008), 19–101.
60. Krohmer, *Verwischte Spuren*, 121ff; Helmer, "Tornister," vol. 2, 36. Cf. Edith Sheffer, *Burned Bridge: How East and West Germans Made the Iron Curtain* (New York, 2011).
61. Johannsen, *Ein Leben*, 90, 101; Fest, *Not I*, 360; Koch, *Edelweiß*, 251; Alenfeld, *Warum seid*, 429ff; Mahlendorf, *Shame of Survival*, 290; Bork, *Jedes Unglück*, 83f. Cf. Lutz Niethammer, *Die Mitläuferfabrik: Die Entnazifizierung am Beispiel Bayerns* (Berlin, 1982).
62. Schirmer, "Erinnerungen," 28f; Koch, *Edelweiß*, 244; Eyck, *Historian's Pilgrimage*, 324ff; Fehr, "Erinnerungen," 102f; Alenfeld, *Warum seid*, 463f.
63. Fest, *Not I*, 358f; Johannsen, *Ein Leben*, 77; Tausch, "Mein Lebensbericht," 37; and Baehrenburg, "Maikäfer flieg," 100.
64. Schultheis, *Kindheit und Jugend*, 116; Bork, *Jedes Unglück*, 89; Koch, *Edelweiß*, 250; Schöffski, "Erinnerungen," 102ff; Johannsen, *Ein Leben*, 91ff; Helmer, "Tornister," vol. 2, 22, and so on. Cf. Axel Schildt and Arnold Sywotteck, eds, *Modernisierung im Wiederaufbau: Die westdeutsche Gesellschaft der 50er Jahre* (Bonn, 1998).
65. Sieg, *Im Schatten*, 104ff; Schultheis, *Kindheit und Jugend*, 106ff; Eyck, *Historian's Pilgrimage*, 288ff; and Helmer, "Tornister," vol. 2, 37. Cf. Steven Remy, *The Heidelberg Myth: The Nazification and Denazification of a German University* (Cambridge, MA, 2002).
66. Mahlendorf, *Shame of Survival*, 278–85; Helmer, "Tornister," vol. 2, 46ff; Härtel, "Leben in grosser Zeit," 330ff; Baehrenburg, "Maikäfer flieg," 128. Cf. Andrew Haeberlin, "Towards a Post-Nazi Education: Administrators Rebuild the German School System 1945–1949" (Diss., Chapel Hill, 2015).

67. Hanns to Amanda, April 17, 1955, "Papas Briefe"; Neumaier, "Mein Leben," 68ff; Helmer, "Tornister," vol. 2, 59; Schultheis, *Kindheit und Jugend*, 118. Cf. Härtel, "Leben in grosser Zeit," 337ff; and Sieg, *Im Schatten*, 117–22.
68. Baucke, *Das Buch gehört dazu*, 103; Bulwin, *Spätes Echo*, 187ff; Huber, "Das war mein Leben," 103; Bork, *Jedes Unglück*, 89f; Johannsen, *Ein Leben* , 112; Andrée, *Stationen*, 57, 62, 71; Baehrenburg, "Maikäfer flieg," 132ff; Debus, *Ein Leben*, 135f; Frenzel, *40 verlorene Jahre*, 134f; Sieg, *Im Schatten*, 99, 119; Helmer, "Tornister," vol. 2, 22; Grothus, "Horst," 143ff; Neumaier, "Mein Leben," 75ff; Schultheis, *Kindheit und Jugend*, 119ff.
69. Mahlendorf, *Shame of Survival*, 280, 299; Fest, *Not I*, 348ff; and Helmer, "Tornister," vol. 3, 8.
70. Helmer, "Tornister," vol. 3, 3ff; Sieg, *Im Schatten*, 102–14; Mahlendorf, *Shame of Survival*, 294; Fest, *Not I*, 376.
71. Sieg, *Im Schatten*, 109ff; Mahlendorf, *Shame of Survival*, 294; Baehrenburg, "Maikäfer flieg," 134. Cf. Dirk Moses, *German Intellectuals and the Nazi Past* (Cambridge, UK, 2007), passim.
72. Oral communications by Gertrud Krapf and Fred Flessa; Thamm, *Boy Soldier*, 1ff; Alenfeld, *Warum seid*, 466f; Krapf, "Recollections," 960f; Mahlendorf, *Shame of Survival*, 330f.
73. Helmer, "Tornister," vol. 2, 7; Kolesnyk, "Alte Zeiten," 138–55. Cf. Anna Holian, *Between National Socialism and Soviet Communism: Displaced Persons in Postwar Germany* (Ann Arbor, MI, 2011).
74. Ingeborg Hecht, *Als unsichtbare Mauern wuchsen: Eine deutsche Familie unter den Nürnberger Rassengesetzen* (Hamburg, 2010), 148ff; Alenfeld, *Warum seid*, 463ff; and Marie Simon, *Underground in Berlin: A Young Woman's Extraordinary Tale of Survival in the Heart of Nazi Germany* (New York, 2015), 342f. Cf. Michael Meng, *Shattered Spaces: Encountering Jewish Ruins in Postwar Germany and Poland* (Cambridge, MA, 2011).
75. Judith Magyar Isaacson, *Befreiung in Leipzig: Erinnerungen einer ungarischen Jüdin* (Witzenhausen, 1991), 162ff, Ilse Polak, *Meine drei Leben: Die Geschichte einer Papenburger Jüdin* (Papenburg, 2013), 46–50; Ruth Klüger, *Weiter leben: Eine Jugend* (Göttingen, 1992), 203–23. Cf. Atina Grossmann, *Jews, Germans, and Allies: Close Encounters in Occupied Germany* (Princeton, NJ, 2007).
76. Ganor, *Wer bist du, Annuschka?*, 120ff; and Mandelstam, "Memoirs," 34; Elias, *Die Hoffnung*, 310.
77. Fritz Stern, *Five Germanys I Have Known* (New York, 2007), 193; Georg Iggers, *Zwei Seiten einer Geschicte: Lebensbericht aus unruhigen Zeiten* (Göttingen, 2002), 81ff; Albert Gompertz, "Experiences of Albert Gompertz: From Nazi Germany to America" (Palm Beach, 1998), 45ff; Werner T. Angress, *Witness to the Storm: A Jewish Journey from Nazi Berlin to the 82nd Airborne, 1920–1945* (Durham, NC, 2012), 328ff; Eyck, *Historian's Pilgrimage*, 356; Peter Gay, *My German Question* (New Haven, CT, 1998), 189ff.
78. Fest, *Not I*, 372f; Frenzel, *40 verlorene Jahre*, 126ff. Cf. Christoph Klessmann, *Die doppelte Staatsgründung: Deutsche Geschichte 1945–1955* (Göttingen, 1982).
79. Fritz Klein, *Drinnen und Draußen: Ein Historiker in der DDR; Erinnerungen* (Frankfurt, 2000), 119ff; Carola Stern, *In den Netzen der Erinnerung: Lebensgeschichten zweier*

Menschen (Hamburg, 1986), 250f; Helmer, "Tornister," vol. 2, 12; Joachimsen, *Ein Leben* , 108ff.

80. Mahlendorf, *Shame of Survival*, 273; Johannsen, *Ein Leben*, 115; Baehrenburg, "Maikäfer flieg," 134f; Fest, *Not I*, 378f.
81. Neumaier, "Mein Leben," 70; Bulwin, *Spätes Echo*, 147f; Andrée, *Stationen*, 69; Bork, *Jedes Unglück*, 89. Cf. Anthony J. Nicholls, *Freedom with Responsibility: The Social Market Economy in Germany, 1918–1963* (Oxford, UK, 1994).
82. Baucke, *Das Buch gehört dazu*, 122; Baehrenburg, "Maikäfer flieg," 136f; Eyck, *Historian's Pilgrimage*, 365. Cf. Michael D. Haydock, *City under Siege: The Berlin Blockade and Airlift, 1948–1949* (Washington, DC, 1999).
83. Fest, *Not I*, 375ff; Stern, *In den Netzen*, 249; Baehrenburg, "Maikäfer flieg," 135; Weigelt, *Mein langes Leben*, 354ff.
84. Huber, "Das war mein Leben," 66f; Grothus, "Horst," 130ff; Schöffski, "Erinnerungen," 100; Mahlendorf, *Shame of Survival*, 267f; Klüger, *Weiter leben*, 203ff; Krapf, "Recollections," 960f.
85. Martin Broszat, Klaus-Dietmar Henke, and Hans Woller, eds, *Von Stalingrad zur Währungsreform: Zur Sozialgeschichte des Umbruchs in Deutschland* (Munich, 1990), and Lutz Niethammer, ed., *Lebensgeschichte und Sozialkultur im Ruhrgebiet 1930 bis 1960* (Bonn, 1983).
86. Homeyer, "Die letzten Stunden," passim; Baehrenburg, "Maikäfer flieg," 135; Schöffski, "Erinnerungen," 94ff; Helmer, "Tornister," vol. 2, 21ff; Bulwin, *Spätes Echo*, 137. Cf. Herfried Münkler, *Die Deutschen und ihre Mythen* (Berlin, 2009).
87. Dieter Schoenhals, "Betrogener Idealismus oder unglaubliche Naivität" (Uppsala, 1985), preface; Christel Beilmann, *Eine katholische Jugend in Gottes und dem Dritten Reich* (Wuppertal, 1989), 345ff. Cf. Eva Sternheim-Peters, *Habe ich denn allein gejubelt? Eine Jugend im Nationalsozialismus* (Berlin, 2015), 114–18; and Lore Walb, *Ich, die Alte, ich die Junge: Konfrontation mit meinen Tagebüchern 1933–1945* (Berlin, 1998), 353ff.
88. Fest, *Not I*, 364; Mahlendorf, *Shame of Survival*, 289ff; Sieg, *Im Schatten*, 110–14; Tausch, "Mein Lebensbericht," 49.
89. Baehrenburg, "Maikäfer flieg," 125f; Mahlendorf, *Shame of Survival*, 295; Fest, *Not I*, 357; Sieg, *Im Schatten*, 108; and Krohmer, *Verwischte Spuren*, 127.

CHAPTER 8. DEMOCRATIC MATURITY

1. Ruth Bulwin, *Spätes Echo: Erzählungen aus Großmutters jungen Jahren* (Wismar, 2014), 153–83.
2. Ibid, 137; Hellmut Raschdorff, "Mein Leben von 1922 bis Ende 2003" (Freiburg, 2003), 80f.
3. Joachim Fest, *Not I: Memoirs of a German Childhood* (New York, 2013), 381f; Ursula Mahlendorf, *Shame of Survival: Workingt through a Nazi Childhood* (University Park, PA, 2009), 308f; Helmer, "Tornister," vol. 3, 45.
4. Mahlendorf, *Shame of Survival*, 310f; Martin Greiffenhagen, *Jahrgang 1928: Aus einem unruhigen Leben* (Munich, 1988), 55–63. Cf. Wolfgang Benz, *Die Gründung der Bundesrepublik: Von der Bizone zum souveränen Staat* (Munich, 1999).

5. Martin Sieg, *Im Schatten der Wolfschanze: Hitlerjunge auf der Suche nach Sinn—Autobiographische Skizze eines Zeitzeugen* (Münster, 1997), 108f; Hans Tausch, "Mein Lebensbericht" (Forchheim, 1984), 60. Cf. Arnd Bauerkämper, Konrad H. Jarausch, and Marcus M. Payk, eds, *Demokratiewunder: Transatlantische Mittler und die kulturelle Öffnung Westdeutschlands, 1945–1970* (Göttingen, 2005).
6. Ulrich Herbert, *Deutsche Geschichte im zwanzigsten Jahrhundert* (Munich, 2015), passim.
7. Klaus Dietmat Henke, *Die amerikanische Besetzung Deutschlands* (Munich, 1995).
8. Helmer, "Tornister," vol. 2, 22; Raschdorff, "Mein Leben," 71; Edith Schöffski, "Erinnerungen: Nur in der Rückschau, in der Zusammenfassung alles Erfahrenen, besitzen wir unser Leben ganz" (Berlin, n.d.), 102ff; Mahlendorf, *Shame of Survival*, 317.
9. Horst Andrée, *Stationen meines Lebens* (Boxberg, 2000), 57; Hermann Debus, *Ein Leben im Wandel der Zeiten* (Dörscheid, 1998), 135; Horst Grothus, "Horst in seiner Zeit," 3rd ed. (Dorsten, n.d.), 142; Huber, "Das war mein Leben," 103; Schöffski, "Erinnerungen," 103; Helmer, "Tornister," vol. 2, 59f; Mahlendorf, *Shame of Survival*, 316.
10. Mahlendorf, *Shame of Survival*, 321; Grothus, "Horst," 142ff; Fest, *Not I*, 378; Helmer, "Tornister," vol. 3, 1ff.
11. Heinz Schultheis, *Kindheit und Jugend zwischen den Kriegen und Erwachsenwerden danach* (Leverkusen, 2007–2010), 119; Andrée, *Stationen*, 84; Grothus, "Horst," 145; Ursula Baehrenburg, "Maikäfer flieg: Lebenserinnerungen 1920–2005" (Lautertal, 2005), 157; Helmer, "Tornister," vol. 3, 57f. Cf. Konrad H. Jarausch, *Deutsche Studenten 1800–1970* (Frankfurt, 1984), 213ff.
12. Andrée, *Stationen*, 85ff; Grothus, "Horst," 168ff; Neumaier, "Mein Leben," 76ff; Baehrenburg, "Maikäfer flieg," 159ff; Helmer, "Tornister," vol. 3, 30.
13. Debus, *Ein Leben*, passim. Cf. Gunter F. Moeser, *Die Entwicklung der Marktformen in der deutschen Rheinschiffahrt und deren Auswirkungen auf die Wettbewerbslage der Rheinschiffahrt* (Munich, 1959).
14. Andrée, *Stationen*, 69–102; Huber, "Das war mein Leben," 100–23; Benno Schöffski, "Meine Familiengeschichte von 1835 bis 1980" (Berlin, 1980), 84. Cf. Jeffrey K. Wilson, *The German Forest: Nature, Identity, and the Contestation of a National Symbol, 1871–1914* (Toronto, 2012).
15. Tausch, "Mein Lebensbericht," 51–61; Baehrenburg, "Maikäfer flieg," 156–224. Cf. Konrad H. Jarausch, *The Unfree Professions: German Lawyers, Teachers, and Engineers, 1900–1950* (New York, 1990), 202ff.
16. Helmer, "Tornister," vol. 2, 49ff, vol. 3, 1–36; Sieg, *Im Schatten*, 102–67. Cf. Dorothee Sölle, *Gegenwind: Erinnerungen* (Hamburg, 1995), 29ff.
17. Gerhard Baucke, *Das Buch gehört dazu: Gute Seiten—Schlechte Seiten: Spiegelbild erlebter Zeiten 1919–1999* (Berlin, 2002), 103–21; Fest, *Not I*, 495ff. Cf. Christina von Hodenberg, *Konsens und Krise: Eine Geschichte der westdeutschen Medienöffentlichkeit, 1945–1973* (Göttingen, 2006).
18. Karl Härtel, "Leben in grosser Zeit: Von den goldenen 20ern bis zum Zusammenbruch des Deutschen Reiches und dem beginnenden Wiederaufbau" (Leopoldshafen, 1996), 434–45; Neumaier, "Mein Leben," 75–89; Schultheis, *Kindheit und Jugend*, 119ff.

19. Erika Taubhorn, "Mein Leben: Erinnerungen" (Wuppertal, 2000), 74; Huber, "Das war mein Leben," 124f; Bulwin, *Spätes Echo*, 150; Gisela Grothus, "Mein Leben" (Dorsten, n.d.), 51. Cf. Christine von Oertzen, *The Pleasure of a Surplus Income: Part-Time Work, Gender Politics, and Social Change in West Germany, 1955–1969* (New York, 2007).
20. Grothus, "Horst," 169; Neumaier, "Mein Leben," 77.
21. Raschdorff, "Mein Leben," 84–118; Baucke, *Das Buch gehört dazu*, 135ff.
22. Bulwin, *Spätes Echo*, 184–98.
23. Grothus, "Horst," 170–90; Grothus. "Mein Leben," 51ff.
24. Debus, *Ein Leben*, 373–89.
25. Tausch, "Mein Lebensbericht," 61; Helmer, "Tornister," vol. 3, 60, 70ff; Debus, *Ein Leben*, 257; and Raschdorff, "Mein Leben," 118f.
26. Schultheis, *Kindheit und Jugend*, 120f; Grothus, "Horst in seiner Zeit," 172, 197; Neumaier, "Mein Leben," 79ff, 92, 135. Cf. Kees Gispen, *New Profession, Old Order: Engineers and German Society, 1815–1914* (Cambridge, UK, 1989).
27. Grothus, "Horst," 157ff, 207ff; Neumaier, "Mein Leben," 88–103.
28. Hans-Gerd Neglein, *. . . und die Verantwortung trage ich! Aus der Chefetage der Wirtschaft zum Naturschutz in Andalusien* (Frankfurt, 2008), 61ff.
29. Mehmet Ünaldi, *Mehmet—Ich Gastarbeiter und Türke: Erinnerungen eines Gastarbeiters der ersten Generation* (Münster, 2014), 170.
30. Debus, *Ein Leben*, passim; Baucke, *Das Buch gehört dazu*, 136f; Neumaier, "Mein Leben," 79; Grothus, "Horst," 201; Christel Groschek, *Die totgemachte Seele* (Egelsbach, 1999), 29ff.
31. Raschdorff, "Mein Leben," 89, 92, 94f; Bulwin, *Spätes Echo*, 187, 197; Grothus, "Horst," 184; and Härtel, "Leben in grosser Zeit," 487.
32. Baucke, *Das Buch gehört dazu*, 136ff; Neumaier, "Mein Leben," 106f. Cf. Mark E. Spicka, *Selling the Economic Miracle: Reconstruction and Politics in West Germany, 1949–1957* (New York, 2007).
33. Mahlendorf, *Shame of Survival*, 306f. Cf. Hanna Schissler, ed., *The Miracle Years: A Cultural History of West Germany, 1949–1968* (Princeton, NJ, 2001).
34. Fest, *Not I*, 388ff; Neumaier, "Mein Leben," 71f; Mahlendorf, *Shame of Survival*, 293ff. Cf. Sölle, *Gegenwind*, 29ff, 142ff.
35. Huber, "Das war mein Leben," 111; Raschdorff, "Mein Leben," 72ff; Taubhorn, "Mein Leben," 72ff; Grothus, "Mein Leben," 41; Grothus, "Horst," 148ff.
36. Grothus, "Mein Leben," 45f; Grothus, "Horst," 164f; Neumaier, "Mein Leben," 78; and Tausch, "Mein Lebensbericht," 56f. Cf. Huber, "Das war mein Leben," 123; Schöffski, "Familiengeschichte," 85; Schöffski, "Erinnerungen," 143; and Bettina Fehr, "Erinnerungen" (Bonn, 2005), 192.
37. Baehrenburg, "Maikäfer flieg," 169–282. Cf. Baucke, *Das Buch gehört dazu*, 120.
38. Groschek, *Die totgemachte Seele*, 54–104; Neglein, *Die Verantwortung*, 81ff. Cf. Dirk Blasius, *Ehescheidung in Deutschland 1794–1945: Scheidung und Scheidungsrecht in historischer Perspektive* (Göttingen, 1987).
39. Neumaier, "Mein Leben," 78; Raschdorff, "Mein Leben," 80f; Huber, "Das war mein Leben," 124f; Grothus, "Horst," 165; Schöffski, "Erinnerungen," 143.

40. Grothus, "Mein Leben," 47–49; Huber, "Das war mein Leben," 125–28; Neumaier, "Mein Leben," 105; Grothus, "Horst," 165. Cf. Raschdorff, "Mein Leben," 78, 81; Taubhorn, "Mein Leben," 75; and Fehr, "Erinnerungen," 204ff.
41. Huber, "Das war mein Leben," 136f; Grothus, "Horst," 215ff; Neumaier, "Mein Leben," 88f; Winfried Weigelt, *Mein langes Leben* (Schwerin, 2017), 365–70.
42. Schöffski, "Erinnerungen," 146; Mahlendorf, *Shame of Survival*, 306f; Huber, "Das war mein Leben," 132; Weigelt, *Mein langes Leben*, 380. Cf. Wolfgang König, *Geschichte der Konsumgesellschaft* (Stuttgart, 2000).
43. Neumaier, "Mein Leben," 104f, 122f; Raschdorff, "Mein Leben," 116ff; and Debus, *Ein Leben*, 327.
44. Raschdorff, "Mein Leben," 116; Baucke, *Das Buch gehört dazu*, passim; Debus, *Ein Leben*, 496ff.
45. Huber, "Das war mein Leben," 133; Raschdorff, "Mein Leben," 98ff, 164.
46. Neumaier, "Mein Leben," 110–14; Härtel, "Leben in grosser Zeit," 482. Cf. Rudy Koshar, *German Travel Cultures* (Oxford, UK, 2000).
47. Grothus, "Horst," 238f; Taubhorn, "Mein Leben," 65–69; Raschdorff, "Mein Leben," 91f; Huber, "Das war mein Leben," 134ff.
48. Debus, *Ein Leben*, passim; Baehrenburg, "Maikäfer flieg," 281; Neumaier, "Mein Leben," 135; Raschdorff, "Mein Leben," 165ff; Grothus, "Horst," 183.
49. Paul Frenzel, *40 verlorene Jahre: Erinnerungen an die Diktatur des nationalen und des realen Sozialismus* (Stuttgart, 1994), 282ff; Krause, "Mein Leben in der DDR," 18ff; Gerhard Joachim, "Wundersame Reise des Odysseus des XX. Jahrhunderts: Von Hitlers Aufstieg bis zum Untergang der Stalinistischen Ära" (Rostock, 1998), 164.
50. Raschdorff, "Mein Leben," 167–170; Debus, *Ein Leben*, passim; Baucke, *Das Buch gehört dazu*, 174f; Weigelt, *Mein langes Leben*, 384ff.
51. Baucke, *Das Buch gehört dazu*, 174; Debus, *Ein Leben*, 585ff ; Raschdorff, "Mein Leben," 170ff, 230–36; Weigelt, *Mein langes Leben*, 407–24. Cf. Pat Thane, *A History of Old Age* (Los Angeles, 2005).
52. Huber, "Das war mein Leben," 137ff, 161; Raschdorff, "Mein Leben," 170; Bulwin, *Spätes Echo*, 198; Debus, *Ein Leben*, passim; Andrée, *Stationen*, 106; Neumaier, "Mein Leben," 121f; Weigelt, *Mein langes Leben*, 370ff.
53. Neumaier, "Mein Leben," 138. Cf. Hanno Hochmuth, *Kiezgeschichte: Friedrichshain und Kreuzberg im geteilten Berlin* (Berlin, 2017).
54. Sieg, *Im Schatten*, 97; Günter Krause, "Unschuldig zu 10 Jahren Arbeitslager verurteilt vom sowjetischen Geheimdienst" (n.p., 2006), preface. Cf. Konrad H. Jarausch, *After Hitler: Recivilizing Germans, 1945–1995* (New York, 2008), 19ff.
55. Sölle, *Gegenwind*, 34–38; Raschdorff, "Mein Leben," 123; Helmer, "Tornister," vol. 3, 4.
56. Mahlendorf, *Shame of Survival*, 294; Grothus, "Horst," 154–63; Greiffenhagen, *Jahrgang 1928*, 103–9. Cf. Anselm Doering-Manteuffel, *Wie westlich sind die Deutschen? Amerikanisierung und Westernisierung im 20. Jahrhundert* (Göttingen, 1999).
57. Carola Stern, *In den Netzen der Erinnerung: Lebensgeschichten zweier Menschen* (Hamburg, 1986), 243ff; and Krause, "Unschuldig," passim. Cf. Stefan Creuzberger and Dierk

Hoffmann, eds, *"Geistige Gefahr" und "Immunisierung der Gesellschaft": Antikommunismus und politische Kultur in der frühen Bundesrepublik* (Munich, 2014).

58. Greiffenhagen, *Jahrgang 1928*, 81ff; Sieg, *Im Schatten*, 104ff; Stern, *In den Netzen*, 244; and Sölle, *Gegenwind*, 38ff.
59. Mahlendorf, *Shame of Survival*, 310f. Cf. Deutscher Bundestag, ed., *Basic Law for the Federal Republic of Germany* (Berlin, 2012).
60. Fest, *Not I*, 344f; Irene Alenfeld, *Warum seid Ihr nicht ausgewandert? Überleben in Berlin 1933 bis 1945* (Berlin, 2008), 425, 463. Cf. the forthcoming study of Christian Democracy by James Gregory Chappel.
61. Harro Matthiessen, "Günter Hagemann," *Unser Farmsen* 429 (1995). Cf. Peter Merseburger, *Der schwierige Deutsche: Kurt Schumacher: Eine Biographie* (Stuttgart, 1995), passim.
62. Grothus, "Horst," 222. Cf. Jörg Michael Gutscher, *Die Entwicklung der FDP von ihren Anfängen bis 1961* (Königstein, 1984).
63. Gerard Braunthal, *Right-Wing Extremism in Contemporary Germany* (Basingstoke, 2009); and Patrick Major, *The Death of the KPD: Communism and Anti-Communism in West Germany, 1945–1956* (Oxford, UK, 1998).
64. Debus, *Ein Leben*, passim. Cf. Jost Küpper, *Die Kanzlerdemokratie: Voraussetzungen, Strukturen und Änderungen des Regierungsstiles in der Ära Adenauer* (Frankfurt, 1985).
65. Mahlendorf, *Shame of Survival*, 312f; Schöffski, "Familiengeschichte," 87; Raschdorff, "Mein Leben," 79. Cf. Holmgren. "Gateway to Freedom," passim.
66. Mahlendorf, *Shame of Survival*, 320f; Härtel, "Leben in grosser Zeit," 490ff. Cf. Michael Hughes, *Shouldering the Burdens of Defeat: West Germany and the Reconstruction of Social Justice* (Chapel Hill, NC, 1999).
67. Peter Gay, *My German Question* (New Haven, CT, 1998), 195; Ruth Klüger, *unterwegs verloren: Erinnerungen* (Vienna, 2008); Mandelstam, "Memoirs," 49; "Experiences of Albert Gompertz: From Nazi Germany to America" (Palm Beach, 1998), 47f. Cf. Constantin Goschler, *Schuld und Schulden: Die Politik der Wiedergutmachung für NS-Verfolgte seit 1945* (Göttingen, 2005).
68. Gompertz, "Experiences," 43ff; Gerhard Krapf, courtship correspondence from the early 1950s in private possession; Klüger, *unterwegs verloren*, 72ff; Werner T. Angress, *Witness to the Storm: A Jewish Journey from Nazi Berlin to the 82nd Airborne, 1920–1945* (Durham, NC, 2012), 330f; George L. Mosse, *Confronting History: A Memoir* (Madison, 2000); Fritz Stern, *Five Germanys I Have Known* (New York, 2007), 210ff.
69. Sölle, *Gegenwind*, 34, 51, 70–105. Cf. Timothy Scott Brown, *West Germany and the Global Sixties: The Antiauthoritarian Revolt, 1962–1978* (Cambridge, UK, 2013).
70. Baehrenburg, "Maikäfer flieg," 255–58. Cf. Nikolas Wehrs, *Protest der Professoren: Der "Bund Freiheit der Wissenschaft" in den 1970er Jahren* (Göttingen, 2014).
71. Greiffenhagen, *Jahrgang 1928*, 153–74. Cf. Martin Klimke, *The Other Alliance: Student Protest in West Germany and the United States in the Global Sixties* (Princeton, NJ, 2010).
72. Grothus, "Mein Leben," 131f; Grothus, "Horst," 231f. Cf. Stephen Milder and Konrad H. Jarausch, eds, "Green Politics in Germany," special issue of *German Politics and Society* 33, no. 4 (2015).

73. Sölle, *Gegenwind*, 221–229; Grothus, "Mein Leben," 132f. Cf. Benjamin Ziemann, ed., *Peace Movements in Western Europe, Japan and the USA during the Cold War* (Essen, 2007).
74. Baehrenburg, "Maikäfer flieg," 227; Grothus, "Mein Leben," 63–89. Cf. Karen Hagemann and Sonya Michel, eds, *Gender and the Long Postwar: The United States and the Two Germanys, 1945–1989* (Washington, DC, 2014).
75. Grothus, "Mein Leben," 91–128; Grothus, "Horst," 225. Cf. Angelika von Wahl, *Gleichstellungsregime: Berufliche Gleichstellung von Frauen in den USA und in der Bundesrepublik Deutschland* (Opladen, 1999).
76. Neglein, *Die Verantwortung*, 5ff, 24. Cf. Frank Uekötter, *"The Greenest Nation?" A New History of German Environmentalism* (Cambridge, UK, 2014).
77. Grothus, "Horst," 225–30; Grothus, "Mein Leben," 129–31. Cf. Jürgen Kocka, *Civil Society and Dictatorship in Modern German History* (Hanover, NH, 2010).
78. Helmer, "Tornister," vol. 2, 58; Grothus, "Horst," 231. Cf. Edgar Wolfrum, *Die geglückte Demokratie: Geschichte der Bundesrepublik Deutschland von ihren Anfängen bis zur Gegenwart* (Stuttgart, 2006).
79. Grothus, "Horst," 223. Cf. Konrad H. Jarausch, *The Rush to German Unity* (New York, 1994).
80. Kolesnyk, "Alte Zeiten," 155; Tausch, "Mein Lebensbericht," 61. Cf. Konrad H. Jarausch and Michael Geyer, *Shattered Past: Reconstructing German Histories* (Princeton, NJ, 2003), 317ff.
81. Andrée, *Stationen*, 69ff; Baucke, *Das Buch gehört dazu*, passim; Neumaier, "Mein Leben," 79–130; Grothus, "Horst," 207ff; Raschdorff, "Mein Leben," 244.
82. Schöffski, "Erinnerungen," 85ff; Grothus, "Mein Leben," 53; Baehrenburg, "Maikäfer flieg," 169ff; Huber, "Das war mein Leben," 167; Weigelt, *Mein langes Leben*, 361ff.
83. Weigelt, *Mein langes Leben*, 365. Cf. Jarausch, *After Hitler*, 14–17. Cf. Paul Nolte, *Was ist Demokratie? Geschichte und Gegenwart* (Munich, 2012).
84. Hans-Harald Schirmer, "Erinnerungen an die Familie Hans und Luise Schirmer aus Wolfenbüttel," 78; Stern, *In den Netzen*, 254f; Krause, "Unschuldig," 20. Cf. Charles S. Maier, *The Unmasterable Past: History, Holocaust, and German National Identity* (Cambridge, UK, 1988).

CHAPTER 9. COMMUNIST DISAPPOINTMENT

1. Carola Stern, *In den Netzen der Erinnerung: Lebensgeschichten zweier Menschen* (Hamburg, 1986), 242ff. Cf. Thomas Abhe, "Autobiographische Erzählungen aus der 'Integrierten Generation' und die Darstellung der DDR," in *Autobiographische Aufarbeitung: Diktatur und Lebensgeschichte im 20. Jahrhundert* (Göttingen, 2012), 87–109.
2. Werner Braune, *Abseits der Protokollstrecke: Erinnerungen eines Pfarrers an die DDR* (Berlin, 2009), 33–38.
3. Fritz Klein, *Drinnen und Draußen: Ein Historiker in der DDR; Erinnerungen* (Frankfurt, 2000), 143; Günter Krause, "Mein Leben in der DDR" (n.p., 2006); Werner Hübschmann, *Trotzdem—(m)ein pralles Leben in der DDR* (Berlin, 2015), 183ff. Cf. Corey

Ross, *The East German Dictatorship: Problems and Perspectives in the Interpretation of the GDR* (London, 2002).

4. Werner Feigel, *Mission Gerechtigkeit: Ein Leben für die DDR* (Ribnitz-Damgarten, 2014), 102, 142; Paul Frenzel, *40 verlorene Jahre: Erinnerungen an die Diktatur des nationalen und des realen Sozialismus* (Stuttgart, 1994), 159ff. Cf. Konrad H. Jarausch, ed., *Dictatorship as Experience: Towards a Socio-Cultural History of the GDR* (New York, 1999).
5. Horst Johannsen, *Ein Leben von Diktatur zu Diktatur* (Bromskirchen, 2003), 150. Cf. Dirk Spilker, *The East German Leadership and the Division of Germany: Patriotism and Propaganda 1945–1953* (Oxford, UK, 2006).
6. Gerhard Joachim, "Wundersame Reise des Odysseus des XX. Jahrhunderts: Von Hitlers Aufstieg bis zum Untergang der Stalinistischen Ära" (Rostock, 1998), 55–61. Cf. Lorn Hillacker's forthcoming dissertation on the East-West competition for "a better Germany" (Chapel Hill, 2018).
7. Johannsen, *Ein Leben*, 83ff. Cf. Norman Naimark, *The Russians in Germany: A History of the Soviet Zone of Occupation, 1945–1949* (Cambridge, MA, 1995), passim.
8. Günter Manz, *Aufstieg und Fall des Landes DDR: Erinnerungen und Ansichten* (Berlin, 2002), 71ff versus Albert Leithold, *Notizen aus "tausendjährigen Reichen"* (Delitzsch, 1994), 25ff. Cf. Klaus Schroeder, *Der SED-Staat: Geschichte und Strukturen der DDR 1949–1990* (Cologne, 2013).
9. Joachim, "Wundersame Reise," 61; Feigel, *Mission Gerechtigkeit*, 21; Johannsen, *Ein Leben*, 87; Härtel. "Leben in grosser Zeit," 319; Klein, *Drinnen und Draußen*, 107, 141.
10. Frenzel, *40 verlorene Jahre*, 144, 171ff; Johannsen, *Ein Leben*, 90ff, 114, 124. Cf. Andre Steiner, *The Plans That Failed: An Economic History of the GDR* (New York, 2010).
11. Joachim, "Wundersame Reise," 63; Klein, *Drinnen und Draußen*, 115, 143; Johannsen, *Ein Leben*, 119. Cf. Christoph Klessmann, *Arbeiter im "Arbeiterstaat" DDR: Deutsche Traditionen, sowjetisches Modell, westdeutsches Magnetfeld 1945–1971* (Bonn, 2007).
12. Johannsen, *Ein Leben*, 110; Feigel, *Mission Gerechtigkeit*, 30; Hübschmann, *Trotzdem*, 88; Gerhard Baucke, *Das Buch gehört dazu. Gute Seiten—Schlechte Seiten: Spiegelbild erlebter Zeiten 1919–1999* (Berlin, 2002), 104; Klein, *Drinnen und Draußen*, 115. Cf. Ulrich Mählert and Rüdiger Stephan, *Blaue Hemden, Rote Fahnen: Die Geschichte der Freien Deutschen Jugend* (Opladen, 1996).
13. Feigel, *Mission Gerechtigkeit*, 23, 36; Frenzel, *40 verlorene Jahre*, 135, 167; Hübschmann, *Trotzdem*, 97; Joachim, "Wundersame Reise," 67; Klein, *Drinnen und Draußen*, 167, 198.
14. Karl Härtel, "Leben in grosser Zeit: Von den goldenen 20ern bis zum Zusammenbruch des Deutschen Reiches und dem beginnenden Wiederaufbau" (Leopoldshafen, 1996), 351; Frenzel, *40 verlorene Jahre*, 135ff; Braune, *Abseits der Protokollstrecke*, 173; Hübschmann, *Trotzdem*, 92ff. Cf. Mary Fulbrook, *The People's State: East German Society from Hitler to Honecker* (New Haven, CT, 2005).
15. Braune, *Abseits der Protokollstrecke*, 56, 67, 74, 85f, 104; Joachim Gauck, *Winter im Sommer, Frühling im Herbst: Erinnerungen* (Munich, 2009). Cf. Rudolf Mau, *Der Protestantismus im Osten Deutschlands, 1945–1990* (Leipzig 2005).

16. Joachim, "Wundersame Reise," 62; Feigel, *Mission Gerechtigkeit*, 27, 33, 37, 57; Johannsen, *Ein Leben*, 137. Cf. Thomas Lindenberger, *Volkspolizei: Herrschaft und öffentliche Ordnung im SED-Staat, 1952–1968* (Cologne, 2003).
17. Günter Krause, "Unschuldig," 3–26; Härtel, "Leben in grosser Zeit," 362. Cf. Günter Morsch, *Sachsenhausen: "Das Konzentrationslager bei der Reichshauptstadt"* (Berlin, 2014).
18. Johannsen, *Ein Leben*, 109; Klein, *Drinnen und Draußen*, 131f; and Joachim, "Wundersame Reise," 89ff. Cf. Esther von Richthofen, *Bringing Culture to the Masses: Control, Compromise and Participation in the GDR* (New York, 2009).
19. Joachim, "Wundersame Reise," 52ff; Feigel, *Mission Gerechtigkeit*, 81, 94; Hübschmann, *Trotzdem*, 91; Stern, *In den Netzen*, 248; Johannsen, *Ein Leben*, 139.
20. Hübschmann, *Trotzdem*, 47ff; Feigel, *Mission Gerechtigkeit*, 50, 59; Härtel, "Leben in grosser Zeit," 337ff, 367ff, 434–43; Joachim, "Wundersame Reise," 96; Klein, *Drinnen und Draußen*, 225.
21. Joachim, "Wundersame Reise," 89; Frenzel, *40 verlorene Jahre*, 149; Feigel, *Mission Gerechtigkeit*, 89ff; Hübschmann, *Trotzdem*, 97; Johannsen, *Ein Leben*, 140.
22. Hübschmann, *Trotzdem*, 59, 116; Feigel, *Mission Gerechtigkeit*, 44; Härtel, "Leben in grosser Zeit," 328, 355; Johannsen, *Ein Leben*, 125ff; and Klein, *Drinnen and Draußen*, 133. Cf. Jürgen Kocka, "Eine durchherrschte Gesellschaft," in *Sozialgeschichte der DDR*, edited by Hartmut Kaelble et al. (Stuttgart, 1994), 547–53.
23. Braune, *Abseits der Protokollstrecke*, 120; Johannsen, *Ein Leben*, 148; Frenzel, *40 verlorene Jahre*, 169, 215; Joachim, "Wundersame Reise," 88; Hübschmann, *Trotzdem*, 83ff. Cf. Stefan Wolle, *Die heile Welt der Diktatur: Alltag und Herrschaft in der DDR 1971–1989* (Berlin, 1998).
24. Frenzel, *40 verlorene Jahre*, 152ff; Heinrich Johann Buschmann, *Erinnerungen aus meinem Leben in der DDR* (Berlin, 2010), 37ff. Cf. Thomas Klein, *"Für die Einheit und Reinheit der Partei": Die innerparteilichen Kontrollorgane der SED in der Ära Ulbricht* (Cologne, 2002).
25. Frenzel, *40 verlorene Jahre*, 173–77; Joachim, "Wundersame Reise," 78; Feigel, *Mission Gerechtigkeit*, 48; Manz, *Aufstieg und Fall*, 77–82; and Leithold, *Notizen*, 28ff. Cf. Roger Engelmann and Ilko-Sascha Kowaczuk, eds, *Volkserhebung gegen den SED-Staat: Eine Bestandsaufnahme zum 17. Juni 1953* (Göttingen, 2005).
26. Joachim, "Wundersame Reise," 91; Frenzel, *40 verlorene Jahre*, 185; Klein, *Drinnen und Draußen*, 185–93. Cf. Siegfried Prokop, "Zwischen Tauwetter, Frühling und Frost—die DDR in den Monaten nach dem XX. Parteitag der KPdSU," *Jahrbuch für Forschungen zur Geschichte der Arbeiterbewegung* 2 (2006).
27. Joachim, "Wundersame Reise," 91; Johannsen, *Ein Leben*, 145, 162; Klein, *Drinnen und Draußen*, 138; Braune, *Abseits der Protokollstrecke*, 86, 146.
28. Johannsen, *Ein Leben*, 158ff; Hübschmann, *Trotzdem*, 80; Härtel, "Leben in grosser Zeit," 423–52; Braune, *Abseits der Protokollstrecke*, 91.
29. Joachim, "Wundersame Reise," 67; Feigel, *Mission Gerechtigkeit*, 40f; Härtel, "Leben in grosser Zeit," 343; Braune, *Abseits der Protokollstrecke*, 55. Cf. Konrad H. Jarausch and Hannes Siegrist, eds, *Amerikanisierung und Sowjetisierung in Deutschland, 1945–1970* (Frankfurt, 1997).

30. Johannsen, *Ein Leben*, 228; Hübschmann, *Trotzdem*, 189. Cf. Jeannette Maderasz, *Working in East Germany: Normality in a Socialist Dictatorship, 1961–1979* (Basingstoke, 2006).
31. Feigel, *Mission Gerechtigkeit*, 47; Frenzel, *40 verlorene Jahre*, 208–16; Klein, *Drinnen und Draußen*, 210. Cf. Michael Lemke, *Vor der Mauer: Berlin in der Ost-West Konkurrenz, 1948–1961* (Cologne, 2011).
32. Buschmann, *Erinnerungen*, 169; Johannsen, *Ein Leben*, 158, 177; Braune, *Abseits der Protokollstrecke*, 91, 104; Gabriel Berger, *"Mir langt's, ich gehe": Der Lebensweg eines DDR-Atomphysikers von Anpassung zu Aufruhr* (Freiburg, 1988), 33.
33. Johannsen, *Ein Leben*, 160ff; Berger, *"Mir langt's,"* 34ff; Frenzel, *40 verlorene Jahre*, 226; Braune, *Abseits der Protokollstrecke*, 94. Cf. Hope Harrison, *Driving the Soviets up the Wall: Soviet–East German Relations, 1953–1961* (Princeton, NJ, 2003).
34. Frenzel, *40 verlorene Jahre*, 225ff; Berger, *"Mir langt's,"* 35ff; Klein, *Drinnen und Draußen*, 213; Feigel, *Mission Gerechtigkeit*, 70. Cf. Klaus-Dietmar Henke, ed., *Die Mauer: Errichtung, Überwindung, Erinnerung* (Munich, 2011).
35. Frenzel, *40 verlorene Jahre*, 227ff; Johannsen, *Ein Leben*, 161; Braune, *Abseits der Protokollstrecke*, 101ff. Cf. Hans-Hermann Hertle and Maria Nooke, *Die Todesopfer an der Berliner Mauer 1961–1989: Ein biographisches Handbuch* (Berlin, 2009).
36. Joachim, "Wundersame Reise," 100f; Frenzel, *40 verlorene Jahre*, 237ff. Cf. Mario Frank, *Walter Ulbricht: Eine deutsche Biografie* (Berlin, 2001).
37. Johannsen, *Ein Leben*, 152, 250; Gauck, *Winter im Sommer*, 177; and Erich Hasemann, *Als Soldat in der DDR* (Berlin, 1997), 39ff. Cf. Daniel Giese, *Die SED und ihre Armee: Die NVA zwischen Politisierung und Professionalismus, 1956–1965* (Munich, 2002).
38. Klein, *Drinnen und Draußen*, 216ff; Joachim, "Wundersame Reise," 100ff; and Johannsen, *Ein Leben*, 201f. Cf. Simone Bark, Martina Langermann, and Siegfried Lokatis, *"Jedes Buch ein Abenteuer": Zensur-System und literarische Öffentlichkeiten in der DDR bis Ende der sechziger Jahre* (Berlin, 1997).
39. Johannsen, *Ein Leben*, 174; Frenzel, *40 verlorene Jahre*, 182ff; Leithold, *Notizen*, 50ff. Cf. The forthcoming dissertation by Larissa Stiglich about the model city of Eisenhüttenstadt (Chapel Hill, 2018).
40. Feigel, *Mission Gerechtigkeit*, 109; Braune, *Abseits der Protokollstrecke*, 96, 142; Hübschmann, *Trotzdem*, 110; Frenzel, *40 verlorene Jahre*, 198; and Leithold, *Notizen*, 44ff, 116ff. Cf. David Crew, ed., *Consuming Germany in the Cold War* (Oxford, UK, 2003).
41. Braune, *Abseits der Protokollstrecke*, 121f; Manz, *Aufstieg und Fall*, 88ff. Cf. Armin Mitter and Stefan Wolle, *Untergang auf Raten: Unbekannte Kapitel der DDR-Geschichte* (Munich, 1993).
42. Joachim, "Wundersame Reise," 106ff. Cf. Monika Kaiser, *Machtwechsel von Ulbricht zu Honecker: Funktionsmechanismen der SED-Diktatur in Konfliktsituationen 1962 bis 1972* (Berlin, 1997).
43. Carole Fink and Bernd Schaefer, eds, *Ostpolitik, 1969–1974: European and Global Responses* (Washington, DC, 2009).
44. Johannsen, *Ein Leben*, 172ff; Braune, *Abseits der Protokollstrecke*, 178ff; Frenzel, *40 verlorene Jahre*, 249. Cf. Wolle, *Heile Welt der Diktatur*, 64ff.

45. Klein, *Drinnen und Draußen*, 287ff; Frenzel, *40 verlorene Jahre*, 193ff; Hübschmann, *Trotzdem*, 193ff. Cf. Jens Giesecke, *The History of the Stasi: East Germany's Secret Police, 1945–1990* (New York, 2014).
46. Hübschmann, *Trotzdem*, 89; Klein, *Drinnen und Draußen*, 198ff; Frenzel, *40 verlorene Jahre*, 250–62. Cf. Konrad H. Jarausch, "Das Ringen um Erneuerung," in *Sozialistisches Experiment und Erneuerung in der Demokratie: Die Humboldt Universität zu Berlin, 1945–2010*, edited by Konrad H. Jarausch, Mattias Midell, and Annette Vogt (Berlin, 2012), 555ff.
47. Frenzel, *40 verlorene Jahre*, 155; Klein, *Drinnen und Draußen*, 170; Johannsen, *Ein Leben*, 164, 201.
48. Johannsen, *Ein Leben*, 190, 247. Cf. Eli Rubin, *Amnesiopolis: Modernity, Space and Memory in East Germany* (New York, 2016).
49. Hübschmann, *Trotzdem*, 110, 172ff; Leithold, *Notizen*, 41ff. Cf. Günter Gaus, *Wo Deutschland liegt: Eine Ortsbestimmung* (Hamburg, 1983).
50. Johannsen, *Ein Leben*, 111; Feigel, *Mission Gerechtigkeit*, 52, 62; Braune, *Abseits der Protokollstrecke*, 134f; Hübschmann, *Trotzdem*, 63, 123ff. Cf. Lewis H. Siegelbaum, ed., *The Socialist Car: Automobility in the Eastern Bloc* (Ithaca, NY, 2011).
51. Johannsen, *Ein Leben*, 167f, 242; Feigel, *Mission Gerechtigkeit*, 80, 84; Hübschmann, *Trotzdem*, 164f. Cf. Christopher Görlich, *Urlaub vom Staat: Tourismus in der DDR* (Cologne, 2012).
52. Johannsen, *Ein Leben*, 139; Frenzel, *40 verlorene Jahre*, 255; Hübschmann, *Trotzdem*, 63, 142; Cf. Martin Diewald, Anne Goedicke, and Karl Ulrich Mayer, eds, *After the Wall: Life Courses in the Transformation of East Germany* (Stanford, CA, 2006).
53. Hübschmann, *Trotzdem*, 155; Braune, *Abseits der Protokollstrecke*, 146, 152; Klein, *Drinnen und Draußen*, 127. Cf. Klessmann, *Arbeiter im "Arbeiterstaat,"* passim.
54. Feigel. *Mission Gerechtigkeit*, 86ff; Joachim, "Wundersame Reise," 91f, 111; Klein, *Drinnen und Draußen*, 292; Frenzel, *40 verlorene Jahre*, 152. Cf. Hans-Hermann Hertle and Konrad H. Jarausch, eds, *Risse im Bruderbund: Die Krim Gespräche Honecker-Breschnew, 1974 bis 1982* (Berlin, 2006).
55. Klein, *Drinnen und Draußen*, 133ff, Feigel, *Mission Gerechtigkeit*, 44ff. Cf. Donna Harsch, *Revenge of the Domestic: Women, the Family, and Communism in the German Democratic Republic* (Princeton, NJ, 2007).
56. Joachim, "Wundersame Reise," 113; Frenzel, *40 verlorene Jahre*, 245; Johannsen, *Ein Leben*, 253, 258. Cf. Jaap Sleifer, *Planning Ahead and Falling Behind: The East German Economy in Comparison with West Germany 1936–2002* (Berlin, 2006).
57. Johannsen, *Ein Leben*, 215, 219; Feigel, *Mission Gerechtigkeit*, 113; Frenzel, *40 verlorene Jahre*, 249. Cf. Hartmut Berghoff and Uta Balbier, eds, *The East German Economy, 1945–2010: Falling Behind or Catching Up?* (Washington, DC, 2013).
58. Frenzel, *40 verlorene Jahre*, 251ff; Härtel, "Leben in grosser Zeit," 397; Johannes, *Ein Leben*, 232; Braune, *Jenseits der Protokollstrecke*, 120; Alfred Kosing, *Innnenansichten als Zeitzeugnisse: Philosophie und Politik in der DDR: Erinnerungen und Reflexionen* (Berlin, 2008), 350ff.

59. Braune, *Jenseits der Protokollstrecke*, 183f; Berger, "*Mir langt's*," passim; Joachim, "Wundersame Reise," 123ff. Cf. Jan Philipp Wölbern, *Der Häftlingsfreikauf aus der DDR, 1962/63–1989: Zwischen Menschenhandel und humanitären Aktionen* (Göttingen 2014).
60. Braune, *Abseits der Protokollstrecke*, 60f; Joachim, "Wundersame Reise," 122–39. Cf. Uta Poiger, *Jazz, Rock, and Rebels: Cold War Politics and American Culture in a Divided Germany* (Berkeley, 2000).
61. Johannsen "Wundersame Reise," 233ff; Braune, *Abseits der Protokollstrecke*, 152. Cf. Erhart Neubert, *Geschichte der Opposition in der DDR, 1949–1989* (Berlin, 1997).
62. Härtel, "Leben in grosser Zeit," 384, 408; Braune, *Abseits der Protokollstrecke*, 108ff; Johannsen, *Ein Leben*, 240–50. Cf. Julia Ault, "Saving Nature in Socialism: East Germany's Official and Independent Environmentalism, 1968–1990" (Diss., Chapel Hill, 2015).
63. Braune, *Jenseits der Protokollstrecke*, 185–204; Johannsen, *Ein Leben*, 261. Cf. Ned Richardson-Little, "Between Dictatorship and Dissent: Ideology, Legitimacy, and Human Rights in East Germany, 1945–1990" (Diss., Chapel Hill, 2013).
64. Krause, *Mein Leben in der DDR*, 19f; Frenzel, *40 verlorene Jahre*, 281–93. Cf. Uwe Spiekermann, "The Stasi at Home and Abroad: Domestic Order and Foreign Intelligence," *Bulletin of the German Historical Institute*, Supplement 9 (2014).
65. Joachim, "Wundersame Reise," 138. Cf. Renate Hürtgen, *Der Schein der Stabilität: DDR-Betriebsalltag in der Ära Honecker* (Berlin, 2001).
66. Manz, *Aufstieg und Fall*, 105ff; Johannsen, *Ein Leben*, 191; Härtel, "Leben in grosser Zeit," 387; Braune, *Abseits der Protokollstrecke*, 148; Leithold, *Notizen*, 115f. Cf. Steiner, *The Plans That Failed*, passim.
67. Klein, *Drinnen und Draußen*, 315ff; Joachim, "Wundersame Reise," 117ff; Frenzel, *40 verlorene Jahre*, 274ff, Johannsen, *Ein Leben*, 261. Vladislav Zubok, *A Failed Empire: The Soviet Union in the Cold War from Stalin to Gorbachev* (Chapel Hill, NC, 2007).
68. Joachim, "Wundersame Reise," 116, 138; Klein, *Drinnen und Draußen*, 315ff, 334; Frenzel, *40 verlorene Jahre*, 275; Feigel, *Mission Gerechtigkeit*, 121, 125; and Manz, *Aufstieg und Fall*, 99ff.
69. Klein, *Drinnen und Draußen*, 285, 337; Feigel, *Mission Gerechtigkeit*, 133; Johannsen, *Ein Leben*, 263. Cf. Stephen Pfaff, *Exit-Voice Dynamics and the Collapse of East Germany: The Crisis of Leninism and the Revolution of 1989* (Durham, NC, 2006).
70. Klein, *Drinnen und Draußen*, 338ff; Joachim, "Wundersame Reise," 149ff; Feigel, *Mission Gerechtigkeit*, 134; Johannsen, *Ein Leben*, 264. Cf. Konrad H. Jarausch, *The Rush to German Unity* (New York, 1994), passim.
71. Johannsen, *Ein Leben*, 267ff, Feigel, *Mission Gerechtigkeit*, 130; Klein, *Drinnen und Draußen*, 342f. Cf. Charles S. Maier, *Dissolution: The Crisis of Communism and the End of East Germany* (Princeton, NJ, 1997).
72. Klein, *Drinnen und Draußen*, 340ff; Johannsen, *Ein Leben*, 268ff; Feigel, *Mission Gerechtigkeit*, 135; Hübschmann, *Trotzdem*, 208ff. Cf. Hans-Hermann Hertle, *Der Fall der Mauer: Die unbeabsichtigte Selbstauflösung des SED Staates* (Cologne, 1996).
73. Klein, *Drinnen und Draußen*, 343; Johannsen, *Ein Leben*, 271ff; Feigel, *Mission Gerechtigkeit*, 136f. Cf. Heinrich Bortfeld, *Von der SED zur PDS: Wandlung zur Demokratie?* (Berlin, 1992).

74. Johannsen, *Ein Leben*, 273ff; Feigel, *Mission Gerechtigkeit*, 137, Joachim, "Wundersame Reise," 153. Cf. Jarausch, *Rush to German Unity*, 115ff.
75. Johannsen, *Ein Leben*, 276ff; Feigel, *Mission Gerechtigkeit*, 140f; Leithold, *Notizen*, 122f. Cf. Wolfgang Seibel, *Verwaltete Illusionen: Die Privatisierung der DDR-Wirtschaft durch die Treuhandanstalt und ihre Nachfolger 1990–2000* (Frankfurt, 2005).
76. Braune, *Abseits der Protokollstrecke*, 211. Cf. Andreas Rödder, *Deutschland einig Vaterland: Die Geschichte der Wiedervereinigung* (Munich, 2009).
77. Feigel, *Mission Gerechtigkeit*, 142; Joachim, "Wundersame Reise," 153; Hübschmann, *Trotzdem*, 208; Braune, *Abseits der Protokollstrecke*, 211f. Cf. Volker Benkert, "Biographien im Umbruch. Die um 1970 in der DDR Geborenen zwischen Geschichte und Erinnerung" (Diss., Potsdam, 2016), passim.
78. Feigel, *Mission Gerechtigkeit*, 153; Hübschmann, *Trotzdem*, 92ff ; Krause, "Unschuldig," 1; Joachim, "Wundersame Reise," 165; and Buschmann, *Erinnerungen*, 114. Cf. Sabrow, "Autobiographie und Systembruch im 20. Jahrhundert," in: *Autobiographische Aufarbeitung*, 9–24.
79. Buschmann, *Erinnerungen*, 135; Braune, *Abseits der Protokollstrecke*, 220; Joachim, "Wundersame Reise," 154ff; Kosing, *Innenansichten als Zeitzeugnisse*, 20.
80. Feigel, *Mission Gerechtigkeit*, 137; Buschmann, *Erinnerungen*, 41–51; Johannsen, *Ein Leben*, 174; Hübschmann, *Trotzdem* 73; Braune, *Abseits der Protokollstrecke*, 158; Manz, *Aufstieg und Fall*, 45. Cf. Bernd Faulenbach, *Halbherziger Revisionismus: Zum postkommunistischen Geschichtsbild* (Munich, 1996).
81. Joachim, "Wundersame Reise," 165; Buschmann, *Erinnerungen*, 129; Klein, *Drinnen und Draußen*, 348ff; Feigel, *Mission Gerechtigkeit*, 146, 152. Cf. Konrad H. Jarausch, ed., *United Germany: Debating Processes and Prospects* (New York, 2015).
82. Feigel, *Mission Gerechtigkeit*, 145ff; Kosing, *Innenansichten als Zeitzeugnisse*, 17; Buschmann, *Erinnerungen*, 127; Stern, *In den Netzen*, 255.

CONCLUSION: MEMORIES OF FRACTURED LIVES

1. Ruth Bulwin, *Spätes Echo: Erzählungen aus Großmutters jungen Jahren* (Wismar, 2014), 5; Horst Johannsen, *Ein Leben von Diktatur zu Diktatur* (Bromskirchen, 2003), preface; Manz, *Aufstieg und Fall*, 11; and Huber,"Das war mein Leben," 1.
2. Joachim Fest, *Not I: Memoirs of a German Childhood* (New York, 2013), 423f; Fritz Klein, *Drinnen und Draußen: Ein Historiker in der DDR; Erinnerungen* (Frankfurt, 2000), 7–13; Benno Schöffski, "Meine Familiengeschichte von 1835 bis 1980" (Berlin, 1980), 2. Cf. Volker Depkat, "Autobiographie und die soziale Kontruktion von Wirklichkeit," *Geschichte und Gesellschaft* 29 (2003): 441–76; and Christiane Lahusen, *Zukunft am Ende: Autobiographische Sinnstiftungen von DDR-Geisteswissenschaftlern nach 1989* (Bielefeld, 2014), passim.
3. Carola Stern, *In den Netzen der Erinnerung: Lebensgeschichten zweier Menschen* (Hamburg, 1986), 12; Günter Krause, "Unschuldig zu 10 Jahren Arbeitslager verurteilt vom sowjetischen Geheimdienst" (n.p., 2006), preface. Cf. Konrad H. Jarausch, "A Double Burden: The Politics of the Past and German Identity," in Jörn Leonhard and Lothar

Funk, eds, *Ten Years of German Unification: Transfer, Transformation, Incorporation* (Birmingham, UK, 2002), 98–114.

4. Ulrich Herbert, *Deutsche Geschichte im zwanzigsten Jahrhundert* (Munich, 2015), passim. Cf. Konrad H. Jarausch, *After Hitler: Recivilizing Germans, 1945–1995* (New York, 2008), 269ff.
5. Brigitte Krieg-Oberlader, preface to Neumaier, "Mein Leben"; Erich Hasemann, *Als Soldat in der DDR* (Berlin, 1997), 7; Gerhard Baucke, *Das Buch gehört dazu: Gute Seiten—Schlechte Seiten: Spiegelbild erlebter Zeiten 1919–1999* (Berlin, 2002), 166; and Hellmut Raschdorff, "Mein Leben von 1922 bis Ende 2003" (Freiburg, 2003), 1.
6. Neumaier, "Mein Leben," 135f; Fest, *Not I*, 413f; Gisela Grothus, "Mein Leben" (Dorsten, n.d.), 65ff; Hermann Debus, *Ein Leben im Wandel der Zeiten* (Dörscheid, 1998), 327f; Huber, "Das war mein Leben," 141ff; Krause, "Mein Leben," 20.
7. Huber, "Das war mein Leben," 125–41; Bulwin, *Spätes Echo*, 198ff; Erika Taubhorn, "Mein Leben: Erinnerungen" (Wuppertal, 2000), 75; Raschdorff, "Mein Leben," 120ff.
8. Debus, *Ein Leben*, 486ff; Huber, "Das war mein Leben," 163ff; Krause, "Mein Leben in der DDR," 21.
9. Raschdorff, "Mein Leben," 244; Baucke, *Das Buch gehört dazu*, 176; Horst Grothus, "Horst in seiner Zeit," 3rd ed. (Dorsten, n.d.), 244.
10. Ursula Mahlendorf, *Shame of Survival: Working through a Nazi Childhood* (University Park, PA, 2009), 3–5. Cf. Lu Seegers and Jürgen Reulecke, eds, *Die "Generation der Kriegskinder": Historische Hintergründe und Deutungen* (Giessen, 2009).
11. Baucke, *Das Buch gehört dazu*, 166; Klein, *Drinnen und Draußen*, 333ff. Cf. Jarausch, *Rush to German Unity*, passim.
12. Hasemann, *Als Soldat*, 344; Kosing, *Innenansichten als Zeitzeugnisse*, 510ff; Manz, *Aufstieg und Fall*, 240ff; Feigel, *Mission Gerechtigkeit*, 155ff; Buschmann, *Erinnerungen*, 61ff; and Johannsen, *Ein Leben*, 278f.
13. Neumaier, "Mein Leben," 138; Huber, "Das war mein Leben," 166; Ursula Baehrenburg, "Maikäfer flieg: Lebenserinnerungen 1920–2005" (Lautertal, 2005), 377; Winfried Weigelt, *Mein langes Leben* (Schwerin, 2017), 442; and Raschdorff, "Mein Leben," 242.
14. Heinz Schultheis, *Kindheit und Jugend zwischen den Kriegen und Erwachsenwerden danach* (Leverkusen, 2007–2010), 121, versus Edgar Wolfrum, *Welt im Zwiespalt: Eine andere Geschichte des 20. Jahrhunderts* (Stuttgart, 2017).
15. Schöffski, "Familiengeschichte," 3ff; Thomas Mann, *Reflections of a Nonpolitical Man* (New York, 1983). Cf. the negative image in Hans-Ulrich Wehler, *The German Empire, 1871–1918* (Leamington Spa, 1985).
16. Gerhard Krapf, "Recollections" (Edmonton, 1990s), 7ff; Bettina Fehr, "Erinnerungen" (Bonn, 2005), 134; Alfred Döblin, *Berlin Alexanderplatz: The Story of Franz Biberkopf* (New York, 1931). Cf. Eric D. Weitz, *Weimar Germany: Promise and Tragedy* (Princeton, NJ, 2009), passim.
17. Christa Wolf, *A Model Childhood* (New York, 1980); and Melita Maschmann, *Account Rendered: A Dossier of My Former Self* (London, 1964).
18. See Walter Kempowski's series of montages called *Echolot* or Peter Bamm, *The Invisible Flag* (New York, 1956). Cf. Nicholas Stargardt, *The German War: A Nation under Arms, 1939–1945* (London, 2015), passim.

19. Matthias Strässner, *"Erzähl mir vom Krieg!" Wie vier Journalistinnen 1945 ihre Berliner Tagebücher schreiben: Ruth Andreas-Friedrich, Ursula von Kardorff, Margret Boveri und Anonyma* (Würzburg, 2014). Cf. the Poenichen trilogy of novels by Christine Brückner.
20. Victor Klemperer, *"Ich will Zeugnis ablegen bis zum letzten": Tagebücher 1933–1945*, 2 vols. (Berlin, 1995). Cf. Nikolaus Wachsmann, *KL: A History of the Nazi Concentration Camps* (New York, 2015), passim.
21. Heinrich Böll, *Der Engel schwieg: Roman* (Munich, 1997). Cf. Tony Judt, *Postwar: A History of Europe since 1945* (New York, 2005), passim.
22. Karl Jaspers, *The Question of German Guilt* (New York, 1947). Cf. Günter Grass, *Die Blechtrommel: Roman* (Darmstadt, 1959).
23. Hans Modrow, *Ich wollte ein neues Deutschland* (Berlin, 1998). Cf. Eugen Ruge, *In Times of Fading Light: The Story of a Family* (Minneapolis, 2013).
24. Aleida Assmann, *Geschichte im Gedächtnis: Von der individuellen Erfahrung zur öffentlichen Inszenierung* (Munich, 2007). See the dissertation by Peter Gengler on the establishment of a master narrative of flight and expulsion (Chapel Hill, 2018).
25. Joachim Bässmann, "Bericht eines SS-Mannes über Dienst in Auschwitz," 84; Kosing, *Innensichten als Zeitzeugnisse*, 5ff; Mandelstam, "Memoirs," passim; Krauss, "Unschuldig," preface; Baehrenburg, "Maikäfer flieg," passim.
26. Martin Sieg, *Im Schatten der Wolfschanze: Hitlerjunge auf der Suche nach Sinn—Autobiographische Skizze eines Zeitzeugen* (Münster, 1997), 1f; Will Seelmann-Eggebert, *Weder Narren noch Täter—der Schock kam erst später* (Ahlhorn, 2004), 91–96; Gerhardt B. Thamm, *Boy Soldier: A German Teenager at the Nazi Twilight* (Jefferson, NC, 2000), 2f; Haertel, "Leben in grosser Zeit;" 16, 51f; Debus, *Ein Leben*, passim.
27. Buschmann, *Erinnerungen*, 19f; Grothus, "Horst," 66ff; Bulwin, *Spätes Echo*, 5.
28. Lore Walb, *Ich, die Alte, ich die Junge: Konfrontation mit meinen Tagebüchern 1933–1945* (Berlin, 1998), 18ff; Eva Sternheim-Peters, *Habe ich denn allein gejubelt? Eine Jugend im Nationalsozialismus* (Berlin, 2015), 114ff; Renate Finckh, *Sie versprachen uns die Zukunft: Eine Jugend im Nationalsozialismus* (Tübingen, 2002), 7.
29. Albert Leithold, *Notizen aus "tausendjährigen Reichen"* (Delitzsch, 1994), 11f; Härtel, "Leben in grosser Zeit," 4f; Moosmann, *Barfuß*, 132. Cf. Eric A. Johnson, *What We Knew: Terror, Mass Murder and Everyday Life in Nazi Germany* (Cambridge, UK, 2005); Longerich, *"Davon haben wir nichts gewusst"*; and Mary Fulbrook, *Reckonings: Legacies of Nazi Persecution* (Oxford, UK, 2018).
30. Mahlendorf, *Shame of Survival*, 325ff; Grothus, "Horst," 154ff. Cf. Konrad H. Jarausch, "Selbstkritik als Erinnerungskultur: Grundlagen moralischer Politik in Deutschland?," first annual Sachsenhausen lecture, June 2016.
31. Martin Sieg, *Im Schatten*, 102ff; Klein, *Drinnen und Draußen*, 107ff. Cf. Jeffrey Herf, *Divided Memories: The Nazi Past in the Two Germanys* (Cambridge, UK, 1997), passim.
32. Bässmann, "Bericht eines SS-Mannes," 47. Cf. Patrick Tobin, "Crossroads at Ulm: Postwar West Germany and the 1958 Ulm Einsatzkommando Trial" (Diss., Chapel Hill, 2013); Hannah Arendt, *Eichmann in Jerusalem: A Report on the Banality of Evil* (New York, 2006 [1963]); Peter Weiss, *Die Ermittlung: Oratorium in elf Gesängen* (Frankfurt, 2005).

33. Gerhard Joachim, "Wundersame Reise des Odysseus des XX. Jahrhunderts: Von Hitlers Aufstieg bis zum Untergang der Stalinistischen Ära" (Rostock, 1998), 55ff, 118ff; Klein, *Drinnen und Draußen*, 117ff, 316ff; Kosing, *Innenansichten als Zeitzeugnisse*, 427ff, 535ff. Cf. Jon Olsen, *Tailoring Truth: Politicizing the Past and Negotiating Memory in East Germany, 1945–1990* (New York, 2015).
34. Mahlendorf, *Shame of Survival*, 337ff; Walb, *Ich die Alte*, 21ff; and Fehr, "Erinnerungen," 98, 157. Cf. Grothus, "Mein Leben," 63ff; Grothus, "Horst," 225ff; Sölle, *Gegenwind*, 57f, 70ff; Braune, *Abseits der Protokollstrecke*, 147ff.
35. Albert Gompertz, "Experiences of Albert Gompertz: From Nazi Germany to America" (Palm Beach, 1998), 56ff; Ganor, *Wer bist Du Annuschka?*, 125ff; Ilse Polak, *Meine drei Leben: Die Geschichte einer Papenburger Jüdin* (Papenburg, 2013), 62; Mandelstam, "Memoirs," 52ff; Fritz Stern, *Five Germanys I Have Known* (New York, 2007), 208ff; Georg Iggers, *Zwei Seiten einer Geschichte: Lebensbericht aus unruhigen Zeiten* (Göttingen, 2002), 137ff; Ruth Klüger, *Weiter leben: Eine Jugend* (Göttingen, 1992), 269ff; Werner T. Angress, *Witness to the Storm: A Jewish Journey from Nazi Berlin to the 82nd Airborne, 1920–1945* (Durham, NC, 2012), 331ff; and Judith Magyar Isaacson, *Befreiung in Leipzig: Erinnerungen einer ungarischen Jüdin* (Witzenhausen, 1991), 209.
36. Tom W. Smith and Seokho Kim, "National Pride in Comparative Perspective: 1995/96 and 2003/04," *International Journal of Public Opinion Research* 18 (2006) 127–36; Claudia von Salzen, "Dieses Land hat heute den Beifall der Welt gewonnen," *Tagesspiegel*, January 27, 2016; and Niraj Chokshi, "These Are the World's Best Countries," *Washington Post*, January 21, 2016.
37. Härtel "Leben in grosser Zeit," 6. Cf. Jarausch, *After Hitler*, passim.
38. Schultheis, *Kindheit und Jugend*, 121; Finckh, *Sie versprachen*, 268f. Cf. Volker Berghahn, "The Generation of '32 and the Re-Civilizing of Post-Hitler West Germany," in *German Zeitgeschichte: Konturen eines Forschungsfeldes*, edited by Thomas Lindenberger and Martin Sabrow, 128–43 (Göttingen, 2016).
39. Martin Sabrow, "Höcke und wir," January 25, 2017, http://www.zeitgeschichte-online.de/kommentar/hoecke-und-wir.
40. Schoenhals, "Betrogener Idealismus," preface; Grothus, "Horst," 244. Cf. Konrad H. Jarausch, Harald Wenzel, and Karin Goihl, eds, *Different Germans, Many Germanies: New Transatlantic Perspectives* (New York, 2017).
41. Timothy Garton Ash, "In gewisser Hinsicht wäre ein Kanzler Schulz für Europa sogar besser," *Tagesspiegel*, April 2, 2017.

List of Sources

ABBREVIATIONS

DTA	Deutsches Tagebucharchiv, Emmendingen, Germany
LBA	Leo Baeck Institute Archive, New York City
Priv.	In private possession
Pub.	Published
SK	Sammlung Kempowski in Akademie der Künste

AUTOBIOGRAPHIES

Alenfeld, Irene. *Warum seid Ihr nicht ausgewandert? Überleben in Berlin 1933 bis 1945*. Berlin, 2008. Pub.

Andrée, Horst. *Stationen meines Lebens*. Boxberg, 2000. DTA.

Angress, Werner T. *Witness to the Storm: A Jewish Journey from Nazi Berlin to the 82nd Airborne, 1920–1945*. Durham, NC, 2012. Pub.

Baehrenburg, Ursula. "'Maikäfer flieg,' Lebenserinnerungen 1920–2005." Lautertal, 2005. DTA.

Baucke, Gerhard. *Das Buch gehört dazu! Gute Seiten—schlechte Seiten: Spiegelbild erlebter Zeiten, 1919–1999*. Berlin, 2002. SK.

Beilmann, Christel. *Eine katholische Jugend in Gottes und dem Dritten Reich: Briefe, Berichte, Gedrucktes 1930–1945; Kommentare 1988/89*. Wuppertal, 1989. Pub.

Berger, Gabriel. *"Mir langt's, ich gehe": Der Lebensweg eiens DDR-Atomphysikers von Anpassung zu Aufruhr*. Freiburg, 1988. Pub.

Bork, Ingrid. *Jedes Unglück hat ein Glück in sich. Friedrichshainer Lebenserinnerungen*. Berlin, 2010. Pub.

Braune, Werner. *Abseits der Protokollstrecke. Erinnerungen eines Pfarrers an die DDR*. Berlin, 2009. Pub.

Bruhns, Wibke. *My Father's Country: The Story of a German Family*. New York, 2008. Pub.

Bulwin, Ruth. *Spätes Echo: Erzählungen aus Großmutters jungen Jahren*. Wismar, 2014. Pub.

Buschmann, Heinrich Johann. *Erinnerungen aus meinem Leben in der DDR*. Berlin, 2010. Pub.

Debus, Hermann. *Ein Leben im Wandel der Zeiten*. Dörscheid, 2002. SK.

Ehrle, Gustav. "Lebenserinnerungen," Anlagen 2 and 3. SK.

Elias, Ruth. *Die Hoffnung hielt mich am Leben: Mein Weg von Theresienstadt und Auschwitz nach Israel*. Munich, 1990. Pub.

Eyck, Frank. *A Historian's Pilgrimage: Memoirs and Reflections*, edited by Rosemarie Eyck. Calgary, 2009. Pub.

Fehr, Bettina. "Erinnerungen." Bonn, 2005. Priv.

Feigel, Werner. *Mission Gerechtigkeit: Ein Leben für die DDR*. Ribnitz-Damgarten, 2014. Pub.

Fest, Joachim. *Not I: Memoirs of a German Childhood*. New York, 2014. Pub.

Finckh, Renate. *Sie versprachen uns die Zukunft: Eine Jugend im Nationalsozialismus*. Tübingen, 2002. Pub.

Fischer, Gudrun. "Mein 14. Geburtstag und dann . . . Eine Allensteinerin berichtet." SK.

Frenzel, Paul. *40 verlorene Jahre: Erinnerungen an die Diktatur des nationalen und des realen Sozialismus*, edited by Jürgen Schneider. Stuttgart, 1994. Pub.

Ganor, Niza. *Wer bist Du Anuschka? Die Überlebensgeschichte eines jüdischen Mädchens*. Munich, 1999. Pub.

Gay, Peter. *My German Question: Growing Up in Nazi Berlin*. New Haven, CT, 1998. Pub.

Gompertz, Albert. "Experiences of Albert Gompertz: From Nazi Germany to America." Palm Beach, 1998. LBA.

Grah, Ingeborg. "Die rote Käthe." SK.

Greiffenhagen, Martin. *Jahrgang 1928: Aus einem unruhigen Leben*. Munich, 1988. Pub.

Gros, Günter. "Flucht und Heimkehr aus russischer Gefangenschaft." Giessen, 1945. DTA.

Groschek, Christel. *Die totgemachte Seele*. Egelsbach, 1999. Pub.

Grothus, Gisela. "Mein Leben als glückliche Mutter, Großmutter, Medizinisch Technische Assistentin, Büromanagerin, Verlegerin, Zeugin der Weltkatastrophe und des Wiederaufbaus, Feministin und Aktivistin für gleiche Rechte und Chancen aller Frauen." Dorsten, n.d. Priv.

Grothus, Horst. "Horst in seiner Zeit auf dem Wege zum Nationalsozialisten, Militaristen, Patrioten, Flieger, Heldentod, Hungertod, Amputierten, Ehegatten über sechs Jahrzehnte, in Liebe und einer neuen Kultur, Vater, Ingenieur, Manager, Freiberufler, Managementguru, Wissenschaftler, Sozialisten, Kosmopoliten, Politiker, Zivilbürger, Intellektuellen, Weltverbesserer, Störer, Liberalen." Dorsten, n.d. Priv.

Grün, Max von der. *Wie war das eigentlich? Kindheit und Jugend im Dritten Reich*. Darmstadt, 1979. Pub.

Härtel, Karl. "Leben in grosser Zeit: Von den goldenen 20ern bis zum Zusammenbruch des Deutschen Reiches und dem beginnenden Wiederaufbau." Leopoldshafen, 1996. DTA.

Hasemann, Erich. *Als Soldat in der DDR: Erinnerungen aus über dreißigjähriger Dienstzeit in den bewaffneten Organen der DDR*. Berlin, 1997. Pub.

Hecht, Ingeborg. *Als unsichtbare Mauern wuchsen: Eine deutsche Familie unter den Nürnberger Rassengesetzen*, 3rd ed. Hamburg, 2010. Pub.

Helmer, Erich. "'Der Tornister': Autobiographie 1922–1983." 3 vols. Braunschweig, 1983. DTA.

Hubbe, Wolfgang. "Übernen Graben: Protokoll einer Fahnenflucht." SK.

Huber, Anneliese. "Das war mein Leben." Freiburg, 2000. DTA.

Hübschmann, Klaus. *Trotzdem—(m)ein pralles Leben in der DDR*. Berlin, 2015. Pub.

Iggers, Wilma, and Georg Iggers. *Zwei Seiten einer Geschichte: Lebensbericht aus unruhigen Zeiten*. Göttingen, 2002. Pub.

Isaacson, Judith Magyar. *Befreiung in Leipzig: Erinnerungen einer ungarischen Jüdin*. Witzenhausen, 1991. Pub.

Jarausch, Bruno. "Erinnerungen in einer schlesisch-märkischen Familie." Berlin, n.d. Priv.

Joachim, Gerhard. "Die wundersame Reise des Odysseus des XX. Jahrhunderts: Von Hitlers Aufstieg bis zum Untergang der stalinistischen Ära." Rostock, 1998. SK.

Johannsen, Horst. *Ein Leben von Diktatur zu Diktatur*. Bromskirchen, 2003. DTA.

Klein, Fritz. *Drinnen und Draußen: Ein Historiker in der DDR; Erinnerungen*. Frankfurt, 2000. Pub. Manuscript in Akademie der Wissenschaft.

Klüger, Ruth. *Unterwegs verloren: Erinnerungen*. Vienna, 2008. Pub.

———. *Weiter leben: Eine Jugend*. Göttingen, 1992. Pub.

Koch, Gertrud. *Edelweiß: Meine Jugend als Widerstandskämpferin*. Reinbeck, 2006. Pub.

Kolesnyk, Sonja. "Alte Zeiten." Ingolstadt, 1987. SK.

Kolesnyk, Wilhelm. "Wie es dazu kam, dass ich Nationalsozialist wurde." N.p., n.d. SK.

Kosing, Alfred. *Innenansichten als Zeitzeugnisse: Philosophie und Politik in der DDR*. Berlin, 2008. Pub.

Krapf, Gerhard. "Recollections." 9 vols. Edmonton, 1990s. Priv.

Krause, Günter. "Unschuldig zu 10 Jahren Arbeitslager verurteilt vom sowjetischen Geheimdienst (NKWD) 1946–1950: Gera, Weimar, Sachsenhausen, Waldheim." 2006. DTA.

Krohmer, Fritz. *Verwischte Spuren: Erinnerungen eines Kriegskindes 1933–1945*. Erdmannhausen, 1992. Pub.

Lehmann, Helmi. *Verwehte Spuren: aus dem Leben unseres Vaters Friedrich Wilhelm Lehmann*. Schliersee, n.d. Priv.

Leithold, Albert. *Notizen aus "tausendjährigen Reichen."* Delitzsch, 1994. Pub.

Mahlendorf, Ursula R. *Shame of Survival: Working through a Nazi Childhood*. University Park, PA, 2009. Pub.

Mandelstam, Lucy. *Memoirs*. Netanya, 1998. LBA.

Manz, Günter. *Aufstieg und Fall des Landes DDR: Erinnerungen und Ansichten*. Berlin, 2002. Pub.

Meyerstein, Heinz Jehuda. *Gehetzt, gejagt und entkommen: Von Göttingen über München und das KZ Dachau nach Holland, Deutschland, Holland und durch Frankreich über die Pyrenäen in Spanien gerettet*. Konstanz, 2008. Pub.

Moosmann, Agnes. *Barfuß aber nicht arm: Kindheit und Jugend in Bodnegg*. Sigmaringen, 1985. Pub.

Neglein, Hans-Gerd. *. . . und die Verantwortung trage ich! Aus der Chefetage der Wirtschaft zum Naturschutz in Andalusien*. Frankfurt, 2008. Pub.

Neumaier, Robert. "Das war—Das ist mein Leben 1924–2006." DTA.

Petzold, Joachim. *Parteinahme wofür? DDR-Historiker im Spannungsfeld von Politik und Wissenschaft*. Potsdam, 2000. Pub.

Polak, Ilse. *Meine drei Leben. Geschichte einer Papenburger Jüdin*. Papenburg, 2013. Pub.

Queiser, Hans R. *Du gehörst dem Führer! Vom Hitlerjungen zum Kriegsberichter: Ein autobiographischer Bericht*. Cologne, 1993. Pub.

Raschdorff, Hellmut. "Mein Leben von 1922 bis Ende 2003." Freiburg, 2003. DTA.

Richter, Hans Peter. *I Was There*. New York, 1973. Pub.

Schirmer, Hans-Harald. "Erinnerungen an die Familie Hans und Luise Schirmer aus Wolfenbüttel: Von den Lebensbedingungen einer Arbeiterfamilie und ihrer Verwandten in den Krisenjahren nach der Inflation 1923, unter der Nazidiktatur ab 1933 bis zum Kriegsende 1945 und vom Neubeginn." SK.

Schoenhals, Dieter. "Auch ich war in Arkadien geboren . . . oder erstens kommt es anders, zweitens als man denkt." Stockholm, 1985. Priv.

———. "Betrogener Idealismus oder unglaubliche Naivität" Stockholm, 1985. Priv.

Schöffski, Benno. "Meine Familiengeschichte von 1835 bis 1980." Berlin, 1980. Priv.

Schöffski, Edith. "Erinnerungen: Nur in der Rückschau, in der Zusammenfassung alles Erfahrenen, besitzen wir unser Leben ganz." Berlin, n.d. Priv.

Scholz-Eule, Eberhard, ed. *Wir Scholz-Kinder vom Herrnvorwerk: Aus dem Leben einer schlesischen Familie daheim und in der Zerstreuung*, 3rd ed. St. Georgen, 2008. DTA.

Schultheis, Heinz. *Kindheit und Jugend zwischen den Kriegen, Erwachsenenwerden danach: Gießener Erinnerungen aus den Zwanziger und Dreißiger Jahren und weiter bis 1950*. Leverkusen, 2010. DTA.

Seelmann-Eggebert, Will. *Weder Narren noch Täter—der Schock kam erst später: Eine glückliche Jugend und erfüllte Jahre in bewegter Zeit*. Ahlhorn, 2004. Pub.

Sieg, Martin. *Im Schatten der Wolfschanze: Hitlerjunge auf der Suche nach Sinn—Autobiographische Skizze eines Zeitzeugen*. Münster, 1997. Pub.

Simon, Marie. *Underground in Berlin: A Young Woman's Extraordinary Tale of Survival in the Heart of Nazi Germany*. New York, 2015. Pub.

Sölle, Dorothee. *Gegenwind: Erinnerungen*. Hamburg, 1995. Pub.

Stern, Fritz. *Five Germanys I Have Known*. New York, 2006. Pub.

Sternheim-Peters, Eva. *Habe ich denn allein gejubelt? Eine Jugend im Nationalsozialismus*. Berlin, 2015. Pub.

Taubhorn, Erika. "Mein Leben: Erinnerungen." Wuppertal, 2000. DTA.

Tausch, Hans. "Mein Lebensbericht." Forchheim, 1984. SK.

Thamm, Gerhardt B. *Boy Soldier: A German Teenager in the Nazi Twilight*. Jefferson, NC, 2000. Pub.

Ünaldi, Mehmet. *Mehmet—Ich Gastarbeiter und Türke: Erinnerungen eines Gastarbeiters der ersten Generation*. Münster, 2014. Pub.

Walb, Lore. *Ich, die Alte, ich, die Junge: Konfrontation mit meinen Tagebüchern 1933–1945*. Berlin, 1998. Pub.

Warmbrunn, Werner. "The Terrace Memoirs." Laguna Beach, CA, 1999–2000. LBA.

Weigelt, Winfried. *Mein langes Leben*. Schwerin, 2017. Pub.

Witolla, Jakobine. "Tagebuch, 1923–1990." Hameln, 1990. SK.

MEMORY FRAGMENTS

Anonyma. *Eine Frau in Berlin: Tagebuchaufzeichnungen vom 20. April bis 22. Juni 1945*. Frankfurt, 2003. Pub.

Bässmann, Joachim. "Bericht eines SS-Mannes über Dienst in Auschwitz." SK.

Botz, Gerhard, ed. *Schweigen und Reden einer Generation: Erinnerungsgespräche mit Opfern, Tätern und Mitläufern des Nationalsozialismus*, 2nd ed. Vienna, 2007. Pub.

Bronnen, Barbara. *Geschichten vom Überleben: Frauentagebücher aus der NS-Zeit*. Munich, 1998. Pub.

Bulwin, Ruth. "Briefe an ihre Eltern, 1937–1945," transcribed by Brigitte Stark. Priv.

Busch, Marianne. "1. September 1943 bis 21. Januar 1945." DTA.

Dörr, Margarete. *"Wer die Zeit nicht miterlebt hat . . ." Frauenerfahrungen im Zweiten Weltkrieg und in den Jahren danach*. 3 vols. Frankfurt, 1998. Pub.

Hagemann, Günther. Interview with Harro Matthiessen. Hamburg, 1995. Priv.

Hagenauer, Johanna. "Flucht aus Würzburg 1945." Munich, 2015.
Homeyer, Wilhelm. Letters from Russian prison camp. SK.
———. "Die letzten Stunden." Medenau, 1945. SK.
Keil, Jack Baruch. "Untitled Memoirs." LBI.
Lindauer, Inge. "Tagebuch der Flucht aus Oberschlesien." 1945. SK.
Marlens, Hanna. "Untitled Memoirs." Huntington, 1970. LBI.
Mueller, Irmgard. Repeated oral communication. Chapel Hill, NC, 1990s.
Stekeler-Weithofer, Pirmin. "Papas Briefe und andere." Leipzig, 2017. Priv.
Weinberg, Gerhard. Oral communication. Chapel Hill, NC, 2016.

Index

Abeles-Iggers, Wilma, 200, 432
Abitur (high school diploma), 74, 87, 268
Ackermann, Anton, 331
Adenauer, Konrad, 266, 274, 281, 306–8, 310, 315, 375f
Agricultural Production Cooperative (LPG), 335
air force (*Luftwaffe*), 107, 108, 111, 122, 125, 139, 164, 237, 244
air raids: by Allies, 139, 158, 173, 175, 177; defense against, 102, 105, 148, 158 160, 167; firestorms of, 175
airlift, 275
Albers, Hans, 122
Alenfeld, Erich, 203, 205, 260, 266, 271, 307
Alenfeld, Irene, 207, 260, 271
American army, 141, 229, 241, 242; anti-Nazi propaganda of, 252; émigré volunteers in, 226; military intelligence of; occupation government of, 252
Amundsen, Roald, 104
ancestors, legacies of, 17–41
Andersen, Lale, 123
Andrée, Horst, 19, 21, 47, 57, 85f, 116, 241–43, 245, 247f, 269, 283–85, 303, 317, 362f
Angress, Werner "Tom," 6, 30, 47, 59, 60, 63f, 70 74, 84, 87, 94, 194, 197–201, 204, 219, 223, 225, 227–30, 242, 273, 310, 378
Anschluss (annexation of Austria), 83, 152, 198, 201
anti-Fascism, 4, 245, 322, 373, 376
anti-Semitism: Austrian, 201; German, 62, 74; racial, 62, 74, 83
Apitz, Bruno, 306, 320
apprenticeship, 23, 55, 86, 87, 88f, 153, 269, 284, 291
Ariès, Philippe, 43
Aryan descent, 20f, 89
Aryanization, 200
Assmus, Erika, 66, 274, 275, 305. *See also* Stern, Carola
atrocities: of Nazis, 103, 134f, 141, 148, 163, 179, 186, 215, 218, 221, 226, 231f, 239, 244f, 246, 270, 365, 370; of Red Army, 139, 141, 179
Auschwitz, 169, 186, 208–14, 216, 218, 244, 278, 376, 378, 431, 434; Birkenau subcamp, 191, 209, 211, 215; *Stammlager*, 209, 214f. *See also* Holocaust
Autobahn (superhighway), 75
autobiographies, 1–14, 65, 95–97, 144–46, 186–89, 231–33, 276–78, 316–19, 357–59, 360, 380; apologetic, 65, 67, 144–46, 214, 238, 372–78; self-reflexive, 8, 374; as source, 5–12; writing of, 5–14, 360–80
Axis, 128

Backhaus, Wilhelm, 269
Baeck, Leo, 7, 209, 361
Baehrenburg, Ursula, 6, 56, 154, 163f, 168f, 176, 178, 181–83, 252–54, 257–61, 263, 268–70, 275–78, 284f, 296, 301, 311, 313, 318, 366, 373, 361
Barth, Karl, 286
Basic Treaty, 340
Bässmann, Joachim, 209, 211f, 214f, 218, 373, 376
Baucke, Gerhard, 27, 69, 74, 86, 101, 110, 114, 120, 127f, 133–35, 241, 246, 262, 269, 286, 288, 292–94, 299, 302f, 317, 325, 362, 364f
Bauer, Fritz, 376
Baum, Herbert, 94, 220
BBC broadcasts, 172, 219, 226

Beck, Ludwig, 221
Beilmann, Christel, 162, 185, 187, 277
Belgium, 22, 143, 203
Berger, Gabriel, 336
Berlin, 5, 7, 18, 22, 26, 29, 34–36, 47, 50, 61, 63, 75, 90, 94, 155, 163, 184, 194, 203, 204, 208, 214, 220f, 223, 229, 233, 241, 296, 301f, 316, 320, 326–28, 331, 333–37, 431f, 434; blockade of, 275, 286; destruction of, 173, 175f, 247, 267; as metropolis, 35, 58, 156, 334
Bildung (cultivation), 26, 55
Bismarck, Otto von, 22, 28, 32, 36f, 82
black market, 207, 241, 252, 258, 275
Blitzkrieg (lightning warfare), 115, 126, 133
Bochow, Herbert, 204
Böll, Heinrich, 3, 270, 306, 371
Bondy, Kurt, 200
Bonhöffer, Dietrich, 221, 306
Borchert, Wolfgang, 270, 306
Bork, Ingrid, 69, 83, 174, 182, 187, 257–61, 269
Boy Scouts, 61, 78
Brandt, Willy, 220, 230, 274, 316, 340, 355, 375
Braune, Werner, 320, 326, 339, 345, 348–50, 377
Brezhnev, Leonid, 345
Bruha, Antonia, 169
Bruhns, Wibke, 221
Buchenwald, 169, 193, 218, 320, 377
Bultmann, Rudolf, 286
Bulwin, Rolf, 106, 108, 111, 113f, 125, 165, 241, 247–50, 269, 279, 288, 293, 303, 363
Bulwin, Ruth, 9, 29, 31, 44f, 47, 51, 63, 72, 75, 77, 85f, 88, 90, 92, 95, 104, 113, 154–57, 159f, 162, 165f, 181, 188, 240, 259, 261, 263–65, 275, 277, 279, 287, 303, 360
Bund deutscher Mädel (BdM, female Hitler Youth), 77f, 82, 85, 92, 95, 122, 125, 143, 148, 151–54, 156–62, 167, 170, 175, 177, 179, 185f, 188, 360, 365, 369, 374
Bürgertum (middle class): educated (*Bildungs-*), 26; grand (*Gross-*), 31; petite (*Klein-*), 5, 31
Busch, Marianne, 168, 210, 212, 215f, 218
Buschmann, Heinrich, 331, 335, 358f, 366, 374
Busse, Emil, 203
Butler, Nicholas Murray, 225

cadre system, 329, 331
CARE packages, 258
Catholics, 5, 22, 28, 32–34, 53, 56, 61, 63f, 69, 86, 93, 95, 167, 258, 277, 280, 296f, 302, 304, 306–8, 333; subculture of, 32, 36f
censorship, 38, 121f, 338f; of Nazis, 38, 121f; of SED, 338
Center Party, 37, 53
Central Association of German Citizens of Jewish Faith (CV), 33, 195
Choltitz, Dietrich von, 136
Christian Democratic Union (CDU), 274, 306f, 355
Clay, Lucius, 275
Cold War, 2, 4, 9, 12, 102, 273, 286, 312, 322, 327, 347, 358, 361, 373
collaboration, 119f, 149, 187, 267, 278, 304, 325; cost of, 149, 278, 304; motives of, 120, 149, 325
collective biography, 3, 9
Communism, 37, 215, 278, 319–59, 365; attraction of, 226, 245, 273; disappointment in, 320–59; persecution of, 194; resistance of, 193, 245, 305
Communist Party of Germany (KPD), 192, 273f, 308, 323, 326
concentration camp (KZ), 4, 10, 69, 190f, 208–19, 328, 373, 375; capos of, 212; crematoria in, 190, 212, 214, 251; death marches from, 216f; escapes from, 213f; guards of, 148, 168f, 193, 214f, 376; labor in, 194, 210, 212f; liberation from, 216–18, 228, 371; medical experiments in, 213; plunder in, 214f; selection in, 190, 210, 212f, 215
consumer society, 294
Cramer, Ernst, 227
Cuba, 202–4, 222
currency reform, 274f, 280, 298
Czechoslovakia, 34, 201f

Dachau, 191, 222, 433
dancing lessons, 90f, 156, 159
Danzig, 180
Datsche, 343
de Gaulle, Charles, 115
Debus, Hermann, 7, 34f, 71, 110, 132, 141, 145, 238, 249, 261f, 269, 285, 289f, 292, 299, 301f, 309, 362, 364
Deiters, Heinrich, 29, 376

democratization, 310, 318, 352; inner, 281; socialist, 353
demonstrations, 92, 316, 350, 353, 355
denazification, 257, 264–66, 274, 324, 375
Deutsche Allgemeine Zeitung, 35, 69
Deutsche Mark (DM), 356
dismantling, 249, 252, 282, 323
Displaced Persons (DPs), 271, 309, 371
dissidents, 94, 168, 221, 230, 330, 349; Initiative Peace and Human Rights (IFM), 350; New Forum, 353
Döblin, Alfred, 369
Dubček, Alexander, 339

economy, 87, 159, 176, 249, 305; market, 301, 308, 316, 331, 352; planned, 301, 324, 337–40, 346f, 351; scarcity, 339
ego documents, 7f; shared experiences, 10f, 372. *See also* autobiographies
Eichmann, Adolf, 201, 376
Einsatzgruppen (Nazi murder units), 102, 206, 218
Einstein, Albert, 224, 230
Elias, Ruth, 169, 213, 217, 260, 273
Equalization of Burdens Law (LAG), 309
Eretz Israel, 84, 222, 272f
Erhard, Ludwig, 275, 308
ethnic cleansing, 2, 135, 191, 206, 232f, 370
eugenics, 157, 167
euthanasia, 93, 157, 370
expellees, 254, 294; claim to homeland, 304; dispossession in, 254–56; expulsion, from East, 2, 33, 277; integration of, 256, 309, 371f; as pressure group, 372; resentment against, 256; revenge during expulsion, 12, 97, 188, 254, 256, 305, 370; violence in, 12, 97, 188, 254, 256, 305, 370
Eyck, Erich, 36, 224
Eyck, Frank, 26, 50, 63, 66, 73f, 90, 96, 199, 222, 225f, 229f, 266, 268

families, 17–41, 42–65; childcare of, 46f; destruction of, 188; divorce in, 30, 205, 297, 346; ideal of, 17f; orphans of, 157, 263, 309; reassembly of, 247, 250, 256, 259
Faulhaber, Cardinal Michael von, 95
Federal Republic of Germany (FRG), 279–19. *See also* Germany, West
Feigel, Werner, 321, 325, 327, 329f, 339, 344f, 352f, 357–59, 366
femininity, volkish, 188; and Weimar "new women," 149
Fest, Joachim, 21f, 37, 73, 84, 93, 106f, 132, 138, 142, 239, 240–42, 247, 251, 263, 266, 269, 275, 277f, 280, 283, 286, 307, 360, 362
Finckh, Renate, 150f, 153, 156–59, 161f, 168, 170–72, 175, 177f, 185–87, 189, 379
flak, 173, 187, 240
Flessa, Friedrich, 109
flight, 2, 114; from GDR, 336f, 348; from Red Army, 12, 97, 142, 149, 179–82, 188, 245, 263, 277, 296, 305, 333, 336, 370; from Third Reich, 196, 199, 222
Flügge, Elisabeth, 200
France, defeat of, 114
Fränkel, Anna, 190, 207f, 213f, 217, 230, 272
Free Democratic Party (FDP), 274, 307f, 355
Free German Labor Union (FDGB), 344
Free German Youth (FDJ), 325, 328, 336, 341, 348
Freischar (youth group), 61, 77f
Freisler, Roland, 221
Frenzel, Paul, 47, 50, 53, 55, 60f, 77f, 84, 88–90, 92, 106, 111, 118–20, 124f, 128, 145, 244, 249, 269, 273, 301, 321, 325f, 330f, 334, 341f, 346f, 350
Friedan, Betty, 148
Friedrich, Sabine, 11
Fröhlich, Peter, 191, 199, 202–4, 222f. *See also* Gay, Peter
Führer, cult of, 81f, 93. *See also* Hitler, Adolf

Galen, Cardinal Clemens von, 157
Ganor, Niza, 272, 377. *See also* Osimok, Anna
gardens, 24, 31, 47f, 50, 160, 257, 259, 282, 299, 362
Garton Ash, Timothy, 380
Gay, Peter, 195, 198, 200, 223–25, 310. *See also* Fröhlich, Peter
generational rebellion (1968), 315; critique of, 310–12; as cultural revolution, 311f; motives of, 311f; violence of, 311
genocide, 96, 135, 218, 233, 379. *See also* Holocaust
German Communist Party (DKP), 308
German Democratic Party (DDP), 36
German Democratic Republic (GDR), 320–59. *See also* Germany, East

German Labor Front (DAF), 89
German National People's Party (DNVP), 36
German People's Party (DVP), 35
Germanization, 103, 120, 232
German-Soviet Friendship Society (DSF), 329, 333
Germany, East (GDR), 320–59, 372; anti-fascism of, 4, 321–23, 325, 328, 334, 336, 338, 372f, 376f; dictatorship of the proletariat, 281, 306, 321, 323, 327; disenchantment in, 320–59; nostalgia for, 359
Germany, Imperial, 17–41, 367f
Germany, West (FRG), 279–319; Basic Law of, 281, 306, 356; chancellor democracy of, 308; economic miracle of, 287f, 293, 303f, 308, 317, 372; magnetism of, 341
Gestapo, 201, 204, 220–22, 240; brutality of, 93, 96, 138f, 169, 193, 208, 231, 250; denunciation to, 95, 138, 168f
Globke, Hans, 274
Goebbels, Joseph, 71, 112f, 118, 125, 128, 132, 139, 172, 179, 202, 219f, 230, 305
Goerdeler, Carl, 221
Gogarten, Friedrich, 286
Goltz, Isa von der, 180
Gompertz, Albert, 21, 69f, 86f, 194, 200, 223–26, 229f, 273, 310, 377
Gompertz, Leo, 21, 194, 201f, 224
Gomułka, Władysław, 332
Gorbachev, Mikhail, 291, 351f
Göring, Hermann, 114, 125
grandparents, 7, 9, 19–28, 31, 39, 47, 50, 75, 197, 303, 363, 367
Grass, Günter, 3, 10, 372, 377
Great Britain, 22f, 61, 101, 114, 119, 125, 131, 160, 199, 203, 219, 222, 226f, 270, 299, 305; Battle of Britain, 114
Great Depression, 2, 11, 43, 61, 150, 158, 192, 194, 199, 340, 369, 378
Green Party, 312, 355
Greiffenhagen, Martin, 240, 305, 311f
Gros, Günter, 243
Groschek, Christel, 256, 292, 296
Grothus, Gisela, 25, 53, 58, 60, 64, 73, 84, 87f, 90–92, 154, 163, 187, 263, 287, 295, 297f, 312–14, 317
Grothus, Horst, 25, 29, 49, 60, 80, 82f, 85, 97, 107, 111, 114, 127, 131, 139, 143, 244, 262, 269, 276, 283f, 287, 289–93, 296–98, 300f, 305, 307, 315–17, 362, 364, 374, 377
Grothus, Ulrich, 7
guest workers (*Gastarbeiter*), 291f, 434

Härtel, Erna, 26, 262, 330, 333
Härtel, Karl, 7, 18, 26, 31, 38, 42, 44, 48, 50, 54, 56, 60, 65, 78f, 86, 87, 89, 94f, 106, 109, 111, 123, 125, 135, 143, 238, 241–43, 245f, 248, 251, 268, 287, 309, 326, 329, 333, 345, 351, 373, 379
Haffner, Sebastian, 219, 230. *See also* Pretzel, Raimund
Hagemann, Günter, 307, 318
Hager, Kurt, 352
Hall, G. Stanley, 67
hamstern (scavenge), 257
Harbig, Rudolf, 110
Harich, Wolfgang, 332
Hasemann, Erich, 338, 365
Hauptmann, Gerhard, 34
Hecht, Ingeborg, 197f, 203, 205f, 271
Hedin, Sven, 104
Heimat (homeland), 22, 124
Helmer, Erich, 7, 17, 21, 57, 59f, 72, 74, 93, 96, 107f, 111, 122f, 125f, 135, 137f, 140, 143–45, 237, 243, 247–50, 257f, 262, 265, 268f, 274, 277, 280, 283f, 286, 290, 304
Helsinki Declaration, 341
Heuss, Theodor, 281, 307, 375
Heydrich, Richard, 206
Heym, Stefan, 227
Hierl, Konstantin, 105
Hillers, Marta, 184, 370
Himmler, Heinrich, 125, 140f, 167, 205, 219, 242
Hindenburg, Paul von, 42, 53, 62f, 65f, 68
Hitler Youth (HJ), 9, 66–68, 71–74, 76–85, 89–94, 107f, 111f, 139, 143, 148, 151, 161, 186, 192, 237, 250, 304, 325, 365, 374; activities of, 71f, 77–81, 83–85, 92, 104f, 112, 369; indoctrination in, 67f, 71f, 77–85, 92, 96, 104f, 112, 156f, 369, 101; peer pressure of, 68, 76–85, 96
Hitler, Adolf: assassination attempt of, 137, 177, 221, 284; charisma of, 82, 156; as commander in chief, 109, 113f; as orator, 62, 80f, 374; suicide of, 141. See also Führer
HIWIS (Nazi auxiliaries), 120

Holland, 35, 114, 141, 199–205, 222, 229
Hochmuth, Katharina, 7
Holmer, Uwe, 321
Holocaust, 190–233; assembly line murder in, 206–12; by bullets, 133–35, 179, 206f, 216; death by labor in, 194, 210, 212f; remembrance of, 218f, 231–33, 310, 376–79
home, 42–65, 85–95
home front, 9, 148, 158f, 171, 173, 187, 370
Homeyer, Wilhelm, 141f, 245f, 276
Honecker, Erich, 193, 219, 320, 340, 343, 345, 347, 353, 376
housing, 28, 31, 37, 241, 248, 264, 334, 339; building of, 19, 282, 324, 343; crisis of, 259, 297, 309, 343; destruction of, 259
Hubbe, Wolfgang, 138
Huber, Anneliese, 88f, 91, 122, 155f, 163–65, 263, 269, 276, 283, 285, 287, 295, 297f, 300f, 303, 318, 363, 366
Huber, Paul, 261, 300, 364
Hübschmann, Klaus, 321, 325f, 330f, 334, 339, 343–45, 357f
hyperinflation, 2, 38, 40, 50, 369

identity, 8, 32, 37, 195, 198, 203, 208f, 217f, 223, 227, 232, 333; German, 21, 23; regional, 28, 34
Iggers, Georg, 197f, 201, 223–26, 273, 378
imprisonment, 111, 138, 203, 244, 249, 262, 306, 326, 338, 341, 348, 350, 375; American, 241f, 246; British, 242f, 247, 260, 307; correspondence from, 245; flight from, 246; French, 243; homecoming from, 247f, 250; reeducation during, 242; release from, 241, 243, 245–48, 251, 260, 328, 348; Russian, 243f, 300, 370, 435
intermarriage: Catholic-Protestant, 37; Jewish-gentile, 20, 33, 195
Isaacson, Judith Magyar, 378
Italy, 41, 130, 142, 241f, 272, 285, 291, 300

Janka, Walter, 332
Jannings, Emil, 172
Japan, 128, 291
Jaspers, Karl, 306, 372
Jewish emigration, 4, 94, 201f, 205, 219, 223f, 271f, 272, 300; decision for, 74, 192, 197, 199; papers for, 199, 203; preparation of, 87, 198, 199f, 222; safe havens for, 199, 202, 222, 232
Jewish persecution: boycott of Jewish businesses, 69, 83, 195f; civil service purge of Jews, 20f, 195; deportation of Jews, 178, 205, 207f, 224; ghettoization of Jews, 205–9, 371; loss of citizenship of Jews, 191, 197; pogrom of (*Kristallnacht*) Jews, 152, 157, 202; racial laws of, 191, 197–99, 205–7; resistance against, 194f, 197f, 220f, 230, 232; underground survival of Jews, 207–9, 219, 232; yellow star of, 170, 206, 208
Jewish refugees, 196, 199–206, 222; adjustment of, 200, 204, 223–25, 273; Americanization of, 223, 225–27, 273; finding jobs, 199f, 223–25; name change of, 222f
Jews: assimilation of, 36, 63, 84, 94, 191, 194f, 197–99, 223; from Eastern Europe, 194; friends with, 194f, 199f, 203; *Geltungsjuden*, 205; of mixed descent, 194, 197, 205; orthodox, 194; reconciliation of, 310; reform, 195, 223; self-defense of, 194f, 197f, 220f, 230, 232; veterans, 194f, 205; youth groups of, 84, 197f; Zionists, 84, 191, 195, 197, 272
Joachim, Gerhard, 111, 138, 245, 323, 325–30, 332, 337f, 340, 346, 348, 351f, 356–59, 376
Joachim, Waiko, 348
Johannsen, Berndt, 349
Johannsen, Horst, 78, 140, 249f, 253, 257, 261, 266, 269, 322, 325, 330, 333–35, 338f, 343f, 346f, 349, 351, 353, 355, 358, 360
Jugendweihe (youth consecration), 326
June 17, 1953 uprising, 316, 331f
Junkers, 321

Kaiser, 17, 27, 37f. *See also* Wilhelm II
Kant, Immanuel, 21, 33
Katterwe, Erna, 125, 263
Keil, Jack Baruch, 197, 201, 203
Keil, Samuel, 196
Kempowski, Walter, 7
Khrushchev, Nikita, 332, 334, 336
kindergarten, 47, 285
Kinderlandverschickung (sending children to countryside), 154, 173
Klein, Dorle, 47, 346
Klein, Fritz, 6, 29, 35, 47, 63f, 69, 87, 92, 96, 106f, 110, 145, 274, 321, 325f, 328f, 332, 337f, 341f, 345f, 351f, 359, 361, 365, 376

Klier, Freya, 350
Klüger, Ruth, 192, 198, 204, 206f, 209–13, 216, 218, 230, 272, 276, 310, 377f
Koch, Gertrud, 27, 38, 170, 220, 259, 266
Koch, Ilse, 169
Koeppen, Anne Marie, 150
Kohl, Helmut, 3, 233, 291, 355
Kolb, Ruth, 125
Kolesnyk, Sonja, 162, 271
Kolesnyk, Wilhelm, 81, 85, 96, 108, 113f, 134
Kopelev, Lev, 184
Kosing, Alfred, 347, 359, 365, 373, 377
Krapf, Gerhard, 6, 32, 42, 46, 59, 61, 63, 71, 73, 79f, 82, 84–86, 93–96, 106, 110, 112, 116–18, 121–24, 128, 130f, 137, 139f, 142f, 146, 244, 247f, 271, 276, 310
Krause, Günter, 301, 305, 319, 321, 327, 350, 357, 361f, 364, 373
Krawczyk, Stephan, 350
Krenz, Egon, 353
Kühlem, Gertrud, 93
Kulturbund (League of Culture), 328, 338
Künneke, Evelyn, 123

labor movement, 322f, 329, 346; subculture of, 37; trade unions of, 37
Landjahr (farm duty), 148, 154
Lebensborn (SS nurseries), 167
Lehmann, Wilhelm, 30
leisure, 28, 37, 68, 77, 79, 85, 110, 155, 294, 299, 343, 350, 362, 369
Leithold, Albert, 329, 332, 375
Lenge, Kurt, 193
Lengsfeld, Vera, 330
Lenin, Vladimir I., 40, 325, 344
Leningrad, siege of, 127f
Liberalism, 22, 43, 307, 380
Lichti, Gertrud, 310
Lichti, Walter, 270
Liddell Hart, Sir Basil H., 115
life stages: adolescence, 65–97; adulthood, 101–360; birth, 42f; childhood, 43–65; death, 366; old age, 300–303, 362–66
Lilje, Hanns, 267, 306, 376
Lindauer, Inge, 180
living space, 81, 103, 112, 162, 206
Löwith, Karl, 306
Lüders, Marie Elisabeth, 256
Luxemburg, Rosa, 350, 377

Maginot Line, 114
Mahlendorf, Ursula, 34, 47, 53, 62, 68, 92, 151–53, 155–58, 160f, 163, 168f, 171, 173, 178–80, 182f, 185–87, 254, 256, 259, 264, 269–71, 274, 276–78, 280, 283, 294, 298, 305f, 309, 365, 375, 377
Mandelstam, Lucy, 67, 197, 201–7, 209f, 212, 216f, 224, 229, 271–73, 310, 373, 377
Mann, Thomas, 230, 368
Manstein, Field Marshal Erich von, 130
Manz, Günter, 323, 332, 340, 358, 366
marriage, 5, 9, 20, 30, 37, 89, 125, 151, 153, 156, 165f, 170, 195, 197, 204f, 209, 261–62, 271, 283, 285, 287, 296f, 311f, 315, 318, 371
Marshall Plan, 282
masculinity, martial, 102, 148
maternalism, 148
Meinecke, Friedrich, 267
memories: communicative, 372, 377; contested, 321, 372–78; fractured, 12, 187, 360–80; guilty, 13, 277f, 369, 374, 379; public, 231, 372–78; tropes of, 10f; of war, 144–46, 312
Mengele, Josef, 213
Merkel, Angela, 378
Mewis, Karl, 332
Meyerstein, Heinz Jehuda, 219, 222
Mielke, Erich, 332, 341
military police (MPs), 134, 138f, 142, 185, 240
military service: basic training of, 102, 109–11, 121, 144, 227; conscription in, 103, 106f, 167, 172, 338; desertion from, 106, 111, 138, 240, 245; officer training in, 110, 118; physical for, 108, 111; promotion in, 122; swearing in to, 109
Millett, Kate, 148
miracle weapons (V2), 137–39, 176
miscegenation, 162, 205
misogynism, 149
Mitläufer (follower), 257
Mittag, Günter, 347
Mittlere Reife (junior high graduation), 86f
mobility, social, 22
Model, Walter, 141
modernism, 269

Modrow, Hans, 3, 372
Moosmann, Agnes, 35f, 78, 97, 185, 187, 239
Mosse, George L., 310
Mueller, Irmgard, 200, 207, 212
Müller, Rudi, 123
Mussolini, Benito, 41, 126, 130

nannies, 30, 46f
narratives, 1–14; of adventure, 5, 84, 103f, 107, 144–46, 369f; of failure, 357–59; of gender, 5, 187–89; of heroism, 10, 103, 107, 143–46, 158, 171, 231, 276; of success, 10, 281–94, 316–19; of survival, 10, 103, 144, 231–33; of victimhood, 10, 231–33, 373
National Committee for a Free Germany (NKFD), 245
National People's Army (NVA), 336, 338
National Socialism: ideology of, 70–73, 80–82, 149, 192, 194, 374; indoctrination in, 66, 68–76, 77–79, 96f, 101, 112, 121, 151, 154, 369f; movement of, 62–65, 68
nationalism, 27f, 41, 56f, 76, 215, 267, 307f
NATO, 312, 322, 330
Nazification, 66f, 68–76, 85, 93, 96
Nazi-Soviet Pact, 113, 205
Neglein, Hans-Gerd, 291, 297, 314
neighborhood, 44, 54, 57–64, 69, 85, 194
Nemmersdorf, 139, 179
neo-Nazis, 322–23; National Democratic Party (NPD), 308; Socialist Reich Party (SRP), 308
Neue Wache, 233
Neues Deutschland, 286, 326
Neumaier, Hanne, 297, 300
Neumaier, Robert, 87–90, 92, 96, 107, 110, 116, 118, 120, 129f, 134–36, 141, 145, 243, 257, 262, 268f, 284, 287f, 290–92, 294, 297–99, 301, 317, 362, 366
new social movements, 315f; of environmentalism, 312, 314, 355; of feminism, 147, 232, 264, 312–14; of pacifism, 307, 313, 380
NKVD, 323, 327
normalization, 264, 268f, 277, 371
Normandy landing, 135, 227
Norway, 114, 119, 144, 168, 220
NÖSPL (New Economic Policy), 337
NSDAP, 64, 66, 71, 79, 148f, 247; old fighters of, 66, 68, 70; opportunists in, 68, 73, 177, 186, 218; seizure of power of, 3, 65f, 68f, 77f, 190, 323. *See also* anti-Semitism
NS-Frauenschaft (Nazi Women's League), 151
NSV (Nazi People's Welfare), 154, 173, 180, 185, 217
Nuremberg, 109, 270, 289; Nuremberg Laws, 197, 199, 219, 274; party congresses in, 75; Nuremberg Trials, 250, 266, 277, 375
nursing, 163, 167, 187, 218

occupation, 9, 38, 118–20, 166, 229, 238, 247, 252, 258f, 264, 268, 273f, 277, 282, 305, 308, 323, 333, 371; American occupation government, 227; zones of, 242, 246f, 250, 252f, 264f, 274f, 280–82, 337
Oder River, 34, 141, 178
Olympic Games of 1936, 75
Osimok, Anna, 208. *See also* Ganor, Niza
Osteinsatz, 162. *See also* Germanization
Oster, Hans, 221
Ostpolitik (reconciliation with the East), 340

Palach, Jan, 340
parents, influence of, 28–39
partisans, 102, 134f, 145, 179
Party of Democratic Socialism (PDS), 355
paternalism, 28, 43, 315
Paulus, Field Marshal Friedrich, 130
peace movement: in the East, 348f; in the West, 313
peaceful revolution (*Wende*), 357, 359, 365
people's police, 325, 327, 332, 338
perestroika, 351
Peters, Eva, 56, 61, 67, 78, 81, 83, 91, 95, 97, 141, 147, 152, 157, 159, 163, 175, 177, 186–88
Plattenbauten (prefab apartments), 343
Polak, Ilse, 217, 272, 377
Poland, 34, 120, 126, 170, 203, 205f, 247, 352; corridor through, 119, 159; defeat of, 101, 113f, 159, 170
pollution, 314, 349
Potsdam, 18, 74, 254, 264, 308, 321
POWs, 5, 11, 114, 120, 127, 178, 182, 226f, 229, 237, 240–51, 253, 255f, 260f, 276, 294, 300, 309, 370. *See also* imprisonment
Prague Spring, 340
Pretzel, Raimund, 219. *See also* Haffner, Sebastian

private lives, 2f, 7, 9, 53, 154, 160, 173, 175, 205, 240, 267, 273, 315, 318, 322, 326, 330, 338, 367, 375, 377; rewards of, 294–303, 317, 343, 357; spaces for, 85–95, 303, 327
propaganda, 112, 226, 277, 308; Communist, 219, 275, 327, 334, 337; Nazi, 64, 68, 70–72, 74, 79, 81–83, 91, 94, 101f, 104f, 107, 112, 119, 121, 125, 128, 132, 137, 140, 145, 153, 161, 172f, 179, 182, 194, 219f, 230, 239, 305, 374
prosperity, 2, 4, 10, 18, 22, 26, 28, 40, 44, 274, 281f, 291f, 294, 296–99, 301, 308, 317, 345, 316, 367f, 379
Protestants, 32f, 36f, 53, 326, 349; Confessing Church, 93, 96, 153; German Christians, 93, 153
Prussia, 22, 28, 30, 32–34, 36, 40, 47, 51, 87, 110, 137, 206, 237; East, 23, 139, 141, 178f, 181, 248, 254, 260, 285; legacy of, 18, 74; patriotism of, 56
public engagement, 304–16

Queiser, Hans R., 22, 25, 52, 82f, 95, 102, 105, 107, 109, 111, 114–16, 119, 121, 123, 131, 138, 143f, 245
Quisling, Vidkun, 120

Raschdorff, Anne, 32, 295, 300, 303
Raschdorff, Hellmut, 7, 32, 65, 69, 75, 89, 107, 119, 127, 134, 246f, 279, 288, 290, 292, 294f, 297, 299–304, 317, 362–64, 366
rationing, 160, 171f, 248, 257f
Ravensbrück, 169, 216f
rearmament, 73, 102f, 115, 308, 311, 316
reconstruction, 264, 266f, 278f, 281, 286, 294, 309, 343; of housing, 4; of infrastructure, 4, 267, 282, 324; labor for, 246, 249, 371; of personal lives, 2
Red Army, 133, 139, 142, 178, 214, 230, 260, 271, 274, 320, 322, 329, 336, 338, 370, 373; advance of, 127, 129f, 137, 141, 180f, 205, 216; brutality of, 141, 179, 182f, 253, 305, 323; casualties of, 129; manpower of, 127, 130, 333; plunder by, 182f, 253; rapes by, 97, 149, 183f, 188, 305; weapons of, 127, 129–31, 137
reeducation, 186, 191, 194, 242, 327
Reich Labor Service (RAD), 89, 105f, 107, 185
Reichsbanner (republican militia), 62
Reichstag fire, 69
resistance, 219–30; Edelweiss Pirates, 93, 170, 220; female, 170, 183; inner emigration, 97, 220, 269, 281; officer's plot, 137, 177, 221; political, 93; swing youth, 92f; White Rose, 94
restitution, 21; for Jewish victims, 232, 271, 280, 307, 310, 376; for slave laborers, 310
retirement, 2, 5, 9, 296f, 301f, 345, 352, 362–66
reunification, 316, 331, 355–58, 365, 379; Ten Point Plan for, 355; Two-Plus-Four Agreement for, 356f; Treaty for, 356
Reuter, Ernst, 219, 275
Rhine River, 34, 141, 178, 241f, 249, 281, 283f, 299
Rhineland, 32, 36, 38, 103, 308, 333
Ribbentrop, Joachim von, 74
Richthoven, Manfred von, 104
Richter, Hans Peter, 105
Riefenstahl, Leni, 75
Riesengebirge, 34
Ritter, Gerhard, 283
Rosenberg, Jesse, 278
Roter Frontkämpferbund (Communist militia), 62
Ruge, Eugen, 372
Ruhr Basin, 21, 34, 141, 222, 284, 288, 293

SA (*Sturmabteilung*, Nazi militia), 62, 68, 70, 73, 77, 93, 108, 158, 170, 190, 192, 195f, 201f, 369f
Saar, 22, 92, 246
Sartre, Jean-Paul, 269, 306
Sauckel, Fritz, 172
Sauerbruch, Ferdinand, 95
Schabowski, Günter, 354
Schalck-Golodkowski, Alexander, 347
Scheller, Theo, 150
Schelsky, Helmut, 273
Schirach, Baldur von, 77
Schirmer, Hans-Harald, 37, 41, 63, 70, 78, 91, 96, 251, 266, 318
Schmeling, Max, 198
Schmidt, Helmut, 3, 102
Schneider, Paul, 194
Schoenhals, Dieter, 246, 277, 379
Schöffski, Benno, 21, 23–25, 33, 48, 60, 69f, 78, 85, 129, 285, 298
Schöffski, Edith, 17f, 24f, 33, 38, 47, 48, 69, 95, 153f, 163, 173, 183, 187, 258, 260, 276f, 283, 297f, 317
Scholz-Eule, Erika, 253
Scholz-Eule, Traudel, 253
schools, 51–57; *Berufsschule* (trade), 55f; *Gymnasium* (classical), 26f, 30, 54–56, 72, 215; polytechnical, 329, 334; *Realschule* (modern), 54f, 87; *Volksschule* (primary), 54f
Schultheis, Heinz, 34, 45, 58, 61, 65, 76, 79, 84, 87,

89, 92, 104–6, 115, 118, 126f, 249, 268f, 283, 287, 290, 366, 379
Schumacher, Kurt, 196, 281, 306f, 323, 375
Schwarzer, Alice, 148
Schwerin, Ernst, 201
scorched earth: by Red Army, 133; by Wehrmacht, 133
Seelmann-Eggebert, Will, 61, 373
segregation, 253; by gender, 52, 54, 90; by religion, 94, 191, 198, 207
Seidel, Ina, 95
sexuality, 54, 91, 123, 152, 184, 194, 205, 252, 256, 295, 346, 370
siblings, 42, 44, 46, 50f, 59, 126, 153, 159, 245, 261, 317
Sieg, Martin, 238f, 242f, 250, 261, 269f, 281, 286, 304, 373, 376
Silesia, 21f, 34, 36, 115, 141, 157, 163, 173, 178, 180f, 183, 185, 200, 206, 253–55, 327
Simon, Marie Jalowicz, 208, 272
skeptical generation, 280
slave labor, 117, 119, 138, 145, 149, 171f, 178, 181, 183, 185, 187, 191, 194, 217, 241, 243, 249, 271, 370
Social Democratic Party (SPD), 37, 192, 273–75, 307f, 316, 323, 326, 355
Socialist Unity Party (SED), 4, 274, 286, 304, 315f, 321–22, 324–38, 340–42, 345–50, 352–55, 357–60, 365f, 372f, 376f
Sölle, Dorothee, 304, 311f, 377
Sonderweg (special path), 10
Soviet Military Administration (SMAD), 324
Soviet Union, 131, 193, 220, 243f, 249, 320f, 329, 332, 351, 358; invasion of, 126f, 204; victory of, 322, 329
Sovietization, 333
SS (*Schutzstaffel*, Nazi elite guard): KZ guards, 148, 168f, 193f, 210, 214, 216f, 228, 304, 376; Waffen SS, 107f, 125, 134, 227, 229
"stab-in-the-back-legend," 56
Stahlhelm (conservative militia), 62
Stalin, Joseph, 114, 126, 192, 254, 325, 331f
Stalingrad, 129f, 169, 171, 177, 374
Stalinism, 184, 244, 323, 327, 329, 337f, 351, 355, 358, 372; destalinization, 332
Stark, Brigitte, 6
starvation, 38, 70, 128, 212, 243f, 370
Stasi, 301, 321, 327, 347–50, 353, 357; files of, 350; informal informants of (IM), 330, 341; Ministry for State Security (MfS), 341, 350; surveillance of, 327, 332, 341f, 350, 353
Stauffenberg, Claus Schenk von, 219, 221
Stern, Carola, 318, 359, 361. *See also* Assmus, Erika
Stern, Fritz, 34, 190, 198, 201, 204, 223–26, 273, 310, 378
Strauss, Richard, 95
Streicher, Julius, 194
Stresemann, Gustav, 35
Stukas (dive bombers), 115, 131
Sudetenland, 152, 256

teachers, 72, 171, 173, 210, 212, 215f, 261, 263, 268f, 284–87, 290, 292, 307, 311, 330, 335; authoritarian, 51–53, 57, 70f, 73, 278, 280, 284f, 324; progressive, 51–53, 57, 59, 61, 86, 92, 200, 311
Taubhorn, Erika, 29, 49, 52, 154f, 174, 187, 257, 259, 261–63, 287, 295, 300, 362
Tausch, Hans, 55, 106, 118, 120, 122, 124, 129, 131, 135, 256, 267, 278, 285, 290, 317
Thälmann, Teddy, 62, 68
Thamm, Gerhardt B., 21, 109, 113–15, 118, 128, 130, 137, 141, 143, 373
Theresienstadt, 209
Third Reich. *See* National Socialism
Third Way, 355–57
total war, 132, 148, 171, 188; mobilization for, 148, 172, 187
Trabant (Trabi), 339
travel: in GDR, 301, 347, 354, 359, 362; restrictions against, 333, 341, 347f, 353; travel cadres, 341, 347;
trench warfare, 117
Treskow, Henning von, 221
Troschke, Frauke von, 7

Ukraine, 85, 108, 126f, 134, 162, 181, 183, 190, 208, 271
Ulbricht, Walter, 274, 323, 326, 330–32, 336–38, 340, 346, 376
United States, 22, 128, 131, 200, 202f, 222f, 226, 230, 244, 253, 264, 271–73, 284, 291, 305, 378
Unrechtsstaat (illegitimate state), 321, 359

vacations, 9, 25, 47, 50, 61f, 75, 79, 156, 292, 295, 299, 317, 330, 344
VEB (people's owned factory), 324

Versailles, 35, 38, 40, 56, 80, 92, 103, 112, 122, 206, 373
Vichy, 119
victimhood, 373; competition about, 191f; varieties of, 231–33
Vogel, Wolfgang, 348
Volksgemeinschaft (people's community), 80, 95, 150, 172, 238
Volkssturm (last ditch militia), 140

Walb, Lore, 154, 156, 158, 166, 170f, 173, 175, 177, 181, 185–88, 374, 377
Wall, 337f, 340, 351; building of, 335, 336f; fall of, 316, 353–58, 365; victims of, 337, 358
war production, 125f, 128, 131, 172, 176, 187, 205, 222, 370
Warmbrunn, Werner, 32, 54, 84, 199, 203, 224f
Warsaw Pact, 322, 338
Weber, Alfred, 267
Weber, Max, 82
Weddingen, Otto von, 104
Wedekind, Frank, 67
Wehler, Hans-Ulrich, 18
Wehrmacht: bordellos of, 123; censorship of, 121f; chaplains in, 123; combat experience of, 101f, 115f; comradeship in, 112, 117f, 139; death toll of, 115, 125, 145; decorations of, 122, 127; defeats of, 103, 114, 125, 126–44, 239–51; entertainment in, 122f; furloughs of, 118, 123–25, 140, 164; hospitals of, 124, 132, 163, 178f, 183, 185, 227; mail service in, 122; offensives of, 113, 126, 129; retreats of, 127, 132f, 136–38, 142; surrender of, 125, 137f, 141–43, 179, 185f, 226f, 239, 241, 251; victories of, 112–26, 127, 144; wounds in, 111, 115f, 118, 122, 124f, 128, 140f, 144f, 163–65, 179, 183–85, 227, 244
Wehrmacht Exhibition, 102
Weigelt, Ruth, 19, 34, 64, 68, 88, 90, 95, 156, 165f, 180, 185, 255, 276, 302f, 318, 366
Weimar Republic, 2f, 9, 11, 38, 43, 50f, 54, 56f, 61, 63f, 147, 149f, 158, 281, 306, 307, 359, 368 children of, 42–65; civil strife during, 62f; cultural innovation of, 60; progressive reforms of, 44, 56f
Weinberg, Gerhard, 222, 224
Weizsäcker, Richard von, 3, 6
Wessely, Paula, 172
Westernization, 305
Wilhelm I, 22, 26
Wilhelm II, 37
Wilhelmine Empire, 9, 27, 37. *See also* Germany, Imperial
Wilson, Woodrow, 40
Winter Aid, 80
Witolla, Jakobine, 14, 180, 182, 245
Wolf, Christa, 3, 42, 274, 345, 369, 377
Wolf, Friedrich, 245
women: careers of, 150f, 155, 167, 346; education of, 153–55, 167, 346; equality of, 263f, 313, 346; fraternization with, 252; hour of, 232, 251–64; of the rubble, 256–58, 282; struggles of, 147–89; war brides, 252; war duty of, 172; war widows, 166, 260–63, 294
working class, 5, 40, 61, 90, 125, 154, 187, 220, 274, 325, 327, 331, 345, 350
World War I (also First World War), 3, 9, 12, 35, 43, 64f, 104, 113f, 122, 133, 147, 194f, 307; loss of, 38, 40, 56, 231, 378; suffering during, 38, 40
World War II (also Second World War), 101–41; aims of, 103; as annihilation, 2, 96, 102, 115, 133, 135, 144, 159; as attrition, 126, 133; crimes in, 145, 239; defeatism in, 125, 130, 132, 138, 164, 169; destruction of, 133, 137, 140, 146, 175f, 229, 238, 258f, 270, 323, 367, 369; disillusionment in, 103, 109; outbreak of, 101f, 112f; preparation for, 102, 103–12; reporting about, 103, 121; survival through, 103, 110, 112, 115–18, 128, 140, 143–45, 165, 178, 238, 277; violence of, 102, 115f, 132–35, 141
Wriedt, Lotte, 260

youth groups, 32, 41, 105, 197
Youth Movement, 61, 76f, 79, 84, 105, 193, 197

Zahnwetzer, Moritz, 193
Zerbony, Edgar von, 201
Zöger, Heinz, 193, 205, 220, 359, 361
Zuckmayer, Carl, 270, 306